Mr John Hyland
1105 Priscilla Ln
Alexandria, VA 22308-2545

MW00453544

China Goes to Sea

China Goes to Sea

Maritime Transformation in Comparative Historical Perspective

edited by Andrew S. Erickson, Lyle J. Goldstein,
and Carnes Lord

NAVAL INSTITUTE PRESS
Annapolis, Maryland

Naval Institute Press
291 Wood Road
Annapolis, MD 21402

Library of Congress Cataloging-in-Publication Data

Erickson, Andrew S.
  China goes to sea : maritime transformation in comparative historical perspective /
Andrew Erickson, Lyle Goldstein, and Cary Lord.
    p. cm.
  Includes bibliographical references and index.
  ISBN 978-1-59114-242-3 (alk. paper)
  1. China—History, Naval. 2. Sea-power—China—History. 3. Naval art and
science—China—History. 4. History, Naval. 5. Sea-power—History. 6. Naval art
and science—History. I. Goldstein, Lyle. II. Lord, Cary. III. Title.
  DS739.E75 2009
  359.00951—dc22

                              2008055202

Printed in the United States of America on acid-free paper

14 13 12 11 10 09   9 8 7 6 5 4 3 2
First printing

Contents

Maps

Acknowledgments

IN A PROMINENT LOCATION IN WESTERN BEIJING, next to the Military Museum, stands the China Millennium Monument. In the words of the Organizing Committee for the 2008 Olympic Games, the monument is designed to "promote the national spirit by . . . expressing [aspirations for] the future" as "new opportunities, challenges, and hopes are emerging over the horizon of [the] China of the 21st century."[1] "The Chinese nation, with its splendid civilization of 5,000 years," the Committee declares, "is on the threshold of an epoch of great renewal, as a future of yet greater splendor is arising in the East of the world." Many share this assessment, or at least acknowledge its possibility. But what will be the nature of China's resurgence, how will it be accomplished, and what will it mean for the world?

As befits an edifice of such national significance, the monument (also known as the Grand Altar to Chinese Patriotism) is redolent with symbolism, offering tantalizing hints of answers to these questions. Beneath a massive sundial, museums display a panorama of Chinese history dating from Neolithic times to the monument's construction in 2000 AD At the southern entrance, where "the gentle . . . rise of the ground suggest[s] the rise of the Chinese nation," the Plaza of Holy Fire is 960 square meters in area, embodying explicitly China's 9,600,000 square kilometers of land territory. Along either side of the elongated plaza, a constant stream of water represents the Yangzi and Yellow Rivers, cradles of Chinese civilization. An engraved "Map of the Chinese Native Land" depicts Taiwan and the other offshore islands that Beijing claims, though not the sea surrounding them.

Rumors that the China Millennium Monument has been hotly contested make this abstract demarcation of time and territory all the more fascinating. To some Chinese, the monument's relative lack of water underscores the traditional conception of China as a continental power. Yet it is also said that China's State Oceanic Administration specifically criticized the monument for not having sufficient water. Even in the decade since the monument's construction, China has made previously unthinkable strides in the maritime direction. Years from now, when it is refurbished, will there be some symbolic acknowledgement that China has gone to sea?

⸙

Many individuals have contributed to the success of this project. The authors are indebted to Ken Allen, Dennis Blasko, Ja Ian Chong, John Corbett, Peter Dutton, Tobie Meyer-Fong, M. Taylor Fravel, George Gilboy, John Hattendorf, Nan Li, Alexander Liebman, William Murray, Stephan Platt, Michael Szonyi, and David Yang for their helpful suggestions and inputs. Christopher Robinson worked tirelessly to produce the detailed maps for this volume. Patricia Brower made our prose far more cogent and accessible. As always, the Naval Institute Press team—including Susan Corrado, Tom Cutler, George Keating, Chris Onrubia, Marla Traweek, and Judy Heise—were excellent partners in this effort.

All ideas expressed in this volume are solely those of the authors and editors and do not represent the official designations, interpretations, or estimates of the U.S. Navy or any other element of the U.S. government. Any errors are solely the responsibility of the editors. While every effort was made to verify the authenticity of data before this volume went to press, all cartographic illustrations, nomenclature, and boundary and maritime claim representations may be subject to disagreement and even, in some cases, to change. Depictions thereof in this volume are for unofficial scholarly purposes only. They must therefore be interpreted with extreme caution.

When possible, the maps in this volume portray clearly all territorial disputes and maritime claims relevant to China, the focus of this study. Any failure to note territorial disputes or to characterize them in a certain way (either inside or outside of China) does not imply a failure to acknowledge them or a judgment concerning the relative validity or state of claims among the parties involved (or the political status of those parties).

Given the wide range of historical periods covered by this volume, it is particularly important to emphasize that previous empires (e.g., the Chinese imperial system) operated quite differently from the centralized states with which we are familiar today. Such empires often exercised sovereignty and authority in a more diverse fashion and with a wider array of affiliated polities than is the case with present nation states. The "borders" of such empires, and the "boundaries" within them, must therefore be understood in a more complex sense as well.

Some concepts addressed in this volume have never been defined officially or depicted graphically in a definitive manner by the People's Liberation Army Navy, or any other element of China's government, to the outside world. A prime example is the "Island Chains" in the Western Pacific that, while described in such important sources as Adm. Liu Huaqing's memoirs, are still subject to various interpretations among scholars of China. Other examples include Beijing's various maritime claims, such as the one in the South China Sea, whose precise nature is still under debate in China. Such concepts are therefore introduced notionally and should not be overinterpreted.

Notes

1. Unless otherwise specified, data for this and the next two paragraphs are derived from Beijing Organizing Committee for the Games of the XXIX Olympiad, "The China Millennium Monument" [中华世纪坛世界艺术馆, *Zhonghua Shijitan*], Official Website of the Beijing 2008 Olympic Games, http://en.beijing2008.cn/spectators/beijing/tourism/list/n214068432.shtml.

RUSSIA

Lake Baikal

KAZAKHSTAN

KYRGYZSTAN

MONGOLIA

Changchun

Shenyang

NORTH KOREA

XINJIANG

Beijing

Tianjin *Bohai Sea*

SOUTH KOREA

Chinese line of control

Indian claim

XIZANG/ TIBET

Possible Chinese claims

Indian line of control

Chinese claim

NEPAL

Lhasa

BHUTAN

INDIA

Yellow River

Zhengzhou

C H I N A

Nanjing

Wuhan

Chengdu

Yangtze River

Changsha

Nanchang

Guiyang

Fuzhou

Kunming

Nanning

Macau

Hong Kong

Haikou

HAINAN

XISHAI PARACEL IS.

South China Sea

NANSHAI SPRATLY IS.

BRUNEI

Yellow Sea
(see note in legend)

JAPAN

Shanghai

East China Sea

OKINAWA/RYUKYU IS.

DIAOYU/ SENKAKU IS.

TAIWAN

PHILIPPINES

BURMA

VIETNAM

LAOS

THAILAND

CAMBODIA

INDONESIA

MALAYSIA

MALAYSIA

INDONESIA

China's Territorial and Maritime Claims, c. 2009

━━ China's South China Sea Claim. There is no consensus, even in China, concerning the precise nature of this claim.

---- Maritime Boundary Delimitation with Vietnam

•••••• China's Continental Shelf Claim

-- -- China's 200NM Exclusive Economic Zone Claim

▨ Disputed Status

▨ Disputed Territory

Note: Taiwan's status is disputed. China claims the Bohai Sea as internal waters and has not published its maritime claims in relation to North Korea in the Yellow Sea.

0   250   500 Kilometers

0   250   500 Miles

Andrew S. Erickson and Lyle J. Goldstein

Introduction
Chinese Perspectives on Maritime Transformation

IT HAS BEEN OBSERVED THAT THERE EXIST "massive differences in the assumptions of European nations and Asian nations about the significance of sea power, today and into the future."[1] This represents the reversal of a great historical trend that began six hundred years ago, in which China withdrew from the seas and European naval expansion spread Western influence around the globe.[2] Now, while the U.S. Navy is diminishing quantitatively and European naval powers are in substantial decline, many nations in Asia are prioritizing naval development. For many observers, China's rise and America's relative decline are the central dynamic forces within this great divergence.[3]

In modern history, China has been primarily a land power, dominating smaller states along its massive continental flanks. But China's turn toward the sea is now very much a reality, as evident in its stunning rise in global shipbuilding markets, its vast and expanding merchant marine, the wide offshore reach of its energy and minerals exploration companies, its growing fishing fleet, and indeed its increasingly modern navy. Yet, for all these achievements, there is still profound skepticism regarding China's potential as a genuine maritime power. Beijing must still import the most vital subcomponents for its shipyards, maritime governance remains severely challenged bureaucratically, and the navy evinces, at least as of yet, little enthusiasm for significant blue water power projection capabilities.

This volume presents a comprehensive assessment of prospects for China's maritime development by situating these important geostrategic phenomena within a larger world historical context. It accepts the premise that geography matters but explores precisely how and under what circumstances it matters. In the words of Alan Wachman, "Geography . . . does condition the choices made by policy makers, presenting both opportunities and constraints" but it "does not determine the strategic ambitions or policies of a state."[4] We use the terms "maritime power" and "sea power" to mean not only explicit naval strength but also the commerce and shipping that underpin it. Sea power is not an end in itself but rather both a medium for trade and a source of national security. China is hardly the only land power in history to attempt transformation by fostering sea power. Moreover, China was not always only a land power—quite the contrary: watertight bulkheads, rudders, and even the compass are thought to have originated there.

This book examines each of these vital perspectives in turn. Too many works on China view the nation in isolation. Of course, China's history and culture are to some extent exceptional, but building intellectual fences actually hinders the effort to understand China's current development trajectory. Historically, China has been profoundly influenced by external religions, ideologies, and sociopolitical models. The need to compare, moreover, is additionally highlighted by the realization that such macrohistorical comparisons are currently ongoing in China—and potentially affecting state policy in Beijing. Some of these current and influential People's Republic of China (PRC) studies are surveyed in the penultimate chapter of this volume. Finally, when undertaking comparative historical studies, there is an imperative to take note of major illustrative differences between cases that may be just as analytically significant as various similarities in the cases. Comparative history has been a rewarding method for the study of international politics and strategic studies, and the present work is inspired by a variety of successful studies relying on these methods.[5]

This present work would be incomplete, however, if it did not grapple directly and intensively with the enigmatic phenomena of Chinese maritime development itself. Comparison in the absence of direct knowledge regarding a given subject raises the specter of crude and inappropriate analogy. The editors of the present volume are fully aware that historical parallels can, when misapplied, lead to a false sense of certainty and sometimes to grave errors in judgment.[6] Any seasoned observer of international relations understands that history never repeats itself in identical patterns. To guard against the misapplication of historical analogies, the comparisons are wide-ranging, but they are also balanced by ample analyses in the second part of this volume that review both historical and contemporary developments in China's maritime sector. These analyses review in detail both the high points of Chinese sea power (e.g., the Ming Voyages of Zheng He) as well as the low points (e.g., Mao's Cultural Revolution). It is emphasized in the second part of this volume that contemporary China is not the only case of attempted maritime transformation in Chinese history. Detailed knowledge presented by the distinguished group of China-watchers highlighted here safeguards the integrity of the comparative analytical effort that is the heart of this volume. This volume's contributors include historians, political scientists, industry consultants, and sinologists, not to mention a variety of naval officers, both active and retired. They represent a wealth of talent that holds the potential to yield the best results from such multidisciplinary endeavors. It must be emphasized that the opinions expressed in this volume are solely those of the authors and editors and do not represent the official policies or estimates of the U.S. Navy or any other agency of the U.S. government.

As a foundation for the comparative section on maritime transformations outside China, the volume examines carefully several cases of attempted transformation from the ancient world that may prove illuminating for those considering China's maritime prospects. Gregory Gilbert describes the case of Persia, which initially viewed the sea "as a barrier" but through devoting major financial resources was subsequently able to build "the first truly substantial navy in world history." In contrast, Barry Strauss' description of Sparta's efforts in the maritime realm illustrate that "the maritime option was problematic for Sparta. . . . It ran against the grain of an austere, inward-looking, arrogant, conservative, continental power." Like Persia, Rome saw some considerable success in maritime transformation, described by Arthur M. Eckstein as "simply stunning" in its dimensions. Eckstein also concludes, however, that Rome's maritime transformation was "superficial for a very long time [and] occurred at first only under the extreme pressure of circumstances." Jakub Grygiel, in evaluating the Ottoman Empire's exertions on the sea, suggests that "the most striking fact of Ottoman history is in fact the rapidity of the Ottoman naval rise . . . [and that they] succeeded in challenging, and defeating, the main Mediterranean naval power . . . [Venice]." This case reveals a continentalist approach to sea power, which stands in marked contrast to that of the classic maritime powers of Europe.

As the center of naval competition moved into the Atlantic and beyond during the modern era, a number of the major continental powers made earnest attempts at maritime transformation with limited success, however. According to James Pritchard, "French maritime transformations were characterized by enormous effort that yielded limited benefits and led generally to outright failure." Perhaps implying some vital strategic choices for Beijing, he concludes, "It seems clear that France could be a land power or a sea power but not both simultaneously." In another chapter with strong implications for China's evolving maritime strategy, Holger H. Herwig reflects on Adm. Alfred von Tirpitz's initiative to build a fleet by the "patient laying of stone upon stone," expressing Germany's yearning for a navy "as a symbol of industrial progress . . . [that] would be forward looking and progressive . . . [and] would "show the flag around the globe" while preventing Britain from severing Germany's sea-lanes. But he cautions strenuously against the temptation to "build first, design a strategy later" that had disastrous results for Germany. In discussing Russia's maritime development before World War I, Jacob W. Kipp asserts, "In contravention of Mahan's concept of sea power evolving out of a nations' civilian maritime calling, Russian naval power had to be planted and nurtured by an absolutist state directing a continental power," but this had rather mixed results. A final extremely relevant case for contemporary China concerns Soviet attempts to wield maritime power during the Cold War despite its "extremely unfavorable geostrategic position" with respect to maritime strategy. It remains to be seen whether China will embrace, as Milan Vego outlines, the eventual Soviet perspective that "any country that intends to be a major power must also be strong at sea"— whether Beijing will find its own naval exponent equivalent to the Kremlin's Adm. Sergei Gorshkov. These historical cases provide ample lessons— lessons that are presently being studied by Chinese strategists as they debate potential blueprints for Chinese sea power.

The volume's second section, "Chinese Maritime Transformations," examines selected Chinese attempts to become a more capable maritime power. Andrew R. Wilson recounts that "with the last of the great voyages commanded by the eunuch official Zheng He [郑和] in 1433, the Ming state . . . made a series of conscious decisions to step back from the maritime realm, shifting from a concerted agenda of aggressive navalism to a defensive continental focus." As Bruce A. Elleman demonstrates, Qing China initially focused on stabilizing its northern and western land frontiers. Suddenly confronted with the threat of rising British, French, and Japanese naval power in Asia, in addition to its internal political problems, it eventually purchased ships from abroad but had neither the reliable infrastructure nor the professional navy to operate them effectively in battle, with disastrous results. Thus, Qing "China's maritime defeats were directly due to the Qing decision not to modernize and Westernize its navy following the first Opium War." During the Cold War, Bernard Cole relates, China's naval development was constrained by U.S. dominance of maritime East Asia and later by internal policy debacles and deterioration of relations with the Soviet Union: The People's Liberation Army Navy (PLAN) was "viewed by its military and civilian masters as an organization with the primary mission of supporting army forces. Beijing's maritime concerns were defensive."

Looking to the Deng era and beyond, then, is China finally overcoming its historical difficulties to achieve enduring maritime development? While hardly discounting the challenges that Beijing continues to face, three chapters suggest that this may indeed be the case. In their review of China's ship-building and other marine industries, Gabriel Collins and Michael Grubb reveal that "China's current maritime transformation is to a large extent led by an exceedingly dynamic commercial maritime sector, which is in turn creating ample synergies for naval development," thereby offering a sound basis for transformation that was frequently lacking in other cases examined in this volume. In his chapter on the current state of PLAN development, Rear Adm. Eric A. McVadon, USN (Ret.), assesses that China "has moved dramatically over the last decade or so to modernize its naval forces . . . and is now advancing . . . toward making those forces a truly operational modern navy." In their chapter on the Chinese government-inspired historical study *The Rise of Great Powers*, Andrew S. Erickson and Lyle J. Goldstein suggest that Beijing is learning from other nations' historical experiences with maritime development: "a major conclusion . . . is the fundamental value of the market and international trade as drivers for national development and consequently national power." Finally, in his concluding chapter, Carnes Lord offers insights into the larger factors that have tended to influence the success or failure of maritime transformations. The sobering implication for China is that, while it is making dramatic and in some ways unprecedented progress, maritime transformation is a difficult and treacherous process that no modern land power has fully accomplished: "With the two (partial) exceptions [of Persia and Rome] . . . the historical record has not been kind to powers attempting maritime transformations."

Certain key questions with respect to maritime transformation will form the core intellectual threads found in each of the chapter case studies.

- What factors affect a continental state's decision to develop significant naval and maritime capabilities?
- What strategic objectives does it serve?
- What are the political or bureaucratic processes that make such a decision possible?
- How important is visionary political or military leadership?
- To what extent is a continentalist strategic culture an impediment to such a decision, and how is it overcome?
- To what extent do economic or commercial considerations drive maritime transformations?
- How does a transforming power understand and assess the trade-offs between land and naval strength?
- What are the operational handicaps that transforming maritime powers face, and how are these handicaps addressed?
- How do maritime transformations develop over time?
- What strategies do rival powers employ to counter transforming maritime states, and which of these strategies are most successful?

These questions will be examined in a series of historical case studies framed by thematic discussion and analysis.

It is also important to understand what this volume is not. It is not a treatise on sea power generally. Thus, the reader may be surprised to see rather little discussion of the conventional sea powers: Portugal, Holland, England, Japan, and the United States.[7] While some tendencies in these states are relevant, the intentional focus of the chosen case studies is rather on continental states with pronounced land-focused strategic orientations. Persia, Sparta, Rome, the Ottoman Empire, Germany, France, and Russia all fit this mold well and serve as useful test cases in which to examine the processes of attempted maritime transformation. In exploring both ancient experiences as well as non-European cases as part of this wide-ranging comparative analysis, the volume attempts to break substantial new ground, thus adding to the more conventional case studies of strategy in continental powers. The chapters in part 2 that address Chinese maritime development directly aim to cover China's modern maritime history comprehensively. Unfortunately, because of space constraints, there are some gaps. Thus, the foundations of Chinese sea power established during the Song and Yuan dynasties are not discussed in detail in this volume. Nevertheless, the crucial Ming case is treated in appropriate detail—and this case emerges as an interesting example, among the others, of a genuine maritime power undergoing reverse transformation. The Qing and Cold War cases fit the more conventional pattern illustrated in this volume. Three chapters at the end of the volume describe in considerable detail the actual processes of maritime transformation that are ongoing today in China: commercial, military, and intellectual.

To set the stage for deeper comparison and analysis of China's contemporary development in subsequent chapters, this introduction will briefly survey the intense debate now under way in Beijing regarding China's future trajectory and the role of maritime power in that development process.

China as Land or Sea Power?

It has long been widely acknowledged that China's squandering of its nascent maritime potential in the Ming and successive dynasties represented a tragic mistake of macrohistorical proportions. The following Chinese interpretation is quite typical:

> The enterprise of China's ocean development has a splendid history dating back to [Ming Dynasty admiral] Zheng He's seven voyages to the West. But its previous feudal rulers locked their doors against the world. They fettered the Chinese Nation's vigorous ocean-based development. This included especially the Ming and Qing Dynasty's severe prohibition of maritime [focus] for over 400 years. This repeatedly caused the Chinese Nation to miss favorable opportunities [that would have stemmed from] developing civilization from the sea. Then the Western battleships bombarded their way through the gate that China's feudal rulers had locked. Thenceforth, a succession of wars of invasion from the sea visited profound suffering as well as galling shame and humiliation on the Chinese Nation. The beautiful, abundant ocean gave forth only sorrow and tears.[8]

Unquestionably, China's "Century of National Humiliation" (百年国耻) is a powerful motivating force in Beijing's current drive to achieve maritime transformation. In 1995 an Academy of Military Science researcher argued that, in contrast to that of the West, "Chinese geostrategic thinking . . . is characterized by land power." More than a decade later, as China's power, influence, and openness have increased dramatically, a genuine debate regarding China's land/sea-power orientation is emerging in China. For the first time, a substantial number of analysts and officials contend that China is already a major maritime power and that its development in this realm should be further prioritized.

Yet it is far from certain that this will soon become a majority view and, hence, a decisive driver of national policy and military strategy. While even advocates of a continentalist school of thought accept the need for sea power "consciousness" and development, they nevertheless maintain that China must accept that historical and geostrategic conditions have made it a land power. In between these extremes, a number of analysts believe that China is both a land and a sea power, and that its strategic development must proceed accordingly. Given the mix of challenges and opportunities that China faces on its continental and maritime flanks, and increasingly in the wider world, these strategic choices for Beijing will become even more acute in the coming decades.

The Maritime Faction

As might be expected, the PLAN leadership is a strong proponent of China becoming a major maritime power. Writing in the official journal of the Communist Party of China Central Committee, PLAN commander Wu Shengli and political commissar Hu Yanlin review China's past two centuries of maritime history to argue that lack of naval power exposed China to disastrous attack by the "strong vessels and sharp cannons" of the West. "Only when the navy is strong can the maritime rights rise," they write, "which will bring the rise of the nation."

Moreover, China's sea power development can address the Taiwan issue, which "involves our national security and development—the full unification of our nation. It is also the key interest of the Chinese nation and one of the three important historical missions for our Party. To ensure the unification of our nation is the holy mission of our army. A powerful navy is a key force that can shock the 'Taiwan independence' separatists, and defend the unification of our nation."[9] Wu and Hu envision PLAN missions beyond and in addition to reunification with Taiwan, however: "In order to protect normal fishing, oceanic resource development, oceanic investigation and scientific tests, to maintain the safety of the oceanic transportation and the strategic passageway for energy and resources, ensure the jurisdiction of our nation to neighboring areas, continental shelf, and exclusive economic zones, and effectively safeguard our national maritime rights, we must build a powerful navy."[10]

This conception of China facing both challenges and opportunities from the sea is prevalent among Chinese analysts:

> As the democratic revolutionary pioneer Dr. Sun Yat-sen himself pointed out, in terms of world trends, a nation's rise and fall often lies not on land but at sea. It is maritime power that produces victors. . . . At present, the world's population is increasing severely, land resources are acutely decreasing, [and] environmental pollution is severe. One after another, nations have trained their sights on the sea. The strategic status and use of the sea are of obvious importance. Contradictions and contention for maritime rights and interests are increasingly violent. The 21st century is a Maritime Century. Facing the Maritime Century's call, the Chinese Nation's desire for resurgence has never been as strong, and its maritime connection has never been more inseparable.[11]

China's reliance on the seas has been growing constantly throughout the post-1978 reform period.[12] "The navy is concerned with China's sea power, and sea power is concerned with China's future development," states Zhang Wenmu, a prominent professor at the Center for Strategic Studies at the Beijing University of Aeronautics and Astronautics.[13] "If a nation lacks sea power, its development has no future."[14] Zhang allows that the sources of sea power have evolved over time: "In military history, command of the sea was at one point an important factor behind the rise and fall of nations. Today, in the 21st century, command of the sea based on the mastery of satellite communications technology, guided missile long-range attacks, and precision intercepting technology is still a decisive factor in determining a nation's rise and fall."[15] The lesson for China, in Zhang's view, is that "with its aviation and space undertakings taking big strides forward, China today is a flying dragon. But that is not enough, not by a long shot. China must also be a dragon in the deep pool of the western Pacific. Otherwise, it will not achieve the great revitalization of the entire Chinese nation."[16] This theme is echoed by two PLAN officers who argue forcefully that sea powers are more economically vital and less militarily vulnerable than land powers.[17]

A former member of the Chinese People's Political Consultative Conference and director of China's State Oceanic Administration has emphasized the need to "build a strong maritime nation [海洋强国]."[18] PLAN senior captain Xu Qi builds on this theme, emphasizing that "the country's long period of prosperity [as well as] the Chinese nation's existence, development, and great resurgence [all] increasingly rely on the sea."[19] Xu notes, "Historically, great powers struggling for supremacy have invariably focused their attention on the ocean and spared no efforts in pursuing their maritime geostrategic rivalries."[20]

In a major naval history treatise, which has reportedly entered the curriculum of China's naval academies,[21] PLAN deputy commander Vice Adm. Ding Yiping and his coauthors write, "In order to uphold national rights and resist foreign invasion, China must build a powerful navy, so as to solidify national defense and safeguard maritime rights and interests."[22]

The individuals cited above appear to see rapid PLAN development as an urgent priority. This is hardly unprecedented. As early as 1997, the director of a PLAN headquarters research institute wrote, "Establishing a Chinese maritime strategy has become a task of top importance."[23] In 2001 Adm. Zheng Ming, then director of the PLAN Armament and Technology Department, reportedly "stressed that the PLA must speed up the modernization of its naval forces so that China can transform from a large oceanic country into a strong ocean power at an early date."[24] Another article frames the issue in stark terms: "China faces a grim naval strategic environment in the 21st Century. If the unfavorable maritime situation is allowed to continue deteriorating, if we continue to be surrounded in our coastal waters, then how can we speak of China rising to prominence? How can Chinese naval power be promoted? How can China's maritime rights and interests be guaranteed? How can a country with just a 'brown water' navy win the respect of other countries for its naval power, or have any right to prattle on about becoming a world power or to carry out an Asia-Pacific strategy, let alone a global one?"[25] Zhang Wenmu contends that "what China is doing today in exercising its maritime rights falls far short of 'pursuing sea power.'"[26]

If the aforementioned views carry the day, to what uses might a strengthened PLAN be put? There is a wide variety of opinion on this matter. An article in the PLAN publication *Modern Navy* lists as possible threats "fishery disputes, controversies regarding continental shelves, fights over islands and reefs, ownership disputes over deep-sea resources, conflicts regarding maritime surveys, and disagreements related to maritime anti-terrorism."[27] Among advocates of Chinese sea power, there is a strong sense that China must have an independent military capability to defend its growing maritime interests. Since the seas are a "lifeline for the future existence and development of the nation," opines a recent article, while China does "not want to become an overlord, . . . neither can we let an overlord control our oceans."[28]

Safeguarding trade and economic development is a major theme of Chinese sea power proponents. According to Ni Lexiong, director of Shanghai Normal University's War and Culture Institute, "In the last decade or so, overseas trade has become more critical within our economic structure. 'The maritime lifeline' has become increasingly important. It has become necessary to establish a powerful naval force."[29] Two Logistics Command Academy specialists maintain that "the Navy is a necessary investment for a nation to safeguard and develop its overseas trade.[30] A nation's overseas trade requires strong naval support. This positive interaction is the basic rule of sea power development."[31] This economic rationale for PLAN development is seconded by Vice Adm. Feng Liang, deputy director of the Naval Command Academy's Strategy Teaching and Research Office.[32] Many analysts stress that China's coastal economic development has shifted its strategic center of gravity eastward.[33] Protecting seaborne energy is another major rationale for the expansion of Chinese sea power. Zhang strongly believes that China must control its sea-based oil supplies: "We must build up our navy as quickly as possible. . . . We must be prepared as early as possible. Otherwise, China may lose everything it has gathered in normal international economic activities, including its energy interest, in a military defeat."[34]

Maritime territorial sovereignty remains a major theme. A magazine published by the Academy of Military Science has called for a strong PLAN to defend China's more than 6,961 islands, which "are symbols of a nation's sovereignty, and the legal basis to delimit a nation's territorial sea," potentially creating situations in which—like their analogs around the world—"every island must be fought for, and every inch of sea must be owned."[35] In this vein, a Naval Command College analyst contends that China must fortify the Spratlys and Paracels as bases for forward deployment.[36]

The Continentalist Faction

China's growing sea power faction confronts a massive and well-established array of "continentalists," however, who maintain that China's geopolitical situation remains relatively unchanged, fear military confrontation with other powers, and believe that critical remaining challenges in China's internal development demand renewed prioritization. Perhaps the most visible representative of this school of thought is Ye Zicheng, a prominent Beijing University international relations scholar.[37] As part of his major theoretical key project for China's Ministry of Education, "Research on the International Environment of China's Peaceful Development: The Geopolitics of China's Peaceful Development Environment," Ye has specifically called for Beijing to "focus on peaceful development in its land space" and "not engage in armed expansion overseas." While some sea power advocates might dismiss the later scenario as hyperbole, Ye strongly believes that maintaining a "land power" strategy will "lower the possibility of a head-on clash" among "great powers competing for maritime supremacy."[38] Aircraft carriers permeate the maritime-continentalist debate, with members of the former faction often advocating their construction by China and members of the latter faction typically opposed. Ye is no exception: He questions the utility of China building vessels for a "blue water navy" and contends that advances in precision strike make aircraft carriers a poor investment for China.[39]

Ye maintains that "in the current stage we must regard the building of China's land homeland as the central task and develop land power as the strategic focus, [while] the development of sea power should be limited and should serve and be subordinate to the development of land power." China's strategists must remember "the lesson of the late Qing: When there are major problems in the building of a country's system, it is impossible to become a sea power just by developing maritime military forces."[40]

In sum, Ye contends,

> when choosing whether to focus on sea or land power or a balance of both, quite big arguments and differences are prone to arise in those countries that are both sea and land powers, and although many viewpoints of so-called balance of sea and land are produced, very few can truly achieve such a balance; the second is that those countries that were originally maritime and wanted to change their maritime nature and become both sea and land powers due to the limits of maritime space are all powerful countries. . . . [The histories of Russia, Japan, and the United States] tell us that mankind can to a certain extent overcome the constraints formed by the natural situation, but there is a limit here, and one will encounter defeat by going beyond the limit.[41]

Ye's interpretation of China's century of humiliation is quite different from that of China's maritime theorists: "The reason why China suffered aggression and bullying from western countries at the time—although the backwardness of sea power was an important factor—was first of all caused by the relative decline of China's land power, which meant that the western powers could win battles not only at sea but also on land." More broadly, "China's historical and cultural traditions and its national condition determine that China was a great land power for a long time in the past, and in the future it can only have the basic strategic orientation of being a great land power."[42] In an argument similar to that of American sinologist Robert Ross,[43] Ye asserts: "China's land power development strategy helps to ease the strategic contradictions between China's rise and the United States; the strategic special nature of Sino-U.S. geopolitics determines that the two countries can avoid the tragedy of strategic confrontation."[44]

In a similar vein, Feng Zhaokui contends,

> In the future, land, rather than the sea, will continue to be a main source of wealth to China, and will continue to be the most important space and the most important venue that the Chinese people rely on for survival and for seeking a greater development. Viewing from this perspective, we can say that it is true that we need to work hard to enhance our sea power and safeguard our maritime rights and interests, yet we must never ignore the need for protecting and utilizing more effectively the resources on our own land.[45]

Given these larger realities, the U.S. enjoys "absolute dominance" at sea. Beijing has "no intention, neither does it have the ability, to challenge the maritime hegemony of the United States."[46]

The "Maritime-Continental" Faction

Some Chinese analysts embrace a "middle-of-the-road" approach of developing both sea power and land power. Beijing University professor Li Yihu appears to have developed the intellectual basis for this school of thought most thoroughly thus far. China, Li explains, "is a geopolitical entity with a relatively high sea/land ratio, having a dual identity as both a land and sea power." This dual identity gives China independence and geostrategic flexibility. Yet China's dualistic identity poses dangers as well. While "in terms of maximum integration of geopolitical potential and power, China has the endowment conditions for being a world power . . . China is also very greatly geopolitically constrained, and if the situation of sea-land dichotomy cannot be changed, it will be driven by geopolitical inertia to a stage where it is forced to ward off blows." To make the best use of China's position, "we must replace the traditional simple mentality of attaching much importance to the land and little to the sea with the all-round mentality of overall sea and land planning. . . . [The PLAN] must switch from coastal water defense to ocean defense; their capability cannot just be limited to the first island chain but break through beyond it." The new strategic posture Li envisions requires "maintaining strong land power, and . . . developing strong sea power; for a certain time, however, developing strong sea power can be given a more priority status."[47]

Li Yihu believes that his nation is well placed to avoid the worst of a critical historical dynamic. China's "location on the eastern fringe of the Eurasian continent means that China is unlike 19th century Prussia and Austria, restricted to being surrounded by land powers, or countries like Germany and Russia that have struggled hard to find sea outlets, thus incurring lack of forceful land power backing."[48] Yet Li cautions that

> as a large country with both sea and land, when coveting the continental hinterland and developing in depth toward the Pacific, China is always facing a typical "historical predicament": Giving priority to developing land power will cause other powers such as Russia and India to feel insecure; giving priority to developing sea power will arouse suspicion among maritime countries such as the United States and Japan (a similar problem has in the past encumbered geopolitical powers possessing both sea and land: France, Germany, and the Soviet Union. Their external strategy always hovered between the continent and the ocean, to the extent that they would lose one out of concern for the other, and would fail in different geopolitical tussles).[49]

As with the other factions, there is a wide range of thinking within this one. Some maritime–continental advocates caution against overemphasizing sea power. "The present argument over the status of land and sea, centering on building aircraft carriers, somewhat emphasizes the importance of the sea, and there is no need at all to doubt this; what we need to guard against is the trend of boundlessly elevating the status of the sea and the navy, in which case we may go to another extreme."[50]

Some military analysts are also advocating for balanced development. A decade ago, former Academy of Military Sciences director Lt. Gen. Mi Zhenyu wrote that "China is a nation of both land and sea . . . [with] needs and opportunities in two directions, and also faces security challenges on two fronts. Having historically emphasized land and taken sea development lightly, China needs to foster a maritime consciousness among its citizens, develop a maritime economy, and develop its naval security forces."[51] Similarly, an article in *Modern Navy* (当代海军) suggests that "As a nation comprised of both land and sea, China can neither ignore the sea nor neglect the land."[52] On this point, PLAN Commander Wu Shengli has called for Beijing to "research and formulate our country's maritime security strategy."[53]

Undergirding these debates are the difficult trade-offs that China, like many continental powers surveyed in this volume, faces regarding maritime development. Factors competing for China's investment of capabilities and resources include the need to develop and purchase new high-technology weapons systems while improving salaries and benefits to attract and retain technically capable military personnel to operate them; the need to secure China's land borders (especially with the rise of Islamic fundamentalism and the appearance of a U.S. presence in Central Asia); and the need to maintain internal stability, in part by addressing China's social problems (e.g., income inequality, unemployment, social safety net, environmental protection). While some of these issues do not relate directly to naval or even military matters, they do present competition for China's vast (but still limited) resources and the attention of China's leaders.

Conversely, unless it wants to depend permanently on the goodwill of the U.S. Navy—something it seems reluctant to do—China may decide to secure militarily its seaborne trade and energy imports. Already, a major study led by Rear Adm. Yang Yi, PLAN, and advised by such influential bureaucrats as Dr. Qiu Yanping, deputy director of the Chinese Communist Party Central Committee's national security leading small group office, emphasizes the importance of securing China's sea lines of communication.[54] Other factors that may fuel PLAN development include the long-simmering issue of Taiwan's political status and the potential challenge of a strong Japanese Maritime Self-Defense Force.

Beijing's Emerging Maritime Orientation

While intense debate is ongoing among academics and also military analysts, a range of leadership pronouncements, state media statements, and official documents appear to reflect a gradually increasing maritime perspective at the highest levels of China's government. In recent years, Beijing has increased its naval and civil maritime capabilities, developed an increasingly broad-based maritime surveillance and security network, signed a variety of international conventions, and passed relevant domestic laws.

Statements by China's top leaders appear to focus increasingly on the nation's maritime interests. According to former PLAN political commissar Yang Huaiqing, "Comrade Deng Xiaoping unequivocally pointed out that seas and oceans are not a moat and China must face the world and go beyond seas and oceans in order to become prosperous and strong. Comrade Jiang Zemin has taken a further step and put forward a new outlook on seas and oceans that combines the outlook on territorial waters, outlook on marine economy and outlook on maritime security."[55] As President Jiang declared during a 1995 inspection of a PLAN unit on Hainan Island, "Developing and using the sea will have more and more significance to China's long-term development. We certainly need to understand the sea from a strategic high-point, and increase the entire nation's sea consciousness."[56] In a 1999 speech to the PLAN, Jiang stated, "the people's navy shoulders the sacred mission of safeguarding the sovereignty of our country's territorial waters and defending the state's maritime rights and interests."[57]

President and Central Military Commission chairman Hu Jintao appears to conceptualize China as a growing sea power. In a speech to China's powerful CMC (Central Military Commission) in September 2004, Hu introduced the "historical mission of the army" concept, which states that the PLA must "provide a security guarantee for national interests" for the party, and for ensuring national development.[58] According to a subsequent article in *Liberation Army Daily*, this included maritime rights and interests. Specifically, Hu Jintao "further enrich[ed] and expand[ed] the contents of the PLA's historical mission . . . [by] requir[ing] our military to not only pay close attention to the interests of national survival, but also national development interests; not only safeguard the security of national territory, territorial waters, and airspace, but also safeguard electromagnetic space, outer space, the ocean, and other aspects of national security."[59] On 27 December 2006, Hu reportedly "stressed, since our nation is a great maritime power [海洋大国],[60] our Navy plays an important role in defending our national sovereignty and security, as well as safeguarding our marine rights and interests, and hence is undertaking an honorable mission. . . . We must . . . solidly make good preparations for military competition so as to ensure effective fulfillment of tasks at all times."[61]

The Five Year Plan is an authoritative expression of overall national priorities. Whereas the outline for Beijing's 10th Five Year Plan made the general statement that China needed to "strengthen ocean resources surveys, development, protection, and management," and to "use and management of sea areas and protection of our maritime rights and interests," the 11th

Five Year Plan contained an entire section titled "Protect and Develop Ocean Resources." It called on China to "strengthen the protection of islands, . . . improve the demarcation of maritime areas, regulate the orderly use of the sea, [and to] develop in a focused way the resources in the exclusive economic zone, continental shelf, and international seabed."[62]

Chinese white papers reflect an increasing maritime focus. A "White Paper on Maritime Programs," promulgated by Beijing in 1998, laid out a "sustainable marine development strategy" to "safeguard the new international maritime order and the state's maritime rights and interests" and to improve management of maritime resources.[63] China's defense white papers provide increasing detail concerning naval issues. China's 2000 Defense White Paper alluded to "maritime rights and interests" as part of "border defense."[64] According to China's 2002 Defense White Paper, "taking effective defensive and administrative measures to defend national security and safeguard maritime rights and interests" were among the "goals and tasks of China's national defense."[65] Instead of merely mentioning China's maritime interests, the 2006 Defense White Paper explained how they might be defended. China "endeavors to strengthen its border and coastal defense, administration and control, and to build a modern border and coastal defense force," it stated. Beijing has promulgated "relevant laws and regulations and updated its border and coastal defense policies and regulations pursuant to international laws and practices." In an unprecedented statement, it charged the PLAN with achieving "gradual extension of strategic depth for offshore defensive operations and enhancing its capabilities in integrated maritime operations and nuclear counterattacks."[66] Given this record of commitment to maritime affairs dating back to Deng Xiaoping, China's new turn to the sea should not be underestimated.

Sailing into a Strategic Headwind?

China's uniqueness is often overstated. Moreover, stereotypes have the debilitating effect of hindering the ability of scholars and analysts to foresee change in the international system. The inertia of centuries of decline leads many to subject China's seapower prospects to significant skepticism.

The comparative approach taken in this volume, from one perspective, can serve to reinforce that skepticism. Almost all the cases in this volume illustrate the series of failures that have ensued when land powers attempted to transform themselves into genuine maritime powers. Whether in the form of the Ottoman fleet's failed attempt to project power into the Indian Ocean,

Germany's catastrophic lunge for sea power prominence, or the Soviet ambition that exposed itself as a "house of cards" in 1991, major land powers have encountered seemingly insuperable difficulties in trying to accomplish maritime transformation. In this sense, China's new maritime orientation is itself sailing into a strategic head wind—the obstacles, material and intellectual, that stand in the way of Beijing's emergence as a genuine maritime power are immense.

Still, this volume is not an indictment of China's new maritime orientation. In fact, a close reading of the cases presented herein reveals distinct differences between China and other historical powers that have attempted maritime transformation. Beijing has impressive commercial maritime dynamism, is discovering that it has a robust historical maritime tradition that predates the modern period and has recognized that stable relationships with continental neighbors will be a prerequisite for the growth of maritime power.[67] Given the security of China's eastern seaboard, its trade routes, and the delicate Taiwan issue, China also has vital national interests that are impelling its new maritime orientation. This is not simply a matter of the Kaiser or the Kremlin fancying big, shiny toys.

Because Chinese maritime development is a phenomenon of great complexity, however, readers are invited to draw their own conclusions with respect to the appropriateness (or lack thereof) of the various historical cases presented in this volume. In that sense the book may have greatest value as a heuristic tool that brings a variety of significant data and analysis together, offering insights to generations of future strategists.

China's evolution as a maritime power (or, alternatively, failure in that regard) will give rise to macropolitical phenomena in the twenty-first century of epic proportions—with the potential to overturn the balance of power in East Asia that has endured since the end of World War II. Of late, serious economists are beginning to entertain the possibility of a Chinese economy that one day outstrips that of the United States. Though perhaps still unlikely given the many constraints enumerated in this volume, it may not be too early to consider the possibility of some future era in which China (again) dominates the world's oceans.

Notes

This chapter represents only the authors' personal opinions and not the policies or analyses of the U.S. Navy or any other element of the U.S. government. The authors thank Ian Chong for his detailed reviews of this and several other chapters in this volume.

1. Paul Kennedy, "The Rise and Fall of Navies," *International Herald Tribune*, 5 April 2007, http://www.iht.com/articles/2007/04/05/opinion/edkennedy.php.

2. Ibid.

3. See, for example, Robert D. Kaplan, "America's Elegant Decline," *Atlantic Monthly* (November 2007), http://www.theatlantic.com/doc/prem/200711/america-decline; G. John Ikenberry, "The Rise of China and the Future of the West: Can the Liberal System Survive?" *Foreign Affairs* (January/February 2008): 23–37.

4. Alan M. Wachman, *Why Taiwan? Geostrategic Rationales for China's Territorial Integrity* (Stanford, CA: Stanford University Press, 2007), 41.

5. In the field of international relations, there is, for example, Paul M. Kennedy, *The Rise and Fall of the Great Powers: Economic Change and Military Conflict from 1500 to 2000* (New York: Vintage Books, 1989); John J. Mearsheimer, *The Tragedy of Great Power Politics* (New York: Norton, 2001); Peter J. Katzenstein, *A World of Regions: Asia and Europe in the American Imperium* (Ithaca, NY: Cornell University Press, 2005); John Ikenberry, *After Victory: Institutions, Strategic Restraint, and the Rebuilding of Order after Major Wars* (Princeton, NJ: Princeton University Press, 2001); Hendrik Spruyt, *The Sovereign State and Its Competitors: An Analysis of Systems Change* (Princeton, NJ: Princeton University Press, 1994); Stephen M. Walt, *The Origins of Alliances* (Ithaca, NY: Cornell University Press, 1987); Jack L. Snyder, *Myths of Empire: Domestic Politics and International Ambition* (Ithaca, NY: Cornell University Press, 1991); William C. Wohlforth, *The Elusive Balance: Power and Perceptions during the Cold War* (Ithaca, NY: Cornell University Press, 1993); Niall Ferguson, *Empire: The Rise and Demise of the British World Order and the Lessons for Global Power* (New York: Basic Books, 2003). The method finds increasing resonance in China studies: see, for example, Thomas J. Christensen, *Useful Adversaries: Grand Strategy, Domestic Mobilization, and Sino-American Conflict, 1947–1958* (Princeton, NJ: Princeton University Press, 1996); and Mingxin Pei, *From Reform to Revolution: The Demise of Communism in China and the Soviet Union* (Cambridge, MA: Harvard University Press, 1996).

6. For a brilliant exposition of this danger, see Yuen Foong Khong, *Analogies at War: Korea, Munich, Dien Bien Phu, and the Vietnam Decisions of 1965* (Princeton, NJ: Princeton University Press, 1992).

7. Some might argue that the United States is an example of a continental power that successfully transformed itself into a global naval power. Indeed, it was not until the late nineteenth and early twentieth century and Theodore Roosevelt's construction of the Great White Fleet that the United States became a full-fledged naval power. It is true that the United States was initially preoccupied with continental expansion westward, that the British were able to burn Washington, D.C., in the War of 1812, and that much of the Civil War was fought on land. One reason the

United States supported the Open Door policy in China, in fact, was the recognition that it lacked the naval and force projection capabilities to compete militarily against Japan and Russia.

Unlike the continental powers surveyed in this volume, however, the United States had a robust tradition of domestic shipbuilding and overseas maritime commerce that predated its founding as a nation. Moreover, thanks to its uniquely favorable land borders, the United States is not a continental power in the traditional sense because it has not faced substantial continental threats—in the same way that Portugal and Holland are not, despite possessing nontrivial land borders. As a maturing power, therefore, the United States did not face the difficult choices in geostrategic prioritization that so beset the true continental powers studied in this volume. As such, scrutinizing its course of naval development would not be particularly instructive in elucidating this volume's central questions. The issue is addressed to some extent, however in the "United States" section of the chapter on "China Studies the Rise of Great Powers" by Erickson and Goldstein.

8. 李兵 [Li Bing], 海军英豪: 人民海军英模荟萃 [*Naval Heroes: An Assembly of Heroic Models from the People's Navy*] (Beijing: Sea Tide Press, 2003), 1.

9. 吴胜利, 胡彦林 [Wu Shengli, Commander of the Navy, and Hu Yanlin, Political Commissar of the Navy; edited by Wang Chuanzhi], "锻造适应我军历史使命要求的强大人民海军" ["Building a Powerful People's Navy That Meets the Requirements of the Historical Mission for Our Army"], 求事 [*Seeking Truth*], 16 July 2007, no. 14, http://www.qsjournal.com.cn/qs/20070716/GB/qs^459^0^10.htm, OSC# CPP20070716710027.

10. Ibid.

11. Li Bing, *Naval Heroes*, 1–3.

12. 徐立凡 [Xu Lifan], staff reporter for *Caijing* Magazine, "三大现实挑战要求中国从海洋大国成为海洋强国" ["Three Big, Actual Challenges that Require China to Go from a Great Maritime Nation to a Strong Maritime Nation"], 华夏时报 [*China Times*], 12 July 2005, www.china.com.cn/chinese/zhuanti/zhxxy/913118.htm.

13. For similar sentiment, see 姚文怀 [Rear Adm. Yao Wenhuai], Deputy Director of the PLAN Political Department, "建设强大海军, 维护我国海洋战略利益" ["Build a Powerful Navy, Defend China's Maritime Strategic Interests"], 国防 [*National Defense*], no. 7 (2007): 1–2.

14. 张文木 [Zhang Wenmu], "经济全球化与中国海权" ["Economic Globalization and Chinese Sea Power"], 战略与管理 [*Strategy & Management*], no. 1 (2003): 96.

15. 张文木 [Zhang Wenmu], "现代中国需要新的海权观" ["Modern China Needs a New Concept of Sea Power"], 环球时报 [*Global Times*], 12 January 2007, http://www.people.com.cn/GB/paper68/, OSC# CPP20070201455002.

16. Ibid.

17. 郝廷兵, 杨志荣 [Hao Tingbing and Yang Zhirong], 海上力量与中华民族的伟大复兴 [*Sea Power and the Chinese Nation's Mighty Resurgence*] (Beijing: National Defense University Press, 2005), 30–33.

18. 张登义 [Zhang Dengyi], "管好用好海洋, 建设海洋强国" ["Manage and Use the Ocean Wisely, Establish a Strong Maritime Nation"], 求实 [*Seeking Truth*], no. 11 (2001): 48.

19. *China Military Science* is published by the PLA's Academy of Military Sciences. Unless otherwise indicated, quotations in this paragraph are from 徐起 [Xu Qi], "21世纪初海上地缘战略与中国海军的发展" ["Maritime Geostrategy and the Development of the Chinese Navy in the Early 21st Century"], 中国军事科学 [*China Military Science*] 17, no. 4 (2004): 75–81. Translation by Andrew Erickson and Lyle Goldstein published in *Naval War College Review* 59, no. 4 (autumn 2006).

20. Ibid.

21. Chin Chien-li, "A Core Figure in the Communisty Party of China's Fight with Taiwan—A Profile of Vice Admiral Ding Yiping, First Deputy Commander of the PLA Navy," *Chien Shao* [*Frontline*], no. 194 (1–30 April 2007): 58–62, OSC# CPP20070418710009.

22. 丁一平, 李洛荣, 龚连娣 [Ding Yiping, Li Luorong, and Gong Liandi], 世界海军史 [*The History of World Navies from the Chinese Perspective*] (Beijing: 海潮出版社 [Sea Tide Press], 2000), 429.

23. PLAN Senior Colonels Yan Youqiang and Chen Rongxing, "On Maritime Strategy and the Marine Environment," [*China Military Science*] no. 2 (May 1997): 81–92, OSC# FTS19971010001256.

24. Wang Cho-chung, "PRC Generals Call for Reinforcing Actual Strength of Navy," 中國時報 [*China Times*], 26 March 2001, OSC# CPP20010326000046.

25. 谢值军 [Xie Zhijun], "21世纪亚洲海洋: 群雄争霸, 中国怎么办" ["Asian Seas in the 21st Century: With So Many Rival Navies, How Will China Manage?"], 军事文摘 [*Military Digest*], 1 Feb 2001, pp. 20–22, OSC# CPP20010305000214.

26. 张文木 [Zhang Wenmu], professor at the Center for Strategic Studies, Beijing University of Aeronautics and Astronautics, "现代中国需要新的海权观" ["Modern China Needs a New Concept of Sea Power"], 环球时报 [*Global Times*], 12 January 07, http://www.people.com.cn/GB/paper68/, OSC# CPP20070201455002.

27. 刘江平, 追月 [Liu Jiangping and Zhui Yue], "21世纪经略海洋: 中国海军将何去何从" ["Management of the Sea in the 21st Century: Whither the Chinese Navy?"], 当代海军 [*Modern Navy*], June 2007, pp. 6–9, OSC# CPP20070628436012.

28. 展华云 [Zhan Huayun], "经略海洋—叩响大战略之门" ["Strategic Use of the Seas—Knocking at the Door of a Grand Strategy"], 当代海军 [*Modern Navy*], May 2007, pp. 17–19, OSC# CPP20070626436011.

29. Chiang Hsun, "China's New Strategy to Strengthen Its Maritime Awareness," 亞洲週刊 [*Asiaweek*], 11 June 2006, pp. 38–40, OSC# CPP20060609715028.

30. For a similar argument on this point, see 何家成, 邹芳, 赖志军 [He Jiacheng, Zou Lao, and Lai Zhijun], Naval Command Academy, "国际军事安全形势及我国的国防发展战略" ["The International Military Situation and China's Strategy of National Defense Economic Development"], 军事经济研究 [*Military Economic Research*], no. 1 (2005): 12.

31. 朗丹阳, 刘分良 [Lang Danyang and Liu Fenliang], "海陆之争的历史检视" ["Historical Exploration into the Land-Sea Dispute"], 中国军事科学 [*China Military Science*], no. 1 (2007): 46.

32. 冯梁 [Feng Liang], professor and deputy director, and 张晓林 [Zhang Xiaolin], professor in the Strategy Teaching and Research Office, Naval Command Academy, "论和平时期海军的战略运用" ["A Discussion of the Navy's Strategic Use in Peacetime"], 中国军事科学 [*China Military Science*], no. 3 (2001): 78.

33. See, for example, Zhang Huayun, "海上安全环境对战略的影响与虎视" ["Impact and Inspiration of Maritime Security Environment on Strategy"], 当代海军 [*Modern Navy*], no. 8 (August 2007): 10.

34. 张文木 [Zhang Wenmu], "中国能源安全与政策选择" ["China's Energy Security and Policy Choices"], 世界经济与政治 [*World Economics & International Politics*], no. 5 (May 2003): 11–16, FBIS# CPP20030528000169.

35. 高新生 [Gao Xinsheng], 沈阳炮兵学院 [Shenyang Artillery Academy], "岛屿与新世纪中国海防建设" ["Islands and China's Coastal Defense in the New Century"], 国防 [*National Defense*] (November 2006): 45–47.

36. 刘一建 [Liu Yijian], Naval Command Academy, "中国未来的海军建设战略" ["The Future of China's Naval Development and Naval Strategy"], 战略与管理 [*Strategy & Management*], no. 5 (May 1999): 98.

37. For Ye's most thorough argument yet of why China developed as a land power, see 叶自成 [Ye Zicheng], 陆权发展与大国兴衰: 地缘政治环境与中国和平发展的地缘战略选择 [*Land Power Development and the Rise and Fall of Great Powers: The Geopolitical Environment and Geostrategic Choices for China's Peaceful Development*] (Beijing: 新星出版社 [New Star Press], 2007). This book is affiliated with China's Ministry of Education Project on Resolving Major Theoretical Issues (国家教育部重大理论攻关课题) and two other projects.

38. 叶自成 [Ye Zicheng], "中国的和平发展: 陆权的回归与发展" ["China's Peaceful Development: The Return and Development of Land Power"], 世界经济与政治 [*World Economics & Politics*] (February 2007): 23–31, OSC# CPP20070323329001.

39. 叶自成 [Ye Zicheng], "中国海权须从属于陆权" ["China's Sea Power Must Be Subordinate to Its Land Power"], 国际先驱导报 [*International Herald Leader*], 2 March 2007, OSC# CPP20070302455003.

40. 叶自成 [Ye Zicheng], "从大历史观看地缘政治" ["Geopolitics from a Greater Historical Perspective"], 现代国际关系 [*Contemporary International Relations*], 20 June 2007, OSC# CPP20070712455001.

41. Ibid.

42. 叶自成 [Ye Zicheng], "中国的和平发展: 陆权的回归与发展" ["China's Peaceful Development: The Return and Development of Land Power"], 世界经济与政治 [*World Economics & Politics*] (February 2007): 23–31, OSC# CPP20070323329001.

43. Robert S. Ross, "The Geography of the Peace: East Asia in the Twenty-first Century," *International Security* 23, no. 4 (Spring 1999): 81–118.

44. Ye, "China's Peaceful Development."

45. 冯昭奎 [Feng Zhaokui], "中国崛起不能只靠走向海洋" ["China's Rise Cannot Rely Only on Heading towards the Sea"], 环球时报 [*Global Times*], 23 March 2007, http://www.people.com.cn/GB/paper68/, OSC# CPP20070402455001.

46. Ibid.

47. 李义虎 [Li Yihu], "从海陆二分到海陆统筹—对中国海陆关系的在审视" ["Sea and Land Power: From Dichotomy to Overall Planning—A Review of the Relationship between Sea and Land Power"], *Contemporary International Relations* (August 2007): 1–7, OSC# CPP20070911329003.

48. Ibid.

49. Ibid.

50. 程亚文 [Cheng Yawen], "欧洲大陆是中国利益中心" ["The Eurasian Continent Is the Center of Gravity of China's Interests"], 环球时报 [*Global Times*], 15 November 2007, OSC# CPP20071211587001. For a range of related views, see 冯梁 [Feng Liang], 战略教研室 [Strategy Teaching and Research Section], and 段廷志 [Duan Tingzhi], 第二政治理论教研 [Political Affairs Teaching and Research Section No. 2], Naval Command College, "Characteristics of China's Sea Geostrategic Security and Sea Security Strategy in the New Century," 中国军事科学 [*China Military Science*], January 2007, pp. 22–29; 王淑梅, 石家铸, 徐明善 [Wang Shumei, Shi Jiazhu, and Xu Mingshan], "履行军队历史使命, 树立科学海权观" ["Carry Out the Historic Mission of the Military and Establish the Scientific Concept of Sea Rights"], 中国军事科学 [*China Military Science*] (February 2007): 145–46; 张炜 [Senior Col. Zhang Wei], Navy Research Institute Researcher, "国家海上安全理论探要" ["Exploring National Sea Security Theories"], 中国军事科学 [*China Military Science*] (January 2007): 84–91.

51. Lt. Gen. Mi Zhenyu, "A Reflection on Geographic Strategy," *China Military Science* (February 1998): 6–14, OSC# FTS19980616000728.

52. Zhan, "Strategic Use of the Seas."

53. 刘文英 [Liu Wenying], "吴胜利司令员在十届全国人大五次会议上审议 '政府工作报告' 时强调: 制定国家海洋安全战略, 加大军事设施保护力度" ["When Deliberating on the 'Government Work Report' at the Fifth Session of the 10th NPC, Navy Commander Wu Shengli Calls for Formulating the State's Maritime Security Strategy, Enhancing Protection of Military Facilities"] 人民海军 [*People's Navy*], 12 March 2007, p. 2.

54. 杨毅, 主编 [Yang Yi, Chief Editor], 国家安全战略研究 [*Research on National Security Strategy*] (Beijing: 国防大学出版社 [National Defense University Press], 2007), 274, 289, 323–24. For the importance to China of maritime development in general, see also 276, 292, 294–95.

55. 杨怀庆 [former PLAN political commissar Yang Huaiqing], "指导人民海军建设的强大思想武器" ["A Powerful Ideological Weapon for Guiding the Building of the People's Navy in the New Period—On Studying Jiang Zemin's Important Thinking on Navy Building"], 求实 [*Seeking Truth*], no. 15 (August 2000): 26, OSC# CPP20000816000070. For a similar argument, see Zhan, "Strategic Use of the Seas," 19.

56. 焦永科 [Jiao Yongke], "弘扬海洋文化, 发展海洋经济" ["Enhance Maritime Culture, Develop the Maritime Economy"], 中国海洋报 [*China Maritime Report*], no. 1407, 国家海洋局海洋发展战略研究所 [Ocean Development Strategy Research Institute, State Oceanic Administration], http://www.soa.gov.cn/hyjww/hyzl/2007/03/20/1174354271537153.htm; "名人论海洋—中国领导人对海军建设的指示" ["Famous People Debating the Sea—The Instructions of China's Leaders Regarding Naval Construction"], Working Paper of the Ocean Development Strategy Research Institute, 国家海洋局网站 [Office of the State Oceanic Administration website], available online 8 December 2005, http://www.soa.gov.cn/zhanlue/hh/index.html; gongxue.cn/guofangshichuang/ShowArticle.asp?ArticleID=7086.

57. Xinhua News Agency, 27 May 1999.

58. "Earnestly Step Up Ability Building within CPC Organizations of Armed Forces," 解放军报 [*Liberation Army Daily*], 13 December 2004, http://www.chinamil.com.cn/site1/xwpdxw/2004-12/13/content_86435.htm.

59. 刘明福, 程钢, 孙学富 [Liu Mingfu, Cheng Gang, and Sun Xuefu], "人民军队历史使命的又一次与时俱进" ["The Historical Mission of the People's Army Once Again Advances with the Times"], 解放军报 [*Liberation Army Daily*], 8 December 2005, p. 6. See also Yang, *Research on National Security Strategy*, 323.

60. A state-owned Chinese periodical interprets the phrase "great sea nation" to mean that China has massive maritime areas, economic interests, and "sea rights." 秦皇 [Qin Huang], "航母与国家健康指数" ["Aircraft Carriers and the Index of National Health"], 环球人物 [*Global People*] (1 March 2007): 48, OSC# CPP20070326332003.

61. 丁玉宝, 郭益科, 周根山 [Ding Yubao, Guo Yike, and Zhou Genshan], "胡锦涛在会见海军第一次党代表会代表时强调: 按照革命化现代化正规化相统一的规则, 锻造适应我军历史使命要求的强大人民海军" ["When Hu Jintao Met with the Naval Delegates at the 10th Party Congress, He Emphasized Building a Powerful People's Navy That Meets the Requirements to Accomplish Historical Missions of Our Army in Accordance with the Principle of Unifying Revolutionization, Modernization, and Standardization"], 人民海军 [*People's Navy*] (28 December 2006): 1.

62. Xinhua, 15 March 2001.

63. Xinhua, 28 May 1998.

64. Xinhua, 16 October 2000.

65. Xinhua, 9 December 2002.

66. See "China's National Defense in 2006," Information Office of the State Council, People's Republic of China, 29 December 2006, http://www.fas.org/nuke/guide/china/doctrine/wp2006.html.

67. On this last point, see Jakub Grygiel, *Great Powers and Geopolitical Change* (Baltimore, MD: Johns Hopkins University Press, 2006), 169–70; M. Taylor Fravel, *Strong Borders, Secure Nation: Cooperation and Conflict in China's Territorial Disputes* (Princeton, NJ: Princeton University Press, 2008).

China Goes to Sea

PART I

Premodern Era

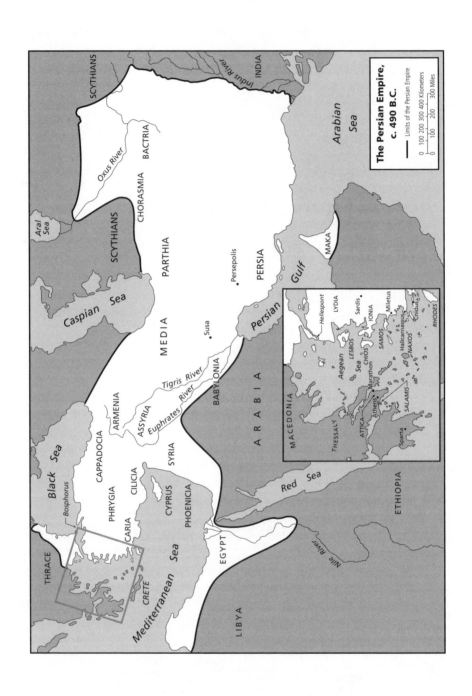

The Persian Empire, c. 490 B.C.

— Limits of the Persian Empire

0   100 200 300 400 Kilometers
0   100   200   300 Miles

SCYTHIANS

Indus River

INDIA

Oxus River

BACTRIA

CHORASMIA

SCYTHIANS

Aral
Sea

PARTHIA

Arabian
Sea

Persepolis

PERSIA

Caspian
Sea

MAKA

MEDIA

Susa

Persian
Gulf

Tigris River

Euphrates River

BABYLONIA

ARABIA

Black
Sea

ARMENIA

ASSYRIA

CAPPADOCIA

Bosphorus

PHRYGIA

CILICIA

SYRIA

CYPRUS

PHOENICIA

Red Sea

CARIA

THRACE

CRETE

Mediterranean
Sea

EGYPT

Nile River

LIBYA

ETHIOPIA

Inset:

Hellespont

LYDIA

Sardis

IONIA

Miletus

SAMOS

Halicarnassus

Cnidus

RHODES

LESBOS

CHIOS

NAXOS

Aegean
Sea

MACEDONIA

THESSALY

Marathon

ATTICA

Athens

SALAMIS

Sparta

Gregory Gilbert

Persia: Multinational Naval Power

I am trained in my hands and in my feet: as a horseman, I am a good horse-man; as a bowman, I am a good bowman, both on foot and on horseback; as a spearman, I am a good spearman, both on foot and on horseback.

—Darius I[1]

SO CLAIMED THE PERSIAN "KING OF KINGS" Darius in an inscription found on his monument at Naqš-i Rustam.[2] This is typical of the royal inscriptions that established the ideology of ancient Persian kingship. Military prowess, both physically and mentally, emphasized the image of the king as a good warrior and a divine majesty. The ideology does not, conversely, reflect the changing nature of the Persian realm, for although the Persian Empire was traditionally and ideologically a land power, it underwent a maritime transformation between 550 and 490 BC, from which time it became a first-rate sea power. Indeed, it has a strong claim to being the first truly great maritime power in world history.

Despite the lack of evidence for maritime traditions or nautical skills in the Persian written record, it is possible to reconstruct the rise of Persian sea power from other surviving historical documents and archaeological remains.[3] This chapter examines such evidence to describe the nature of the Persian maritime transformation and then interprets the evidence to improve our understanding of how and why the ancient Persians became a formidable sea power.

Precursors to the Persian Empire

The Persian Empire was the successor to a series of ancient Near Eastern empires that, from at least 1100 BC, had grown in sophistication, complexity, and size to effectively control much of the civilized world. The Neo-Assyrian Empire (883–612 BC) effectively used military force to dominate the neighboring great kingdoms. The Assyrians used military terror as a political weapon. They conducted annual campaigns to collect tribute and acquire new subject states. Any resistance or reluctance by these new states to pay tribute was overcome using extreme violence, and such methods acted as a deterrent for any other states that may have considered opposing Assyrian rule.[4] This form of psychological warfare was reinforced by forced displacement of rebellious subjects within the Assyrian empire, most famously the deportation of a Jewish community to Babylon.[5] At its height the Neo-Assyrian Empire included Mesopotamia, Syria, Phoenicia, and (for a short time) Egypt, as well as much of the highlands of Anatolia (modern Turkey) and Persia (modern Iran). The Assyrian subject states soon evolved into provinces in which subject rulers were replaced with Assyrian governors and a centralized bureaucracy reported regularly to the Assyrian king.

The Assyrian Empire originated in the land-locked kingdom centered upon the city of Assur in northern Mesopotamia. As with all other empire-builders in the ancient Near East, it was a land-based military power, lacking the maritime capabilities and nautical skills required to effectively utilize the sea. Nevertheless, the genesis of Persian sea power may be found in the interaction between the Assyrian rulers and the maritime communities of the eastern Mediterranean—particularly the Phoenicians and the Egyptians.

The Phoenicians occupied a strip of the Syrian-Palestinian coast, including much of the modern coastline of Lebanon. Although connected by a common language and cultural traditions, Phoenicia did not consist of a single state; rather it contained numerous coastal city-states, each with its own ruler and trade routes, and trading colonies throughout the Mediterranean. The Assyrian army incorporated the Phoenician cities into their empire in a series of swift campaigns along the Syrian-Palestinian coastline, with little military opposition. The Assyrians were initially content to leave the Phoenician cities in relative political autonomy so they could use Phoenician expertise in maritime trade to obtain the goods they required. In effect, the Assyrian kings relied upon the flow of Phoenician maritime communications as a major source of their own commercial power. Occasionally one or a few of the Phoenician city-states would rebel against Assyrian rule, and the Assyrian army would crush the rebellion and introduce direct rule by an Assyrian governor.

On the one hand, Phoenician shipping continued to trade throughout the Mediterranean to help finance the Assyrian Empire. On the other hand, the Phoenician city-states were levied to provide specialist services for the empire. Phoenician mariners were requisitioned as skilled labor for imperial projects along the eastern Mediterranean coast as well as in the Assyrian heartland. Phoenician ships were used to transport the Assyrian army on a number of campaigns along the Mediterranean coast (after 734 BC).[6] While the Assyrians' expansion did not extend to the islands of Cyprus or the Aegean, it is clear that they relied upon Phoenician ships during their campaigns in Egypt. There is also evidence that Phoenician ships and sailors were used to help transport Assyrian troops on campaign to the vicinity of Elam in the Persian Gulf.[7] The movement of troops and supplies by ship was an obvious advantage to the Assyrians, even if they may not have fully understood the flexibility and opportunities that the maritime environment gave them. Their strategies remained land-based. Phoenician mariners and shipping were also used to their advantage in the maritime trade along the Euphrates and Tigris rivers.[8]

The Egyptians had a long association with the coastal city-states of Syria-Palestine, and they competed with the Assyrians for hegemony in this area. Egyptian interference eventually prompted the Assyrians to invade Egypt, which they did for the first time in 674 BC, marching overland through the Sinai;[9] in subsequent campaigns they burnt the Egyptian capital at Memphis, conquered the northern provinces, and put down several rebellions.[10] But the Assyrians were unable to dominate all of Egypt. Like the Phoenicians, the Egyptians had a long maritime tradition and substantial naval resources.[11] It would appear that the Assyrians did not understand that the control of Egypt was in significant part a maritime endeavor; hence, despite a series of campaigns and the capture of numerous cities, they were unable to solidify their hold on the country. The Assyrians were forced to rely upon one of their Egyptian vassals, the Prince of Sais in the western Nile delta, to help overcome resistance elsewhere in Egypt, but this policy ultimately led to a dramatic increase in Saite power. In 664 BC, the Saite ruler Psamtek I finally drove the Assyrians out and proclaimed himself king of Egypt.

The native Egyptian Saite kings of the 26th dynasty ruled Egypt until they were conquered by the Persians in 525 BC.[12] The Saite dynasty managed a resurgence of Egypt's power in the ancient Near East, much of which was based upon a strengthening of trade links with Greece and Phoenicia, and the development of Egyptian sea power. The Egyptian kings hired Ionians and Carians, from Asia-Minor, as mercenaries and used their warships as part of the Egyptian navy.[13] The Saite Egyptians were "friends of the Greeks."[14] King Psamtek I (664–610 BC) was able to project Egyptian military forces far inland along the coast of Syria-Palestine in opposition to the Babylonians (the major Near Eastern empire at the time). Psamtek's successor, Nekau II (610–595 BC), constructed a fleet of war galleys with rams (most likely biremes) for use in both the Mediterranean and the Red Sea. He also began the construction of a canal running from the Nile to the Red Sea, and he sponsored exploration of the African coast. King Apries (589–570 BC) continued to oppose the Babylonian Empire with a series of campaigns against Cyprus and Phoenicia, in which good use was made of the fleet. King Amasis (570–526 BC) is recorded as the first foreigner to conquer Cyprus and to make it a tribute-paying subject state,[15] and he defeated the Babylonians when they attempted to invade Egypt. The Egyptians, however, became alarmed at the rapid rise of the Persians after Cyrus II (559–530 BC) ascended the Persian throne. To deal with the rising Persian menace, the Saite king formed a grand alliance in defense of the east Mediterranean consisting of Egypt, Croesus of Lydia (in Anatolia, part of modern Turkey), Sparta (in Greece), and the Babylonians.[16]

By the time the Assyrians were expelled from Egypt, the Assyrian Empire was in gradual decline. By 512 BC it had imploded following numerous internal revolts and the consolidation of the rival Median kingdom (northwest Iran). Most of Mesopotamia, Syria, and Phoenicia became part of a new empire formed by the kings of Babylon. Although a number of kingdoms resisted Babylonian rule, they were soon overcome by the same methods the Assyrians had used. Massacres, destruction, and deportations soon convinced the surviving rulers to agree to Babylonian domination. The Babylonians also used Phoenician maritime resources in support of their empire, and although the evidence is sparse, it is most likely that the Phoenicians were left as semiautonomous entities, as they had been under the Assyrian Empire. In the north, the Medes inherited what was left of the Assyrian domain to form their own Median Empire. The Egyptians, always wary of the most powerful empire of the ancient Near East, then changed their policy from opposing the Assyrians to opposing the Babylonians while they courted alliance with the kingdom of Lydia and the Greek city-states.

The important points to note from this summary are that the Assyrian and Babylonian empires both used the maritime resources of the Phoenician city-states in support of their imperial goals, albeit in mostly land-based strategies, and that the Egyptian opposition to these Near Eastern empires had traditionally relied upon the use of sea power. Both of these factors significantly influenced the Persian maritime transformation that commenced during the last quarter of the sixth century BC.

Establishing the Land-based Empire

Prior to 560 BC the Persian kingdom, with its capital Persepolis (modern Takht-i Jamshid, near Shiraz in southwest Iran), was a relatively insignificant kingdom consisting of farmers and nomads organized into a number of tribal groupings.[17] The Persians were subjects of the Median Empire, but they were also closely related to the Medes, being cultural descendants of the same Iranian people and speaking a dialect of the same Iranian language. As such, Cyrus was able to unite the Persian tribes under his rule while at the same time attaining high command within the Median army.[18] In time his military and political skills also gained him many admirers and supporters among the Medes as well as the other Iranian subject peoples.

Cyrus effectively usurped the Median kingship between 553 and 550 BC, and in a rapid series of decisive battles subjugated his opponents within the Median Empire, while his supporters—whether Medes or Persians—retained their positions within the newly created Persian Empire.[19] Initially Cyrus' imperial administration was able to capitalize on the valuable experience in imperial statecraft gained by the Medes and the Assyrians before them. The makeup of Cyrus' military forces was also inherited from the Medes and the Assyrians; it emphasized elite cavalry, archers, and spearmen, supported when required by levy spearmen.[20] Consolidation of the new Persian Empire was not enough for Cyrus, however. After mastering the Iranian plateau, he turned the Persian army against Croesus of Lydia, and in another quick campaign conquered much of Anatolia.[21] With Sardis (modern Sart in Turkey) under Persian control, the Ionian Greeks as well as the indigenous peoples of the Mediterranean coasts of Turkey (Phrygians, Carians, and Lycians) felt exposed and quickly sought an accommodation with the Persian king; the mainland Ionian Greeks were allowed to retain some political control as semiautonomous city-states within the empire.

The offshore Greek cities, such as Chios, Mytilene, and Samos, did not feel threatened because the Persians did not have naval forces capable of projecting their land forces into the Mediterranean.[22] Cyrus then turned toward the Babylonian Empire, the other successor to the Assyrian Empire. In 539 BC he defeated the Babylonians and was given entry into Babylon, not as a conqueror but—at least according to his propaganda—as the savior of the Babylonian god Marduk.[23]

This leads us to consider the Persian view of empire, which differed significantly from the Assyrian and Babylonian views. Each city or district of the Persian "known world" was idealized as either within the realm of "truth" (ruled by the Persian king of kings) or under the agents of anarchy and darkness. Darius expressed the ideal when he represented his power as "a force for good." As his inscription states: "Much of the evil that had been committed, I turned into good. The countries that fought each other, whose peoples killed each other, I fixed, by the grace of Ahura-Mazda, so that their peoples did not kill each other, and I restored each one to its place."[24]

How did this image of the benign Persian Empire translate into reality? There are many instances in which the traditional political and cultural structures of the conquered peoples were left unchanged under Persian rule even though there is also evidence for the introduction of strong imperial controls and the exercise of administrative authority. Persian subjects were given a remarkable degree of autonomy and were allowed, in particular, to continue to worship their own gods. Compared with the Assyrians' deliberate use of terror, Persian rule was one of tolerance, provided their subjects did not challenge Persian policies or administrative decisions.

In addition to his conquests in the west, Cyrus attacked the Bactrians and Scythian kingdoms in northeast Iran, Afghanistan, and Central Asia (modern Turkistan).[25] These were mostly light cavalry affairs, campaigns involving skirmishes and maneuver rather than battles of attrition. It was during one of these campaigns that a Persian army was destroyed and the king killed (530 BC).[26] In fewer than twenty years, the Persian Empire under Cyrus had grown to include the complete Iranian plateau, Afghanistan and much of Central Asia, Anatolia, Mesopotamia, Syria, Palestine, and parts of Arabia. The Persian Empire was ruled through a philosophy of cooperation and order; the Persian king was "king of kings" rather than a despotic dispenser of centralized violence. Cyrus had truly earned the epitaph "the Great."

The expansion of the Persian Empire up to the death of Cyrus had been achieved through the application of a land-based military strategy, which was not unlike the strategies adopted by the Assyrian, Babylonian, and Median empires before it. To conquer new lands, it was necessary to sustain large military forces on the frontiers, and it became evident that over time this mode of expansion would be unsupportable.[27] Unless an alternative strategy was adopted, the Persian Empire would ultimately burst like a bubble that is blown too large.

When the Persian armies first reached the sea in the Persian Gulf, the Mediterranean, and the Black seas, they saw it as a barrier. Yet the cooperative methods habitually used by the Persians suggested a different possibility. They soon came to see these maritime frontiers not as barriers at all but rather as communication highways permitting the maneuvering of potentially decisive military forces over great distances. They developed a new maritime strategy, in addition to their traditional land-based one, as the most effective means to continue expanding the empire and otherwise influencing events on the empire's periphery.

A Maritime Alliance

Cyrus' inability to dominate the offshore Greek city-states of Ionia was not an accident. The initial response to the rise of Persia was an alliance consisting of Egypt, Croesus of Lydia, Sparta, and the Babylonians.[28] Nevertheless, as we have seen, Lydia was the first to fall to Persian land power, and it was soon followed by Babylon. Meanwhile, the Spartans, protected by the Aegean Sea, soon retreated into a strategy of isolation. As the Phoenician city-states were incorporated into the Persian Empire, the whole continental land mass of the ancient Near East became secure under the Persians. Once again Egypt was isolated. Accordingly, it now turned to the Greek city-states of Ionia and the Aegean islands, seeking a new maritime alliance against Persia's expansion and influence in the east Mediterranean.

Although maritime trade was important throughout much of the history of the Mediterranean, there is particularly strong evidence of commercial trade between the Ionian Greeks and Egypt during the Saite period, and especially during the reign of the Egyptian king Amasis. He favored the Greek community in Egypt and gave preferential treatment to the important Greek city-states of Chios, Teos, Phocaea, Clazomenae, Rhodes, Cnidos, Halicarnassus, Phaselis, Mytilene, Aegina, Samos, and Miletus.[29] These trade links are confirmed by the archaeological remains of Greek imported pottery vessels found in ancient Egyptian contexts.[30] Such evidence reinforces the maritime nature of the anti-Persian alliance but also highlights the potential source of wealth for the alliance. The tyrant of Samos, Polycrates, became a close friend of Amasis, and with Egyptian support led a series of successful campaigns against Greek communities on the Ionian mainland and among the Aegean islands friendly to Persia.[31] Polycrates acquired a fleet of one hundred warships (penteconters[32]) with an army of one thousand archers and is recorded as having defeated a rival fleet in a sea battle off Miletus on the Ionian coast.[33]

Some controversy exists over the timing and origin of the development of the large galley warships (triremes) that transformed naval operations in the ancient world.[34] The evidence appears to support a long gestation period, during which a three-tiered oar-bank for propulsion was combined with the longer (approximately forty-meter) hulls used to transport larger cargoes. In the east Mediterranean, pirates and trading communities alike used the penteconter to ram and capture or sink other ships at sea. Speed, maneuverability, and robustness were the main driving factors for the new ramming tactics, and it was not long before a smaller warship with two banks of oars, the bireme, was developed. Phoenician biremes dated to 702 BC are depicted in Assyrian reliefs found in the palace at Nineveh.[35] By the middle of the sixth century BC, however, practical experience had shown that a long thin warship with three oar banks could outrun and outmaneuver the smaller biremes and penteconters. Thus the best solution for naval ramming tactics, the trireme, evolved.[36]

Although minor advances in technology did enable gradual improvements in trireme performance, the trireme remained the standard warship for at least two hundred years. The trireme had 170 oarsmen arranged in three rows, one staggered above the other, with each oarsman wielding his own individual oar. A captain, 15 sailors, and 14 marines were onboard, adding up to a crew of 200. Often the trireme carried up to 40 marines, used to board other ships or as a part of a landing force.[37] Each trireme had a typical sprint speed of 9 knots (up to 30 minutes), and averaged 6 knots over long distances.[38] Their lightweight construction and lack of storage space, especially for water, meant that a trireme was brought ashore on a gentle sloping beach each evening so that the crew could eat, drink, and rest. Trireme operations were limited to fine weather because they were unstable in choppy seas or adverse weather conditions; there were many instances where a fleet of warships was lost in a storm.

Importantly for present purposes, the construction, maintenance, and crewing of a trireme was a resource-intensive business. During much of the sixth century BC, the maritime city-states (Phoenician or Greek) were incapable of operating a permanent fleet of penteconters or biremes, let alone a fleet of triremes. In practice, important and wealthy cities provided only one or two warships at public expense. When required, available merchant ships were used to supplement this meager permanent naval force. Only the greater resources of the Egyptian kingdom were able to develop a large fleet, as well as allowing the Egyptians to help their maritime allies develop their own navies. The rise of Polycrates' Samian navy is a prime example of such Egyptian aid.[39] Individually, the Phoenician and East Greek city-states may have constructed and crewed a handful of triremes; nevertheless, it was the critical financial support of the Persian king that ultimately led to the creation of the large trireme fleets capable of projecting power across the Mediterranean.

The Sea-based Empire

The transformation of the Persian empire from a land-based to a maritime power may be traced to the earliest part of the reign of Cambyses. As stated previously, by 530 BC the western borders of the Persian Empire were threatened by the maritime alliance between Egypt, Samos, and other offshore Greeks.[40] Essentially, the control of maritime trade in the east Mediterranean, from Libya in the west to the Black Sea in the east, was in the hands of the enemies of Persia. The Phoenicians were effectively excluded from this lucrative trade while the Egyptian occupation of Cyprus was an open wound in their side and the whole Syrian-Palestinian coastline was susceptible to raids by the Egyptians and their allies. Experience had also demonstrated the difficulty of invading Egypt with land forces alone because it was impossible to conquer Egypt without using the Nile for communications and supplies. Cambyses must have sought the advice of his Phoenician subjects, and probably also those Greek and Egyptian traitors who sought gain from Persian rule.[41] What the Persian empire needed was a large fleet, consisting of the most advanced warships ever constructed—triremes, capable of controlling the waters of the east Mediterranean and projecting military power across water to overcome Persia's opponents in their homelands. This was a truly revolutionary change. Cambyses was the first to use the financial, personnel, and material resources at his command to effect a maritime transformation of the Persian Empire. This transformation was doubly significant because it involved building the first truly substantial navy in world history, as well as developing many of the fundamental ideas of naval strategy.[42] The extent of this transformation and the changes to Persian grand strategy were made much clearer by the start of the Greco-Persian wars in 490 BC. Within a period of less than fifty years, the Persian navy experienced almost every role known to the navies of today.[43] Its commanders witnessed the advantages of using navies in certain situations, and they were confronted with the limitations associated with the use of navies.[44]

Herodotus reports that it was a matrimonial squabble between the Persian and Egyptian kings that led to Cambyses' invasion of Egypt in 525 BC.[45] Such trivial proximal causes tend to hide real causes, which in this case certainly involved Persian prestige, the extent of Egyptian influence, and the control of trade in the east Mediterranean. The invasion of Egypt required approximately five years of planning and preparation, including the formation of the Persian navy itself.[46] The Phoenicians "had joined the Persian forces of their own accord and the whole navy depended on them."[47] A number of Greek triremes formed part of this navy, as is suggested by the record of a ship from Mytilene (a city on the Aegean island of Lesbos) that was used to send a Persian herald to Memphis in Egypt.[48] The appointment of Oroetes as satrap (provincial commander) of Sardis and supreme commander in Persia's Anatolian provinces was intended to re-exert Persian authority in that area.[49] Oroetes effectively used deception to eliminate Polycrates of Samos and remove Samian sea power from the anti-Persian maritime alliance. The Persians then managed to conquer Cyprus and neutralize or bring to their own side the Ionian Greeks. These measures destroyed the northern part of the maritime alliance and left Egypt isolated.

Cambyses secured the overland route into Egypt by capturing Gaza and forming an alliance with the Sinai Arabs. He then marched his army across the Sinai desert and attacked the Egyptians at the mouth of the Nile. The Egyptian forces, including Carian and Greek auxiliaries, were defeated at Pelusium and retreated into the citadel at Memphis (the ancient capital near Cairo), which Cambyses besieged successfully.[50] There is almost no mention of the Egyptian navy in the historical sources, although it may probably be assumed that the Egyptians put up at least some resistance to the Persians at sea. A later authority states that Cambyses laid siege to Pelusium and that the Egyptians were thus able to block entry into Egypt for some time.[51] This may have been a preliminary to the arrival of the Persian army overland. In any case, the Persian navy cooperated with the Persian army when they met up at Pelusium and for the remainder of their campaign along the Nile. An inscription on a statue of an Egyptian, Udjahorresnet, describes how he commanded the Egyptian fleet under Amasis and then Psamtek III (hence proving its existence). He also retained command of the Egyptian fleet (which thus continued to exist) under the Persians.[52] Although Udjahorresnet later presented himself as the favorite of Cambyses, there is no definitive evidence that the Egyptian navy under his leadership deliberately abandoned Psamtek III.

After conquering Egypt, Cambyses wanted to extend the Persian Empire to the west and the south. The Libyans and the Greeks of Cyrene and Barca surrendered without a fight; it is likely that their decision was influenced by the presence of the Persian navy along the North African coast. It is said that Cambyses wanted to extend Persian power even farther west and conquer the Phoenician colony of Carthage, near modern Tunis, but the expedition was apparently cancelled because the Phoenicians in the Persian navy were unwilling to make war on their own colony.[53] This report, however, may have been a later Greek invention because there was really no need for the Persians to capture Carthage. Carthage was already closely tied to the Phoenicians and thus virtually an ally of the Persians.

The Persian forces, probably now incorporating parts of the Egyptian navy, next campaigned south along the Nile to defeat the "Ethiopian" kings who ruled the upper reaches of the Nile (actually the Meroë kingdom in modern Sudan). The archaeological evidence from the fortress of Dorginarti, dating to the Persian period, confirms that Cambyses was able to extend his power into the northern Sudan, despite Herodotus stating that Cambyses' expedition against the "Ethiopians" ended in disaster.[54]

King Cambyses stayed in Egypt until 522 BC, when he was forced to return to Persia to put down a rebellion. He was injured in Syria on the way home and soon died of gangrene.[55] This resulted in a contest for succession to the Persian throne involving Bardiya, a usurper who claimed to be the brother of Cambyses, and Darius, a successful general who was distantly related to the Persian royal family. Darius I (522–486 BC) gained control during a brief but violent civil war.[56] Although one provincial commander, Oroetes, the powerful satrap of Sardis, rebelled against Persian rule at this time, he too was soon overcome by Darius.[57] Regaining control over the provinces of the Persian Empire of his forebears, Darius also earned the title "the Great": "Darius the king says: 'These are the countries which belong to me. By the favor of Ahura-Mazda I was their king: Persia, Elam, Babylonia, Assyria, Arabia, Egypt, the People-by-the-Sea, Lydia, Ionia, Media, Armenia, Cappadocia, Parthia, Drangiana, Aria, Chorasmia, Bactria, Sogdiana, Gandara, Scythia, Sattagydia, Arachosia and Maka, altogether twenty-three countries.'"[58]

The system of imperial provinces, established under the strong centralized authority of Cyrus and Cambyses, was fundamentally important for the maintenance of power within the Persian Empire. Darius was an exceptional leader with strong organizational skills and almost unlimited energy. He reorganized the tribute system, constructed new capitals, promoted maritime trade, and organized exploratory expeditions from the Indus to the Nile.[59] But like his predecessors, Darius was also interested in territorial expansion, and it was at this stage that he too adopted and adapted the maritime strategies that had been so successful under Cambyses. The Persian Empire's chief planners did advise Darius not to extend the empire farther because expeditions on the extreme periphery of the empire against the Scythians and the Greeks were fraught with great risk and were seen as having little economic benefit.[60] For Darius, though, Persian prestige demanded further expansion, and he recognized that maritime forces could help him achieve his objectives.

During 519 BC, Darius advanced against the Scythians (*Saka Tigrakhauda*) living adjacent to the Caspian Sea (in modern Turkestan), and successfully used Persian ships to maneuver part of his troops behind the Scythians to cut them off and force them to submit.[61] These vessels were purpose-built for these Persian naval operations in the Caspian Sea.

The Persian navy's participation during Darius' 513 BC invasion of the European Scythians (*Saka Paradraya*), living along the northern coast of the Black Sea (in modern Ukraine), is described in much more detail by the ancient sources.[62] "Darius was getting ready to invade Scythia. He sent out messengers in all directions, ordering his subjects to supply him with foot-soldiers, and ships, and others to build a bridge over the Thracian Bosporus."[63] The invasion force included a large Persian army (between 70,000 and 150,000 men) accompanied by "six hundred ships."[64] It is unlikely that this fleet consisted of six hundred triremes, as this would have added another 120,000 men to the invasion force. The Persian fleet probably consisted of around four hundred triremes (40,000 men) and four hundred merchant vessels. Darius marched his army overland through Thrace, but he also "ordered the Ionians to take the navy into the Euxine [Black] Sea and sail to the River Ister [Danube], where they were to bridge the river and wait for him. For the navy was commanded by the Ionians, Aeolians, and Hellespontine Greeks."[65] The Persian invasion thus was, using the modern parlance, a joint maritime operation. The Persian army met the fleet at the bridge they had built across the Danube and used the opportunity to regroup and resupply before the force advanced into the Ukrainian interior against the Scythians. The Greeks were first ordered to abandon the fleet and join the invasion force, but in spite of this, an Ionian general convinced Darius that it was preferable to leave a Greek force with the fleet on the Danube to protect their communications. The Scythians withdrew in front of the Persian advance, adopting a scorched earth policy, and used horse archers in an early form of guerrilla warfare. After two months, it was clear that the Persian advance into the Ukraine was fruitless, so Darius elected to withdraw back to the Danube. The Scythians turned to the offensive as the Persians withdrew. The Persian land force would have been destroyed if not for the steadfastness of the Persian navy and its Greek ship-captains on the Danube. Although the Scythian campaign was not successful, the territorial gains across the Bosphorus and in eastern Thrace were absorbed into the Persian Empire and were to serve as stepping stones in later Persian invasions of the west.[66]

In 499 BC, the Persian Empire had to deal with the Ionian Revolt. This revolt was triggered by the actions of Aristagoras, the tyrant of the Ionian city of Miletus, who, having failed once to capture the Aegean Island of Naxos on behalf of King Darius, decided his future would be better served if he cast off his allegiance to the Persians and instead assumed the leadership of a rising democratic movement in Ionia. Aristagoras saw that his prestige with the Persian court was declining, and his position in command of the East Greek ships within the Persian navy could be used to advantage. Aristagoras convinced the Persian "East Greek" fleet (approximately three hundred triremes) to revolt from its Persian commanders, and at one stroke he gave the Ionian rebels control of the sea and denied the Persians the use of it.[67]

The conflict lasted from 499 to 493 BC. Aristagoras, with the help of the Ionian cities near Miletus, managed to overthrow many tyrants and replace them with rule by the people. The growing democratic movement was probably linked to the rise of the Persian navy in East Greek waters. As the Persians built more triremes and employed more oarsmen, the political influence and power of the poorer elements in Greek society (i.e., those who manned the oars) also grew. However, the Persians' desire to be a "force for good" often meant that they supported the status quo; hence they continued to favor the Greek tyrants who ruled the East Greek city-states, even though their own policies contributed to social and political change in these cities.

Aristagoras knew that Persian forces would plan to reconquer the Ionians, so he traveled to mainland Greece to convince the Greek city-states there to support the revolt. The Spartans refused; the Athenians and Eretrians agreed to send ships.[68] They joined a force of Ionians that disembarked near Ephesus and marched on the Persian satrapy capital of Sardis. The Persians, having sent most of their army to besiege Miletus, were surprised by this early example of "operational maneuver from the sea." The Persian garrison was able to retreat to the citadel of Sardis and hold it while the Greeks pillaged the town and then burnt it to the ground. As the Persian land forces regained the initiative, the Greeks withdrew toward Ephesus. Nevertheless, they were caught by the Persians before they could return to the coast and were defeated.[69] The surviving Athenians and Eretrians fled to their ships and returned to Greece.

The burning of Sardis was a political victory for the Greeks. Much of Asia Minor and many of the offshore island cities threw off Persian rule and joined the revolt. The revolt spread to include most cities of East Greece, the Aegean, the Hellespont, Propontis, and Cyprus. However, the Persian Empire could not be disabled so easily. On land, the Persians were able to assemble large military forces that reconquered the coastal cities piecemeal, although the cities located on the offshore islands were safe as long as the rebel fleet remained the only naval force in the area. The Persians, however, were determined to crush the rebellion, so the Phoenician and Egyptian fleets of the Persian navy were assembled and gradually moved westward, ultimately crushing all naval opposition at sea. Persian troops were then landed to reconquer each island city that had joined the revolt.

As a Persian fleet of 600 triremes moved closer to Miletus, the rebel East Greek fleet of 363 triremes challenged them for sea control.[70] They could not land their triremes along the mainland coast due to fear of attack by Persian land forces, so the rebel East Greek fleet was assembled on an island off the coast of Miletus, where they were decisively defeated at the Battle of Lade in 494 BC. Following that battle, Miletus was captured, the rebel leaders overthrown, and the remaining rebel cities quickly defeated.[71] Always open to peaceful settlements, the Persians removed the tyrants whose abuse of power helped spur the Ionian Revolt, and replaced them with democratic leadership.[72] By such conciliatory actions, the Persians regained control of Ionia and quickly rebuilt the East Greek fleet as part of the Persian navy.

Darius next turned his attention toward the mainland Greeks, in particular the Athenians and Eretrians who had participated in the burning of Sardis. There was much more to these campaigns, though, than Darius' desire for revenge against Athens; rather, they formed part of the Persians' ongoing strategy to extend their empire in Europe. "The Persians intended to subjugate as many Greek towns and cities as they could."[73] In the spring of 492, the king sent his son-in-law Mardonius sailing with a joint maritime force along the Thracian coast to gain the allegiance of the Greek cities in the area and lay waste any that might instead oppose him. The Persians spent much of 491 making arrangements for a joint maritime campaign directly across the Aegean, the object of which was to secure the allegiance of Athens, Sparta, and the other mainland Greek city-states.[74] Diplomatic efforts were repulsed by the Athenians and Spartans, although many other Greek cities and the northern Greek kingdom of Macedonia agreed to the demands and joined the Persian side—"medized," as the saying went. In the meantime, Persian naval and land forces were mobilized in Cilicia (on the southern coast of Anatolia), consisting of six hundred triremes (80,000 to 120,000 men) and some 25,000 soldiers, including spearmen, archers, and cavalry, all under the command of two Persians, Datis and Artaphernes.[75]

The Persian expedition sailed from Cilicia via Samos in 490 BC. The route took them first to Naxos, which had resisted the Persian fleet under Aristagoras back in 500 BC. "The Naxians did not stay to fight the Persians, but fled to the hills."[76] The fleet proceeded from island to island across the Aegean, and any resistance—notably at Eretria on the large island of Euboea, modern Évia—was crushed. In a telling move, the religious sanctuary on the island of Delos was taken under Persian protection as a symbol of the new power in the east Mediterranean. This helped to make Persian policy clear to all: Only those who resisted the Persians would have their temples destroyed.[77] The presence of the Persian fleet in the Aegean and off the Greek mainland convinced many more Greek city-states to medize, and even an oligarchic faction within Athens preferred Persian rule to Athenian democracy. Internal dissent was often fostered by the Persians to achieve their political ends without physical military means, the Persian fleet being effectively used as a floating symbol of the power of the Persian Empire.

Of course, the expedition to Athens ended with the well-known Battle of Marathon, where a force of mostly Athenian citizen solders defeated the large Persian invasion force. Only a few points need to be raised here concerning this famous Greek victory.[78] On the day of the battle, much of the fleet was rowing around the southern coast of Attica toward Athens; hence it is quite possible that the Athenian attack may have been precipitated by a Persian strategy to maneuver into a more powerful position by landing outside the walls of Athens. This maneuver did not pay off for the Persians, and the defeat of their land forces (those left to guard the Marathon shoreline) led to their withdrawal and return to Asia Minor.

Darius' invasion of Greece was only the first of two major attempts to incorporate the mainland Greeks within the Persian Empire. After Darius' death, his successor, Xerxes I (486-465 BC), organized and led a massive invasion force along the east Mediterranean coastline, through Thrace, Macedonia, Thessaly, Central Greece, and on into Attica. For this operation, the Persian navy had brought together all the naval forces available in the Mediterranean, including the astounding number of 1,380 triremes (more than 25,000 men) and 1,800 auxiliary vessels. The auxiliaries included penteconters, thirty-oared vessels, other light vessels, provision ships, and horse-transports. For Xerxes' invasion, the triremes were allocated to five fleet units consisting of an Egyptian fleet (200 ships), a Phoenician fleet (300 ships, including Syrians), a central fleet (330 ships, including Cypriots, Cilicians, Pamphylians, and Lycians), an East Greek fleet (270 ships), and a northern fleet (280 ships, including Aeolian and Hellespontine Greeks and Thracians).[79]

In 480 BC, Xerxes' joint maritime force overcame all opposition until it arrived in Attica, where it captured and burned Athens. But the Persian fleet suffered a severe defeat in the Battle of Salamis, perhaps the most famous naval victory in the history of the ancient world.[80] The Persian land forces that remained in Greece were defeated decisively in the following year at the Battle of Plataea, and at about the same time, the remaining Persian fleet in Ionian waters was destroyed on the shoreline at the Battle of Mycale. Even after these reverses, which left the Greeks (mostly the Athenians) in control of the Aegean, Ionia, and the Black sea, the Persian navy managed to retain sea control in much of the east Mediterranean (the waters adjacent to Cyprus, Phoenicia, and Egypt).[81]

The Persian navy was never a spent force. But after these reverses, its activities became more circumspect, in support of Persian policy that used political influence and economic rewards to play one Greek city off against another, in effect preventing the dominance of any single power in the Greek world. Even during the late fourth century BC, the famous king of Macedonia, Alexander the Great, was forced to use the land route to reach the Persian Empire and to destroy Persian sea power by capturing their ports and harbors from the land.[82]

Whereas Cyrus the Great's victories were the result of an effective continental strategy of expansion, Cambyses and Darius the Great achieved their victories through the use of a maritime strategy with the Persian navy operating as part of a joint maritime force. Darius had extended his empire by seizing islands, coastlines, and waterways using the power of his fleet.[83] It was only after the defeat of Xerxes' expedition in 479 BC that the Persian Empire's grand strategy changed from one of expansion to one of containment.

The Nature of Persian Sea Power

Up to this point it may seem that the Persian maritime transformation between 550 and 490 BC was a natural consequence of the desires of the

Persian king and his military commanders. The Persian navy did not grow out of the king's words alone, and no matter what the king willed, he would have been unable to transform the Persian Empire's military forces absent a few key conditions. Persia's maritime transformation is perhaps the earliest example where such conditions came together. Persian sea power grew from advances in imperial administration; tribute, royal gifts, and currency; maritime trade and communications; and good governance with a belief in fair and just rule.

Warships have always been expensive, and the number of warships that a maritime power can build is limited by the need for regular funding. During the period examined here, the number of triremes that could be built, maintained, and crewed also depended directly on the resources available. A powerful trading city-state, Phoenician or Greek, could afford between 1 and 5 triremes. The largest commercial states, such as Corinth or Athens, could stretch this to perhaps 40 triremes.[84] A large territorial monarchy such as Egypt could afford—in the right circumstances—more than 100 triremes. With their well-organized satrapies, conversely, the Persian Empire was able to allocate resources to support fleets numbering many hundreds of triremes (in the east Mediterranean, typically 300 to 600 triremes, although Xerxes' fleet in 480 BC numbered more than 1,200). Such numbers were beyond the reach of any of the Persian Empire's adversaries.

The Persian Empire of 500 BC was vast—stretching from India to Thrace and from Libya to the Caspian Sea.[85] The Persian satrapies were each subject to royal assessments and tribute, consisting of direct payments in talents (a monetary unit equal to about 30 kilograms in silver), annual gifts of special value, and military levies (permanent garrisons as well as expeditionary forces). Darius reorganized the Persian Empire into twenty permanent satrapies and reformed the administration of taxation within each satrapy. As a result, the empire collected a regular income of well over 10,000 talents annually, and this was in addition to the gifts and services also provided.[86] For example, the fifth satrapy, encompassing the whole of Phoenicia, Palestinian Syria, and Cyprus, not only paid an annual tribute of 350 talents but also crewed and maintained a fleet of the Persian navy comprising approximately three hundred triremes.[87] As one scholar puts it, "In fact, the organization of the navy was based upon a simple principle: the royal administration built the ships (with the help of requisition of manual labor), while the tributary coastal peoples (Greeks, Carians, Lycians, Cilicians, Cypriots, and Phoenicians) provided the oarsmen."[88] For operations in the east Mediterranean, the Persian navy was able to deploy one or more of its main fleet units.[89] Thus the satrapies contributed the resources necessary to implement the Persian maritime strategy.

Moreover, the introduction of coinage in Lydia in the mid-sixth century BC started a financial revolution that promoted trade and economic invest-ment. Following the conquest of Lydia, currency spread throughout the Persian Empire, at least among its wealthier classes, and for the first time in history a standardized currency was established, based upon the Persian gold *daric*. Even though coinage was not in everyday usage throughout the empire, a financial standard was created that gave a major boost to interre-gional and international trade.[90]

Maritime trade and communications were a significant factor in the economy of the Persian Empire by the time of Darius.[91] We have already heard of the use of Phoenician maritime expertise under the Assyrians; this Phoenician role expanded rapidly under Persia. The river systems of Mesopotamia continued to take advantage of Phoenician nautical exper-tise, with ships being transported overland from Phoenicia to Babylonia. The ancient trading routes within the Persian Gulf, along the southern coast from Mesopotamia, past Bahrain, and to Oman, were supplemented by a chain of Persian ports along the northern route.[92] Under Darius the Persian Gulf trade was expanded into the Indian Ocean, the Arabian Sea, and the Red Sea.[93] A canal linking the Red Sea with the Mediterranean—effectively an ancient Suez Canal—was first completed during the reign of Darius, thereby providing a direct maritime link between the empire's eastern and western parts. The utility of this canal for merchant vessels may have been limited due to the lack of suitable winds in the northern Red Sea, but the canal did facilitate the transfer of naval vessels—not dependent on sail—to and from the Mediterranean when required.[94]

The east Mediterranean has a long tradition of sea communications, going back at least five millennia. The geography of the Mediterranean means that it is much easier to communicate and move people and goods by sea than to do the equivalent overland.[95] Phoenician maritime trade continued to prosper in the Mediterranean under Persian rule, as much of the west Mediterranean, given the dominant position of Carthage, remained a Phoenician lake. There is even some evidence to suggest that the Phoenicians helped establish a Persian trading colony on the Calabrian coast in southern Italy around 500 BC.[96] The Egyptian and Cyprian maritime trade also continued under Persian rule, although there is less evidence surviving that is clearly attributable to these times. The East Greeks, of Ionia and the adjacent parts of Asia Minor, had controlled a large part of the maritime trade in the east Mediterranean, with trade routes extending from the Greek cities in the Black Sea to Egypt; however, the Ionian Revolt and the Greco-Persian wars effectively stopped Persian commerce in these areas. Subsequently, after 479 BC, the Athenians controlled maritime trade in the Aegean and the Black Sea. The archaeological evidence also shows that the Athenians were able, at times, to dominate much of the maritime trade with Egypt under Persian rule.[97]

Good governance was an unplanned consequence of the Persian belief in the value of "truth" as characterized by fair and just rule.[98] "The covenant embodied by Persian rule could not have been made any clearer: harmony in exchange for humility; protection for abasement; the blessings of a world order for obedience and submission."[99] The teachings of the religious leader Zoroaster, as applied by the Persian elite, were fundamental to this new approach to imperial administration in the ancient Near East.[100] Without overstating the practical bearing of all this on day-to-day management of the empire, it nevertheless seems clear that Persia represented a new sort of empire in the ancient Near East, one much more reliant than its predecessors on the willing collaboration of its subjects.

But how, in practical terms, did the Persians achieve their maritime transformation? In fewer than fifty years, they changed from an empire without a navy into one that could field as many as 1,380 warships with crews numbering more than twenty-five thousand men. The classical historian Diodorus Siculus described the Greek ships forming part of Xerxes' fleet: "the crews were furnished by the Greeks, the ships supplied by the king."[101] Indeed, this concisely describes the arrangement for each of the main fleet units of the Persian navy: the crews were provided by the king's subjects, and the Persians supplied the ships.[102] Command was in Persian hands, with the support of Persian marines, but the crew and oarsmen were supplied by the subject maritime populations.

The large fleets of warships were built by the maritime subjects—the Phoenicians, Egyptians, Cilicians, Cypriots, and Greeks—under the direction of the Persians. Persian gold and silver paid for the triremes, they were constructed from shipbuilding materials supplied by the Persians, and they were put together by a labor force assembled by the Persians. Of course, when it came to shipbuilding, the Persians were essentially managers who were able to redistribute the necessary resources from around their empire to achieve the needed results. The minor differences between triremes from different regions within the empire confirms that each maritime people designed and built their own vessels. The materials required for ship construction were transported from a number of areas within the empire, each renowned for a particular component of the process. The biblical prophet Ezekiel describes a warship built at Tyre (Phoenicia) that fits well with other descriptions of ships built for the Persian navy: The Tyrian ship was built with cypress trees from Senir, cedar from Lebanon, oak from Bashan, with decoration in ivory from Kittim's isles, and a fine linen sail from Egypt. The inhabitants of Sidon and Arvad (Phoenician cities) were the rowers, and the troops carried were from Persia, Lud, and Put (the latter two places have not been positively identified).[103] Herodotus states that the Greek triremes at Salamis were heavier than their Persian counterparts, and he also confirms that there were significant differences in speed between the triremes within each fleet.[104]

Herodotus mentions a few instances in which specific ships were supplied by individual cities, including Mytilene, Myndos, Samothrace, and Iasos.[105] The sailors (including captains, navigators, and helmsmen), as experienced mariners, were typically provided by the city that was required to crew each trireme. The manning of the oars was much more difficult, for most of the oarsmen were professionals capable of maintaining time and balance within the somewhat light and unstable warships. The large numbers of rowers required would have drained maritime trade if they were levied from the merchant fleet by the Persian satraps. It is more likely that the Persians introduced regular pay for their time at the oar, a measure that other powers could not afford to do until well after 490 BC. At the time, only the Persian Empire had the mechanisms to create and develop the personnel necessary for maritime transformation.[106]

In light of this evidence, the Persian navy can be visualized as a coalition of navies working as a "force for good" under the control and direction of the Persian king. Indeed, using modern terminology, it was the "maritime partnership" of the fifth century BC.

The Persian Navy Experience

The Persian maritime transformation between 550 and 490 BC was extraordinary. The development of the Persian navy and the subsequent applications of Persian sea power were early stepping stones on the long path that has led to the rise of modern navies and the use of maritime power worldwide. The Persian experience of maritime transformation was always a top-down management process. The Persian kings, their advisors, and senior commanders exercised visionary but sound leadership within the confines of their particular religious and cultural setting. This enabled them to freely seek and listen to advice from specialists from any number of fields from within and outside their empire. They had the uncanny ability to sort good advice from bad without having access to any specialist subject matter expertise. They adapted the best technologies (triremes), allocated and managed resources, and gathered the right people to provide the right leadership and incentives to meet their broad strategic goals. These characteristics of Persian rule were applicable to all the empire's endeavors; hence their impact was not limited to the Persian navy.

This maritime transformation was largely invisible to the majority of subjects under the Persian Empire. Agricultural communities, the mainstay of the imperial population, continued to produce a meager surplus that helped to underwrite the satrapy system, and they retained their land-based myths and traditions. It was the populations of the maritime cities and towns located on the empires' peripheries, those with long-held nautical traditions, that provided the expertise and personnel necessary to fuel the Persian maritime transformation. The Persians purposely adopted ideas from all the regional maritime cultures forming part of their empire—and not just the Phoenicians, the Greeks, or even the Egyptians but also maritime communities of the Persian Gulf (from southern Mesopotamia, the southern coast of Persia, the southern Gulf coast, and coastal Oman), the Indian Ocean, and the Caspian Sea.[107] In some ways, their lack of maritime traditions may have helped the Persian elite to select the best solutions for the Persian navy's maritime transformation without having to overcome entrenched views or narrow-minded opponents. It was the interplay of ideas and the collective cooperation of these maritime peoples, under strong leadership, that created the Persian navy and transformed maritime affairs forever.

The Persian Empire's maritime transformation of 550–490 BC involved a large continental power adopting a practical approach to the use of maritime forces. This included the rapid construction of large fleets of warships; the recruiting and training of large numbers of ship's captains, marines, sailors and rowers; and the collection and redistribution of large quantities of shipbuilding materials, supplies, labor, and money. These activities used the specialist knowledge and experience of almost all the available mariners living under Persian rule in a manner that relied more upon cooperation and rewards than upon force or coercion. The belief that they were acting as a "force for good" and the philosophical underpinnings of the teachings of Zoroaster made a crucial difference to the rise of Persian sea power. But above all, their understanding of the advantages of maritime operations and the practical application of seapower was the great enabler for the ancient Persians.

Notes

1. A chronology of the Persian kings with their regnal years follows, for convenience:

Cyrus II (the Great)	559–530 BC
Cambyses II	530–522 BC
Bardiya (the Usurper)	522 BC
Darius I (the Great)	522–486 BC
Xerxes I	486–465 BC

2. The second inscription from Darius' tomb in Naqš-i Rustam, 6 km north of Persepolis in Iran, comes from P. Lecoq, *Les inscriptions de la Perse achéménide* (Paris: Gallimard, 1997). The full text is repeated in Pierre Briant, *From Cyrus to Alexander: A History of the Persian Empire* (Winona Lake, IN: Eisenbrauns, 2002), 212; and Maria Brosius, *The Persian Empire from Cyrus II to Artaxerxes I*, LACTOR 16 (London: The London Association of Classical Teachers, 2000), 64–65.

3. The textual evidence includes classical Greek sources as well as numerous inscriptions from the ancient Near East. Much recent work undertaken in Achaemenid studies has tried to counter the Greek bias of much of the surviving evidence, and this chapter follows this pro-Persian school. General works on ancient Persia include Lindsey Allen, *The Persian Empire: A History* (London: British Museum Press, 2005); Maria Brosius, *The Persians: An Introduction* (London: Routledge, 2006), chap. 2; and A. R. Burn, *Persia and the Greeks: The Defence of the West, c. 546–478 BC*, 2nd ed. (London: Duckworth, 1984). Briant, *From Cyrus to Alexander*, is highly recommended.

4. A. K. Grayson, "Assyrian Civilization," in John Boardman et al., eds., *The Cambridge Ancient History*, vol. 3, pt. 2 (2nd ed., Cambridge, U.K.: Cambridge University Press, 1992), 219–21.

5. See the Biblical reference in 2 Kings 17:6, 18:11.

6. P. Amiet, *Art of the Ancient Near East* (New York: H. N. Abrams, 1980), plate 105.

7. J. Reade, "Ideology and Propaganda in Assyrian Art," in M. T. Larsen, ed., *Power and Propaganda: A Symposium on Ancient Empires*, Mesopotamia 7 (Copenhagen: Akademisk Forlag, 1979), 330–32.

8. A. L. Trakadas, *Skills as Tribute: Phoenician Sailors and Shipwrights in the Service of Neo-Assyria*, MA thesis, Texas A&M University, 1999, pp. 92–94.

9. See the "Sendjirli Stele" in Daniel D. Luckenbill, *Ancient Records of Assyria and Babylonia, Volume II—Historical Records of Assyria from Sargon to the End* (Chicago: University of Chicago Press, 1926), 580.

10. John Taylor, "The Third Intermediate Period (1069–664 BC)," in Ian Shaw, ed., *The Oxford History of Ancient Egypt* (Oxford: Oxford University Press, 2000), 358–59; and Karol Mysliwiec, *The Twilight of Ancient Egypt: First Millenium B.C.E.* (Ithaca: Cornell University Press, 2000), 105–9.

11. Gregory P. Gilbert, *Ancient Egyptian Seapower and the Origin of Riverine and Littoral Operations* (Canberra: Sea Power Centre–Australia, 2008).

12. Allan B. Lloyd, "The Late Period (664–332 BC)," in Shaw, ed., *Oxford History of Ancient Egypt*, 369–83. A chronology of the Egyptian kings of the 26th (Saite) dynasty including their regnal years follows:

Psamtek I	664–610 BC
Nekau II	610–595 BC
Psamtek II	595–589 BC
Apries	589–570 BC
Amasis	570–526 BC
Psamtek III	526–525 BC

13. Herodotus, 2.154.

14. There are numerous examples within Book II of Herodotus' *Histories*; in particular, King Amasis is described as a philhellene by Herodotus, 2.178–182.

15. Herodotus, 2.182.

16. Lloyd, "The Late Period," 382.

17. Briant, *From Cyrus to Alexander*, 18–19.

18. Ibid., 27–28.

19. Ibid., 31–35.

20. Kaveh Farrokh, *Shadows in the Desert: Ancient Persia at War* (Oxford: Osprey Publishing, 2007), 39–40.

21. Briant, *From Cyrus to Alexander*, 35–38.

22. Herodotus, 1.143; Thucydides, 1.13.6.

23. Briant, *From Cyrus to Alexander*, 40–49.

24. Persian Royal Inscription—Darius inscription from Susa, part e, (DSe) 001, quoted in Briant, *From Cyrus to Alexander*, 166. Zoroastrianism formed the basis for Persian rule, with Ahura-Mazda (Supreme Angel) as the all-powerful single god who represented all that was good and truthful. His rival, Ahriman, may be equated with the devil in the Christian faith. For an overview see John R. Hinnells, *Persian Mythology* (London: Chancellor Press, 1997); and Mary Boyce, *Zoroastrians: Their Religious Beliefs and Practices* (London: Routledge, 2001).

25. Briant, *From Cyrus to Alexander*, 38–40, and 49.

26. Herodotus, 1.215.

27. This applies to land-based territorial expansion only. It was necessary to maintain military and constabulary forces in the "pacified" satrapies to keep order and help prevent rebellions. Imperial military levies were used in emergencies to supplement the small, elite Persian military forces that were spread throughout the empire. Farrokh, *Shadows in the Desert: Ancient Persia at War*, 39–40.

28. Lloyd, "The Late Period," 382.

29. Herodotus, 2.178–179.

30. See R. M. Cook and Pierre Dupont, *East Greek Pottery* (London: Routledge, 1998), 1–7, for a number of Egyptian excavations that have unearthed East Greek transport amphorae; and 142–45 where the trade links with the Black Sea region

are also evident. For the workings of Greek trade in Egypt, see also Astrid Möller, *Naukratis: Trade in Archaic Greece* (Oxford: Oxford University Press, 2000). For details of maritime traders before 490 BC, see C. M. Reed, *Maritime Traders in the Ancient Greek World* (Cambridge, U.K.: Cambridge University Press, 2003), 69–74.

31. Herodotus, 3.39–40.

32. Penteconters were fifty-oared galleys.

33. Herodotus, 3.39; H. T. Wallinga, "The Ancient Persian Navy and Its Predecessors," in H. Sancisi-Weerdenburg, ed., *Achaemenid History I* (Leiden: Nederlands Instituut voor het Nabije Oosten, 1987), 61.

34. M. Amit, *Athens and the Sea: A Study in Athenian Sea Power*, Collection Latomus, Vol. 74 (Brussels: Revue d'Études Latines, 1968); J. S. Morrison and R. T. Williams, *Greek Oared Ships 900-322 BC* (Cambridge, U.K.: Cambridge University Press, 1968); J. S. Morrison, J. F. Coates, and N. B. Rankov, *The Athenian Trireme: The History and Reconstruction of an Ancient Greek Warship*, 2nd ed. (Cambridge, U.K.: Cambridge University Press, 2000); and relevant chapters in Robert Gardiner, ed., *The Age of the Galley* (London: Conway Maritime Press, 1995).

35. A. H. Lanyard, *The Monuments of Nineveh I* (London: John Murray, 1849), 71, reprinted in H. T. Wallinga, "The Ancestry of the Trireme 1200-525 BC," in Gardiner, *Age of the Galley*, 36–48. In general, Wallinga is to be preferred to J. Morrison, "Introduction" and "The Trireme," in Gardiner, *The Age of the Galley*, 8 and 54–57. Wallinga's views are detailed in H. T. Wallinga, *Ships and Sea-Power before the Great Persian War: The Ancestry of the Ancient Trireme* (Leiden: E. J. Brill, 1993).

36. Hans van Wees, *Greek Warfare: Myths and Realities* (London: Duckworth, 2004), 203–9, presents a recent summary of these developments.

37. The use of separate terminology for "marine" and "soldier" is often misleading in the Persian context. The elite troops of the Persian army were not separated into "naval" and "military" forces, rather they were essentially joint forces, equally capable of operating from ships or by land. This is particularly noticeable when we consider the Persians' ability to move large numbers of cavalry by ship over some distance, and the cavalry's ability to rapidly deploy, move, and fight ashore.

38. J. Morrison, "The Trireme," in Gardiner, *Age of the Galley*, 57–59; and J. Coates, "The Naval Architecture and Oar Systems of Ancient Galleys," in Gardiner, *Age of the Galley*, 127–29.

39. Herodotus, 3.39; and Briant, *From Cyrus to Alexander*, 52.

40. Wallinga, "Ancient Persian Navy and its Predecessors," 66–67.

41. Herodotus, 3.4. The mercenary Phanes fled Egypt by sea, was chased by an Egyptian trireme, was captured, and escaped again before agreeing to assist Cambyses.

42. Contra George Cawkwell, *The Greek Wars: The Failure of Persia* (Oxford: Oxford University Press, 2005), 258: "Persians remained, navally speaking, unadventurous and inert." Unfortunately Cawkwell lacks an understanding of sea power and appears to suffer the common misconception that naval forces are used to "dominate the seas" rather than cooperate with land forces in joint maritime operations.

43. For an introduction to the modern roles of navies, see Geoffrey Till, *Seapower: A Guide to the 21st Century* (London: Frank Cass, 2004).

44. The Greco-Persian Wars are described in Peter Green, *The Greco-Persian Wars* (Berkeley: University of California Press, 1996); and Tom Holland, *Persian Fire: The First World Empire and the Battle for the West* (London: Little Brown, 2005). The Persian evidence is examined in Briant, *From Cyrus to Alexander*, 139–64 and 515–68. Of course, the best source remains Herodotus' classic *Histories*. A readily available translation is Robin Waterfield, trans., *Herodotus: The Histories* (Oxford: Oxford University Press, 1998).

45. Herodotus, 3.1–2.

46. Although the evidence for the Persian navy's formation is meager, there are a number of references to Cambyses' navy during and after the Egyptian campaign.

47. Herodotus, 3.19.

48. Ibid., 3.13.

49. Briant, *From Cyrus to Alexander*, 52.

50. Herodotus, 3.13.

51. Polyaenus, *Stratagems of War,* 7.9; see R. Shepherd, trans., *Polyaenus: Stratagems of War* (Chicago: Ares, reprinted 1974).

52. Brosius, *The Persian Empire from Cyrus II to Artaxerxes I*, 15–17; Briant is correct when he suggests "Egypt could not be entered without controlling the town [Pelusium] or having naval superiority." Briant, *From Cyrus to Alexander*, 54.

53. Herodotus, 3.17 and 19.

54. Briant, *From Cyrus to Alexander*, 55; and Herodotus, 3.25. Greek troops forming part of the invasion force traveled home by ship after they returned to Memphis.

55. Briant, *From Cyrus to Alexander*, 61.

56. A translation of Darius' Bisitun inscription (DB) is found in Brosius, *The Persian Empire from Cyrus II to Artaxerxes I*, 27–40; for the nineteen battles, see §52, p. 36.

57. Herodotus, 3.126.

58. Brosius, *The Persian Empire from Cyrus II to Artaxerxes I*, §6, p. 30. Compare with the Greek version of the Persian Empire's tribute list, which includes twenty provinces (satrapies), in Herodotus, 3.89–97.

59. Briant, *From Cyrus to Alexander*, 137–40.

60. Herodotus, 4.83. This is perhaps part of the Greek tradition that the Persians overextended their power in their attempts to conquer the territories on the European mainland.

61. He proclaimed his victory in an inscription on Mount Bisitun along the Royal Road, which ran from Babylon to Ecbatana (modern Hamadan in Iran). See the Bisitun inscription in Brosius, *The Persian Empire from Cyrus II to Artaxerxes I*, §74, p. 39. See also Farrokh, *Shadows in the Desert*, 56–57.

62. Briant, *From Cyrus to Alexander*, 141–44; Farrokh, *Shadows in the Desert*, 57–59. The original sources include Herodotus, *The Histories*, 4.83–143.

63. Herodotus, *The Histories*, 4.83.

64. Herodotus, 4.87, gives seven hundred thousand men for the army (not including the fleet), but this seems excessive. See also Farrokh, *Shadows in the Desert*, 58.

65. Herodotus, 4.89.

66. Briant, *From Cyrus to Alexander*, 144.

67. Herodotus, 5.35–36.

68. Athens sent twenty triremes (some four thousand men) while Eretria sent another five; Herodotus, 5.97–99.

69. For the burning of Sardis see Herodotus, 5.99–103; and Briant, *From Cyrus to Alexander*, 148, 153–54.

70. "As for the navy, the Phoenicians formed the most willing contingent, and they were supported by the Cyprians (who had recently been reconquered), the Cilicians and the Egyptians." Herodotus, 6.6 and 9.

71. In contrast to this chapter, Peter Green presents the wars as a part of a larger traditional conflict between east and west. He describes the results of the debacle at Lade in terms of burning townships, refugees, and young boys and girls "sent off to servitude as palace eunuchs and members of the Royal Harem." Green, *The Greco-Persian Wars*, 21–22.

72. It is interesting that after the Ionian Revolt, the Persian general Mardonius overthrew the East Greek tyrants who were under Persian rule and replaced them with more democratic institutions. Herodotus, 6.43.

73. Ibid., 6.44.

74. Ibid., 6.47–49, 94–95.

75. The six hundred triremes mentioned by Herodotus (6.95) probably did not have their full complement; rather, a proportion would have temporarily carried troops or horses. The number of soldiers carried is a modern estimate, although such numbers would apply to the heavily armed troops only, and the crew of the fleet would have also contributed numerous light troops to the force. As an interesting aside, the Greek sources only recognise their heavy soldiers (hoplites) during campaigns and almost always ignore the relatively large numbers of light troops that were also involved. See van Wees, *Greek Warfare*, 65.

76. Herodotus, 6.96.

77. Briant, *From Cyrus to Alexander*, 159.

78. For the conventional narrative see Alan Lloyd, *Marathon: The Crucial Battle that Created Western Democracy* (London: Souvenir Press, 2005); Holland, *Persian Fire*, 171–201; and Green, *The Greco-Persian Wars*, 30–40. Unfortunately there is no detailed equivalent that avoids the bias of the largely Greek sources, although Briant (*From Cyrus to Alexander*, 156–61) and Farrokh (*Shadows in the Desert*, 69–73) have made a start.

79. Herodotus, 7.89–99. There has been much discussion of the size of Xerxes' fleet, but these figures are the best estimates available.

80. The role of the Athenian Themistocles is pivotal in the Greek victory; it was he who turned the Athenians from steadfast hoplites into sea-tossed mariners: "Themistocles," in I. Scott-Kilvert, trans., *Plutarch: The Rise and Fall of Athens*, (London: Penguin, 1960), 77–108, esp. 81. For a general overview of the battle see Barry Strauss, *Salamis: The Greatest Naval Battle of the Ancient World, 480 BC* (New York: Simon & Schuster, 2004). Apparently the Persians did not believe in the centrality of decisive battle, and their actions suggest that they much preferred to achieve their strategic goals through application of intimidation or the use of naval presence, or both.

81. In many ways the conquering Athenians underwent their own maritime transformation after 479 BC, one that often mimicked certain Persian cultural attributes and traits. At the beginning of the Peloponnesian War in 431 BC, the Athenian navy was much more professional, with greater regulation, standardization, training, and efficiency than the Persian navy was ever able to achieve. Amit, *Athens and the Sea*, 20–30.

82. Arrian, *Anabasis*, 2.17; and N. G. L. Hammond, *Alexander the Great: King, Commander and Statesman* (London: Bristol Press, 1980), 111–20, for the conquest of Phoenicia and Egypt. The Athenians had attempted to defeat the Persians using a small professional fleet, but they could never overcome the economic depth of the Persian Empire, which could rebuild and equip fleets more readily than Athens. The Macedonians, under Alexander, instead elected to destroy the bases of the Persian navy and in this way gained control of the east Mediterranean.

83. Thucydides, 1.16.1.

84. At the height of the Athenian empire in the mid-fifth century BC, the Athenian fleet could muster two hundred triremes with the tribute from the Athenian dependencies and allied city-states.

85. "Darius the king says: This is the kingdom which I hold: from the Scythians who are beyond to Ethiopia, from Sind to Sardis." An inscription from Persepolis quoted in Brosius, *The Persian Empire from Cyrus II to Artaxerxes I*, 76. For information on the geographical locations mentioned in this chapter, refer to J. Haywood, *The Penguin Historical Atlas of Ancient Civilizations* (London: Penguin, 2005).

86. Herodotus, 3.89–97; and Briant, *From Cyrus to Alexander*, 389–94.

87. Herodotus, 3.91.

88. Briant, *From Cyrus to Alexander*, 405.

89. Between 490 and 480 BC, when the Persian Empire was at its greatest extent, the Persian navy in the Mediterranean included an Egyptian fleet, a Phoenician fleet, a central fleet (including Cyprian, Cilician, Pamphylian, and Lycians crews), an East Greek fleet (East Greek Ionians and Dorians, Carians, and Aegean Islanders), and a northern fleet (Aeolians, Hellespont, and Thracians); Herodotus, 6.47–49, 94–95.

90. Briant, *From Cyrus to Alexander*, 406–10; and Farrokh, *Shadows in the Desert*, 65–66.

91. For an overview, see Briant, *From Cyrus to Alexander*, 377–87; and Farrokh, *Shadows in the Desert*, 66–67.

92. Direct evidence comes from Alexander the Great's generals, who sailed from India to Susa over five months in 325–324 BC; see Arrian, *Indica*, 21–40; George F. Hourani, *Arab Seafaring*, exp. ed. (Princeton, NJ: Princeton University Press, 1995), 13–17; and Mark A. Smith, *The Development of Maritime Trade between India and the West from c. 1000 to c. 120 BC*, MA thesis, Texas A&M University, 1995, 62–70.

93. Details may be found in Smith, *Development of Maritime Trade*, 26–53.

94. Brosius records the inscription written on a stele found near the original Red Sea canal: "Darius the king says: 'I am a Persian. From Persia I seized Egypt. I ordered the digging of this canal from a river called Nile, which flows in Egypt, to the sea which begins in Persia. Afterwards this canal was dug just as I ordered, and ships passed through this canal from Egypt to Persia, as I had wished'"; Brosius, *The Persian Empire from Cyrus II to Artaxerxes I*, 47.

95. The overland route from the Ionian coast to the king's palace in Susa was a three-month journey; Herodotus, 5.50–54. Fast messengers, traveling by day and night, would have reduced this time by at least half if not by two-thirds; however, the time between Susa and Sardis would still be some thirty days or so. See Xenophon, *Cyropaedia*, 8.6.17–18, available in W. Ambler, trans., *Xenophon: The Education of Cyrus* (Ithaca: Cornell University Press, 2001).

96. A possibility raised by the Calabrian art historian Nik Spatari in *L'enigma Delle Arti Asittite: Nella Calabria Ultramediterranea* (Mammolo, Italy: Museo Santa Barbara, 2003), 321.

97. Möller, *Naukratis*, 191. However, the Athenian trade was not necessarily due to "Persian rule breaking down in the western Delta."

98. For example, see Hinnells, *Persian Mythology*, 48. Khshathra Vairya, (the Desired Kingdom) is the personification of God's might, majesty, dominion, and power. On Earth he represents "that kingdom which established God's will on earth by helping the poor and weak and by overcoming all evil." His opponent is Saura, the arch-demon of misgovernment, anarchy, and drunkenness.

99. Holland, *Persian Fire*, 60.

100. Zoroaster was "the first to teach the doctrines of an individual judgment, Heaven and Hell, the future resurrection of the body, the general Last Judgment, and life everlasting for the reunited soul and body. These doctrines were to become familiar articles of faith to much of mankind, through borrowings by Judaism, Christianity and Islam." Boyce, *Zoroastrians*, 29.

101. Diodorus Siculus, 11.3.7.

102. Only a few scholars have dealt specifically with the Persian navy (in the English language): Wallinga, "The Ancient Persian Navy and its Predecessors," 47–76; Wallinga, *Ships and Sea-Power before the Great Persian War*, 103–29; and, briefly, Farrokh, *Shadows in the Desert*, 66–67. The views expressed in Cawkwell, *The Greek Wars*, 255–73, are problematic.

103. See the biblical reference in Ezekiel 27.

104. Herodotus, 8.23 and 60.

105. Ibid., 3.13–14, 5.33, 8.90, and 7.99. For Iasos, see Arrian, *Anabasis* 1.9.

106. Wallinga, "The Ancient Persian Navy and its Predecessors," 70–71.

107. Although the Western bias of our sources emphasizes the Phoenician and Greek contributions, there is increasing archaeological evidence, dating to the Persian Empire, for ancient maritime trading communities operating across the Persian Gulf, the Red Sea, the Arabian Sea, and the Indian Ocean. For instance, see Daniel Potts, "Persian Gulf in Antiquity," at www.iranica.com/newsite/articles/ot_grp7/ot_pers_gulf_ant_200503223.html (accessed 21 January 2008). Almost nothing is known of the Scythian peoples located beside the Caspian Sea. For instance, very little is known of the maritime Dahistăn, who apparently provided the Scythian marines in Xerxes, fleet, mentioned in I. M. Diakonoff, "Media," in William B. Fisher, ed., *The Cambridge History of Iran, Volume 2: The Median and Achaemenian Periods* (Cambridge, U.K.: Cambridge University Press, 1985), fn on p. 128. The lack of surviving evidence for many of the Persian Empire's maritime peoples means that much of their contribution remains unrecorded and undervalued.

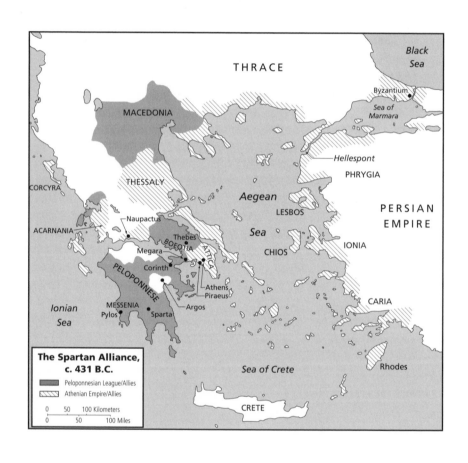

THRACE

Black
Sea

MACEDONIA

Byzantium

Sea of
Marmara

THESSALY

Hellespont

PHRYGIA

CORCYRA

Aegean

PERSIAN
EMPIRE

LESBOS

Naupactus

ACARNANIA

Sea

Thebes

BOEOTIA

Megara

ATTICA

CHIOS

IONIA

PELOPONNESE

Corinth

Athens
Piraeus

Ionian
Sea

MESSENIA

Pylos

Argos

Sparta

CARIA

Rhodes

**The Spartan Alliance,
c. 431 B.C.**

Sea of Crete

Peloponnesian League/Allies

Athenian Empire/Allies

0   50   100 Kilometers
0   50   100 Miles

CRETE

Barry Strauss

Sparta's Maritime Moment

THE RISE AND FALL OF ATHENS and its sea power is one of the most dramatic narratives in ancient history. Thanks to Thucydides, it is also one of the best known. Sparta often gets overlooked when it comes to the sea, yet its meteoric rise and fall are even more striking. Ancient Greece's land power par excellence, Sparta turned itself into a naval power and defeated Athens, the nautical titan of the Eastern Mediterranean. Then, within a decade, Sparta lost its maritime empire as quickly as it had gained it. Failure may be disappointing, but it can be revealing. For historians of maritime transformation, the Spartan case is rich in lessons.

At the outbreak of the Peloponnesian War in 431 BC, Sparta had a tiny navy. Athens held a great overseas empire while Sparta presided over a largely land-bound military alliance. By the end of the war, in 404 BC, Sparta had replaced Athens as the Greek maritime hegemon. But just ten years later, in 394 BC, the wheel turned again and the Spartan fleet was crushed in a naval battle off southwestern Anatolia. Sparta's maritime empire was over, though not its naval power; Sparta remained a significant force at sea for another two decades.

The heyday of the Spartan fleet—between 411 and 394—was brief but decisive. Sparta transformed itself from a continental power with a minor navy into a power with a great fleet. Sparta's navy was tactically inelegant

and historically short-lived, but it got the job done. Athens had been confident that Sparta could never challenge it at sea, much less defeat it. But Sparta
won the Peloponnesian War and dismantled the Athenian Empire, replaced
it with an empire of its own, and then proceeded to project its power across
the Aegean Sea and wage war against the Persian Empire—Sparta's former ally
against the Athenians. This proved to be a step too far, however, and ultimately
led to Sparta's undoing. But Sparta lacked nothing in maritime ambition.

In defeating Athens, Sparta beat the greatest sea power the Greek world
had ever known. And Sparta managed it without Athens' various strategic and
technical advantages: without the presence of philosophers, historians, a bus-
tling port, a huge infrastructure of dockyards and ship sheds—generations'
worth of naval experience spread widely among its population or the dynamism of democracy.

How did Sparta do it? The great Greek historian Thucydides' answer is
that in a sense, it did not: Athens defeated itself. As he writes: "Yet after losing most of their fleet besides other forces in Sicily [413 BC], and with faction already dominant in the city, they could still for three years make head
against their original adversaries, joined not only by the Sicilians, but also
by their own allies nearly all in revolt, and at last by the King's son, Cyrus,
who furnished the funds for the Peloponnesian navy [407 BC]. Nor did they
finally succumb till they fell the victims of their own internal disorders [404
BC]."[1] But that is true only up to a point. True, if Athens had not faltered in
Sicily, Sparta would not have been able to build a navy. Furthermore, without help from Greek allies in the Aegean and Sicily and from Persia, its naval
power could not have been sustained. The "Spartan" navy never had more
than a small number of Spartans; most of the ships and labor were supplied by allies or were mercenaries. But although Athens itself provided the
bulk of the Athenian navy's ships, it too needed allied and mercenary labor.
More important, Sparta deserves credit for its shrewdness and opportunism.
When opportunity knocked, it did not hesitate; it knew just what was needed
to defeat Athens.[2]

There are three reasons for Sparta's good judgment. The Peloponnesian
War gave Sparta a lesson in naval warfare: a painful but salutary education.
The Athenians taught the Spartans how to innovate. Failure drove home the
message: Peloponnesian naval initiatives against Athens during the first ten-
year phase of the Peloponnesian War (431–421 BC) had resulted in humiliation and defeat. But Sparta was as honor-driven a culture as the Greek world
would know; there is nothing like the sting of defeat to provoke change.[3]

Spartan society, furthermore, was in flux. To fight the Peloponnesian War, Sparta had been forced to address shortages in military labor. The Spartan elite saw no choice but to concede a degree of power and responsibility to large numbers of low-status individuals. Sparta's hungry new men saw golden opportunities in maritime adventures. Let the old guard concern themselves with traditional infantry battle on the Greek mainland: The new Spartan was going down to the sea.

Most important, however, Sparta was not quite the landlubber that it is usually imagined to be. It did not build a navy ex nihilo. Sparta may have had few ships of its own, but it had used its allies' ships for overseas expeditions on numerous occasions from the mid-500s on. And, at least as early as the 470s BC, the evidence suggests that there was a vocal navalist faction in Sparta.

Thucydides emphasizes the conservative nature of Sparta's land power and compares it to the dynamic sea power of Athens: "The Spartans proved the most convenient people in the world for the Athenians to be at war with. The wide difference between the two characters, the slowness and want of energy of the Spartans as contrasted with the dash and enterprise of their opponents, proved of the greatest service, especially to a maritime empire like Athens."[4] But this is caricature. It took nearly a decade after Athens' defeat in Sicily, but in the end Sparta made the case for the tortoise.

The following pages trace the rise and fall of Sparta's maritime power. A combination of narrative and analysis is offered. The story is divided into three stages: the period before the Peloponnesian War (ca. 550–432 BC), the Peloponnesian War (431–404 BC), and the period after the Peloponnesian War, when the Spartan Empire briefly flourished and then collapsed (404–371 BC).

One word of warning before proceeding: Secrecy was public policy in Sparta. The authorities, helped by much of the free population, tried to keep foreigners out of their land and Spartan resources hidden. Knowing that fear is a force multiplier, Spartans cultivated a powerful image. Spartans were laconic in discourse; they said little and wrote less. Theories about Sparta, therefore, are always somewhat more speculative than one might wish.[5]

Sparta before the Peloponnesian War

There were hundreds of Greek poleis (city-states), but Sparta was unique. Sparta was even more dependent on an armed citizenry than was the average polis owing to its large subject population. Spartan society was structured around a class system consisting of three main parts. Helots, unfree laborers who worked the land, were at the lowest level. At the top stood *Spartiates* (the "Similars" or "Peers," as they were also known), who were the only full citizens. Somewhere in between were those called *Perioikoi* (roughly, the "Neighbors," because most lived on the periphery of Spartan territory), who were free but had no political rights. The term "Lacedaemonian" is used to include both Spartiates and Perioikoi. We do not know the number of Helots, but we do know that they vastly outnumbered the other two classes.[6]

Spartiates were privileged people. Each of them received a minimum allotment of land; some were quite wealthy and owned considerably more than the minimum. Every Spartiate had to pay dues in kind to support the mess where adult males had meals in common with their companions. Thanks to the land allotments and Helot labor, Spartiate men were free to devote themselves to one main activity: soldiering. There was no alternative.

As a result, though, Sparta faced a permanent internal security problem. The restive Helots had to be policed. Sparta needed a crack army; to get that, it needed to train, support, and glorify its soldiers. Whether Spartiates should be considered civic-minded soldiers or militarized citizens is a matter of debate. In any case, they paid a great deal of attention to war. To discourage consumption, Sparta issued no coins; the official "currency" consisted of heavy and clumsy iron skewers. Since the outside world was considered corrupt and corrupting, Sparta engaged in little trade and admitted few foreigners to its territory—and those who were admitted were subject to periodic expulsion.[7]

Most important, Spartan boys went through a unique education, the famous *agogê* ("upbringing"), which created by far the best soldiers in Greece. Spartan girls were trained to be mothers and wives tough enough to accept sacrifice and inspire their men. The result was a military machine that was the wonder of the Greek world.[8]

Beginning around 550 BC, Sparta used its military might to establish a leadership position in Greece and build up a network of alliances. This loose confederacy of some two dozen states in the Peloponnese and Central Greece is known to modern scholars as the Peloponnesian League; to the ancients it was simply "the Lacedaemonians [Spartans] and the allies." Each of these states had pledged "to have the same friends and enemies and to follow the Lacedaemonians wherever they might lead."[9] In return the Spartans would protect these states from external threats and from internal revolt. Most of the allies were, like Sparta, oligarchies—conservative, generally agrarian regimes. Although a few, like Corinth, were commercial centers and had navies, the main strength of the Peloponnesian League was in infantry, particularly the soldiers of Sparta and Thebes. The structure of the alliance was informal. Assemblies would be called, if needed, to debate important subjects, above all, questions of war. Sparta, the hegemon, collected no tribute, and there was no standing legislature.

Sparta was generally a conservative hegemon, tending to intervene abroad only to prevent threats from arising on the horizon, and usually only after much debate. The Spartans feared that if they sent their soldiers too far from home, the Helots would revolt.[10]

And yet, now and then some Spartans showed signs of interest in overseas expansion and naval affairs. In 546 BC, for example, Sparta sent a warship with an ambassador to the Persian King Cyrus the Great. The Spartans demanded a hands-off policy regarding the Greek cities of the east (the Ionian coast of present-day Turkey). Cyrus was unimpressed by mere words, and perhaps he knew that Sparta had rejected an eastern Greek plea for military assistance. In 524 BC, however, the Spartans did send a seaborne force eastward, to the island of Samos, where they tried to depose the tyrant Polycrates. Arguably, Corinth provided the ships, while Sparta provided only soldiers. After a siege of forty days, the Spartans admitted failure and went home.[11] In 517 BC the Peloponnesian League under Sparta's King Cleomenes successfully deposed the tyrant Lygdamis in the island of Naxos. One ancient tradition claims that Sparta controlled the central Aegean Sea for two years at that time.[12] Around 512, a Spartan naval expedition landed in Attica in hopes of deposing the Athenian tyrant Pisistratus, but this too was defeated.

Sparta was very active during these years (ca. 550–500 BC) as a land power. We might imagine that Spartan majority opinion then favored a continental strategy of using the Spartan army to maintain Spartan preeminence and security on the Greek mainland. But there seems also to have been a maritime party with grander ambitions of expanding Spartan power overseas and perhaps of building a substantial navy. We might guess that they were also interested in wealth, as opposed to Sparta's traditional austerity. Someone in Sparta, after all, was meant to be impressed by the purple cloak worn by the ambassador from Phocaea, an eastern Greek city in 546. Meanwhile, King Cleomenes was tempted by a huge bribe offered by another eastern Greek ambassador in 499, or at least Cleomenes' daughter feared this.[13]

If there was a Spartan maritime party, it almost achieved a breakthrough early in the fifth century BC, during the great Persian invasion of 480–479 BC. Sparta is usually remembered for its heroic last stand at Thermopylae in 480 and for its leadership of the Greek infantry at the land battle of Plataea in 479. In fact, Sparta was in principle Greece's hegemon (leader) at sea as well as on land. This was true even though Sparta contributed only sixteen ships to the Hellenic navy, compared to two hundred Athenian ships.[14]

In 480, the Spartan Eurybiades was the nominal commander of the Greek fleet at Salamis, although the Athenian Themistocles really called the shots. In 479, the Spartan King Leotychides II shared command of the Greek forces at the Battle of Mycale with another Athenian, Xanthippus. But the consensus of opinion in Sparta (we do not know if Leotychides shared it) was to liquidate the war overseas by resettling the Ionian Greeks on the Greek mainland. In any case, a year later Leotychides was recalled on charges of bribery and corruption. The great Spartan general Pausanias the Regent, victor at the land battle of Plataea in 479, replaced him as commander of the Greek fleet, now based at Byzantium.

Pausanias was indeed an advocate of overseas expansion, and he led a combined Greek naval offensive against Persian-held ports in Anatolia. His tenure of office revealed various fault lines in Sparta's reach for naval power, however. For one thing, he illustrates the need in Sparta for a great leader— a king, a regent or, in the case of Lysander, a kingmaker—for the maritime faction to make headway. In a conservative polity like Sparta, innovation was always suspect. Success required patronage from above. For another thing, the maritime faction could be easily stopped by decapitation, as Pausanias also reveals. He was eventually recalled and charged with treason, because of alleged pro-Persian behavior; with corruption, because of having allegedly dressed and dined on the grand scale, Persian style; and with tyranny, because of his undoubtedly violent actions toward other Greeks.

This was the third fault line in Sparta's bid for naval hegemony: arrogance. Spartans were proud men. They were taught from boyhood to lord it over the rest of mankind, including the other Greeks. They were used to giving orders and to enforcing them with spears. Although perhaps a desirable quality in battle, arrogance was not the most useful tool for building an alliance.

Pausanias the Regent was acquitted, for the time being. Not long afterward, the Spartan authorities obtained clear proof that he was plotting a Helot revolt in collusion with Persia. Pausanias was caught while fleeing arrest and was forced to starve to death. Well before that happened, he had been replaced in command of the fleet with another Spartan, Dorcis. It was too late, however. The other Greeks insisted on an Athenian commander, and so naval hegemony passed from Spartan hands. Athens founded a new naval confederacy known today as the Delian League (founded in 478–477 BC on the Aegean island of Delos). Many Spartans breathed a sigh of relief, fearful that any other leaders they sent out might "become worse men," as had happened with Pausanias.[15]

But they had second thoughts. In 475 BC a majority of the Spartans in assembly nearly approved a proposal to go to war against Athens to take back the command of the sea. They were pushed in this direction by a group of younger men who sought opportunities to increase Sparta's public wealth and power as well as their private profit. They might have had their day, too, if not for the opposition of Hetoemaridas, a prominent and noble member of the council of elders. His advice was suitably laconic: "It was not in Sparta's interest to dispute over the sea."[16] There is perhaps more here than meets the eye, but arguably, without a Pausanias to champion it, the maritime strategy option was too fragile politically to survive conservative opposition.

And that opposition had a point. The political and economic costs of a maritime strategy would have been high. Navies are expensive; the Spartans prided themselves on their relative poverty. Sparta had very few ships and little shipbuilding capacity. Its economy was agrarian and autarchic, and its public finances were primitive. A navy would have required considerable concessions to the subordinate classes in Sparta's extremely stratified social system. For example, Sparta's naval port, Gytheion, was inhabited not by Similars but by Perioikoi. Perioikoi and Helots would have been needed to row, and possibly also to serve as light naval troops.[17] And the financial requirements of maintaining a navy would almost certainly have forced the Spartans to create a new dependence on commerce and trade with the larger Greek world.

It took decades before the wheel turned again. During an extended period of cold war and then actual fighting between Athens and Sparta (the so-called First Peloponnesian War, ca. 460–445 BC), Sparta did not build a major fleet.

Sparta during the Peloponnesian War[18]

The conflict between Athens and Sparta for hegemony in Greece lasted for a hundred years. It began after these two states had led Greece to victory in the Persian invasion of 480–479. Athens incited Spartan fear and jealousy by its refusal to subordinate its newly won sea power to Sparta's traditional hegemony on land. By 431, Sparta had been the dominant land power in Greece for about a century. Since 480, Athens had been the dominant sea power. The conflict between Athens and Sparta in the Peloponnesian War of 431–404 BC is a classic clash between an elephant and a whale—between a great land power and a great sea power. The fleet of Athens and its allies ruled the seas, while the armies of Sparta and its allies dominated the land. Neither side could reach the enemy's center of gravity, and so the war dragged on for twenty-seven years and involved virtually all of the Greek world (which included the coastal cities of Anatolia, southern Italy, and Sicily as well as Greece) and the Persian Empire.

In 431 Athens had the best navy in the eastern Mediterranean. Her superb fleet included at least three hundred warships as well as a number of older ships that could be repaired and launched, if necessary. Athenian allies Chios, Lesbos, and Corcyra could provide more ships, perhaps another one hundred. Athens had an excellent harbor in Piraeus, a rich infrastructure of dockyards and ship sheds, and experienced shipwrights and architects. She had access to northern Greek sources of raw materials (timber, tar, and pitch) needed for shipbuilding. And Athenian financial resources were great because most of the allied or subject cities of Athens' empire paid tribute rather than providing military resources in kind.

With all of this, the Peloponnesians could not compete. At the outbreak of the Peloponnesian War, the Peloponnesian navy consisted of about one hundred ships, most of them Corinthian. Unlike the sea-going Athenians, the Spartans were deficient in experience of the sea, and their allies were unable to compensate for this. King Archidamus, known for his caution and moderation, recognized the hopelessness of Sparta's position. Unless they could defeat the Athenian navy or deprive Athens of its imperial revenues, they could not win; without a competitive fleet of their own, the Peloponnesians could achieve neither of these goals. Hence, failure was assured. The Corinthians argued that help from the treasuries of Delphi and Olympia (the key Greek religious shrines), as well as taxes levied on the Peloponnesian allies, could fund a fleet; after a single victory, Athens' mercenary rowers would defect to the Peloponnesian side. Archidamus rightly saw this as special pleading and advised against going to war with Athens, but the Spartans voted against him.

But by the end of the war, one side had decided to meet the enemy on its own terms. Remarkably, it was not the dynamic, democratic Athenians but the hidebound Spartans who proved flexible enough to alter fundamentally their strategic orientation. Sparta built a fleet and, although it faced a steep learning curve, eventually defeated an overextended and divided Athens and won the war. In short, Sparta became a maritime power.

The Peloponnesian War may be conveniently divided into four phases: the Archidamian War (431–421 BC), the Peace of Nicias (421–415), the Sicilian

Expedition (415–413), and the Ionian or Iono-Decelean War (412–404).[19] Sparta flirted with naval expeditions in the Archidamian War, but it never made a commitment to a full-blown maritime strategy. In 432, as Sparta prepared for war, it did little in terms of building ships or collecting money to finance a navy.[20] Sparta expected to win the war by overawing the Athenians with a land invasion by Peloponnesian armies. Athens expected to win by sitting out the invasion behind the city's long walls (connecting Athens proper to the port of Piraeus) and by harassing the Peloponnesians with a series of raids. Neither plan proved successful.[21]

Although Sparta's efforts at sea may have been insufficient, nevertheless, they did exist. In the second year of the war, for example, the Athenians raided the Peloponnese again, as they had done the year before. They were surprised to discover, however, that far from being daunted, the Spartans launched a naval attack on the island of Zacynthus, an Athenian ally off the western Peloponnese. This attack was unsuccessful, but it marked the beginning of a new Peloponnesian strategy of offensives outside of Attica. Another side of this policy was a Spartan overture to Persia for help against Athens. Though a failure this time—Athens captured and executed the Spartan emissaries—this would later prove a key component of Sparta's winning strategy.

In the summer of 429 the Peloponnesians continued their policy of offensives outside of Attica, this time launching a seaborne attack on Acarnania, an Athenian ally northwest of the Corinthian Gulf. From a base in the Corinthian Gulf, however, a detachment of the Athenian navy, taking advantage of its vast tactical superiority to the Peloponnesian fleet, was able to interfere effectively with these operations. The Athenian base was at Naupactus, on the north shore of the Gulf, where Athens had planted a colony of renegade Spartan Helots. The Athenian commander there, Phormio, had been sent to Naupactus in the winter of 430 to protect the port and to attempt to close off the Corinthian Gulf. His two naval victories in the Gulf in 429 against larger Peloponnesian fleets demonstrated that there is no substitute for experience and good leadership, and effectively demoralized the enemy. Consequently, Athens was able to establish effective local control of the seas surrounding the territories of the Spartans and their allies.[22]

Athenian control of the seas was maintained for the rest of the Archidamian War. In spite of this, the Peloponnesians were capable of occasional, daring challenges to Athens at sea, but these generally proved to be tactical failures. Immediately after their second defeat by Phormio in 429, for example, they organized a naval raid on Piraeus from the port of Megara. At the eleventh hour, however, frightened by the risk, they set out for the less important target of the island of Salamis—until the first sighting of an Athenian naval force, at which point the Peloponnesians fled. Two years later, in 427, they sent out a fleet of forty-two triremes under Alcidas in support of the people of Mytilene, a town on the island of Lesbos, then in rebellion against Athens. With good leadership, even so small a fleet could have caused serious trouble for Athens, either by helping the Mytilenian rebels or by stirring up a new rebellion on the coast of Asia Minor, which might bring in Persian help. Athens faced a potentially dangerous situation. Alcidas indeed landed on the Asia Minor coast, yet when the news came that the Athenian fleet was in pursuit, he fled—all the way back to the Peloponnese![23]

There was still one possibility of action for this fleet. When it returned to the Peloponnese, bolstered by thirteen additional ships, the Peloponnesian fleet sailed north to Corcyra (modern Corfu) to intervene in a civil war there in the hopes of detaching an important Athenian ally. They easily defeated a force of sixty Corcyrean ships, whose crews were ill-disciplined and even fought among themselves. The presence of twelve Athenian ships, however, as well as Alcidas's timidity prevented the Peloponnesians from taking advantage of their victory. A day later, when the news came that a relief fleet of sixty Athenian ships was on its way, the Peloponnesians fled.

One of the ship's trierarchs (captains) in this fleet was Brasidas. Then obscure, he would go on to become Sparta's most aggressive and innovative general on land in the Archidamian War. He would also play a hard-hitting role on the one other occasion in which the Peloponnesian fleet was used during the Archidamian War, this time in response to an Athenian initiative. In the spring of 425 under the command of Demosthenes (not the famous orator of a later century), Athens seized and fortified Pylos, a rocky, uninhabited promontory in the southwestern Peloponnese. Pylos was in Messenia, the Spartan-controlled homeland of the Helots. Any fort there might be a refuge for runaway Helots and was potentially, therefore, a serious threat to Sparta. It had the additional advantage of being located on the northern edge of the excellent harbor of Navarino Bay.

The Spartans did not wait long to attack the small Athenian force of five ships and several hundred men at Pylos. They gathered sixty ships to use against the expected Athenian reinforcements. Perhaps they considered closing off the two entrances to Navarino Bay, north and south of the island of Sphacteria, which lies just south of Pylos and runs along the western, seaward side of the bay. At any rate, they left a detachment of elite Spartan infantrymen (hoplites) on Sphacteria. In the meantime, they attacked the fort at Pylos with land forces and with forty-three of their ships. Brasidas purposely ran his ship aground and encouraged others to do so, in order to make a landing. The Athenians, however, held their ground for two days until Sparta called off the attack. Thucydides is impressed by the irony of the situation: "It was a strange reversal of the order of things for Athenians to be fighting from the land and from Laconian land too, against Spartans coming from the sea; while Spartans were trying to land from shipboard in their own country, now become hostile, to attack Athenians, although the former were chiefly famous at the time as an inland people and superior by land, the latter as a maritime people with a navy that had no equal."[24]

The next day saw the arrival of an Athenian fleet of fifty ships. After a brief withdrawal in the early demonstration of the power of the offensive at sea, they attacked the Peloponnesian fleet, which occupied a defensive position line abreast in Navarino Bay, and routed it thoroughly. Worse yet for Sparta, 420 hoplites were isolated on Sphacteria. Some of these men belonged to the first families of Sparta, and the government took their plight seriously enough to sue for peace with Athens. In the meantime, a truce handed over to Athens not only all the ships at Pylos but also all the triremes in Spartan territory, a total of sixty. In the end, the two sides were not able to agree upon peace terms. After a considerable delay, caused in no small part by fear of even a small force of Sparta's formidable soldiers, Athens managed to storm Sphacteria and take 292 of these men alive.

The Peloponnesian navy was not a factor again until the Sicilian Expedition, Athens' ill-fated attempt to conquer the wealthy island's Greek cities and, in particular, Syracuse. Prodded by an Athenian defector, the rogue politician and general Alcibiades, Sparta sent a military advisor, Gylippus, to Syracuse in 414. He played a crucial role in stiffening Syracusan resistance. Although a full Spartiate, Gylippus had risen from the inferior status of *mothax*. Whether *mothakes* were illegitimate sons of Helot mothers or sons of impoverished Spartiates is unclear. What is certain is that a mothax had something to live down. In Sparta that might have made him more conservative than the conservatives or, alternatively, left him open to new methods and policies. Gylippus seems to have taken the latter route, to judge by the skill at overseas campaigning that he displayed in Sicily and later.

But Gylippus had more to shake off than his legal status. His father, Cleandridas, had been convicted of taking Athenian bribes in 446 BC. Exiled from Sparta, Cleandridas moved to Thurii, a pan-Hellenic colony in southern Italy. Cleandridas bears all the signs of a Spartan navalist: a connection with Athens, an interest in money, and a willingness to settle in a cosmopolitan port city overseas. Perhaps Gylippus inherited from his father a taste for maritime activity as well as a connection to the western Greeks. Unfortunately, Gylippus was eventually tarred with the same brush as Cleandridas. After Sparta's victory in 404 Gylippus was entrusted with a huge sum of money to bring back to Sparta. But he was accused of stealing some of it and he fled before he could be tried, convicted, and condemned to death in absentia. He died in exile.

Back in 414, Sparta's Peloponnesian ally, Corinth, also sent help to Syracuse. Eventually a Corinthian technical innovation in ship design enabled Syracuse (itself a significant naval power) to win a major naval victory. Syracuse now dominated the Great Harbor. It went on utterly to smash the Athenian invading force.[25]

Neither the Sicilian disaster nor the revolt of key Athenian allies could win the war for Sparta because Athens could and did build a new fleet. To win, Sparta would have to destroy that fleet. True, from 413 on, the Peloponnesians had a permanent garrison at Decelea, in the hills above Athens, which did great damage to the countryside. The garrison at Decelea would not win the war, however, because it could not reach Athens' center of gravity.

Athens' defeat in Sicily revolutionized Spartan opinion. Buoyed by enthusiastic allies and eager neutrals, in 413 Sparta concluded that it was possible to defeat the Athenians once and for all. The hope of a big navy from Sicily coming to their aid gave the Spartans particular confidence—an exaggeration, as it turned out, because Syracuse was too exhausted for more than a small effort in the Aegean. The outcome, the Spartans believed, would leave them "in quiet enjoyment of the supremacy over all Hellas." Hence, they decided to go for broke in the pursuit of victory. One of Sparta's two kings, Agis, now made a considerable effort to collect money for their fleet.[26]

Agis was a rallying point for Sparta's advocates of overseas expansion. Much of the support for this, however, came from the opposite end of the social spectrum. Sparta's society—closed, stratified, and depleted by war and natural disasters (a devastating earthquake had struck ca. 465 BC)—was subject to great strain. Various groups of inferior status appear in Sparta during the Peloponnesian War or shortly afterward. The details are murky, but it appears that they included illegitimate sons, men whose resources had sunk below the minimum level needed to support a warrior's way of life, and even freed Helots. Their financial needs gave them a reason to support a vigorous foreign policy.[27]

Sparta's allies in Greece and Sicily provided ships and crews for the new fleet, as did Sparta itself. In 413 the Spartans were no longer dreaming of the massive fleet that some in 431 had hoped to build, but they still wanted a major effort. The biggest members of the Peloponnesian League were expected to make significant contributions: The Spartans and Boeotians were each expected to provide twenty-five ships, and the Corinthians fifteen ships. The other states were expected to pool their resources in regional consortia: In central Greece, the Phocians and Locrians together were to provide fifteen ships; in the central and northern Peloponnese, the Arcadians, Pellenians, and Sicyonians were to furnish ten ships; and in the northeastern Peloponnese and Isthmus, the Megarians, Troezenians, Epidaurians, and Hermionians were to provide another ten ships. It is not known how many of these ships were ever built.[28]

The most important source of funding for shipbuilding and paying crews was Persia. The Persians decided to open their vast treasury and fund a new navy to fight Athens. The "barbarians," as the Greeks called them, would give Sparta the tools to destroy the Athenian Empire. This was not an offer to turn down.[29]

Very few ships in the new Spartan navy were in fact Spartan. It has been suggested that during the remainder of the Peloponnesian War there were never more than ten Spartan ships in the fleet. The admiral of the fleet, the *navarch*, was a Spartiate. The ship captains (trierarchs) were probably all Lacedaemonians, either Spartiates or Perioikoi. It is likely that the chief marine of the Spartan ships was a Spartiate; on allied ships, he was a Perioikos. The rowers were either Helots, allies, or mercenaries. Sparta was known for its military discipline; Spartan officers trained their crews hard, which probably contributed greatly to their eventual success at sea.[30]

The price of Persia's help was steep: In 411 Sparta surrendered the Greek city-states of the Asia Minor coast to at least de facto and possibly de jure Persian sovereignty. The Persians had never fully reconciled themselves to the loss of the Ionian cities following the defeat of Xerxes' invasion of Greece in 480–479 BC. Previously, fear of Athens had kept Persia neutral. Now Athens' defeat in Sicily weakened her so greatly in the Aegean that Persia reawakened.

The strategic objective of Spartan policy was the destruction of Athenian naval power. In the short term, that could be achieved in partnership with Persia. In the long term, that alliance was fragile. It depended in large part on personality; change the players, and the long-standing enmity between Sparta and Persia would resurface quickly. Few on either side could be happy about an alliance with the men whom their ancestors had fought at Thermopylae and Plataea. Even worse for the Spartans, the nation that had gone to war in 431 to liberate the Hellenes had now agreed to a loss of Hellenic freedom. This could hardly stand.

By summer 411, Athenian and Spartan fleets faced each other in the Aegean. Building a fleet had imposed sacrifices on the Athenian treasury. Athens had lost important allies and was short of labor. Nevertheless, recognizing that everything depended on control of the Aegean, Athens pressed on. The Athenian fleet was based on the island of Samos while the Spartans were a short distance away in the mainland city of Miletus.

Sparta's strategy had two parts. The first thing was to secure the islands of Chios and Lesbos, former Athenian allies and important naval powers now in revolt. The second and more important step was to take control of the Hellespont (i.e., the Dardanelles), probably the weakest link in Athens' vital chain of supply to Ukrainian grain. It was a good strategy, but for years Sparta proved singularly inept at carrying it out. The Spartans allowed themselves to be manipulated and cheated by Persian politicians. The Persians wanted a Spartan navy that was strong enough to challenge Athens but weak enough to keep the Greeks fighting each other indefinitely—leaving Persia to enjoy the spoils. From 411 to the end of the war, the Spartan fleet did not win a single major victory over Athens in a regular battle. In fact, the Athenians crushed the Spartans in three major naval engagements, yet the Spartans won the war.

In the summer of 411 a Peloponnesian fleet of eighty-six ships challenged an Athenian fleet of seventy-six ships. The battle took place in the narrow waters of the western Hellespont, off the Cynossema promontory. Despite a promising Spartan initiative, Athens once again demonstrated tactical skill and superb training, which ensured composure in battle and enabled a decisive victory.

The next year, 410 BC, Athens won a second major naval victory at Cyzicus. This time eighty-six Athenian ships defeated eighty (or sixty, according to a variant source) Peloponnesian ships and killed the Spartan navarch, Mindarus. If the Spartans now made an offer of peace, as one source claims, Athens rejected it. It took the Spartans three years to recover at sea. Even after Sparta's resurgence with a new fleet in 407, it still lost the big battles. The third great Athenian victory took place four years later, in 406, at the Arginusae Islands, off the Asia Minor coast across the strait from the island of Lesbos. Once again, there is evidence of another Spartan peace offer, also rejected.

But what proved to be decisive was the emergence of a new Spartan navarch in 407. The Spartan navy reached its greatest success under this visionary leader, Lysander. He proved to be able, brilliant, and ruthless. If the sources are to be believed, he bragged of his callousness. Dice were for cheating boys, said Lysander, and oaths were for cheating men. And Lysander was immensely powerful. Aristotle might have been thinking of Lysander when he described the navarch as virtually a third king of Sparta. The navarch had great authority on campaign, including the power of life and death and immense patronage power. Like Gylippus, Lysander was a mothax and, hence, a Spartan who would probably not have had the opportunity to rise in normal times; war was his path upward.[31]

Lysander's forte was not battle but diplomacy. His key move was to win the support of Persia's new representative on the Aegean coast of Anatolia, the royal prince Cyrus. Cyrus was a teenager, and perhaps impressionable, although Machiavellian might be an equally apt description. Within a few years, Cyrus would fight his older brother Artaxerxes for the throne and Sparta would support Cyrus. Who knows whether Lysander hinted at such support already in 407? In any case, Lysander convinced Cyrus to raise the pay of a Peloponnesian rower to a level about 25 percent above the Athenian rate. The result was a large-scale desertion of rowers from Athenian ships.[32]

Lysander added a naval victory to this financial one in 407, at Notium, on the coast near Ephesus. Taking a leaf from Athens' book, he lured an Athenian fleet out against a superior Peloponnesian force and sank twenty-two ships. An unexpected benefit was that the Athenian assembly blamed the defeat on Alcibiades, the commander in chief, who was absent on another mission. This popular politician and clever general was forced into exile, thereby depriving Athens of a major leader.

Lysander had no intention of suffering a similar fate. He built up personal ties among oligarchs in the Greek cities of the eastern Aegean. He and they showed their colors the next year, in 406, when Callicratidas (another mothax) replaced Lysander as navarch. Where Lysander had been cunning and effective, Callicratidas was straightforward, honorable, and a failure. Lysander had no interest in seeing Callicratidas succeed, so he returned to Cyrus what was left of the money that the Persian prince had given him. Callicratidas proved unequal to the task of getting the funds back: He refused to do business with Cyrus, saying it was beneath his dignity as a Greek to flatter and wait at the gates of barbarians.[33] He resolved to try to reconcile the Greeks one day so that they could join forces against Persia, as in the past. But he died in the Battle of Arginusae (406 BC), where he led the Peloponnesian fleet to defeat against the Athenians.

Despite a legal prohibition against serving more than one term, in 405 Lysander reappeared as vice admiral but de facto navarch. It was now that he effected his masterstroke. In September 405 Lysander caught the Athenian fleet napping in the Hellespont. The Peloponnesians and Athenians each had massive fleets there of about 180 ships. The Peloponnesians had the advantage of a secure harbor at Lampsacus, an important Athenian ally whom they had brought over to their side. The Athenians were forced to beach their ships at the small town of Aegospotami. Incautious and overconfident, the Athenians were taken unawares one afternoon by the Peloponnesian fleet. Sweeping down on the enemy while he was dispersed ashore, the Peloponnesians captured virtually the entire Athenian armada with hardly a fight; only about ten ships escaped. Otherwise, Athens had no navy.[34]

With no money to build a new fleet or allies to help them, the Athenians were finished. They held out against a Peloponnesian siege at home for several months, but in spring 404 Athens surrendered. The Athenian Empire was finished and the Peloponnesian War was over. The Spartan Empire, however, was just beginning.

The Spartan Empire

Beginning in 405 BC the dominance of the Spartan fleet in the Aegean enabled the Spartans to inherit Athens' maritime empire.[35] Sparta's bid for overseas empire would be the dramatic and disastrous story of the next generation. Wealth, power, and glory would accrue to Sparta but unguided by wise strategy. It was, as one historian has recently put it, a case of "victory without a concept of a blueprint for a lasting peace."[36] Sparta made many mistakes—none more glaring than its failure to maintain command of the sea. But we are getting ahead of the story.

After Aegospotami, Lysander sailed the Aegean. He sent Athenians packing. He ousted pro-Athenian democracies and replaced them with narrow governments run by ten men (*decarchies*) who were favorable to Sparta but loyal personally to Lysander. Athens was allowed to have thirty rather than ten oligarchs in charge (the so-called Thirty Tyrants), but it was still a narrow group of Lysander's men. Most cities had to accept a Spartan commander or governor (*harmost*). Tribute was also imposed on Sparta's new allies, in imitation of Athenian practice.

Lysander engaged in self-promotion on a grand, indeed, shocking scale, given Sparta's communal mores. It is hard to say which looked worse: Was it the huge statue group, which he had erected in Delphi depicting Sparta's admirals and, chief among them, himself, being crowned with a victory wreath by Poseidon? Or was it the divine honors that he allowed the city-

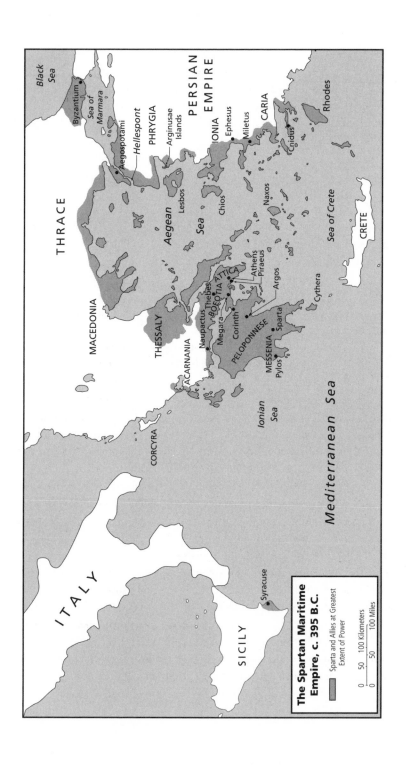

The Spartan Maritime Empire, c. 395 B.C.

Sparta and Allies at Greatest
Extent of Power

0   50   100 Kilometers
0   50   100 Miles

Black Sea

Byzantium

Sea of Marmara

Hellespont

Aegospotami

PHRYGIA

Arginusae Islands

PERSIAN EMPIRE

Rhodes

IONIA

Ephesus

Miletus

CARIA

Cnidus

THRACE

Lesbos

Chios

Aegean Sea

Naxos

Sea of Crete

CRETE

MACEDONIA

THESSALY

ACARNANIA

Naupactus

Thebes

BOEOTIA

ATTICA

Athens

Piraeus

Argos

Cythera

Megara

Corinth

PELOPONNESE

Sparta

MESSENIA

Pylos

CORCYRA

Ionian Sea

Mediterranean Sea

ITALY

SICILY

Syracuse

state of Samos to bestow on him? The big monument at Delphi would have required a budget far beyond the bounds of Spartan austerity. As for deification, Lysander is the first Greek mortal known to have received this honor. (In later years, after Alexander the Great, deification became relatively common.) Deification was a sign of Lysander's personal power, his achievement, and his egotism.

Many Greeks both in and outside of Sparta shuddered. Sparta's old Peloponnesian League allies, Corinth and Thebes, each worried about the colossus that their old hegemon had become. Thebes supported Athenian rebels against the Thirty—for that matter, so, in effect, did Sparta's King Pausanias. Perhaps in part because of their scruples and certainly in large part because of their fears of Lysander, Pausanias and his allies within Sparta abolished the decarchies (and accepted the restoration of democracy in Athens) and withdrew the harmosts. But they did not abandon the policy of maintaining an overseas presence. It was a policy of "indecisive aggressiveness," as it has aptly been called, and it merely emboldened Sparta's enemies. Persia became the first among them.[37]

Sparta gave naval support to Prince Cyrus's attempted revolt in 401 BC against his brother, King Artaxerxes II (404–359 BC). Cyrus's failure, after nearly succeeding, left Sparta with an enemy on the Persian throne. Artaxerxes declared that the Spartans were the "most shameless of men."[38] Already in 400, Persia began to take over the Greek cities of the Aegean coast, in retaliation for their support of Cyrus. These cities in turn sent ambassadors to appeal to Sparta to help free the Greeks, and Sparta agreed. The partners who had won the Peloponnesian War at sea now turned on each other.

It is either a tribute to Sparta's ambition or a sign of Sparta's overextension that it barely stopped to catch its breath while also dealing with a serious threat of domestic revolt around the same time (399 or 398). A Spartan of inferior rank named Cinadon mobilized the "Inferiors" (*hypomeiones*) and "New Citizens" (*neodamodeis*) against the Spartiates and their privileges. The authorities moved quickly to execute Cinadon and his associates. But Cinadon's revolt pointed to a potentially fatal problem. The very basis of Sparta's strength was in trouble: The number of Spartiates was constantly shrinking. While scholars disagree about the causes, the likeliest explanation is the distribution of wealth. Spartan property had always tended to concentrate in fewer and fewer hands. That left ever more Spartiates "below the poverty line." Unable to meet the requirements of their messes, they lost Spartiate status; they and their sons were no longer trained as elite soldiers. The new wealth and power won after 404 might have been distributed to the poor in an effort to replenish the number of Spartiates. But it was not. Sparta's elite military was hanging by a thread. Yet no one in the leadership was willing to face this problem.[39]

Instead, in 399 BC Sparta launched a campaign across the Aegean Sea to drive the Persians out of western Anatolia. They sent an expedition commanded by Thibron, who was followed in command by Dercyllidas (399–397 BC). The Spartans fully understood the naval dimension of the war. Their fleet operated off Caria (in southwestern Anatolia) under the navarch Pharax. Caria played a crucial strategic role because it was the gateway to the interior, via the valley of the Maeander River. Off Caria lay the island of Rhodes, which also assumed great strategic significance.[40]

But the effort was too ambitious. In response, Persia organized and funded an anti-Spartan alliance among the major land powers of the Greek mainland. At the same time, it built a new fleet in 397, commanded and staffed in large part by former Athenian sailors. Artaxerxes appointed an Athenian as admiral: Conon, a general who had survived Aegospotami. The Persian satrap Pharnabazus served with him. The navy was a tool to use against Sparta, with the right men at the helm. Sparta held the advantage at first; then, as the full complement of Persia's new fleet became available, Conon began to prevail. At this point, in 396, Rhodes revolted against Sparta. By 395 Conon was in charge in Rhodes.[41]

In the meantime, Sparta sent a third commander and new troops to the Anatolian mainland, this time led by King Agesilaus. Agesilaus had been Lysander's handpicked successor to the throne, chosen in place of the heir apparent, whom Lysander arranged to have declared illegitimate. (Rumor made the heir into the son of the Athenian exile Alcibiades.) But Agesilaus proved to be his own man, for better and worse. He dismissed Lysander and with him Lysander's skill in naval affairs.

Agesilaus was successful on land—at first. He tried to broker an agreement with Artaxerxes to grant autonomy to the Greeks of the Anatolian coast, under Spartan hegemony, but the Persian refused. A Spartan victory in a battle near Sardis made the Persians reconsider, but they insisted that the Greeks pay tribute to Persia. This time, Agesilaus refused. His policy is unclear. One suggestion is that he planned to build buffer states between the Greeks of the coast and the Persians farther inland. But he never got the chance because of the outbreak of the Corinthian War. In 395 BC Athens, Corinth, and Thebes declared war on Sparta, and Agesilaus was recalled home.[42]

Sparta prevailed in land battle on the Greek mainland during the Corinthian War (395–386 BC), despite certain setbacks. Lysander was removed quickly from the military equation after he died in battle in central Greece in 395. His political legacy lived on, if mainly as a warning. After Lysander's death, his political enemies claimed to find among his papers plans for a coup that would make him king. Whether genuine or not, the discovery might have hurt Lysander's friends; perhaps it also had a chilling effect on the policy of maritime expansion that he had championed.

Despite successes on land, Agesilaus failed disastrously at sea mainly because he neglected sea power. He had been appointed in the first place because of Persia's naval buildup. But Agesilaus did nothing to prevent Conon from bringing about the revolt of Rhodes or intercepting supplies sent to Agesilaus by Egypt. Agesilaus committed a fatal error of nepotism in appointing his brother-in-law Pisander as navarch. Although Pisander built up a large fleet, he was an incompetent battle commander.[43]

In August 394 the Persian and Spartan fleets fought off Cnidus, a city in Caria. Eighty-five Spartan triremes under the command of Pisander faced 170 Persian triremes under Conon and Pharnabazus. Sparta suffered the crushing loss of 50 ships as well as five hundred men. For the rest of the summer of 394, Conon and Pharnabazus sailed triumphantly around the Aegean, driving out pro-Spartan regimes and installing pro-Athenian democracies. The next spring they crossed the Aegean and sailed for the Peloponnese. They occupied the island of Cythera and used it as a base for raiding the Spartan mainland, to devastating effect.[44]

Cnidus was a turning point. Never again would Sparta be the master of the Aegean Sea. But the story of Sparta's naval power was not quite finished. Before 411 BC Sparta's navy had been relatively insignificant because of the massive scale of the competition. When Athens or Persia each had hundreds of ships at their disposal, Sparta's paltry few dozen ships mattered little. From 411 to 394, Sparta too could send out massive armadas. Then came the crash. And yet between 391 and the date of Sparta's last major naval expedition in 372, Sparta's opponents were unable to muster significantly larger fleets, which made Sparta's small navy an important and sometimes victorious player in international affairs. Sparta's naval comet, at its zenith between 411 and 394, had a long tail.

After Cnidus, democracies arose again in the Aegean, with Athens as their champion. Even earlier, in 395, the democrats of Rhodes had expelled their oligarchs. In 391, the oligarchs requested Spartan aid for a counterrevolution. Sparta agreed and in autumn 391 sent eight ships under the navarch Ecdicus. But when Ecdicus reached Cnidus, he heard that the democrats in Rhodes had twice as many ships as he did, so he wisely spent the winter at

Cnidus. In spring 390 Sparta sent another fleet to Rhodes under Teleutias, with twelve ships. He captured ten Athenian ships en route to help Evagoras of Cyprus. By the time he reached Rhodes, Teleutias had thirty-seven ships.

In the Aegean and Saronic Gulf, naval power seesawed between Athens and Sparta and the two fleets that each could muster. Athens sent a fleet of forty ships against Teleutias at Rhodes, but their commander, Thrasybulus, decided to go instead to the Hellespont. In that strategic region he made an effort to rebuild Athens' empire. Although Thrasybulus was killed, he had achieved some success, so Sparta sent out a new fleet to challenge Athens in the Hellespont. But under the brilliant Athenian commander Iphicrates, Athens parried effectively. Meanwhile, a second Spartan fleet sailed the Saronic Gulf from its base on the island of Aegina. From here they attacked Athenian ships and raided Piraeus and the coast of Attica. Athens attacked Spartan ships in turn and landed on Aegina, although it failed to take the island.

At this point, Spartan diplomacy proved decisive. Sparta's job was to persuade Artaxerxes that the specter of revived Athenian empire was even worse than Spartan "shamelessness." Antalcidas, a Spartan statesman, proved equal to the task. He could point not only to Athenian naval activity in and around the Hellespont but also to Athenian support for Persian rebels in Cyprus and Egypt. As Xenophon noted, in a Thucydidean vein, Athens was hurting itself.[45]

As both navarch and ambassador to Artaxerxes in summer 388, Antalcidas persuaded the Persians to finance a new Spartan fleet. Sparta also had aid from Dionysius of Syracuse. Back in the Hellespont in summer 387 after his mission to Persia, Antalcidas defeated the Athenians and took control of the waterway with a fleet grown to eighty ships. Afraid of a second Aegospotami, Athens surrendered.

The result was the treaty known as the King's Peace or the Peace of Antalcidas. Under this treaty, Athens was excluded from the eastern Aegean (with a few exceptions), but so was Sparta; Persia was granted authority over the Aegean coast of Anatolia and Cyprus. Sparta was given, in effect, a free hand to exert its military power and assert its hegemony on the Greek mainland.

On first sight, Persia and Sparta were the winners from this arrangement, but Athens benefited as well. Athens had surrendered in 404 to the one-two punch of the Persian-financed Spartan navy and the Spartan-led Peloponnesian army. Then Persia found itself on the defensive in western Anatolia against a series of Spartan invasions in 399–395 BC. But a coalition of great powers, led by Persia and Athens and including Corinth and Thebes, was able to destroy the Spartan navy and free Persia of the threat of Spartan invasion after 394.

True, Athens was outmaneuvered by Sparta, which made a deal with Persia that allowed Sparta to re-impose its continental hegemony on the Greek peninsula by 385 BC. But Athens could maneuver too. Within a decade, she had launched a new naval alliance in the Aegean, which would have not been possible without Persia's prior help in crushing Sparta's navy. So, in one way or another, Persia and Athens each profited from their joint enterprise against the Spartan fleet.

With the King's Peace of 386, both sides demobilized their armies and navies. But neither Sparta nor Athens was done with naval power yet. In 378–377 BC, Athens launched a new naval league, the so-called Second Athenian Confederacy. Although never a success on the scale of Athens' fifth-century empire, the Confederacy gave Athens considerable power at sea. For most of the next two decades, Athens and Sparta competed again at sea.[46]

Historians tend to subordinate the details to the story of Sparta's conflict on land with Thebes. And rightly so, since the land war proved decisive— indeed, fatal. Beginning in 378 BC Thebes led a revived Boeotian confederacy in opposition to Sparta. For most of the 370s Athens joined the Boeotians against Sparta until Athens grew alarmed at the growth of its ally's power.

At the battle of Leuctra in 371 Thebes killed Cleombrotus, one of Sparta's two kings, and destroyed Spartan land power permanently. This proved surprisingly easy to do, for the simple reason of Sparta's shortage of military manpower. The chickens of Sparta's social and economic problems had come home to roost. Over the following few years, the Boeotians invaded the Peloponnese repeatedly and reestablished Messenia as an independent state. It marked the liberation of the Helots and the destruction of the economic and territorial basis for Spartan supremacy.

In contrast, Sparta's naval activities in the 370s merely confirmed its inability to defeat Athens at sea. The details are as follows. A year after Athens' foundation of the Second Athenian Confederacy, in 376, Sparta struck at sea after a decade of neglecting the fleet. Under the navarch Pollis, Sparta sent sixty ships to take control of the waters around Aegina, Ceos, and Andros, off the coast of Attica. Pollis was also able to interfere with the import of grain from the Black Sea to Athens in summer 376. But Sparta's victories were temporary. Athens broke the blockade, and in September the Athenian commander Chabrias sailed with eighty-three ships to besiege the island of Naxos and to challenge Sparta to battle. Naxos was a great Athenian victory despite the loss of eighteen Athenian ships, about one-fourth of its fleet. Sparta was deprived of more than half of its fleet: Twenty-four ships were lost and eight more were captured.

Still, Sparta was not finished at sea. The naval struggle between Sparta and Athens now shifted from the Aegean to the waters off northwestern Greece. In 375 Sparta mustered a fleet of fifty-five ships, but it too was defeated, this time at the battle of Alyzia (in Acarnania). Both victories brought new members to the Second Athenian League. In 375–374 small Spartan fleets went on expeditions to the islands of Zakynthos and Corcyra to support anti-Athenian factions in both places.

Sparta's last known navarch was Mnasippus. In autumn 373 Mnasippus was in control of the island of Corcyra, where he commanded a fleet of sixty ships and a force of fifteen hundred mercenaries. Mnasippus treated the mercenaries miserably, with the arrogance of which only the Spartans were capable. In spring 372 they suffered a crushing defeat at the hands of the Athenians, in which Mnasippus was one of the fallen.

Conclusion

Sparta's imperial navy did great things in its short life. Although innovative, it was less of a departure from Spartan tradition that it might seem at first. Long before 411 BC, Sparta had its own proponents of a maritime strategy. And yet when all is said and done, the maritime option was problematic for Sparta. It ran against the grain of an austere, inward-looking, arrogant, conservative, continental power. True, from 411 BC on, that state sought supreme power in Greece. But when the going got rough, Sparta was quick to go back to old continental habits. The navy was dispensable.

The maritime option was popular among many in Sparta, but not generally among the Spartiate elite, where it had only a toehold. From the point of view of the leading Spartan statesmen, the Spartan navy was the natural outlet for misfits. Ambitious men who were denied the chance of reaching the top in Sparta's military-political hierarchy turned to the navy and made their own way in it. Pausanias the Regent, who could not be king in his own right, and Lysander, a commoner and mothax who could not be king at all, not by accident, are the two greatest names in Sparta's maritime history. Other mothakes such as Gylippus and Callicratidas also played important roles in Sparta's overseas operations. The fleet was an outlet for diplomats as well— Lysander or Antalcidas. And it is somehow fitting that Brasidas, the avatar of a risky and innovative overland mission to northern Greece, should have served as a trierarch in the Spartan fleet.

For Sparta the navy was a luxury, but it was also a temptation. And it is in the nature of austere oligarchies to crack down on temptation. For every Spartan who was attracted by maritime expansion, there was another and more powerful oligarch who was determined to maintain the old ways of a land power. It is not surprising that navalists like Pausanias the Regent and Gylippus ended up condemned to death, or that Lysander was disgraced posthumously. Nor is it surprising that the most influential man in Sparta, King Agesilaus, could neglect the indispensable naval foundation of Sparta's newly won imperial power.

The Spartan elite was small, and personal influence was key. In such a system, a very talented individual could accomplish quite a lot. But the other side of the coin was cronyism, back-scratching, and incompetence. If Lysander showed what one Spartan could do with ships, so did Callicratidas and Pisander.

The fleet that won the Peloponnesian War proved to hang on the fate of the man who had built it: Lysander. Sparta's commitment to naval power was never more than skin deep. The result was the brief duration of Sparta's naval empire: born 405 BC, died 394 BC—one year after the death of Lysander.

Spartan culture was both a spur to naval expansion and a weight that dragged it down. Spartans were taught to put Sparta first: the good of the state came before private life, and Sparta came before the rest of the Greeks. The result was a spirit of pragmatism that shaded easily into opportunism. Given an opportunity such as Athens' failure in Sicily and Persia's offer of aid, Sparta was quick to respond. It had little trouble selling out the Anatolian Greeks in exchange for vital Persian help against Athens. But Sparta had equally little trouble selling out the Persian state for a rebel prince, Cyrus, and when that venture failed, for turning and turning again in a seemingly endless cycle of friendship and enmity.

Perhaps surprisingly, Sparta's oligarchy proved more flexible than Athenian democracy when it came to doing what had to be done to win. Sparta won the Peloponnesian War and did so by beating democracy at its own game: versatility. But Sparta lacked the institutional mechanisms to build on its achievements. Neither Athens nor Persia was as versatile as Sparta, but they each had deeper "bench strength," so to speak. Persia had not been an Aegean naval power since at least 449 BC, if not 479. Beginning in 412, however, it began funding fleet after fleet to make war on first one Greek naval power, then another. Athens lost its entire navy in the Peloponnesian War, but about twenty-five years later it founded a second naval confederacy.

Sparta's interest in the maritime option proved durable enough for it to remain active as a naval power for three decades after the Peloponnesian War. But the massive effort needed to maintain a naval empire was sustained by Sparta for only ten years. In the end it was not all that difficult for Sparta's enemies to drive Sparta from command of the seas. They had only to join forces and do what they each did naturally and best. Sparta, by contrast, would have had to behave unnaturally to succeed.

As Aristotle comments, "Yet while they [the Spartans] preserved themselves as long as they were at war, they came to ruin when they were ruling [an empire] through not knowing how to be at leisure, and because there is no training among them that has more authority than the training for war."[47] In the end, Sparta survived naval disaster. It could not overcome a catastrophe on land. Theban-led Boeotia crushed the Spartan land army at Leuctra in 371 BC. Boeotia did what Athens had failed to do in the Peloponnesian War—defeat Sparta in its own element. But by 371 Sparta had been bled dry by Athens and Persia and squeezed of manpower by its own brittle social system. The ancient world would have to await the coming of Rome to see a continental power achieve and maintain mastery of the sea, and survive—at least for a time—the burdens of empire.

Notes

1. Thuc. 2.65.12. This and all translations from Thucydides are taken from Robert B. Strassler, ed. *The Landmark Thucydides. A Comprehensive Guide to the Peloponnesian War* (New York: Simon & Schuster, 1998). I use the standard abbreviations for the names of classical authors, found in Simon Hornblower and Antony Spawforth, eds. *The Oxford Classical Dictionary*, 3rd edition (Oxford, U.K.: Oxford University. Press, 1999), xxix–liv.

2. J. F. Lazenby, *The Peloponnesian War: A Military History* (London: Routledge, 2004), 252–54. For an assessment of the war's outcome that is much less impressed by Sparta, see Victor Davis Hanson, *A War Like No Other: How the Athenians and Spartans Fought the Peloponnesian War* (New York: Random House, 2005), 309–12.

3. On Spartan honor, see J. E. Lendon, "Spartan Honor," in Charles D. Hamilton and Peter Krentz, eds. *Polis and Polemos. Essays on Politics, War, and History in Ancient Greece in Honor of Donald Kagan* (Claremont, CA: Regina Books, 1997), 105–26.

4. Thuc. 8.96.5.

5. For a good discussion of Spartan secrecy in military matters, see Anton Powell, "Mendacity and Sparta's Use of the Visual," in Anton Powell, ed. *Classical Sparta: Techniques behind Her Success*, foreword by Paul Cartledge (Norman: University of Oklahoma Press, 1988), 173–92.

6. The scholarly literature on Sparta is not small. A general-audience introduction is Paul Cartledge, *The Spartans: The World of the Warrior-Heroes of Ancient Greece* (New York: Vintage Books, 2003). Short but perceptive is W. G. Forrest, *A History of Sparta 950–192 BC* (New York: W. W. Norton & Co, 1968); for more detail, see H. Michell, *Sparta* (Cambridge, U.K.: Cambridge University Press, 1952, repr. 1964); or J. T. Hooker, *The Ancient Spartans* (London: J. M. Dent, 1980). Valuable recent collections of scholarly essays are Stephen Hodkinson and Anton Powell, eds., *The Shadow of Sparta* (New York: Routledge for the Classical Press of Wales, 1994); Hodkinson and Powell, *Sparta: New Perspectives* (London: Duckworth, 1999); Hodkinson and Powell, *Sparta: Beyond the Mirage* (London: Classical Press of Wales and Duckworth, 2002); Thomas J. Figueira, ed., *Spartan Society* (Swansea: The Classical Press of Wales, 2004); Hodkinson and Powell, eds., *Sparta & War* (Swansea: The Classical Press of Wales, 2006).

7. On the Spartan army, see J. F. Lazenby, *The Spartan Army* (Warminster, U.K.: Aris & Phillips, 1985); Nicholas Sekunda, *The Spartans* (London: Osprey Pub. Ltd., 1998). On Sparta's militarism (or lack thereof), see Stephen Hodkinson, "Was Classical Sparta a Military Society?" in Hodkinson and Powell, eds., *Sparta & War*, 11–163.

8. See Nigel M. Kennell, *The Gymnasium of Virtue: Education and Culture in Ancient Sparta* (Chapel Hill: University of North Carolina Press, 1995); Jean Ducat, *Spartan Education: Youth and Society in the Classical Period*, trans. Emma Stafford, P.-J. Shaw, and Anton Powell (Swansea: University Press of Wales, 2006).

9. On the Peloponnesian League, see Donald Kagan, *The Outbreak of the Peloponnesian War* (Ithaca: Cornell University Press, 1969), 8–30.

10. On the nature of the Peloponnesian League and of Spartan hegemony, see G. E. M. de Ste. Croix, *The Origins of the Peloponnesian War* (Ithaca, NY: Cornell University Press, 1972), 89–166, 333–42.

11. Cyrus: Hdt. 1.152–53; Polycrates: Hdt. 3.54–56; Paul Cartledge, *Agesilaos and the Crisis of Sparta* (Baltimore: Johns Hopkins University Press, 1987), 47.

12. "Thalassocracy List" in Eusebius, *Chronographia* 1.225, ed. Schoene. Pisistratus: Hdt. 5.63.

13. Phocaea: Hdt. 1.152; Cleomenes' daughter: Hdt. 5.51.

14. On Sparta's naval actions in 480 BC, see Barry Strauss, *The Battle of Salamis: The Naval Encounter that Saved Greece—and Western Civilization* (New York: Simon & Schuster, 2004).

15. Thuc. 1.95.7.

16. Diodorus Siculus 11.50.6; Kagan, *The Outbreak of the Peloponnesian War*, 51–52; Ste. Croix, *Origins of the Peloponnesian War*, 169–78.

17. Cartledge, *Agesilaos*, 47.

18. Among one-volume histories of the war are Donald Kagan, *The Peloponnesian War* (New York: Viking, 2003); and Lazenby, *Peloponnesian War*. I offer an overview of the war's naval history in Barry Strauss, "Athens and Sparta," in C. Gray and R. W. Barnett, eds., *Seapower and Strategy* (Annapolis, MD: Naval Institute Press, 1989), 77–99. The indispensable commentary to Thucydides' history is A. W. Gomme, *A Historical Commentary on Thucydides*, vols. 1–4 (vols. 4–5 with A. Andrewes and K. J. Dover; Oxford: Clarendon Press, 1945–70), now supplemented by two volumes of commentary, on Thucydides' first four books as well as the first twenty-four chapters of the fifth book, by Simon Hornblower, *A Commentary on Thucydides* (Oxford: Clarendon Press, 1991).

19. On these divisions, see "The Problem of Periodization: The Case of the Peloponnesian War," in Mark Golden and Peter Toohey, eds., *Inventing Ancient Culture: Historicism, Periodization, and the Ancient World* (Routledge, 1997), 165–75.

20. Thuc. 1.125.2, cf. 7.28.3. On the finances of war in this era, see Lisa Kallet-Marx, *Money, Expense, and Naval Power in Thucydides' History 1–5.24* (Berkeley: University of California Press, 1993).

21. On Spartan actions in the Archidamian War, see P. A. Brunt, "Spartan Policy and Strategy in the Archidamian War," *Phoenix* 19 (1965): 255–80; Donald Kagan, *The Archidamian War* (Ithaca, NY: Cornell University Press, 1974); Thomas Kelly, "Thucydides and Spartan Strategy in the Archidamian War," *American Historical Review* 87 (1982): 25–54.

22. Thuc. 2.83–92.

23. See Joseph Roisman, "Alkidas in Thucydides," *Historia* 36 (1987): 385–421.

24. Thuc. 4.12.3.

25. Books 6 and 7 of Thucydides are devoted primarily to the subject of Athens' ill-fated attempt to conquer Syracuse (and with it, the island of Sicily, or so the Athenians hoped).

26. Syracusan squadrons took part in several naval actions of the Ionian War. After the losses of Cynossema and Cyzicus, the Syracusans built twenty-five new triremes for Lysander in the eastern Aegean; Xen. *Hell.* 1.1.25–26; J. S. Morrison, J. E. Coates, and N. B. Rankov, *The Athenian Trireme: The History and Reconstruction of an Ancient Greek Warship,* 2nd ed. (Cambridge, U.K.: Cambridge University Press, 2000), 82, 87–88. "In quiet enjoyment": Thuc. 8.2.4. On Agis' money-raising efforts, see Thuc. 8.5.3; and Lisa Kallet, *Money and the Corrosion of Power in Thucydides: The Sicilian Expedition and Its Aftermath* (Berkeley: University of California Press, 2001), 238–42.

27. Donald Kagan, *The Fall of the Athenian Empire* (Ithaca: Cornell University Press, 1987), 11–13.

28. Thuc. 1.82–83, 8.3.2. For Sparta as hegemon of the Peloponnesian League during the Peloponnesian War, see Barry Strauss, "The Art of Alliance and the Peloponnesian War," in Hamilton and Krentz, eds., *Polis and Polemos,* 127–40.

29. The best discussion of Sparta's relationship with Persia is David M. Lewis, *Sparta and Persia: Lectures delivered at the University of Cincinnati, Autumn 1976 in Memory of Donald W. Bradeen* (Leiden, The Netherlands: E. J. Brill, 1977).

30. Luigi Pareti, "Ricerche sulla potenza marittima degli Spartani e sulla cronologia dei nauarchi," *Memorie della Accademia delle scienze di Torino. 2, Classe di scienze morali, storiche e filologiche* 59 (1908/09): 71–159, reprinted in *Idem, Studi minori di storia antica,* vol. 2 (Rome: Edizioni di Storia e Lettteratura, 1961), 36–38. On Sparta's navarchs, see Raphael Sealey, "Die Spartanische Navarchie," *Klio* 58 (1976): 335–58. On Spartan training, see F. S. Naiden, "Spartan Naval Officers: An Overlooked Factor in the Peloponnesian War," paper delivered at the annual conference of the Association of Ancient Historians, Tampa, Florida, April 2008.

31. Dice: Plut. *Lysander* 8.5. Aristotle, *Pol.* 1271a40. On Lysander see Detlef Lotze, *Lysander und der Peloponnesische Krieg* (Berlin: Akademie-Verlag, 1964); Paul A. Rahe, Jr., "Lysander and the Spartan Settlement," PhD diss., Yale University, 1977; Jean-François Bommelaer, *Lysandre de Sparte: Histoire et Traditions* (Athens: École Française d'Athènes, 1981).

32. Morrison, Coates, and Rankov, *Athenian Trireme,* 178–80.

33. Plut., *Lysander* 6.4.

34. The bibliography on Aegospotami includes Christopher Ehrhardt, "Xenophon and Diodorus on Aegospotami," *Phoenix* 24 (1970): 225–28; Bommelaer, *Lysandre,* 101–15; Barry Strauss, "Aegospotami Reexamined," *American Journal of Philology* 104 (1983): 24–35; *Idem,* "A Note on the Tactics and Topography of Aegospotami," *American Journal of Philology* 108 (1987): 741–45; Lazenby, *Peloponnesian War,* 240–44.

35. For a narrative history of Greco-Persian war and diplomacy from 404 to 362 BC, see John Buckler, *Aegean Greece in the Fourth Century BC* (Leiden, The Netherlands: Brill, 2003), 1–350.

36. Karl-Wilhelm Welwei, *Sparta: Aufstieg und Niedergang einer Antiken Grossmacht* (Stuttgart, Germany: Klett-Cotta, 2004), 268.

37. Forrest, *History of Sparta,* 123.

38. Plut. *Artaxerxes* 22.1.

39. For an introduction to the subject of Sparta's socioeconomic problems in the decades after the Peloponnesian War, see Cartledge, *Agesilaos*, 395–412, and Stephen Hodkinson, "Inheritance, Marriage and Demography: Perspectives upon the Success and Decline of Classical Sparta," Anton Powell, ed., *Classical Sparta: Techniques behind Her Success*, foreword by Paul Cartledge (Norman: University of Oklahoma Press, 1988), 79–121.

40. On these points, see Simon Hornblower, "Persia," in David M. Lewis, John Boardman, Simon Hornblower, et al., *The Cambridge Ancient History*, 2nd ed., vol. 6, *The Fourth Century* BC (Cambridge, U.K.: Cambridge University Press, 1994), 65–67.

41. Hornblower, "*Persia*," 67.

42. Hornblower, "*Persia*," 71–72. For an assessment of Spartan policy in the Corinthian War, see Charles D. Hamilton, *Sparta's Bitter Victories: Politics and Diplomacy in the Corinthian War* (Ithaca, NY: Cornell University Press, 1979).

43. Xen. *Hell.* 4.3.10–12, cf. 3.4.27–29; Plut. *Agesilaus* 10.5–6; Cartledge, *Agesilaos*, 357–58; Charles D. Hamilton, *Agesilaus and the Failure of Spartan Hegemony* (Ithaca, NY: Cornell University Press, 1991), 109.

44. Losses at Cnidus: Diod. *Sic.* 14.83; Conon's expedition to Greece: Guido Barbieri, *Conone* (Rome: A. Signorelli, 1955).

45. Xen. *Hell.* 4.8.24.

46. Jack L. Cargill Jr., *Second Athenian League: Empire or Free Alliance?* (Berkeley: University of California Press, 1981).

47. Aristotle, *Pol.* 1271b1, trans. Carnes Lord, *Aristotle, The Politics* (Chicago: The University of Chicago Press, 1984), 78.

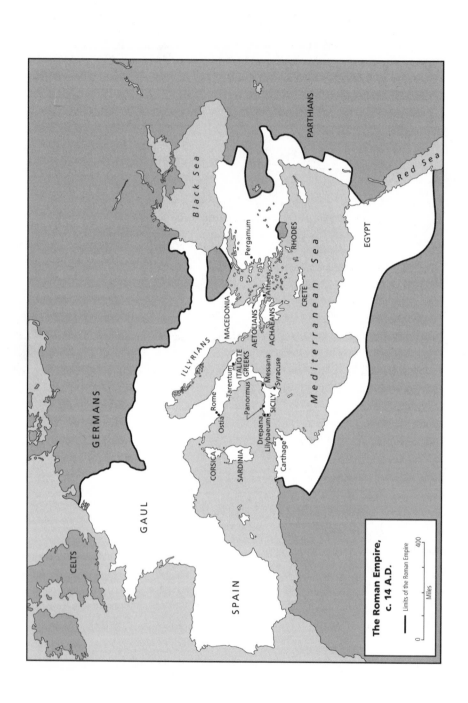

**The Roman Empire,
c. 14 A.D.**

— Limits of the Roman Empire

0   400

Miles

GERMANS

CELTS

GAUL

SPAIN

CORSICA

SARDINIA

Rome
Ostia

Tarentum
ITALIOTE
GREEKS

Panormus

Drepana
Lilybaeum
SICILY

Messana
Syracuse

Carthage

ILLYRIANS

MACEDONIA

AETOLIANS

ACHAEANS

Athens

Pergamum

RHODES

CRETE

Black Sea

PARTHIANS

Red Sea

EGYPT

Mediterranean Sea

Arthur M. Eckstein

Rome Dominates the Mediterranean

THE PRESENT VOLUME EXPLORES the nature and impact of "maritime transformation"—that is, how and why great states that have previously been purely or almost purely land powers become important sea powers as well, and how the gaining of sea power impacts their worldview, policies, and even culture. The Roman Republic in the age of the Punic Wars seems at first glance a good candidate for this topic. For hundreds of years in their early history, the Romans were purely a land power, and their primary military weapon always remained the heavy infantry legion, and not warships. But it is also true that Rome in the end became a sea power as well as a land power, and eventually Rome became the sole surviving and uncontested sea power in its world. Roman fleets came to patrol all of the Mediterranean Sea from Spain to Syria, and a look at a map suggests immediately that it was around the Mediterranean that Rome constructed its empire, with the sea acting not as a barrier but as a central communications link to the constituent parts of that empire. The Romans came to call the Mediterranean Sea *mare nostrum*, "Our Sea." And eventually squadrons of Roman warships even patrolled the Atlantic coasts of Spain, Gaul (France), and Britain—"The Outer Sea."

Yet it is also the case that the trajectory of the seafaring of the Romans was not a simple and unidirectional development from land power to sea power. "Maritime transformation" in Rome was superficial for a very long time; it occurred at first only under the extreme pressure of circumstances and was even reversed for long periods. The establishment of permanent fleets to patrol the seas was exceptionally long delayed, not occurring until after 30 BC—more than two hundred years after the Senate ordered the building of the first war fleet. And the phrase *mare nostrum* dates only from the mid-first century BC, more than a century after the obvious founding (or so one would have thought) of Roman maritime supremacy throughout the Mediterranean.[1]

To be sure, Rome after three hundred years as a purely land power in Italy suddenly built and began deploying large war fleets to contest control of the western Mediterranean with Carthage in two great wars after 264 BC. Large Roman fleets also played an important role in the great wars Rome fought with the Hellenistic monarchies at the end of the third century and beginning of the second—the wars that established Rome as the dominant power throughout the Mediterranean. Again, almost a century and a half later, around 70 BC, large Roman war fleets began clearing the eastern Mediterranean of pirates, and war fleets sometimes played a vital role in the civil wars that destroyed the Republic after 50 BC. The founding victory of the New Order, the Principate of the Emperor Augustus, was in fact a naval victory: his victory over Antony and Cleopatra in the Bay of Actium off western Greece in 31 BC.

Nevertheless, in spite of the improvisational character of Roman naval war making in the period of Rome's struggle for survival and power with the other great Mediterranean states (264–188 BC), after winning naval supremacy in the Mediterranean by 188 BC, the government at Rome allowed the almost complete decay of Roman naval resources and engaged in no major naval activity for a century between 168 BC and 70 BC. The civil wars of the late Republic did bring a return to vigorous naval warfare, this time between Roman political factions, but it was still essentially improvisational naval warfare. Fleets were not in being but were hurriedly constructed for the crisis, and although the fleets were large in numbers of warships, the ships were crude, the sailors ill trained, and the tactics unsophisticated. Only under Augustus, the first emperor, did the Roman government finally create a permanent naval establishment, with squadrons of Roman warships regularly patrolling the Mediterranean and even the Atlantic coasts of Europe. This was part of Augustus' general reorganization of Rome's disorderly government on a more rational (if more dictatorial) basis, but this came after two centuries of delay.

In premodern times the sources of naval expertise, and eventually of military shipping, lay with the merchant marine, and here it appears that the Romans and Latins were always weak. They might engage in investments overseas (e.g., in the farming of taxes in provinces), but they rarely engaged personally in overseas shipping as investments during the Republic. In fact, a law of 218 BC forbade senators to invest in large-scale merchant ships.[2] To judge from the inscriptions preserved from the great entrepôt at Delos in the central Aegean, most of the Italians active in the Aegean were *Italiotes* (that is, citizens of Greek-speaking towns in southern Italy), and the "Romans" who appear on Delos are mostly freedmen. A classic example is the shipping magnate Trimalchio in Petronius' comic novel *Satyricon* (ca. AD 60): Trimalchio is a freed slave of Syrian origin, although now he is legally a Roman citizen (and a fabulously rich one). Similarly, after the imperial fleets in being were institutionalized by Augustus, they were manned primarily by non-Romans who came from cultures with a strong naval heritage. Both in commerce and in the imperial fleets, then, the secret to Roman success lay not so much in a maritime transformation of Roman culture but in the ability of the Romans to attach to themselves those polities and cultures that did have strong naval traditions. Moreover, in the great wars with Carthage, Rome's "naval allies," the *socii navales* (primarily Greek polities and a few Etruscan polities of Italy), contributed substantially to the Roman fleets, and in the slightly later great wars against the Hellenistic monarchies, the important fleets of Rhodes and Pergamum were equal partners in Roman naval endeavors. The Romans came to dominate the Mediterranean by building— out of necessity—their own large fleets, but equally by employing as their instruments the ships and men of more naval-oriented cultures.[3]

The reason for this lack of Roman interest in the sea was not that Rome was geographically a "continental" power. The city of Rome was located only some fifteen miles inland from the coast of Latium, and many Romans worked farms near or along the coastline. This coast has few good harbors, but a significant potential port existed at Ostia, a town in existence by the fourth century BC on the coast just west of Rome; Ostia thus could have played a role in early Roman history similar to that of the Piraeus to Athens, but it did not. Eventually Antium (Anzio) was also available. As Thiel points out, the coast of Holland is a terribly difficult one, with treacherous shoals and swept by sudden and dangerous gales, but that did not stop the Dutch from taking to the sea. The Roman situation in terms of access to a sailable coast was not nearly so difficult.[4]

The explanation for Roman lack of interest in seafaring seems to have been economic, not geographical. In antiquity, it was often those polities whose agricultural hinterland was not very fertile whose denizens took to the sea to make a living or to supplement what could be gotten from farming. The sea was always a second choice, for given the primitive character of ancient sailing technology, the sea was a place of high risk: Petronius' Trimalchio once lost almost his whole fortune in a storm. But the Roman heartland of Latium south of the Tiber River was immensely fertile, and it could support a population that was very large in comparison to most city-states. Given an agricultural bounty that was immediately available and could be gotten without chancing the sea, it is no wonder that Roman culture remained focused on the land, or that our sources say that farming was the most honorable way to make a living.[5]

One final introductory point: Over the past generation, it has become general scholarly opinion that the key to understanding the exceptional success of Rome in expanding its power and influence and eventually coming to dominate the entire Mediterranean basin was the fact that Rome was an exceptionally militaristic and aggressive state—in fact, a ferocious international predator, and not merely in our terms but in ancient terms as well.[6] This conclusion seems to me to be based on a misunderstanding of the brutal character of ancient international relations. The Roman state appears to us today to be extraordinarily militaristic and aggressive in its diplomacy, but its behavior was not exceptional within its own environment. The ancient Mediterranean world was a harsh multipolar anarchy, in which all polities—large, medium, and small; monarchies, republics, democracies, or federal leagues—were in our terms exceptionally militaristic, bellicose, and aggressive. The lack of international law and their own fragility as states forced all these polities in the same brutal direction and made them all functionally similar. Rome's neighbors—at first the Latins and Etruscans, later the Celts and the Samnites and the Italiote Greeks, later still the Carthaginians and the great Hellenistic kingdoms—were as militaristic and bellicose and aggressive as Rome.[7]

But if Rome's exceptional international success cannot be explained by its militarism, bellicosity, and aggressiveness—qualities that it shared with many other states—what, then, explains it? The answer was given by Theodor Mommsen long ago: the ability of Rome to attach to itself, and eventually even to absorb, other (i.e., non-Roman) peoples, a flexibility that allowed Rome access to unusually large resources with which to conduct the savage interstate struggle for survival and power.[8] This Roman quality is specifically shown in the development of Roman sea power, which always depended in good part not on Romans but on Italiote Greeks, and later on other extra-Italian peoples more habituated to seafaring than were the Romans.

We hear little of Romans on the sea before the third century BC. The situation began to change as Roman influence expanded southward beyond Campania (the region south of Latium) and the Republic began to take the Greek cities of southern Italy under its protection. Rome found a source of potential naval strength among these Italiote polities. The Greek coastal cities had a long maritime tradition, both merchant marine and military, and because they assumed the role of allies of Rome, they became allies of a special sort. When states in Italy swore treaties of alliance with Rome, their primary obligation was military support of Roman war efforts, overwhelmingly in the form of land troops. But when Rome needed warships or transports, the Greek coastal towns—the socii navales—now provided them.

From 311 BC the Senate appointed a board of *duumviri navales* (literally, "the two men for dealing with naval matters") who probably had control over a squadron of twenty ships when such a squadron was necessary. In this way the Romans could assert some sort of naval power along the coasts of Italy.[9] But it was not a substantial naval power. In a famous incident, one such squadron of ten triremes was defeated by the war fleet of Tarentum in 282 when it entered the Gulf of Tarentum.[10] It is likely that these squadrons, including the squadron defeated in 282, neither put to sea every year nor were truly Roman ships but rather were drawn from ships (fifty-oared vessels—*penteconters*—and triremes) loaned to Rome on an ad hoc basis by the Italiote Greek socii navales and manned and captained by Italiotes, although under the overall command of a Roman official. This was still the situation in 264 BC.[11] So although the creation of the duumviri navales indicates that by the turn of the third century BC naval matters had become an occasional element of senatorial concern, the sea still received only minimal attention.

It is possible that in 267 the duumviri navales were allowed to lapse, replaced by a board of four annually-elected Roman *quaestores classici* ("supervisors of the fleet"), but the evidence is disputed. Some scholars argue that this development shows a profound change in the Roman attitude toward naval warfare, an indication that the Romans were preparing for a permanent warfleet—and hence a war with the great naval power Carthage—three years before the first great conflict with Carthage began.[12] In any case, it is certain that down to 264 BC the only naval resources Rome had available were triremes and fifty-oared ships, light vessels in Hellenistic terms (i.e., not line-of-battle ships), drawn from and manned by the Italiote naval allies.

The Roman state had no heavy warships (*quinquiremes*—see later discussion), nor even any warships built and manned by Romans. Thus Polybius of Megalopolis, the great Greek historian of the rise of Rome, writing around 150 BC, is explicit that at the start the First Punic War in 264 BC, "not only did Rome possess no kataphraktoi [decked ships, triremes or heavier] but Rome had no warships at all, not even a single lembos [light craft]." Any squadrons operating on behalf of Rome before 264 BC, then, must have been gathered on an ad hoc basis from the socii navales.[13]

The resultant Roman weakness at sea is clear from accounts of the crisis at the Straits of Messana (separating Sicily from southern Italy) in 264 BC. The crisis originated in an appeal to Rome from the Mamertine rulers of Messana, on the Sicilian side of the Straits, for protection against the great Siceliote Greek city of Syracuse. The Carthaginians, who had long dominated the western Mediterranean with their fleet, took advantage of the Mamertine crisis to throw their own garrison into Messana, but the Mamertines clearly preferred Rome. They soon threw the Punic garrison out, inviting in the Romans, but this led to the creation of an alliance between Carthage and Syracuse against Messana, and a joint siege of the town.[14] A Roman army arrived at the straits, determined to break the siege, but the Carthaginian commander warned the Romans not even to attempt a crossing, for Punic enmity would mean that "the Romans would not be allowed even to wash their hands in the sea."[15] The insult shows how weak Rome's naval reputation was in 264, and Polybius explicitly says that in the crisis the Romans had only a squadron of Italiote light ships under their command.[16] This Italiote squadron was defeated in the straits by the Carthaginian fleet; yet the Roman consul Ap. Claudius Caudex managed by a trick and under cover of night to slip his army in transports across the two miles of open water into Messana. His legionaries then defeated both the Syracusan and Punic forces besieging the town, and broke the siege. It is significant that the victory was won on land by the legions. Syracuse soon made its peace with Rome, but the Punic government would not allow Rome to gain predominant influence in eastern Sicily and instead poured both naval and land reinforcements into the island. The result was a large-scale war between Carthage and Rome for control of Sicily—the First Punic War.[17]

The complete lack of a Roman navy in 264 BC, or even Roman access to naval allies who possessed the standard Hellenistic heavy warship the quinquireme, is striking. As noted earlier, the Romans' main weapon throughout this period was, and would remain, the heavy infantry legion. But although the fertility of Latium meant that Roman society had previously felt no great need to engage in seafaring, the war with Carthage created necessities of its own—military ones. The problem was that Rome after 264 was in the untenable position of contending with Carthage in a war for control of a huge island (Sicily) while possessing no fleet except the light vessels of its Italiote allies. Moreover, the Carthaginians now began to use their naval bases in Sicily, Sardinia, and Corsica to launch seaborne raids on Italy itself. The city-states of the Italiote south had only recently come under Roman hegemony (in the 280s and 270s), which meant that their allegiance to Rome was still unstable. If Rome was unable to provide them with protection from seaborne raids (and, equally important, protection for their vital seaborne commerce), not only would Sicily be a lost cause, but Roman control of southern Italy itself would be in danger.

It was this threatening situation—combined, however, with the possibilities opened by evidence that on land Roman armies were clearly superior to Punic ones—that led the Senate in 261 to order the construction of the first Roman war fleet. We have a detailed account of the building of this fleet, in Polybius, and the account underlines how little the Romans knew of the sea at this point. They employed as a model from which to work a Carthaginian quinquireme that had run aground in the Straits of Messana. They had no carpenters trained as shipwrights, and no trained crews, "for the Romans had never given a thought to the sea";[18] but they pressed ahead and built one hundred quinquiremes on the Carthaginian model, as well as twenty triremes. The novice crews were trained on land, sitting on rowers' benches as they would in an actual quinquireme (three benches high, with two men on each of the top two benches), with a boatswain calling out the strokes so that they learned to do the oarstrokes in unison.[19] Polybius was greatly impressed with the energy displayed by the Roman state in this project. The Senate immediately ordered this new fleet to challenge the Carthaginians, who had controlled the western Mediterranean for more than two hundred years.[20]

It is appropriate to admit how little we know about the crucial elements that would have constituted a distinct naval "culture" at Rome. We have little detailed knowledge of the skills and personal qualities needed in the officers and men of the warships, only generalities such as "intelligence" and "courage" and (for ship pilots) "knowledge of the sea." For the First Punic War, we have no information about the ethnic origins of the crews. In contrast to the trireme fleets of fifth-century Athens, which were oared by Athenian citizens,[21] it is probable that the navigators and helmsmen of "Roman" ships of this period were Italiote Greeks even if the ship captain was a Roman. And to judge from the situation in the Second Punic War (218–201 BC), the rowing and deck crews were not always Romans either but were drawn from the socii navales of the Italian coast.[22]

Similarly, we know almost nothing of the skills, knowledge, and personal qualities needed for the administrators who must have run the state dockyards where warships were built and where they received maintenance and dry-docking when not in use (and storage over the winter nonsailing season). And we know nothing about the merchants and contractors who must have supplied those dockyards. But we have some idea of the vast variety of materiel that was needed for the maintenance of a Hellenistic war fleet even in harbor.[23] We know something about the training of oarsmen (discussed earlier), but almost nothing about the training of navigators (*proretae*), helmsmen (*gubernatores*), or ship captains (*navium magistri*).[24] We have little idea of the cost of building Hellenistic warships or the cost of maintaining them, either while on campaign or in harbor—although the costs of both building and maintenance must have been higher for the Hellenistic quinquireme than it had been for the trireme of the Classical period because the quinquireme was significantly larger than the earlier warship. Moreover, the cost of crews must have been much higher because the quinquireme took 400 men to the trireme's 240 or so.[25] We do know something about how Hellenistic warships were employed strategically to seize and maintain what we can call control of the sea, and what the purpose of doing so was. And we actually know a great deal about the limitations on warship usage both on campaign and in battle imposed by the unusual design of the ships (see later discussion) and quite a bit about the tactics these ships employed.

Still, in terms of the development of a Roman naval culture, it appears that few members of the crew of any Roman quinquireme of the Punic Wars were actually Latin-speaking Romans, perhaps only the captain and the marines. This "bi-ethnic" nature of the warships employed by the Republic in this period was actually not so unusual, for in the great Macedonian kingdoms the rowers and deck crews of the quinquiremes were (again) Greeks, whereas the marine contingents were Macedonian soldiery, and Macedonian fleets (such as Roman fleets of the period) employed boarding tactics to take advantage of the qualities of the Macedonian soldiery. The Macedonians, like the Romans, had little experience of the sea and were an overwhelmingly agricultural society; like the Romans, this remained true of them even when the fleets of the Macedonian monarchies came to dominate the eastern Mediterranean. This naval achievement was, it seems, accomplished primarily via the employment of maritime peoples under Macedonian control. The Romans were similar.

Whatever Rome's limitations in maritime experience, their strategic foundations of naval warfare in the third and second centuries BC and the difficulties in the projection of naval power over distance were not lost on the men in the Roman Senate. The basic warship of the third and second century was the quinquireme. Although such ships had sails, their primary motive power came from oarsmen. Instead of the famous three banks of single oarsmen for the earlier trireme, the quinquireme contained three banks of larger oars, with two men working the oars of the upper two tiers.[26] The rowing crew numbered about three hundred, which meant that the ships had thirty files of oars on each side, in three banks rowed by five men on a file. The rowing crew was thus double or more the number of oarsmen employed in a trireme, but all these men were still crammed onto and into a long narrow vessel. Triremes of the fifth century had measured about 115 feet long by 15 feet wide; quinquiremes measured about 130 feet long by 20 feet wide, only somewhat larger in size, yet filled with double the oar crew.[27] Quinquiremes also carried about double the number of marine infantry soldiers than triremes—ninety or so marines was the ordinary complement on the new sort of ship—and these men too had to be crammed aboard. Because of the development of marine catapults and the increased use of arrow-weapons, the rowing areas were roofed over for protection. The result was that quinquiremes, while only somewhat larger than triremes, were significantly heavier and less maneuverable. Such ships were designed more for ramming and boarding—hence the large contingent of marines—than they were for ramming and quick withdrawal to maneuver against another ship (the famous tactic of the triremes of the fifth century). An exception was the Rhodian fleet, renowned seamen who continued to pursue the ramming tactic more than any other navy.[28] A similar exception was the Carthaginian fleet as it existed at the beginning of the First Punic War, a fleet that could deal with boarding tactics but which was also trained to ramming as maneuver rather than as a mere preliminary to boarding the enemy.[29]

Thus, most Greek navies of the period tended to turn sea battles into land battles, as the Romans were later famous for doing; it is a popular misconception that such naval tactics were unique to Rome and demonstrate that they were "landlubbers." Given the Roman access to high-quality infantry, of course, the widespread tactic of the quinquireme as a boarding platform in battle, rather than a maneuver vessel, worked to the Roman advantage.[30] Yet it is still striking that the Romans—in contrast to the Greeks—did not develop a specialized terminology for naval battle tactics, but used the terminology of army and land warfare for naval battle. The approach of ships in line-ahead toward the enemy fleet was simply the *agmen* (the column, as in a column of infantrymen), and the charge of ships in line-abreast against the enemy—a common tactic—was simply the *acies* (the battleline, as in a phalanx of infantrymen).[31]

The main strategic consequence of these developments is that quinqueremes crammed with their large crews required nearby land bases from which to operate. Long sea voyages to battle were impossible. Most important was the situation facing the oarsmen: rowing in crammed conditions is tremendously hard work, either in the hot Mediterranean sun or in the stifling conditions created after the oarsmen were decked over for their own protection from missile-weapons; oarsmen especially needed a great deal of water to function. Triremes had been unable to carry enough water (or food) for the crew; conditions in quinqueremes were even more crowded and overloaded.[32] The needs of the crew for water (and food) meant that for Hellenistic oared warships to function, they needed friendly bases close by at which they could put in for water, rest, and supplies. In fact, crews normally expected and needed to beach their galleys for a noon meal, as well as for the night. This meant that for fleets to function and naval power to be projected over distance, naval bases could not be situated far from each other but had to be mutually supportive. The best situation was to establish bases that were only a day's voyage from one another.[33]

These facts determined the strategy that had to be followed in engaging in naval warfare on a large scale. Because both Rome and Carthage had access to bases in Sicily in the First Punic War, the clash of large forces at sea in great battles was possible: Rome had Messana and Syracuse (although use of the latter required diplomacy with the Syracusan government); Carthage had Panormus at first (it was seized by Rome in the late 250s) and Drepana and Lilybaeum. By contrast, in the Second Punic War, Carthage's lack of bases within range of Italy meant not only that Hannibal had to invade Italy overland but also that reinforcement by sea from Carthaginian-held territory was difficult and risky. In fact, the Punic government only attempted such reinforcement directly from Africa once; the operation was successful but was not tried again. That was a reasonable decision, but it meant that Hannibal, after his invasion of Italy stalled, was cut off. The Carthaginian government did attempt to regain the bases in Sicily and Sardinia from which a challenge might be mounted to Rome in the seas surrounding Italy and from which reinforcements might be brought to Hannibal. The absolute need for bases from which to conduct naval operations with large ships under Hellenistic conditions explains the Punic strategy. The strategy should not be thought of as the foolish diversion of forces that should have gone to Hannibal because in fact such forces could not get safely to him.[34] The Carthaginians failed in this effort; although it was carried through with great persistence, they never managed to gain permanent control of a single port city in Sicily or Sardinia that could act as naval base.

Meanwhile, the Romans, in possession of many such naval bases—Messana, Syracuse, Panormus, Lilybaeum, Cagliari, Pisa, Massilia, Corcyra—dominated the western Mediterranean seas. These bases allowed the relatively swift dispatch of Roman reinforcements by sea to Spain, for instance, where P. Cornelius Scipio was dismantling the Punic Empire that had been established in the far west in the 230s and 220s. And meanwhile Hannibal remained cut off, his army a wasting asset. His war against Rome had to be fought on land, and although he was a brilliant general, his resources were never large enough to inflict a fatal blow on Rome.

It is clear that the men in the Senate in Rome soon came to understand the logistical constraints under which war fleets operated, the need for bases to fight the Sicilian naval war, and the need to deprive Carthage of such bases, hence the early establishment of Messana as the main naval base in Sicily and the willingness of the Senate to engage in diplomacy with the Syracusans to gain the occasional use of Syracuse as a base. Hence, too, the adoption of a strategy to deprive Carthage of its own naval bases by conquering the main ports in western Sicily (Panormus, Lilybaeum, Drepana) and attacking the bases in Sardinia and Corsica. Strategic vision is shown most obviously by the extraordinarily rapid development of a large navy, which was a huge investment in materiel, and the training of an enormous number of sailors and marines to man that navy. Even if most oarsmen and crew for the great new fleet came from the Italiote allies, the large warship that now became the Roman standard warship was itself not of a type or size that the Greeks of Italy had ever used before, and the Romans of course had never had large warships at all or fought as marines before.

Just how rapid the learning curve of the Senate was in this period about the possibilities of sea power is shown by several startling facts. First was the large and increasing size of the Roman navy. Whereas in 264 Rome possessed no war fleet, in 261 the Senate ordered the building of 100 quinquiremes of the most modern kind with which to contest Sicily with Carthage. Polybius stresses that this was a stunningly large project for a previously nonnaval power to undertake;[35] the senatorial order meant that the fleet of Roman quinquiremes that took to the sea a year later was already almost twice as large as the fleet of Rhodes. And the building did not stop there: by 256, just four years later, the Roman war fleet numbered an astounding 330 quin-quiremes. The number rose to 364 quinquiremes by the summer of 255 BC.[36]

Moreover, this rapid learning curve in terms of the number of war-ships needed against Carthage was paralleled by a rapidly expanding Roman geographical and strategic vision. Whereas in 264 the Romans had almost no experience in naval warfare, by 256 Rome had won control of the seas around Sicily with its enormous new fleet of quinquiremes. Furthermore, Rome was using this fleet to harass the traditional naval bases of Carthage on Sardinia and Corsica (thus entering yet another new geographical arena) but was actually using naval bases in Sicily to prepare for a massive cross-sea invasion of Africa itself to besiege Carthage from both the landward and sea-ward sides. Meanwhile, at the level of the Roman populace, the oarsmen in the Roman quinquiremes may have mostly been Italiotes (and perhaps some Italians), but tens of thousands of Roman soldiers now took to the sea for the first time as marines. The rapidity of the transition from a purely Italian land power into a power that had large capabilities of power projection both on land and far at sea is simply stunning. And what is more, a naval power pos-sessing a huge fleet of large modern warships capable not merely of challeng-ing but also of dominating Carthage at sea, even off the African coast itself (and all this accomplished within the space of four or five years), is maritime transformation indeed.

But the invasion of Africa, visionary as it was, ended in disaster. The expeditionary force, having defeated the Punic navy off southern Sicily in the great battle of Ecnomus (summer 256), and having then achieved a lodg-ment on the North African coast and pushed the Punic army back inside the walls of Carthage (autumn), was itself decisively defeated on land the follow-ing spring. And the war fleet sent to complete the siege of Carthage, which became instead a rescue mission for the survivors of the African expedition-ary force, was itself destroyed in a storm off southern Sicily in the summer of 255 as it returned from Africa. Of the 364 quinquiremes in this great fleet, some 280 were lost in a single day.[37] The loss of life was enormous, and the loss of experienced crews a brutal blow. Polybius stresses that the disaster was caused by Roman inexperience at sea. The Greek ship pilots had warned the Roman consuls who commanded the fleet that the southern coast of Sicily in summer was dangerous because of high winds and gales that came from Africa, combined with the lack of coastal landing places. But a consul is not necessarily an admiral, and the response to the Greeks was that Roman willpower would see the fleet through.[38] This shows that, although the Senate had come to understand the strategic opportunities for projecting Roman power over distance offered by a great fleet and had come to understand the strategic dangers posed by an enemy that possessed a great fleet (as is shown by the Roman demand in winter 256–255 that Carthage give up both Sicily and Sardinia-Corsica in exchange for peace), the techniques of sailing a war fleet in complex conditions remained beyond the capacities of most Roman aristocrats.[39]

The failure of the African invasion combined with the loss of the veteran Roman fleet changed what had been an increasingly clear Roman victory over Carthage into a stalemate. The Senate did authorize major naval efforts over the next few years, but they all proved disastrous. A painfully rebuilt Roman war fleet of 300 quinquiremes suffered the loss of 150 ships in a storm between Sicily and Italy in 253.[40] Rebuilt again, the new fleet now numbering 200 quinquiremes was decisively defeated off Drepana in western Sicily in 249, and two-thirds of it lost; Polybius explicitly says this was because the Carthaginians' ships were faster and superior in construction, their crews better trained.[41] Soon thereafter another storm off the southern coast of Sicily resulted in the destruction of the Roman ships that were left.[42] As Thiel says, the mark of a culture that has not adapted to sea-faring is not excessive fear of the sea but lack of fear of the sea; the Carthaginian admiral who had been advancing to meet the Roman fleet had read the weather signs and put into port.[43]

This series of disasters in fact led the Senate to abandon the attempt to create Roman sea power altogether. Over the next few years, the Romans sought to conquer the fortresses of Punic western Sicily—all on the coast— via sieges solely from the landward side; it was an impossible task, for the fortresses could be continuously revictualled and reinforced from the sea. In desperation, the Senate in 242 finally authorized the building of yet another war fleet. Fleets cost a great deal of money, and the Roman treasury was now exhausted by the expenses of the war. The fleet, so tradition has it, was paid for by the private wealth of the senatorial class—which at least demonstrates that the Romans still understood the importance of sea power, even if they had not yet shown an ability to use it well. The new ships were paid for by one wealthy man, or a small group of wealthy men, with the understanding that the money would be repaid if victory over Carthage was attained.

In fact, the private investment paid off. In the spring of 241 the new Roman war fleet of 200 decked warships caught the Punic fleet loaded down with reinforcements headed for western Sicily and, in a battle in heavy seas off the Aegates Islands, utterly defeated it, sinking or capturing 120 ships.[44] With a Roman fleet now controlling the seas around western Sicily, the position of the Punic fortresses suddenly became untenable (reinforcement and resupply being almost impossible) and so the Punic government—itself without the cash to construct a new fleet—was forced to sue for peace. But the Carthaginians proved tough negotiators, and the Roman populace was itself war-weary; in the subsequent peace treaty, the Carthaginians thus managed to retain Sardinia and Corsica although they had to evacuate Sicily.[45]

In the period between the First Punic War and the Hannibalic War, the Senate showed evidence of continued naval-strategic thinking. First, in 238–237 BC, it authorized the seizure of Sardinia and Corsica. These two great islands had had a complex history over the previous four years: left to Carthage by the peace of 241, the islands had been seized by rebel mercenaries against Carthage in 240, and then the rebels had in turn been expelled by a massive indigenous rebellion. The Romans could thus present a good case that in 238–237 Sardinia and Corsica belonged to no state and were free for the taking; of course, the Carthaginians—and Polybius—thought differently.[46] For us, however, the seizure of Sardinia and Corsica, whatever its morality, shows the broadened horizon of the Senate resulting from the Punic War and the senators' awareness of naval geography: the seizure of the islands was clearly put in train to create, along with Sicily, a permanent "barrier reef" between Italy and Africa. With the three great islands all in Roman hands, Italy was now safe from Punic naval raids—for without the existence now of friendly naval bases, warships could only reach Italy directly from Africa with great difficulty. Moreover, any aid that Carthage might render the Celtic peoples of the Po Valley, who had become very threatening to Rome from around 238, was now made immensely more difficult. Equally important, the transport of a large invasion force from the west coast of Italy all the way to Sardinia (a distance of some 150 miles across the open sea) was carried through with good efficiency; it was an impressive naval achievement. This is—again—maritime transformation.

Similarly, in 229 the Senate sent the fleet of two hundred warships into the Adriatic for the first time to put down the pirate-state of the Illyrian Ardiaei (on the coast of what is now Croatia), opening up a new region for Roman naval operations. Polybius does emphasize that the Senate was reluctant to authorize this expedition despite the pleas from Italiote merchants about the increasing Illyrian piracy;[47] and he makes clear that the Senate (in about 230 BC) was far more concerned with the Celtic threat overland from the Po Valley across the Appennine Mountains against Roman central Italy.[48] Nevertheless, the Roman naval expedition into Illyria, when finally mounted, was decisively victorious: The Illyrian kingdom was broken up, the Illyrians forbidden to sail for purposes of war into the Straits of Otranto (the main mercantile thoroughfare between Italy and Greece), and a range of Greek coastal towns in the region now established friendship with Rome. A decade later the Senate had to send another large naval expedition into the region to put down Demetrius of Pharus, who had reunited the Illyrian kingdom and was threatening the Roman sphere of influence; this expedition, too, was large and spectacularly successful. Rome now was not merely the dominant naval power in the seas around Sicily, Sardinia, and Corsica but in the Adriatic as well.[49]

When war with Carthage broke out again in 218, the Senate approached the large-scale employment of sea power with similar confidence. A fleet of 220 quinqueremes was launched immediately; many of these warships (though not all of them) must have dated from 242. This was essentially the same fleet that Rome had employed in 238–237 against Sardinia and Corsica, and in 229 and 219 in Illyria. For comparison with Roman naval power here, the famous fleet of Rhodes in this period did not number more than 50 decked warships, that of Pergamum about 35, that of Macedon (after the building program of Philip V) about 50, and that of Antiochus III about 100. The Carthaginians were able to launch only about 100 quinqueremes themselves.[50]

The senatorial plan was strategically visionary: While sixty quinqueremes were detailed to Spain, the rest of the fleet was sent to Lilybaeum in western Sicily in preparation for another invasion of Punic North Africa and a siege of Carthage—a repeat of the strategy followed at the height of Roman naval power in 256–255 BC. This was senatorial confidence in Roman naval domination. The Senate continued to worry about naval attacks on Italy, however. It thus assigned 25 quinqueremes to guard the coasts near Rome itself in 215, after the Roman disaster at Cannae,[51] and there was a true "naval panic" in 208 when the Senate heard rumors that the Carthaginians were about to raid Latium with a fleet of two hundred quinqueremes.[52] But in fact large-scale Punic raids on Italy were very difficult without intermediate bases, as we see in the story of the failure in 215 of the expedition of Hasdrubal Calvus.[53]

Hannibal's perception of Roman domination of the sea meant that in pursuing his own strategic offensive—the invasion of Italy from his bases in Spain—he had no choice but to take his army overland, and eventually over the Alps, instead of the easier course of going by ship along the coast from Spain into northern Italy. It took Hannibal's army the entire summer of 218 to make this overland journey, and his forces suffered significant losses along the way.[54] Despite these difficulties, Hannibal's brilliant battlefield leadership (and the adherence of tens of thousands of Celtic warriors from the

Po Valley) resulted in a strategic offensive that brought Rome and its control of Italy into far more danger than had ever occurred in the first war, when the Carthaginians had remained mostly on the defensive. Yet even when confronted by Hannibal's overland invasion and the massive damage it caused in Italy, and even when Hannibal's early victories almost brought the Roman government and the Roman alliance system in Italy to its knees, the advantages of Roman control of the sea must have been forcefully brought home to the Senate in these years. That is, it must have been crystal clear that without Roman control of the sea, the military situation would have been far worse.

The Punic government is sometimes criticized by modern scholars for its focus on fighting in Spain, Sardinia, and Sicily, instead of on reinforcing Hannibal after he had invaded Italy. But here, too, a good case can be made that control of the sea was a vital consideration. Although the government in Carthage aimed to preserve Spain because of its great resources in men and gold necessary for prosecuting the war (in itself a reasonable strategy), the government also aimed at gaining control of significant naval bases either on Sardinia and Corsica or in Sicily because only possession of such bases could ensure a regular and relatively low-risk reinforcement of Hannibal in Italy. In other words, Hannibal was not cynically abandoned by the Senate at Carthage, nor was the Punic Senate childishly distracted during the war from what should have been the primary focus in Italy by an interest in merely "secondary" goals such as Sardinia or Sicily. Rather, the Punic strategy was coherent and was founded on conquering a string of naval bases from which Hannibal's expeditionary force could be supplied and reinforced. It was an intelligent strategy and persistently followed; it simply failed in implementation in the face of Roman superiority both on land and at sea.[55]

Similarly, Hannibal's seizure of the ports of Heraclea, Metapontum, and Thurii in southern Italy shows that he was trying to link hands with Africa. The problem was that as long as Rome held the great fortresses of Lilybaeum and Messana, so that Sicily blocked the naval route north, the seizure of the smaller Italiote ports meant little: Without a safe landing place in Sicily, even southern Italy remained out of range from Carthage.[56] There was certainly Punic venturesomeness at sea—shown by several bold attempts to raid the coasts of Italy via Sardinia, which the Carthaginians did not control, and even brief expeditions into the Adriatic to support Hannibal's ally, Philip V of Macedon, against Rome.[57] But the hard fact of Roman superiority at sea is shown in 211 by the failure of the large fleet of Bomilcar (130 quinqueremes), detailed to bring aid to Syracuse, which was in rebellion against Rome, to stand and fight when confronted by a Roman fleet under M. Claudius Marcellus off southern Sicily.[58] Syracuse fell into Roman hands shortly thereafter. And the naval panic at Rome in 208 was followed by twin Roman naval victories over the Punic fleet (which was half its rumored size of 200 quinqueremes) in preemptive attacks off the coast of North Africa.[59]

Earlier Hannibal's great victory at Cannae in 216 had led King Philip V of Macedon to believe that Rome would lose the war and, hence, to an alliance with the Carthaginian general (215); Philip built a fleet of light ships with which to seize Illyria and perhaps to invade Italy itself. Such predatory conduct, one must emphasize, was typical of the brutal multipolar anarchy that constituted the Hellenistic Mediterranean. The Senate, upon learning of the alliance, ordered more warships built and launched against this new enemy, and a watch was established in the Adriatic against Philip's naval depredations. Members of the Senate again underwrote the cost of launching the new fleet, for the Roman treasury at this point was once more close to bankruptcy; in this risky financial transaction one could not have a better sign of senatorial understanding of the importance of naval power.[60] The Senate also sanctioned an alliance against Philip with the Aetolian League, old Greek enemies of Macedon; the purpose was to keep the king so busy with war in Greece that he would have no thought of joining Hannibal in Italy. Under the alliance, Roman naval squadrons appeared now for the first time in the Aegean—where they wreaked significant damage on Philip's Greek allies. The conduct of the Senate here shows again how the struggle with Carthage was itself broadening Roman strategic horizons, and how senators were willing to risk the fleet built from their private loans on projects enormously far away. By 209 Roman geopolitical goals could be pursued as far as the coast of northeastern Greece. In the end, the war against Philip ended in 206 (for Aetolia) and 205 (for Rome) in a compromise peace with neither side victorious. But since the Romans' strategic purpose had been limited to keeping Philip away from Italy, that was sufficient for Roman purposes.[61]

The Hannibalic War was eventually brought to an end by the fulfillment of the Roman plan of 256–255, which Hannibal's invasion of Italy had cut short in 218: A large expeditionary force operating from bases in Sicily landed on the coast of North Africa in 204. Commanded by the brilliant General P. Cornelius Scipio, this force—continually resupplied and reinforced by sea—was able to establish a secure lodgment near Carthage.[62] The concept of the expedition was opposed by many in the Senate, led by the elderly Q. Fabius Maximus (who could remember the disaster of 256–255). But Scipio's successes forced the Punic government to recall Hannibal from Italy in 203 to defend Carthage itself. And in the climactic battle at Zama in 202, Roman forces for the first time decisively defeated Hannibal on the battlefield. By the peace of 201, Carthage was demilitarized, its navy was reduced to a few ships, and Carthage was permanently restricted within the boundaries of its domain in North Africa.[63]

The victorious end of the Punic War, which had exhausted Rome and carried away perhaps half the citizen manpower available for the fighting forces in 218, was immediately followed by a new crisis. Envoys from no less than four important Greek states (and possibly five) arrived at Rome in autumn 201 to report that Philip V of Macedon and Antiochus III of the Seleucid Empire had joined together to destroy the domain of the Ptolemies in Egypt, which was then under the rule of a child (Ptolemy V). If successful, this would have meant the gain of enormous power by these vigorous and expansionist monarchs (or worse, the eventual concentration of stupendous power in the hands of one of them).[64] The Roman government, having just experienced Hannibal, had no wish to see such a geopolitical threat emerge in the East. And one specific argument that the Greek envoys may have used in autumn 201 deserves note. It is likely that the Greek envoys warned the Senate that Antiochus III's formidable navy (one hundred quinqiremes) might soon be joined by Philip V's own large and newly built navy, now numbering more than fifty quinqiremes—and in summer 201 it had just shown itself to be highly effective off the coast of Asia Minor.[65] The Greek envoys, to arrive at Rome in autumn 201, would have been dispatched to Italy while the fierce naval fighting between Philip on the one side and Pergamum and Rhodes on the other was at its height. Whatever had happened afterward in the southeast Aegean, this was the situation they would have reported at Rome.[66] Such a report would have had an impact upon the Senate, which understood that sea power had previously been vital in preventing Philip from attacking Illyria and even coming to Italy. Now Roman control of the seas immediately east of Italy was potentially at risk again. The Senate took several concrete steps to strengthen the naval watch on the eastern coast, and Rome declared war on Philip unless he made peace with the Greeks, while an embassy was sent to warn Antiochus off invading Egypt proper.[67]

Antiochus III acquiesced for the moment and satisfied himself with seizing all the Ptolemaic possessions in Lebanon and Judaea (although in 196, upon hearing a rumor that Ptolemy V was dead, he readied himself again for the conquest of the Nile).[68] Philip V, on the other hand, rejected the Roman ultimatum, and soon the two states were at war. Rome took the offensive: A large Roman expeditionary force was landed in Greece while a significant

Roman war fleet, joined by Pergamene and Rhodian squadrons, swept the Aegean and battered the Greek allies of Macedon. The allied fleet was one hundred quinquiremes strong, of which the Romans supplied slightly more than half.[69] Philip, outnumbered two to one, did not dare to confront the naval forces of the coalition. The resulting situation is summarized by the elected leader of the Achaean League in autumn 198, just before the League voted to switch sides from Macedon to the coalition: "The Romans have the sea in their power" (*mare in potestate habent Romani*).[70] Thus the decisive battles of the war were fought on land, and although Philip gave a good account of himself, the war eventually ended in an allied victory (fought mostly but not completely with Roman troops) at Cynoscephalae in Thessaly in 197.

With the advice of the Senate, the Roman commander on the spot, T. Quinctius Flamininus (victor of Cynoscephalae and a man in the mold of Scipio Africanus), dictated in 196 a new political structure for European Greece in which Macedon would continue to exist, but no Greek state would be powerful; none would have hegemony over other states; and the Romans—having achieved a satisfactory balance of weakness in the Aegean—would withdraw back to Italy. This was the policy called "The Freedom of the Greeks," and it was likely sincere on the part of the Romans, at least in the sense that Flamininus himself believed that such a system would guarantee Rome good support from the Greek states, should Antiochus threaten them. The Greek governments understood that any system of hegemony that Antiochus imposed would be far harsher than the Roman sphere of influence established in 196.[71]

In fact, Antiochus did constitute a threat to the Aegean. By the late 190s his empire stretched from Ionia to Afghanistan and included part of northern Greece. He had gone to war every year for thirty years, but his ambitions were not at an end. The Aetolian League, allies of Rome who felt they had received inadequate territorial compensation for their role in the war against Philip, called in Antiochus to be the new champion of the Greeks, and Antiochus eventually came (autumn 192). The Romans had repeatedly warned him away, yet they had also completely withdrawn their military presence back to Italy (as promised in 196); so Antiochus' invasion of Greece, stepping into what must have seemed to him a power vacuum, was a natural act given the harsh Mediterranean anarchy. What is more, he now had Hannibal—exiled from Carthage—as one of his military advisors.[72]

The Roman response to the crisis in Greece was to transport an army across the Adriatic, and this army drove Antiochus from Europe in 191. The

Senate also dispatched into the Aegean a fleet that eventually numbered eighty quinqueremes (only thirty of which were new). To this force would soon be added the sixty or so quinqueremes of Pergamum and Rhodes; old allies of the Romans now, they had joined the anti-Antiochus coalition because Antiochus threatened them even more than he threatened the Romans—and threatened them more directly than the Romans did. Although, based on his experience, Hannibal advised Antiochus that "the Romans were as strong at sea as they were on land," it is interesting that this was not the view of Antiochus' chief admiral, Polyxenidas.[73] He urged Antiochus to send his own fleet of one hundred quinqueremes against the Roman fleet before it merged with that of the Greek allies, for the Romans' ships were "inexpertly built, clumsy and slow."[74] One aspect of the Roman maritime transformation is clear here: The individual units in the Roman fleets of this period were still not as impressive as Greek ships.

Because Antiochus possessed a powerful fleet, the pattern of this war was not that of the war with Philip; there were major battles fought at sea as Antiochus contested control of the Aegean with the fleet of the coalition. A key role on the coalition side was played by the fleet of Rhodes—acknowledged to be the best trained in the Mediterranean. The Rhodian fleet participated in the minor victory at Korykos in late 191 and then, operating on its own, won a strategically important victory at Side (summer 190), blocking the attempt of Hannibal to sail with Seleucid naval reinforcements into the Aegean. A few weeks later the Rhodians formed a key section of the coalition fleet at Myonessus, where the Rhodian admiral Eudamas, through a daring maneuver, saved the hard-pressed Roman fleet from Polyxenidas' attack. Without Eudamas and the Rhodians, the Romans might well have been crushed by Polyxenidas, and if that had occurred the Roman invasion of Asia Minor in pursuit of Antiochus would have been delayed for at least a year. Instead, a great naval victory was won, and the Roman army was transported across the Hellespont (Gallipoli) Straits unimpeded.[75]

Without underemphasizing the Romans' own large and stalwart contribution to these naval victories, they demonstrate a Roman principle we have encountered before: One way the Romans multiplied their power at sea was to depend upon Greek states with a longer and better naval tradition. That had been true early on with the Italiote polities, and it was true in the East. Thus the Roman success at sea against Antiochus was not merely a naval success but also a fundamental diplomatic success.

This diplomatic success was in turn based on the fact that the Romans in this period appeared in the Aegean world as a counterhegemonic force (much as China may appear to some today). This aspect of the diplomatic situation seems ironic in view of the outcome—namely, the Roman Empire; but it is important to understand this source of Roman diplomatic—and eventually military—strength. It is not an accident that the Rhodians contributed so strongly to the Roman naval victories over Antiochus or that, similarly, Eumenes II of Pergamum contributed so strongly to the great land victory won against Antiochus at Magnesia in western Asia Minor in January 189, which ended the war in a triumph for the coalition. The governments of the Greek polities were not naive about the ambitions of great states, but it is striking that they believed Rome to be the least-threatening of the great powers they faced. Because Philip V (with or without Antiochus) and then Antiochus had appeared more directly threatening to them, the Greek states had used the Romans in a balancing strategy against the kings.[76]

And so the Romans in the East at the turn of the second century were able to multiply their own naval power via the Greeks, a naval power that Antiochus' admirals saw had weaknesses on its own. And the Greek allies of Rome were not disappointed. In the peace with Antiochus that the coalition struck in 188 BC—the Peace of Apamea—the frontiers of the Seleucid realm were pushed back three hundred miles to the Taurus Mountains (between what is today Turkey and Syria) while the Seleucid fleet was scuttled. These measures eliminated the Seleucid pressure on the second-rank Greek states that had existed for almost twenty years. Moreover, the settlement brought great territorial rewards to Pergamum and Rhodes at Antiochus' expense, while in Europe both the Achaean League and even Macedon (where Philip had sided with the Romans against Antiochus) benefited territorially. And then—strikingly—the Romans disappeared back beyond the Adriatic again. No Roman forces, garrisons, bases, political overseers, or even diplomats were left among the Greeks. Rome had certainly turned the Aegean region into a sphere of influence in which no other great power would be allowed to interfere; in essence, the Romans now left the Greeks to themselves. In that sense, the states that had allied with Rome in the crisis that began with the collapse of the Ptolemaic regime had chosen wisely from the unpleasant alternatives the crisis had presented to them.

It is already noticeable that in both the war with Philip and the war with Antiochus, the Roman naval effort was substantially smaller than the naval effort called forth in the Hannibalic War, let alone the stupendous efforts of the First Punic War. To be sure, with the help of their naval allies, the Romans controlled the sea from the start in the war against Philip and fought successfully to gain control of the sea against Antiochus. But the maximum

Roman naval effort in the East in this period, against Antiochus, involved just approximately half the number of warships employed in the Hannibalic War. Moreover, after the threat from Antiochus was ended by the Peace of Apamea, the Romans dry-docked their fleet. No Roman squadrons appeared in the Aegean—nor were there large Roman squadrons at work anywhere else in the Mediterranean. When in 171 a new crisis arose with Macedon because of the alleged aggressions of Philip V's son Perseus, there was no Roman fleet in being to deal with the crisis. The Senate instead had to order out of storage the warships that had been laid up for seventeen years, only some of which were now seaworthy.[77]

This decline of the Roman war fleet after 188 has been taken as a sign of special Roman "landlubberliness."[78] In itself, this is somewhat unfair. War fleets, with their large crews and fragile ships, were expensive to maintain, and not even the government of Rhodes, with its great naval reputation, kept a full fleet in being; on the contrary, most of its large warships were, as in Rome's case, in dry dock until needed.[79] Nevertheless, it is noticeable that the fleet Rome sent to the Aegean for the war against Perseus numbered only about forty quinquiremes, about half the size of the fleet sent to confront Antiochus, and that this moderately sized fleet, even with some help from the navies of Rhodes and Pergamum, was unable to stop the grain trade to Macedon or put a stop to Macedonian naval raids in the Aegean carried on by lighter ships.[80] But such Macedonian activity was itself hardly a major threat, and Perseus—although his land army was larger than the army of his father, Philip—did not dare to contest overall maritime supremacy with Rome and her allies. Perhaps that explains the diminished size (and elderly character) of the Roman fleet sent to the East in 171: Roman involvement at sea was ad hoc and purely a matter of dealing with the size (in this case, the diminished size) of the threat. After Perseus' defeat, the Romans withdrew once more to Italy, and no large Roman war fleets were to appear east of the Adriatic for another one hundred years.[81]

A sign of Roman weakness at sea in the East is the ease with which King Mithridates VI of Pontus was able to sweep the Aegean of any Roman ships in 88 BC, eventually blockading the Romans in the Piraeus, the fortified port of Athens to which they had withdrawn. Nor did the Roman general L. Cornelius Sulla arrive in Greece accompanied by a war fleet to confront Mithridates (as had been the usual Roman procedure with expeditionary forces in 214, 200, 192, and 171). Sulla eventually did receive aid from a fleet under L. Licinius Lucullus, but this fleet was drawn primarily from Greek polities in the Aegean.[82] To be sure, Mithridates was finally defeated, but that was accomplished on land, by the legions. The absence of Roman war fleets from the East and the pathetic Roman naval showing in the First Mithdridatic War suggest that there is good reason to maintain doubts about (in our terms) the depth of any Roman maritime transformation caused by the Punic Wars a century before.[83]

Similarly, there was little Roman naval effort in the western Mediterranean after Hannibal. Rome certainly made use of the sea for the regular transport of troops from Italy to the provinces in Spain, but even in the Third Punic War (149–146 BC) the Roman naval effort involved only fifty quinquiremes. And even when aided by one hundred lighter ships, these warships were unable to prevent besieged Carthage from being occasionally resupplied at sea; maintaining station off Carthage proved to be too difficult technically for them.[84] Carthage did eventually fall, after a siege that lasted fully three years, but only to a land assault. And it took seventy-five years before the Senate decided to take to the sea in force again. That decision, in 70 BC, was in good part provoked by the fact that the large fleets of pirates that had already infested the chaotic eastern Mediterranean for decades with no Roman response were now operating off the coasts of Italy itself. The Roman operations against the pirates were eventually successful under the command of Cn. Pompeius Magnus (Pompey) starting in 67, but not even the decision of 70 BC meant the creation of a Roman fleet in being.[85] The constant maintenance of ships and payment of crews were still considered by the Senate too expensive for such a measure. Thus, in the civil wars that followed Caesar's death in 44, it is clear that Roman war fleets had to be built up again on an ad hoc basis; Octavian's warships were notoriously poorly built and clumsy, although his resources enabled him to overwhelm his naval enemies numerically.[86] Yet it was Octavian who fundamentally transformed the naval situation after his victory over Antony and Cleopatra at Actium. In the following decades, the first emperor funded the establishment of the first permanent squadrons of warships to patrol the Mediterranean and the Atlantic coasts. It is noticeable, however, that these ships were not the great quinquiremes of the age of the Punic Wars but smaller and more maneuverable vessels. It was less expensive that way.[87]

On the instrumental level, the Roman government quickly adapted to the needs of naval warfare when they were confronted with the conflict with Carthage, and one can talk about a maritime transformation at Rome in the age of the Punic Wars. Yet this transformation was only functional; it did not penetrate Roman society or culture deeply, and it had little permanent cultural impact. Nevertheless, the men in the Senate showed themselves flexible in developing their strategic thinking; they saw how—under the pressing circumstances of the period—naval power was both a necessity and an advantage for Rome and did not hesitate under those circumstances to build war fleet after war fleet, even at their own private expense. Meanwhile, they also continued the traditional Roman dependence on allies as a force multiplier. And if the maritime transformation at Rome did not penetrate very far into society and culture, the transformation in Roman thinking at the pragmatic and instrumental level was impressive indeed, and the Roman effort strenuous and sufficient for war fleets to become a vital factor that allowed the Roman Republic to win control over the Mediterranean world.

Notes

1. The phrase *mare nostrum* first appears only in the works of Caesar and Sallust; see, for instance, Sallust, *Jugurthine War*, e.g., chapters 17 and 18.

2. On this law, *lex Claudia*, see Livy 21.63.3; cf. Cicero, *Second Oration against Verres*, 5.45.

3. On the sources of recruitment into the Roman naval forces during the Second Punic War, see John S. Morrison (with John F. Coates), *Greek and Roman Oared Warships* (Oxford: Oxbow Books, 1996), 352. Pergamene and Rhodian major contributions at sea to the wars against Philip V of Macedon and Antiochus III of Syria: see Evelyn V. Hansen, *The Attalids of Pergamum* (Ithaca, NY: Cornell University Press, 1971), 57–69 and 74–88; and Richard M. Berthold, *Rhodes in the Hellenistic Age* (Ithaca, NY: Cornell University Press, 1984), chaps. 6 and 7.

4. J. H. Thiel, *Studies on the History of Roman Seapower in Republican Times* (Amsterdam: North Holland Publishing Co., 1946), 31.

5. Alan E. Astin, *Cato the Censor* (Oxford: Oxford University Press, 1978), 255 (with sources).

6. The path-breaking work here is William V. Harris, *War and Imperialism in Republican Rome* (Oxford: Oxford University Press, 1979). See also Peter S. Derow, "Rome, the Fall of Macedon, and the Sack of Corinth," in *Cambridge Ancient History*, vol. 8, 2nd ed. (Cambridge, U.K. : Cambridge University Press, 1989), 290–323; and idem, "The Arrival of Rome: From the Illyrian Wars to the Fall of Macedon," in Andrew Erskine, ed., *The Hellenistic World* (Oxford: Blackwell, 2003), 51–70; Kurt R. Raaflaub, "Born to Be Wolves? Origins of Roman Imperialism," in Robert W. Wallace and Edward M. Harris, eds., *Transitions to Empire: Essays in Greco-Roman History, 360–146 BC in Honor of E. Badian* (Norman: Oklahoma University Press, 1996), 273–314; and Brian Campbell, "Power Without Limit: The Romans Always Win," in Angelos Chaniotis and Pierre Ducrey, eds., *Army and Power in the Ancient World* (Stuttgart, Germany: Franz Steiner, 2002), 167–80.

7. See Arthur M. Eckstein, *Mediterranean Anarchy, Interstate War, and the Rise of Rome* (Berkeley and Los Angeles: University of California Press, 2006), chaps. 2–6.

8. See Theodor Mommsen, *Römische Geschichte*, vol. 1, 9th ed. (Berlin: Bertelsmann, 1903), 412–30, and Eckstein, *Mediterranean Anarchy*, chap. 7.

9. See Frank W. Walbank, *A Historical Commentary on Polybius*, vol. 1 (Oxford: Oxford University Press, 1957), 74.

10. This was evidently in violation of a treaty that Rome had sworn with Tarentum a generation previously to stay out of the Gulf; but the affair is mysterious. See Livy, *Periocha (Summary)* of Book 12; Zonaras 8.2; Appian, *Samnite Wars*, 7.1 (suggesting a squadron of ten triremes), with discussion in Christopher L. H. Barnes, *Images and Insults: Ancient Historiography and the Outbreak of the Tarantine War* (Stuttgart, Germany: Franz Steiner, 2005).

11. See Polyb. 1.20.14.

12. The establishment of the quaestores classici: Lydus, *de Magistratibus*, 1.27; cf., even more briefly, Livy, *Periocha (Summary)* of Book 15. Taken as evidence that the Romans were laying the groundwork for a large and permanent fleet: Filippo Cassola, *I gruppi politici romani nel III. Secolo A.C.* (Trieste, Italy: Instituto di Storia Antica, 1962), 179; Harris, *War and Imperialism*, 184. But the main source on the quaestores classici is a brief notice in John Lydus, in the sixth century AD, and recent research suggests that Lydus may be confused both as to the number and the function of the new quaestors, who may have had nothing to do with naval matters. See E. S. Staveley, "Rome and Italy in the Early Second Century," *Cambridge Ancient History*, vol. 7:2, 2nd ed. (Cambridge, U.K.: Cambridge University Press, 1989), 438; and B. Dexter Hoyos, *Unplanned Wars: The Origins of the First and Second Punic Wars* (Berlin: Walter de Gruyter, 1998), 19 and n. 5.

13. Polyb. 1.20.13–14, with the important comments of Walbank, *Commentary I*, 74–75; on kataphraktoi as triremes, see Morrison, *Oared Warships*, 43. The lembos was a fifty-oared ship, not capable ordinarily of confronting kataphraktoi.

14. On the complex crisis of 264 BC, see Arthur M. Eckstein, *Senate and General: Individual Decision Making and Roman Foreign Relations, 264–194 BC* (Berkeley and Los Angeles: University of California Press, 1987), chap. 2; and Hoyos, *Unplanned Wars*, chaps. II–VI.

15. Diodorus of Sicily 23.2.1; Cassius Dio fragment 43.8–9, cf. Zonaras 8.9.

16. Polyb. 1.20.14.

17. On the gradual escalation of the crisis of 264 into a savage struggle between Rome and Carthage, see the classic study of Adolf Heuss, "Der erste punische Krieg und das Problem des römischen Imperialismus (zur politischen Beurteilung des Krieges)," *Historisches Zeitschrift* 169 (1949): 457–512.

18. Polyb. 1.20.12.

19. Polyb. 1.21.2.

20. Polyb. 1.20.11–12.

21. See Aristotle, *Constitution of the Athenians*, 2.19–20.

22. For the evidence on the Second Punic War, see Morrison, *Oared Warships*, 352. For P. Cornelius Scipio's invasion of Africa in 204, inland central Italian peoples such

as the Marsi and Marrucini not only provided deck soldiers but even volunteered as oarsmen (Livy 28.45.13)—but that was an unusual situation in part motivated by personal ties with Scipio. But even in the 170s BC the Romans depended strongly (though not totally) on Italiote socii navales; see Livy 42.48.4 (though at 42.37.3–8 we may have a reference to rowing crews from Latium).

23. This comes to us from the account in Polybius 5.90 of the material needed for the war fleet of Rhodes in the mid-220s BC, which included enormous amounts not only of ship timber of various sizes but also such things as tow for caulking, sail-cloth, iron, solid and liquid pitch, resin and large amounts of fresh human hair for the rope used for catapults.

24. Morrison, *Oared Warships*, xv. We know nothing about the training and little about the detailed functions of catapult-men, archers, marines—or the flute-players and drum-men who crucially kept time for the oarsmen's strokes (on these parts of the crew: ibid., 350).

25. For the Hellenistic and Roman Republican periods, we have nothing like the par-tially preserved dockyard maintenance inscriptions from the Piraeus at Athens.

26. This was what our sources mean when they speak of "fives" or larger ships, and not evermore numerous banks of oars, proven by Pliny, *Natural History*, 7.207, which is explicit that the nickname by number refers to the number of files of oarsmen on each side of a ship. See Morrison, *Oared Warships*, xiv.

27. For the comparative measurements, see Morrison, *Oared Warships*, 345.

28. See Morrison, *Oared Warships*, 358–59. Greek training in battle tactics in the Classical age, including rapid maneuvers of ships en masse, was more sophisticated than that of the Romans; see Herodotus, 6.11.2–21.1. The Rhodians followed this tradition; see Polyb. 16.4.14; Appian, *Civil Wars*, 4.71.

29. See, e.g., Polyb. 1.51, which is explicit in drawing the contrast between the Carthaginians and the Romans, with their cruder and less maneuverable warships, and their less well-trained crews.

30. Not that the Romans made the best marines. Polybius believed the Macedonians were individually better soldiers than the Romans both on land and on sea; see Eckstein, *Mediterranean Anarchy*, 202. As noted, the navies of the Macedonian kingdoms employed Macedonians as marines in ships otherwise manned and crewed by people from stronger maritime cultures. The parallel with Rome is clear and shows that one did not need a strong seafaring tradition to construct a naval force capable of projecting significant military power across the sea.

31. Noted, but without comment, by Morrison, *Oared Warships*, 359–60.

32. The constraints which these logistical considerations put on naval strategy were first pointed out by Arnold W. Gomme, "A Forgotten Factor of Greek Naval Strategy," *Journal of Hellenic Studies* 53 (1933): 16–24. See also the important observations of John F. Coates, "The Naval Architecture and Oar Systems of Ancient Galleys," in Robert Gardiner and John F. Morrison, eds., *The Age of the Galley* (London: Chatwell Books, 1995), 138–41; and Boris Rankov, "The Second Punic War at Sea,"

in Timothy Cornell, Boris Rankov, and Philip Sabin, eds., *The Second Punic War: A Reappraisal* (London: Institute of Classical Studies, 1996), 51.

33. Discussion in John S. Morrison and John F. Coates, *The Athenian Trireme* (Cambridge, U.K.: Cambridge University Press, 1986), 94–106 (for triremes); J. E. Dotson "Economics and Logistics of Galley Warfare," in Gardiner and Morrison, *Age of the Galley*, 217–23; Rankov, "Second Punic War," 51.

34. Emphasized by Rankov, "Second Punic War," 52–55.

35. Polyb. 1.20.10–12.

36. The 100 quinqueremes of 261 BC: Polyb. 1.20; the 330 quinqueremes of 256: Polyb. 1.25.7; the 364 quinqueremes of summer of 255: Polyb. 1.37.1.

37. Polyb. 1.37.1.

38. Polyb. 1.37.5–9.

39. On the meaning of Polyb. 1.37, see Eckstein, *Mediterranean Anarchy*, 200–201.

40. Polyb. 39.1–6.

41. Polyb. 1.51.

42. Polyb. 1.54.

43. Thiel, *Roman Seapower*, 4. Polybius' explicit comparison of the wise Punic commanders and the foolish Roman consul: 1.54.6–8.

44. On the battle of the Aegates Islands, see Morrison, *Oared Warships*, 53–54.

45. On the peace of 241, see Hoyos, *Unplanned Wars*, 118–23.

46. For the Roman case, see William Carey, "*Nullus Videtur Dolo Facere*: The Roman Seizure of Sardinia in 238 B.C.," *Classical Philology* 91 (1996): 203–22. For Polybius' judgment (conforming to that of the Carthaginians themselves)—"theft"—see Polyb. 3.28.2–3 and 30.4, with Arthur M. Eckstein, *Moral Vision in the Histories of Polybius* (Berkeley and Los Angeles: University of California Press, 1995), 100–101.

47. Polyb. 2.8.2.

48. Polyb. 2.22–24.

49. On the origins and geopolitical impact of these two naval expeditions into Illyria, see Arthur M. Eckstein, "The Pharos Inscription and the Question of Roman Treaties of Alliance Overseas in the Third Century B.C.," *Classical Philology* 94 (1999): 395–418.

50. Rhodes: see Berthold, *Rhodes*, 118; Pergamum: ibid; Antiochus: Livy 33.19.9. Carthage: see Morrison, *Oared Warships*, 64.

51. Livy 23.23.18.

52. Discussion and sources in Morrison, *Oared Warships*, 63–64.

53. Livy 23.40–41.

54. See the comments of Rankov, "Second Punic War," 53.

55. Ibid., 53–54.

56. Ibid., 53.

57. See Polyb. 3.96; Livy 23.40–41; cf. Livy 28.46 (from Spain via the Balearic Islands) and 29.4.6 (directly from North Africa).

58. Livy 25.27.

59. Discussion and sources in Morrison, *Oared Warships*, 63–64.

60. In fact, the loans took a very long time for the state to repay. See Livy 26.36 (the original loan); 31.3.4–9; 33.42 (196 BC, the loans were still not paid back).

61. On the Roman goals in this war, compare the analysis of Arthur M. Eckstein, "Greek Mediation in the First Macedonian War (209–205 BC)," *Historia* 52 (2002): 168–297, with that of John W. Rich, "Roman Aims in the First Macedonian War," *Proceedings of the Cambridge Philological Society* 210: 126–80.

62. Resupply and reinforcement of Africanus by sea: see Livy 30.24–25, with the comments of Morrison, *Oared Warships*, 68.

63. For discussion of Scipio's invasion of Africa, see Eckstein, *Senate and General*, chap. 8.

64. The envoys came from Rhodes, Pergamum, Athens, the Ptolemies in Egypt, and perhaps the Aetolian League. See Eckstein, *Mediterranean Anarchy*, chap. 7.

65. On the size of Antiochus' navy ca. 197 BC, see John D. Grainger, *The Roman War of Antiochus the Great* (Leiden: Brill, 2002), 36–37. On the size of Philip's navy after his seizure of Samos in early summer 201, see Frank W. Walbank, *Philip V of Macedon* (Cambridge, U.K.: Cambridge University Press: 1940), 117 and n. 2.

66. G. T. Griffith "An Early Motive for Roman Imperialism," *Cambridge Historical Journal* 5 (1935): 6–9.

67. See Griffith, "Motive," 8–9 and 12–13.

68. See Eckstein, *Mediterranean Anarchy*, chap. 7.

69. Livy 32.21.27.

70. Livy 32.21.32; the speech as it appears in Livy is based on material from Polybius, who was himself an Achaean; see Arthur M. Eckstein, "Polybius, the Achaeans, and the 'Freedom of the Greeks,'" *Greek, Roman, and Byzantine Studies* 51 (1990): 45–71.

71. On "the freedom of the Greeks," see Erich S. Gruen, *The Hellenistic World and the Coming of Rome* (Berkeley and Los Angeles: University of California Press, 1984), chap. 4; and Eckstein "Freedom of the Greeks."

72. On the complex story of Roman relations with Antiochus in the 190s, see Eckstein, *Mediterranean Anarchy*, chap. 7. The least one can say about the Roman withdrawal from Greece in 194, as they had promised, was that it was not the act of a savagely aggressive power; rather, it was the act of a power with very limited strategic aims east of the Adriatic at this point.

73. Livy 34.1.1.

74. Livy 36.43.1.

75. On the battle of Side (summer 190), see Berthold, *Rhodes*, 157–58. On the battle of Myconessus (late summer), ibid., 159–61 (with sources).

76. Greek conduct here thus conforms to the paradigm of alliance making (with the least-threatening great power) suggested by Stephen Walt, *The Origins of Alliances* (Ithaca, NY: Cornell University Press, 1984), chaps. 1 and 2. See also the comments of Eckstein, *Mediterranean Anarchy*, chap. 7.

77. Livy 42.27.

78. Thiel, *Roman Seapower*, 11–14.

79. See Morrison, *Oared Warships*, 109 and 356. Rhodian naval reputation in the 160s (greater than that of Rome): Livy 44.23.

80. See Livy 44.23.

81. This insight into the ad hoc and purely functional nature of Roman involvement with the sea is owed to Thiel, *Roman Seapower*, 11–14.

82. Appian, *Mithridatic War*, 56; emphasized by Thiel, *Roman Seapower*, 13.

83. On the course of the First Mithridatic War, see Morrison, *Oared Warships*, 115–16.

84. Appian, *Punic Wars*, 120.

85. See Appian, *Mithr. Wars*, 92–99.

86. Discussion in Morrison, *Oared Warships*, 149–53 (with sources).

87. This new type of ship, called by moderns Liburnians, had already begun to make an appearance during the Third Punic War: see Appian, *Punic Wars*, 75.

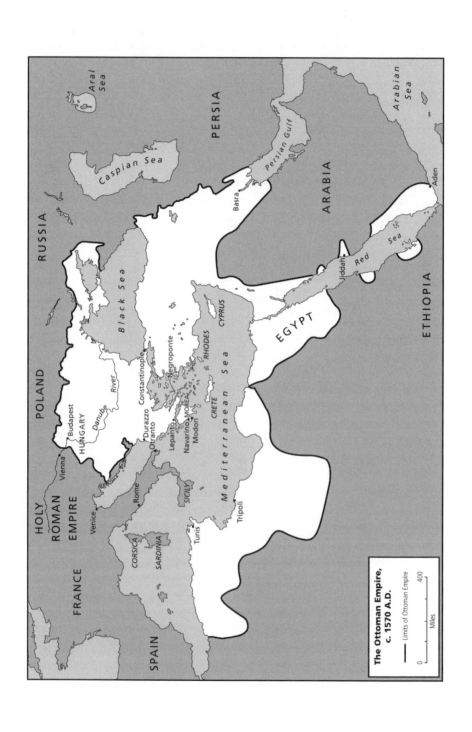

The Ottoman Empire, c. 1570 A.D.

Limits of Ottoman Empire

0   400

Miles

Jakub Grygiel

Ottoman Sea Power and the Decline of the Mediterranean World

THE EARLY EXPANSION OF OTTOMAN POWER occurred exclusively on land. The maritime theater was at best a secondary concern for the Osmanli tribe. Between the early fourteenth century and the second half of the fifteenth century, the Ottomans conquered Anatolia, nibbled on Byzantine territories, and, after crossing the straits into Europe, rapidly pushed toward the Danube and Belgrade. By the mid-fifteenth century, Ottoman-controlled territories had completely enveloped Constantinople. The city, the Second Rome, capital of a by-then nonexistent empire, fell in 1453 after a siege. It is only then that the Ottomans began a considerable and rapid shipbuilding program, rising to challenge in the following century the Venetians in the Mediterranean and the Portuguese in the Indian Ocean. Why and how did they become a naval power capable of instilling terror among European states and of projecting power across the Mediterranean and as far as India?

The answer is complex, and there is no clear consensus among historians regarding the reasons for, as well as the strategic impact of, Ottoman naval power. For instance, it can be argued that Ottoman sea power presented a serious threat to Europe (Italy and Spain in particular), and only the Battle of Lepanto (1571) succeeded in stopping Ottoman expansion. At the same time, however, a plausible argument can be made that the Battle of Lepanto was strategically irrelevant because the main thrust of Ottoman expansion was by land, and only the defeat at the gates of Vienna in 1683 arrested the sultan's ambition and capabilities.

My goal here is not to settle definitely these historical debates but to try to examine the broad conditions under which a state such as the Ottoman empire needs to, and is able to, transform itself from an almost exclusively land-based power to one grounded also in a large and formidable naval force. In what follows, I analyze three features that characterized the early Ottoman state and its approach to sea power.

First, the larger geopolitical context of the Ottoman rise to power influenced when and why the Ottomans decided to build a naval force. The eastern Mediterranean, which became the seat of Ottoman power, had been for centuries the key link between the Asian and European markets, and the Ottomans simply replaced the previous holders of this position. Moreover, the period of the late fifteen and early sixteenth century is characterized by dramatic geopolitical changes, fueled by technological advances and geographic discoveries, and the Ottoman naval rise is in many ways a response to this "Age of Discoveries."

Second, there were two main maritime vectors of Ottoman expansion: the Mediterranean and the Red Sea/Indian Ocean. The former was dictated by a strategy of defense and consolidation while the latter was characterized by an offensive posture aimed at recapturing a connection with Asia. There were profound differences between these two theaters, and the Ottomans failed to adapt their Mediterranean tactics and technology to the demands of the Indian Ocean.

Third, building a navy is a difficult process, and the Ottomans were not exempt from the technical challenges of shipbuilding, developing navigation skills, and training a competent body of seamen. While the Ottomans had easy access to shipbuilding material, they lacked technical expertise and were often forced to rely on Western (often Italian) shipbuilders. Yet, their main technological weakness was that the core of the Ottoman navy was a fleet of galleys, excellent at navigating the narrow straits, long coastlines, and often windless waters of the Mediterranean but unsuited for the rough open oceans.

Although an analysis of these features will not resolve historical debates, it will shed some light on the rise of Ottoman sea power and, by analogy, on the broader questions of how and why a land power redirects its resources toward the sea.

Geopolitical Context

Every state faces a unique geopolitical situation that circumscribes its strategic possibilities and prioritizes its needs and objectives. On a very broad level, this determines whether the state focuses its resources on land expansion and defense of its continental frontiers, or on the development and projection of maritime power.[1] To understand the role of the navy of the early Ottoman state it is therefore necessary to examine the geopolitical situation that it faced. The maritime power of the Ottomans in the fourteenth and fifteenth centuries was in fact severely constrained by the geopolitical imperative to concentrate on land power. And it was only from the last decades of the fifteenth century on that the Ottoman sultans could—indeed were forced to—devote their energies and attention to developing a considerable naval power.

There are two key features of the geopolitical situation of the early Ottoman Empire. First, the geopolitical characteristics of the immediate Ottoman neighborhood, roughly coinciding with the eastern Mediterranean, encouraged a rapid continental expansion and limited the need for and feasibility of substantial Ottoman maritime power. Second, the larger, global context contributed to spur the rise of Ottoman naval power. From the early sixteenth century on, the Mediterranean was deeply affected by dramatic geopolitical changes brought about by the discovery of America and of new routes linking Atlantic Europe with Asia, the result of which was a slow decline of the Mediterranean—and thus a growing irrelevance of Ottoman sea power.

The Eastern Mediterranean

The vectors of early Ottoman expansion in the fourteenth century were almost exclusively on land, beginning in Anatolia.[2] The territories of the decaying Byzantine Empire in Asia Minor as well as in southeastern Europe presented a valuable and easy objective for the Ottoman forces. The wealth of these territories, combined with the fact that they were nominally ruled by a Christian power, attracted numerous groups from as far as the Caucasus and Central Asia seeking plunder and glory. The small Osmanli tribe rapidly augmented its manpower by incorporating the *ghazis*, holy warriors eager to assault the "Second Rome."[3] The expansion took these groups through Asia Minor, rapidly taking over key Byzantine cities (Bursa, Nicea, Nicomedia) by the mid-fourteenth century, and then jumping over the Bosphorus and invading the European territories.[4]

Ottoman expansion at the expense of the Byzantine Empire was further aided by the weakness of the heir of Roman glory. Financially exhausted, internally corrupted, and politically separated from the main European powers, the Byzantine Empire was simply incapable of offering a coherent and effective defense against the growing Ottoman forces. In the fourteenth century it was a hollow power. In several instances disgruntled actors inside the Byzantine Empire sought Ottoman support to achieve their own narrow interests that undermined even further the security of Constantinople. In 1308 a band of mercenaries, the Catalan Grand Company, engaged a group of Ottomans to fight on their side, helping them to cross the straits. Similarly, in the 1340s a pretender to the Byzantine throne allied himself with the Ottomans, which allowed them to cross the Sea of Marmara and establish the first siege of Constantinople.[5]

Byzantium was also weakened by its inability to muster European support in its defense. The relationship between the Eastern Roman Empire and the Western Christian powers (such as Venice, France, Poland) was often strained. The Fourth Crusade of 1204, which conquered Christian Constantinople instead of attacking Muslim powers in Palestine, was a low point in this relationship, and it had the effect of not only undermining Byzantine power but also exacerbating the bad feelings between East and West. Moreover, from the fourteenth century on, Europe was splintering politically, often because of religious tensions. The resulting disunity, combined with the weakening of Papal authority, made an anti-Ottoman coalition effectively impossible—a situation that would benefit the Ottomans throughout their history.[6]

The absence of a strong maritime component in the early Ottoman expansion is therefore not surprising. There was certainly a growing interest in maritime affairs, and the Ottoman expansion of the fourteenth and early fifteenth century built some of the conditions necessary for its future sea power. By controlling cities such as Brusa or Nicomedia, and especially by extending their control over the two shores of the Dardanelles Straits, the Ottomans established a presence on the eastern Mediterranean. These developments led to more than a symbolic interest in the sea and had increasingly important strategic ramifications. For instance, after their 1354 conquest of Gallipoli on the European shore of the straits, the Ottomans could control shipping between the Mediterranean and the Black seas, threatening to cut off Constantinople from its few likely allies in the West. Nevertheless, the early Ottoman expansion occurred almost exclusively on land, and if it had an impact on the maritime sphere, it did so indirectly by controlling the shores and limiting access to ports and straits to Venetian or Genoese ships. When a direct naval clash occurred, such as one between the Ottomans and Venetians in 1391 on the waters facing Gallipoli, the Ottoman ships were soundly defeated.

In brief, until the mid-fifteenth century, the principal objective of the Ottomans was to consolidate their power in Asia Minor and Europe and direct it against the decaying empire of Byzantium. The main threats to this expansion were not European navies, which could control the seas but could not translate their strength into power effective on land, nor even European land armies, which were soundly defeated in several instances. For instance, in the 1440s the Europeans, led by Poland and Hungary, organized a massive expedition, later renamed the Crusade of Varna. The initial successes of the European powers ended ignominiously at the Battle of Varna in 1444 where the bulk of the Polish and Hungarian nobility was wiped out by Ottoman forces, effectively ending any serious attempt by Christian powers to oppose Ottoman expansion for at least a century.[7]

The most serious challenge to the early Ottomans came instead from the east in the early fifteenth century. Tamerlane's hordes expanded swiftly from Central Asia to the Caucasus and Persia, and in 1402 defeated the Ottoman army, taking the sultan as prisoner. The resulting political chaos in the Ottoman state lasted for several decades, effectively until the rise of Mehmed II the Conqueror, who was able to restore a central authority among the Ottomans and then organize the final assault on Constantinople in 1453.

In this early period the main Ottoman preoccupation was clearly the expansion and defense of the continental frontiers of the young state. It was only with the complete defeat of Byzantium, the stabilization of the frontier on the Danube, and the removal of the threats from the east and south that the Ottomans could consider a greater role on the sea. In other words, the birth of the Ottoman naval power saw its beginning in the changing geopolitical situation of the Ottoman state. Before the 1450s the Ottomans did not need a navy to expand and could not afford one given their main strategic concerns. But from 1450 on, the Ottoman empire needed a navy to maintain control over its eastern Mediterranean sphere of influence and, perhaps most importantly, to respond to slow but dramatic changes in the larger strategic situation of Eurasia.

The Global Geopolitical Situation

This wider geopolitical context is the second broad feature that is important for understanding how and why the Ottoman empire became a naval power. The end of the fifteenth century, in fact, saw the beginning of massive geopolitical changes that resulted in a gradual marginalization of the Mediterranean and the globalization of the strategic map faced by states. Beginning with the discoveries of America and of the route circumnavigating Africa, the Atlantic powers in Europe (the Dutch Republic, Portugal, Spain, and Great Britain) gained a considerable advantage over the Mediterranean states. First, the routes linking Europe and Asia through the Mediterranean Sea and the Middle East had to compete with those crossing the Atlantic (which created new links between Asia and America) and circumnavigating Africa. This meant that a key source of wealth and strategic leverage for Byzantium, Venice, and, later, the Ottoman empire—the successive powers controlling the eastern Mediterranean—was weakened by the shift in trade routes to the Atlantic Ocean.[8] Although some historians doubt that these new routes diverted substantial amounts of trade away from the Mediterranean, it is clear that Venice, Genoa, and then the Ottomans had to compete with Western European powers for access to Asian markets. For instance, beginning in 1507 the Portuguese often blockaded the Red Sea and the Persian Gulf, interrupting the flow of goods (mainly spices) to Alexandria and other Mediterranean ports. The link between the Mediterranean and Asia was therefore threatened, and its various trading cities, from Venice to the cities on the Syrian and Palestinian coast, began to decline.[9]

From the early sixteenth century on, states such as Portugal or the Dutch Republic started to have direct access to the Asian markets. With the establishment of Spanish colonies in the Philippines, a world market linking all the continents began to take shape, putting the Atlantic European powers at its center.[10] The Mediterranean played at best a secondary role in this first example of global commercial interaction, and the states on its shores (with the exception of Spain, which was both an Atlantic and a Mediterranean actor) were incapable of participating in the new lucrative exchanges between Europe and America as well as between Asia and America (through Manila).[11]

Furthermore, the Mediterranean powers, including the Ottomans, were left out of the colonial expansion in Asia and the Americas and thus could not benefit from the resources developed there. The wealth derived directly from the American territories built the Spanish empire, strengthening its military capabilities and giving it an edge over those states, such as the Ottomans, that had no direct access to these colonies.[12] As one historian observes, Spanish access to silver mines (such as the ones, perhaps the largest in the world, in Potosí) and the ability to sell bullion in Asia and China allowed Castile to finance "simultaneous wars for generations against the Ottomans in the Mediterranean; Protestant England and Holland and the French in Europe, the New World, and Asia; and against indigenous peoples in the Philippines."[13] The abundance of silver certainly also had negative effects in the form of massive inflation that took its toll on both Spain and Ming China, therefore mitigating the long-term relative gains of Atlantic Europe versus the Ottomans.[14] Yet the rapid enrichment of Western Europe from the early 1500s on put considerable pressure on the Ottomans to reassert their position as an intermediary between Europe and Asia. It also created a new set of powers (mainly the Hapsburg Empire) that had the will and capability to challenge Ottoman expansion both on land and at sea.

In brief, the Age of Discoveries was not kind to the Mediterranean region, and by extension, to the young Ottoman Empire. It altered in a dramatic way the geopolitical context, forcing the Ottomans to respond not only to its traditional opponents, such as Venice and Hungary, but also to new, rapidly rising powers such as Spain and Portugal. The sixteenth century, therefore, expanded the map that the Ottomans had to consider when formulating their policies, extending their strategic interests from the straits and the Aegean coastline to the Mediterranean Sea as well as the Red Sea and Indian Ocean. Such an outlook demanded the construction of a considerable naval force and the development of a maritime empire. By the end of the 1400s, sea power was no longer a secondary objective and tool but a crucial and indispensable part of the arsenal of the Ottoman Empire.[15]

Two Maritime Theaters

The geopolitical context described above established two distinct, yet obviously linked, maritime theaters of Ottoman activity. First, the most immediate and pressing concern for the Ottoman sultans was to secure the Aegean and eastern Mediterranean seas in order to solidify their control over Southeastern Europe, Anatolia, and the Syrian coastline. Second, the Portuguese entry into Asia in the early 1500s not only put pressure on the Ottoman southern frontier but also threatened Ottoman access to the Asian markets, forcing the sultan to project power to the Red Sea and Indian Ocean to challenge Portuguese influence there. The former maritime theater was indispensable for defensive purposes to maintain internal coherence and stability of the land empire built until then by the Ottomans. The latter was crucial if the Ottomans wanted to compete with the rising Atlantic powers, and it was characterized by a more aggressive Ottoman policy.[16]

A brief description of Ottoman activities in both maritime theaters from the late fifteenth century until the early seventeenth—the period of the rapid rise and the pinnacle of Ottoman sea power—illustrates the motivations as well as the challenges of developing a navy while being preoccupied with land frontiers.

Mediterranean

The 1453 conquest of Constantinople concluded the Ottoman expansion at the expense of the Byzantine empire.[17] By taking over the imperial capital of the "Second Rome," the Ottomans assumed also a certain appearance of legitimacy. They were no longer a loose band of ghazi warriors or tribesmen but a power that spanned two continents and had to be treated as a serious political counterpart. As a result, there was a change, characterized by a marked decrease in crusading spirit, in Europe's diplomatic approach to the Ottoman Empire. It was inconceivable at this point to push the Ottomans back to some desolate valley in Anatolia and restore Christian control over the region. Furthermore, beginning in the early sixteenth century the growing split within Christianity made crusades impossible to organize in Europe because often there was more desire and interest in fighting against other Europeans than against the Ottomans.[18] A testament of this change was the fact that, only a year after the fall of Constantinople, Venice signed a commercial agreement with the Ottomans, both parties more eager to maintain the flow of trade than to fight for religious predominance.[19]

By conquering Constantinople, however, the Ottomans gained more than tacit recognition of their power. With the city under their control, the Ottomans inherited not only a strategically located position dominating the straits but also a center of naval power. The port served as a key commercial entrepôt linking the Black Sea with the Mediterranean. Moreover, the shipyards of Constantinople, together with their skilled labor, remained mostly untouched by the siege and the conquest. The Ottoman Empire now had both the ability and the need to turn its attention to the sea, and Sultan Mehmed II began a concerted effort to expand and strengthen the Ottoman fleet.

The first effort was directed toward the Mediterranean and brought mixed results. By the second half of the fifteenth century, the Aegean and Eastern Mediterranean seas were effectively internal seas of the Ottoman

Empire. Extending from Southeastern Europe to Asia Minor, and pushing southward toward Palestine and Egypt, Ottoman power surrounded these waters without controlling them directly. The challenge was that Venice, and to a smaller degree the Knights Hospitaller (to be precise, the Knights of the Order of St. John of Jerusalem, later known as Knights of Malta) based in Rhodes, had sufficient naval strength and control over strategic islands to threaten Ottoman shipping and communication.

Despite attempts at coexistence, the Venetian presence in the Aegean was deemed to be too threatening to the Ottomans, who directed their power against the Republic's outposts in the region. The long 1463–79 war marked the beginning of Ottoman maritime ascendancy in the Aegean, but it also showed serious limitations of the sultan's fleet. The Ottomans were still lacking naval skills and during the entire war "considered a superiority of at least four to one necessary to tackle the Venetians."[20]

In 1470 a massive Ottoman fleet of three hundred to four hundred ships was sent against Negroponte (ancient Euboea), a key Venetian-controlled island. This Ottoman "forest on the sea" in the end pushed the Venetians out of the island, ending their two-century-long control.[21] Despite European (and in particular Venetian) fears of Ottoman naval supremacy, it was the sultan's land army more than his fleet that was responsible for this military success. To attack Negroponte, for instance, the sultan built a bridge of ships between the Greek mainland and the island, rather than using his fleet to attack Venetian ports or ships.[22] In fact the Ottoman fleet, despite its impressive size, did not manage to win a single naval battle against the Venetians in this war and played only a supporting role to the land armies. The strategy pursued by Sultan Mehmed II did not differ substantially from that pursued by his predecessors, who leveraged their superiority on land to hinder and even block European naval forces but avoided direct clashes between fleets. By holding key points, such as Gallipoli at the entrance to the Dardanelles or, after 1470, Negroponte, the Ottomans could control the sea by denial and did not have to confront directly the navies of Venice, Genoa, or the Knights of Rhodes and their French and Spanish supporting naval forces. As the historian John Pryor observes, "the eventual consolidation of Ottoman maritime dominance in the eastern Mediterranean was achieved not by pitched naval battles but by a slow, relentless, and exhausting drive to gain possession of the bases and islands from which war galleys could control shipping along the sea lanes."[23]

A decade after taking over Negroponte, the Ottomans tried to conquer Rhodes, situated strategically close to the Anatolian shore and between the

Greek mainland and Cyprus. But after a prolonged siege, the Ottoman army failed to conquer the fortified city and retreated. They were more successful against other Venetian outposts, such as Lepanto, Modon, Koron, Navarino, and even Durazzo on the Dalmatian coast. Their success against these ports was in large measure again due to their ability to project large land armies there without having to rely, as had been the case in their attack on Rhodes, on extensive maritime support.

The war of 1499–1503 between the Ottomans and Venice was more decisive, ending in a clear recognition by all parties involved of Ottoman maritime preponderance in the Eastern Mediterranean. At the very outset of the war, in the Battle of Zonchio (near Modon, on the Ionian coast of Greece), the Venetian fleet was clearly defeated by the Ottoman ships in a bloody encounter that involved naval artillery. The rest of the war continued along similar lines, leaving Venice, the main maritime opponent of the Ottomans, shocked and considerably weaker. A foray of Ottoman land forces even reached northeastern Italy, wreaking havoc within sight of the Venetian lagoon. In the peace of 1503, Venice was forced to give up most of its colonies, and most importantly, lost control over the mouth of the Adriatic. Its access to the Mediterranean routes was from now on in the hands of the sultan who was effectively unchallenged in the Eastern Mediterranean.

Yet the maritime supremacy of the Ottoman Empire was not without limits. The continental nature of the empire with its long frontiers presented a serious strategic problem. From 1503 until the 1520s Ottoman interest in the Mediterranean had to compete with the unstable situation in the eastern frontier region, where the Persian Safavi dynasty had extended its control over modern-day Iran, projecting its power even farther to the north, around the Caspian Sea. Only after the defeat of the Safavis, and the succeeding conquest of Mamluk Egypt in 1517, could the Ottomans devote their full attention and resources again to the Mediterranean. Similarly, the northern frontier with Hungary and the Habsburg lands required constant military and diplomatic attention, making the Mediterranean a secondary front.

Clear evidence of the supporting role played by the Mediterranean in Ottoman strategy was the conquest of Rhodes in 1522. This stronghold continued to be held by the Knights of St. John, who resisted several Ottoman attacks over the previous decades. The naval power of the Knights was relatively small but was still capable of endangering Ottoman shipping in the region. But the "threat which Rhodes posed to Ottoman shipping did not suffice to divert, to any great degree, the attention of the Ottoman state from its two primary objectives during this time, Iran and Egypt."[24] Only after the conquest of Egypt in 1517 did the Ottomans concentrate on evicting the Knights from Rhodes, which by then was located on a key logistical link between Anatolia and Egypt, a maritime route that was preferable to the unstable and lengthy roads of Mesopotamia and Syria.

The policies of the Knights did not strengthen their already weak and lonely position. In the early 1500s, Rhodian ships, often manned by privateers, disrupted Mediterranean commerce and impacted negatively not just the Ottomans but also the Venetians, the most likely allies of the Knights. Because of the common interest in accessing Asian markets, Venice and the Ottoman Empire had a rapprochement after the 1499–1503 war, which left Rhodes an isolated Christian outpost that could not expect any help from Europe. In 1522 the Ottoman sultan Suleiman the Magnificent finally succeeded in defeating the Knights and expelling them to Sicily.

The fall of the Venetian strongholds and of Rhodes generated great fears among Europeans. The Ottomans appeared to have established a thalassocracy comparable to that of Byzantium in the tenth century or of Venice from the thirteenth century on. In Italy, many expected an Ottoman invasion aimed at conquering the other half of the former Roman territories. For instance, in a 1521 letter to a friend, Niccolò Machiavelli wrote that an Ottoman attack was a hotly debated topic in the piazza (public square).[25] A 1545 Venetian map of the Mediterranean showed six Ottoman galleys off the Tuscan coast, ready to plunder.[26]

These fears were not completely unfounded. In 1480 the Ottomans briefly held Otranto in southern Italy and in the succeeding years solidified their control over the Greek and Dalmatian coastline, appearing poised for a continued westward expansion. Their forays to the outskirts of Venice terrified the inhabitants of northern Italy. And Muslim pirates based in North Africa and under the nominal authority of the sultan ravaged Italian coastal cities, threatening even Rome.

Yet the fears of an Ottoman onslaught and maritime monopoly remained only fears. The sultan did not translate the maritime power achieved in the early sixteenth century into a long-lasting strategic gain. While by the mid-sixteenth century Ottoman naval forces were considerably more numerous than those of Venice or (perhaps, briefly) even of Spain, Ottoman sea power in the Mediterranean remained a secondary front for the sultans who were preoccupied with their long and unstable land frontiers in Europe and the Middle East.

Moreover, in the Mediterranean three broad factors limited Ottoman maritime success. First, the sultan relied heavily on Muslim pirates based in

North Africa. An unintended consequence of the Spanish *Reconquista* was that many of the Muslim rulers who had been pushed out of the Iberian Peninsula took to the sea their religious zeal and continued to harass Spanish territory throughout the sixteenth century. In other cases, such as the infamous Barbarossa brothers, adventurers who were seeking plunder but who were also motivated by the desire to spread Islam joined forces in North Africa and conducted a persistent *guerre de course* against the Christian powers. These Muslim pirates were formidable and able to project power to distant coastal areas, as in the case of a 1544 raid on Toulon. They were firmly based by the mid-sixteenth century in Algiers and Tunis, from which European powers tried unsuccessfully several times to evict them.[27] The Ottomans supported these pirates by supplying them with arms as well as bestowing upon them honors and often the official imprimatur of the state. As Hess observes, "behind the corsairs, the Ottoman sultan, who claimed to be the champion of the Islamic world in the Holy war, added the support of a great state. For those corsairs who won fame in frontier wars, the Ottoman administration, by the late fifteenth century, could offer state positions that went well beyond the rewards of a privateer."[28]

The pirates, however, did not bring significant strategic advantages to the Ottoman sultan. They could not defeat any of the European powers in the Mediterranean and were simply a nuisance, however terrifying, for the Italian cities. Moreover, the connection between them and the Ottoman authorities was thin, despite the great honors bestowed on some of the pirates (especially Barbarossa, who became an admiral of the Ottoman navy). Maritime actions were mostly seasonal; therefore the Ottoman navy coordinated its activities with the pirates only in the summer.[29] On top of this sporadic coordination, the allegiance of the pirates to the sultan was very weak. They were interested in plunder or, when motivated by religion, in simply attacking the Christian powers and their vessels, regardless of the strategic utility of their actions. The sultan, therefore, could not rely on them to take concerted action that could seriously affect the fortunes of the Spanish or the Italian maritime states.[30]

The second feature that limited Ottoman sea power in the Mediterranean was the rise of Spain, which replaced Venice as the key Christian naval power in the region. The Ottoman expansion in the Mediterranean coincided with the rise of Spain as a unified state in control of the Western Mediterranean, putting a serious check on the sultan's ability to extend his influence farther on the seas. By the end of the fifteenth century, the Reconquista was complete and the Muslims were expelled from the Iberian Peninsula, making the

Spanish kingdom the principal champion of Christian Europe and thus in direct opposition to the Ottomans. Although the Atlantic, with its recently discovered American lands and its competing powers (mainly British), attracted most of the attention of Spain, the Mediterranean continued to play an important role in the strategic outlook of Castile, and in particular of Philip II. The emperor was also king of Naples and Sicily and thus had a strong interest in keeping the sea-lanes between Spain and southern Italy open and firmly in Spanish hands. The raids of the Barbarossa brothers and other Muslim pirates constantly harassed these sea-lanes, and Spanish possessions in Southern Italy were under constant threat from Ottoman naval forces as well.

From the 1550s on, Spain began to mobilize its considerable military capabilities and diplomatic influence to counter Ottoman expansion in the Mediterranean. Because of these efforts, a coalition of European powers led by Spain inflicted a spectacular defeat on the Ottoman fleet at Lepanto in 1571. The victory of the Christian powers at Lepanto was astounding and represented the first real military success against the Ottomans, who were deemed almost invincible since the 1444 battle of Varna and the conquest of Constantinople. As Braudel rightly described it, Lepanto represented "the most spectacular military event in the Mediterranean during the entire sixteenth century."[31] The long string of European losses seemed to be over.

Yet, the Spanish victory was a tactical success with limited immediate strategic benefits for Europe. The Christian coalition collapsed soon after the battle, with Venice choosing to preserve its commercial relations with the sultan and signing a separate peace.[32] The Spanish king, Philip II, had also a plethora of other preoccupations ranging from the management of his growing overseas empire to the Protestant revolt in the Netherlands and the worsening fiscal condition of his kingdom.[33]

Moreover, the core of the Ottoman Empire was on land, along the Danube and in the Middle East, and the naval defeat at Lepanto did not affect the sultan's power there.[34] However spectacular a battle, Lepanto had no impact on the ability of the Ottomans to maintain or even project power on land, and ultimately only the defeat at Vienna in 1683 and the ratification of that defeat in the 1699 Treaty of Karlowitz arrested the expansion of the empire.[35]

Finally, the Ottomans rebuilt their navy with great speed, even conquering a Spanish stronghold near Tunis three years after Lepanto. With some exaggeration but also with a grain of truth, the Ottoman grand vizier argued in 1572 that the "Ottoman state is so powerful, if an order was issued to cast anchors from silver, to make rigging from silk, and to cut the sails from satin, it could be carried out for the entire fleet."[36] By 1574 the Ottoman navy had returned to its pre-Lepanto strength and was capable of sending to Tunis a fleet so large that Spain preferred not to oppose it.

Despite these advantages, the Ottoman navy could not compete in the long term with the wealth of Spain. Lepanto did not destroy Ottoman sea power, but it showed that the sultan's fleet could not remain unchallenged in the Mediterranean.

Finally, the third factor that constrained Ottoman maritime power in the Mediterranean was the growing irrelevance of the Mediterranean and the resultant diminishing Ottoman interest in it. Whereas Lepanto by itself had at best only a psychological impact by showing that the Ottomans could be defeated, Ottoman sea power in the Mediterranean had in fact reached a peak by the end of the sixteenth century. By 1580, the sultan recognized the futility of further expansion in the Mediterranean. Despite the rapid rebuilding of the Ottoman navy, Spanish power was also growing. In 1580–81, Spain annexed Portugal, an event that not only augmented its navy, making it the largest in the world, but also gave it "a long Atlantic seaboard at a moment when the Atlantic was becoming the major battlefield between the Spanish Monarchy and the powers of northern Europe."[37]

From the Ottoman perspective, not only was it clearly impossible to dislodge Spain from its position in the region, it was also useless. The broader geopolitical context within which the battle of Lepanto took place was decreasing the strategic value of the Mediterranean, thereby diminishing the importance of a victory or a defeat in this theater. The Mediterranean, as discussed earlier, was being gradually displaced as a key strategic theater by the Atlantic and Indian oceans. It is toward this new theater—the Red Sea, the Persian Gulf, and the Indian oceans—that the Ottomans directed their sea power after the first decades of the sixteenth century. The rise of the Ottoman thalassocracy coincided with the shift away from the Mediterranean, the main theater of the Byzantine power that they replaced, toward the Indian Ocean, where the Portuguese were developing their own imperial maritime dominion. The European powers, Braudel writes, "abandoned the fight, tiring suddenly of the Mediterranean, but the Turks did precisely the same, at the same moment; they were still interested, it is true, in the Hungarian frontier and in naval war in the Mediterranean, but they were equally committed in the Red Sea, on the Indus and the Volga."[38]

The Indian Ocean

The arrival of the Portuguese in the Indian Ocean at the turn of the sixteenth century threatened the connection between the Mediterranean (and, thus, the Ottoman Empire) and the Asian markets. In 1507, for instance, no Asian goods arrived in the Red Sea, closed at its entrance by the Portuguese fleet.[39] To maintain that access and be able to compete with Portuguese power, the Ottomans had to direct their attention to the southern frontier (Persia, Egypt, the Red Sea, the Persian Gulf, and farther, the Indian Ocean), which until the early 1500s was of very limited interest to them. The Mamluks of Egypt tried in the first decade of the sixteenth century to oppose the Portuguese naval forays into the Red Sea, but they failed to achieve great successes, even with the military support of the Ottoman sultan. Moreover, the relationship between the Mamluks and the Ottomans was unstable because of the competition between them for the role of protector of Muslim populations and holy sites in the Middle East. Starting in 1514, the Ottomans pushed southward, rapidly expanding in southern Anatolia, then Syria, and finally in 1517 conquering Cairo and deposing the Mamluk rulers.

This victory put the Ottomans on the Red Sea, establishing a new maritime front for them. In 1538 they organized a massive naval expedition to regain full control over the Red Sea and push the Portuguese back. They succeeded in conquering coastal areas in Yemen, including the port of Aden, and crossed the Indian Ocean, reaching India itself. Once in India, however, the Ottomans failed to take the Portuguese stronghold of Diu and had to retreat by land to Constantinople.[40]

A second direction of Ottoman expansion was toward the Persian Gulf. In 1534 the Ottomans conquered Baghdad and a few years later reached Basra on the Gulf. But their control over the region was feeble because the local population was opposed to their rule and the Safavid dynasty, despite a peace agreement, continued to wage a low-level guerrilla war against them. Moreover, the Gulf was a de facto closed sea because the Straits of Hormuz were under Portuguese control.

The Ottoman expansion toward the south—both to the Red Sea and the Persian Gulf—is instructive because it is part of the larger story of the rise of Ottoman maritime power. It was no longer sufficient for the Ottomans to supplant Byzantine sea power in the Mediterranean theater. To maintain a position of power vis-à-vis the other European powers, the Ottomans had to project their influence toward Asia. But this new strategic direction required a set of skills and capabilities—namely, the ability to conduct long voyages on open waters as well as to conquer and administer noncontiguous territories—that the Ottomans lacked.

In fact, the Ottomans pursued a maritime strategy in the Red Sea and Indian Ocean that was analogous to the one they pursued in the Mediterranean. More precisely, they built their maritime power not by controlling a few strategically located outposts but by gradually expanding by land. This reflected a strategic mentality, as well as an administrative and social structure, which was profoundly different from those of the Venetians in the Mediterranean and the Portuguese (and later on, the Spanish, Dutch, and British) in the Atlantic and Indian oceans. While the Venetians, in the thirteenth to fifteenth centuries, and the Portuguese, in the late fifteenth and sixteenth centuries, concentrated their efforts on building widely dispersed strongholds along key sea routes and controlled commercial flows from them, the Ottomans attempted to counter such expansion by effectively enveloping the contested waters by land. As Hess puts it, "While Portugal rejected the conquering tradition of her warrior aristocracy to lean almost entirely upon maritime commerce as the primary reason for imperial naval expansion in the East, the Ottomans, in contrast, sought to conquer territories in order to gain tax revenues from newly acquired agricultural and commercial economies. Thus the conquest system of the Ottomans reflected the desire to administer and tax numerous lands and peoples, for only ample resources could support the vast armies and bureaucracies that ruled the Muslim Empire."[41]

A corollary feature of this strategic posture was that the Ottomans rarely focused on defeating the enemy's fleet and limited themselves instead to controlling the shore and hindering its operations. This was in part a conscious decision taken from a position of naval weakness, but it continued even after the Ottoman navy achieved considerable strength and mastered the necessary skills to conduct naval operations effectively. The key to Ottoman sea power was not the fleet (or, from the Ottoman perspective, the destruction of the enemy's fleet) but control over the land surrounding the seas. That is why Lepanto, where the sultan's fleet was annihilated, did not end Ottoman control of the sea. In other words, the maritime strategy of the Ottoman Empire maintained a strongly land-centric focus.[42]

The problem for the Ottomans was that the Indian Ocean was not the Mediterranean, and the strategy that was successful in the latter was not appropriate in the former.[43] In fact, the geographic contours of the Mediterranean made Ottoman maritime strategy feasible because the extensive coastlines in the Aegean, Dalmatia, and North Africa gave enormous power to whoever controlled them. By holding Tunis, for instance, the Ottomans controlled the flow of commerce to Sicily. Similarly, by holding the Greek and Dalmatian coasts (and briefly also Otranto in southern Italy) the Ottomans effectively cut Venice off from the Mediterranean. Such a land-based maritime strategy was, however, impossible in the open waters of the Indian Ocean.

The Ottomans certainly managed to extend their control over a sizeable portion of the Arabian coastline, with forays to East Africa. But control over these shores was insufficient to hinder Portuguese naval operations. This was due in part to the sheer size of the Indian Ocean; it could not be easily encircled by land, as the Mediterranean was. Even when the Ottomans controlled the Arabian coastline, the Portuguese could simply avoid nearby sea-lanes and reach their ports in India without difficulty. Moreover, the Ottomans held only tenuously many of these shores and had to devote more attention to landward challenges than to Portuguese seaborne threats. This was true in the Persian Gulf, where the Safavids continued to challenge Ottoman dominance of Mesopotamia, and along the East African shores. For instance, a telling anecdote is the 1588 expedition of an Ottoman corsair, Mir Ali Beg, to modern-day Somalia. With only a few small galleys armed with artillery he sailed along the East African coast and in one place set up a fort defended by artillery on land and by the armed galleys at sea. The goal was to repel a Portuguese fleet sent there to force the Ottomans out and to extend the sultan's control over the East African shores and sea-lanes. This was meant to be "a classic showdown between Ottoman artillery and Portuguese sea power," which had brought a crucial success to the Ottomans in 1517 in their defense of Jiddah against Portuguese naval forces.[44] Although this particular expedition ended poorly for the Ottomans, who were attacked from the sea by the Portuguese and from land by indigenous cannibals, it conveys very well the Ottoman approach to sea power and the difficulties of adapting it to the requirements of this vast maritime theater.[45]

Technological Challenges

Having looked at the reasons for, and the directions of, Ottoman maritime expansion (the "why" and "where"), it is important to examine now the ways (the "how") the Ottomans built their naval power. The development of a navy was not easy, especially for a state that focused its attention on land conquests. It required technical expertise, skilled labor, and sufficient material (mainly wood). The development, coordination, and administration of all of these, on a scale that would result in a navy that could match the power of Venice or Spain or Portugal, could not have occurred without a concerted effort of the central government and, more precisely, of the sultan himself.[46] This occurred only after the conquest of Constantinople in 1453.

Mehmed the Conqueror was the first Ottoman head of state to recognize the need for a navy and to devote his attention to building one. The city of Constantinople gave him not only a symbolic seat of power but also a strategic port and a working shipyard. His navy increased quite rapidly thereafter. We lack clear numbers, but it is evident that, from the second half of the fifteenth century on, the Ottomans no longer had to rely on the sporadic and short-lived maritime support of others to satisfy their needs for naval forces (as, for instance, when they had to cross the straits to project their power in Europe).[47] The numbers seem to indicate an exponential growth of the Ottoman navy in the 1453–1500 period. For instance, the Ottoman sultan had about 100 ships at his disposal in 1453, but twenty years later he could muster around 500 (in the 1475 conquest of Kaffa, the Ottomans used 380 ships, of which 120 were galleys).[48]

The quality of the Ottoman navy was unremarkable in this first period. As noted earlier, Ottoman fleets avoided direct engagements with the Venetian galleys, even though numerically they were equal if not superior to the fleets Venice was able to field. But Ottoman shipbuilding improved and most likely came to match the high technical standards of the best Venetian galleys. Frederic Lane writes, for instance, that by the end of the sixteenth century, Venetian galleys were slower and more prone to damage in storms than Ottoman ships.[49] Others, however, argue exactly the opposite. For instance, Pryor writes that "Ottoman galleys were still reputed to be inferior to Venetian ones and were said to be poorly built of inferior materials, to be poorly maintained, and to be less manageable."[50] Conducting a net assessment of Ottoman naval strength was difficult then and is doubly arduous now in large measure because the size and quality of Ottoman ships was either exaggerated or denigrated by Western observers throughout the fifteenth and sixteenth centuries either to stir fear and thus stimulate an anti-Ottoman coalition or to support notions of European superiority and disdain for the Ottomans.[51]

In part, however, the conflicting estimates of the quality of the sultan's navy were due to the different design of Ottoman ships, reflecting again the different strategic mentality of this continental power. Guilmartin writes, "The Ottoman galley . . . was designed for a strategic role which was profoundly offensive and a tactical role which was profoundly defensive. Its job was to get the siege forces to their objectives and to prevent interference with their activities by enemy naval forces once there. This might mean receiving an attack from an enemy fleet; but it rarely meant delivering one. An Ottoman fleet victory could do little to help the progress of the siege, but a defeat could do much to impair it."[52]

Even assuming technical parity, by the mid-sixteenth century the Ottoman navy had two clear advantages over its Venetian and other Christian counterparts. First, the Ottomans controlled most of the east Mediterranean coastline, as discussed earlier. This allowed the Ottomans to hinder, and if necessary block, European shipping, to control access to key shipbuilding resources (especially timber, which was in short supply in Italy), and in short, to make the eastern Mediterranean an Ottoman lake.

The second advantage stemmed from the sultan's reliance on North African Muslim corsairs, who supplied him with labor as well as new technologies. Human power was essential for a Mediterranean fleet. The galley, the principal vessel of war in the Mediterranean, remained effectively similar across centuries, and an Ottoman pilot most likely would have been capable of sailing an Athenian galley.[53] Its key feature was that it was oar-powered, thereby requiring many sailors. The oarsmen often turned into sword-wielding soldiers when boarding the enemy's galleys or when disembarking and leading charges on ports or other land fortifications. The challenge was that every time a fleet had to be manned, the naval authorities had to find a large number of men. The Ottomans tended to recruit their oarsmen among their conquered populations, in many cases avoiding forced conscription and relying on volunteers. But this method was insufficient when facing large Christian fleets in the sixteenth century. The North African ghazis, however, could supply large numbers of slaves, obtained during their raids on the Italian shores, and attracted Muslim populations from Spain (after the Reconquista).[54]

Furthermore, the North African corsairs proved to be more adaptable and introduced new types of ships in the sixteenth and seventeenth centuries. They were in constant contact with Portuguese ships in North and East Africa, and with the Spanish navy in the Mediterranean, and these continuous clashes forced them to introduce new ship designs to compete with the technologically more advanced Atlantic powers. Having reached a naval peak in the late sixteenth century, the Ottomans instead remained wedded to the galley as their principal ship, and despite their defeats in the Indian Ocean did not attempt to compete technologically with the Portuguese. The advances in cartography and ship design (combined with artillery) that were achieved by the Portuguese (as well as the Spaniards) allowed these powers to send their navies across open oceans, a feat that would remain impossible to Ottoman fleets.[55] The Muslim corsairs did not have the resources to match Portuguese and Spanish overseas expansion but maintained enough capabilities, in large measure aided by technological innovation, to keep an uneasy status quo in the Mediterranean, thereby protecting the Western maritime frontier of the Ottoman Empire.[56]

The Ottomans' inability or unwillingness to improve their naval technologies in the sixteenth century severely impaired the growth of their sea power.[57] While the Atlantic European powers developed the carrack (a "remarkable vessel, the full-rigged ship, which married technology of both the northern seas and the Mediterranean in one vessel"[58]) and the caravel, the Ottomans continued to use the oar-powered galley, which had an advantage in narrow straits and along the coastline but was completely ineffective in oceanic waters.[59] As a result, Ottoman maritime expansion ended in the Red Sea and the Persian Gulf, which "became the southern limit of effective Mediterranean galley warfare, while the Indian Ocean became the home of the Atlantic sailing ship."[60] The Ottomans would never overcome these technological limitations, imposed on them by the geographic theater where their maritime power began. Their inability to control the key sea-lanes of the world, which established for the first time in history a truly global market, made the Ottoman power a large but increasingly weak and regional actor.[61]

As a result, the Ottoman Empire, despite its impressive naval capabilities, remained essentially a continental power. An Ottoman Turk in the late seventeenth century is said to have asserted that "God hath given the sea to the Christians and the land to them [the Muslims]."[62] Such fatalism was not fully warranted. The Ottomans deliberately chose not to pursue a more aggressive strategy in the Indian Ocean, failed to introduce fundamental technological innovations into their naval forces, and focused more on their Danube frontier than on access to Asia and the growing global markets. On a more positive note, sea power allowed the Ottomans to subdue the Venetians, challenge the Spaniards, and expand to Egypt.[63] Yet this Ottoman fatalism is also based on the hard facts of geography. The geographic position of the Ottoman Empire constrained its expansion and prevented it from benefiting from the Age of Discoveries. Long land frontiers, no matter how well defended and stable, were a constant source of threat and demanded resources that could not then be devoted to overseas adventures.

Conclusion

It is always dangerous to draw enduring lessons from history, which after all is as much the realm of contingency as of eternal principles. Yet it would be equally dangerous and shortsighted not to examine the lessons of history that can be derived from the rise of Ottoman maritime power. Two sets of lessons, broadly concerning the ease and the difficulty of developing sea power, come to mind.

First, naval power is not an exclusive property of a few states. It can be developed very rapidly in part because naval technology, however difficult to master, cannot be confined to a few powers: As the Ottomans showed, technology can be copied, bought, or conquered. The most striking fact of Ottoman history is in fact the rapidity of the Ottoman naval rise. The Ottoman state was for more than a century focused only on territorial conquests, and then in the second half of the fifteenth century it developed a growing and increasingly effective fleet. The Ottomans very quickly succeeded in challenging and defeating the main Mediterranean naval power, Venice, and continued to be a serious threat to the other European powers.

Second, states are also severely limited in their ability to develop sea power and to use it. The Ottomans are a great example of the constraints imposed upon naval power by the nature of a state. The long land frontiers of the Ottoman Empire and the numerous powers pressuring their borders (Hungary, Poland, Russia, Safavids, and more) indelibly shaped their strategic mentality. The way that the Ottomans expanded reflected their continental outlook with its focus on controlling territory; this was in direct contrast to the modality of Portuguese (but also Venetian) expansion, which depended on a network of widely scattered ports. As Nicholas Spykman observed decades ago, "A land power thinks in terms of continuous surfaces surrounding a central point of control, while a sea power thinks in terms of points and connecting lines dominating an immense territory."[64] Such a continental mentality is difficult to overcome and perhaps impossible to change given the strategic concerns of a power with long land borders.

The challenge was that, for those facing rising Ottoman sea power, it was impossible to predict which trend—the ease or the difficulty of sea power—would come to characterize Ottoman history. In the end, I argue, the Ottomans were so severely hampered by their continental concerns that they were unable to compete with the rising global maritime powers of Spain and Portugal and thus remained a powerful land empire. But if you were a Venetian, Portuguese, or Spanish strategist at the turn of sixteenth century, you did not have this certainty of history, and you would have been perhaps correct to worry and fear an Ottoman naval onslaught, as did those Italians in the piazza described by Machiavelli.

There is an inherent tension in the rise of a sea power. On the one hand, it is possible to build a naval force with relative ease, and even quite quickly. Technology can be bought, stolen, and so on—and it allows a state (such as the Ottoman Empire) to put an impressive fleet on the sea. On the other hand, some serious difficulties or limitations are not easily overcome. The easiest are perhaps the technological expertise, the skills, and the workforce. The most difficult are the political conditions, notably whether the principal threat and interest of the state lies on the sea or on land. This challenge applies to China—namely, how it will deal with its continental nature and its long frontiers.

Notes

1. See A. T. Mahan, *The Influence of Sea Power upon History, 1660–1783* (New York: Dover, 1987), 29.

2. For a brief description of the early Ottoman expansion, see Bernard Lewis, *Istanbul and the Civilization of the Ottoman Empire* (Norman: University of Oklahoma Press, 1963), 3–35.

3. On the "ghazi" factor in early Ottoman history, see Paul Wittek, *Rise of the Ottoman Empire* (London: Royal Asiatic Society, 1938), 2.

4. On the pattern of Ottoman conquests in Anatolia and the Balkans, see Halil Inalcik, *The Ottoman Empire: The Classical Age, 1300–1600* (London: Weidenfeld & Nicolson, 1973), 11 and 14.

5. See Mark C. Bartusis, *The Late Byzantine Army* (Philadelphia: University of Pennsylvania Press, 1992), 103–19.

6. Kelly DeVries, "The Lack of a Western European Military Response to the Ottoman Invasions of Eastern Europe from Nicopolis (1396) to Mohács (1526)," *Journal of Military History* 63 (3) 1999: 539–60.

7. Edward Potkowski, *Warna 1444* (Warsaw: Wydawnictwo Bellona, 1990); Edwin Pears, "The Ottoman Turks to the Fall of Constantinople," in *The Cambridge Medieval History*, vol. 4, ed. J. R. Tanner, C. W. Previté-Orton, and Z. N. Brooke (New York: Macmillan, 1926), 675–76.

8. See Robert Finlay, "Crisis and Crusade in the Mediterranean: Venice, Portugal, and the Cape Route to India (1498–1509)," *Studi Veneziani* 28 (1994): 45–90.

9. For a dated but concise summary of the main trade routes and the effects of Portuguese expansion on them, see A. H. Lybyer, "The Ottoman Turks and the Routes of Oriental Trade," *The English Historical Review* 30, no. 120 (October 1915): 577–88. Good treatments of this period and of the rise of the Atlantic powers can also be found in J. H. Parry, *The Establishment of the European Hegemony, 1415–1715* (New York: Harper & Row, 1961); G. V. Scammell, *The First Imperial Age: European Overseas Expansion, c.1400–1715* (London and New York: Routledge, 1992).

10. Dennis O. Flynn and Arturo Giraldez, "Born with a 'Silver Spoon': The Origin of World Trade in 1571," *Journal of World History* 6, no. 2 (Fall 1995): 201–21; J. H. Parry, *The Age of Reconnaissance* (New York: Mentor Books, 1963), 211–13.

11. In 1580 an Ottoman advisor to the sultan even suggested the idea of digging a canal at Suez to restore the flow of goods from Asia. See Bernard Lewis, *The Muslim Discovery of Europe* (New York: W. W. Norton & Co.), 34.

12. In addition, beginning in the sixteenth century parallel changes in the European state system further undermined Ottoman position. The emergence of what is now called the "modern nation state," which occurred at the same time as these geopolitical changes of the "Age of Discoveries," contributed to the move of Europe's center of power to Western Europe. See Charles Tilly, *Coercion, Capital, and European States: AD 990–1992* (Cambridge, MA: Blackwell, 1992).

13. Flynn and Giraldez, "Born with a 'Silver Spoon,'" 211. For a history of Spanish imperial expansion and its effects, see also J. H. Parry, *The Spanish Seaborne Empire* (Berkeley: University of California Press, 1990); J. H. Elliott, *Imperial Spain, 1469–1716* (New York: Penguin Books, 1990).

14. For the effects of silver trade on Ming China, see William Atwell, "Some Observations on the 'Seventeenth-Century Crisis' in China and Japan," *Journal of Asian Studies* 45, no. 2 (1986): 223–44; William Atwell, "Ming China and the Emerging World Economy, c. 1470–1650," in *The Cambridge History of China*, vol. 8, *The Ming Dynasty, 1368–1644*, ed. Frederick W. Mote and Denis Twitchett (New York: Cambridge University Press, 1998), part 2, 376–416.

15. Abbas Hamdani, "Ottoman Responses to the Discovery of America and the New Route to India," *Journal of the America Oriental Society* 101, no. 3 (1981): 323–30.

16. Palmira Brummett, *Ottoman Seapower and Levantine Diplomacy in the Age of Discovery* (Albany: State University of New York Press, 1994), 107–8.

17. Steven Runciman, *The Fall of Constantinople, 1453* (New York: Cambridge University Press, 1990).

18. Braudel argues that the 1571 Battle of Lepanto was the last crusading effort because it managed to unite most of Europe under the Spanish banner against the Ottomans. But the decline of European unity preceded that. Neither Venice nor Rhodes succeeded in organizing a larger European coalition against the Ottomans in the second half of the fifteenth century in large measure because of growing political divisions within Europe. In fact, it is probably more correct to argue that the 1444 Battle of Varna marked the end of the crusades. See Fernand Braudel, *The Mediterranean and the Mediterranean World in the Age of Philip II*, vol. 2 (New York: Harper & Row, 1973), 842–84.

19. See also Robert Schwoebel, "Coexistence, Conversion, and the Crusade against the Turks," *Studies in the Renaissance* 12 (1965): 164–87. For further indications of attempts at coexistence, see Louis Thuasne, *Gentile Bellini et Sultain Mohammed II* (Paris: Ernest Leroux, 1888).

20. Niccolo Capponi, *The Victory of the West: The Great Christian-Muslim Clash at the Battle of Lepanto* (Cambridge, MA: Da Capo Press, 2007), 36.

21. Frederic C. Lane, *Venetian Ships and Shipbuilders of the Renaissance* (Baltimore: The Johns Hopkins University, 1934), 138.

22. Franz Babinger, *Mehmed the Conqueror and His Time* (Princeton, NJ: Princeton University Press, 1978), 281.

23. John Pryor, *Geography, Technology, and War* (Cambridge, U.K.: Cambridge University Press, 1988), 177.

24. Palmira Brummett, "The Overrated Adversary: Rhodes and Ottoman Naval Power," *The Historical Journal* 36, no. 3 (September 1993): 540.

25. Letter of 18 May 1521, in Niccolò Machiavelli, *Letter a Francesco Vettori e a Francesco Guicciardini* (Milano, Italy: Rizzoli, 1989), 295. In his comedy *Mandragola*, Machiavelli strikes a less serious note on this subject. A woman who goes to con-

fession shares with the priest her fears of an Ottoman invasion. The priest responds that this will happen if she does not pray. There is an indication here of the irrational nature of some of these fears that nonetheless were sweeping through Italy. See Machiavelli, *Mandragola* (Prospect Heights, IL: Waveland Press, 1981), Act 3, Scene 3, p. 30.

26. Capponi, *Victory of the West*, 8.

27. On Algiers as a base of Muslim pirates, see Braudel, *The Mediterranean and the Mediterranean World*, 884–87. See also E. Hamilton Currey, *Sea Wolves of the Mediterranean* (New York: Stokes, 1910); Pryor, *Geography, Technology, and War*, 193–96.

28. Andrew C. Hess, "The Evolution of the Ottoman Seaborne Empire in the Age of the Oceanic Discoveries, 1453–1525," *American Historical Review* 75, no. 7 (December 1970): 1906. See also Andrew C. Hess, "The Battle of Lepanto and Its Place in Mediterranean History," *Past and Present*, no. 57 (November 1972): 57–58.

29. The Ottoman state had similar relations with other bands of ghazis or even mercenaries based on land. See Karen Barkey, *Bandits and Bureaucrats* (Ithaca, NY: Cornell University Press, 1997), 189–228.

30. On the role of pirates in the strategy of states, including the relationship between the Barbary corsairs and the Ottoman authorities, see also Janice Thompson, *Mercenaries, Pirates, and Sovereigns* (Princeton, NJ: Princeton University Press, 1996).

31. Braudel, *The Mediterranean and the Mediterranean World*, 1088.

32. Jack Beeching, *The Galleys at Lepanto* (London: Hutchinson, 1982), 231–32.

33. For a fascinating study of Philip II, see Geoffrey Parker, *The Grand Strategy of Philip II* (New Haven, CT: Yale University Press, 1998).

34. See also John Francis Guilmartin, *Gunpowder and Galleys: Changing Technology and Mediterranean Warfare at Sea in the 16th Century* (Cambridge, U.K.: Cambridge University Press, 1980), 221–52.

35. See Angelo Tamborra, "Dopo Lepanto: Lo spostamento della lotta antiturca sul fronte terrestre," in *Il Mediterraneo nella seconda metà del '500 alla luce di Lepanto*, ed. Gino Benzoni (Florence: Leo S. Olschki Editore, 1974), 371–91.

36. Quoted in Hess, "The Battle of Lepanto," 54.

37. Elliott, *Imperial Spain*, 276.

38. Braudel, *The Mediterranean and the Mediterranean World*, 844.

39. George Stripling, *The Ottoman Turks and the Arabs* (Philadelphia: Porcupine, 1977), 15. See also Hess, "Evolution of the Ottoman Seaborne Empire," 1907–8.

40. Stripling, *Ottoman Turks and the Arabs*, 92–96; André Cot, *Suleiman the Magnificent* (London: Saqi Books, 1989), 194–95; Andrew C. Hess, "The Ottoman Conquest of Egypt (1517) and the Beginning of the Sixteenth-Century World War," *International Journal of Middle East Studies* 4, no. 1. (January 1973): 55–76.

41. Hess, "Evolution of the Ottoman Seaborne Empire," 1916. In part this difference between the Ottomans and the Portuguese (as well as the Venetians) can be
explained by the fact that, by the sixteenth century, the latter derived most of their
resources from taxing the revenues of large swathes of territory while the former
sought wealth from maritime commerce. See also Cot, *Suleiman the Magnificent*,
192 and 198.

42. A good discussion of the differences between the Ottoman and Venetian (and to a
degree Spanish) maritime strategy, as well as of the inability to understand Ottoman
sea power from a Mahanian perspective, is in Guilmartin, *Gunpowder and Galleys*,
16–41.

43. The differences between the Mediterranean Sea and the oceans had been known
since Roman times. As Julius Caesar observed in the description of his military
campaigns in Gaul and Britain (the latter being quite unsuccessful), "sailing in a
wide ocean was clearly very different matter than sailing in a land-locked sea like the
Mediterranean." Yet, knowing that there was a difference was insufficient to adapt
quickly and effectively, as the Ottomans found out. See Caesar, *Gallic War*, 3.9.

44. A detailed analysis of the 1517 Jiddah battle, which truly marked the frontier
between the Mediterranean and the oceanic sea powers, is in John F. Guilmartin,
Gunpowder and Galleys (Cambridge, U.K.: Cambridge University Press, 1974),
7–15.

45. Giancarlo Casale, "Global Politics in the 1580s: One Canal, Twenty Thousand
Cannibals, and an Ottoman Plot to Rule the World," *Journal of World History* 18,
no. 3 (September 2007): 267–73.

46. This is part of a much broader story of the rise of the modern state, with its central-
ized administration of resources that became a requirement for the political sur-
vival of polities. See for instance J. R. Hale, *War and Society in Renaissance Europe,
1450–1620* (Baltimore: Johns Hopkins University Press, 1985); Hendrik Spruyt,
The Sovereign State and Its Competitors (Princeton, NJ: Princeton University
Press, 1994); Tilly, *Coercion, Capital, and European States*; Brian M. Downing, *The
Military Revolution and Political Change: Origins of Democracy and Autocracy in
Early Modern Europe* (Princeton, NJ: Princeton University Press, 1992).

47. A similar story could be told about other military technologies of the Ottomans.
For instance, Ottoman artillery, which was key in the 1453 siege of Constantinople,
was built by a Western renegade, a Hungarian who defected from Byzantium. See
Bernard Brodie and Fawn M. Brodie, *From Crossbow to H-Bomb* (Bloomington:
Indiana University Press, 1973), 46–47.

48. Babinger, *Mehmed the Conqueror and His Time*, 449.

49. Lane, *Venetian Ships*, 13.

50. Pryor, *Geography, Technology, and War*, 187.

51. See for instance the exhaustive study of Venetian opinions of Ottoman power,
Lester J. Libby Jr., "Venetian Views of the Ottoman Empire from the Peace of 1503
to the War of Cyprus," *Sixteenth Century Journal* 9, no. 4 (Winter 1978): 103–26.

52. Guilmartin, *Gunpowder and Galleys*, 219.

53. See also William Ledyard Rogers, *Naval Warfare under Oars, 4th to 16th Centuries: A Study of Strategy, Tactics and Ship Design* (Annapolis, MD: Naval Institute Press, 1967).

54. Guilmartin, *Gunpowder and Galleys*, 118–19.

55. Ibid., 257.

56. The challenge of relying on corsairs (e.g., lack of effective control over them, their inability and unwillingness to extend control over land) was examined earlier, but it was also compounded by the difficulty of managing a large maritime theater. In the sixteenth century, the Ottomans had to decentralize their naval command to respond rapidly to local threats, which were often increased by the interference of European powers. The Ottoman admiral of Gallipoli, who at least nominally controlled the navy, was supplemented by semiautonomous regional commands (e.g., Rhodes, Lesbos, Alexandria, Suez, the Black Sea, and even the Danube).This decentralization may have had the effect of further weakening Ottoman ability to respond to the growing maritime power of Spain and other Atlantic European states. See Capponi, *The Victory of the West*, 35.

57. The Ottomans, like any other state, also faced budgetary constraints. The expense of the navy was often covered by extraordinary levies because the regular budget was insufficient. This reliance on other nonbudgetary sources to pay for the fleet seems also to indicate that the main strategic preoccupation of the Ottomans remained on land, and the navy—especially from the late sixteenth century on—was a secondary concern, if not a luxury. See also Rhoads Murphey, *Ottoman Warfare, 1500–1700* (New Brunswick, NJ: Rutgers University Press, 1999), 17–19.

58. Archibald R. Lewis, "The Islamic World and the Latin West, 1350–1500," *Speculum* 65, no. 4 (October 1990): 839.

59. On the differences between the Mediterranean and Atlantic ships, see also Parry, *Age of Reconnaissance*, 67–84. The 1571 battle of Lepanto was the last battle between oar-powered ships, a sign of the declining importance of the Mediterranean naval technology. Brodie and Brodie, *From Crossbow to H-Bomb*, 64.

60. Hess, "Evolution of the Ottoman Seaborne Empire," 1917.

61. For a discussion of whether it was superior military technology (namely gunpowder) or control over sea-lanes and transportation that made Atlantic Europe so powerful, see George Raudzens, "Military Revolution or Maritime Evolution? Military Superiorities or Transportation Advantages as Main Causes of European Colonial Conquests to 1788," *Journal of Military History* 63, (no. 3): 631–42.

62. Quoted in Hess, "Evolution of the Ottoman Seaborne Empire," 1895.

63. See Brummett, *Ottoman Seapower*, 179.

64. Nicholas Spykman, "Geography and Foreign Policy, II," *American Political Science Review* 32, no. 2 (1938): 224.

PART II

Modern Era

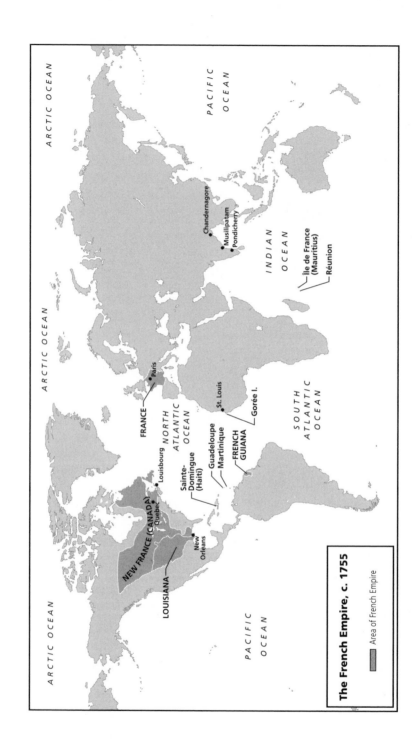

The French Empire, c. 1755

Area of French Empire

James Pritchard

France: Maritime Empire, Continental Commitment

A BASIC CONTINUITY HAS MARKED the several maritime transformations that France has experienced during the last half millennium. From the early sixteenth century to the outbreak of World War II and the collapse of the Third Republic in 1940, French maritime transformations were characterized by enormous effort that yielded limited benefits and led generally to outright failure. France never benefited from these transformations to the extent that French merchants, politicians, statesmen, and sailors believed it should. French efforts to expand overseas and develop maritime defenses were marked by nearly insoluble problems that were geopolitical, socioeconomic, and strategic in nature. Each maritime transformation arose out of a different set of contingent circumstances, yet each failed for approximately similar reasons.

The first maritime transformation, which occurred during the sixteenth century, was unique in being almost entirely the product of private rather than state resources. It was part of a European-wide phenomenon arising as more people produced more goods and services and the growing division of labor within industrial communities led to increased international trade. This first transformation could be excluded from this discussion for that reason

but is included to show that a maritime transformation without state participation is possible and indeed has occurred. Although quite remarkable in its
own way, perhaps owing to the absence of direct state involvement, this first
maritime transformation was destined to fail in the face of actions at sea by
opposing states.

The second and greatest maritime transformation occurred during the
last thirty years of the seventeenth century and the first decade of the next,
during which France built what was then the world's largest navy. But it
ended in exhaustion and defeat arising from a failure to recognize that successful state sea power must be integrated with a vigorous seaborne trade
and an active foreign policy. France's reach had exceeded its grasp. A third
maritime transformation, extending roughly from 1745 to 1815, was paradoxically the most successful in French history, yet conferred few benefits
on the nation. Finally, in the late nineteenth and early twentieth centuries
the fourth maritime transformation occurred when France and the French
navy entered the modern industrial age, which forced it to adjust to massive
political, technical, and economic changes while attempting to compete with
overwhelming maritime, naval, and economic capabilities of several rival
states. This maritime transformation, too, provided few benefits and proved
no more successful than preceding ones.

The history of these marine transformations, like that of France's overseas empire, is one of disjuncture and contradictions.[1] They were not only
products of accident, error, and special interests as well as of national or
state design, they were also a drag on France's economic and political development. It was, moreover, a common feature during these centuries that
France's maritime transformations did not succeed in linking its empire to
the nation.

From the sixteenth century onward, French overseas expansion was a
product of chance rather than design. The efforts of individuals, merchants,
or small business groups who possessed a vision of profit and the energy to
pursue it, or often-fiercely individualistic soldiers or messianic missionaries
pursuing their own visions, normally left the French state to deal with faits
accomplis. The French government was generally a peripheral force; troops,
ships, and funds needed to secure overseas territories were rarely forthcoming and, when they did arrive, often proved to be too little, too late, to seize
fully the opportunity. Overseas attractions and maritime transformations
also competed at home with a host of demands upon scarce resources in the
face of continental wars and the call of domestic politics. The French overseas empire, like the French navy, was constructed in fits and starts. Both

were, however, amazing achievements; resiliency was a measure of their success. In spite of indifference and tepid support at home, the French once built the world's largest navy and French men and women established an imposing presence overseas. Since then the once global empire has shrunk to a few islands in the sea.

Unique among European empires, ambiguity surrounds the idea of the French imperial state. There are two distinct views of the meaning of empire in the French case: in one, empire refers to Europe, and in the other, alludes to the world overseas. Although our present focus is France overseas, it is worth remembering that France—the eternal hexagon—has itself been viewed as an empire: "A complex of territories, conquered, annexed, and integrated in a political and administrative whole, many of them with strongly developed national or regional personalities, some of them with traditions that were specifically anti-French."[2] The French Empire, it may be argued, was the continental creation of the kings of France (and Napoleon Bonaparte) much more than it was the disparate collection of French colonies overseas. Moreover, Napoleon actually crowned himself emperor, and although the term "empire" fell into disuse with his demise, it was revived in the middle of the nineteenth century when his nephew Louis-Napoléon declared France an empire and himself emperor. The term "empire" appeared again in the draft Vichy constitution, which was never adopted. More recently, some French scholars have presented a third concept of "informal empire" incorporating areas and nations such as Russia, Latin America, and the Ottoman Empire where French capital investment predominated.[3] Such a notion may be salted to one's own taste.

In the sixteenth century, long wars in Italy preoccupied the weak French state, and civil war at home nearly bled it dry. France's involvement with navies and overseas expansion remained occasional and intermittent for more than a century and a half. Its initial modern maritime transformation had nothing to do with the state and everything to do with fishing, trade, and privateering. Undertaken by private individuals, these activities were all more important than anything sponsored by the state. Early voyages of exploration, such as those by Giovanni da Verrazzano in 1524 along the coast of North Carolina, and by Jacques Cartier in 1534 and 1536–1537 in the gulf and river of Saint Lawrence, received royal permissions but were privately sponsored and financed.

From the earliest years of the century, fishing interests from many towns in the provinces of Normandy, Brittany, Poitou, and Saintonge financed and fitted out private ventures to the northwest Atlantic in pursuit of codfish.

The Basque whaling industry employed hundreds of men in the Gulf of St. Lawrence and along the Labrador coast before Cartier ventured up the St. Lawrence River in 1536. By the end of the century, five hundred or more ships annually employing twelve thousand fishermen from French ports worked on the Grand Banks.[4]

The New World was also well known to France's merchants and sailors. Early in the century, French ships from Channel and Atlantic ports ventured south to Africa and across the Atlantic to Brazil, where they discovered a prized commodity variously known as brazilwood, dyewood, or logwood and—despite the wrath of the Portuguese—quickly began exploiting the area. Soon after the first recorded French voyage to Brazil in 1504, there were as many French ships on the coast as there were Portuguese vessels.[5] Pushing into the Caribbean, other merchants found a growing market for French textiles and African slaves in Spanish America. Finally, French privateers led the way across the Atlantic to plunder the wealth of the Indies. French sailors quickly grasped the importance of attacking Spanish lines of communication between Spain and America. Between 1522 and 1523 French corsairs captured nearly all of Montezuma's treasure sent to Spain by Hernán Cortés, and in 1529 the king of Portugal complained that he had lost three hundred ships to French privateers and pirates.[6] Nevertheless, the French state played an insignificant part in all of this activity compared to private interests both noble and mercantile.

The effect of fishing, trade, and privateering was that the French maritime transformation leading to overseas expansion contributed to urban growth and promoted rivalry among coastal ports at home rather than unity centering on the state, which after 1559 became increasingly caught up in the throes of religious and political civil war. From 1532, when Brittany was definitively attached to France, the duchy sought to extend its special privileges while the state attempted to integrate it into the kingdom, thus giving rise to additional rivalry and much strife.[7] None of these overseas activities required or was conducive to settlement, nor did they need naval assistance. Instead, towns such as Bayonne, La Rochelle, Morlaix, Saint-Malo, Honfleur, Rouen, and Dieppe carried out French overseas expansion, all competing furiously against one another. Protestant merchants of Rouen, for example, were primarily behind French attempts to settle Brazil while Dieppe merchants invested in the Florida venture.

The quasi-religious settlements in Brazil and Florida, located on the shoulders of the Spanish Empire, were weak and quickly destroyed by the Portuguese and Spanish. French settlement attempts in the next century shifted farther away from Spanish possessions to Canada, while interurban competition continued between merchants from Saint-Malo and La Rochelle who obtained royal monopolies to exploit the fur trade at the expense of their rivals. It cost the crown nothing to grant monopolies. Nor did it cost much to issue royal charters granting proprietary ownership to private investors interested in exploiting the several West Indian islands and New France.

Although the French state built a small royal navy during the middle of the sixteenth century, it quickly shriveled away, becoming only a vague memory by the next. The construction of a navy by Cardinal Richelieu during the 1630s failed to leave a legacy, and the history of French overseas expansion in the seventeenth century resembles the previous period at least until the 1660s. Although Richelieu was the first French statesman to articulate the need for a naval strategy to protect France's Atlantic and Mediterranean coasts from attacks, overriding internal problems at home— chiefly the imperatives of consolidating royal power—and long continental wars directed against Spain militated against significant state involvement after his death in 1642.[8] The French crown become directly involved in overseas colonial development only after 1663, when France was at peace and the king financed seaborne expeditions to India and revoked the ownership of the proprietary colonies of Martinique, Guadeloupe, and New France, making them royal provinces.[9]

The subsequent half century, extending from 1663 to 1713, witnessed France's greatest maritime transformation and a degree of political, social, and economic stability never before seen in France and its overseas possessions. Yet basic geopolitical, socioeconomic, and strategic factors then began to come into play that made it impossible for France to sustain Europe's largest navy. The authority of the early French state was not well developed, elaborate, or effective. The absolutism of Louis XIV, which arose from the monarch's successful collaboration with provincial elites rather than their coercion, was less effective than is usually claimed.[10] French geography and a noncapitalist social structure also limited early naval development and overseas expansion. Moreover, France's governing classes possessed anticommercial attitudes, and overseas expansion continued to promote interregional rivalry and discourage national unity. Merchants from different ports thwarted competitors by obtaining monopolistic privileges to exploit trade with North America, Africa, the West Indies, the East Indies, and the southern sea. Overseas expansion, which fostered national unity in England, thus did exactly the opposite in France. The fact that the national capital was far inland coupled with a lack of a uniform central authority in the kingdom further encouraged this interregional rivalry.

During the maritime wars of Louis XIV, the strategic focus of the French navy changed completely, from being an ally of the English against the Dutch in the 1670s to fighting the combined Anglo-Dutch fleet in the 1690s, and from fighting the Spanish in the 1680s to protecting the Spanish in the 1700s. Between 1702 and 1713, for example, French naval forces abandoned France's colonies to escort Spanish gold shipments across the Atlantic. These complex alterations of alliances had the effect of placing the French and British in direct opposition later in the eighteenth century, thereby altering the strategic situation yet again.

During the long period of a century and a half, from 1665 to 1815, the French adopted three general naval strategies. These were to strike across the English Channel at Great Britain, to send forces elsewhere in the world (to the West Indies, North America, India, or Egypt), and to make war on enemy commerce. Although details varied over time, these three options or combinations of them remained at the heart of French maritime strategy. The strategies largely failed—chiefly because they were not normally integrated with French foreign policy and in fact often operated independently of it.

Absolutism contributed in a major way to the failure of French colonies to evolve beyond a collection of scattered, isolated towns and territories. Although much was accomplished, and by the end of the seventeenth century an imperial vision appeared to hold glowing promise of world dominion, limits to imperialism were already qualifying state involvement; by 1713 the imperial vision of fifteen years earlier lay in ruins. The six decades between 1670 and 1730 were crucial in the formation of the first Bourbon Empire, but the state's role remained minimal. French royal absolutism was less a unifying force than a process of co-opting powerful provincial political, legal, and social forces in the interests of the crown.[11] Nowhere did the king's writ run unimpeded.

A major limitation to early French imperialism was the lack of migration overseas to colonies of settlement between 1600 and 1800. This is all the more significant when we recall that during these centuries France was the most populous country in Europe. Why the migration of French men and women overseas should have been a mere trickle in comparison to broad Spanish, Portuguese, and English migration flows is a matter of debate. But the explanation is probably that there were few incentives to leave France. In particular, peasants, who owned nearly half the land in France, enjoyed the most secure land tenure in Europe, so that as long as their hold on productive land remained firm, nothing existed to push them overseas.[12]

Despite an apparently successful maritime transformation, the young, inexperienced navy of Louis XIV and his successors never found an imperial role. The navy took part in many campaigns between 1670 and 1730 in the Caribbean and North America, first against the Dutch and then against the English, Spanish, and Portuguese. But after each encounter, the navy did not fulfill the expectations placed upon it. The lessons learned during the Franco-Dutch War (1672–1678) lie at the heart of the navy's failure to find a role in imperial defense.[13] Although French naval action successfully drove the Dutch out of the French West Indies, excluding them from French commerce, other developments—weak institutional boundaries between the army and navy overseas, insufficient provisions and inability to acquire any from local sources, sickly crews, and the rapid deterioration of warships in warm tropical waters—meant that naval support overseas proved expensive and difficult to maintain for any length of time. Overseas losses also undermined Louis XIV's confidence in his navy and left his naval minister diminished in his rivalry with the war minister. Logistical problems were not easily solved owing to a lack of overseas bases where squadrons could revictual, refit, and repair. Strikingly, no naval establishment—not a dockyard or even a careening wharf—was ever constructed in the West Indies.[14]

The strategic problem of defense was another limit to French imperialism. It seems clear that France could be a land power or a sea power but not both simultaneously, at least not without a maritime strategy closely integrated with an active foreign policy. Under Louis XIV, France constructed Europe's largest navy, as well as its largest army.[15] It could not support both forces on the foundations of noncapitalist agriculture and the rickety, medieval financial system that left the state's revenues and expenditures in the hands of private financiers.[16] These distinctly ancient financial arrangements directly affected French naval strategy in 1693: Following the defeat of the fleet at Barfleur-La Hougue in May–June 1692, the navy was unable to mount any further fleet actions during the Nine Years' War (1688–1697). The navy was forced to alter its strategy from *guerre d'escadre*, or fleet action, to *guerre de course*, attacks on trade. This change involved more than dividing the fleet into penny packets to attack commerce. It required leasing the king's ships to private interests to attack trade.[17] The fleet continued to remain a formidable threat in being, but no money was available to permit it to go to sea, and after 1693 it never again engaged the enemy. Royal privateering, *la course royale*, was not an effective means to support French strategy overseas. It ran directly counter to the commercial need for convoys and escorts for merchant shipping, undermining the entire (if unacknowledged) question of imperial defense.[18]

The navy attempted to return to fleet actions during the opening years of the War of the Spanish Succession (1702–1713), but following a humiliating defeat at Vigo in 1702 and the brief encounter of Velez-Malaga in 1704 (when both sides claimed victory), the fleet never again opposed the Anglo-Dutch forces during the remainder of the war. Instead, lack of human, material, and financial resources forced the navy to return to its strategy of *guerre de course* against English, Dutch, and Portuguese trade.[19] The sole exception to plundering attacks and commerce raiding was the provision of warships to escort critically important Spanish treasure fleets across the Atlantic in 1708, 1710, and 1712.[20] Naval weakness coupled with financial exhaustion at home and military defeat in Europe forced France in 1713 to give up the fight and surrender possessions in the New World (Hudson Bay, Newfoundland, Acadia, and St. Christopher) to preserve French conquests made earlier in the reign. The maritime transformation of the 1660s had ended in ignominy because it had never been integrated with the monarchy's main concerns.

With the coming of peace in 1713, the French fleet faded away as the nation's need to recover made it impossible to restore the navy for many years.[21] Indeed, in the wake of Louis XIV's wars, some French naval officers came to believe that fleet actions had cost France far too much and had decided nothing.[22] During the eighteenth century, French colonial trade grew independent of naval protection. From 1716 to 1744, the value of goods exchanged between the West Indies and France grew by at least four times, representing 25 to 30 percent of all French foreign trade. This unprecedented growth in maritime trade was accompanied by similar growth in merchant shipping; the number of vessels increased by three times between 1704 and 1743.[23] Such maritime mercantile expansion was not accompanied by concurrent increases in the number of naval warships. Although colonies and colonial trade flourished, neither Louis XV nor his senior ministers gained any appreciation of the navy's function as it related to imperial defense. Indeed, until his death in January 1743, Cardinal André-Hercule de Fleury, France's capable foreign minister, maintained that the key to French independence abroad lay in preserving peace through diplomacy and alliances rather than French military and naval power.[24]

In addition to the weakness of the French navy in the early 1740s, its officer and manpower reserves were also slim. The French naval officer corps was quite separate from the civilian officer corps that administered the navy, its arsenals, and the colonies; built, repaired, and victualled its ships; and recruited its sailors. Moreover, French naval arsenals were located far apart, were largely independent of one another, and were far from Paris and the court. French naval officers were not in positions to advise ministers, who lacked any firsthand knowledge of what navies could and could not do. French statesmen, with few exceptions, never understood the strategic role that the navy might play in defense of France and its colonies. They came instead to rely on a mixture of fixed fortifications, native alliances, metropolitan troops, and local militias for colonial defense.

But the chief reason for France's failure to use its navy to defend the Bourbon Empire was geographic. West Indian colonies proved incapable of reprovisioning naval squadrons. Dedicated to commercial agriculture based on slavery, colonists had neither land nor labor nor inclination to grow provisions for the navy. Unlike the English and Spanish, the French had no mainland American colonies that produced agricultural surpluses in sufficient quantities to revictual naval forces.[25] French authorities did not build naval facilities in the Americas during the eighteenth century because they did not understand until too late the possible role that naval defense of the colonies might play in the defense of France.[26]

Between 1745 and 1805, a period of sixty years, the French navy experienced a series of renewed transformations that, paradoxically, eventually led to its destruction. Several features distinguish this period from the maritime transformation that occurred under Louis XIV. First, this third maritime transformation was about colonial trade and overseas possessions. Second, unlike the previous transformation, when the French navy had largely fought alone against a grand alliance of European powers, the French frequently fought in alliance with Spain. True, the French had been protector of a mistrustful Spain after 1700, but during the seventeenth century the French had largely fought alone. During this third maritime transformation, the geostrategic problem of dealing with a divided fleet became more acute, as British possession of Gibraltar and the Mediterranean island of Minorca and France's need to cooperate with its Spanish ally to protect coastal shipping in Europe placed great strains upon the navy. Finally, this third transformation, characterized by destruction and renewal, also witnessed the most successful employment of a maritime strategy in French history.

The War of the Austrian Succession (1744–1748), during which the French lost Louisbourg in North America yet recovered it after agreeing to give up the army's occupation of the Low Countries, appeared to reinforce a strategic lesson the French had taken from the Treaty of Utrecht thirty-five years earlier—namely, that colonies were won and lost in Europe. The errors of this lesson were brutally learned during the Seven Years' War (1756–1763), when, following the destruction of the navy in 1759 at Lagos and Quiberon Bay, France lost territories in America, Africa, and India to superior British naval forces. For twenty years after 1763, however, for the first and only time in French history, the navy became the primary instrument to project French power overseas and to reinforce its position in Europe. This succeeded because the French actively pursued a policy of securing peace in Europe in order to attack Great Britain at home and overseas. By a supreme irony, however, the greatest beneficiary of French naval power was the United States of America, whose newly won independence it guaranteed.[27]

Another limit to French imperialism at this time, and at least as strong and often superior to contemporary empire-building ideology, was the presence of a strong anticolonial tradition. As early as the sixteenth century, when Montaigne raised doubts about France's overseas enterprise in Brazil, French writers and statesmen generally opposed the idea of France overseas.[28] During the eighteenth century, philosophers frequently denounced colonial expansion and slavery. One must be careful in assessing their views, however, because many French writers cared little about colonies, employing them chiefly as settings to project their own desires for reform of contemporary French life.[29] By the mid-eighteenth century, imperial ideology had been reduced to little more than a collection of strategic insights on the part of a few politicians and naval officers and plaintive calls of colonial governors for support. The sentiment expressed in Napoleon's famous aphorism "damn sugar, damn coffee, damn colonies," following the loss of thousands of soldiers sent to Saint-Domingue (present-day Haiti) in the 1790s, foreshadowed his sale to the United States of France's claim to the North American interior in 1802; but this sentiment also had a long history.[30]

At the beginning of the nineteenth century, after Saint-Domingue had joined other colonies in the lost column and Louisiana was sold, little remained of empire beyond chimeras. Nothing remained of the French navy. France's idea of "empire" reverted to Europe; Napoleon's ambitions in Egypt were attached to his search for imperial glory rather than colonial conquest. His move there (in 1798) reflected a long-standing French strategy of sending fleets and expeditionary forces abroad to draw British fleets away from the French coast, enabling greater freedom of action (including the invasion of Ireland and England) at home.[31]

The Congress of Vienna in 1815 left France with French Guiana, Martinique, and Guadeloupe in the West Indies, the small islands of St. Pierre and Miquelon off Newfoundland in the Western Hemisphere, the island of Réunion near Madagascar, and a few trading posts in Senegal and India. French naval strategy remained committed to *guerre de course*, but during the decades after 1815, the sheer enormity of Great Britain's maritime trade made this French strategy infeasible. A battlefleet emerged slowly under Napoleon III (1852–1870), but its purpose was chiefly to assist commerce raiding, conduct coastal raids, and deter threats of invasion. Its appearance recalls earlier seventeenth-century developments under Cardinal Richelieu. New possessions overseas were added slowly: Algeria in the 1830s and West Africa and Indochina in the 1850s and 1860s.[32] The growth of empire quickened during the 1880s, however, when the French presence grew in Tunisia, Morocco, and China.[33]

Late nineteenth-century French imperialism and its accompanying maritime transformation differed in several significant ways from earlier versions. The navy was entering the modern industrial age and had to adjust to large changes in technology, strategic thought, and the political environment. Major continental rivals, Germany and Italy, had not even existed in the eighteenth century. The empire also differed in several respects from its earlier mercantilist guises. First, it was part of a worldwide competition for territory. Between 1875 and 1895, half a dozen European countries seized more than one-quarter of the land surface of the globe. France claimed more than one-third of the African continent.[34] Second, colonies became viewed as integral parts of advancing industrial economies, supplying raw materials, cheap labor, and semifinished goods for the benefit of metropolises.[35] Third, racism was a pronounced feature of late nineteenth-century imperialism and was accompanied by a conscious cultural mission to civilize or Europeanize overseas colonial populations in the image of the metropolis.[36] Fourth, the militarization of colonial populations was a new feature of imperialism. More than eight hundred thousand colonial conscripts served France during World War I as soldiers and defense workers.[37] Like imperialism's predecessor, however, this also created the preconditions of international conflict in Europe.

In general, the French navy responded well to the challenges of new materials and new weapons. Early technical excellence appeared under Napoleon III with the construction of the first fast steam line-of-battle ship, the first seagoing ironclad, and the first iron-hulled capital ship. Later pioneering work continued with new submarines and torpedo boats. But as in the eighteenth century, industrial and financial deficiencies rendered this *marine de prestige* ineffective by the 1860s, and naval strategy became a subject of unresolved quarrels in ensuing decades.[38]

The host of technological changes in naval warfare—screw propeller, iron hulls, shell-fire, ram, armor, turrets, and gunboats—that gave rise to enormous confusion in naval architecture during this period also stimulated new theories of naval warfare. The French had long faced the dilemma of seeking command of the sea to be able to attack the enemy's coasts and commerce. During the 1870s and 1880s, naval officers began to argue that new technologies had changed the nature of naval warfare and would allow France to overcome the old dilemma by developing cruiser and coastal warfare in lieu of blue water warfare or fleet actions. The advocates of attacking undefended coasts and pursuing open warfare against unarmed merchant ships became known as *la jeune école* (the "young school"). They were also strong advocates of colonial expansion. Their ideas, which reflected the social Darwinism of the period, were never tested and failed to reckon with the contradiction between warfare against English trade and against new continental enemies such as Germany and Italy.[39]

Lack of internal French unity was another limit to imperialism. The French were not, and had never been, a single people; what outsiders think of as French is chiefly the French bourgeoisie or middle class. At most, only half the French population in 1900 spoke standard French as a native language; the rest first learned Celtic, Germanic, and Romance dialects.[40] During the century following 1845, French domestic history reads like colonial history: authority imposed by outside forces; elaborate development schemes; contempt for locals, their languages, and their customs; suppression of armed rebellion; and talk of the civilizing mission. In the words of Theodore Zeldin, "The French nation had [yet] to be created."[41] This was especially the case after the most traumatic event of the late nineteenth century: the Franco-Prussian War (1870–1871) and the defeat of the French army at Sedan.

The growth of French imperialism and the colonial lobby was, at least partially, a response to defeat at home. By advocating expansion overseas, French imperialism in the age of the "scramble" was a psychological form of denial, a refusal to face the reality of declining French birth rates and growing German ones. The history of the French navy paralleled this development. During the Third Republic, between 1871 and 1940, the navy became very closely associated with France overseas. The naval officer corps, whose members were traditionally drawn from privileged, aristocratic, and Catholic backgrounds, provided many colonial governors and high ministry officials.[42] But the close association between the navy and the colonies during the period was less a reflection of France's concern for empire than the irrelevance of both at a time when France accounted for less than 5 percent of the world's shipping and the military budget concentrated on rebuilding the army. During the first decades of the Third Republic, France had no coherent maritime policy; the navy developed in isolation from the rest of the nation, largely by directing its energies toward Asia, Indochina, and the Far East.[43]

Military ambition, Roman Catholic apostolic zeal, and an organized political party drove late nineteenth- and early twentieth-century French imperialism and reveal indirectly another of the French empire's limitations, namely, the weak economic connections between France and its colonies. Economic arguments are of limited use to explain French imperialism. There is little evidence that imperialism aided the French economy to develop and some evidence that it retarded French development.[44] During the years 1908 to 1912, for example, only 11.3 percent of French imports came from the colonies, which in turn received just 13 percent of France's exports.[45] In 1913 the French Empire received only 8.8 percent of French investment abroad compared to 47.3 percent in the British case.[46] Colonies were expensive luxuries that made little or no economic sense. French exports and capital investment to both Russia and Latin America were far greater than to France's overseas possessions. Commercial gain had little to do with the late nineteenth-century scramble for territories, which coincided with a depression in world trade that lasted from 1874 to 1896.

With the exception of technology, for many years the French navy did not meet the challenges of the new industrial age. Advocates of the newest naval tactics were curiously opposed to necessary institutional reforms. Naval strategies continued to remain independent of French foreign policy concerns and provided for war against either the continental powers or Great Britain, which led to confusion as one or another potential enemy predominated. Obsession with its imperial mission during the late nineteenth century allowed the navy to ignore its European mission and the appearance of not one but three new navies with global ambitions: American, German, and Japanese.[47] Only after the *entente cordiale* of 1904 did moderates prevail sufficiently to overcome the ambiguities and contradictions of the previous three decades and integrate naval strategy with diplomacy as the navy grew to see itself as an instrument of national defense. Although commerce raiding remained the essence of naval strategy, a battlefleet was now available for active defense and offense.[48] Nevertheless, during World War I the French fleet was confined chiefly to the Mediterranean.[49] Despite the navy's involvement with Indochina, World War I exposed the tenuous nature of maritime

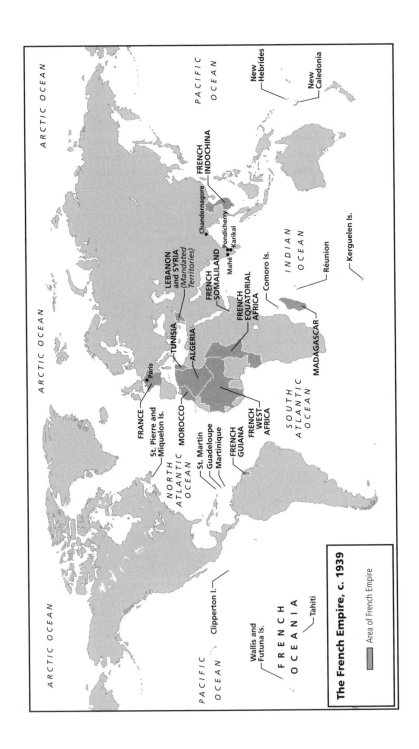

The French Empire, c. 1939

Area of French Empire

communication between France and Asia—so much so that Clemenceau, an outspoken opponent of colonial expansion, proposed offering Indochina to Japan.[50] In 1930 France's leading naval strategist, Adm. Raoul Castex, advocated getting rid of France's empire in the east as quickly as possible.[51]

In brief, few French people were ever attracted to the colonies or the navy during the Third Republic, and turnover among administrators there was high. Whether or not the divided administration of France overseas limited imperialism is moot, but it is hard to argue that it provided strong support. By 1900 Algeria was a department of France whose governor-general reported to the minister of the interior. Tunisia and Morocco were protectorates whose residents-general reported to the ministry of foreign affairs. The rest of the empire reported to the minister of the colonies, which came into existence only in 1893 when it was separated from the naval ministry. The new colonial ministry was perhaps the least important element of French imperial administration. Finally, colonial troops everywhere were responsible to the ministry of war.

Promoters of French imperialism after 1871 relied heavily on the experience of the earlier Bourbon Empire to inspire and guide the new empire builders. Indeed, their commitment to contemporary empire building profoundly shaped their interpretation of France's past glories overseas. But despite their argument that a unique genius for colonization—*la génie coloniale*—was inherent in the French race and made manifest in the moral qualities of French settlers, the effectiveness of military and political leadership, and the success of French relations with indigenous peoples around the world, the great majority of Frenchmen had no interest in France overseas. Despite the fervid nationalism that inspired the naval thinkers of *la jeune école* and French imperialism, France overseas never replaced the lost provinces of Alsace and Lorraine in the hearts and minds of the French people between 1870 and 1914.

During World War I and immediately afterward, France completed building the second largest empire in world history. New territories came from the breakup of both German and Ottoman empires in Africa and the Middle East, respectively. During these years, however, the French government lost control not only of the soldiers and colonial administrators in the outposts of empire but also of policy at the center of empire. Imperial policy fell into the hands of enthusiasts motivated chiefly by ideas about France's civilizing mission and national honor rather than any geopolitical strategy or ideas about economic exploitation for France's greater security or development.[52] Ideas resembling seventeenth-century notions of Roman Catholic apostolic zeal and *la gloire* more commonly associated with the reign of Louis XIV predominated over economic and political ambition.

While the great increase in French investment in empire between the world wars stood in sharp contrast to the prewar period, this economic activity was in part a delusion. It owed much to the collapse of the French franc in 1919, the loss of half of all French foreign investment following the collapse of Russia and the Bolshevik Revolution, and the need to constrain French investment within French territory. Between 1914 and 1940 French capital invested in the empire, the bulk of it in North Africa, increased four-fold, and the empire's share of total French foreign capital investment grew from 9 percent to nearly 45 percent. But in 1929 the empire still accounted for only 12 percent of France's imports and purchased less than one-fifth of its exports. While the relative importance of imperial trade may have grown during the 1930s, it did so largely because world trade had collapsed.[53]

The empire and the navy remained marginal to France's national concerns. The revival of French imperial enthusiasm as World War II approached was chimerical. French imperialists' claims to meet German demographic and economic strength with a renewed empire of colonial soldiers and workers proved to be nothing more than wishful thinking. Yet French imperialism was not merely a product of self-delusion. At its apogee, Greater France (*la plus grande France*) encompassed 11 million square kilometers and more than 100 million people on several continents.[54] But today all that remains is *la francophonie*, which does seem little more than an illusion. During decolonization in the 1960s General de Gaulle, ever the realist, referred to France's African colonies as the dust of empire. The lack of postimperial success stories in Algeria, Indochina, and sub-Saharan Africa may make the French Empire look less real than it was. From the perspective of the twenty-first century, it seems clear that the French Empire was chiefly the product of individuals, explorers, traders, sailors, missionaries, and soldiers who set out for an overseas destination hoping for a groundswell of government and public support that only occasionally appeared.

The maritime transformations of France that began in the sixteenth century and were renewed in each subsequent century never fully integrated the navy into national policy. Despite the extent of some transformations, the French navy was never responsible for the defense of France nor was it responsible for French prosperity. Like the empire, it was never central to the government's concern or to its policies. The French state has always been primarily interested in itself and its place in Europe. Only occasionally has it looked overseas. To seek independent action in foreign policy, French naval strategy had to be pursued concurrently with other considerations of economic and political realism, whether alone or in alliance with others. This occurred only once and briefly. Too often French naval strategy developed independent of considerations of national interest and consequently proved ineffective when applied. Despite building and operating a large navy for more than two centuries, France never became a world maritime power, and the empire failed to attract the support imperialists sought.

In summarizing the failures of France's maritime transformations, several observations may be relevant to consideration of the modern Chinese situation. Indeed, the French case may have greater relevance than any other example drawn from modern history because it evolved over four centuries and because, like China today, France faced both hostile land and sea powers. First, internal national consolidation appears to be a prerequisite for any successful maritime transformation. France's long struggle to consolidate political power in the state weakened the effectiveness of maritime transformations. Without a centralized authority, overseas maritime activity became a form of ill-coordinated, costly adventurism best left to individuals. Geopolitical challenges cannot be ignored but can be successfully met. While states have become simultaneously both land and sea powers, this is not easily accomplished by states confronting aggressive land and sea powers.

The French experience shows that regardless of the period, navies are very expensive to build and to maintain. They place enormous burdens on the state. Of the many challenges, however, the technical may the easiest to master. From the seventeenth to the nineteenth centuries the French virtually invented the science of naval architecture and built some of the finest warships of their time.[55] The greatest challenges to successful maritime transformations are social, economic, political, and administrative. Social unity is necessary to provided manpower, but it is not a sufficient condition of success. Developing a vigorous, sophisticated economy to support the burdensome demands of a navy is clearly a vital prerequisite to success. Just as important is the need for a law-based system of government to permit that economy to continue to develop and a concomitant, internal system of administration and taxation to enable the state to appropriate efficiently the human, material, and financial resources needed to support a maritime transformation.[56] Finally, the essential ingredient of a successful maritime transformation is a realistic appraisal of its possibilities and integration of naval strategy into foreign policy and overall national defense strategy.

Notes

1. Three recent all-encompassing and very different French colonial histories are the collaborative efforts by Jean Meyer, Jean Tarrade, Annie Rey-Goldzeiguer, and Jacques Thobie, *Histoire de la France coloniale*, vol. 1, *Des origins à 1914* (Paris: Armand Colin, 1991); Jacques Thobie, Gilbert Meynier, Catharine Coquery-Vidrovitch, and Charles-Robert Ageron, *Histoire de la France coloniale*, vol. 2, *De 1914 à 1990* (Paris: Armand Colin, 1990); and Pierre Pluchon, *Histoire de la colonization français*, Tome 1, *Le Premier empire coloniale des origins à la Restauration* (Paris: Fayard, 1991).

2. Eugene Weber, *Peasants into Frenchman: The Modernization of Rural France, 1870–1914* (Stanford, CA: Stanford University Press, 1976), 485.

3. For more on ideas of empire see Robert Aldrich, *Greater France: A History of French Oversea Expansion* (London: Macmillan, 1996), 89–121.

4. Laurier Turgeon, "Le temps des pêches lointains, permanences et transformations 1500-vers 1850," in *Histoire des pêches maritimes de France*, ed. Michel Mollat (Toulouse: Privat, 1987), 137–38.

5. N. P. Macdonald, *The Making of Brazil: Portuguese Roots, 1500–1822*, (Sussex: The Book Guild, 1996), 63–65.

6. Lyle McAlister, *Spain and Portugal in the New World, 1492–1700* (Minneapolis: University of Minnesota Press, 1987), 200, 259–60.

7. Alain Boulaire, "La Bretagne maritime de 1492 à 1592," in *La France et la mer au siècle des grandes découvertes*, ed. Philippe Masson and Michel Vergé-Franceschi (Paris: Tallandier, 1993), 155–61.

8. Étienne Taillemite, *L'histoire ignorée de la marine française* (Paris: Librairie Académique Perrin, 1988), 42–67; and E. H. Jenkins, *A History of the French Navy: From Its Beginnings to the Present Day* (London: Macdonald and Jane's, 1973), 15–37.

9. See Glenn Ames, *Colbert, Mercantilism and the French Quest for Asian Trade* (DeKalb: Northern Illinois University Press, 1996).

10. This argument is developed in James Pritchard, *In Search of Empire: The French in the Americas, 1670–1730* (Cambridge, U.K.: Cambridge University Press, 2004), 231–34.

11. See William Beik, *Absolutism and Society in Seventeenth-Century France: State Power and Provincial Aristocracy in Languedoc* (Cambridge: Cambridge University Press, 1985); and Sharon Kettering, *Patrons, Brokers and Clients in 17th-century France* (Oxford, U.K.: Oxford University Press, 1986).

12. Pritchard, *In Search of Empire*, 16–27.

13. James Pritchard, "The Franco-Dutch War in the West Indies, 1672–1678: An Early 'Lesson' in Imperial Defense," in *New Interpretations in Naval History, Selected Papers from the Thirteenth Naval History Symposium* (Annapolis, MD: Naval Institute Press, 1998), 3–22.

14. Pritchard, *In Search of Empire*, 267–300.

15. Daniel Dessert, *La Royale, vaisseaux et marins du Roi-Soleil* (Paris: Fayard, 1996).

16. Henri Legohérel, *Les Trésoriers généraux de la Marine, (1517–1788)* (Paris: Éditions Cujas, 1965); and James C. Riley, *The Seven Years' War and the Old Regime in France: The Economic and Financial Toll* (Princeton, NJ: Princeton University Press, 1986).

17. Geoffrey Symcox, *The Crisis of French Sea Power, 1688–1697: From guerre d'escadre to guerre de course* (The Hague: Martinus Nijhoff, 1974).

18. Pritchard, *In Search of Empire*, 356.

19. For the best discussion of *la guerre de course*, see the collection of essays in J. S. Bromley, *Corsairs and Navies, 1660–1760* (London and Ronceverte: The Hambledon Press, 1987).

20. Pritchard, *In Search of Empire*, 372–74.

21. Jan Glete, *Navies and Nations, Warships: Navies and State Building in Europe and America, 1500–1800*, 2 vols. (Stockholm: Almquist & Wiksell International, 1993), 1: 256–62.

22. See James Pritchard, *Anatomy of a Naval Disaster: The 1746 French Expedition to North America* (Montreal and Kingston: McGill-Queen's University Press, 1995), 20.

23. Paul Butel, *Les Négociants bordelais, l'Europe et les Iles au XVIIIe siècle* (Paris: Aubier-Montaigne, 1974), 48, and 392–93 graphs.

24. Pritchard, *Anatomy of a Naval Disaster*, 16–20.

25. This is clearly spelled out in Christian Buchet, *La Lutte pour l' espace Caraïbe et la façade Atlantique de l'Amérique Centrale et du Sud (1672–1763)*, 2 vols. (Paris: Librarie de l'Inde, 1991).

26. James Pritchard, *Louis XV's Navy, 1748–1762: A Study of Organization and Administration* (Montreal and Kingston: McGill-Queen's University Press, 1987); also Jonathan R. Dull, *The French Navy and the Seven Years' War* (Lincoln: University of Nebraska Press, 2005).

27. Jonathan R. Dull, *The French Navy and American Independence: A Study of Arms and Diplomacy, 1774–1787* (Princeton, NJ: Princeton University Press, 1975); and James Pritchard, "French Strategy and the American Revolution: A Reappraisal," *Naval War College Review* 48, no. 4 (Autumn 1994): 83–108.

28. See Michel de Montaigne, "Of Cannibals," in *The Complete Essays of Montaigne*, trans. Donald E. Frame (Stanford, CA: Stanford University Press, 1979), 150–59.

29. Frederick Quinn, *The French Overseas Empire* (Westport, CT: Praeger, 2000), 96–100.

30. Quoted in ibid., 77.

31. Jenkins, *History of the French Navy*, 226–28.

32. Annie Rey-Goldzeiguer, "La France coloniale de 1830 à 1870," in Meyer et al., *Histoire de la France coloniale*, 1: 315–552; Aldrich, *Greater France*, 24–67.

33. Rey-Goldzeiguer, "La France coloniale," 338–44; Milton E. Osborne, *The French Presence in Cochinchina and Cambodia, 1895–1905* (Ithaca, NY: Cornell University

Press, 1969); Douglas Porch, *Conquest of the Sahara* (New York: Random House, 1984); and William Hoisington Jr., *Lyautey and the Conquest of Morocco* (New York: St. Martin's Press, 1995).

34. A. S. Kanya-Forstner, *The Conquest of the Western Sudan: A Study in French Military Imperialism* (Cambridge, U.K.: Cambridge University Press, 1969); and David L. Lewis, *The Race to Fashoda: European Colonialism and African Resistance in the Scramble for Africa* (New York: Weidenfeld and Nicholson, 1987).

35. Henri Brunschwig, *French Colonialism, 1871–1914: Myths and Realities*, rev. ed., trans. William Glanville Brown (London: Pall Mall Press, 1966), [1960] 87–96.

36. William B. Cohen, *The French Encounter with Africans: White Response to Blacks, 1530–1890* (Bloomington: Indiana University Press, 1980); David Prochaska, *Making Algeria French: Colonialism in Bône, 1870–1920* (Cambridge, U.K.: Cambridge University Press, 1990); Alice L. Conklin, *A Mission to Civilize, the Republican Idea of Empire in France and West Africa, 1895–1930* (Stanford, CA: Stanford University Press, 1997).

37. Quinn, *French Overseas Empire*, 186; Myron Echenberg, *Colonial Conscripts, the Tirailleurs Sénégalais in French West Africa, 1857–1960* (Portsmouth, NH: Heinemann, 1991).

38. Theodore Ropp, *The Development of a Modern Navy: French Naval Policy, 1871–1904*, ed. Stephen S. Roberts (Annapolis, MD: Naval Institute Press, 1987), 6–25.

39. Taillemite, *Histoire ignorée de la marine française*, 354–68, and Ropp, *Development of a Modern Navy*, 155–80, 210–16, and 254–80 contain excellent summaries of the confusion arising from the tactical ideas of *la jeune école*.

40. Patrick Geary, *The Myth of Nations: The Medieval Origins of Europe* (Princeton, NJ: Princeton University Press, 2002), 31; also see Geary for a discussion of ethnicity, language, and nationalism in the nineteenth century.

41. Theodore Zeldin, *France, 1848–1945: Intellect and Pride* (Oxford: Oxford University Press, 1980), 1.

42. Ropp, *Development of a Modern Navy*, 48–50; and Ronald Chalmers Hood III, *Royal Republicans: The French Naval Dynasties between the Wars* (Baton Rouge: Louisiana State University Press, 1985).

43. Taillemite, *Histoire ignorée de la marine française*, 343–88.

44. Aldrich, *Greater France*, 195–98; Brunschwig, *French Colonialism*, 87–96.

45. Pierre Guillaume, *Le Monde colonial, XIXe–XXe siècle* (Paris: Armand Colin, 1974), 256.

46. Ibid., 258; Aldrich, *Greater France*, 196.

47. Ropp, *Development of a Modern Navy*, 141–54.

48. Ibid., 327–28.

49. Paul G. Halpern, *A Naval History of World War I* (Annapolis, MD: Naval Institute Press, 1994), 11–13, 67.

50. Quinn, *French Overseas Empire*, 115; and Christopher M. Andrew and A. S. Kanya-

Forstner, *France Overseas: The Great War and the Climax of French Imperialism* (London: Thames and Hudson, 1981), 237.

51. Ropp, *Development of a Modern Navy*, 142.

52. This is cogently argued by Andrew and Kanya-Forstner, *France Overseas*; see also Martin Thomas, *The French Empire between the Wars and during the Vichy Regime: Imperialism, Politics and Society* (Manchester, U.K.: University of Manchester Press, 2005).

53. Andrew and Kanya-Forstner, *France Overseas*, 248; Aldrich, *Greater France*, 196–97, presents a more positive view.

54. Aldrich, *Greater France*, 1.

55. See Larrie D. Ferreiro, *Ships and Science: The Birth of Naval Architecture and the Scientific Revolution, 1600–1800* (Cambridge, MA: MIT Press, 2006); and James Pritchard, "From Shipwright to Naval Constructor: The Professionalization of 18th-Century French Naval Shipbuilders," *Technology and Culture* 28, no. 1 (January 1987): 1–25.

56. On this matter, see the excellent study by John Brewer, *The Sinews of Power: War, Money and the English State, 1688–1783* (New York: Alfred A. Knopf, 1989).

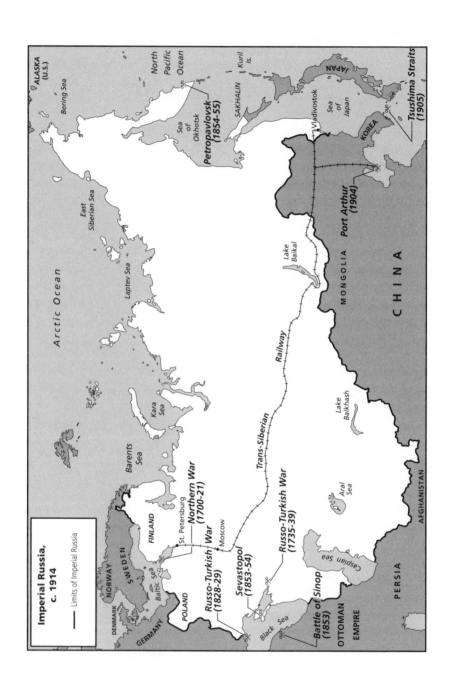

Imperial Russia, c. 1914

— Limits of Imperial Russia

Jacob W. Kipp

Imperial Russia: Two Models of Maritime Transformation

THE RUSSIAN NAVY CELEBRATED its three hundredth anniversary in 1996. In St. Petersburg—once again carrying the name of its founder, Peter the Great—naval exhibitions and reviews abounded, with warships flying the St. Andrew's cross, once the naval ensign of Imperial Russia. No object got more attention than the *botik* ("little boat") of Peter the Great—the *St. Nicholas*, a small craft that Peter himself called the "Grandfather of the Russian Navy" and on which the tsar had learned to sail on the lakes and rivers round Moscow in his youth.[1] The celebration came at a time when the navy was still in disorder and only beginning to recover from the collapse of the Soviet state, a time when many of its ships were rusting in port, with many waiting for breakers to salvage them, while naval officers were seeking to persuade their fellow Russians that Russia did indeed need a navy.

The editors of the three-volume history of the navy published to mark the anniversary began their work with a plea for the revival of the state's naval power:

The history of the navy and the history of the state are inseparable like the crown and roots of a tree. Periods of growth and decline of any of the former or current great powers are to one degree or another connected with their victories or defeats in naval wars, with periods of the rise or weakening of their naval power. The examples of this are many in classical antiquity, Greece, Carthage, and Rome, in the middle ages, Spain and Portugal, in early modern history, Holland, the Ottoman Empire, and France, and in the modern era, Great Britain.[2]

The authors went on to note the Soviet criticism of Alfred Thayer Mahan and John H. Colomb as ideologues of "the reactionary imperialist theory" of command of the sea as the foundation of empire and prosperity. But they then praised the same authors for their correct assertion that, in the global balance of power, states with the naval capability of dominating strategically important regions across the world ocean had played and would continue to play a decisive role. The authors made a plea for their countrymen to appreciate the importance of naval power for the Russia state, even as the country's historical experience, continental extent, economic self-sufficiency, and traditional landward threats had given the army a dominant position in both strategic considerations and access to the nation's resources. The decline of the Soviet Navy was not a case of a navy destroyed in war but a result of state collapse in which the very burden of defense spending contributed mightily to its final decline. Defeat or victory in war usually provides the acid test of a successful maritime transformation, but the Soviet case is different. Adm. Sergei Gorshkov's navy, which emerged during the three decades during which he was its commander in chief, was a force shaped by the major technological innovations transforming warfare after 1945—nuclear weapons, nuclear propulsion, ballistic missiles, and cruise missiles. Its capital ships were nuclear-powered ballistic missile submarines (SSBNs). Its combat fleets, built around guided missile cruisers, destroyers, and attack submarines, ultimately even included several generations of aircraft carriers, each with enhanced deck aviation. In short, the Soviet Navy was a complex institution composed of many systems and subsystems requiring increasingly sophisticated means of command and control. Indeed, Gorshkov's navy was on the cutting edge of the application of computer technology to automated systems of command and control. Senior Soviet naval theorists were, like their American counterparts, applying systems theory to guide future naval developments. The navy was locked in an intense competition with the U.S. Navy but with considerable geostrategic and economic disadvantages. As Admiral Gorshkov asserted, "Our state—a great continental and maritime world power—at all stages of its history has needed a powerful fleet as an essential element of the armed forces."[3]

The navy's decline came quickly. But its harbingers were already evident in the wake of just one minor test of some of these technologies in a distant clash between foreign navies—the British and Argentine—over the Falkland Islands. Soviet naval officers labeled that conflict the first modern naval war since 1945.⁴ The results of that conflict set off a domestic debate over the impact of electronic warfare and precision-strike systems on the conduct of naval combat and raised the prospect of another spiral in a costly naval arms race.⁵ This subdebate became part of what Marshal Nikolai Ogarkov, the chief of the Soviet General Staff, had labeled the Revolution in Military Affairs (RMA).⁶ Ultimately the projected costs of military modernization associated with the RMA became a critical factor leading to geostrategic disengagement and halting attempts at reform of the Communist command economy and mobilization state. Those attempts led to the loss of empire in Eastern Europe and the collapse and dismemberment of the Soviet Union.⁷

This juxtaposition of the Petrine origins of the navy and its nadir in 1996 raises a host of issues relating to Russia's efforts in the course of its history to transform itself from a continental to a maritime power. Between the Petrine origins and Soviet decline stands the intriguing problem of the relationship between Russian modernization and revolutionary upheaval. The recent attention shown to Peter's *botik* calls to mind one approach to maritime transformation—one linked to external threats, autocratic power, and charismatic leadership. But there is another model of maritime transformation that also has relevance for Russian history. It is an interesting coincidence that Peter's sailboat was on display at the Central Naval Museum, which had served down to the Bolshevik Revolution as the St. Petersburg Stock Exchange (*Birzha/Bourse*), which operated from 1865 to 1917 as part of the transformation of the Russian economy following the Crimean War. For a brief period in the late nineteenth century, as Russia struggled with the implications of its defeat in that war and the pressing need to modernize to face the growing military and industrial strength of the great European powers, a new, quasi-liberal model of societal renovation emerged. This would provide the context for a second maritime transformation for Russia, and one that has perhaps greater relevance for the situation of that country today.

The Petrine model had at its base a Russia that would mobilize its human and natural resources on the model of a well-ordered police state under the absolute power of the tsar. That model accepted the concept of universal service for the nobility through the Table of Ranks for military, civil, and court service, and for the "tax-paying" strata of the nation as obligated labor in the form of state peasants or the nobility's serfs. For the Petrine elite this model demanded an education to prepare them for such service. The model proved sufficient to guarantee Russia the status of great power in the post-Westphalian order in Europe. It allowed Russia to operate on a plane with the other great powers. Neither Peter nor his successors, however, created a functioning bureaucratic order to run a police state (*Polizeistadt*) on the German model, and the nobility escaped the demand of universal service in the middle of the eighteenth century. But Peter's system with modifications remained the model. Autocratic Russia suffered from underadministration and faced increasing backwardness as the West carried forward its own social transformation, even as her autocrats claimed a monopoly on power within the state and over society. By the middle of the nineteenth century, circumstances made it evident that Peter's solutions would no longer meet the challenge of dynamic economic change and technological innovation in the West.

The Imperial Russian Navy was born in 1696. That was the beginning of the first great transformation of Russia from a regional land power into a great power with a regular army and a standing navy. In that year, Peter the Great responded to defeat in the first Azov campaign of 1695 by initiating development of a squadron of galleys to support the investment and siege of the Ottoman fortress at Azov.[8] Success in this campaign ensured that an instrumental interest in naval forces would become a general strategic requirement in Peter's subsequent wars and would foster the growth of urban complexes to support the navy's yards and works. Even before embarking on his contest with Sweden, Peter demonstrated an appreciation for the technological transformation that had shifted the balance of naval power from Mediterranean powers to those of Northern Europe, especially England and Holland. During Peter's grand embassy to Western Europe in 1697, this giant of a man traveled incognito, worked as a humble shipwright in Holland, and observed English shipwrights at Deptford, seeking to master the art of building larger ships. The Great Northern War against Charles XII's Sweden (1700–21) witnessed the appearance of the Russian Navy in the Baltic, first in battles for control of the Gulf of Finland and later for command of the Baltic. Russia built a fleet composed of ships-of-the-line and galleys to contest Swedish naval power and established the yards and works to support their building and maintenance. Peter established the Imperial Navy. One need look no further than the spire of St. Petersburg's Admiralty and remember that the first yard founded there in 1704 and the fortress complex and yards at Kronshtadt became the foundations of a permanent Russian naval power in the Gulf of Finland. The symbol of the town/fortress at Kronshtadt makes this point evident with representation of a lighthouse and fortress wall. With the conquest of the Baltic provinces, Revel became the maneuver base for the fleet's operations in the Baltic. Without this infrastructure there could be no navy. Vasilii Tatishchev, statesman, historian, and ideologue of the Petrine autocracy, presented Peter's naval transformation as nothing less than creating Russian naval power on four seas (the White, Baltic, Black, and Caspian seas), which would bring victory in war and commercial success.[9] The costs of this infrastructure include the untold numbers who perished in the building of the tsar's "Window on the West," St. Petersburg. Peter built his navy rapidly to meet the immediate challenge of the war with Sweden. By 1725 Russia was the dominant littoral power in the Baltic, with twenty-seven thousand men, thirty-four ships-of-the line, nine frigates, thirty-four smaller sailing ships, and several hundred galleys supported by an annual expenditure of 1.5 million rubles. The ships and galleys, built of green timber, had a short service life—Russia built more than one thousand short-lived vessels of all classes during the Great Northern War—but the infrastructure—the Admiralty College, the Naval Academy, Peter's Naval Regulations, and the yards, works, and supporting fortress complexes—remained.

During his long struggle with Sweden for access to the Baltic during this period, Peter formulated a military strategy that used naval forces—sailing and galley fleets as well as Gen.-Adm. Count F. M. Aprakhsin's marines or "landing corps" (*desantnyi korpus*)—to support the advance of the Russian Army. Peter took a leading role in the navy's operations, including its first major victory at Gangut (Hankö). The raids that Russian naval and military forces launched against the Swedish coasts in 1719, 1720, and 1721 brought the war home to the government in Stockholm. Peter's *Naval Regulations* (*Kniga morskogo ustava*) defined this strategy: "A sovereign who has an army has only one arm, but a sovereign who has an army and navy has two." The prince brings his arms to bear in the service of specific strategic objectives.[10] As the prominent historian Evgenii Tarle has pointed out, the navy had a major role in Petrine foreign policy, especially in forging and sustaining the alliances that supported Russian influence in the Baltic, finally secured by the Treaty of Nystad in 1721.[11] However, such was not the case with the naval infrastructure in the south. After the end of the Northern War, Peter I moved to counter the advance of the Ottomans in the Caucasus and Caspian region, where a number of Persian provinces had risen in rebellion against their Shah. Peter I's intervention here in 1722 brought a significant expansion of Russian naval presence on the Caspian and enjoyed initial success until the Ottoman Empire intervened. The war with the Turks, for which

Russia was not prepared, began and ended with a military disaster on the river Pruth and a negotiated peace in 1724. Following Peter's death in 1725, the naval infrastructure in the south languished until the reign of Catherine the Great, who incorporated the Crimea into the empire and established the Black Sea Fleet with its main base at Sevastopol and its shipbuilding yards at Nikolaev on the Dnieper.

In contravention of Mahan's concept of sea power evolving out of a nation's civilian maritime calling, Russian naval power had to be planted and nurtured by an absolutist state directing a continental power, where naval power was the supporting instrument of national power. Peter's personal signet gave artistic manifestation to this transformation by showing Peter as an imperial Pygmalion whose passion animates the statue of his beloved Russia, complete with the symbols for the army, navy, and the all-seeing eye of reason in the background.[12]

Peter, the artisan tsar with a passion for sailing and a talent for joint campaigning, thus inaugurated Russian naval power, but the foundations of that power remained weak. Naval power had to compete for influence and resources before successive national leaders who saw Russia as a continental power primarily, and naval power as an auxiliary instrument. The three centuries of Russian naval history are marked by the waxing and waning of naval power in accordance with particular crises, geostrategic reorientations, and technological changes. Military historians of early modern Europe have spoken of a military "revolution" which would contribute centrally to the global hegemony eventually achieved by Europeans.[13] Peter's transformation is the first evidence of a sustained response to this military challenge of the West. Peter's embracing of Western forms is combined with distinct domestic socioeconomic structures to challenge the West's hegemony. Absolutism and enlightenment—an educated and westernized service elite ruling over an enserfed peasantry—became the hallmarks of the new order. This model evolved over the next century and a half but remained the foundation of Russian military power and state organization. It was sufficient to ensure Russia's place in the European balance of power down to and through the wars of the French Revolution and Napoleon.

Successive Russian rulers might appreciate or ignore naval power depending upon their personal orientation and strategic circumstances. Naval declines were followed by periods of recovery. Each period of recovery began with a necessary reappraisal of the role that naval power should play in Russia's national strategy. Geography was not kind to Russian naval strategists. Continental land theaters of great extent and threats of foreign invasion by land armies gave the Russian Army the dominant role in national defense. Naval theaters dominated by choke points and separated by great distance from one another made for a history of individual fleets rather than a unitary navy. Geostrategic priorities in these divergent theaters put a premium on developing infrastructure to support each fleet at different times and according to very different requirements. The fate of the Russian Navy would wax and wane over the next century and a half until the Crimean War—when new circumstances brought about another naval transformation, with profound consequences for the navy as well as the Russian state and society.

For Nicholas I, the Baltic and the Black Sea fleets were instruments for intervention in regional conflicts. Nicholas pursued naval forces in each theater that would be superior to the navies of the other littoral powers (i.e., Sweden in the Baltic and the Ottoman Empire in the Black Sea). Russia's overall naval strength would ensure it third place among the European naval powers behind England and France. In this fashion naval power was supposed to be an instrument in support of Russian diplomacy by making Russia more appealing as a potential alliance partner in case of a general European conflict involving the great maritime powers.[14] Under favorable circumstances, as developed for example during the Greek revolt against the Ottoman Empire, Russia's fleet could join the European maritime powers England and France in common action, as it did at the Battle of Navarino in 1827.[15] Following Navarino, the Baltic Fleet declined into a kind of naval parade force in the absence of an immediate maritime threat. Its best sailors took part in long-range cruises around the world, but the bulk of the fleet was a hollow force. Prince Alexander Menshikov, the confidant of Nicholas I and the de facto naval minister from 1833 until he assumed command of ground forces in the Crimea in 1854, emphasized external appearances and not combat capabilities. Mindful of the empire's chronic fiscal crises, he did not press for new technologies, including screw-propelled warships. The Black Sea Fleet fought its own war with Turkey in support of the advance of Russian forces through the Balkans in 1828–29.[16] At the same time, the professionalization of the Black Sea Fleet developed apace as a result of superior leadership (notably that of Adm. M. P. Lazarev) and continuous operations in support of Russia's protracted war with Caucasian mountaineers. As a young officer, Admiral Lazarev served for five years with the Royal Navy in the Atlantic and Indian oceans. He retained a deep respect for the Royal Navy and its traditions, celebrating the anniversary of Trafalgar with his junior officers.[17] On occasion, the Black Sea Fleet would conduct landing operations and provide fire support to infantry ashore. For more than two decades small craft were involved in blockading arms shipments to the mountaineers and supporting the coastal garrisons along the Caucasian coast. Lazarev considered the cruiser squadrons operating there an important training group for officers and men. Vice Adm. P. S. Nakhimov's overwhelming victory against a Turkish squadron at Sinope in late 1853, which brought Anglo-French intervention in the Crimean War, was, in fact, a continuation of the Black Sea Fleet's mission to isolate the Caucasian theater of operations from maritime resupply.[18]

Changing international conditions, rapid technological innovations with which Russia did not keep pace, and a combination of imperial miscalculation and aggressive policies toward the "Sick Man of Europe" combined to bring about a war that Russia was poorly positioned to win.[19] The victory of Nakhimov's squadron over the Ottomans at Sinope, the swan song of the sailing navy, provided the justification for Anglo-French intervention against Russia in the Black Sea. The immediate objective of the war for the allies was the destruction of Russian naval power in the Black Sea. But the war took on a global character, with naval operations in the Baltic and Barents seas and the Pacific Ocean as well. In the Arctic, British ships raided Russian ports and shipyards but failed in their attempt to take Arkhangelsk. In the Pacific, Russian naval and ground forces successfully defended Petropavlovsk from assault by a superior Anglo-French squadron in 1854, and when allied forces returned to Petropavlovsk in 1855, they found that Russian forces had withdrawn. As Andrew Lambert has suggested, British grand strategy also included the destruction of Russian naval power in the Baltic, an objective not achieved by the time the war ended in 1856.[20]

On paper, Russia began the Crimean War with the third largest navy in the war, but the Russian fleet was facing block obsolescence. The Baltic Fleet boasted twenty-six sailing ships-of-the-line in service and seven in reserve; the Black Sea Fleet had fourteen ships-of-the-line in service and two in reserve. Only one screw-propelled ship-of-the-line and two frigates were under construction in the Baltic and Barents seas, and their engines were on order from England. Russian steam warships were predominantly side-wheel frigates carrying few cannon: the Baltic Fleet had nine such frigates carrying 103 guns; the Black Sea Fleet had seven such frigates with 49 cannon.[21]

The liberal transformation of the Russian Navy began during the Crimean War. In the Black Sea, the initial victory of the Russian fleet had made the navy popular with Russian society. The scuttling of the same sailing fleet left Russian naval operations in the Black Sea to a few paddle-wheel steamers supporting the defense of Sevastopol. The overwhelming numerical and technological superiority of Anglo-French naval forces, based upon screw-propelled ships-of-the-line and frigates, dictated the decision of Adm. V. A. Kornilov to scuttle the fleet. He wrote in his order: "You have observed the enemy steamers and have seen that his ships do not rely upon sails. He has achieved a two-to-one advantage over us in just such ships and can attack us from the sea. We must give up any idea of engaging the enemy in the water. Furthermore, we are needed for the defense of the city, our homes, and families."[22]

Naval personnel marched into the entrenchments at Sevastopol and became the immortal defenders of the fortress-city. Vice Admiral Kornilov was in a unique position to appreciate the advantages of steam propulsion in naval tactics. On 5 November 1853 (OS) Kornilov was aboard the Russian eleven-gun, paddle-wheel frigate *Vladimir* when that ship met and engaged the Turkish ten-gun, paddle-wheel frigate *Pervaz Bakhri* in a three-hour battle. Captain-Lieutenant Butakov, commander of the *Vladimir*, outmaneuvered the Turkish frigate and directed precise fire of solid shot and exploding shells to seriously damage the enemy vessel, which surrendered.[23] Thus the Crimean War, which began with victory for the Russians in the first naval battle between steam warships, also exposed the backwardness of Russian naval power.

The maritime situation in the Baltic was no better than in the Black Sea. The Baltic Fleet began the Crimean War with sailing ships-of-line and frigates and nine paddle-wheel frigates. Russia's Naval Ministry had undertaken the construction of one screw-propelled warship, the frigate *Archimedes*, which was launched in 1848 and lost in a storm off Bornholm in 1850. Admiral Kornilov and others had proposed a shipbuilding program to meet the naval revolution involved in the acquisition of screw-propelled ships-of-the-line and frigates in England and France. But the plans had not borne fruit when war began.[24] One of the reasons for Russia's lack of progress in this area was the absence of plants and works to produce steam engines and boilers of sufficient size and quality for large warships.

To direct naval administration, Nicholas I had turned to one of his most trusted officers, Prince A. S. Menshikov, who had served as general-adjutant and army officer during the 1812 campaign against Napoleon, and appointed him chief of the Naval Staff in 1827. From 1836 to 1855 Menshikov led both the Main Naval Staff and the Naval Ministry and oversaw further rationalization of the naval administration, which strengthened the tendency toward bureaucratic centralization and control. Reform-minded officers characterized the era as one in which the navy existed for the ministry, and not the ministry to support the fleet.[25] Even Nicholas I was aware that Menshikov emphasized appearance, which he associated with the Baltic Fleet, over combat effectiveness, which he had come to expect from the Black Sea Fleet.[26] One searches in vain through Menshikov's very brief report on the development of the navy during the first twenty-five years of Nicholas I's reign (1825–50) for any evidence of the need for naval modernization or technological innovation.[27]

Two years later, in 1852, a fresh wind blew into the Naval Ministry in the form of the Grand Duke Konstantin Nikolaevich, who was named Menshikov's deputy and who became de facto naval minister after 1853. Menshikov thereafter had little time to oversee the Naval Ministry. Nicholas I dispatched him as special envoy to the Porte on the eve of the Crimean War and then appointed him commander in chief of Russian Army and Naval Forces in the Crimean War (1853–56). Nicholas I had dedicated the life of his second son, the Grand Duke, to the navy, entrusting his education to a leading naval officer, making sure that he took part in various naval events and cruises, and granting him the rank of general admiral of the Russian Navy, thus emphasizing the tie between the dynasty and the navy. Admiral Lazarev and his subordinates sought during the young grand duke's summer cruise in 1844 aboard the frigate *Flora* to recruit him as a supporter of naval professionalism as it had developed in the Black Sea Fleet.[28] Konstantin Nikolaevich proved to be a good pupil and an ardent champion of naval reform, using the Black Sea Fleet's experience as a model. One of the first official acts of Gen. Adm. Konstantin Nikolaevich was to organize a major project for the reform of naval regulations. In the years 1850–53 he oversaw a systematic study of foreign naval regulations and a review of existing Russian naval regulations. A committee met more than fifty times to examine 2,400 articles from naval regulations in English, French, Dutch, Danish, and Italian as well as Russian.[29] A. V. Golovnin, the son of a famous admiral, served as secretary for the project and described the process of publicizing the reform and inviting comments from professional officers as artificial publicity (*iskusstvennaya glasnost*), by which he meant the use of the Naval Ministry's recently established professional journal, *Morskoi sbornik* (Naval Review), to conduct a discussion among the "public" (i.e., professional naval officers) about an issue in which they had a vested interest.[30]

One feature of this review was the development of a team of young, experienced naval officers and civil servants to undertake the reform of naval regulations.[31] These junior officials brought an investigative bent to their task and applied statistical tools to assess the situation with the navy. One such investigation addressed the rate of illness and death within the Baltic and Black Sea fleets during the decade, 1842–51. On the basis of information provided by the staff-doctor of the Naval Ministry, the report listed 23,547 deaths in the Baltic Fleet and 11,529 for the Black Sea Fleet for the decade, or more than 3,400 deaths per year in what were years of largely peacetime service.[32] The statistics underscored how cheap a sailor's life was in the Russian Navy. Commentary on these depressing statistics emphasized the demand placed upon commanders and senior officers to ensure the health of naval personnel in earlier Russian naval regulations and in foreign regulations. The difference in this project was the willingness to address the causes of such losses and to propose remedies that would place the responsibility for reducing such deaths on senior naval commanders.[33] In Russian military service, in which enlisted personnel were treated as uniformed serfs and uncompensated labor, such concepts meant a fundamentally different way of regarding servicemen. Such efforts would be the hallmark of naval reform over the next three decades. The new naval regulations were accepted and published in 1853.

After the war began and a maritime threat in the Baltic appeared, Nicholas I learned how ineffective his fleet would be in open battle with the Anglo-French squadron that appeared in 1854. In a war council with his senior naval commanders aboard the ship-of-the-line *Peter I*, Nicholas I had to listen to his admirals advise against going to sea to meet the Anglo-French fleet in the Gulf of Finland. The tsar expressed his frustration: "Was the Navy created and maintained so that at this very minute when it is most needed, they would say to me that the Navy is not ready for action?"[34]

The Naval Ministry under the reformist leadership of Gen.-Adm. Konstantin Nikolaevich found itself facing the same problem of technological backwardness that had led to the scuttling of the Black Sea Fleet. A modest construction program for screw-propelled capital ships, which had begun in 1852, was now suspended because plans for their completion had depended upon the delivery of advanced steam engines from England. These circumstances demanded an asymmetric response that would leverage new technologies to overcome the enemy's overwhelming naval superiority. In the Baltic, Russia did have a network of state shipyards and private yards and engine works that could be mobilized to meet the threat. One of Konstantin Nikolaevich's technical experts published in *Morskoi Sbornik* an analysis of the Anglo-French naval race to build screw-propelled capital ships and concluded that Britain had the advantage because of its ability to mobilize such private yards and works to build advanced warships. In a state where public finances were unknown, Reutern used the British and French naval budgets to analyze the British advantages derived from enlisting private shipyards and works in its race with the state-dominated shipbuilding industry in France.[35] What worked for Britain could be used by a Russia under immediate threat of attack. The general admiral accordingly arranged to organize St. Petersburg's and other Baltic ports' shipyards and engine and boiler works to produce screw-propelled gunboats for the immediate defense of St. Petersburg, Kronshtadt, and the Gulf of Finland. The engine works could produce smaller reliable engines for Russia's gunboats. In the course of two years, this project produced thirty-eight such 170-ton gunboats.[36] Success of the gunboat program led to the building of six screw-propelled "clippers" (1,500 tons, 24-gun) at Archangel equipped with Russian engines and fourteen corvettes (2,500 tons, 32-gun) during the same period.[37]

Too small an addition to Russian naval power to allow the Baltic Fleet to meet the Anglo-French squadron (which deployed there again in 1855) on anything approaching equal terms, the gunboats became part of an evolving system of maritime defense, the "mine-artillery position," which sought to deny the opposing fleet the opportunity to engage Russian naval forces and shore positions with impunity. The naval mines were placed to restrict the maneuvers of British and French ships and force them into designated fields of fire for Russian shore batteries, fortress guns, and ships. The gunboats were used to cover the minefields and inhibit the Allies' primitive efforts to sweep the fields. Naval minefields were laid at Kronshtadt in 1854 and at Sveaborg, Vyborg, and Tolbukhin Lighthouse in 1855.[38] In the summer of 1855, six gunboats under the command of Rear Adm. S. I. Mofet fought a two-hour battle with a screw-propelled frigate and two other steamers at Tolbukhin Lighthouse. Mines played a prominent role in the Russian defense of the Sveaborg Fortress and Helsinki in August 1855 during an Anglo-French bombardment. As Lambert has suggested, the failures of the Anglo-French naval expeditions in 1854 under Vice Adm. Charles Napier and in 1855 under Vice Adm. James Dundas led Her Majesty's government to plan an even larger and better-equipped naval expedition for 1856, which was not mounted because of the end of hostilities.[39]

In early 1855, Nicholas I died a broken man. The gendarme of Europe had seen his imperial ambitions smashed by the Allied coalition. It fell to his successor, Alexander II, to assess Russia's weak diplomatic position, empty treasury, and ill-equipped military and seek peace on the best terms available.[40] Alexander II began his reign with a weak hand and played it somewhat successfully through the spring, summer, and fall of 1855. Kars fell to Russian arms in the Caucasus; the Anglo-French Fleet withdrew from the Baltic with the approach of winter and the sea ice; and on the Crimean front there was little more than minor exchanges of shots. Strains among the Allies and the deteriorating state of Russian finances brought the powers to Paris, where the treaty ending the war was signed in March 1856.

What followed the Crimean War was an unstable international system in which Russia would seek peace to carry out pressing domestic reforms. Meanwhile, Alexander II and his foreign minister, Alexander Mikhailovich Gorchakov, sought to ensure Russia's gradual reintegration into the European balance of power and create the conditions for the undoing of the most onerous provisions of the Treaty of Paris.[41]

For the navy, the costs of the war were particularly high. The loss of the Black Sea Fleet, the destruction of Sevastopol, and the forced demilitarization of the Black Sea and the Aland Islands in the Baltic under the Treaty of Paris forced the Russian Naval Ministry to concentrate its efforts in the Baltic. There Konstantin Nikolaevich continued a capital ship program begun prior to the war to arm the Baltic Fleet with screw-propelled ships-of-the-line.[42] At the same time, he embarked upon a program of naval modernization, internal reforms, and strategic transformation. In 1857 Konstantin Nikolaevich's response to a question posed by Vice Admiral Napier, the commander of the Anglo-French Baltic expedition of 1854, as to why the Russian Baltic Fleet had not met the Anglo-French Fleet at sea suggested the direction of this transformation: "If I had had screw frigates I would have countered you."[43] As any naval historian knows, frigates, carrying 44–60 cannon in two decks, do not engage ships-of-the-line, carrying 72–120 cannon on three decks. The verb "counter" here reflects the key strategic shift. Following the Crimean War the Naval Ministry embarked upon a shipbuilding program to transform the Baltic Fleet and make it an effective instrument of policy and a means of deterring maritime intervention against Russia. In 1855 the general-admiral informed the State Council that the Naval Ministry would require funding for a modern steam navy: "Owing to the transformation taking place in the fleets of all nations with the introduction of the screw mechanism all our old sailing ships must be replaced by steamships and the naval administration already faces [the task] not of supporting and completing the existing fleet with new vessels but to create a new screw fleet and to train qualified officers and mates for it."[44]

Russia did complete nine screw ships-of-the-line, but these numbers did not restore Russia to the position of third naval power of Europe. Plans were drawn up to add additional modern ships-of-the-line under a twenty-year program, but budgetary constraints slowed the process and technological innovations forced a radical reconsideration of priorities. As table 1 indicates (below), by 1860, as Konstantin Nikolaevich reported to the State Council, England and France had, respectively, seventy-three nonscrew and thirty-seven screw ships-of-the-line—built, in reserve, or under construction.[45] Instead of emulating them, the Naval Ministry shifted its construction program to powerful frigates, other smaller screw-propelled combatants, and the acquisition of ironclads, which Konstantin Nikolaevich had proposed to the State Council in the same year that the *General-Admiral*, one of the first "overdressed" frigates—like U.S. Navy frigates, which carried many more cannon than their 44-gun rating implied—was launched in New York. The first such craft, a converted gunboat, the *Opyt* (Experiment), carrying a single large cannon, entered service in 1861.[46]

Table 1: Development of Russia's Steam-Screw Navy

Type	1856	1860
Ships-of-the-line	1	9
Frigates	1	7
Corvettes	—	19
Clippers	—	7
Schooners	1	24
Gunboats	40	75
Transports	—	8
Barks	—	2
Side-wheel Frigates	10	10
Side-wheelers	43	47
Yachts	—	2
Total	96	210

The new building program and naval strategy represented a profound change in Russian naval culture. The model was not the Petrine navy, designed to support the army in offensive operations in littoral seas, but rather a more modest force to balance the naval forces of the Baltic states and provide for coastal defense in case of intervention by the maritime powers. Internal development of railroads to unite the coastal regions with the heartland of the empire would make it possible to counter relatively quickly any amphibious landing with overwhelming ground forces. To preclude such intervention, the Russian Navy would be postured so it could engage in *guerre de course*—commerce raiding by smaller, fast, well-armed combatants deployed around the world in peacetime so that they might act as a deterrent should the maritime powers consider war with Russia. As Konstantin Nikolaevich wrote, Russia needed naval forces that "can inspire in the great powers such respect that will force them to seek either an alliance with Russia or her neutrality in their wars among themselves, and which will force [them] to undertake greater preparations and undergo greater costs in a struggle with Russia."[47] The symbol of this new strategy and posture was the frigate *General-Admiral*, built by Webb & Company in New York and launched in 1858. At 5,600 tons and 800 horsepower, the *General-Admiral* was as large as a ship-of-the-line and carried a very heavy armament of seventy large-caliber cannon. She was thus "overdressed" in terms of engines and armaments and designed to outrun any ship-of-the-line and to defeat any other frigate. The *General-Admiral* and the *Svetlana*, another large frigate built in France, became the models of a new class of Russian super frigates designed for commerce raiding.[48] Foreign purchases in these cases served to acquire a technological base, which Russian yards and works could then master and provide domestic production capability.

The new frigates, corvettes, and clippers were to be the instruments of a new naval strategy based upon long-range cruises to train the crews and to provide Russia with the naval means on distant stations in the Mediterranean, Atlantic, and Pacific to influence the balance of power.[49] Konstantin Nikolaevich had given up the ideas of a huge navy and decisive naval victories for a strategy of deterrence. As Captain Likhachev observed, getting to sea before a declaration of war was the only alternative to being trapped "like fish in a barrel" by the maritime powers.[50] The new ships would serve as commerce raiders that could operate alone or as squadrons to threaten the interests of the maritime powers, especially England, and thereby deter their intervention. Capt. A. A. Popov made this point in a memorandum to

Konstantin when he deployed as commander of Russia's Pacific Squadron. A threat to British commerce had to be taken seriously in London.[51]

With the pace of technological modernization accelerating following the introduction of ironclads, the Naval Ministry faced a serious dilemma. Russia did not have the capacity at home to build ships such as Britain's HMS *Warrior*, with its iron hull and cast-iron, 4.5-inch plates. The Naval Ministry adapted the model used with the *General-Admiral* and ordered one such battery ironclad, the *Pervevenets*, in England in 1862, negotiated for a British firm to build a second at St. Petersburg, and sought to have a third built at a Russian yard. However, the appearance of a new class of ironclads during the American Civil War led the Naval Ministry to shift its priority to the construction of monitors, which were quick to build, cheap in comparison with ironclad batteries, based on readily available iron-casting technology, and of superior fighting characteristics for coastal defense.[52] Ten monitors were ordered, eight from Russian yards and two from Belgium. The shift to the monitor class of ironclad further reinforced the strategic direction of seeking to develop a national technological and industrial infrastructure to execute naval modernization as demanded.[53]

The Russian Navy would continue to look for new ship designs in the West and adapt them to Russia's maritime defense requirements. Admiral Popov, chair of the shipbuilding section of the Naval Ministry's Technical Committee from 1870 to 1880, designed Russia's first modern battleship, the *Petr Velikii*, and a series of armored cruisers for long-range operations.[54]

Of the most exotic design were the infamous "circular ironclads" built by Popov for the Black Sea Fleet in the 1870s, after Russia regained the right to maintain a fleet there but lacked the yards, metalworks, and engine factories to build warships in theater. The "popovkas" were floating batteries designed to provide artillery support in shallow coastal waters. Each carried two heavy guns in a barbette. The *Novgorod*, the first ship of the class, was built in parts in St. Petersburg and transported by rail to the Black Sea for assembling at Nikolaev. The second, *Vitse-Admiral Popov*, was built at Nikolaev. They never proved as effective, unfortunately, as their designer had forecasted.[55] The navy also continued to pursue the development of mine/torpedo weapons and developed the mine-cruiser as a specific type of warship, leading to the development of the torpedo boat and the *minonosets*/destroyer.[56]

A key ingredient in this shipbuilding policy was the active promotion of a partnership between the state and the private yards, with the government fostering development in capital-intensive industries such as shipbuilding, engine works, and ordnance manufacture. Where Nicholas I's

Russia had been hostile to private enterprise, open finances, and commercial banking, the reformers around Konstantin Nikolaevich embraced the liberation of capital to speed Russia's economic development. Their model was the laissez faire capitalism of the United States with its boom and bust cycles. M. Kh. Reutern, who was one of Konstantin Nikolaevich's key reformers and, as Minister of Finance, the champion of private railroad development in Russia, spoke of the end of the police state and the liberation of capital to unleash the power of science and technology in Russia.[57] The great industrial enterprises that would dominate St. Petersburg's economy into the twentieth century—the Baltic Yards of Carr & McPherson, the Putilov Metal Works, and the Obukhov Steel Mill and Ordnance Works—were the product of naval reform and modernization. While the private–state partnership underwent periodic crises because of the business cycle and tight state budgets that battered the Russian economy over the next decades, the idea of national economic growth on the basis of market relations survived.[58] Naval forces could not be created overnight in case of the threat of war but required the maintenance of an advanced national infrastructure capable of creating warships that employed the latest scientific and technological innovations.

Naval development involved more than technological change and a partnership with private enterprise. Naval reformers sought to create a smaller and more professional naval service. The circle of reform-minded officials and officers around the Grand Duke Konstantin Nikolaevich combined bureaucratic skills, naval professionalism, and a keen sense of court politics in Alexander II's St. Petersburg. The purge of old school bureaucrats in the Naval Ministry began during the war. The emphasis was on youth and talent.[59] Every effort was made to streamline paperwork and simplify administrative procedures. In 1860 the ministry was reformed to permit greater decentralization of authority and more direct support to naval operations.[60]

One problem that troubled the reformers was the low morale among naval personnel. Cases of desertion, petty crimes, drunkenness, and disorderly conduct were particularly high among shore personnel.[61] Konstantin Nikolaevich responded to this problem by proposing to rid the navy of such obligated labor and replace it with salaried employees. Naval service would be for those who served at sea on warships.[62] The Naval Ministry abolished the obligatory service of the so-called "admiralty serfs" at Okhta Yards and replaced them with wage labor.[63] Konstantin Nikolaevich stressed the need to treat the navy as an elite force. The common seamen were, in fact, "universal soldiers" combining the skills of the seaman, technician, artillerist, and infantry man.[64] The navy needed literate sailors; a program of "Sunday schools" led by junior officers sought to teach the men reading and writing. V. I. Dal,' the famous lexicographer and official in the Naval Ministry, composed a small book of readings for the ratings titled *A Seaman's Leisure Time*.[65]

With the fate of Russia and the navy hanging in the balance, *Morskoi Sbornik* became a forum for patriotic mobilization and support for the navy. An editor of this journal observed in 1853: "The belief in the benefit of a navy has never appeared in the nation and because of this the development of the navy, deprived of the support of public opinion, has always been a difficult and unsound task." To stimulate interest in the navy, the war, and reform, Konstantin Nikolaevich transformed the publication into a mass-circulation periodical that was read widely beyond the Naval Ministry. Between 1848, the year of its founding, and 1853, when Konstantin Nikolaevich took over the Naval Ministry, subscriptions had climbed gradually from 500 to 800. In 1854 Konstantin Nikolaevich decreed that all naval officers would subscribe, and the circulation climbed to 3,100 for officers and 500 for voluntary subscribers. By 1857 there were 3,500 officer-subscribers and 1,677 civilian subscribers. Officers were drawn to the official section of the journal, which provided information on the Naval Ministry and the fleet. Officers and civilians followed the public issues addressed in the unofficial section.[66] Those pages carried critical articles on all aspects of imperial administration, educational reform, reform of the university system, censorship reform, court reform, and the abolition of corporal punishment.[67] The worldview of the reformers was summed up by the surgeon N. I. Pirogov, a member of the Russian Academy of Sciences, a medical innovator, and hospital director in Crimea during the war. Pirogov referred to education as "questions of life" and promoted public education for all and a broad liberal education for Russia's elite, rejecting the idea of specialized military schools for the very young. The function of education was not to create mindless cogs for the state's bureaucratic machine but to allow for the individual's development and integration into society.[68] Ultimately the civilians associated with naval reform were drawn into the great issue of the age—the emancipation of the serfs—and became active proponents of the abolition of serfdom.[69] The naval reforms became the basis of much more systemic reforms reshaping Russian society and institutions over the next three decades.

The test of the reformers' naval strategy came twice. In 1863, when war with England threatened over the January Insurrection in Poland, the Naval Ministry deployed Vice Adm. S. S. Lesovsky's Atlantic Squadron to the East Coast of the United States and Capt. A. A. Popov's Pacific Squadron to San Francisco. While it is difficult to assess the impact of these deployments on the actual course of the diplomacy surrounding the Polish Question, it is clear that the navy saw the outcome as confirmation of the strategy.[70] By deploying to American ports before the Polish crisis led to war, the navy's leadership saw the threat to British interests in case of a U.S.-Russian alliance to be a constraint upon Her Majesty's government. More recent Russian military theorists have assessed the deployments as a success. In a discussion of direct and indirect means for achieving strategic objectives, Gen. Makhmut Gareev, president of the Russian Academy of Military Sciences, noted the deployment of the squadrons as a success for an indirect strategy.[71] The more difficult test came in the 1870s after Russian diplomacy had won back the right to remilitarize the Black Sea, and when Russian foreign and military policy looked toward an aggressive strategy to resolve another Balkan crisis by decisive military action. The navy, lacking the yards and works in the south to build modern capital ships, found itself forced to make use of armed steamers, coastal defense craft, and mine cruisers. While the navy neutralized the Turkish naval advantage in the Black Sea by aggressive use of mine/torpedo warfare, it could not prevent the possible intervention of the Royal Navy to counter the Russian Army's advance to Straits.[72] In his assessment of the naval reforms, Shevyrev argues that the Naval Ministry failed to use the years between 1870 and 1877 to build a modern battlefleet in the Black Sea. He does note the reformers' claims that such a project would have taken years, would have depended upon the development of sufficient infrastructure, including railroads, to support such an endeavor, and would not have been realized by the time war broke out.[73] Moreover, such a "fleet in being" would not have speeded the Russian advance through the Balkan Mountains and would only have made British naval intervention to protect the Porte more likely in another crisis over the Eastern Question.

For Russia, as for other continental powers, naval power without sufficient infrastructure to support its creation, maintenance, and development in a particular theater is a dangerous luxury. The Russo-Japanese War of 1904–5 confirmed that lesson at the cost of much of the Russian Navy. Imperial Russia in the late nineteenth century embarked upon a naval expansion in the Far East in response to the growth of Japanese naval power in the aftermath of the Sino-Japanese War of 1894–95. While Russia was in the process of tying European Russia to its Far Eastern domains via the Trans-Siberian railroad, its statesmen rushed into the acquisition of naval stations in China and began a naval rivalry with Japan for which Russia was unprepared. Isolated, without maritime allies in the theater, Russia provoked a war for which neither its army nor its navy were prepared. Russia's main naval forces at Port

Arthur were damaged by surprise attack by Admiral Togo's fleet and then placed under blockade by Japanese naval and ground forces. Failing to break the combined land and sea blockade, that fleet was lost when Port Arthur fell in January 1905. The dispatch of the Russian Baltic Fleet, an act of patriotic enthusiasm and strategic miscalculation, came too late to affect the outcome at Port Arthur, and the Russian fleet of mixed warships and no combat experience sailed to its destruction in the Tsushima Straits at the hands of the Japanese Navy in May 1905. Although a spectacular naval defeat by all measures, it did not affect the outcome of the war. The tsarist government of Nicholas II, already facing a revolution at home, had no stomach for war, and Japan with naval hegemony could not annihilate Russian land forces in Manchuria. A precipitous rush to acquire naval power before the foundations have been laid ashore diplomatically and economically can only invite the dominant naval power in a region to practice the art of preemptive attack à la Nelson at Copenhagen.

For Russian statesmen and naval officers contemplating another naval transformation in the twenty-first century, there is much appeal in the Petrine model of autocratic reform and qualitative change leading to military victories. But the twenty-first century seems to be an age closer to that of the nineteenth century when the primary need is to find the social organization to master new technology, accelerate scientific innovation, and integrate the national economy into global markets and the information age. Chinese statesmen and naval officers would do well to grasp the key lessons of naval transformation from Russia's example.

Notes

This essay draws upon Jacob W. Kipp, "The Imperial Russian Navy," in Robin D. S. Higham and Frederick W. Kagan, eds., *The Military History of Tsarist Russia* (New York: St. Martin's Press, 2002), 151–82.

1. On Peter's own account of his early interest in sailing, see A. V. Obukhov and G. I. Demin, *Istoriya Rossiiskogo voenno-morskogo flota* (Moscow: Izdatel'stvo TsenrKom, 1996), 94–98.

2. F. M. Gromov, ed., *Tri veka Rossiiskogo flota* (St. Petersburg: LOGOS, 1996), I, p. 5.

3. S. G. Gorshkov, *The Sea Power of the State* (Annapolis, MD: Naval Institute Press, 1979), 154. See also Jacob W. Kipp, "Sergei Gorshkov and Naval Advocacy: The Tsarist Heritage," *Soviet Armed Forces Review Annual* (1979), III, 225–39. Russia and China share the common fate of being Eurasian powers with the challenges of controlling vast continental territories and seeing sea power as a secondary tool of statecraft, necessary for geopolitical influence but useful primarily to support land power.

4. Jacob W. Kipp, *Naval Art and the Prism of Contemporaneity: Soviet Naval Officers and the Falklands Conflict* (College Station, TX: Center for Strategic Technology Stratech Paper Series, 1984).

5. V. S. Pirumov and R. A. Chervinsky, *Radio-elektronika v voine na more* (Moscow: Voenizdat, 1987), 77. For a more complete treatment of Soviet naval transformation, see the chapter in this book by Milan Vego.

6. Nikolai Ogarkov, "The Defense of Socialism: The Experience of History and the Present Day," *Krasnaya zvezda*, 9 May 1984; and Jacob W. Kipp, "The Labor of Sisyphus: Forecasting the Revolution in Military Affairs during Russia's Time of Troubles," in Thierry Gongora and Harold von Riekhoff, eds., *Toward a Revolution in Military Affairs?* (Westport, CT: Greenwood Press, 2000), 87–104.

7. N. N. Moiseev, *Sotsializm i informatika* (Moscow: Izdatel'stvo politicheskoi literatury, 1988), 62ff; and Jacob W. Kipp, "The Soviet Military and the Future: Politico-Military Alternatives," in John Hemsley, ed., *The Lost Empire* (London: Brassey's/Pergamon, 1992), 67–90.

8. Jacob W. Kipp, "Peter the Great, Soldier-Statesman of the Age of Enlightenment: A Naval Perspective," in Abigail T. Siddall, ed., *Acta No. 7* (Washington, DC, 25–30 July 1982), International Commission for Military History (Manhattan, KS: Sunflower University Press, 1984), 113–39.

9. I. I. Firsov, *Petra tvoren'e* (Moscow: Molodaya Gvardiya, 1992), 3.

10. *Rossiya. Vtoroe otdelenie Sobstvennoi Ego Imperatorskago Velicheestva Kantselarii, Polnoe Sobranie Zakonov Rosssiiskoi Imperii*, Series I, Vol. VI, No. 3485, p. 3.

11. E. V. Tarle, "Russkii flot i vneshnyaya politika Petra I," in Evgenii Viktorovich Tarle, *Sochineniya* (Moscow: Izdatel'stvo Akademii Nauk SSR, 1962), XII, 115–201.

12. V. Iu. Matveev, "K istorii vozniknoveniya i razvitiya siuzheta 'Petr I, vysekaiushchii statyiu Rossii,'" in G. V. Villenbakhov et al., *Kul'tura i iskusstvo Rossii XVIII veka: Novye materialy i issledovaniya.* (Leningrad: Iskusstvo, 1981), 26–43.

13. Geoffrey Parker, *The Military Revolution and the Rise of the West, 1500-1800* (Cambridge, U.K.: Cambridge University Press, 1988). Peter, Russia, and its army and navy receive only passing reference in this work.

14. N. Korguev, *Russkii flot v tsarstvanie Imperatora Nikolaia I-go* (St. Petersburg, 1896), 86-87.

15. V. G. Oppokov, ed., *Morskie srazheniya russkogo flota: Vospominaniya* (Moscow: Voenizdat, 1994), 270-91.

16. V. A. Zolotarev and I. A. Kozlov, *Rossiiskii voennyi flot na Chernom more and Vostochnom Sredizemnomore* (Moscow: Nauka, 1988), 48-52.

17. V. D. Dotsenko, ed., *Admiraly Rossiiskogo flota: Rossiya podnmaet parusa* (St. Petersburg: Lenizdat, 1995), 378-79.

18. Ibid., 53-55.

19. John C. K. Daly, *Russian Seapower and "The Eastern Question"* (Annapolis, MD: Naval Institute Press, 1991); and Philip E. Mosley, "Englisch-russische Flotten Rivalitat," *Jahrbuecher fuer Geschichte Osteuropas* I (1936): 549-68.

20. On the global character of the Crimean War, see Andrew D. Lambert, *The Crimean War: British Grand Strategy against Russia, 1853-1856* (Manchester, U.K.: Manchester University Press, 1990).

21. K. A. Mann, ed., *Rossiya, Morskoe Ministerstvo, Obzor deiatel'nosti morskago upravleniya v pervoe dvadtsatipiatiletie tsarstvovaniya Gosudarya Imperatora Aleksandra Nikolaevicha* (St. Petersburg: Morskoe Ministerstvo, 1880), I, 396-99.

22. N. B. Novikov and P. G. Sofinov, eds., *Vitse-Admiral Kornilov* (Moscow: Voennoe Izdatel'stvo Ministerstva Vooruzhennykh Sil Soiuza SSR, 1947), 258.

23. Ibid., 206-13.

24. V. D. Dotsenko et al., *Istoriya otechestvennogo sudostroeniya* (St. Petersburg: "Sudostroenie," 1994), I, 398-99.

25. On the Menshikov era, see Jacob W. Kipp, "Imperial Russia: The Archaic Bureaucratic Framework, 1850-1863," in Ken J. Hagan, ed., *Naval Technology and Social Modernization in the Nineteenth Century* (Manhattan, KS: Military Affairs, 1976), 32-67.

26. A. Zaionchkovskii, "Poslednii smotr Imperatorom Nikolaem Pavlovichom Chernomorskago flota v 1852 godu," *Istrocheskii vestnik*, no. 3 (1900): 1054-59.

27. A. S. Menshikov, "Obzor minushago dvadtsipyatiletiya v otnoshenii k ustroistvu morskikh sil Rossiiskoi Imperii," *Sbornik imperatorskago Russkago istoricheskogo obshchestva* XCVIII (1896): 448-56.

28. Novikov and Sofinov, eds., *Vitse-Admiral Kornilov*, 80.

29. "Novyi morskoi ustav," *Morskoi sbornik* IX (May 1853): 406.

30. *Gosudarstvennaya Publicheskaya Biblioteka* (hereafter GPB), Otdel, Rookies, fond 208 (A. V. Golovnin), delo 2./149.

31. Jacob W. Kipp and Maia A. Kipp, "The Grand Duke Konstantin Nikolaevich: The Making of a Tsarist Reformer, 1827–1853," *Jahrbuecher fuer Geschichte Osteuropas* XXXIV (1986): 4–18.

32. Rossiya, Morskoe Ministerstvo, *Proekt morskago ustava* (St. Petersburg: Morskoe Ministerstvo, 1853), 28–29.

33. Ibid., 30.

34. Evgenii Viktorovich Tarle, "Krymskaya voina," in *Sochineniya* (Moscow: Izdatel'stvo Akademii Nauk SSR, 1959), IX, 418–19.

35. M. Kh. Reutern, "Opyt kratkago sravnitel'nago izsledovaniya norskikh budzhetov Angliiskago I Frantsuzskago," *Morskoi sbornik* XI (January 1854): Uchen-Lit., 1–36.

36. These gunboats carried three large cannon on their main decks with each gun having a large arc of fire. Dotsenko et al., *Istoriya otechestvennogo sudostroeniya*, II, 10–11. Putilov went on to become a major industrialist and the founder of the Putilov Works in St. Petersburg.

37. Rossiya, Morskoe Ministerstvo, *Obzor deiatel'nosti morskago upravleniya v pervoe dvadtsatipiatiletie tsarstvovaniya Gosudarya Imperatora Aleksandra Nikolaevicha*, I, 424–25.

38. Ibid., 10. On Russian naval mine development and employment see Tarle, "Krymskaya voina," in *Sochineniya*, IX, 420–28; and A. A. Razdolgin and Iu. A. Skorikov, *Kronshtadtskaya krepost'* (Leningrad: Stroizdat Leningradskoe Otdelenie, 1988), 173–219.

39. Lambert, *The Crimean War*, 309–27.

40. W. Bruce Lincoln, *Nicholas I: Emperor and Autocrat of All the Russias* (Bloomington: Indiana University Press, 1978), 347–50.

41. W. E. Mosse, *The Rise and Fall of the Crimean System, 1855–1871: The Story of a Peace Settlement* (New York: Macmillan, 1963).

42. For a complete discussion of this program, see Jacob W. Kipp, "Consequences of Defeat: Modernizing the Russian Navy, 1856–1963," *Jahrbuecher fuer Geschichte Osteuropas* XX (June 1972): 210–25.

43. Tarle, "Krymskaya voina," 49.

44. Rossiya, Morskoe Ministerstvo, *Obzor deiatel'nosti morskago*, I, 3.

45. GPB, fond 208, delo 23/5–6.

46. Dotsenko et al., *Istoriya otechestvennogo sudostroeniya*, II, 16, 25, 60.

47. GPB, fond 208, delo 10/259–260.

48. Rossiya, Morskoe Ministerstvo, *Obzor deiatel'nosti morskago*, I, 450–51; See also Dotsenko et al., *Istoriya otechestvennogo sudostroeniya*, II, 14–15.

49. GPB, fond 208, delo 10/259–63; and Rossiya, Morskoe Ministerstvo, *Obzor zagranichnykh plavanii sudov russkago flota s 1850 po 1868 god* (St. Petersburg: Morskoe Ministerstvo, 1870), II, 481–82.

50. K. G. Zhitkov, "Vitse Admiral Ivan Fedorovich Likhachev," *Morskoi sbornik*, no. 11 (1912): neof., 6.

51. M. M. Malkin, *Grazhdanskaya voina v SShA i tsarskaya Rossiya* (Moscow, 1939), 242.

52. Jacob W. Kipp, "The Russian Navy and the Problem of Technological Transfer: Technological Backwardness and Military-Industrial Development, 1853–1876," in John Bushnell, Benjamin Eklof, and Larisa Zakharova, eds., *Studies on the Great Reforms: A Colloquium of Soviet-American Historians* (Bloomington: Indiana University Press, 1994), 115–38.

53. Dotsenko et al., *Istoriya otechestvennogo sudostroeniya*, II, 25–29.

54. Ibid., II, 76–85, 94–109.

55. Ibid., II, 86–93; and Edward James Reed, *Letters from Russia* (London: Murray Company, 1875).

56. Ibid., II, 130–38. Russia remains a leader to this day in the development and manufacture of naval mines and other underwater weapons, a distinction clearly noted by Chinese analysts.

57. M. Kh. Reutern, "Vlianie ekonomicheskogo kharaktera naroda na obrazovanie kapitalov," *Morskoi sbornik* XLVI, no. 5 (April 1860): neof., 55–70. See also Jacob W. Kipp, "M. Kh. Reutern on the Russian State and Economy: A Liberal Bureaucrat during the Crimean Era," *Journal of Modern History* XLVII, no. 3 (September 1975): 437–59.

58. Jonathan A. Grant, *Big Business in Russia: The Putilov Company in Late Imperial Russia, 1868–1917* (Pittsburgh: University of Pittsburgh Press, 1999), 19ff.

59. GPB, fond 208, delo 2/124.

60. A. P. Shevyrev, *Russkii flot posle Krymskoi voiny: Liberalnaya biupokratiya i morskie reformy* (Moscow: Izdatel'stvo Moskovskogo universiteta, 1990), 49–86.

61. M. P. Golitsyn, "Izvelechenie iz otcheta ispravyaiushskago dolzhnosti flota General-Auditora sovetnika Kniazya Golitsyna za 1854 goda," *Morskoi sbornik* XIV, no. 2: (February 1855) of., 248–55.

62. GPB, fond 169, D. A. Miliutina, delo 42, papka 15/7–8, Letter to F. P. Wrangel, 23 July 1855.

63. B. Mansurov, *Okhtenskie admiralteiskiya seleniya: Proekt preobrazovaniya byta Okhtenskikh poselian,* (St. Petersburg: Morskoe Ministerstvo, 1856), 1–9.

64. GPB, fond 208, delo 2/119–20, 236–38.

65. Ibid., 104–5.

66. S. F. Ogorodnikov, "50-letie zhurnala *Morskoi sbornik* (1848–1898 gg.)" (St. Petersburg: Morskoe Ministerstvo, 1898), 18–28; E. D. Dneprov, "*Morskoi sbornik* v obshchestvennom dvizhenii perioda pervoi revoliutsionnoi situatsii v Rossii," in M. V. Nechkina, ed., *Revoliutsionnaya situatsiya v Rossii v 1859–1861 gg.* (Moscow: Nauka, 1965), 229–58; and E. D. Dneprov, "Proekt ustava morskogo suda i ego rol' v podgotovke sudebnoi reformy (Aprel' 1960 g.)," in M. V. Nechkina, ed., *Revoliutsionnaya situatsiya v Rossii v 1859–1861 gg.* (Moscow: Nauka, 1970), 57–70. Eduard Dmitrievich Dneprov, a retired naval officer, historian, and educator, served as Russian Minister of Education from 1990 to 1992. See "Leaders and Prominent Figures in Russian

Educational Reform, 1985–1995," http://faculty.washington.edu/stkerr/sovswww.
htm#dneprov, accessed 20 May 2007.

67. Shevyrev, *Russkii flot posle Krymskoi voiny*, 14–48. Shevyrev provides an in-depth
discussion of the major naval reforms and correctly characterizes them as liberal,
that is, oriented toward a market economy and an open society under a reformed
autocratic system.

68. N. I. Pirogov, "Voprosy zhizni," *Morskoi sbornik* XXIII, no. 9 (September 1856):
neof., 559–97.

69. G. Dzhanshiev, *Iz epokhi velikikh reform*, 5th ed. (Moscow: Tovarishchestvo
Tipografii A. I. Mamontova, 1894), 560–88.

70. Jacob W. Kipp, "Russian Naval Reformers and Imperial Expansion, 1856–1863,"
Soviet Armed Forces Review Annual I (1977): 118–39.

71. Makhmut Gareev, *Esli zavtra voina? (Chto izmenitsya v kharaktere vooruzhennoi
bor'by v blizhaishie 20–25 let)* (Moscow: VlaDar, 1995), 115–16.

72. Jacob W. Kipp, "Tsarist Politics and the Naval Ministry, 1876–1881: Balanced Fleet or
Cruiser Navy," *Canadian-American Slavic Studies* XVII, no. 2 (Summer 1983): 151–79.

73. Shevyrev, *Russkii flot posle Krymskoi voiny*, 163–64.

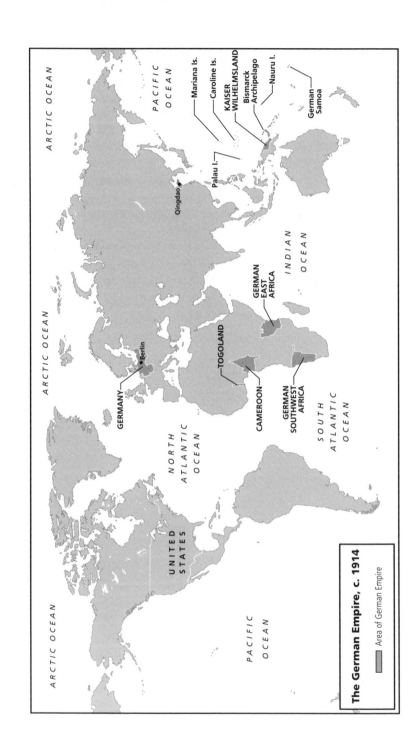

The German Empire, c. 1914

Area of German Empire

Holger H. Herwig

Imperial Germany: Continental Titan, Global Aspirant

We struggled unconsciously for world dominion before we had secured our continental position. This, of course, I can say only in the most intimate circles, but anyone who looks at the issue relatively clearly and historically cannot remain doubtful of it.

—Gen. Wilhelm Groener, 19–20 May 1919

WITH THESE WORDS GENERAL GROENER, who had succeeded Erich Ludendorff as first quartermaster-general of the German General Staff at the end of October 1918, attempted to draw the grand strategic "lessons" of World War I. In a confidential address to members of his staff at general headquarters in Kolberg six months after Germany's defeat, he concluded that the Reich had failed to prepare its "bid" for world power on the basis of a "long-term vision" and to conduct it with "ruthless consistency." Neither its domestic policy nor its foreign policy had remained "firm and unshakable." Both had vacillated between extremes. Thus without firm direction, the Reich had failed at "completely conducting power politics." Consequently, it had ceased to be a "European Great Power." Implicit in Groener's critique was an admonition that if and when a future generation undertook another bid for world power, it do so only after it had first established hegemony on the Continent.[1]

Groener's comments, of course, raise basic questions: What policies had Germany pursued? How had it tried to implement them? Had there been central strategic direction? Had the Reich's leadership understood the trade-offs between land and naval strength? Had the issue of cost effectiveness been thoroughly analyzed? Had military and diplomatic initiatives been coordinated? And had the political leadership secured a firm financial basis for the pursuit of its global maritime aspirations?

At heart, Groener's comments addressed historical parallels, some of which he raised in the Kolberg speech. France under Louis XIV, in the famous words of Alfred T. Mahan, had pursued a "false policy of continental expansion" at the expense of its "colonies and commerce." Its squadrons at sea had been destroyed by "vastly superior force," and its merchant shipping "swept away."[2] Britain and the Netherlands, on the other hand, had "advanced to power at sea" through their "quick instincts" as businessmen, negotiators, producers, shopkeepers, and traders. "The instinct for commerce, bold enterprise in the pursuit of gain, and a keen scent for the trails that lead to it" had allowed these two nations, unlike France, to break the shackles of pure land strategies.[3] What about Germany? Would its future lie on the broad sweeps of the world's oceans or would it be content to remain a dominant continental land power?

Bismarck: Continentalist Strategic Culture

By 1871 Germany had emerged from Chancellor Otto von Bismarck's three wars of unification with a position that historian Ludwig Dehio has described as "semi-hegemony"—that is, it was the Continent's premier power without, however, striving to be a hegemonic power.[4] For a half dozen years thereafter, Bismarck had heeded George Washington's and Thomas Jefferson's warnings against "permanent" or "entangling" alliances. But several diplomatic crises and "war scares" in the 1870s had revealed to him that the European powers regarded German unification—the "German revolution," as Benjamin Disraeli had put it—as the end of a historical development; and that they would not condone any new expansion of the German power base in the heart of the Continent. Bismarck in 1877 had used the occasion of his annual "spa cure" to weigh his options and to chart Germany's future. The resulting "Bad Kissingen Memorandum" remains a model of clarity and vision.[5]

The Iron Chancellor singled out France as Germany's most likely major adversary. It had accepted neither the defeat of 1871 nor the loss of Alsace and parts of Loraine. It constantly taunted Germany with a *cauchemar des coalitions*. This "nightmare of coalitions" could come about through a coalition of France, Britain, and possibly Austria-Hungary. Or, it could come about by what the chancellor called an even "greater danger," namely, a union of France, Russia, and Austria-Hungary. What to do?

First, Bismarck defined Germany's national policy interests. He ruled out the further "acquisition of territory," that is, an expansionist military policy designed to achieve European hegemony, as had been pursued in the past by Charles V, Philip II, Louis XIV, and Napoleon I. The Reich was "satiated," he noted, and it could not absorb any more non-German ethnic groups. Second, he refused to pursue an anti-British course of naval building. Germany needed at best a small coastal defense force to protect its harbors, fisheries, and trade routes in the North and Baltic seas; hence, the Iron Chancellor kept a damper on naval aspirations.[6] Third, Bismarck rejected the acquisition of a colonial empire—despite a brief and failed attempt to play the colonial card to "trump" Britain by bringing about a "Franco-German entente."[7] As he brusquely put it when pushed by the explorer Eugen Wolf to define a bold German colonial policy in Africa, "Your map of Africa is all very fine, but my map of Africa lies in Europe. Here lies Russia . . . and here lies France, and we are in the middle; that is my map of Africa."[8] Fourth, the chancellor grudgingly accepted the fact that Germany, geographically wedged between two great land powers, could no longer afford to bask in "splendid isolation."

Bismarck's solution to the French-driven *cauchemar des coalitions* was bold and simple. Two cardinal axioms drove his national security policy: no conflicts among the major powers in Central Europe, and German security without German hegemony. Having rejected wars of "acquisition," fleet building, and global empire, he decided to restore a conservative, preservationist Metternichian order—one that he had earlier helped to destroy. Germany would assume the role of "honest broker" in Europe. As a "satisfied" player, Germany would maintain the European balance of power as established in 1871. To uphold that balance—by force, if need be—he decreed that the Reich's armed land forces would be set at 1 percent of the population (45 million in 1880) and automatically funded at the rate of 225 Thaler per man—the so-called *Äternat*, or "eternal" budget.

In terms of international relations, he set out to create a "political landscape in which all the Powers, except France, need us and are prevented, by virtue of their relations towards each other, from the possibility of coalescing against us." Put differently, alliance security for Germany; alliance denial for France. Thus, after Bad Kissingen he wove a web of alliances to Austria-Hungary (1879), Italy (1882), Romania (1883), and finally Russia (1887). As long as Germany did not build a powerful battlefleet, he could ignore Britain in his geostrategic calculus. In the words of historian William L. Langer, Bismarck made Berlin "the focal point of international relations."[9] Denied future ties to Vienna, Rome, and St. Petersburg, France was left with only Belgium, Luxembourg, and the Netherlands as potential continental allies.

It was an amazing piece of clearheaded thinking on the part of a man who had never attended a war college and who felt "ashamed" that he had never read Carl von Clausewitz's opus *On War*. Over an afternoon, Bismarck had undertaken a classic Clausewitzean top-down, policy-strategy-means analysis. He had first defined Germany's policy, then laid out a strategy to achieve that policy, and finally established the means by which to realize that strategy. Still, his remaining fear was whether this vision of a peaceful Europe with a powerful, united Germany at its center could be permanently institutionalized and whether future German leaders would have the foresight to maintain it. A "nightmare of coalitions" at times haunted Bismarck.

Industrial-Economic Transformation

The fact of the matter is that Bismark's *Pax Germanica* could not be preserved over time as the very foundations on which it was based began to erode. The Germany of Bismarck's lifetime (1815–1898) was dramatically changing, especially during his last two decades in office. Largely an agrarian country for much of the century, Germany became a highly urbanized and industrialized one by the 1890s. The Prussian semifeudal agrarian state was being transformed into the German bourgeois industrial-commercial state, one that featured concentration of capital, cartel formations, banking syndicates, and revolutionary technology. As well, the German population rose by 60 percent (to 67 million) between 1871 and 1914 while those of Britain and France remained stagnant.

During the last three decades of the nineteenth century, Germany became the industrial engine of Europe.[10] Coal and lignite output shot up from 89 million tons in 1890 to 269 million tons by 1913, a mere 23 million behind that of the world's leader, Great Britain. Pig iron production during that same period climbed sharply from 4.7 to 19 million tons. On the eve of World War I, Germany was Europe's greatest steel producer, second globally only to the United States. Other areas of the economy such as chemicals, electricity, machine making, shipbuilding, and textiles witnessed four- and fivefold expansions during that same period. Overall exports by Germany increased from 3.3 billion Goldmark (GM) in 1890 to 10.1 billion by 1913; exports of finished products alone leaped from 2 billion to 4 billion GM during those years. Economists have estimated overall global trade in 1914 at 150 billion GM: Britain led with 20, Germany was second with 16, and the United States was third with 14 billion GM. Britain, the world's financial, commercial, and industrial leader, became so alarmed at this meteoric growth that in 1896 it appointed an official blue-ribbon panel to investigate a widely perceived "Made in Germany" scare. The parallel to China's industrial-commercial "engine" of the first decade of the twenty-first century is glaringly obvious.

Furthermore, Germany reached out across the globe in the fiscal, industrial, and military sectors. Its overseas investments of 5.8 billion GM in 1913–14 lagged behind only those of Britain and of France, and were ahead of those of the United States. German banks funded the Berlin-to-Baghdad railroad and the Great Venezuelan Railroad. The Hamburg-Amerika Line, the North German Lloyd, and the Kosmos Line shipped finished products to all corners of the globe. In terms of oceangoing shipping, Germany, with 5.1 million registered tons in June 1914, was second only to Britain. German military missions and armaments sales penetrated Argentina, Bolivia, Chile, Colombia, Ecuador, Paraguay, Uruguay, and Venezuela in Latin America as well as China, Japan, and the Ottoman Empire. Germans who had emigrated to escape poverty, hunger and repression at home—the so-called diasporas Deutschtum—were now embraced by the new Reich, and their organizations funded by private societies such as the Gustav-Adolf Foundation and by extra-parliamentary pressure groups such as the Colonial League (42,000 members by 1914) and the Pan-German League (20,000 members by 1914).

This sea change brought with it a dramatic psychological reorientation—from the continentalist, land-oriented, and defensive Bismarckian strategy to what historian Fritz Fischer has called the Wilhelmian "grab for world power." It was perhaps best encapsulated by the sociologist Max Weber in his inaugural address at Freiburg University in May 1895. "We must comprehend," he lectured his listeners, that German unification in 1871 would have constituted little more than a "youthful spree" and a "costly extravagance," had it been "the conclusion rather than the starting point of German power politics on a global scale."[11] In other words, German unification had been but the precursor for the Reich's new global aspirations, encapsulated by the slogan Weltpolitik, or global (overseas) policy. Only by breaking the bonds of

Bismarck's self-imposed continental containment could Germany aspire to great-power status and seek a secure future in overseas colonies and global maritime trade, protected by a powerful Mahanian battlefleet concentrated in squadrons of what later came to be called "capital" ships (battleships and battle cruisers).

Tirpitz: The Maritime Vision

Alfred von Tirpitz became the architect of Germany's new global strategy. One of the first of a new class of professional military managers, Tirpitz offered his monarch and the nation a "New Course," a grand Mahanian maritime philosophy, and promise of global prominence. In position papers of 1888 and 1891 and especially in the famous "Service Memorandum IX" of 1894, he had defined that design in powerful, dramatic terms: to annihilate British sea power, if London proved unwilling to accord Germany its newly defined "place in the sun," in a single Armageddon-like battle in the south-central North Sea. In graphic words, historian Paul M. Kennedy has likened Tirpitz's battlefleet to a "sharp knife, held gleaming and ready only a few inches away from the jugular vein of Germany's most likely enemy."[12]

Tirpitz (perhaps like some People's Liberation Army Navy strategists today) was not interested in coastal defense, in protecting German ports and fisheries, or in securing the Reich's sea lines of communication in the Baltic and North Seas. Nor was he interested in pure continental land defense, describing such a policy as a sure recipe for "moral self-destruction" leading to "national ruin."[13] Instead, he was building for the future, looking ahead two decades to a time when he fully expected a new "global order" to emerge in the wake of the anticipated decline and fall of the British Empire (as suggested by its inability to deal swiftly and efficiently with the rebellious Boers in South Africa). Germany, along with Russia, China, Japan, and the United States, Tirpitz repeatedly informed his monarch, had to be prepared for that day if it did not want to be reduced to the ranks of a "poor farming country."[14] Again, the parallel to China today concerning long-term, futuristic planning is patently obvious.

Tirpitz understood that for a lasting maritime transformation to take place in Germany, the first task was to popularize the concept of fleet and overseas expansion with both parliamentary deputies and the nation at large.[15] To make Germans receptive to the Mahanian promise, he had the American's opus, *The Influence of Sea Power upon History*, which had been translated into German in 1898–99, serialized in popular magazines, read from church pulpits, discussed by women's clubs, and placed aboard German ships. He even ordered eight thousand copies to be given away. He transformed the stodgy service journal *Marine-Rundschau* into a popular magazine; and he founded a second popular journal, *Nauticus*, as well. He established a "News Bureau" within his own Imperial Navy Office to handle what he called "spiritual massage," that is, propaganda for fleet building. He recruited some 270 eminent "fleet professors" (mainly university economists, geographers, and historians) to give academic luster and prestige to the gospel of Mahan. He inveigled private industry into funding a Navy League (with 1.1 million members by 1914) and publishing its own journal, *Die Flotte* (with a circulation of three hundred thousand). He routinely invited Reichstag deputies on board warships and took them out into the North and Baltic seas to witness first-hand the glory of Neptune's realm. And he encouraged German families, from the kaiser on down, to dress their offspring in sailor's uniforms.

Tirpitz set out to keep the scope of his fleet building secret—from Parliament (Reichstag), from the government, and especially from the British. Thus, beginning with his first formal audience with Wilhelm II in June 1897, he used vague and innocuous phrases to obscure his ultimate goals. He simply would build ships-of-the-line "in as high a number as possible." He would merely "strengthen" Germany's "will and importance" with regard to Great Britain. He would only elevate Germany into the elite rank of maritime and colonial powers.[16] At no time did he allude to the ultimate size of the fleet he was building or to the strategy that it was to employ. As he informed senior naval commanders during a visit to the naval base at Wilhelmshaven around the turn of the century, it was "impossible to explain actions and motives during this interim phase" of naval building. He was operating, he allowed, as carefully as "the caterpillar before it has grown into the butterfly."[17] In his memoirs he concluded that his master plan had been purposefully "incremental," like the "patient laying of stone upon stone."[18]

Tirpitz worked to create a fleet that was "removed" from constant parliamentary scrutiny. The Navy Laws of 1808 and 1900, as well as the Supplementary Bills of 1906, 1908, and 1912, were designed to create a state-of-the-art battlefleet of forty-one battleships and twenty battle cruisers by the mid-1920s based on an "iron budget," much like the Prussian Army's financial *Äternat*. That is, once authorized by the Reichstag, the ships would be automatically replaced upon expiration of their established service life— at first twenty-five years and later twenty years. In February 1898 Tirpitz famously informed the kaiser that his navy bills would "remove the disturbing influence of the Reichstag on Your Majesty's intentions with regard to the development of the navy."[19] To camouflage the true scope of his intentions—namely, to challenge the Royal Navy's mastery at sea—the admiral clothed his grand design in the garb of a "risk" fleet. This *Risikoflotte*, he maintained, needed only to be sufficiently powerful to deter Britain from risking an all-out naval encounter with Germany in the North Sea, to be left thereafter either critically weakened or at the mercy of a third naval power or a hostile naval coalition. He even tried to sell it as an "alliance" fleet (*Bündnisfähigkeit*), as one that would rally smaller naval powers to its banner against "perfidious Albion."[20] Both, of course, were smokescreens at best; neither made strategic sense.

Tirpitz cleverly tied naval expenditures to the anticipated growth of the German economy, which by the time of the First Navy Law had long broken out of the "Great Depression" of the 1870s. Since the federal government under Article 70 of the Bismarckian Constitution of 1871 was barred from levying direct taxes, the fleet would be financed by indexing construction to indirect taxation—a host of consumer taxes on beer and champagne, cigarettes and raw tobacco, railroad billets and theater tickets; as well as on a range of service taxes on deeds, stamps, property and goods transfers, and registrations. He thus restricted anticipated naval escalation from one design generation to the next in terms of displacement to two thousand tons, and of main armament to 2 cm. Tirpitz saw this as a political necessity, given that the powerful Conservative Party had little love for what one of its leaders called the "hated and horrible" fleet. He even resurrected former Prussian finance minister Johannes von Miquel's "politics of concentration" (*Sammlungspolitik*) into a broad strategy of reciprocation: The agrarian Conservatives would vote for fleet building in return for business and industry agreeing to clamp higher tariffs on cheap Russian grain imports.[21]

Tirpitz offered the navy to the nation as a symbol of industrial progress, and to industrialists as a font of "spillovers" to areas such as metallurgy, machine building, electrical systems, optics, hydraulics, industrial chemistry, and, of course, steel and gun production. It would bring secure employment to the highly skilled working class and immense profits to steelmakers, shipbuilders, and gun manufacturers. Moreover, the navy, in contrast to the barracked land forces, would be forward-looking and progressive. It would be a testimony to Germany's new scientific and engineering prowess. It would be truly national, whereas the various armies were regional (Bavarian, Prussian, Saxon, Württemberg). The navy would show the flag around the globe and thus constitute an outward expression of the Reich's newfound vitality and growth. Again, China's move away from the infantry-heavy ground forces of the People's Liberation Army to the concept of modern, mobile techno-logical land and sea warfare ("local wars under high technology conditions") constitutes another parallel.[22]

Bureaucratic Process

Tirpitz brilliantly understood what historian Stig Förster has called the "polycratic chaos" of the Prussian-German constitutional system, and he cleverly set out to use the existing diffuse administrative structure to his advantage.[23] To this end, he warded off every effort on the part of various chancellors and finance ministers to hammer out a coordinated national strategy and especially a common defense budget. The "Tirpitz plan" was never debated at the highest councils. Land and sea strategies were never weighed and balanced. No common budgetary strategies were ever estab-lished. Diplomatic policy was never reassessed to reflect the radical shift in strategic reorientation brought about by the "New Course." Instead, each ser-vice developed its own separate strategy, submitted its own separate budget requests, and in the last instance appealed to Wilhelm II to resolve all differ-ences in direction and priority.[24]

Given the absence of a German equivalent to the (however flawed) British Committee of Imperial Defence and the French Conseil Supérieure de la Guerre, there was only one chamber in which the national security could be debated: that of Kaiser Wilhelm II. The Constitution of 1871 gave immense power to the Prussian king/German kaiser.[25] Article 63 established him as commander in chief (*Bundesfeldherr*) of the "entire armed land forces of the Reich . . . in war and in peace." Article 64 required all field and for-tress commanders to pledge unquestioning obedience to the *Bundesfeldherr*. Article 53 likewise gave the kaiser "supreme command" over the "Navy of the Empire." Article 11 granted him exclusive powers—with the cosignature of his appointed imperial chancellor—to declare war and to make peace. The Reichstag could not question, and much less challenge, defense policy. Its ability to determine the Reich's national security strategy was restricted to the power of the purse.

In all fairness it should be pointed out that in July 1888 Wilhelm II had given decision making the trappings of centralization when he had estab-lished a "Headquarters of His Majesty the Kaiser and King." But this so-called *maison militaire*, composed of high-ranking adjutants and generals, was given no functions, duties, or responsibilities. Over time, it degenerated into a posh sinecure for officers from Wilhelm's favorite Palace Guards and Life Guards.

More indicative of the monarch's style of personal rule, in 1897 he peremptorily dissolved the Home Defense Commission (*Landesverteidigungskommission*), which had been composed of generals and admirals and entrusted with coordinating joint defense policies.[26] It was never replaced with an analogous planning body. It is almost surprising that Wilhelm II actually conducted one combined army–navy maneuver—in 1904—but even this was limited to the Baltic Sea region. After the Great War, Chancellor Theobald von Bethmann Hollweg quite proudly wrote in his memoirs that "there never took place during my entire period in office a sort of war council at which politics were brought into the military for and against."[27]

Beyond this constitutional centrality, Wilhelm II enjoyed unchallenged military and naval authority in his capacity as "Supreme War Lord" (*Oberster Kriegsherr*). By way of a personal oath of allegiance, military and naval officers accorded him exclusive and unquestionable powers in all "command decisions" (*Kommandogewalt*). In 1898 Admiral von Tirpitz asked one of Germany's leading constitutional experts, Paul Laband, to render an opinion on the extent of, or the limitations on, this power. Laband concluded that "the execution of *Kommandogewalt* is not governed by laws," and that neither the Reichstag nor the Bundesrath (Upper House) nor the government (chancellor) had any "right of co-determination or control over it." Command authority was the "absolutely personal prerogative" of the monarch.[28]

Within his own house, Tirpitz, the consummate bureaucratic infighter, also established his service *Kommandogewalt*. Although only the head of the administrative and fiscal side of the navy—the Imperial Navy Office (*Reichs-Marine-Amt*)—he used his position with the kaiser to exclude the professional strategy makers—the Admiralty Staff—from the decision-making process. Hence it was Tirpitz rather than Admiralty Staff planners who decided the future fleet's squadron tactics, displacement, main armament, battleground (the south-central North Sea), and even its initial basing (Helgoland Island). Furthermore, already in June 1897 Tirpitz had requested (and received) from Wilhelm II carte blanche to execute his maritime transformation: the right to select the offzicers for his staff; to organize the various divisions of the Reichs-Marine-Amt; to handle all press matters; to ban active naval officers from publicly discussing fleet plans; and to stipulate that there would be no major funding increases for the land forces while the fleet was being built.[29]

To exercise that immense authority, the admiral surrounded himself with a modern-day "think tank." He gathered at his headquarters in Berlin the navy's best and brightest (future admirals such as Eduard von

Capelle, Harald Dähnhardt, Max von Fischel, August von Heeringen, Albert Hopman, Friedrich von Ingenohl, Reinhard Scheer, and Adolf von Trotha) to plan down to the minutest detail what the navy needed. Every summer he took this coterie of aides to his residence at St. Blasien in the Black Forest to finalize naval plans—for presentation in the fall first to the monarch and then to Parliament. In the Reichstag, this coterie stood at Tirpitz's elbow, ready to supply any wavering deputies with mountains of statistics and position papers to shore up their support for fleet building.

Maritime Transformation

Major geostrategic transformations on the part of democratic or even semiauthoritarian societies are difficult to conceal. First and foremost, published military/naval estimates and budgets and their subsequent debates in parliaments reveal shifts and rises in funding levels. Second, military and naval attachés routinely visit major arsenals, shipyards, and maneuvers and hence are well positioned to report on such developments. Tirpitz's First Navy Law (*Flottengesetz*) of April 1898 was closely monitored by the British, and it caused little concern in London. The Law called for a fleet by April 1904 consisting of nineteen battleships, eight armored cruisers, and twelve large as well as thirty light cruisers. While impressive on paper, this entailed new construction of only seven battleships and two large and seven light cruisers over the next six years. Such a fleet was perfectly in line with Germany's expanding maritime commerce, its small colonial empire, and its need to defend ports, fisheries, and sea-lanes in the North and Baltic seas. Moreover, the Reichstag placed a spending limit of 408.1 million GM on naval expansion and clearly defined its parameters.

All this changed dramatically in June 1900 with passage of the Second Navy Law. It entailed nothing less than a doubling of the fleet to thirty-eight battleships and twenty armored and thirty-eight light cruisers. It called for the new construction of nineteen battleships as well as eight large and fifteen light cruisers. It temporarily enacted Tirpitz's goal of laying down three keels per annum (*Dreiertempo*) until 1905—when, obviously, a new naval bill could be expected. This time, the Reichstag set no limits on construction costs, thereby according the British little insight into ship displacement or main armament. It was no secret in an age of "navalism" that battleships were not needed for coastal protection or for brown-water operations in the German colonies.

The Second Navy Law was an overt challenge to British naval mastery, most especially in European waters. Such a battlefleet concentrated but two hundred miles off the largely undefended British east coast constituted a clear and present danger. In an internal memorandum, Tirpitz now described Britain as Germany's "most dangerous opponent at sea." He again demanded battleships "in as high a number as possible"—at first forty-five, then forty-eight—as a minimum security requirement concerning "the military situation with regard to England."[30] The "caterpillar" was disgorging the "butterfly."

From this point on, a classic arms race—like the one that would be conducted between the United States and the Soviet Union in the latter part of the twentieth century—ensued. When Adm. Sir John Fisher upped the ante first with the battleship HMS *Dreadnought* (discussed in the following) and then with the battle cruiser HMS *Invincible*, Tirpitz by way of a Supplementary Law (*Novelle*) in June 1906 added six battle cruisers to the fleet and received from the Reichstag the necessary funds to expand existing docks, locks, and canals for the newer, larger vessels to be built. The Novelle further secured the "gap" in the *Dreiertempo* until 1912. Still not satisfied with either the pace or the extent of fleet building, Tirpitz in April 1908 wrung another Novelle from Parliament, this one reducing the service life of capital ships from twenty-five to twenty years—thereby ensuring that antiquated "pre-dreadnought" battleships and large cruisers would be replaced by state-of-the-art dreadnought-class warships. And in May 1912 the Reichstag agreed to yet another Supplementary Law, this one increasing the size of the battlefleet to forty-one battleships, twenty battle cruisers, and forty light cruisers.[31] If all went according to plan, by the mid-1920s Tirpitz would have poised in the North Sea an armada of sixty-one capital ships, to be automatically replaced every twenty years. The "sharp knife," to stay with Kennedy's analogy, was being prepared for the proverbial British "jugular."

For each of the navy bills passed after 1898 Tirpitz had used his "News Bureau" and the Navy League to drum up public support. The Anglo-German-American competition for Samoa in 1899 and the British seizure of two German steamers in Delago Bay one year later during the Boer War whipped up popular demands for the Second Navy Law of 1900—ostensibly to protect German commerce and to curb British naval "arrogance." The Novelle of 1905 was fueled by British pulp "invasion" novels as well as by the First Moroccan Crisis occasioned by the kaiser's maladroit speech on behalf of Moroccan independence from France. The Anglo-French-Russian entente of 1907 was exploited to pass the Novelle of 1908. The Second Moroccan

Crisis of 1911, brought about by the dispatch of the gunboat *Panther* to press German claims in Africa, was used to pass the Novelle of 1912.

But what maritime geostrategic design, it is fair to ask, drove Tirpitz's frantic fleet building? The simple answer is "none." Build first, design a strategy later. For all his labors to translate Mahan and to uphold the American as the modern-day apostle of sea power, Tirpitz failed to understand that Mahan had begun his every work with a "given": free and unhindered access to what he called "the great thoroughfares of the world's traffic."[32] To reach one of those "great thoroughfares"—the Atlantic Ocean—any German fleet had but two avenues of approach: the English Channel or the several waterways between Scotland and Greenland. When in 1908–1910 two chiefs of the Admiralty Staff, Friedrich von Baudissin and Max von Fischel, reminded Tirpitz that Germany was "basically the aggressor" who was "fighting for access to the open seas, whose entrances on the other side of the North Sea are in England's hands," the state secretary had no reply—other than to have Wilhelm II issue an order forbidding such public discussion of maritime strategy.[33] Indeed, Mahan had even made the geographical comparison for Tirpitz when he had noted that just as Ireland potentially blocked Britain's access to the Atlantic by its geographical position, so too Britain blocked Germany's access to it.[34]

In the final analysis, Tirpitz had developed a "power-political" strategy of bluff and bullying. He probably hoped that he would never have to risk the fleet, his life's work, in an afternoon in the south-central North Sea. Its mere existence would suffice to blackmail London into acquiescing to German demands for colonies and coaling stations. Repeatedly, the admiral had used the terms "political power and importance vis-à-vis England" and "political power importance of sea power" to describe his maritime "strategy."[35] He mistakenly took from Mahan the assumption that an attacking fleet required at all times 33 percent numerical superiority; this would mean that Britain would have to base seventy-seven capital ships in the North Sea if it wanted to do battle with the sixty-one-capital-ship High Sea Fleet. Especially the liberal governments of Henry Campbell-Bannerman and Herbert Asquith with their sweeping promises of spending on social programs, Tirpitz opined, would never be able to mount such a Herculean effort at sea.

As well, it must be remembered that Tirpitz built a classic "one-off" weapon. The High Sea Fleet would on its own fight the Royal Navy, if need be, winner take all. Tirpitz never saw it as but one element of a broader strategic grammar. There was no question in his mind that the British fleet, based on tradition and history, would descend into the German Bight and offer

battle at the start of any war. When Fleet Chief Friedrich von Ingenohl que-
ried Tirpitz during fleet maneuvers in May 1914, "What will you would do if
they [the British] do not come?" the state secretary had no response.[36] Nor
did Tirpitz ever attempt to coordinate his maritime transformation with the
strategic design for the land forces—for example, by interrupting anticipated
British cross-Channel troop and supply transports.[37] Thus, when in August
1914 the Great General Staff enacted the high-risk continental land strategy
of the Schlieffen plan, the navy remained in port. And for the next four years
its leaders conducted desultory discussions in an attempt to hammer out a
possible naval operations plan against Britain—either by way of a desperate
all-out fleet sortie, or by an attritional campaign of unrestricted submarine
warfare. That debate ended with mutiny in 1917, revolution in 1918, and scuttling in 1919.

Finally, maritime transformation brought Germany no new allies.
Holland, Belgium, Denmark, and Sweden declined to join Tirpitz's patently
anti-British initiative, as, of course, did the United States and China and
"the Mohammedans," contra to what Wilhelm II had quixotically imagined.
Quite the opposite took place. Germany in 1890 abandoned Bismarck's vital
tie to Russia and under Chancellor Bernhard von Bülow chose to maintain a
free hand, that is, to avoid any new entangling alliances and to use the pressure of Tirpitz's fleet building to force London to come round to the German
camp. It was a dangerous and ill-advised high-risk national policy at a time
when any future war in Europe was bound to be a protracted coalition war.
Britain, by contrast, understood the unilateral German naval challenge as a
threat to its very existence: It buried colonial rivalries with France and Russia
and, in addition to its tie to Japan in 1902, created an *entente cordiale* with
Paris and St. Petersburg by 1907. German leaders thereafter spoke of "encirclement" without ever appreciating that this had been self-imposed.

Limits of Maritime Transformation

Technology is a double-edged sword. It is constantly open to challenge,
innovation, and improvement. It always tends toward escalation in terms
of both quality and quantity. Tirpitz quickly discovered that his conservative approach to German warship displacement and main armament—and
hence cost—could not be sustained. The British decision in 1905 to challenge
the Tirpitz plan qualitatively and financially with the launching of HMS
Dreadnought, the world's first all-big-gun, one-caliber battleship, threw
German naval planning into panic.[38] Existing locks and docks at Kiel and

Wilhelmshaven would have to be vastly expanded to handle an estimated five-thousand-ton increase in displacement, and the Kaiser-Wilhelm-Kanal that linked the Baltic Sea to the North Sea would have to be both widened and deepened (at a projected cost of perhaps as much as 223 million GM) to handle the new dreadnought-class vessels. Tirpitz's staff estimated that to meet Admiral Fisher's so-called dreadnought challenge, the Reich Treasury would have to raise 1,000 million GM in new indirect taxation.

The stunning costs of this technological spiral can be seen most readily in the escalatory outlays for new construction. Before HMS *Dreadnought*, German battleships had come in on average at 24 million and large cruisers at 21 million GM each; thereafter, that per-unit cost shot up to 47 million and 44 million GM, respectively, a dramatic rise of 96 percent for battleships and 107 percent for battle cruisers. The naval estimates of 219 million GM in 1904 skyrocketed to 259 million in 1906, 347 million in 1908, and 434 million GM in 1910.[39] Tirpitz did his utmost to conceal these sharply rising expenditures from the public but in the end conceded that the cost factor gave him "sleepless nights." He expressed doubts and fears to his inner planning circle whether Germany could "sustain permanently the pace of fleet construction" as the costs for individual ships "had reached impossible heights for Reich finances and will continue to do so."[40] Three state secretaries of the treasury (Max von Thielmann, Hermann von Stengel, and Reinhold von Sydow) resigned in protest over the naval estimates; one chancellor (Bernhard von Bülow) succumbed to the financial morass occasioned by the growing gap between indirect tax revenues and defense outlays.

By April 1914 Tirpitz virtually acknowledged financial bankruptcy to his coterie of aides: Only an immediate infusion of 150 million to 200 million GM and a six- to eight-year extension of the navy bills could salvage his blueprint for *Weltpolitik*. Moreover, German shipyards were not up to the task of challenging their British counterparts. "We cannot even build the ships that have been approved," Tirpitz ruefully confessed to his "think tank."[41] In fact, his grand design in 1914 was a shocking eight battleships and thirteen cruisers behind completion schedules. The national debt had climbed to a staggering 4,918 million GM—of which 1,041 million had gone for fleet building, 693 million for suppression of the Boxer Rebellion in China and the Herero Uprising in German Southwest Africa, and 115 million for expansion of the Kaiser-Wilhelm-Kanal.

Parenthetically, it should be noted that the anticipated "spin-off" effects from Tirpitz's maritime transformation had failed to materialize. Trade with the colonies had been disappointing, constituting a mere 0.5 percent of Germany's total between 1903 and 1914. Colonial debts, on the other hand, had risen to 171.5 million GM. German banking and industry placed a mere 3.8 percent of their overseas investments in the colonies.[42] While Krupp, thanks to its virtual monopolies on armor plates and heavy artillery, had managed handsome profits of around 40 percent from fleet building, Germany's major shipbuilders such as Blohm & Voss by 1913 were losing 1 million GM per unit on capital-ship construction in the highly competitive climate fostered by Tirpitz. Their dividends plummeted to a dismal 1.24 percent.[43] In short, maritime transformation had not led to the promised national prosperity.

Perhaps the most crushing blow to German maritime transformation, however, came in the form of renewed calls for vastly enhanced outlays for continental land defense. In raw terms, the Reich spent 32.5 billion GM on defense between 1872 and 1914—25.9 billion on the army and 6.6 billion on the navy. In percentile terms, this constituted between 85 and 90 percent of federal expenditures! The quickening pace of these outlays can be gleaned from one simple statistic: Whereas total annual defense expenditures between 1872 and 1888 had been around 330 million GM, in the last seven years before the Great War they stood at 948 million per annum.[44]

In terms of interservice fiscal rivalry, Tirpitz at first had held the upper hand—just as he had demanded from Wilhelm II in the June 1897 imperial audience. The navy's share of defense expenditures as a percent of army outlays had climbed from less than 20 percent in 1898 to 35 percent by 1905 and to 55 percent by 1911.[45] Already on the eve of the First Navy Law of 1898, Gen. Alfred von Waldersee, a former chief of the General Staff, had raised the basic question: "The navy more and more cultivates the notion that future wars will be decided at sea. But what does the navy propose to do if the army is defeated, be it in the West or in the East?"[46] With the two-front continental war conception developed by Alfred von Schlieffen by 1905, that question had become acute. And when Helmuth von Moltke (the Younger) and Col. Erich Ludendorff in 1912 "war-gamed" the Schlieffen plan and found that it's vital right wing was eight army corps short of requisite forces, that question became alarming. Not surprisingly, the navy's budget fell from 49 percent of the army's budget in 1912 to 32 percent in 1913. State Secretary of the Treasury Adolf Wermuth on behalf of Chancellor von Bethmann Hollweg connected the line between finances and strategy as follows: "As the strength of the army is for us a matter of life and death, so is the fleet for England."[47]

Admiral Fisher's "dreadnought leap" and the ever-greater pinch on German finances combined to occasion a reorientation of German strategic planning. It is hardly a coincidence that around the time of the 1905 dread-nought leap, Chief of the General Staff von Schlieffen developed his bold design: to concentrate seven-eighths of his land forces to destroy France in the West first, and then to shuttle those forces to confront what he perceived would be the slower Russian mobilization in the East. He accorded the navy no role in that desperate design. Nor did he consult the chief of the Admiralty Staff, the chief of the High Sea Fleet, or the state secretary of the navy in drafting his plans. This reorientation of the Reich's security strategy is per-haps again best revealed in the stark language of the defense budget: In 1912 the army was given a special one-time grant of 219 million GM to prop up its 1911 budget as well as a stunning supplementary "modernization" enhance-ment of 612 million GM for the period 1912 to 1917 for guns and equipment alone.[48] It was a stark expression by the chancellor and the Treasury that the Reich's security in the last analysis rested with its land forces.

Beyond Tirpitz (and Mahan)

Ironically, the world's two most powerful battlefleets—Britain with twenty-one dreadnoughts and four battle-cruisers, Germany with thirteen dreadnoughts and three battle-cruisers—faced each other across the North Sea from 1914 to 1918 without either side seeking a decisive victory. After the indecisive Battle of Jutland on 31 May–1 June 1916, Fleet Chief Adm. Reinhard Scheer informed Kaiser Wilhelm II that Germany could never "*force* England to make peace" by way of surface engagements due to the lat-ter's "great material superiority" and the Reich's "disadvantageous military-geographical position." All that remained was "the defeat of British eco-nomic life—that is, by using the U-boats against British trade."[49] Chief of the Admiralty Staff Henning von Holtzendorff on 22 December 1916 provided the calculus for Scheer's decision. Britain had available about 10 million tons of merchant shipping, the admiral argued. If the U-boats could sink six hun-dred thousand tons per month for four months and five hundred thousand tons per month thereafter; if the "unrestricted" submarine campaign could frighten 1.2 million tons of neutral shipping off the seas; if German crews could disable the 1.4 million tons of shipping interred in neutral ports; then Britain would suffer a "final and irreplaceable loss" of 39 percent in available tonnage and be forced to "sue for peace within five months."[50]

Imperial Germany had never intended to fight a submarine war (*guerre de course*) against Britain. It had built its first U-boat only in 1906 and Tirpitz had savagely curtailed the budget for the undersea service for fear of proliferation ("a museum of experiments") that would cut into funding for the battlefleet. Nevertheless, the navy could not remain idle while the army bled profusely in France and Russia; hence the turn to the U-boats. It was to be a war of economic attrition, pure and simple. At first the U-boats surpassed expectations, sinking on average 629,862 tons of enemy shipping for the first four months of the "unrestricted" campaign and then 506,069 tons for the next two months. But Britain was not "forced to sue for peace." The campaign brought the world's most powerful neutral, the United States, into the war. Although overall the Kaiser's "pirate ships" sank 5,000 Allied ships of 12 million tons, only 393 of the 95,000 ships convoyed across the Atlantic were lost. For its part the U-Boat fleet lost 199 boats and 5,249 officers and ratings. The Reich had launched "unrestricted" submarine warfare on 1 February 1917 with 111 boats—of which one-third were undergoing repair and refit at any given time, and another one-third were going to or returning from war zones, which left a mere 32 (500- to 700-ton) U-boats in the Atlantic, the North Sea, the English Channel, and the Irish Sea. A belated attempt in the autumn of 1918 to raise U-boat production (the "Scheer Program") was largely a national placebo, a propaganda effort.[51]

With the scuttling of the High Sea Fleet at Scapa Flow and the banning of submarine development under Article 191 of the Treaty of Versailles in 1919, German naval planners were free to start anew. They mostly eschewed another war of commerce raiding in favor of using the submarine in a traditional role: to attack enemy warships and military transports, to lay mines, and to scout. The first boat, U-1, slid into the water eleven days after the signing of the Anglo-German Naval Agreement of June 1935; thereafter, German yards launched a U-boat every eight days. By September 1938 the new Kriegsmarine had a North and Baltic seas fleet of seventy-two boats. But few naval planners shared the vision of Capt. Karl Dönitz, who in 1937 called for another U-boat war "to menace the enemy's maritime life-lines, the enemy's trade." Not a single senior naval planner shared Dönitz's vision of a submarine fleet of at least three hundred boats ranging from 517 to 740 tons each.[52]

Adm. Erich Raeder, commander in chief Kriegsmarine, was a devout follower of Tirpitz. He planned from the start to fight a Mahanian blue water war for sea control with a symmetrical battlefleet centered on battleships, battle cruisers, heavy cruisers, and aircraft carriers. Throughout the 1930s he depicted the U-boats as "one of the best *defensive* means of the weaker" naval power. The U-boats had failed to alter the strategic outcome of the Great War. They could achieve operational success only if they operated in conjunction with the battlefleet.[53] Thus on 27 January 1939 Raeder gained from

Adolf Hitler approval for the "Z-Plan": the construction within six years of a mighty armada of 684 warships, which by 1948 would give Germany 10 battleships, 15 "pocket" battleships, 4 aircraft carriers, 5 heavy and 44 light cruisers, and 249 U-boats, to be manned by 201,000 officers and men, and to be built at a cost of 33 billion Reichsmark.[54] Raeder developed his so-called double-pole strategy for the "Z" fleet: While one German fleet of battleships tied down the Royal Navy in the North Sea, another faster fleet of "pocket" battleships and heavy cruisers would assault Britain's oceanic maritime lanes. Commodore Dönitz's renewed call of 1 September 1939 for a fleet of 300 U-boats to wage war against the island nation's vital overseas commerce remained a dead letter—for the moment.

As it did in 1914, Germany went to war at sea in 1939 expecting surface actions to decide the issue. And like Tirpitz in 1914, Raeder complained bitterly that in 1939 the war had come five years too early. But this time around, the fleet would not remain idle but rather would understand "how to die gallantly."[55] And die gallantly it did: the pocket battleship *Graf Spee* at Montevideo in December 1939; three cruisers, ten destroyers, and four U-boats in Norway in April 1940; and the battleship *Bismarck* in May 1941. Therewith Raeder's double-pole strategy had suffered shipwreck. All that remained, as after Jutland in 1916, was the assault on British maritime commerce with the U-boats. Again, it was not the war German naval planners had wanted. Again, it was pure attrition warfare—*Tonnagekrieg*, as Dönitz called it. Again, it was based on a simple calculus (like Holtzendorff in 1916) of sinking around 600,000 tons per month to guarantee victory. Again, it was conducted by far too small a force: 57 ocean-going submarines in 1939 and 249 (mostly 750-ton Type VIIC boats) in 1941. Again, a last-minute (June 1943) naval building program to produce 2,400 U-boats was but a grand delusion. And again, the cost–benefit calculus was negative: Whereas the British merchant marine lost 30,248 seamen on board 2,603 freighters and tankers of 13.5 million tons, Germany lost 30,003 submariners (70 percent of all who sailed) on 739 U-boats destroyed. During the decisive period September 1942 to May 1945, the Allies mounted 953 convoys of 43,526 ships on the Atlantic runs; of these, a mere 272 ships (0.6 percent) were destroyed by U-boats.[56]

The two German (reluctant) attempts at unrestricted submarine warfare in the twentieth century suggest caution for any power looking at this type of warfare. It is slow. It is time-consuming. It is costly. It requires futuristic planning well in advance of any conflict on the seas. And it must be sustained by a massive logistical effort across any major body of water such as the Pacific

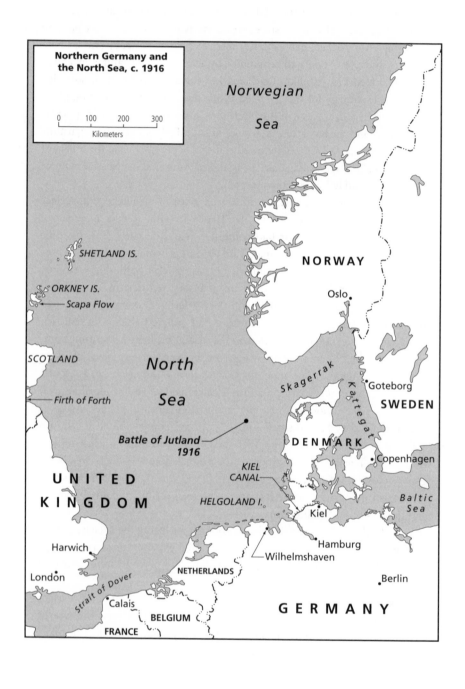

Northern Germany and the North Sea, c. 1916

0   100   200   300
Kilometers

Norwegian Sea

SHETLAND IS.

ORKNEY IS.
Scapa Flow

NORWAY

Oslo

North Sea

SCOTLAND

Skagerrak

Kattegat

Goteborg

SWEDEN

Firth of Forth

Battle of Jutland 1916

DENMARK

Copenhagen

KIEL CANAL

UNITED KINGDOM

HELGOLAND I.

Kiel

Baltic Sea

Harwich

Hamburg

Wilhelmshaven

London

NETHERLANDS

Berlin

Strait of Dover

Calais

BELGIUM

GERMANY

FRANCE

Ocean. Distance is a negative. In light of the German debates over submarine warfare in the past century, it is enticing to speculate on what role China foresees for its twenty older submarines (Han-class SSNs, Romeo- and Ming-class SSs) as well as for its roughly equal number of modern SSNs and SSs (Yuan-, Kilo-, Jin-, and Shang-class). The issue is as complex as it is daunting.

Any serious attempt at major military transformations—whether naval, land, air, or space—requires the systematic planning and conduct of what often are radical shifts in strategic decision making. Objectives have to be clearly laid out. Financial parameters have to be fully understood and accepted. The bureaucratic processes by which the transformation is to be achieved have to be informed and coordinated. Finally, the trade-offs between land and naval strengths have to be firmly appreciated and brought into the nation's fiscal and diplomatic national security objectives.

However bold and revolutionary the Tirpitz plan was, it eventually failed to bring about such a dramatic maritime transformation. Neither its political nor its fiscal base was sufficiently secure. Its ultimate goals and strategy were flawed. The other service (land forces) over time resented its fiscal and strategic implications. No firm central bureaucratic-governmental process guided it to fruition. The fleet that had been created by 1914 was inadequate alone to overcome what Tirpitz had argued was the Reich's continentalist strategic culture.

Simply put, Germany before 1914 had attempted over the life of one generation to become both a continental giant and a global aspirant. Both services had identified their potential adversary—the navy, Britain; the army, France and Russia—and both had devised in-house strategies—the Tirpitz plan and the Schlieffen plan—separately to deal with the Reich's putative security needs. General Groener in 1919 had not been the first in pointing out that the overall timetable had become confused, the national objectives blurred, and the strategic grammar garbled. On the eve of World War I, Kurt Riezler, Chancellor von Bethmann Hollweg's political counselor, had bemoaned what he called "the earlier errors of a Turkish policy against Russia, a Moroccan against France, fleet against England, [thereby] irritating everyone, blocking everybody's way and yet not really weakening anyone. Basic cause: lack of planning, craving for petty prestige victories."[57]

Tirpitz's major miscalculation was that he offered his maritime transformation as an alternative rather than as a complement to the Reich's land forces. It was to be the lone proverbial silver bullet that would allow Germany to shed its narrow continentalist mentality and embrace Mahan's broad philosophy of global commerce and colonial possessions. Colin Gray in his *The*

Leverage of Sea Power has argued powerfully that navies "fight at sea only for the strategic effect they can secure ashore, where people live." In other words, naval forces are primarily the means to gain "strategic leverage in conflict as a whole." They are about "influencing events on land in time of crisis and war."[58] They are in no way autonomous.

In a more recent work, *Modern Strategy*, Gray has refined his language. The "essence of sea power," he suggests repeatedly in the book, historically has been as a "great enabling instrument of strategy." In Gray's "grammar of modern strategy," sea power has to be "adaptable to modern technologies" and to "function at all levels of conflict with enormous flexibility." With regard to second-class navies, such as the Tirpitz fleet, Gray rightly points out that to be strategically useful they have to be able to not only deny the enemy "the ability to use the seas at will," but also "to use the seas for positive purposes."[59] The German High Sea Fleet at no time was in position to undertake either of these tasks, much less both.

Moreover, Germany, as a continentalist land power, inevitably had an unfavorable maritime geography. Mahan's ideal had been that of a nation "so situated that it is neither forced to defend itself by land nor induced to seek extension of its territory by way of the land."[60] That description very obviously failed to apply to Imperial Germany. In fact, Bismarck's "map of Africa," with Germany wedged between two major land powers, France and Russia, had been geostrategically correct. As had Mahan's admonition that just as Ireland potentially blocked Britain's ready access to the "wide common" of the Atlantic, so too did Britain block Germany's access to the critical "thoroughfare." That recognition was made most boldly in 1915 by a German naval officer, Lt. Cdr. Wolfgang Wegener, when he argued that Germany needed to acquire Norway, the Shetland and/or Orkney Islands, and perhaps Iceland as well as its "gates" to the Atlantic.[61] Wegener would spend the next decade of his service career arguing that fleet and geographical position went hand in hand.

In fairness to Alfred von Tirpitz, it should be stated yet again that he did not think in terms of maritime strategy but rather in terms of "power-political considerations." That is, his fleet was to posture as a classic "fleet in being," as one sufficiently powerful to force Britain to recognize and to accept Germany's "place in the sun." For, in addition to Gray's "eight strategic options" available to a continentalist land power attempting to overcome "a sea power foe," Tirpitz had already come up with a ninth option: maritime blackmail.[62] His fleet of sixty-one capital ships positioned just two hundred miles off Britain's east coast would pose such a threat that London would have no alternative but to accede to Berlin's political demands. Whether a continental land power the size of the state of Montana—no matter how powerful it is in terms of industry and land forces—can simultaneously maintain a first-class army and build a first-class navy remains open to debate. History has shown all too many instances where the short answer to that question was "no."

Forty years ago Andreas Hillgruber, the German historian who perhaps did more than any other to assess critically the nation's two bids in the twentieth century to become a global power, came to an all-embracing, if somewhat inelegant, formula of the process required to bring about successful major geostrategic transformations. National security strategy, he argued, consists of the "integration by a state's elite of domestic and foreign policy, of military and psychological war planning and war conduct, of the economy and war industries," to achieve what he termed "an ideological-power political overarching concept."[63] If, in fact, China has embarked on a major course of maritime transformation, it remains to be seen whether it manages to avoid the various pitfalls that brought the Tirpitz plan to ruin strategically by 1905–6 and financially by 1911–12.

Conclusion

Although culturally, politically, and physically a world apart, Imperial Germany and present-day China share a number of national and sea-power commonalities. Both nations believed that they were latecomers as great powers on the international stage. Germany was not unified until 1871, which has led many scholars to argue that it traversed a "special path" (*Sonderweg*) which set it apart from other western powers. China has traveled a modern socialist course only since 1949, with tortuous lurches (Great Leap Forward, Cultural Revolution, Tiananmen Square) en route. It now describes itself, in the words of President Hu Jintao, as a "late-coming great nation."[64] Both states were unified by and saw themselves primarily as continental land powers; both initially regarded the navy as a mere adjunct of the army. Yet both claimed long naval traditions: Germany with the Hanseatic League of the thirteenth to seventeenth century, and China with the Han to Ming Dynasties, culminating in Zheng He's fifteenth-century voyages of exploration into the Indian Ocean and the Red Sea.

Both states thereafter suffered dramatic declines in naval and commercial sea power. Both then used economic growth, technological expertise, and higher education to assist maritime transformation. Banking, industry, seaborne trade, commercial shipping, and overseas investments in both countries drove a robust maritime culture well before either had set out to build an operational blue water navy. In both nations, the government led industrialization "to catch up to earlier modernizers."[65] The U.S. Department of Defense's recent description of China as a "regional political and economic power with global aspirations" perfectly applied to Imperial Germany around 1900.[66]

The obvious major difference is that twice in the twentieth century Germany precipitated devastating wars in the great-power system. Twice, its naval theorists argued that commercial sea power needed to develop under the protection of a blue water navy. Twice they argued that an inferior fleet (that of Germany) could prevail against a superior opponent (Great Britain). Twice, they had to abandon grandiose surface-fleet theories and to fall back on the weapon of the inferior naval power, the U-boats. The question for China, as Eric McVadon has put it in his chapter in this volume, is whether China can (and will) prevail against a superior opponent (the United States) by exercising caution regarding the use of force. Perhaps Beijing's recent criticism in *The Rise of Great Powers* of German "militarism" after unification in 1871 will serve as a powerful example of a course best left untaken.

Notes

1. Bundesarchiv-Militärarchiv, Freiburg, Germany (hereafter BA-MA), Nachlass Kurt von Schleicher, N 42, vol. 12.

2. Alfred Thayer Mahan, *The Influence of Sea Power upon History 1660–1783* (New York: Sagamore Press, 1957), 65.

3. Ibid., 46, 50.

4. Ludwig Dehio, *The Precarious Balance: Four Centuries of the European Power Struggle* (New York: Knopf, 1962), 217–23.

5. "Bad Kissingen Memorandum," 15 June 1877, in Ralph Menning, ed., *The Art of the Possible: Documents on Great Power Diplomacy, 1814–1914* (New York: McGraw-Hill 1996), 185–86.

6. See Lawrence Sondhaus, *Preparing for Weltpolitik: German Sea Power before the Tirpitz Era* (Annapolis, MD: Naval Institute Press, 1997) for a much more positive spin on these naval aspirations.

7. A. J. P. Taylor, *Germany's First Bid for Colonies, 1884–1885: A Move in Bismarck's European Policy* (London: Macmillan, 1938); also, W. O. Henderson, *The German Colonial Empire, 1884–1919* (London: F. Cass, 1993).

8. Eugen Wolf, *Vom Fürsten Bismarck und seinem Haus. Tagebuchblätter von Eugen Wolf* (Berlin: E. Fleischel, 1904), 16.

9. William L. Langer, *European Alliances and Alignments, 1871–1890* (New York: Knopf, 1931), 459.

10. Statistics gleaned from Germany, Statistisches Reichsamt, *Statistisches Jahrbuch für das Deutsche Reich* (Berlin, 1880 ff.), vols. for 1890 to 1914.

11. Max Weber, *Gesammelte Politische Schriften*, ed. Johannes Winckelmann (Tübingen: Mohr, 1958), 23.

12. Paul M. Kennedy, "Tirpitz, England and the Second Navy Law of 1900: A Strategical Critique," *Militärgeschichtliche Mitteilungen* 8 (1970): 38. See also Alfred von Tirpitz, *Erinnerungen* (Leipzig: K. F. Koehler, 1919), 112.

13. Tirpitz laid out his bold design most clearly in an imperial audience on 28 September 1899. BA-MA, Reichs-Marine-Amt (hererafter RMA), Zentralabteilung 2044, PG 66074. See also Jonathan Steinberg, *Yesterday's Deterrent: Tirpitz and the Birth of the German Battle Fleet* (London: Macdonald, 1965); Volker R. Berghahn, *Der Tirpitz-Plan. Genesis und Verfall einer innenpolitischen Krisenstrategie unter Wilhelm II* (Düsseldorf: Droste, 1971); and Michael Epkenhans, *Die wilhelminische Flottenrüstung, 1908–1914. Weltmachtstreben, industrieller Fortschritt, soziale Integration* (Munich: R. Oldenbourg, 1991). The basic documents have been published by Volker R. Berghahn and Wilhelm Deist, eds., *Rüstung im Zeichen der wilhelminischen Weltpolitik. Grundlegende Dokumente* (Düsseldorf: Droste, 1988).

14. Tirpitz, *Erinnerungen*, 167.

15. See Jürg Meyer, "Die Propaganda der deutschen Flottenbewegung" 1897–1900 (PhD dissertation, Bern University, 1967); and Wilhelm Deist, *Flottenpolitik und*

Flottenpropaganda. Das Nachrichtenbureau des Reichsmarineamts 1987–1914 (Stuttgart: Deutsche Verlagsanstalt, 1976).

16. Tirpitz's notes for the imperial audience, 15 June 1897. BA-MA, Nachlass Tirpitz, N 253, vol. 4.

17. Notes of 20 October 1899, BA-MA, RMA, Zentralabteilung 2044, PG 66074. Also, Fürst Bernhard von Bülow, *Deutsche Politik* (Berlin: R. Hobbing, 1916), 120.

18. Tirpitz, *Erinnerungen*, 110, 172.

19. Tirpitz to Wilhelm II, 3 February 1898, BA-MA, RMA, Zentralabteilung 2051, PG 66110.

20. See Ivo Nikolai Lambi, *The Navy and German Power Politics, 1862–1914* (Boston: Allen & Unwin, 1984); and Rolf Hobson, *Imperialism at Sea: Naval Strategic Thought, the Ideology of Sea Power, and the Tirpitz Plan, 1875–1914* (Boston: Brill, 2002).

21. Eckart Kehr, *Schlachtflottenbau und Parteipolitik, 1894–1902: Versuch eines Querschnitts durch die innenpolitischen, sozialen und ideologischen Voraussetzungen des deutschen Imperialismus* (Berlin: E. Ebering, 1930); this theme was taken up much later by Berghahn, *Der Tirpitz-Plan.*

22. See David A. Graff and Robin Higham, eds., *A Military History of China* (Boulder, CO: Westview Press, 2002), especially chapters 14 and 16; Peng Guangqian and Yau Youzhi, eds., *The Science of Military Strategy* (Beijing: Military Science Press, 2005), 409–22.

23. Stig Förster, "Der deutsche Generalstab und die Illusion des kurzen Krieges, 1871–1914. Metakritik eines Mythos," *Militärgeschichtliche Mitteilungen* 54 (1995): 92.

24. See Wilhelm Deist, "Kaiser Wilhelm II in the Context of His Military and Naval Entourage," in John C. G. Röhl and Nicolaus Sombart, eds., *Kaiser Wilhelm II. New Interpretations: The Corfu Papers* (Cambridge, U.K.: Cambridge University Press, 1982), 169–92.

25. Ernst R. Huber, *Deutsche Verfassungsgeschichte seit 1789* (4 vols., Stuttgart: W. Kohlhammer, 1963), III: 989, 821ff.

26. Wiegand Schmidt-Richberg, "Die Regierungszeit Wilhelms II," in *Handbuch zur deutschen Militärgeschichte 1648–1939*, vol. 3, part V, *Von der Entlassung Bismarcks bis zum Ende des Ersten Weltkrieges 1890–1918* (Munich: Bernard & Graefe, 1979), 60–62.

27. Theobald von Bethmann Hollweg, *Betrachtungen zum Weltkriege* (2 vols., Berlin: R. Hobbing, 1919–1921), 2: 7.

28. Deist, "Kaiser Wilhelm II," 171.

29. Tirpitz's notes, 15 June 1897, BA-MA, Nachlass Tirpitz, N 253, vol. 4.

30. Berghahn, *Der Tirpitz-Plan*, 188.

31. Initially outlined by Hansgeorg Fernis, *Die Flottennovellen im Reichstag, 1906–1912* (Stuttgart: W. Kohlhammer, 1934), 53, 92, 148, and 155.

32. Mahan, *Influence of Sea Power*, 28.

33. BA-MA, Admiralstab der Marine, PG 67304, A 1481 IV vom 18.8.1910: Ostsee oder Nordsee als Kriegsschauplatz.

34. Alfred T. Mahan, *Retrospect and Prospect: Studies in International Relations, Naval and Political* (Boston: Little, Brown & Co., 1902), 166. Mahan was so adamant on this point that he frequently reminded his readers that "ready access to the ocean by one or two outlets" was the *sine qua non* for true sea power; Mahan, *Influence of Sea Power*, 286.

35. Tirpitz's notes for Wilhelm II of summer 1897 and winter 1899 in Berghahn and Deist, eds., *Rüstung im Zeichen der wilhelminischen Weltpolitik*, 134–36, 283–85.

36. Cited in Albert Hopman, *Das Logbuch eines deutschen Seeoffiziers* (Berlin: A Scherl, 1924), 393.

37. Gerhard Ritter, *Der Schlieffenplan: Kritik eines Mythos* (Munich: R. Oldenbourg, 1965), 176, 182–92.

38. I have suggested elsewhere that the "dreadnought revolution" was not a classic RMA but rather a coming together and an escalation of existing technologies. Holger H. Herwig, "The Battlefleet Revolution, 1885–1914," in Macgregor Knox and Williamson Murray, eds., *The Dynamics of Military Revolution 1300–2050* (Cambridge, U.K.: Cambridge University Press, 2001), 114–31.

39. Epkenhans, *Die wilhelminische Flottenrüstung*, 465; Peter-Christian Witt, *Die Finanzpolitik des Deutschen Reiches von 1903 bis 1913. Eine Studie zur Innenpolitik des Wilhelminischen Deutschland* (Lübeck and Hamburg: Matthiesen, 1970), 142–43.

40. Cited in Volker Berghahn, "Zu den Zielen des deutschen Flottenbaus unter Wilhelm II," *Historische Zeitschrift* 210 (1970): 91.

41. Cited in Epkenhans, *Die wilhelminische Flottenrüstung*, 361 and 391.

42. Holger H. Herwig, *"Luxury" Fleet: The Imperial German Navy 1888–1918* (London: Humanity Books, 1987), pp. 106–7.

43. Epkenhans, *Die wilhelminische Flottenrüstung*, 453, 455, and 461.

44. *Handbuch der deutschen Militärgeschichte*, vol. 3, part V, 119.

45. Herwig, *"Luxury" Fleet*, 75.

46. Cited in Hans Mohs, ed., *General-Feldmarschall Alfred Graf von Waldersee in seinem militärischen Wirken* (2 vols., Berlin: R. Eisenschmidt, 1929), 2: 388, entry for 25 January 1898.

47. Cited in Berghahn and Deist, eds., *Rüstung im Zeichen der wilhelminischen Weltpolitik*, 360, comment of 28 November 1911.

48. For a brief overview, see Holger H. Herwig, "From Tirpitz Plan to Schlieffen Plan: Some Observations on German Military Planning," *Journal of Strategic Studies* 9 (1986): 53–63.

49. Scheer to Wilhelm II, 4 July 1916, BA-MA, Nachlass Levetzow, N 239, box 19, vol. 2.

50. Holtzendorff's memorandum, 22 December 1916, BA-MA, RM 47, vol. 772.

51. See Holger H. Herwig, "Total Rhetoric, Limited War: Germany's U-Boat Campaign, 1917–1918," in Roger Chickering, ed., *Great War, Total War: Combat and Mobilization on the Western Front, 1914–1918* (Cambridge, U.K.: Cambridge University Press, 2000), 189–206.

52. BA-MA, Nachlass Förste, vol. 15.

53. For interwar submarine developments, see Holger H. Herwig, "Innovation Ignored: The Submarine Problem. Germany, Britain, and the United States, 1919–1939," in Williamson Murray and Allan R. Millett, eds., *Military Innovation in the Interwar Period* (Cambridge, U.K.: Cambridge University Press, 1996), 227–64.

54. See Siegfried Breyer, *Der Z-Plan* (Wölfersheim-Berstadt: Podzun-Pallas, 1996), 8–12.

55. Raeder's comments of 3 September 1939, BA-MA, PG 32023 Case 103, p. 43.

56. See Holger H. Herwig, "Germany and the Battle of the Atlantic," Roger Chickering, Stig Förster, and Bernd Greiner, eds., *A World at Total War: Global Conflict and the Politics of Destruction, 1937–1945* (Cambridge, U.K.: Cambridge University Press, 2005), 71–87.

57. Karl-Dietrich Erdmann, ed., *Kurt Riezler. Tagebücher, Aufsätze, Dokumente* (Göttingen: Vandenhoeck & Ruprecht, 1972), 188, entry for 20 July 1914.

58. Colin S. Gray, *The Leverage of Sea Power: The Strategic Advantage of Navies in War* (New York: Free Press, 1992), 1, 25.

59. Colin S. Gray, *Modern Strategy* (Oxford, U.K.: Oxford University Press, 1999), 218–24.

60. Mahan, *Influence of Sea Power*, 25.

61. See John B. Hattendorf, Wayne P. Hughes, and Wolfgang Wegener, eds., *The Naval Strategy of the World War* (Annapolis, MD: Naval Institute Press, 1989).

62. Gray, *Leverage of Sea Power*, 57.

63. Andreas Hillgruber, "Der Faktor Amerika in Hitlers Strategie 1938–1941," *Aus Politik und Zeitgeschichte. Beilage zur Wochenzeitung "Das Parlament,"* 11 May 1966, 3.

64. See the analysis of the remarkable Chinese study *The Rise of Great Powers* by Andrew Erickson and Lyle Goldstein in this volume.

65. Ibid.

66. Office of the Secretary of Defense, *Annual Report to Congress: Military Power of the People's Republic of China 2007*, I, http://www.defenselink.mil/pubs/pdfs/070523-China-Military-Power-final.pdf.

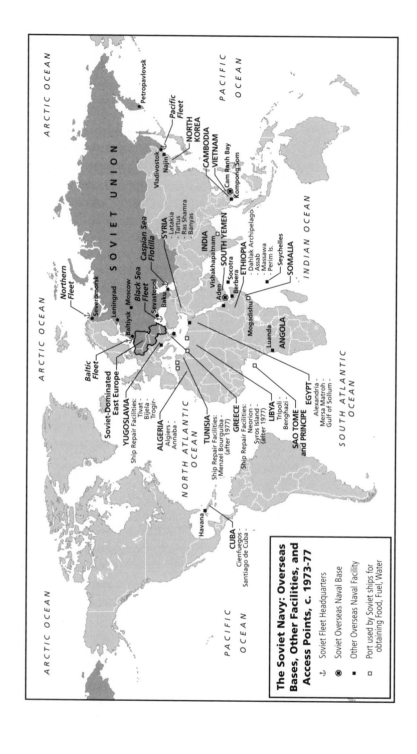

The Soviet Navy: Overseas Bases, Other Facilities, and Access Points, c. 1973-77

⚓ Soviet Fleet Headquarters

◉ Soviet Overseas Naval Base

■ Other Overseas Naval Facility

▢ Port used by Soviet ships for obtaining Food, Fuel, Water

Milan Vego

Soviet Russia: The Rise and Fall of a Superpower Navy

THE SOVIET NAVY UNDERWENT NUMEROUS CHANGES over its seventy-plus-year existence. Its rather abrupt and frequent changes in organization and doctrine must be explained within the broader framework of policy and strategy as determined by the Communist Party's top leadership, the country's economic policies, changes in the international security environment, and the navy's role and influence within the Soviet armed forces as a whole.

The Soviet navy's development was also heavily affected by the country's maritime position. One of the major problems for the development of a strong navy was the extremely unfavorable geostrategic position of tsarist Russia and the new Soviet state that emerged in the aftermath of World War I and the Russian Civil War (1918–20). The Soviet Union stretched for more than nine thousand miles and eleven time zones across two continents. Its seaboard encompassed four regions, each widely separated from the others. Hence, the Soviet navy was divided among four far-flung maritime theaters/fleets: the Arctic, the Baltic, the Black Sea, and the Pacific plus a flotilla in the Caspian Sea. The operating areas of three of these fleets were located near or above the Arctic Circle. To make the situation worse, because of the long distances and choke points dominated by potentially hostile powers, the various Soviet fleets were unable to come to one another's aid in case of war. The Soviet navy had relatively free access to the open ocean in the Arctic. However, the climatic conditions and weather adversely affected the employment of surface ships in Arctic waters.

Compared with what it had been before 1914, Russia's position in the Baltic was seriously weakened in the aftermath of the Bolshevik takeover of power in November 1917. Between 1918 and 1939, the Soviets controlled only Leningrad (St. Petersburg today) and its immediate surroundings in the Gulf of Finland, or about ninety-five miles of coast.[1] This situation changed in June 1940, when Soviet troops invaded the Baltic States and acquired a number of bases for their Baltic Fleet. The Soviets further strengthened their naval position in the Baltic in the aftermath of World War II by virtue of their control over Poland and East Germany. However, after the breakup of the Soviet Union, the former Soviet navy left its naval bases on the island of Rügen (East Germany) and at Świnoujście (Stettin) in Poland. By then the three formerly Soviet Baltic republics (Estonia, Latvia, and Lithuania) had obtained their independence and denied the use of their ports and airfields to the new Russian navy and to Russian land-based aircraft.

The Beginnings, 1921–25

Communist rule was established in Russia in the aftermath of the Bolsheviks' bloody coup d'état against the provisional Russian government established in February 1917. The Russian Baltic Fleet then consisted of four battleships under construction, four battle cruisers in service, and four light cruisers under construction. In the Black Sea, the Russian fleet comprised two battleships (one in service and one under construction). In addition, the Russian navy had in service twenty-four submarines, forty destroyers, and two training cruisers.[2]

The new Bolshevik regime, led by Vladimir I. Lenin, formally disbanded the tsarist army in January 1918 and created the Workers' and Peasants' Red Army (RKKA). About two-thirds of all the commanding officers in the RKKA were former tsarist officers. In fact, the Bolsheviks would not have been successful without having a large number of former tsarist officers and noncommissioned officers (NCOs) fighting on their side during the bloody civil war in 1918–21.[3]

In the aftermath of the civil war, the remnants of the tsarist fleet were in a state of utter chaos and decay due to the turmoil in the country and extremely poor state of the economy. By the end of 1921, naval manpower had been reduced from 180,000 to 35,000 men. Some ships were under-manned by as much as 60 to 80 percent.[4] The Soviets gradually recommis-sioned three (*Gangut*-class) battleships while the remaining large ships were broken up.[5] At that time, some naval offices and sailors demanded a num-ber of reforms in society and the restoration of the Baltic Fleet. After the Bolshevik rulers rejected their demands, the sailors mutinied at the naval base of Kronshtadt (March 1921). The mutiny was brutally crushed by troops led by Mikhail Tukhachevsky, later a marshal; about six thousand muti-neers were killed in the fighting or summarily executed. One result of the Kronshtadt mutiny was that the loyalty of the naval forces to the new regime became highly suspect.[6] This was the main reason that the Bolshevik regime encouraged about ten thousand Komsomol members to enlist in the navy between 1923 and 1927. For example, about 70 percent of the Baltic Fleet sail-ors were Komsomol members in 1928. The junior naval commanders were imbued with communist ideas but were inexperienced and largely unedu-cated.[7] The naval officer corps was still largely composed of former tsarist officers, and they were kept under close surveillance by the political com-missars. They were often called to face so-called tribunals where their loyalty was scrutinized.[8]

In 1921 the Soviet naval forces formally had on the active list 223 combat ships (including 1 battleship, 24 destroyers and torpedo boats, 13 submarines, 101 minesweepers, and 11 gunboats) plus 152 auxiliaries.[9] The navy's budget in 1922–23 was only 1.4 percent of the total state budget (in contrast, the army's share was 14.8 percent).[10] By the end of 1924 the RKKA's naval forces had in service 2 old battleships, 2 cruisers, 17 destroyers, 14 submarines, 45 other warships, and 98 auxiliary ships.[11] The main missions of the RKKA's naval forces were defending the maritime borders of the new state, defending sea communications, and providing support to ground forces on the coast. The main theater in case of war was the Baltic Sea.[12] The new regime did not have naval forces in the Black Sea, the Pacific Ocean, or the Arctic.[13]

A major reason for the neglect of the navy in the early 1920s was a lack of financial resources because of the weak economy and because, as just men-tioned, the top party leaders did not trust the navy.[14] Other negative influ-ences on the development of Soviet naval forces in the early 1920s were the utopian character of Bolshevik doctrine and the lack of a sound theory of naval warfare as well as a systematic collection of lessons learned from World War I. The lack of understanding of the importance of naval power for the development of the Soviet state on the part of the Bolshevik leaders presented a significant problem for the development of the navy.[15]

The Soviet leadership realized early on that the development of modern armed forces including the Navy would require collaboration with their "bourgeois" enemies in the west. Hence, the Soviets tried as early as 1921–22 to establish close cooperation with the German navy (Reichsmarine). In the spring and summer of 1926, Russo-German talks on naval cooperation led to a visit by a German naval mission led by Rear Adm. Arno Spindler. Among other things, the Soviets requested plans of U-boats and operational experience with U-boats. The Germans agreed to provide plans for the B-III-class U-boat, one of the most successful classes in World War I (this design eventually led to the development of the Type VII U-boat, the mainstay of the German U-boat force in World War II). The Soviets based their S-class (also popularly called *Nemka*, or the "German Girl") of submarines on the B-III design.[16]

Consolidation Phase, 1927–32

By the late 1920s the new Communist regime in Russia had consolidated its power. Josef Stalin defeated his main opponents within the party but still did not obtain undisputed control. The Soviet economy began to improve.

The first five-year naval construction program was formally approved by the highest Soviet political leadership in November 1926. It envisioned a fleet comprising one obsolete battleship, two cruisers, four destroyers, twelve submarines, eighteen patrol craft, and thirty motor torpedo boats (MTBs).[17] By the end of 1928 the RKKA's naval forces had in service ninety-eight combatant ships and 28,000 men. The navy's share of total military expenditures was increased from 8.7 to 11–13 percent.[18]

The decision of the XV Party Congress in late 1927 to speed up rapid industrialization also meant that the naval construction program had to be revised to adapt to the country's Five-Year Plan (1928–32). The construction program during the first Five-Year Plan envisaged completion of the unfinished ships of the former tsarist navy and repair and modernization of one battleship and some cruisers and destroyers. This part of the plan was completed. However, the other components of the plan—conversion of one damaged battleship into a fast battle cruiser, and of one battle cruiser and a training ship into aircraft carriers carrying fifty and forty-two aircraft, respectively—were not carried out.[19] In the late 1920s the Soviet navy's budget was too small to start construction of any new ships. Total expenditures for ship repair and construction were less than that for clothing allowances. The Navy's commissar, Romuald Muklevich, complained in a top-secret report on the 1928–29 naval budget that the sums assigned to the navy were completely inadequate for its actual needs. To make the situation worse, in July 1929 Stalin cut naval expenditures by 40 percent, shifting 85 million rubles from its budget to tank production. Muklevich protested the decision personally to Stalin, however, and the funds were restored.[20]

In the late 1920s and the early 1930s the Soviets continued their efforts to obtain badly needed technical assistance for their navy from several western countries. In 1929–30 they obtained some equipment from private German companies although the Reichsmarine was a reluctant partner.[21] The Soviets were more successful in getting technical aid from fascist Italy. In the fall of 1930 a Soviet naval delegation visited Italy. Among other things, the Soviets were interested in obtaining information on Italian torpedoes, antiaircraft guns, and mines as well as plans for modern submarines, destroyers, and cruisers. Another Soviet naval delegation visited Italy in 1932 seeking to obtain plans for submarines, cruisers, and destroyers. Here too, however, the Soviets had only limited success.[22]

Old Versus Young School

In the 1920s, two schools of thought emerged on how best to employ the RKKA's naval forces in defense of the Soviet state. The traditional or "Old School," as embraced by the former tsarist officers, reflected Mahanian views on the command of the sea. The leading proponents of the Old School were the officer Nikolai L. Klado and Soviet Naval Academy professors Boris B. Gervais and Mikhail A. Petrov. Gervais and Petrov contended that a strategy of relying on light surface forces, submarines, and land-based aircraft could not be successful against a strong opponent at sea. Instead, they advocated building a big-ship navy sufficiently strong that it could at least obtain command of Soviet coastal waters in a dispute against a major Western naval power. Although Gervais recognized that aircraft carriers were the new capital ships, he still believed that they could not replace the battleship for gaining and maintaining command of the sea. Petrov initially agreed with Gervais's argument but then sided with those who claimed that the aircraft carrier was the capital ship of the future. Both Mikhail Frunze and Aleksandr A. Svechin supported the eventual building of aircraft carriers for the Soviet naval forces when the country's economy allowed it.[23]

The main ideas of the Old School were clearly unrealistic because such a fleet was impossible to build in view of the extreme weakness of the Soviet economy in the 1920s. The People's Commissar of the RKKA's naval forces, V. I. Zof, in an address to the students of the naval academy in 1925, said, "You speak of aircraft carriers and the construction of the new types of ships . . . at the same time completely ignoring the economic situation of our country and corresponding condition of our technical means."[24] The fleet in the Baltic was so weak that it could be used only for passive defense of the coast in the Gulf of Finland using immobile ships, floating batteries, and the few coastal fortifications.[25] Muklevich warned in 1927 that the classical command-of-the-sea theory was unrealistic to the Soviet situation. In his view, the proper response to the threat of an enemy amphibious landing was to have a small navy to cooperate with the army in executing a common war plan.[26] After Mikhail Frunze replaced Leon Trotsky as People's Commissar for Military Affairs in 1925, he emphasized the Leninist doctrine of the unity of armed forces. This in practice meant that the army would dominate strategic planning. The doctrine of command of the seas as propounded by Mahan was denounced as inherently capitalistic and entirely unacceptable to Soviet naval forces.[27] In the end the Communist party decided that because a big-ship navy as advocated by the Old School was infeasible, the interim solution was to adopt a "small-war" strategy focusing on creating, in key coastal areas, so-called mine-artillery positions supported with light forces to provide defense of the country's sea approaches.[28]

Incompatibility between the strategic concepts propounded by proponents of the Old School and the all-too-evident deplorable condition of Soviet naval forces, combined with the inability of the country's economy to fund a fleet composed of modern surface combatants, led to the emergence of the Soviet Young (or "proletarian") School of naval warfare. The Young School's advocates contended that Communist principles should guide naval doctrine and that the Russian civil war could provide a useful body of experience from which to draw lessons for the future navy. The navy should play a minor role in the country's defense.[29]

The leading proponents of the Young School, such as Ivan S. Isakov, A. P. Aleksandrov, Ivan Ludri, Konstantin Dushenov, and A. Yakimychev, were all recent students of Petrov and Gervais. Yet they attacked the concept of the command of the sea propounded by the advocates of the Old School. In their view naval blockade could not decide questions of sea control. Hence, the fleet should concentrate on taking part in a general battle to be fought largely on the land and in the air.[30] They called for a navy composed of light surface combatants, submarines, mines, and land-based naval aircraft. They also advocated employing submarines jointly with air forces against large surface ships.[31] They believed that both the concept of the naval blockade and the general fleet action between opposing battlefleets as advocated by Mahan for contesting command of the sea had become obsolete, along with the theory of command of the sea itself. In their view, the advent of submarines and aircraft had made big ships obsolete, or at best made them able to play only the subordinate role of providing combat support to the light strike forces.[32] The Young School's ideas were based on a mixture of Marxist-Leninist teachings on dialectic materialism and the principles of "partisan" (guerrilla) warfare at sea. In their view, decisive battles like those of Tsushima in 1904 and Jutland in 1916 were things of the past. They advocated building a fleet composed of submarines and small surface ships. Such a fleet would be cheaper to build and maintain.[33] Despite the shared name, the Soviet Young School's ideas were not identical to the ideas of the French Young School of the 1880s. Some theoreticians argue that the Soviet strategy was defensive, not offensive, as the French strategy was.[34]

Young School Dominant, 1933–36

The Young School was dominant from 1933 to 1936. The proponents of the Old School of strategy were removed from the naval educational institutions. During Stalin's purges in the late 1930s, many vocal advocates of the Old School paid with their lives for the "obduracy of their reactionary thoughts."[35]

The victory of the Young School was shown by the composition of the naval construction program that coincided with the country's second Five-Year Plan (1933–37) drafted in 1932. The Navy's share of the defense budget increased from 4.7 to 8.9 percent in 1933. The first version of the plan called for, among other things, the construction of 281 submarines. The final plan envisaged construction of 8 cruisers, 32 destroyer leaders and destroyers, 355 submarines of various sizes, 194 MTBs, 4 monitors, and 6 minelayers. This program was later scaled down by reducing the number of destroyer leaders and submarines. However, fewer than half of the ships were eventually delivered. They also had poorly designed weapons and protection and inadequate maneuverability.[36]

Stalin's Shift to a Big-Ship Navy, 1937–40

A major change in Soviet naval policy started in the mid-1930s as a result of both internal and external developments. By 1934 Stalin had overcome much of the opposition to his personal dictatorship. At the same time, there was a steady worsening of the political and military situation in Europe and the Far East. The rise of Nazi Germany, the nonaggression pact between Poland and Germany in 1934, the expansionist policies of Japan in the Far East, and the Anti-Komintern pact signed by Germany, Italy, and Japan in November 1936 led Moscow to embark on a policy of seeking closer relations with the Western democracies. Diplomatic relations were established with the United States, United Kingdom, Romania, and Czechoslovakia.

During the Spanish Civil War (1936–39), it was evident that Soviet surface naval forces were inadequate to counter the German and Italian naval presence off the Spanish coast. The new naval race had started by the mid-1930s when Japan and Italy revoked naval treaties they had once signed. Britain and Germany signed a naval agreement in 1935 that allowed Germany to greatly expand its fleet. In addition, the United States, Great Britain, and France adopted new fleet-building programs. Stalin's growing megalomania perhaps played a large role in his decision to embark on a huge naval buildup, including gigantic shipyard construction. Despite many claims to the contrary, the Spanish Civil War was not a major factor in Stalin's decision.[37] In fact, Stalin made that decision in May 1936; it was not based on military needs but on his intent to enhance the Soviet Union's status as a great power.[38] Stalin reportedly did not share his plans about the big-ship navy with others in the Soviet leadership.[39]

By the end of 1935 Stalin became preoccupied with plans to build a mighty oceangoing fleet. In his view, the fleet had to be large enough to obtain sea control in all four fleet areas. Consequently, Stalin decided to assign a rather large share of the defense budget to the navy. By 1939 the navy's expenditures amounted to 7.5 billion rubles out of 18.5 billion for all defense expenditures, or almost 5 percent of the entire state budget (153.1 billion rubles).[40]

The first hint of these changes in Soviet naval strategy was a speech delivered by a junior submarine officer at the 17th Party Congress in Moscow in January 1934 on the need to have an oceangoing fleet.[41] In December 1935 *Pravda* published an article concerning large oceangoing fleets that implied that the temporary weakness of the Soviet navy would soon be overcome.[42] Additional evidence of Stalin's intentions was his decision to restore the navy's status as a separate service of the armed forces. In January 1935 the RKKA's naval forces in the Baltic, the Black Sea, and the Pacific were elevated to the status of independent fleets. The commander of Naval Forces directly controlled all the fleets and flotillas. Naval aviation, part of the air force since 1924, was transferred to the navy's control. In September 1935 the Soviet government reintroduced the system of personal ranks in the armed forces for the first time since 1918. With that decision the Soviet naval officer corps was formally created.[43] At the turn of 1937–38, the Main Naval Staff (Glavny Shtab Voenno-Morskogo Flota) and the People's Commissariat for the Navy (Narodny Kommissariat VMF) were recreated by Stalin. This further enhanced the prestige and role of the navy within the Soviet armed forces.

In February 1936 two alternative plans for a large oceangoing navy were prepared: one by the naval experts of the RKKA's general staff and one by the staff of the commander of Naval Forces. On 15 April the navy high command presented its first draft of the fleet program to be completed by 1947. It included the building of no fewer than 15 battleships, 22 heavy cruisers, 31 light cruisers, 162 destroyers and destroyer leaders, 412 submarines, and many small vessels and auxiliaries totaling 1,727,000 tons.[44] Other sources claim that the first draft of the new naval building program submitted by the navy's commander, Adm. V. M. Orlov, in early February 1936 called for the construction of 16 battleships and 12 heavy cruisers during the next two Five-Year Plans.[45] Chief of the general staff of the RKKA Marshal Alexander I. Yegorov proposed an even larger fleet, some 1,868,000 tons, including 6 aircraft carriers—2 for the Northern Fleet and 4 for the Pacific Fleet. In contrast, Orlov argued that only 2 carriers of 8,000 tons would be sufficient for the Pacific Fleet.[46] In June 1936 the number of battleships was increased to 24 and the number of light cruisers reduced to 20. The revised plan also included construction of 182 destroyers and 344 submarines. By August 1939 the fourth or fifth modification of the plan envisaged construction of about 700 combat ships and 2.5 million tons, plus several hundred auxiliaries.[47] On 27 May 1936 the decision was made to assign about 450,000 tons of the new ships to the Pacific Fleet; 400,000 tons to the Baltic Fleet; 300,000 tons to the Black Sea Fleet; and 150,000 tons to the Northern Fleet, for a total of 1,300,000 tons.[48]

In November 1936 Orlov gave a speech at an extraordinary All-Soviet Congress on the need to have a big fleet comprising all types of warships because of the worsening of the international situation and what he called "imperialist encirclement." He also pointed out the vulnerability of the Soviet maritime borders vis-à-vis Germany, Italy, and Japan.[49] Adm. P. A. Smirnov, the new and short-lived commander in chief of the Soviet navy, stated in 1938 that the main task of the fleet was to ensure the "impregnability of the sea approaches to our sacred land, to guard the motherland from attempts of attack from the sea by the fascist plunderers, to guarantee the travel of trading vessels under the red flag in any part of the world."[50]

By 1937 the Soviets had the largest submarine fleet in the world. Between 1933 and 1938 Soviet shipyards produced about 380 submarines (70 large, 200 medium, and 110 small).[51] However, Stalin was never completely committed to the ideas of the Young School and their emphasis on building a large submarine fleet. Hence, he directed the construction of heavy cruisers (ultimately six were built) and the refitting of three tsarist battleships in the late stages of the second Five-Year Plan.[52] The third Five-Year Plan contemplated the construction of fifteen battleships. In July 1938 the first of these 59,130-ton battleships (*Sovetsky Soyuz*), armed with 16-inch guns, was launched; by 1939 three more battleships of the same class were laid down. The three new 32,870-ton heavy cruisers (*Kronshtadt*-class) armed with 305-mm guns were in fact designed as battleships.[53]

Unfortunately, however, the Soviet shipyards were unable to build ships greater than 30,000 tons. The Soviet steelworks did not have experience in producing high-grade armored plates, and there were problems in producing fire control and communications equipment.[54] The battleship construction program was clearly overly ambitious. Even under the best conditions, none of the battleships laid down in 1938 and 1939 could have been completed within a decade. For example, the construction of the four *Sovetsky Soyuz*–class dreadnoughts required about one-third of the defense budget in 1940. By July 1940 the Soviet naval building program was scaled down; the number of battleships was reduced to ten, battle cruisers from sixteen to eight, and cruisers to only fourteen. However, for the first time, the Soviets included in their plan the construction of two small aircraft carriers, both to be assigned to the Pacific Fleet.[55]

Because of the steadily worsening international situation in Europe after the summer of 1940, the Soviet naval high command wanted to stop construction of all battleships and thereby free yard capacities for building a large number of light forces and submarines. However, Stalin rejected this and refused to scrap two battle cruisers, still two years away from being completed. He also refused to cancel work on the battleship *Sovetsky Soyuz* and ordered the construction of the cruisers to continue.[56]

In the late 1930s the Soviet top political and military leadership discussed the construction of aircraft carriers, but the decision on whether to build them was delayed until the problem of their design was resolved.[57] The former People's Commissar for the Navy, Adm. Nikolai G. Kuznetsov, in his memoirs claimed the construction of carriers in the third Five-Year Plan was postponed until the last years of the plan because of the technical inadequacies of the Soviet shipbuilding industry. He also made clear that the construction of aircraft carriers was fully approved by Stalin but later was cut out of the program for unspecified reasons and would be covered in the third

(1938–41) and fourth plans instead. Stalin, according to Kuznetsov, tended to underrate the role of aircraft carriers. He underestimated the danger to ships from the air.[58] Kuznetsov also claimed that the real reason for the shift to build an oceangoing fleet was the lessons of the Spanish Civil War. In his words, "it became especially clear how important the sea was for us and how badly we needed a powerful fleet."[59]

The Soviets intensified their efforts to obtain modern naval weapons and equipment from several Western countries in the 1930s. They were especially interested in acquiring designs for battleships and heavy cruisers, and later also aircraft carriers. Great Britain did not show any interest in helping the Soviets. The French were reluctant to provide the Soviets with the plans of their cruisers, large destroyers, and submarines or to provide help with the development of torpedoes.[60] However, the Soviets indirectly obtained plans for a submarine built by the German-owned design bureau IvS at The Hague, Netherlands. This design was subsequently used for the construction of the Soviet series IX/N S-class submarines.[61]

Italy was most eager to positively respond to Soviet requests for naval technical assistance. In the 1930s the Italians provided much assistance to the Soviet construction of cruisers and destroyers. Admiral Orlov proposed in 1933 to purchase blueprints of the *Condottieri*-class light cruisers. This request was eventually granted by the fascist Italian regime, and the plans served as the basis for six 9,880-ton *Kirov*-class cruisers (Project 26, built between 1935 and 1944).[62]

Already in 1936 the Soviets began a concerted effort to obtain from the United States, through a private company, the plans, material, and equipment for two or potentially three large battleships. Unfortunately for the Soviets, their intermediary inspired a notable lack of confidence on the part of U.S. shipbuilders. The U.S. Navy also did not want to declassify a large amount of confidential technical information to make this unusual commercial venture a success. The chief of the Bureau of Ordnance and the director of Naval Intelligence took strong and continuing exception to helping a totalitarian regime. They especially opposed any move to strengthen the Soviet navy.[63] By June 1939 negotiations had broken down; after two and a half years of fruitless talks, the Russians lost all hope of getting assistance from the United States.[64]

Soviet–German naval cooperation resumed in the wake of the Non-aggression Pact signed between these two countries in August 1939. The Soviets wanted to obtain German support for their naval buildup, then under way, in exchange for manganese ore and oil.[65] In October 1939 a sixty-member Soviet naval delegation visited Nazi Germany. They came with a long shopping list that included designs for the *Bismarck*-class battleship, the *Scharnhorst*-class battle cruiser, and the never-finished *Graf Zeppelin*–class aircraft carrier. However, the Germans reluctantly sold the Soviets only the half-completed cruiser *Luetzow* in May 1940 (later renamed by the Soviets as *Petropavlovsk*).[66]

In August 1938 the leading proponents of both the Young School and the Old School were publicly indicted in the press and subsequently purged. Stalin, in his typical way, apparently wanted to physically eliminate these proponents and thereby open the way to the so-called Soviet School of naval warfare that would underpin the big-ship navy to be built in the ensuing two Five-Year Plans.[67] This new school of naval warfare emerged just before the beginning of World War II. Its leading proponent, Vladimir A. Belli, professor at the naval academy, was also one of the leading advocates of the Young School. He arbitrarily selected the most important tenets of both the Old and Young schools and in the process repudiated his own views on the subject. The key part of the Soviet School as explained by Belli was gradual attrition of the stronger fleet to bring about equalization in strength. This, in turn, would allow the Soviets to fight a decisive naval engagement with a good prospect of defeating the enemy's main forces and thereby gain full or general command of the sea—hence the need to build a big-ship navy. However, the Soviets would require at least a decade to build such a navy starting in 1937–38. The proponents of the Soviet School argued for applying an active fleet-in-being concept, aimed at obtaining local control of the key sea areas first. This would be followed by obtaining control of ever-larger sea areas adjacent to the country's coast. In contrast to the Young School, submarines and aircraft would be employed to provide support to the main forces, composed of battleships and heavy cruisers. The Soviet School theory was never tested during World War II. None of the battleships was completed, and no keel for an aircraft carrier was ever laid down.[68] By 1940, in fact, the worsening of the strategic situation combined with the perennial problems of the Soviet shipbuilding industry led to additional reductions in the number of large surface combatants to be built. The focus shifted toward construction of smaller ships.[69]

During the Great Patriotic War (as the Soviets refer to World War II), the Soviet navy fought in four maritime theaters and on rivers. However, in none of them did Soviet naval forces make a strategic contribution to the final victory. The navy had a significant role in the defense of Leningrad and in the defense of major bases and ports in the Baltic region and the Baltic Sea in

1941–42. Most actions conducted by Soviet naval forces pertained to protecting the army flank, conducting small-scale amphibious landings, securing communications in coastal waters, and attacking enemy sea communications.[70] This rather poor performance was largely due to poor training and inferiority in materiel. However, perhaps the main reason was the lack of initiative shown by naval commanders or a lack of offensive spirit.[71] This was especially the case in the Baltic region, where the Germans had weak naval forces. The Soviet navy also lost some of its best-educated and experienced commanders in Stalin's purges in 1937–38.

By late 1944 the Soviet navy had in service some 2,490 ships and craft, including 175 submarines, 4 battleships, 9 cruisers, 5 destroyer leaders, and 48 destroyers. Some 118 ships were lost in the conflict.[72]

The End of Stalin's Era, 1946–53

After the end of the war, and in the early Cold War, Moscow considered U.S. and British "imperialism" to be its most probable adversary in the future. This assessment was the core principle of Soviet military policy until the end of the 1980s. The United States became the principal potential enemy of the Soviet Union and all other Communist-ruled countries and "progressive" movements in the world. The United States, in fact, was declared the successor of German fascism in its quest for world domination.[73]

In the aftermath of World War II the Soviet geostrategic position on land was vastly improved over what it had been prior to the war. The Soviets occupied a dominant position in Eurasia by virtue of their enormous land power. A major part of the Soviet ground forces was stationed in western Russia and in Eastern Europe, posing a permanent danger to Western Europe. The Soviets developed a strategic bomber force and modernized territorial air defenses. Stalin also decided to quickly build up deterrent and defensive naval forces in all four Soviet fleets.[74] Strategically the Soviet Union was inferior to Western powers in terms of airpower, nuclear weapons, and naval strength. However, victory over Nazi Germany and Japan only further increased Stalin's interest in creating a navy capable of operating on the ocean. The Soviets also wanted to improve their maritime position in the Black Sea and the Mediterranean. Among other things, they requested access to bases in the Turkish Straits. At the conference of the Allied foreign ministers held in September 1945 in London, Soviet Foreign Minister Molotov, on Stalin's instructions, demanded a Soviet trusteeship of the former Italian colony of Tripolitania (Libya) on the pretext that the British should not have sole control of sea lines of communications in the Mediterranean and that protection for Soviet merchant shipping in the area was needed.[75]

The Soviets acquired a much more favorable maritime position within the Baltic and to some extent in the Far East. However, access to the open waters of the oceans, except in the Arctic, was still controlled by potentially hostile powers. Hence, the USSR's maritime flanks were largely open to attack by Western carrier-borne aircraft and amphibious forces. The Soviet response to the threat of a seaborne invasion would be to deploy in depth a large number of cruiser/destroyer surface attack groups, torpedo-armed aircraft, torpedo boats, and submarines. The Soviets reportedly projected in 1948 that they would have a force of 1,200 submarines, all but 180 of which would be deployed in defense roles in the four fleet areas.[76]

Stalin's prewar big-navy views and the Old School views of the Soviet senior officer corps were confirmed and strengthened by the experiences of World War II.[77] Already in August 1944 the operations staff of the Soviet navy presented the navy's commander, Admiral Kuznetsov, with a draft plan for the development of the navy for the first decade after 1945. This plan provided for the construction of, among other things, 9 battleships, 12 battle cruisers, 30 heavy cruisers, 60 light cruisers, 9 heavy and 6 light aircraft carriers, 485 submarines, 144 large destroyers, and 222 destroyers.[78] In October 1944 Kuznetsov presented to the party's Central Committee a draft plan for naval construction for 1945–47 that envisaged the completion of the ships launched under the provisions of the plan for 1936–40 plus several more.[79] In August 1945 he prepared a ten-year shipbuilding plan sent for the approval of the government. The Soviet navy's staff then planned the construction of 168 large, 204 medium, and 123 small submarines. At that time, only 1 large submarine was under construction and 7 (S-class) medium submarines. Eventually 65 small (M-class) submarines were laid down. However, not all were completed.[80]

The need for the Soviet navy to have aircraft carriers was expressed by a high-ranking naval official writing in the influential journal *Voyennaya mysl (Military Thought)* in 1946. The author stated "the conditions of modern war at sea demand the mandatory participation in the combat operations of navies of powerful carrier forces, using them for striking devastating blows against the naval forces of the enemy as well as for the contest within his aviation. Both at sea and near one's bases these tasks can only be carried out by carrier aviation."[81] The first postwar naval construction program for 1946–55 was essentially based on the proposal Kuznetsov submitted in August 1944. The Soviets then contemplated building 9 battleships, 12 battle cruisers, 60 light cruisers, 9 large carriers, 6 light carriers, 222 destroyers, and about 490 submarines.[82]

The Soviets also introduced new naval technologies that had a significant impact on the construction program then under way. Jet and rocket propulsion for aircraft was adopted. With considerable help from former German scientists, the Soviets introduced ballistic and cruise missiles. They also produced nuclear warheads for bombs and missiles. New electronic sensors and communications equipment were also fitted on board Soviet warships in the early 1950s. The most significant development was the advent of nuclear propulsion for submarines and surface ships. The first nuclear-powered surface ship was a large icebreaker (*Lenin*) completed in 1958.[83] In September 1952 two separate design bureaus were created: one for developing a nuclear submarine and one for a submarine nuclear propulsion plant. The first Soviet nuclear-powered submarine, the 3,110/4,070-ton *November*-class (Project 627), was laid down in September 1955 and completed in 1959.[84]

Khrushchev's Era, 1954–64

In the mid- and late 1950s, Soviet military policy and vision of the future cold war were greatly influenced by U.S. and Western technological advances in developing nuclear-capable carrier-based aircraft, cruise missiles, and nuclear-powered ballistic missile submarines (SSBNs). The Soviets decided to counter these threats to their homeland and to neutralize the possibility of Normandy-scale amphibious landings on their shores.[85] Allegedly, the Korean War awakened Soviet naval planners to the threat posed by the U.S. fast carriers to the Soviet homeland. The power and versatility of these carrier forces was shown in the Anglo-French attack on Suez in 1956 and the U.S. landing in Lebanon in 1958. The strategic mobility of carriers posed serious problems for Soviet naval forces.[86] By the late 1950s, the greatly improved capabilities of U.S. carriers to strike Soviet territory with nuclear weapons from the eastern Mediterranean and the southern reaches of the Norwegian Sea were the main reason for a shift in Soviet naval strategy. In 1957–58 the Soviets made a decision to rely on nuclear submarines, the only platforms capable of operating in the face of Western surface and air superiority; this required many changes in the naval construction program, including the cancellation or reduction of conventional submarines and surface ships projected in 1954.[87]

The introduction of nuclear propulsion for submarines had been delayed by Stalin's purported lack of appreciation for other than conventional forces.

It took almost three years after Stalin's death to formulate, approve, and produce suitable nuclear missiles and other nuclear weapons for the navy and nuclear propulsion for some of its submarines.[88] It was not until 1956 that the modernization program for the navy was given maximum attention. Zhukov told the delegates at the Party Congress that in building the navy "we hold that warfare in naval theaters of a future war will acquire immeasurably greater importance than was the case in the last war."[89]

After Stalin's death in March 1953, a ten-year program that aimed to create a balanced navy was proposed for 1955–64. This plan envisaged the construction of 9 aircraft carriers, 21 cruisers, 118 destroyers, and 324 submarines.[90] However, the Soviet top leadership soon made a decision to shift the focus of naval construction to submarines. Marshal Georgy Zhukov, the Soviet minister of defense, justified the decision by stating that "for the disruption of the sea and oceanic lines of communications a submarine fleet is needed. . . . These objectives cannot be laid upon surface ships. . . . To put forth a goal of strengthening the surface fleet is unreasonable."[91] The Soviets also downgraded the threat of "imperialist" invasion by land and sea. The highest priority was then given to countering the threat of nuclear strikes by U.S. Strategic Command (which comprised some 1,750 bombers in 1959).[92] In 1953 Khrushchev and Zhukov concluded that nuclear weapons would be employed in any general war. In their view, aircraft carriers and other large surface combatants were highly vulnerable to nuclear missiles; hence the Soviet navy should not build any of them. Khrushchev later revealed that it was in 1954 that the Communist Party made a decision to shift from what the Soviet top leadership considered "obsolete" surface ships to a navy based mainly on submarines.[93]

Technological advances, especially in nuclear weaponry, seem to be the primary reason for Khrushchev's decision to drastically reduce the size of the Soviet armed forces (about 5.8 million in 1955), thereby also releasing resources to the civilian economy.[94] During the Khrushchev era, the Soviets made three substantial reductions of their armed forces. In August 1955 Moscow announced the first of three major troop reductions, this one totaling some 640,000 men, to be completed by the end of that year.[95] In May 1956 the Soviet armed forces were reduced by an additional 1.2 million men. The cuts in 1956–57 included 375 naval vessels (mostly obsolete), which were mothballed.[96] The Soviet navy's personnel were reduced to less than 600,000. In January 1960, Khrushchev announced a third and final cut, of about 1.2 million men.[97]

The new Soviet policy announced by Khrushchev in 1960 put heavy emphasis on nuclear weapons. At the same time, the policy further reduced the role of conventional forces. Khrushchev informed the Supreme Soviet that submarine forces had assumed great importance while surface ships could no longer play the part they once had. The Soviet top leadership decided to eliminate from the navy not only the majority of old ships with conventional armament but also bomber, mine-torpedo, and fighter aviation; a large part of the navy's coastal artillery; and naval air defense. The decision was also made to cut up for scrap metal not only all major conventionally armed ships but also ships that had already been built, even ones that had just passed their acceptance trials.[98]

With respect to their submarine program, the Soviets built some 230 Whiskey-class (Project 613) medium and 32 Zulu-class (Project 611) large oceangoing submarines between 1951 and 1958, in addition to the Quebec-class (Project 615) coastal boats. These submarines would be deployed in three layers in defense of the country's sea approaches.[99] The Soviets reportedly planned to build some 1,200 submarines by 1965. However, already in 1954 they had drastically scaled down the construction of the Whiskeys. Eventually only 260 of these submarines were completed. The successor to the Zulus was the Foxtrot-class (Project 641), of which 50 to 60 were built.[100]

The commissioning of the USS *Nautilus* in 1954 led Khrushchev to direct the navy to initiate a crash program of nuclear propulsion for submarines. The first nuclear-powered ballistic missile submarines, the Hotel class (Project 658), were also introduced into service in the late 1950s. The Soviets also designed the first nuclear submarines armed with cruise missiles, the Echo-I class.[101] The propulsion plants of the first generation of nuclear boats, November-class SSNs and Hotel-class SSBNs, were relatively primitive. The Echo-class (Project 659) SSGNs were an interim solution and had limited operational value.[102]

Shift in the Soviet Navy's Mission

In late 1955 Khrushchev appointed as commander in chief of the navy Adm. Sergei G. Gorshkov, a wartime commander of the Azov Flotilla and postwar commander of the Black Sea Fleet. Gorshkov was known as a strong supporter of introducing missile technology into the navy.[103] He was well known for his uncommon strength of will and remarkable intellect.[104] Although it was not immediately apparent, Gorshkov did not share the leadership's new emphasis on a submarine-centric Soviet navy. During his decades-long tenure at the helm of the navy, he attempted and succeeded not only in greatly expanding the resources devoted to it by the Soviet state but also in moving it once again in the direction of a balanced, highly robust blue water navy with a global presence.

Gorshkov had a hard fight. He wrote:

> There were some influential authorities who considered that with the appearance of atomic weapons the navy had completely lost its value as a branch of the armed forces. According to their views, all of the basic missions in a future war allegedly could be fully resolved without the participation of the navy, and even in those circumstances when to do so would require the conduct of combat operations on the broad expanses of the seas and ocean. At that time it was frequently asserted that only missiles emplaced in ground launching sites were required for the destruction of surface striking forces and even submarines.[105]

The ballistic missile proponents even considered that amphibious landings had completely lost their importance and that allegedly the task they had formerly carried out could be accomplished in nuclear war by air assaults or by the armored personnel carriers of the ground troops.

Gorshkov acknowledged in 1961 that large surface ships that had lost their combat value under contemporary conditions had been rightly scrapped, but he was thinking mainly of old battleships, not the new *Sverdlovsk*-class heavy cruisers. Four of these cruisers were indeed scrapped, but fifteen remained in service. Gorshkov clearly believed that cruisers still had a significant role to play in modern naval warfare.[106]

The Cuban missile crisis of October 1962 had a significant effect on Soviet naval policies. The Soviets concluded that their threat of employing submarines had proven ineffective and that they lacked sufficient surface forces to concentrate in Cuban waters. The Soviets were also mistaken in their belief that their nuclear capabilities would deter U.S. interference in such a crisis at sea. The lesson the Soviets drew from the crisis was the necessity of a balanced navy. In their view, if they were able to deploy much larger and more potent forces to Cuban waters, the outcome would have been much more favorable despite Soviet strategic nuclear inferiority.[107] The outcome of the crisis also illustrated that the Soviet policy of relying almost exclusively on nuclear weapons and ballistic missiles and the drastic reduction in the size and funding of conventional forces had been wrong all along.

In the mid-1960s, Gorshkov advocated a balanced fleet, one based on a need for other surface ships to enable submarines to carry out their missions. He emphasized that "modern submarines and missile carrying aircraft comprise the principal strike forces of the navy and are the essence of its power. Yet, there must be other forces besides the long range strike forces both for active defense against any enemy within the limits of the defense zone of a maritime theater, and for the comprehensive support of the operational activities of the main striking force of the navy. To such forces belong surface missile-armed ships and small craft, warships and aircraft for antisubmarine warfare, minesweepers, . . . etc."[108]

By mid-1963, after two years of persistent efforts, Gorshkov had essentially won the argument that surface ships were an indispensable part of the navy. This ensured the survival of the Soviet large surface ships.[109] Not only was he able to complete construction and retain most of the cruisers, but Gorshkov also convinced Khrushchev of the continuing importance of large surface warships in the nuclear era. Gorshkov's successor, Adm. Vladimir N. Chernavin, later revealed Gorshkov's efforts to defend the cruisers from scrapping in order to have a balanced navy, not just a submarine force; efforts that diminished his standing with Khrushchev.[110]

To counter the threat posed by the U.S. submarines armed with Polaris submarine-launched ballistic missiles (SLBMs), the Soviets decided to forwardly deploy their surface forces. Gorshkov explained in February 1963 that maritime defense of the USSR would depend on the outcome of engagements fought far away from Soviet shores. The task of other Soviet forces would be to prevent the launching of nuclear strikes against the "motherland." However, the Soviet navy was ill equipped and ill prepared for such a radical shift to forward deployment.

After the creation of the Strategic Rocket Forces (SRF), the role of the seaborne nuclear deterrent was reduced temporarily. A decision was made to curtail the ballistic missile and cruise missile submarine programs. The last Hotel and Golf-class (Project 629) ballistic missile conventional powered submarines (SSB) were completed in 1962–63; no new ballistic missile submarines were built for another five years. Other planned submarine upgrades were also curtailed.[111]

Brezhnev's Era, 1964–82

Khrushchev lost a power struggle in Moscow and was dismissed as party leader in October 1964. He was replaced by Leonid Brezhnev. The fall of

Khrushchev did not weaken Gorshkov's position. He was promoted in 1967 to fleet admiral and thereby acquired the same standing in the military hierarchy as the commanders in chief of the SRF and the ground forces.[112]

During Brezhnev's term in office, the Soviet Union embarked on the policy of strengthening its rule in Eastern Europe and providing support to various "progressive" movements in the Third World. Soviet military policy under Brezhnev aimed to preserve and, where possible, extend the socialist system. The Soviet realization of the impossibility of defense against nuclear-tipped ballistic missiles led to an emphasis on creating the capabilities to initiate a nuclear first strike. This was, in the Soviet view, the only way to reduce the weight of an enemy attack.

By late 1966 the Soviets had shifted to the view that a new world war would not necessarily be nuclear, and even if it were, that war would not necessarily involve massive strikes. They also scaled down their possible wartime strategic objectives from attacking the United States, which would inevitably lead to strikes against the Soviet homeland, to the less ambitious objective of only seriously weakening the capitalist system without attacking the North American continent with nuclear-tipped ballistic missiles.[113]

The Soviet response to the U.S. Polaris SLBMs and the entrance of the new carriers programmed during the Korean War was to build a much more capable Yankee-class (Project 667) SSBN. Reportedly, about seventy boats were planned to be completed within ten years (1968–77). The Yankees would be held back in home waters, available to the supreme high command for use in a post–nuclear strike exchange phase. The lead boat of the new Yankee-class SSBN was delivered in 1967.[114]

In 1967–68 the Soviets introduced into service a second generation of nuclear-powered submarines. By 1972 some 34 Yankee-class SSBNs were completed. This class was followed by the Delta-I, armed with the 4,200-nautical-mile SS-N-8 missile. These submarines were the first able to operate in Soviet waters and still hit targets in the continental United States. Because of the inadequacies of the older Soviet SSBNs, a decision was made to transfer the Golf and Hotel classes to the anticarrier role.[115]

In the late 1960s and early 1970s the Soviets placed increased emphasis on the navy's oceanic mission and its unique and essential contribution to the country's overall strategy.[116] The Ten-Year Plan for 1971–80 that was adopted on 1 September 1969 committed the Soviets to developing a very long-range SLBM that would allow their SSBNs to operate from the protected areas ("bastions") in the Barents Sea and the Sea of Okhotsk. (The earlier classes of Soviet SSBNs had had to transit through the NATO antisubmarine warfare (ASW) barrier in the Greenland/Iceland/UK gap.) The Tu-142 Bear maritime patrol aircraft was also developed. Another decision in the Ten-Year Plan was to build the three 36,300-ton Kiev-class (Project 1143) heavy aircraft-carrying cruisers with vertical take-off and landing aircraft and helicopters. Four new and powerful Kirov-class (Project 1144.2) heavy missile cruisers would also be built between 1974 and 1996.[117]

After the shift in U.S. strategy from land-based and carrier-based nuclear-armed bombers to land-based intercontinental and submarine-launched ballistic missiles, Gorshkov made a decision to shift emphasis to open-ocean ASW. Hence, the Soviets embarked on the construction of modern *Kresta*- and Kara-class ASW cruisers. The Soviets also made major advances in the capability of their cruise missile submarines after the introduction of the Charlie-I class in the early 1970s. This substantially improved their capabilities against American surface naval forces.[118]

The Soviets deduced some useful lessons from the employment of their 5th Eskadra (squadron) in the Mediterranean during the Yom Kippur War in October 1973. In contrast to the Cuban missile crisis, Soviet naval capabilities in 1973 posed a significant and worrisome threat to the U.S. Navy. Moscow was also able to exploit policy differences between the United States and its NATO allies. Turkey eased the Montreaux Treaty restrictions during the crisis and thereby allowed the Soviets to rapidly reinforce their naval forces in the Mediterranean. This also helped the Soviets to move materiel by air and sea to their clients Syria and Egypt. The United States was forced for political reasons to keep its carrier forces in the eastern Mediterranean, thereby making it easier for the Soviets to target them in case of an outbreak of hostilities. Another major lesson for the Soviets was that, despite a persisting gap in advanced naval technology, Soviet naval forces performed well.[119]

In the early 1970s, Gorshkov published a series of eleven articles collectively titled "Navies in War and Peace" in the leading Soviet naval journal *Morskoy Sbornik (Naval Review)*. The last two articles dealt with current issues facing the Soviet navy. He emphasized that each service had a particular contribution to make but that all must also operate harmoniously. In any major war, final victory demands the occupation of enemy territory by land forces. However, any country that intends to be a major power must also be strong at sea. Gorshkov pointed out the increasing importance of the seas as a source of food, energy, and other vital resources. In his view, the sea had always played a large part in determining the rise and fall of nations. In this, he sent a strong message to the country's political leadership that the Soviet Union must strengthen the maritime component of its strategy.

Many of these leaders' predecessors, both before and after 1917, had failed to recognize this and had neglected the navy. Some leaders even actively resisted the development of sea power, arguing that the country's unfavorable geographic position did not require more than coastal forces for the defense of sea approaches. Gorshkov made it clear that the strategic and economic importance of the oceans and the Soviet Union's need for sea power to protect and further its maritime interests were not always accepted even in his day. His central message was that only a balanced fleet would enable the Soviet state to maintain an effective maritime component in its strategy. Gorshkov argued that the nuclear and conventional capabilities of the Soviet navy removed the threat of nuclear blackmail from the seas and enabled the Soviet Union to provide help to friendly countries against what he called "imperialist aggression."[120]

Whatever the persuasiveness of these arguments, it is clear that Gorshkov's influence had its limits. Another internal debate took place in the early 1970s concerning whether to build full-scale aircraft carriers. According to some recent Russian accounts, the plan was to build a large nuclear-powered carrier carrying sixty to eighty-eight aircraft. The preliminary design was approved in 1973, but Minister of Defense Dmitri F. Ustinov opposed the project because of high costs. A fall-back option of a smaller aircraft carrier capable of carrying fifty aircraft was approved initially, but work on this project stopped in 1976. Less ambitious efforts along similar lines failed to come to fruition in the 1980s.[121]

At the same time, the submarine force was by no means neglected under Gorshkov, and the Soviet made great strides in this area in the waning years of the Cold War. A new titanium-hulled Alfa-class (Project 705 Lyra) SSN was built and was widely regarded as equal if not superior to any equivalent in the West. The first of six new Typhoon-class (Project 941) SSBNs was commissioned in 1981. Oscar-class (Project 949) SSGNs were also introduced into service in the late 1980s and early 1990s, among a number of other new boat types.

Rise of Gorbachev and the Soviet Collapse, 1983–91

By the early 1980s the U.S.–Soviet détente of the early 1970s had ground to a halt and there were increasing tensions in relations with the West. After Brezhnev died in November 1982, Yuri Andropov came to power in Moscow. However, he died after only fifteen months and was succeeded by Konstantin Chernenko, who died in 1985. The new ruler in Moscow was thereafter

Mikhail Gorbachev. From the very beginning, Gorbachev tried to save the Communist system by embarking on a series of reforms aimed to make the system both more efficient and more democratic. Hence, Gorbachev's era was characterized by *glasnost* (openness) and *perestroika* (reform). Gorbachev also initiated a policy of seeking better relations with the United States and other Western countries to end the arms race and thereby shift more resources to the civilian economy.

Soviet military policy in the Gorbachev era was dominated by the assertive and outspoken chief of the general staff, Marshal Nikolai V. Ogarkov. The Soviets adopted an independent conventional war option as a long-term military development. Ogarkov implicitly questioned the validity of nuclear weapons. He and his supporters referred to new technological advances as the new "revolution in military affairs." In fact, he argued that new conventional weapons were in many ways equal to nuclear weapons in terms of their range and lethality. These new weapons would be used in a war that did not involve the territories or nuclear forces of the United States and the Soviet Union. By the late 1980s the Soviets concluded that conventional warfare had fundamentally changed because of the emergence of a global system of reconnaissance, strike-reconnaissance complexes, and high troop mobility. The use of military robotics had contributed to the transfer of an increasing number of functions from people to machines.[122]

Sergei Gorshkov retired in 1985 after an extraordinary thirty years as the commander of the Soviet navy. He was replaced by his chief of staff, Admiral Chernavin. The navy's new commander had served predominantly on submarines; he had become chief of staff of the Northern Fleet in 1975 and two years later its commander. At the time that Chernavin became commander of the navy, top Soviet naval officials were increasingly concerned with the new U.S. "maritime strategy" officially adopted in 1986. Admiral Chernavin accused the United States and several other NATO countries of starting a new naval race with the sharp increase in their maritime activity. This, in turn, had increased the military threat, especially in the world's oceans, where the possibility of a military clash had become likely.[123]

The Soviet Union of the early and mid-1980s was still favorable to large-scale naval shipbuilding and naval aircraft production and to the arming and equipping of submarines, surface ships, and aircraft with missiles and more modern electronics.[124] By early 1985 the Soviet navy was estimated to have about 275 submarines and 2,320 surface ships (though this figure includes about 1,090 coastal combatants and 785 auxiliary ships). Soviet naval air strength was estimated at 1,635 aircraft, but this number included only 375 strike aircraft/bombers and 135 fighters/fighter-bombers.[125]

By the late 1980s the Soviet Union had entered a period of inevitable demise. Gorbachev was moving too fast for the hard-core Soviet elite in his reforms, while the radical reformers perceived him as too slow. Gorbachev tried to remain in control of the reform process. However, he underestimated the depth of the economic problems facing the Soviet Union. Gorbachev also seemed not to fully understand the nationality issues within the Soviet Union. The era of openness led to increasing demands for independence in many of the Soviet republics, and in the Baltic states in particular. Soviet control also became increasingly challenged in the Warsaw Pact countries. In the end the Communist regimes in most Eastern European countries collapsed in 1989–90, and this was followed by the largely peaceful breakup of the Soviet Union. The Soviet Union formally ended on 21 December 1991.

After the dissolution of the Soviet Union, many naval vessels were scrapped or laid up because of a shortage of funds. Since 1991 the overall strength of the Russian navy has declined from 450,000 to 155,000 men (including 11,000 in the strategic nuclear forces, 35,000 naval aviation forces, and 9,500 naval infantry).[126] The number of aircraft fell from 1,666 to 556, submarines from 317 to 61, and surface ships from 967 to 186. Naval bases outside of Russia were evacuated except for Sevastopol, on the Black Sea. Only some two-thirds of 170 factories supporting naval shipbuilding remained in the Russian Federation. The supply of spare parts was also disrupted. The ship construction program was essentially stopped. This situation began to change for the better in 2000 and afterward, when new ships were again being built for the Russian navy. However, the ships are not built in series, as they were in the past. The Russian navy has started to build frigates and corvettes and small ships for the Caspian Flotilla. In 2000–2005, after almost a decade of inactivity, Russian ships are finally going to sea in increased number and for longer missions.[127]

The Russian navy today is organized into four theater fleets: the Baltic fleet in Baltiysk; the Pacific Fleet in Vladivostok; the Northern Fleet in Severomorsk; and the Black Sea Fleet in Sevastopol plus the Caspian Flotilla with headquarters in Astrakhan. (In addition, the Kaliningrad Special Region is subordinate to the Baltic Fleet.) Currently, the Russian navy's sea-based nuclear deterrent force consists of fourteen submarines: two Typhoons, six Delta-IVs (Project 667AT Navaga) and six Delta-IIIs (Project 667 Kalmar). These SSBNs are deployed with the Northern and Pacific fleets, respectively. (In contrast, the Soviets had sixty-two operational SSBNs in 1990.) Three advanced Borey-class SSBNs are under construction. The Russian SSBNs conducted three deterrent patrols in 2005, two each in 2004 and 2003, none in 2002, and only one in 2001. (In contrast, they conducted sixty-one patrols in 1990.)[128] In 2006 the navy's inventories included, besides SSBNs, twenty-two nuclear-powered submarines (six SSGNs and sixteen SSNs), twenty-two SSs, one aircraft carrier, two heavy missile cruisers, five cruisers, fourteen destroyers, ten frigates, eight light frigates, and twenty-three missile corvettes.[129] There were then no plans to build destroyers and cruisers.[130] In a perhaps surprising development, the Russians announced in 2005 a plan to build a class of four new aircraft carriers starting in 2013–14, with initial service in 2017.[131] Russian naval aviation is mainly intended for conducting reconnaissance/surveillance, ASW, and for strikes against ships at sea and on the ground.[132] The inventories include Tu-22s/Tu-95s bombers, Il-38s/Be-12s ASW aircraft, Su-24s/Su-27s fighter-bombers, MiG-31s fighter-interceptors, and Ka-27s/Mi-8s helicopters.[133]

Conclusion

The Soviet navy formally emerged in the last phase of the civil war between the Bolsheviks and their domestic opponents. The sailors of the former tsarist navy joined the Bolsheviks in large numbers. Because of a lack of experts, the former tsarist naval officers were retained in service. Like their counterparts in the army, they played a crucial role in the Bolsheviks' final victory. Nevertheless, the new regime did not trust the former tsarist naval officers. To ensure their continuing loyalty, they were supervised by political commissars.

The Soviet navy's development in the 1920s was greatly hindered by the country's weak economy, combined with the Bolshevik leadership's lack of interest in naval matters in general. Despite the political extremism of the new regime, there was rather open debate on the best direction the navy should take in its future development. Proponents of the Mahanian view of the command of the sea were able to openly and vigorously present their views. Their arguments were clearly divorced from reality because the Soviet economy was absolutely unable to afford the battleships and cruisers for the fleet envisioned by the proponents of the so-called Old School. In contrast, the ideas of the Young School were based on a much more realistic appreciation of the situation. Adherents also fully accepted the view of the RKKA's top leadership that naval forces had to operate in support of the army in any future war.

The naval construction program during the Soviets' first Five-Year Plan was the strongest evidence of the victory achieved by the proponents of the Young School. However, their victory was short-lived. Already by the mid-1930s Stalin apparently had made a decision to build a big navy, one capable of challenging a major power for control of the sea approaches to the Soviet Union. Stalin's decision was in fact an attempt to reconcile the ideas of both the Old and Young schools. (Yet, true to his fashion, he also decided to physically eliminate the leading proponents of both schools of naval warfare.) The new, so-called Soviet School of naval warfare was adopted just prior to the outbreak of World War II. Despite the great industrial progress attained during the first two five-year plans, the Soviet shipbuilding industry was still unable to build the oceangoing fleet Stalin envisioned. Another problem was that the Soviets lacked sufficient expertise in designing super-dreadnoughts, aircraft carriers, and heavy cruisers—hence their persistent, but ultimately not very successful, efforts to obtain the necessary plans and advanced weapons and equipment from Germany, France, Italy, and the United States in the 1930s.

In the aftermath of World War II, Stalin did not abandon his ambitious plans for embarking on the creation of an oceangoing navy. However, because of the poor state of the economy, the emphasis was initially given to the construction of a large number of submarines and smaller surface combatants. The Soviet navy's main mission was to establish a multilayered defense of the country's sea approaches. Stalin apparently intended to complete his plan for a big navy in the early 1950s. Yet his wishes never became a reality before he died in 1953.

Stalin's successors made major changes in Soviet foreign and defense policies. Among other things, they misinterpreted the scope and importance of new technological advances. The so-called Revolution in Military Affairs was used as a rationale to shift the emphasis of the Soviet defense policy to nuclear weapons and ballistic missiles. The size of the Soviet conventional forces was drastically reduced. Large surface combatants were declared essentially useless. The naval construction program shifted toward missile-armed submarines and smaller surface ships. The fallacy of these views did not become apparent until the early 1960s. Admiral Gorshkov had a hard time convincing Khrushchev and the top military leadership of the need to retain large surface ships in service to thereby ensure that the navy was a balanced force.

After the fall of Khrushchev in 1964, the Soviet naval construction program and doctrine were heavily influenced by the rather significant changes in the international security environment and corresponding changes in Soviet defense policies. Until the mid-1980s Soviet foreign policies emphasized the need to spread the country's influence to many parts of the Third World. Naval presence became an indispensable element of these policies. Gorshkov was finally able to realize his idea of having a large and balanced fleet capable of challenging the U.S. Navy in the most important parts of the world's ocean. The need for a balanced fleet was also critical in support of Soviet defense policies in the 1980s when the emphasis shifted toward fighting a limited and conventional war instead of relying on an all-out nuclear exchange.

The end of the Soviet navy came rather abruptly as a result of the chain of internal events in the country. Since 1991 the once-mighty force has entered an era of steady decline. Most of the submarines and large surface combatants have been either decommissioned or scrapped. The navy has become a near replica of the former tsarist navy that existed in 1921. However, the Russian Federation's economic situation has improved significantly over the past few years, which has made it possible to assign larger resources for building new ships for the Russian navy. The prospects for its becoming a larger and more modern force in the near future seem rather better today than they were in the past few years. However, the country's unfavorable maritime position will continue to adversely affect the power projection capabilities of the new Russian navy. The traditionally land-centric focus of the Russian political elite is unlikely to change in the future.

Notes

1. Ritter von Niedermayer, "Nord- und Ostsee: Eine wehrpolitische und strategische Betrachtung," in Th. Arps, R. Gadow, H. Hesse, and D. Ritter von Niedermayer, *Kleine Wehrgeographie des Weltmeeres* (Berlin: E. S. Mittler & Sohn, 1938), 95.

2. Office of Naval Intelligence (ONI), *Russo-German Naval Relations 1926 to 1941: A Report Based on Captured Files of the German Naval Staff* (Washington, DC: Office of Naval Intelligence, June 1947), 8.

3. Gunnar Åsalius, *The Rise and Fall of the Soviet Navy in the Baltic, 1921–1941* (London: Frank Cass Publishers, 2005), 46.

4. G. A. Ammon et al., *The Soviet Navy in War and Peace* (Moscow: Progress Publishers, 1981), 47.

5. ONI, *Russo-German Naval Relations 1926 to 1941*, 8.

6. Eric Morris, *The Russian Navy: Myth and Reality* (New York: Stein and Day Publishers, 1977), 18–19.

7. Ibid., 47.

8. Morris, *Russian Navy*, 18–19.

9. In comparison the Russian Imperial Navy had in 1917 18 battleships, 14 cruisers, 84 destroyers and torpedo boat destroyers, 22 torpedo boats, 41 submarines, 45 mine and net-layers, 11 gunboats, 110 patrol ships, and 42 motorboats; Juergen Rohwer and Mikhail S. Monakov, *Stalin's Ocean-Going Fleet: Soviet Naval Strategy and Shipbuilding Programmes, 1953–1945* (London: Frank Cass Publishers, 2001), 8.

10. George E. Hudson, "Soviet Naval Doctrine under Lenin and Stalin," *Soviet Studies* 28, no. 1 (January 1976): 52.

11. Ammon et al., *The Soviet Navy in War and Peace*, 47.

12. Rohwer and Monakov, *Stalin's Ocean-Going Fleet*, 12.

13. Andrei A. Kokoshin, *Soviet Strategic Thought, 1917–91* (Cambridge, MA: The MIT Press, 1998), 77.

14. Morris, *Russian Navy*, 18.

15. Rohwer and Monakov, *Stalin's Ocean-Going Fleet*, 10.

16. David Woodward, *The Russians at Sea* (London: William Kimber, 1965), 202.

17. Åsalius, *Rise and Fall of the Soviet Navy*, 85.

18. Rohwer and Monakov, *Stalin's Ocean-Going Fleet*, 28.

19. Ibid., 35.

20. Rohwer and Monakov, *Stalin's Ocean-Going Fleet*, 28; quoted in Åsalius, *Rise and Fall of the Soviet Navy*, 126.

21. Ibid., 33.

22. Ibid., 34–35.

23. Robert Waring Herrick, *Soviet Naval Doctrine and Policy 1956–1986*, Book 1, (Lewiston, NY: The Edwin Mellen Press, 2003), 7.

24. Quoted in Bryan Ranft and Geoffrey Till, *The Sea in Soviet Strategy* (Annapolis, MD: Naval Institute Press, 2nd ed., 1989), 94.

25. Morris, *Russian Navy*, 19.

26. Herrick, *Soviet Naval Doctrine and Policy 1956–1986*, Book 1: 7.

27. Ranft and Till, *Sea in Soviet Strategy*, 95.

28. Herrick, *Soviet Naval Doctrine and Policy 1956–1986*, Book 1: 6.

29. Hudson, "Soviet Naval Doctrine," 48.

30. Ibid., 56.

31. Kokoshin, *Soviet Strategic Thought, 1917–91*, 79.

32. Herrick, *Soviet Naval Doctrine and Policy 1956–1986*, Book 1: 7–8.

33. Morris, *Russian Navy*, 20–21.

34. Ranft and Till, *Sea in Soviet Strategy*, 94–95.

35. Morris, *The Russian Navy: Myth and Reality*, 20–21.

36. Åsalius, *Rise and Fall of the Soviet Navy*, 127.

37. Milan L. Hauner, "Stalin's Big-Fleet Program," *Naval War College Review* 57 (Spring 2004): 109.

38. Natalia I. Yegorova, "Stalin's Conception of Maritime Power: Revelations from the Russian Archives," *The Journal of Strategic Studies* 28, no. 2 (April 2005): 158.

39. Quoted in Kokoshin, *Soviet Strategic Thought*, 164.

40. Hauner, "Stalin's Big-Fleet Program," 106.

41. Robert Waring Herrick, *Soviet Naval Strategy: Fifty Years of Theory and Practice* (Annapolis, MD: Naval Institute Press, 1968), 29.

42. Rohwer and Monakov, *Stalin's Ocean-Going Fleet*, 58.

43. Åsalius, *Rise and Fall of the Soviet Navy in the Baltic*, 133–34.

44. Rohwer and Monakov, *Stalin's Ocean-Going Fleet*, 63.

45. Hauner, "Stalin's Big-Fleet Program," 106.

46. Rohwer and Monakov, *Stalin's Ocean-Going Fleet*, 63.

47. Hauner, "Stalin's Big-Fleet Program," 107.

48. Rohwer and Monakov, *Stalin's Ocean-Going Fleet*, 63.

49. Hauner, "Stalin's Big-Fleet Program," 106.

50. Quoted in Hudson, "Soviet Naval Doctrine under Lenin and Stalin," 58.

51. Rohwer and Monakov, *Stalin's Ocean-Going Fleet*, 47.

52. Ranft and Till, *The Sea in Soviet Strategy*, 96.

53. Kokoshin, *Soviet Strategic Thought, 1917–91*, 164.

54. Morris, *The Russian Navy*, 22.

55. Hauner, "Stalin's Big-Fleet Program," 113.

56. Ibid., 113.

57. Ranft and Till, *The Sea in Soviet Strategy*, 96.

58. Herrick, *Soviet Naval Strategy*, 32–33.

59. Quoted in Kokoshin, *Soviet Strategic Thought, 1917–91*, 164.

60. In the search for foreign aid, Britain was uninterested and Japan was excluded. As early 1934–35 negotiation initiated with France for delivery of plans for cruisers and flotilla leaders; however, the French were reluctant to close the deal; see Hauner, "Stalin's Big-Fleet Program," 102.

61. Rohwer and Monakov, *Stalin's Ocean-Going Fleet*, 46. The Soviets also received some help from the engineers of the German company Deschimag at Bremen in obtaining a submarine design that was also used for construction of the German Type I/U-25 class U-boats.

62. In 1935 the Soviets also requested three Italian yards to build a special high-speed destroyer leader (project 20). The lead ship (*Tashkent*) of the new class of 2,830-ton destroyers (the fastest in the world) was built and handed over to the Soviets in May 1939. No other ships of this class were built in Soviet yards because of difficulties in adapting the Italian design in practice. The Soviets also approached the Italian shipyard Ansaldo about purchasing the plans for a 42,000-ton battleship similar to the Italian *Littorio* class. Their request was granted, and the plans were delivered in July 1936. The *Sovetsky Soyuz*–class super-dreadnought was based on this design; ibid., 46, 62–63.

63. Herrick, *Soviet Naval Strategy*, 36–37.

64. Ibid., 38.

65. Hauner, "Stalin's Big-Fleet Program," 88.

66. ONI, *Russo-German Naval Relations 1926 to 1941*, 76–77.

67. Ibid., 11.

68. Ibid., 11–13.

69. Rohwer and Monakov, *Stalin's Ocean-Going Fleet*, 119.

70. George E. Hudson, *The Soviet Navy Enters the Nuclear Age: The Development of Soviet Naval Doctrine, 1953–1973* (Ann Arbor, MI: Xerox University Microfilms, unpubl. PhD. diss., 1975), 72–73; see also Richard T. Ackley, *Soviet Maritime Power: An Appraisal of the Development, Capabilities, and International Influence of the Soviet Navy, Fishing Fleet, and Merchant Marine* (Los Angeles: University of Southern California, unpubl. PhD. diss., 1974), 44.

71. Ranft and Till, *The Sea in Soviet Strategy*, 97.

72. Sergei Chernyavskii, "The Era of Gorshkov: Triumph and Contradictions," *The Journal of Strategic Studies* 28, no. 2 (April 2005): 290.

73. Kokoshin, *Soviet Strategic Thought, 1917–91*, 111.

74. Herrick, *Soviet Naval Strategy*, 59.

75. Yegorova, "Stalin's Conception of Maritime Power," 159; Vladimir O. Pechatnov, "The Allies Are Pressing on You to Break Your Will . . ." Foreign Policy Correspondence between Stalin and Molotov and other Politburo members,

September 1945–December 1946 (Washington, DC: Woodrow Wilson International Center for Scholars, Cold War International History Project Working Paper no. 26, September 1999), 3.

76. Michael MccGwire, "The Soviet Navy and World War," in Philip S. Gillette and Willard C. Frank Jr., *The Sources of Soviet Naval Conduct* (Lexington, MA: Lexington Books, 1990), 198.

77. Herrick, *Soviet Naval Strategy*, 57.

78. Rohwer and Monakov, *Stalin's Ocean-Going Fleet*, 178.

79. Ibid., 178.

80. Stalin cut the program to 40 large submarines because they would interfere with the construction of surface ships. Stalin approved the draft ten-year shipbuilding program on 27 October 1945. Reportedly new designs for the construction of 39 large, 197 medium, and 58 small submarines were prepared in 1946; Yegorova, "Stalin's Conception of Maritime Power: Revelations from the Russian Archives," 160–61.

81. Cited in Herrick, *Soviet Naval Strategy: Fifty Years of Theory and Practice*, 58.

82. Rohwer and Monakov, *Stalin's Ocean-Going Fleet*, 185, 180; A. S. Pavlov, *Warships of the USSR and Russia 1945–1995*, trans. Gregory Tokar (Annapolis, MD: Naval Institute Press, 1997), xviii.

83. The Chinese Navy adopted the *Lenin* icebreaker's nuclear reactor in 1960 as a plant for their first nuclear-power submarine (Han-class); Christopher McConnaughy, "China's Undersea Nuclear Deterrent: Will the U.S. Navy Be Ready?' in Andrew S. Erickson, Lyle J. Goldstein, William R. Murray, and Andrew R. Wilson, eds., *China's Future Nuclear Submarine Force* (Annapolis, MD: Naval Institute Press in cooperation with China Maritime Studies Institute, 2007), 84; Susanne Kopte, *Nuclear Submarine Decommissioning and Related Problems* (Bonn, Germany: Bonn International Center for Conversion, August 1997), 9.

84. Rohwer and Monakov, *Stalin's Ocean-Going Fleet*, 210.

85. Herrick, *Soviet Naval Doctrine and Policy 1956–1986*, Book 1: 67.

86. Ackley, *Soviet Maritime Power*, 53.

87. MccGwire, "The Soviet Navy and World War," 198.

88. Herrick, *Soviet Naval Doctrine and Policy 1956–1986*, Book 1: 92.

89. Quoted in Herrick, *Soviet Naval Strategy*, 76.

90. Chernyavskii, "The Era of Gorshkov," 287.

91. Ibid., 287–88.

92. Michael MccGwire, "The Soviet Navy and World War," 198.

93. Herrick, *Soviet Naval Strategy*, 91, 75–76.

94. Ibid., 131.

95. Herrick, *Soviet Naval Strategy*, 80.

96. Raymond J. Swider Jr. and John Erickson, *Soviet Military Reform in the Twentieth Century: Three Case Studies*, (New York: Greenwood Publishers, 1992), 129–130; Herrick, *Soviet Naval Strategy*, 80.

97. Swider and Erickson, *Soviet Military Reform*, 131, 127.

98. Herrick, *Soviet Naval Doctrine and Policy 1956–1986*, Book 1: 94–95.

99. John Jordan, "Future Trends in Soviet Submarine Development," in Bruce W. Watson and Peter M. Dunn, eds., *The Future of the Soviet Navy: An Assessment to the Year 2000* (Boulder, CO: Westview Press, 1986), 2.

100. Michael MccGwire, "Current Soviet Warship Construction," in Michael McGwire, ed., *Soviet Naval Developments: Capability and Context* (New York: Praeger, 1976), 139.

101. Ibid., 3.

102. MccGwire, "Current Soviet Warship Construction," 139.

103. Herrick, *Soviet Naval Strategy*, 70.

104. Chernyavskii, "The Era of Gorshkov," 298.

105. Herrick, *Soviet Naval Strategy*, 68.

106. Ibid., 72; See Ackley, *Soviet Maritime Power*, 59.

107. Ackley, *Soviet Maritime Power*, 128–29; Andrew Pfister, *Wakeup Call: Soviet Naval Policy and the Cuban Missile Crisis* (Columbus: Ohio State University, unpubl. paper, May 2005), 2.

108. Quoted in Herrick, *Soviet Naval Strategy*, 74.

109. Ibid., 80.

110. Ibid., 71–72, 94.

111. Jordan, "Future Trends in Soviet Submarine Development," 5.

112. Ranft and Till, *The Sea in Soviet Strategy*, 80.

113. MccGwire, "The Soviet Navy and World War," 199–200.

114. MccGwire, "Current Soviet Warship Construction," 204, 138.

115. Michael MccGwire, "The Evolution of Soviet Naval Policy: 1960–1974," in Michael MccGwire, Ken Booth, and John McDonnell, eds., *Soviet Naval Policy: Objectives and Constraints* (New York: Praeger, 1975), 510.

116. Ranft and Till, *The Sea in Soviet Strategy*, 80.

117. Jordan, "Future Trends in Soviet Submarine Development," 6; Pavlov, *Warships of the USSR and Russia 1945–1995*, xxv.

118. Jordan, "Future Trends in Soviet Submarine Development," 8.

119. Lyle J. Goldstein and Yuri M. Zhukov, "A Tale of Two Fleets: A Russian Perspective on the 1973 Naval Standoff in the Mediterranean," *Naval War College Review* 57 (Spring 2004): 57.

120. Ranft and Till, *The Sea in Soviet Strategy*, 81, 85, 87.

121. Norman Polmar, "Soviet Surface Combatant Development and Operations in the 1980s and 1990s," in Bruce W. Watson and Peter M. Dunn, eds., *The Future of the*

Soviet Navy: An Assessment to the Year 2000 (Boulder, CO: Westview Press, 1986), 37–39.

122. Kokoshin, *Soviet Strategic Thought, 1917–91*, 135, 139.

123. Ibid., 143.

124. Robert Waring Herrick, *Soviet Naval Doctrine and Policy 1956–1986*, Book 3 (Lewiston, NY: The Edwin Mellen Press, 2003), 1199.

125. James L. George, Appendix, "Soviet Navy Order of Battle, March 1985," in *The Soviet and Other Communist Navies: The View from the Mid-1980s* (Annapolis, MD: Naval Institute Press, 1986), 423–36.

126. *Jane's Sentinel Security Assessment: Russia and the CIS, Issue Nineteen—2006* (London: Jane's Information Group Ltd, 2006), 601.

127. Yuri Krupnov, *Defense Reform and the Russian Navy* (Rome: NATO Defense College, 2006), 6.

128. Robert S. Norris and Hans M. Kristensen, "Russian Nuclear Forces, 2004," *Bulletin of Atomic Scientists* 60, no. 3 (July–August 2004): 72–74.

129. *Jane's Sentinel Security Assessment*, 601.

130. "Head of Russian Navy outlines plans for new aircraft carrier, Moscow NTV Mir," in Russian, 0500 GMT 28 Oct 06, https://www.opensource.gov/portal/server.pt/ gateway.

131. Russian Navy, http://www.answers.com/topic/russian-air-force.

132. "Russian Naval Aviation Chie Lt-Gen Yuriy Antipov Interviewed, Moscow Krasnaya Zvezda," in Russian, 15 July 2006, https://www.opensource.gov/portal/server.pt/ gateway.

133. Ibid.

PART III

Chinese Maritime Transformations

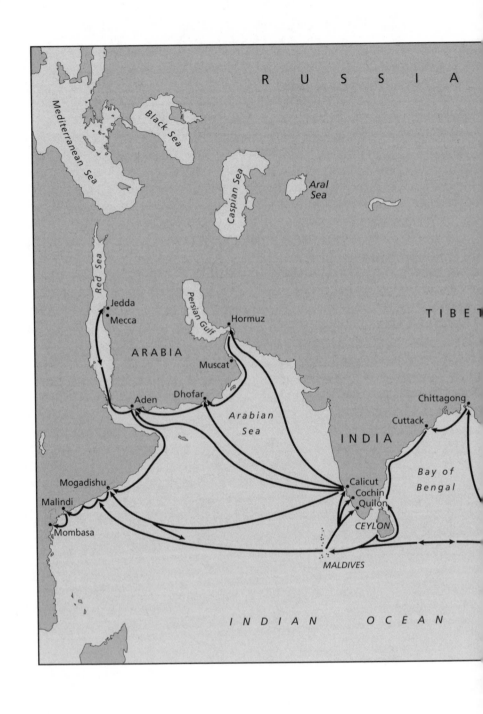

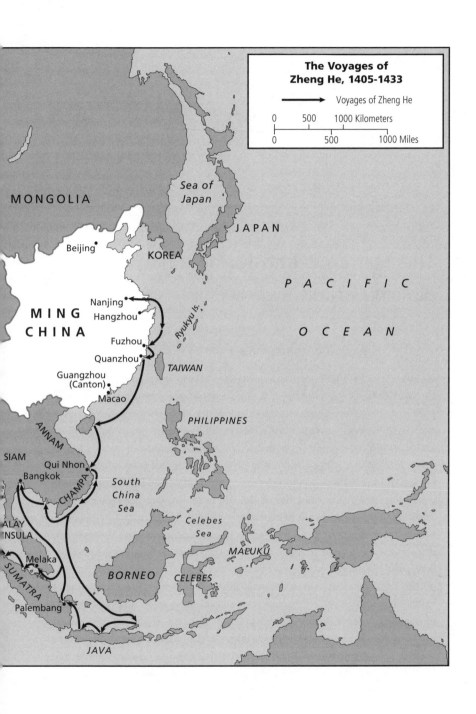

The Voyages of
Zheng He, 1405-1433

→ Voyages of Zheng He

0   500   1000 Kilometers

0   500   1000 Miles

MONGOLIA

Sea of
Japan

JAPAN

Beijing

KOREA

PACIFIC

Nanjing

MING
CHINA

Hangzhou

Fuzhou

Ryukyu Is.

OCEAN

Quanzhou

TAIWAN

Guangzhou
(Canton)

Macao

PHILIPPINES

ANNAM

SIAM

Qui Nhon

Bangkok

CHAMPA

South
China
Sea

Celebes
Sea

MALUKU

ALAY
NSULA

Melaka

BORNEO   CELEBES

SUMATRA

Palembang

JAVA

Andrew R. Wilson

The Maritime Transformation of Ming China

OF ALL THE MARITIME TRANSFORMATIONS covered in this volume, that of China's Ming Dynasty (大明朝, 1368–1644) seems the most out of place. At first glance, the history of the Ming as a maritime power seems exactly the reverse of this book's theme. Unlike those continental powers that have elected or been impelled to transform themselves into significant maritime powers, Ming China, it is generally believed, very rapidly turned its back on the sea and squandered its opportunity to be the dominant maritime power in Asia, if not the world. The standard characterization of the maritime history of China's Ming Dynasty is thus one of early glory followed first by stagnation and then by the precipitous decline of both the maritime economy and Chinese naval power. In other words, a dynasty that had once sent great armadas of hundreds of ships and tens of thousands of men as far as the coast of East Africa in the early fifteenth century was by the midpoint of the sixteenth century incapable of responding effectively to piracy along its own coast. There is a technological corollary to this story line: With China standing at the apex of nautical technology at the beginning of the dynasty in the late fourteenth and early fifteenth centuries, only to decline into a militarily backward state in the seventeenth century, it became wholly dependent on foreign technology in a desperate battle to stave off its inevitable defeat.

As with all conventional wisdom, there is some element of truth to this narrative. With the last of the great voyages commanded by the eunuch official Zheng He (郑和) in 1433, the Ming state, by which I mean the central government in Beijing, made a series of conscious decisions to step back from the maritime realm, shifting from a concerted agenda of aggressive navalism to a defensive continental focus. The reasons for this maritime retreat are many; I will return to them shortly. The Ming's lost maritime opportunity is best typified by a series of strident edicts, generally classed under the rubric of the maritime prohibitions (海禁), first issued in the late fourteenth century and continuing into the mid-sixteenth century. One law in 1500 made it a capital offense to build a ship with more than two masts. Another decree of 1525 called for the destruction of all oceangoing vessels and the imprisonment of Chinese engaged in overseas trade. Yet another writ in 1551 made it illegal for Chinese to sail ships of more than one mast for any reason. What could be more indicative of a myopic disdain for foreign trade and intercourse and of a great opportunity lost than the Ming Dynasty's retreat from the sea? These policies seem all the more misguided in light of the fact that these later edicts coincided with the great global trade boom that followed the European voyages of discovery. This impression of a fundamental retreat from the sea has been reinforced by the tradition in Chinese historiography of marginalizing the maritime environment in the late Imperial period, although this bias has been under assault in recent years.[1]

Even with the end of the Zheng He voyages and the various maritime trade and shipping limits that were subsequently imposed (albeit imperfectly and selectively enforced at the provincial and subprovincial levels), Ming China retained a dynamic maritime trade sector and a large coastal and oceangoing commercial fleet. Although still only a fraction of the domestic economy, Ming export trade was significant and became all the more important over time as silver imports became vital to the wealth and power of the dynasty. Maritime security remained a priority for Chinese coastal officials throughout the long period of relative peace and prosperity of the fifteenth and early sixteenth centuries, and these Mandarins maintained large numbers of naval vessels for counterpiracy and coastal defense missions. Maritime trade and security may have been secondary or even tertiary priorities for the Ming central government, but they were certainly far from marginal, especially in the coastal provinces. This meant that Ming China retained a significant potential of maritime power in all its fundaments— including nautical technology, seamanship, and wealth.

The relative lack of historical attention that the Ming maritime sector has heretofore garnered, other than Zheng He's voyages, can be explained in three ways. First, the scale and audacity of the Zheng He voyages naturally dwarf all subsequent manifestations of Chinese maritime power. It is therefore essential to compare Ming maritime power not against its own apogee in the period between 1405 and 1433, but rather to contemporary peer competitors, such as Japan under Toyotomi Hideyoshi (秀吉豊臣, 1536–98). Second, the official histories of the Ming rightly focus on those matters that were of pressing concern to the imperial court and to senior officialdom, such as continental security and domestic politics, where government attention was consistent. Traditional historiography based on court records therefore tends to concentrate on high politics and ignores the mundane. Lower order issues did not routinely demand the court's attention. Moreover, because China's maritime interactions, extensive though they were—especially in areas such as the porcelain trade, tended to be private rather than official, these activities naturally were not recorded by the court.[2] Even in those aspects of maritime affairs in which the government was involved, we should still not expect the court to have paid much attention. For example, provincial and subprovincial officials along the Chinese coast were responsible for the construction, maintenance, manning, and provisioning of coastal defense vessels. Barring a cross-province security challenge, as with the Wokou (倭寇) crises of the late fourteenth and mid-sixteenth centuries, there was no need for central coordination of or accounting for the Ming navy. In other words, there was no Ming equivalent of the British Admiralty, a centralized administrative structure for managing the fleet. As a result, the maritime sector, with the exception of periods of major maritime crises, is conspicuously absent from the official Ming histories. Any inquiry into the memoirs of coastal officials and the local gazetteers of the major maritime trading regions, however, provides a glimpse of the size and capabilities of both the merchant and naval fleets in late Imperial China. If we can judge by late Ming sources, such as Li Zhaoxiang's *Records of the Shipbuilding Yards on the Dragon River* (龍江船廠志), Mao Yuanyi's *Treatise on Armament Technology* (武備志), and an anonymous Qing era (1644–1911) account titled *Illustrated Explanation of the Coastal Defense Fleet of the Province of Fujian* (闽省水师各标镇协营战哨船只图说), the Chinese throughout this period built a dizzying array of naval and merchant vessels.[3] As for the later source, it is worth noting that the early Qing was as hostile (if not more so) to the maritime sector than was the Ming, and even its very stringent maritime bans could at best only hope to contain commerce—licit and illicit—along the China coast. The third reason for the historiographical elision is that the Neo-Confucian literati who compiled the Ming histories were hostile to military expenditure, overseas adventurism, and state involvement in the maritime economy. Their histories therefore either downplay or deride the scale and nature of the Ming state's interest in overseas trade and naval issues. Ironically, it was these Neo-Confucian literati, whose power base lay in China's lower Yangzi (长江) and southeast coastal regions, who benefited most directly from China's maritime trade and who for obvious reasons wanted to keep an interventionist and predatory state away from their home turf.

These factors should not, however, obscure the fact that in the early fifteenth century the Ming state did consciously retreat from aggressive navalism and direct state intervention in overseas trade, and it imposed a series of policies to confine the maritime economy within manageable boundaries, as the court tried to do with tonnage limits and by licensing foreign merchants. For many reasons this was a prudent and economical choice for the dynasty. By the mid-sixteenth century, however, major security crises and new economic opportunities forced a reappraisal of the Ming maritime outlook. The speed with which the Ming met these challenges shows that while the maritime sector may have been de-emphasized for the preceding century, it had been far from dormant. Between the 1550s and the 1590s, the Ming faced two major maritime threats—coastal piracy and the Japanese invasion of Korea—and it responded successfully to both. Moreover, the Ming military and economic resurgence in the late sixteenth century and its reemergence as regional hegemon were intimately linked with maritime trade and naval warfare. This trend of maritime dynamism continued into the seventeenth century, but the Ming state rapidly lost control over that sector. When all else had been lost on land to a combination of peasant rebellions in the 1630s and 1640s and the Manchu invasion of intramural China in 1644, the last Ming remnants fought on from the sea and even ousted the Dutch from their colony on Taiwan. It would require a massive naval and amphibious campaign against the island in 1683 to finally extinguish the last remnants of Ming maritime power.

Thus, rather than representing the reverse of the other maritime transformations covered in this volume, Ming China is the unique case of a continental power blessed with sufficient wealth, raw materials, technological acumen, and native talent to emerge rapidly as a sea power. This case also highlights the choices that states make about their strategic and economic priorities and the constraints on those choices created by resource limitations, institutional structures, and ideology. Few premodern empires could rival the Ming's wealth, talent, or strategic flexibility, but the Ming was also plagued by systemic flaws and fundamental ideological and institutional paradoxes that prevented it from sustaining a dominant maritime edge.

Finally, while a careful examination of the maritime history of the Ming is a worthy task in itself, I hope that it may also offer some insights into the maritime future of contemporary China. Because the major powers of maritime East Asia still occupy essentially the same geography that they occupied six hundred years ago, many of the patterns of strategic and economic competition and cooperation in the region still pertain. Moreover, today's global and regional trading networks and China's gravitational pull on world trade are very much akin to those of the late Ming, leading me to conclude that maritime China in the twenty-first century will look much more like China in the sixteenth century than China of the recent past. While China has always been primarily a continental power, there is ample historical precedent for China as a major sea power, an innovator in nautical technology, and a significant player in East and Southeast Asia as well as in the Indian Ocean. These are not new phenomena.

Naval and Riverine Warfare in the Founding of the Ming Dynasty

Ming China inherited potent maritime traditions from its two immediate dynastic predecessors. The Southern Song Dynasty (南宋朝, 1127–1279) is the only major Chinese dynasty to have had a seaport as it capital. Hangzhou (杭州), on the lower Yangzi River, was not only the political and cultural center of the Chinese state but also a hub of riverine, coastal, and oceangoing trade and was home to huge shipyards. Under the Southern Song, Chinese nautical technology and seamanship reached new heights. In addition, the military threats to the north, first from the Jurchen Jin Dynasty (金朝, 1115–1234) and then from the Mongols, required that the Song maintain significant naval power. In fact, it was a combination of geography, technological sophistication, and naval skill that allowed the dynasty to survive as long as it did in the face of repeated Mongol assaults. When after forty-five years of resistance the Song finally fell, it was because much of its navy had defected to the Mongols.[4] The Mongol's Yuan Dynasty (元朝, 1271–1368) sought to leverage the oceangoing bent and technological edge of the Chinese in abortive campaigns of conquest by sea. The Mongols' attempted conquests of Japan, Vietnam, and Java would have been inconceivable without Chinese ships and tactics.[5] In fact, the two Mongol invasions of Japan in 1274 and 1281 were likely the greatest amphibious operations of the Middle Ages.

Fourteenth-century China was also at the cutting edge of nautical technology and naval warfare. Over the preceding centuries, the hereditary shipwright households of the lower Yangzi region and the southeast coast had introduced into Chinese shipbuilding transverse bulkheads (potentially allowing for watertight compartments), packed and caulked planking, the axial rudder, stepped masts, and battened sails. Chinese seafarers further benefitted from sophisticated astronomy, cartography, and the magnetic compass. Cross-regional exchange of techniques among the seagoing peoples of East and Southeast Asia also likely contributed to advances in Chinese nautical technology. In addition, many Chinese hulls were built to have the broadest beam aft, making them more seaworthy and more easily navigated at slow speeds.[6] Medieval China was also well endowed with timber, hemp, jute, lime for caulking, tung oil, and sail cloth and had a large and sophisticated internal economy to transport these materials to the shipyards. In terms of combat capabilities, Song and Yuan ships were equipped with a variety of grappling and holing implements, fire weapons, rams, crossbows, and arcuballistae along with defensive armor plating and fire suppression pumps. Larger vessels were equipped with trebuchets and small boats to embark marines.[7] Cannon were used on fourteenth-century Chinese warships as a complement to fire lances and exploding projectiles, as we know from accounts of the Sichuan campaign in 1371, but nowhere near on the scale that we will see later in the Ming.[8]

Emerging from the late-Yuan civil wars, the Ming is one of the few military and political forces in Chinese history to successfully conquer China from south to north, rather than the far more common pattern of conquest from the north. As southern rebels, the Ming founders were far more appreciative of the utility of naval and riverine warfare and were initially far more attuned to the commercial economy of the south than were the more continentally focused northern conquerors such as the Mongols of the Yuan Dynasty or the Manchus of the Qing Dynasty. Two of the central fronts during the Ming's emergence as an imperial contender were the lower Yangzi and the southeast coastal regions. Naturally, especially given the terrain of the region, naval forces played a significant role in the founding of the Ming dynasty. The epic Battle of Lake Poyang (鄱阳湖, August–October 1363) began as a riverine siege of the Ming-held city of Nanchang (南昌) by the Prince of the state of Han (漢王), Chen Youliang (陈友谅). According to different sources, Chen's forces comprised somewhere between three hundred thousand and six hundred thousand men, and his armada included imposing three-decker "tower ships" (楼船, *louchuan*). These served as floating siege engines, were crewed by several hundred men, and featured armor-plated archery towers. The Ming fleet, commanded by Zhu Yuanzhang (朱元璋), later the first emperor of the Ming, arrived in late-August, and Chen withdrew his forces down the Gan River (赣江) into Lake Poyang. Zhu's forces were out-numbered by the Han and their ships were far smaller; nevertheless, the Ming commander chose to engage, relying on the speed and maneuverability of his smaller vessels. The first two engagements (30 and 31 August) proved indecisive, with the Ming forces plagued by command and control problems and many of the larger Ming warships running aground in the shallow lake. A second Ming assault on the 31st, involving fire ships, cannon, and other incendiary weapons, proved more successful and damaged several hundred Han vessels. When the battle resumed on 2 September, the much depleted Han forces spread out their line to decrease their vulnerability to incendiary attack, but this made them more vulnerable to Ming swarming tactics, and several Han ships were boarded and burned. Both fleets broke off, and for the next few weeks Zhu Yuanzhang concentrated on preventing a Han retreat out of the lake and up the Yangzi to their capital at Wuchang (武昌).

In the final engagement on October 4, Chen Youliang was killed and his son (and heir to the Han throne) was taken prisoner. The Han forces rapidly fell into disarray and surrendered later that day. The decisive defeat of the naval power of Han finally secured Zhu Yuanzhang's control of the middle Yangzi region. From there he turned his attention to his downstream rival, the state of Wu (吴), which he exterminated in a series of campaigns in the mid- to late 1360s.[9] These campaigns gave Zhu the momentum to send his fleets south to take the coastal provinces of Guangdong and Fujian in a series of littoral offensives in 1367 and 1368 launched in conjunction with overland assaults on the remaining Yuan outposts in the southeast. At the same time, Zhu dispatched Ming armies north to drive the Mongols from what is now Beijing.[10] Without this critical naval victory at Poyang, which shifted the southern military balance decisively to the Ming, Zhu Yuanzhang's conquest and consolidation of the new Ming Dynasty would have been inconceivable. A final riverine campaign in 1371 reached as far Chongqing (some 1,300 miles upriver) and, combined with an overland campaign against Chengdu, brought Sichuan under Zhu's rule. In addition, if we can take the Poyang campaign as typical, Ming naval forces at the time of the dynasty's founding must have numbered in the hundreds of large combatant ships and hundreds of thousands of men.[11]

Early Ming Maritime Policy and the Emergence of the Coastal Defense System

Despite (or perhaps because of) the centrality of naval warfare to the Ming rise, as emperor, Zhu Yuanzhang (Ming Taizu [明太祖]/Emperor Hongwu [洪武], r. 1368–98) was suspicious of mariners and the maritime economy.[12] This may have been a case of familiarity breeding distrust for the new Ming emperor. From the beginning, Ming leaders appreciated the murky distinction between trade and piracy and the threat that the latter posed to law, order, and good governance. This should come as little surprise given that two of Zhu Yuanzhang's senior naval commanders, Yu Tonghai (俞通海) and Liao Yongzhong (廖永忠, later the victor of the riverine assault at Qutang Gorge [瞿塘峽] in Sichuan in July 1371), had learned their craft as pirates on Lake Chao (巢湖) in the 1340s and 1350s before joining the Ming cause around 1360.[13] The maritime trade policies and coastal defense strategies of the early Ming sought to either co-opt or contain the maritime economy and China's large seagoing population to keep their dynamism from superseding the dynasty's other strategic and economic priorities. Despite being southern Chinese, the Ming founders took many cues from their Mongol predecessors and foes. This included institutions, ruling style, and—most relevant to our purposes—strategic and operational foci (i.e., continental expansion and internal consolidation). The early Ming also differed from its predecessors in significant ways. Whereas both the Song and Yuan had policies that allowed the government to derive income from commerce in legitimate ways, albeit with attendant risks, Zhu Yuanzhang opted for the lower risk, but more stultifying system of a command economy and almost complete reliance on the land tax for state revenue. This was a good match given Zhu's autocratic inclinations, which were in turn reinforced by the Neo-Confucian literati that rallied to his banner in the 1360s.[14] The imperatives of order and the conservative physiocratic ideals that Zhu embraced to legitimate his new regime, however, were naturally at odds with the chaotic and rambunctious nature of maritime society. This was a fluid sector that was difficult for the state to control. The very terrain of the southeast provinces, crossed with rivers and mountains, further limited the Ming state's ability to either control or systematically exploit the oceangoing population.[15] In addition, Ming China was still fundamentally a land power. Throughout the wars that brought the dynasty to power, naval warfare had complemented land warfare but had never supplanted it. An enduring Mongol threat and restive minorities drew Ming energies landward.[16]

Early Ming expansion reached its culmination with a sharp defeat at the hands of the Mongols in 1372 followed rapidly by rebellion of ethnic minorities in the south. After this the Ming shifted to a defensive stance on the northern frontiers. As for overseas and southward expansion, Hongwu explicitly forbade his successors from attempting to conquer any of the major islands or littoral states in East and Southeast Asia.[17] Hongwu's primary objective, to initiate a tributary system in maritime Asia, would define relations between the Chinese state and its neighbors as one of obeisance to Chinese primacy and would have regulated foreign trade under the rubric of periodic gift-laden tribute missions from these subordinate kingdoms to the Ming capital. Zhu appears not to have had the slightest interest in overseas trade or the desires of China's large oceangoing population. He maintained a public posture of indifference to wealth derived from overseas trade, and he was very suspicious of the political and social consequences that might accompany oceangoing commerce. He welcomed tribute missions, but only from truly independent states. He allowed trade to take place only under official auspices and only when tribute was presented. He prohibited private trading between Chinese and "barbarians" and prohibited Chinese from sailing overseas.[18]

Nonetheless, Hongwu could not completely neglect the Chinese maritime sector because there were numerous security threats to be addressed in the early years of the dynasty.[19] Throughout the late Yuan, coastal piracy had been on the rise. The causes of this trend were numerous: The civil wars of Japan's Nambokucho era (南北朝, 1336–92) regularly spilled over into regional waters and were paired with the domestic political and economic chaos in late-Yuan China, and merchant speculators along with displaced soldiers and sailors readily coalesced in a rash of plunder, smuggling, and war profiteering.[20] This spike in piracy was collectively known as Wokou piracy, wo (倭) being the traditional Chinese for Japan and kou (寇), "pirate." Thinking of the Wokou as "Japanese" pirates is misleading, however, because many were Chinese, Korean, or of mixed ethnicity. Moreover, there were Chinese rebels in the late-Yuan era, notably Fang Guozhen (方国珍) and Zhang Shicheng (张士诚), who built powerful coastal domains with both ground and naval forces and posed major threats first to Yuan and later to Ming rule.[21] And even after these men had been killed or co-opted, their displaced followers could go into business for themselves. These threats demanded military and economic countermeasures.[22] During his reign, Zhu Yuanzhang launched a total overhaul of the Chinese military system. The model for this reform was largely carried over from the emperor's methods of organizing and incorporating the soldiers of his vanquished rivals during the civil war in the 1360s. At the same time, the military reorganization was indicative of the new tasks involved in ruling Ming China.[23] During the civil wars, Zhu, his sons, and his lieutenants were on constant campaign and essentially ruled from horseback; therefore, there was no clear delineation between the Ming armies and the Ming government. After the final conquest of Sichuan, Zhu Yuanzhang needed to reorient his regime from a military-centric machine of conquest to a government in which civil administration was coequal with the military.[24] Zhu also needed to maintain a sufficient military power to further consolidate his power and defend the fledgling dynasty without bankrupting his government, and he needed to demobilize and domesticate hundreds of thousands of men then in his ranks.

Zhu's response to this complex dilemma was the introduction of the system of hereditary conscription and the setting aside of land from which the hereditary military families could provide for their own sustenance. This institutional innovation was paired with an organizational scheme called the wei-suo (卫所) system, whereby regional commands were manned by dedicated brigades (卫, wei) numbering between 5,000 and 5,600 men divided into five battalions (所, suo) tasked to defend that region and housed on nominally self-sufficient military agricultural colonies.[25] To meet maritime and riverine threats, Zhu organized the Ming naval forces into their own wei and suo beginning in 1370 and 1371 for Shandong, Nan Zhili, Zhejiang, and Fujian, and later expanding to include some fifty wei (plus an additional eighty to eighty-five suo) patrolling the coast from the Bohai Gulf to the South China Sea. Unlike the ground units, which were clustered on large military colonies, the maritime units were often spread out as individual suo. This change was dictated by terrain, population density, and the inherently diffuse nature of coastal defense.[26] There was also a great deal of variation in the size and composition of the various maritime wei and suo. In some areas, wei fielded as few as 200 men, while in Nan Zhili (literally "The Southern Metropolitan District") at the mouth of the Yangzi there were wei of as many as 11,000 and even 13,000 men.[27] Because the lower Yangzi region was the political and economic heart of the new Ming state, the dedication of so much manpower to its defense seems exceptionally prudent.[28] In addition, coastal and riverine piracy threatened the shipping that transported tax revenues to the capital at Nanjing. In the aggregate, then, the early Ming maritime forces seem to have been a large and potent force that formed the basis of all subsequent coastal defense command structure in the Ming era, but Zhu Yuanzhang's maritime aims were essentially negative. The emperor wanted to pacify China's maritime sector, not exploit it, and he structured his forces accordingly. The naval *wei* were designed to deny key areas of the coast to Wokou predation, whereas offensive amphibious campaigns against pirate strongholds in the Ryukyus and southern Japan may have been a more direct solution to the problem. Although oversea expeditions were certainly within the Ming's military capabilities, and two campaigns were attempted in the 1370s, offensive campaigns in general were explicitly repudiated by the emperor as wasteful of blood and treasure.[29] Even within China, the terrain and porosity of the coastal regions of Fujian and Guangdong proved a consistent impediment to the exercise of effective control. In other words, the dynasty labored to contain the piracy problem, but because of counterproductive trade policy, competing security priorities and the tyrannies of terrain could never eradicate it completely.

In addition to these impressive, albeit wholly defensive, military policies, Emperor Hongwu employed diplomatic overtures and preemptive use of maritime prohibitions [海禁, *haijin*]; the first was promulgated in 1371. In the opinion of Edward Dreyer, the emperor's efforts made the piracy problem worse: "Ming relations with Japan and the maritime countries of Southeast Asia had gone sour in the 1370s after a promising beginning. The underlying cause of the trouble was Hung-wu's [Hongwu's] attempt to suppress private Chinese trade while simultaneously refusing to permit an equivalent volume of trade within the framework of the tribute system."[30] In other words, restrictive government edicts forced maritime merchants (both Chinese and foreign) into piracy and smuggling. By the 1380s, the piracy scourge had abated and it appears that the trading and fishing bans that Hongwu had imposed were loosened, but the maritime sector was still hampered by imperial policies that were hostile to private maritime trade. This may have been doubly damaging because the next century and a half was an era of general peace in East Asia, when more progressive policies might have capitalized on and further encouraged the private commercial boom that was taking place. As the mandates of the Ming founder, however, these strictures would prove difficult to overturn, but because they had to be repeated periodically, the maritime bans are themselves proof of the dynamism of the maritime sector of the early Ming and of the dynasty's attempts to contain that dynamism.[31]

The Voyages of Zheng He: The High Tide of Ming Navalism

The period from 1405–33 was the high-water mark of early Ming interest in the maritime sector and in the maritime economy.[32] Although the western concept of navalism may not be an entirely accurate way to describe the Zheng He (Cheng Ho) voyages,[33] it correctly connotes the construction and deployment of a massive armada designed to intimidate and impress allies, adversaries, and entities of undecided allegiance as well as to open or expand sea-lanes of official trade between Ming China, Southeast Asia, and the Indian Ocean.[34] The seven voyages were initiated by the third Ming emperor, Yongle (永乐, r. 1402–24). Born Zhu Di (朱棣), Yongle was the fourth son of Zhu Yuanzhang and had proven his mettle as a military commander in the Ming rise. He was later enfeoffed as Prince of Yan and established his capital at Beiping (later renamed Beijing). Zhu Di was passed over as Zhu Yuanzhang's successor in favor first of his eldest brother, Zhu Biao (朱标), and then his nephew Zhu Yunwen (朱允炆), who became the Jianwen emperor (建文) upon Hongwu's death in 1398. Zhu Di rebelled against Jianwen, seized Nanjing, and dethroned the emperor in July 1402.[35] Zhu Di's victory would have been unlikely were it not for the fact that Chen Xuan (陈萱, 1365–1433), the commander the of Ming river fleet, defected to the rebels and ferried their army across the Yangzi.[36] Once installed as the Yongle emperor, Zhu Di launched an ambitious array of diplomatic, military, infrastructure, and bureaucratic initiatives, many of them in obvious contravention of his father's mandates. Among these were the rehabilitation and reopening of the Grand Canal, the building of a new capital at Beijing, an invasion of Annam, and numerous campaigns against the Mongols as well as the immense Zheng He voyages. Nor were the Zheng He voyages the only significant naval operations of the Yongle reign.

Prior to the re-opening of the Grand Canal in 1415, grain transport between the lower Yangzi and the northern garrisons followed the coastal route. Its vulnerability to piracy required convoy protection. This was a threat that the Ming took seriously. In 1406 Ming naval vessels returning from escort duty engaged a pirate flotilla off the Liaodong peninsula and pursued them all the way to the Korean coast. The commander of that convoy, the same Chen Xuan who had defected to Zhu Di in 1402, was later involved in major counterpiracy operations off the Fujian and Zhejiang coasts.[37] In addition, the early stages of the invasion and occupation of Annam (1406–27) involved numerous coastal operations in the Gulf of Tonkin and the South China Sea.[38] Needham, Wang, and Lu note that under Yongle, the Ming navy "consisted of some 3,800 ships in all, 1,350 patrol vessels and 1,350 combat ships . . . a main fleet of 400 large warships . . . and 400 grain-transport freighters."[39] These early Ming coastal operations, however, pale in comparison to the feats of the eunuch official Zheng He (1371–1433).

There were three main paths to political influence and power in Ming China: via the civil service exams into the civilian bureaucracy, via the military, or as a eunuch in the retinue of a prince or the emperor. Zheng He followed two of these trajectories. Born into a Muslim family in Yunnan, in China's southwest, Zheng (then surnamed Ma) was taken as a prisoner of war during the Ming conquest of the region, castrated, and assigned to serve in Zhu Di's retinue. He rose to prominence as a military commander during Zhu Di's revolt and was made head of the Directorate of Palace Servants immediately upon Yongle's accession to the Ming throne. Zheng's unique role as both senior palace eunuch and comrade-in-arms put him in direct contact with and made him a trusted confidant of the new emperor.[40] He was an obvious choice to lead one of the emperor's most ambitious projects.

The seven voyages that Zheng He commanded are divided into three groups. The first group comprised the first (1405–7), second (1407–9), and third (1409–11) voyages targeted at reopening the straits of Malacca (Melaka) and reinitiating contacts in the Indian Ocean, especially with Calicut (modern Kozhikode on India's Malabar Coast), a key Indian Ocean trading hub. The second group includes the fourth (1413–15), fifth (1417–19), and sixth (1421–22) voyages that expanded Ming trade and diplomatic contacts to the Middle East and East Africa. A seventh voyage (1431–33) came seven years after Yongle's death and retraced earlier voyages as far as Hormuz and sent out smaller contingents to East Africa.[41] In addition to the huge distances covered on these voyages, the scale and the likely expense of the enterprise is truly astounding. One voyage might involve 250 ships or more and twenty-seven thousand personnel, not to mention livestock, horses, and other draft animals. Among the ships, between 40 and 60 were *baochuan* (寶船), or "treasure ships," the largest of which may have been 440 feet in length and 180 feet abeam and displaced more than twenty thousand tons, making them the largest wooden ships ever built. While truly impressive in the numbers and sizes of the ships and very technologically sophisticated, Zheng He's fleet was relatively slow (with a top speed of no more than 2.5 to 3 knots) and was wholly dependent on favorable monsoon winds because the ships could not beat into the wind. The fleet thus sailed outbound on the northeasterly winter monsoon and returned with the southwesterly summer monsoon; this explains the neat two-year cycles of most of the voyages. In addition, these vessels were not what we might call warships today. Although they were equipped with large numbers of cannon for defense and presumably some offense, this was not a force designed to fight other navies at sea. Rather, they were to overawe any potential adversaries, or barring that, to disembark large numbers of soldiers that constituted the vast majority of the personnel on board.

The overarching motives for the voyages were, in contemporary national security parlance, diplomatic, to open or reopen tributary relations with the coastal and island kingdoms of the South China Sea and Indian Ocean; informational, to advertise the rise, the glory, and the power of the new Ming dynasty; military, to overawe, coerce, or compel; and economic, to lubricate and perhaps expand existing trade links. They were not voyages of exploration to discover new worlds or new markets in the European vein because they travelled along long-established trade routes. Of these four purposes, the diplomatic and informational were foremost. The military aspects, however, cannot be denied. Both Yongle and his confidant Zheng He were soldiers, and the voyages were organized and manned like a military operation. Nor was Zheng He averse to using force, as he did against the Chinese pirate Chen Zuyi (陈祖义) at Palembang in southern Sumatra (rendered as either Sanfoqi [三佛齐] or Jiugang [旧港] in Chinese sources[42]) during the first voyage and against the king of Ceylon on the third voyage. In addition, every voyage stopped at the main Champan port, modern Qui Nhon. Given that Champa was Yongle's key ally in his war against Annam, there may have been some elements of reassuring and reinforcing a strategic partner written into the rationale of the voyages.

The military aspects of Zheng He's missions seem to fly in the face of contemporary Chinese portrayals of the peaceful and "friendly" nature of the voyages. While these were certainly not voyages of conquest and colonization in the European model, they were nonetheless run by the Ming military and in a military fashion. It is important to contrast the overarching purposes with later European expeditions, but erasing the military character almost completely—as many official and nonofficial PRC sources do today—is going much too far.[43] A recent article in the People's Liberation Army's (PLA) foremost official newspaper acknowledges the military aspects of the voyages. Zheng and his men "captured and killed" the "Great Pirate" Chen Zuyi and "dealt a crushing defeat" to the king of Ceylon's armed forces after they tried to "plunder" the treasure fleet. Following these demonstrations of shock and awe with Chinese characteristics, "all countries were shocked and nobody dared to compete." The article concludes that material power—in the form of constructing a fleet and defeating threats—and not diplomatic niceties were what gave the Zheng He voyages their influence. In this vein, it implicitly criticizes Zheng for giving too much and taking back too little, thereby depleting the wealth of Ming and precipitating its resource overstretch and subsequent decline.[44] Moreover, the peaceful versus military distinction is based on a false dichotomy.[45] Because they had come of age during the founding wars of the Ming, neither Yongle nor Zheng He would perceive a clear distinction between the "civil" and the "martial"; rather, these men saw all instruments of Ming power as of one piece. To try to parse the "hard power" and "soft power" aspects of the voyages is therefore anachronistic.[46]

On the economic front, whereas Europeans went out looking for trade, the gravitational pull of the Chinese market brought the trade to it. When this trade was carried out under the tributary system, the Imperial court was the direct beneficiary. This could certainly have been attractive for Yongle, who is said to have been fond of rare and luxury items, but trade cannot be separated from the soft power aspects of the voyages. The economic benefits were secondary to the assertion of Chinese cultural primacy.[47] This is not to say that the voyages did not have an economic rationale or that there was not a significant amount of trading, both personal and official, taking place. Had they continued past the 1430s, these cruises would have represented a permanent insertion of the Ming state into Asian maritime trade. But Zheng He's primary purposes were to advertise the glories of the Ming Dynasty and the power of its new emperor and to smooth, expand, and extend the axes along which Ming China's gravitational pull could be felt, especially within the parameters of the tributary system. In other words, this was one aspect of a larger agenda to legitimate the new Ming dynasty as well as the usurper Yongle, and to repair Chinese foreign relations that had been damaged during the Yuan and that had lapsed during the late Yuan civil wars and the Ming consolidation. Within the framework of the tributary system employed by the Ming, "foreign rulers were to recognize the unique and superior status of the Chinese emperor as the Son of Heaven and the mediator between Heaven, earth and mankind. They were to show this recognition by presenting tribute in the local products of their countries and by accepting and using the Chinese official calendar, at least in their communications with China."[48] For a brief time, Zheng He's fleet became the primary conduit of these reciprocal exchanges between the Ming and its Southeast Asian and Indian Ocean tributaries by ferrying foreign emissaries to and from China and distributing trappings of tributary status to the Ming's new allies. The voyages, however, ceased abruptly in 1422, and only one additional mission was launched in the

1430s. The reasons for this retreat are many.[49] The expense of the missions and the costs of recapitalizing the fleet strained central government coffers already depleted by land campaigns and the construction of a new capital.[50]

The reemergence of the Mongol threat shifted the strategic focus from the coasts and maritime trade routes to the north and northwestern land frontiers. This shift was reinforced by the transfer of the Ming capital from Nanjing in the trade-oriented lower Yangzi region to Beijing, a city vulnerable to steppe nomad predation. This move and the reopening of the Grand Canal as the primary means of grain transport from the Yangzi region to the Northern Capital District naturally deemphasized maritime trade and naval issues among the Ming ruling elite. In addition, defeat in a campaign to annex Annam was further compounded by the innate hostility of the Ming's Neo-Confucian bureaucrats to both military adventurism and expensive central government projects directed and staffed by court eunuchs, such as the Zheng He voyages, of which the now-deceased Yongle emperor had been so fond. The bureaucracy had the additional argument that because the voyages ostensibly contravened the edicts of Zhu Yuanzhang, they were not just wasteful but also unfilial.

In many ways, Yongle was the worst enemy of his own ambitious maritime schemes. His multiple projects, especially the Mongol campaigns and the new capital, competed for Ming resources and strategic focus. The storm of controversy that arose over his plans for another Mongolian incursion in 1421 forced the abbreviation of the sixth voyage. After his death in 1424— which occurred, not surprisingly, while he was on yet another campaign in Mongolia—his successors were hard-pressed to justify the expense. At best, the final voyage of 1431–33 was motivated by the nostalgia of Yongle's grandson and made possible by the fact that the existing fleet was still seaworthy.

Most historians identify the end of the expeditions as a fundamental shift away from the sea. There are many elements of truth to this interpretation, if only for the fact that a focus on the Ming's continental frontiers made both military and economic sense. After the 1430s, the Ming did not devote any less attention to sea power than was rational, given its geostrategic situation. The Ming was the largest, wealthiest, and most powerful land empire in the world at that time. Chinese power extended so far on the mainland and was operating at such a remarkably saturated threshold of control that to expect a new emperor to have taken on a completely new universe of liabilities with respect to the maritime realm is unrealistic, especially in the face of bureaucratic opposition. The Ming kept about as much territory and as many people under its control as it conceivably could, particularly given the limits of both its tax base (tied as it was to more static agricultural levies) and the tyrannies of distance and logistics. This is not to say that the Ming did not miss a historic opportunity with regard to the maritime sector in the fifteenth century, but the political structure of the dynasty meant that the state could try to either contain the maritime sector, as it had under Hongwu, or dominate it, as was the case under Yongle. There was no middle ground between these extremes in which to construct more enlightened and productive ways to shape the relationship between the state and the commercial sector.

There were other impediments as well. In his path-breaking work on the maritime world of the late Ming, John E. Wills Jr. argues that the oceans remained peripheral to the Ming because of the vast and dangerous seas around China and the few significant trade opportunities to be had prior to the sixteenth century. He points to the Ming's lack of interest in colonizing Taiwan, only one hundred miles off the Fujian coast, as emblematic of this marginalization.[51] Policy choices and physical or commercial impediments did not mean, however, that the Ming or its subjects had entirely abandoned the sea. Moreover, the unique riverine environment of China, with much of the domestic trade and tax revenue carried by inland shipping, encouraged the Chinese to maintain a high level of maritime skills even in periods when the dynasty tried to rein in the maritime sector.

The extent of the Ming maritime retreat is overstated, as are the severity and effectiveness of the subsequent controls on maritime trade and shipbuilding. If anything, Yongle's successors came to realize the expense and folly of trying to inject the central government into maritime trade and returned to Zhu Yuanzhang's flawed but far more pragmatic pattern of containing the maritime sector within manageable bounds. The fundamental paradox of the Ming Dynasty, as well as all Chinese dynasties from the Song period onward, was that they had autocratic inclinations but minimal capabilities and limited tax revenues from the agricultural sector. The vast bulk of that revenue was already committed to the upkeep of the Imperial retinue, the maintenance of infrastructure (especially the Grand Canal), bureaucratic expenses, the tributary system, and the ground forces. This made it exceedingly difficult to divide the government's energies among many fronts and severely limited the amount of power it could devote to even its priorities. As a result, there was very little discretionary funding for and bureaucratic interest in becoming more involved in maritime matters. This also meant that what the state could not control directly, it had to either delegate the oversight to a trustworthy stakeholder (as all of the dynasties from the Song era on accomplished by handing off the ideological baton to the Neo-Confucian literati) or attempt to stifle through imperial edict. When it became obvious that maritime trade could not be shoe-horned into the tributary system or run as a government monopoly—one mission of the Zheng He voyages—the Ming chose to try to keep overseas trade at a low enough level that would neither strain government spending nor present a serious security problem.

In the long term, Edward Dreyer sees little tangible benefit of the Zheng He voyages for the Chinese state, especially as the diplomatic gains and expansion of the tributary system rapidly evaporated after the 1430s. However, I am forced to disagree on one point: With Malacca and Palembang in relatively friendly hands, one of the voyages' economic priorities was satisfied. Trade between China and the Indian Ocean region continued. The Ming also returned to the practice of licensing foreign merchants to trade at Chinese ports. While the system penalized Chinese merchants, it nonetheless recognized the value of overseas trade, which was only a fraction of the huge and growing domestic economy. The economic historian Ramon Myers has described the Ming economy as "reticular" or web-like, that is, dominated by neither horizontal nor vertical structures.[52] In other words, the economy was fundamentally parochial and functioned because the state held a mostly laissez-faire economic policy. The role of the government was to make sure that the canals and roads over which trade flowed remained functional.[53] This is in sharp contrast to the maritime European states in the age of discovery, which were compelled to participate in the opening of new markets. Ming China lacked that impetus. Finally, from the mid-fifteenth to the mid-sixteenth centuries there was a conspicuous absence of major war, especially maritime war, in East Asia.[54] For much of this period of the mid-Ming, then, the dynasty had sufficient naval power to meet its needs and a realistic (albeit conservative) degree of maritime awareness.

Ming China's Maritime Frontier in the Early Sixteenth Century

For much of the period between 1433 and the 1550s, the Ming Dynasty did not have a comprehensive maritime strategy and, as we have seen, did not really need one. By the sixteenth century, however, the arrival of Europeans in maritime Asia and the expansion of both the maritime economy and the numbers of Chinese involved in overseas trade would force a reappraisal. The Ming was initially slow to react to these challenges in part because during the preceding century the coastal defense network (as well as

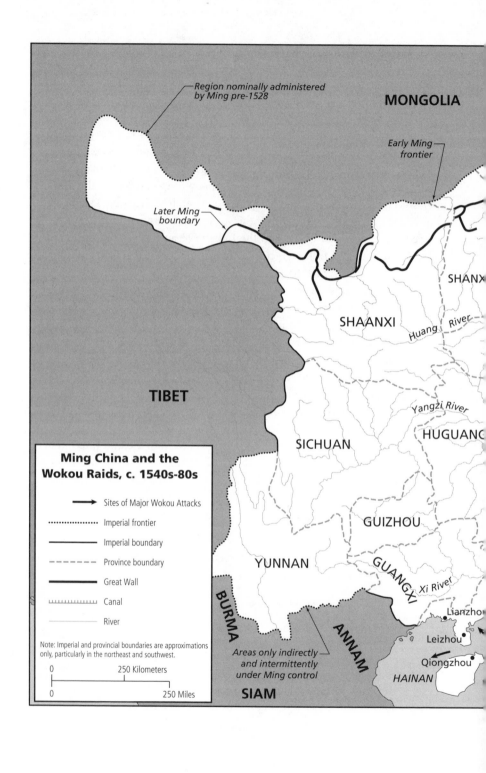

Region nominally administered
by Ming pre-1528

MONGOLIA

Early Ming
frontier

Later Ming
boundary

SHANX

SHAANXI

Huang   River

TIBET

Yangzi River

HUGUANG

SICHUAN

**Ming China and the
Wokou Raids, c. 1540s-80s**

→   Sites of Major Wokou Attacks

·············   Imperial frontier

———   Imperial boundary

– – – –   Province boundary

━━━   Great Wall

⊔⊔⊔⊔⊔⊔⊔   Canal

———   River

Note: Imperial and provincial boundaries are approximations
only, particularly in the northeast and southwest.

0   250 Kilometers
├──────────────┤
0   250 Miles

GUIZHOU

YUNNAN

GUANGXI

Xi River

Lianzho

Leizhou

BURMA

ANNAM

Areas only indirectly
and intermittently
under Ming control

Qiongzhou

HAINAN

SIAM

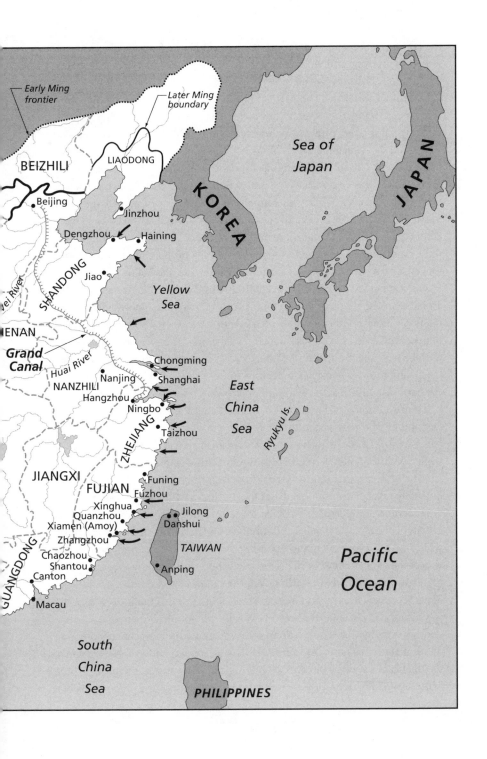

Early Ming
frontier

Later Ming
boundary

Sea of
Japan

JAPAN

KOREA

BEIZHILI

LIAODONG

Beijing

Jinzhou

Dengzhou

Haining

SHANDONG

Jiao

Yellow
Sea

Ryukyu Is.

East
China
Sea

Wei River

ENAN

Grand
Canal

Huai River

Chongming

Nanjing

Shanghai

NANZHILI

Hangzhou

Ningbo

ZHEJIANG

Taizhou

JIANGXI

FUJIAN

Funing

Fuzhou

Xinghua

Quanzhou

Jilong

Xiamen (Amoy)

Danshui

Zhangzhou

TAIWAN

Chaozhou

Shantou

Canton

Anping

GUANGDONG

Macau

Pacific
Ocean

South
China
Sea

PHILIPPINES

the larger *wei-suo* and military estates system) had fallen into disrepair and lacked manpower and resources, and because the inertia of precedent hindered timely policy reform.[55]

Within China, the commercialization and monetization of the economy and a population shift to the south meant that the seafaring population and value of maritime trade were both increasing relative to continental issues and the internal market.[56] In other words, the strategic and economic geography of China was changing fundamentally. With the arrival of the Europeans—drawn to Asia by the gravitational pull of the China market and flush with European and American silver—and the opening of large silver mines in Japan in the 1530s and 1540s, there was additional pressure to open China to less regulated and more multidimensional trade. By the mid-Ming, millions of tons of goods and tens of thousands of merchants and émigrés moved across the sea-lanes of the South China Sea, the Yellow Sea, and the Indian Ocean, and "by the 1540s Ming silks and porcelains were readily available in the shops of Lisbon and Antwerp."[57] Some Chinese officials and many Chinese merchants lobbied hard for an end to the maritime bans, but the initial Ming response was an extension of the bans to include even prohibitions against fishing boats in 1551.[58] The extension of the bans and the prohibitions against all maritime trade yielded the same result as in the early Ming: It drove merchants into piracy. Given the vast scale of the maritime economy and population, not to mention the addition of European technology, the new pirate threat was orders of magnitude greater than it had been in the fourteenth century.[59] It is no surprise, then, that the much-neglected Ming military was ill prepared for this challenge.

The Ming's vulnerability to the mid-sixteenth-century epidemic of piracy is usually taken to be emblematic of the decline of Ming power and military/bureaucratic competence. There is some hint of truth to this because the coastal *wei-suo* system had certainly been neglected in the century prior, which gave the pirates many openings. Conversely, we cannot reasonably expect the Ming to have been able to protect the entire Chinese coast against highly mobile pirate bands. Moreover, the piracy crisis is more indicative of Ming prosperity than it is of a purported Ming decline. Finally, despite some significant early missteps, Ming officials quickly rose to the piracy challenge and implemented a series of military reforms and policy concessions that defused the crisis and contained the threat. As we will see subsequently, the tactical, operational, and technological innovations adopted by the Ming served the dynasty very well later in the Imjin War (壬辰卫国战争).

Thus, rather than indicating decline, the second Wokou crisis reveals a military and economic resurgence.

The Portuguese were the first Europeans to arrive in any significant numbers in maritime Asia. Following Vasco da Gama's voyages in the 1490s, the Portuguese moved progressively across the Indian Ocean in the early 1500s, establishing a base at Goa in 1510 and toppling the Malacca sultanate the following year, thus opening the South China Sea to Portuguese trade. The capture of Malacca also meant that the Portuguese now controlled one of the main linkages between China and the global economy. Soon afterward, Portuguese traders attempted to open direct trade with China but were refused. In 1517 an official Portuguese embassy, including eight warships and commanded by Fernão Peres d'Andrade, tried to establish formal relations with the Ming but was also rebuffed because Portugal was not listed among the Ming's tributaries. Finally in 1520 Tomé Pires, a Portuguese ambassador, was granted—apparently due to some well-placed bribes—an audience with the Zhengde emperor (r. 1506–21) at the southern capital of Nanjing. The audience never took place, however. Pires' party then accompanied the imperial retinue on its return to Beijing but was again denied. On the pretext of Portuguese actions against the Sultanate of Malacca, the court formally rejected the foreigners' requests and imprisoned Pires.[60] Upon taking the throne, the Jiajing emperor (r. 1522–66) reiterated the maritime prohibitions, effectively denying the Portuguese the opportunity to trade legally. Not easily dissuaded, Simao d'Andrade, Fernão's brother, attempted to establish a trading station by force on the Guangdong coast, but his and a subsequent force were repulsed successfully by Ming naval forces.[61] Sino-Portuguese hostilities flared up again in the 1540s when European traders were driven out of coastal enclaves through the zealous actions the Zhejiang governor and commissioner for the coastal defense of Fujian and Zhejiang, Zhu Wan (朱纨). While in the near term the Ming Dynasty was successful in repulsing the Portuguese militarily, there were larger forces at work in maritime Asia, for which standing Ming maritime policy was ill suited. To put it another way, the maritime prohibitions were a decaying dam barely holding back a flood of Chinese commercial dynamism. Merchants, both Chinese and foreign, were eager to breach the dam, but at first the Ming tried to shore up its anachronistic policies. This sparked an immense wave of piracy.

The Second Wokou Crisis

Whereas the first phase of the mid-sixteenth century piracy crisis was homegrown, the second was transnational.[62] In the 1550s, Wang Zhi (王直), just one of many Chinese pirate-merchants of this era, was a frustrated merchant who massed hundreds of ships and thousands of followers to raid the Zhejiang coast and to plunder and pillage official granaries and treasuries. Imperial forces, many of them manned by aboriginal peoples from the southwest, were routed at almost every turn through 1555–56. At one point a negotiated solution seemed possible when Wang Zhi offered to surrender in exchange for a pardon and permission to trade, but others in the pirate business, notably Xu Hai (徐海), were more than willing to continue the fight. Wang Zhi did ultimately surrender in 1557 and was subsequently executed on orders from the Jiajing emperor (嘉靖). In the interim, a policy of appeasement and cooptation and the final defeat of Xu Hai by Hu Zongxian (胡宗宪) in 1556 alleviated the crisis somewhat, but the fundamental causes had not yet been addressed. [63] In addition, there was a great deal of confusion as to how best to respond to piracy. Some officials, such as Hu Zongxian and Zhao Wenhua (赵文华), were advocating a repeal of the maritime ban and offers of pardons to pirate leaders paired with military action against recalcitrants; others completely repudiated any form of appeasement and lobbied for reinforcing the bans. Moreover, Wang Zhi and Xu Hai had revealed the strategic vulnerabilities and commercial opportunities to be had along the China coast, and their defeat simply opened the door for new generations of Chinese and Japanese pirates, who harassed the Ming coasts well into the 1560s. Japanese daimyo were particularly interested in exploiting the lucrative China trade to enhance their wealth and power in their ongoing civil wars of the late sixteenth century.[64]

Finally, in 1563, the Ming military began to get a handle on the problem. Qi Jiguang (戚继光) was dispatched to Fujian to clear out several pirate bases. Qi was born into a hereditary military family and, although fairly young, had commanded coastal defenses in Shandong and served under Hu Zongxian during the antipiracy campaigns in the 1550s.[65] Qi was critical of the system of using nonnative troops; he preferred locals who had a vested interest in regional defense and whom he believed were easier to train and drill. Pirate raiding parties were often trained and led by Japanese warriors who emphasized cohesive small unit actions and close combat. Qi developed drill techniques, organizational innovations, and combined arms formations to counter that tactical advantage.[66] Qi's forces quickly gained the upper hand in combat against landing parties, and his campaign rapidly morphed into amphibious warfare to oust pirates from their offshore bases and to intercept raiding parties at sea. By the late 1560s the Ming was deploying large numbers of naval vessels, almost all armed with cannon, to meet the threat.

Nor was the resurgent Ming "navy" averse to pursuing pirates very far afield; in 1575 Ming forces chased the pirate Lin Feng (林凤) all the way to Luzon. Lin was a native of Guangdong and early in his freebooting career had become a protégé of Lin Daoqian (林道乾), who had bases on the Fujian and Guangdong coasts and at the port of Patani on the east coast of the Malay Peninsula. Ming offensives in 1563, led by Yu Dayou (俞大猷) and Qi Jiguang, had driven both Lins to abandon their coastal bases and set up operations on Taiwan. By late 1572, however, Lin Feng was once again harassing Guangdong and Fujian, and the Board of War launched a campaign to eliminate him and his followers. In 1574 an offensive commanded by Hu Shouren (胡守仁), the Fujian Regional commander, cost Lin Feng several ships and forced him to retreat once more to Taiwan and the Pescadores (澎湖岛). Reeling from this defeat, Lin captured a Chinese merchant junk returning from Luzon. Seeing the silver and gold the merchants had acquired in Manila and hearing of the rather shabby nature of the Spanish defenses, Lin and his fleet embarked from their base in the Pescadores and headed south to Luzon, apparently with the intention of ousting the Spanish and establishing a base at Manila.[67]

On the morning of 30 November 1574, Lin's men, numbering several hundred, landed at Manila and attacked the town. That attack was repulsed, as was a second assault on 2 December, but Lin Feng was determined to establish a base on Luzon, presumably because the islands were beyond the range of Ming naval forces. Accordingly, he left Manila bay and sailed north along the coast of Luzon to Lingayen Bay where he built two heavily fortified settlements. Meanwhile, the Chinese authorities had been alerted to Lin's attack on Manila. In April 1575, a Spanish ship encountered a Chinese embassy commanded by Wang Wanggao (王望高), a military official in the service of the governor of Fujian, Liu Yaohui (刘尧诲). Wang was dispatched to find Lin Feng, and either capture him, convince his subordinates to mutiny, or, if all else failed, offer him a pardon. Lin Feng managed to escape Lingayen and retreat back to the Taiwan straits area before the Ming forces arrived in strength in Luzon, but within a year the Ming had undermined Lin's power base through a combination of military action and by inducing his lieutenants to defect.[68]

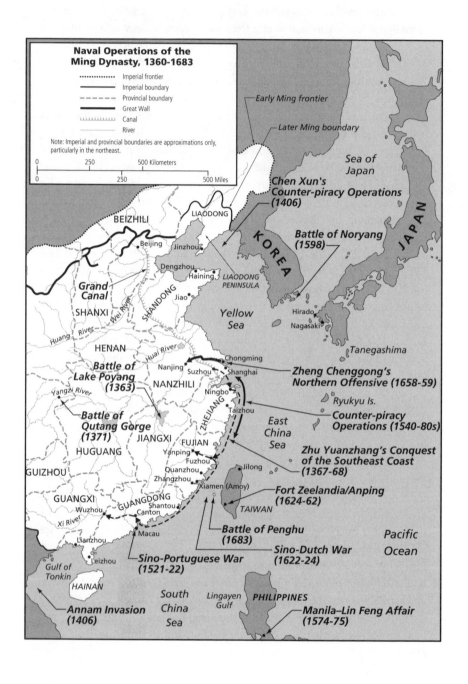

Naval Operations of the Ming Dynasty, 1360-1683

- ·············· Imperial frontier
- —— Imperial boundary
- – – – – Provincial boundary
- ▬▬ Great Wall
- ⊥⊥⊥⊥⊥⊥⊥ Canal
- ········· River

Note: Imperial and provincial boundaries are approximations only, particularly in the northeast.

0 — 250 — 500 Kilometers
0 — 250 — 500 Miles

Early Ming frontier

Later Ming boundary

Sea of Japan

Chen Xun's Counter-piracy Operations (1406)

JAPAN

Battle of Noryang (1598)

BEIZHILI

LIAODONG

KOREA

Beijing Jinzhou

Dengzhou

Haining LIAODONG PENINSULA

Grand Canal

SHANDONG

Jiao

Yellow Sea

Hirado

Nagasaki

SHANXI

Wei River

Huang River

HENAN

Huai River

Tanegashima

Battle of Lake Poyang (1363)

Nanjing Suzhou Shanghai

Chongming

Zheng Chenggong's Northern Offensive (1658-59)

Yangzi River

NANZHILI

Ningbo

Ryukyu Is.

Battle of Qutang Gorge (1371)

JIANGXI FUJIAN

ZHEJIANG

Taizhou

East China Sea

Counter-piracy Operations (1540-80s)

HUGUANG

Yanping

Fuzhou

Zhu Yuanzhang's Conquest of the Southeast Coast (1367-68)

GUIZHOU

Quanzhou

Zhangzhou

Jilong

Xiamen (Amoy)

Fort Zeelandia/Anping (1624-62)

GUANGXI

GUANGDONG

Shantou

Canton

TAIWAN

Wuzhou

Xi River

Battle of Penghu (1683)

Pacific Ocean

Lianzhou

Macau

Sino-Dutch War (1622-24)

Leizhou

Sino-Portuguese War (1521-22)

Gulf of Tonkin

HAINAN

South China Sea

Lingayen Gulf

PHILIPPINES

Annam Invasion (1406)

Manila–Lin Feng Affair (1574-75)

By the early 1570s the Wokou crisis had begun to abate. Ming military successes were abetted by the lifting of the maritime ban in 1567 and the initiation of an "open seas" policy that allowed licensed Chinese merchants to sail abroad for trade. That decision was particularly timely because it closely corresponded to the opening of new trading entrepôts in Macau (1557) and Manila (1571) that would soon be funneling silver into China. The new Ming trade policy did restrict foreign landings at Chinese ports and forbade Chinese trade with Japan, so some of the impetus for smuggling and piracy remained. In the near term, however, the Japan trade ban did not become a problem because the political consolidation in Japan under Oda Nobunaga (織田信長) and Toyotomi Hideyoshi had, at least for the time being, diverted Japanese energies to internal matters. Nonetheless, counterpiracy remained a strategic priority for the dynasty: "Ming vigilance and effectiveness continued for decades thereafter, as even as late as 1588 we read of a massive fleet of pirates being sunk off the coast of Zhejiang, with some 1600 losing their lives in their rout at the hands of the Ming."[69] In the early 1600s, in a clear indication of changed attitudes about maritime defense, the Ming began to fortify the Pescadores as an advance base for counterpiracy operations. The extent of the Ming's maritime resurgence is most clear from the Ming's military performance in the Imjin War.

We can see, then, that when faced with profound maritime security threats—the Wokou Crisis of the 1550s and 1560s and Toyotomi Hideyoshi's invasions of Korea (1592–98), to which I will turn next—the Ming could rise to challenges and deploy significant military power, especially naval forces. In the case of the Wokou, the military surge was mostly an indigenous Chinese response, with some aid from regional as well as European partners.[70] The threat that Hideyoshi posed to Korea, and ultimately to Ming primacy, required something on a much larger scale, compelling the Ming to reach out, both economically and technologically, to relatively new players on the Asian scene—the Dutch, Portuguese, and Spanish. This outreach reflected a fundamental shift both in the regional economy, especially the marked rise of American silver flowing into the region, and in the technological balance as European innovations in gunpowder weaponry played a crucial role in all these campaigns, but especially in the defense of Korea. These shifts were not nearly as lopsided as generally believed. In its dealings with all the actors involved, whether Asian or European, the Ming rightly acted as the hegemon and treated all others as junior partners. This was only natural, given that the gravitational pull of the Chinese market rendered all but the Japanese beholden to good relations with Beijing.[71] Likewise, in the arena of technology, the flow of military sophistication was not merely from West to East. Chinese technological prowess in nautical technology, mass production of gunpowder weapons, and the Ming military's ability to adapt and improve upon European models (which the Westerners then adopted) made this a good deal for Chinese and Europeans alike. In one ironic example of this technological accomplishment, a Spanish military officer serving in Manila was so impressed with Chinese cannon designs that he suggested casting fifty of the guns for use in an invasion of China.[72]

Ming Sea Power during the Imjin War

The late sixteenth century was a period of tremendous dynamism in maritime East Asia. The Dutch, Spanish, and Portuguese were a growing presence in the region, and Asia's indigenous powers were looking to maritime trade and security with great interest. Ming China benefited mightily from the boom in maritime trade. In 1597 alone it was estimated that nearly thirty-five metric tons of silver (more than 8.5 million taels[73]) entered China via Manila, exceeding the total amount produced by Chinese mines in the preceding fifty years. This sum likely amounted to more than twice the entire Ming tax revenue for that same year. For China, the material consequences of foreign trade were spectacular. The discovery and exploitation of overseas markets for Chinese products, dominated by tea, porcelains, and silks, catalyzed commercial expansion along the southeast coast. Demand created a boom in the trade networks of coastal China as suppliers scrambled to provide Fujian and Guangdong merchants with exports. Demand raised prices and created fortunes for the ambitious, talented, and lucky, leading to a significant change in Chinese culture and society in the late Ming era.[74] One of the most significant developments was that the elite families of the south and southeast that had traditionally trained their sons to serve in the bureaucracy were increasingly diversifying into the commercial sector. Classically trained scholars from these southern families still dominated the Ming civil bureaucracy, where they tended to lobby for small government and against imperial activism, but they were also the main beneficiaries of the commercial boom.[75]

In the 1590s, therefore, the Ming Dynasty was not a moribund state tottering toward an inevitable demise, as some have characterized the late Ming and especially the reign of the Wanli emperor (万历), r. 1573–1620.[76] Rather, the Ming was one of the more dynamic states in Asia. Under Wanli, the Ming developed a potent military that had proven its mettle already and would soon rise to the challenge of Hideyoshi's invasion of Korea.[77] The degree of tactical and organizational innovation that took place in these wars revealed the military realities that would characterize seventeenth century warfare across the globe and especially in the "gunpowder empires": professionally led mass infantry armies equipped with standardized firearms, supported by artillery, cavalry, and naval forces, all of which were dependent on immense and complicated logistical structures.[78] Silver was the basis of military power. This fact was not lost on the Ming emperor, who was intent on securing specie for his armies. Wanli's ambitions, however, especially his military campaigns, were under constant assault from the antistatist southern elite, not merely because they were proactive and required enhanced fiscal extraction (i.e., inserting the state into the southern economy, which was the southern elites' stock in trade) but also because they allowed Wanli to promote and reward military officers rather than mainstream bureaucrats.[79] From the Neo-Confucian (i.e., the official orthodox) point of view, "the ideal emperor was to act as an impartial adjudicator of bureaucratic disputes and a passionless vessel for ritual use. . . . [This ideal] served . . . to constrain and hamper emperors' efforts to assert themselves."[80] This model suited neither Wanli's personal style nor the challenges of the late sixteenth century. While their motivations might have been questionable, the southern elites' argument was particularly powerful because it was based on a strict interpretation of the ideological inclinations of Zhu Yuanzhang, the founding emperor. A similar argument had been used successfully in the fifteenth century to reverse many of Yongle's initiatives, notably the Zheng He voyages. Moreover, because the Ming founder had opted out of policies that would have allowed the state to legitimately and consistently draw revenue from commerce, his successors would have to either completely overhaul the system or fall back on interventionist and extortionist measures.

At this juncture it is necessary to muddy the waters somewhat on what some readers might see as a sharp distinction between "Neo-Confucian literati" or "southern elites" and the Ming state. Because the Ming bureaucracy was in large part staffed by Neo-Confucian elites, many of them southerners, while many of the interests of southern elites were analytically distinguishable from those of the imperial state, they were never wholly separable. Elites and the state were effectively joined in a social contract that kept them mutually interpenetrating and codependent. Elites formed the manpower base of the state and served as its proxies in local society; in return the state kept the peace, legitimized elites through the imperial examination system, and guaranteed elite preeminence against such cataclysmic events as peasant rebellion. In this sense elites were not inexorably opposed to state power or expansion of state revenue, especially because all of them hoped to dip into state revenues when it came their turn to don their official robes. They were particularly opposed, however, to any revenue schemes that might circumvent their critical medial role in the operations of the empire. As long as state revenues were tied to agriculture (which always represented the greatest percentage of imperial revenues) and elites sat at the fulcrum of the fiscal system—the state could never access those revenues without farming out their collection to elites—there was no problem. Schemes to involve the state in trade, conversely, implied both an expansion of the state apparatus itself (because trade agents were formal state employees, often court eunuchs whereas rural "tax farmers" remained private individuals) and the collection of revenue outside of the income streams that would afford local elites a cut. Although there were always interest groups within the government (the emperor, the court eunuchs, the military) for whom a renegotiation of the social contract was appealing, these prospects were distressing to elites (even elites serving in the state itself) for obvious reasons. As long as the dynastic state remained one of, by, and for elites, therefore, insurmountable systemic resistance would preclude permanent or profound state penetration of the commercial or maritime economies. It took an existential threat to the dynasty for the court to make any headway against these institutional and ideological impediments.

During the six years of violent struggle waged between Ming China, its Korean ally (the Choson Dynasty), and Hideyoshi's Japan, known as the Imjin War, Wanli seemed to have the upper hand in the contest with his own bureaucracy. Hideyoshi's intention was to use Korea as a springboard for the eventual conquest of the Ming; hence, Chinese intervention was dictated as much by a desire to defend a traditional ally as it was to save the dynasty.[81] In the midst of this crisis, therefore, Wanli was able to initiate a series of policies that would have been almost inconceivable in a time of peace and that allowed the court to tap directly into the foreign trade sector to cover the costs of the war.[82] The Ming's success in the Imjin War is difficult to imagine in the absence of both a vibrant maritime economy and such emergency measures. The most controversial of these fiscal expedients was the 1596 mining-intendant system, which tasked court eunuchs (under the guise of mining intendants) to extort silver bullion directly from local elites and merchants and otherwise insinuate the state into the southern bullion economy.[83] The fiscal apparatus of the Ming state was ill suited to the challenges of the late sixteenth and early seventeenth centuries. Reformers like Zhang Juzheng

(张居正), who had gained the favor of the emperor in the 1570s, tried in vain to overhaul the revenue apparatus by rationalizing agricultural taxes and reasserting the primacy of the state over local elites. Zhang's reforms failed in the face of stiff opposition from many quarters: Local officials resisted the expansion of the center, court eunuchs opposed Zhang's personal power, and Neo-Confucians rallied against any increase in the state's extractive capabilities. Profoundly flawed and divisive though it may have been, in the near term the intendant system placed central government officials at the nexus between foreign trade and the domestic market.[84]

The Ming was victorious in its military campaigns in Korea through a combination of superior leadership, mobilization, and innovation that included the widespread adoption of firearms and gunpowder artillery, and the professionalization of officer and enlisted ranks.[85] Ming success at sea and in amphibious operations was also based on the hard-won experience from the second Wokou crisis as well as a large oceangoing population leveraged for service in the dynasty's fleets and a robust shipbuilding infrastructure. Early in the war Ming commanders realized that they held the advantage in naval warfare and that the Japanese were more proficient at land warfare—an ironic observation given that Japan is an island nation and China a continental power; nevertheless, the Chinese maintained their maritime advantages throughout the conflict while progressively improving their ground combat capabilities.[86] Established Ming naval power and proficiency bought the Ming precious time and were critical enablers in the war itself. Of equal importance is the fact that because Hideyoshi could not deploy sufficient naval forces to expand the war to include attacks on China's northern and southern ports, now stoutly defended, or to harass Chinese maritime trade, the silver flow was not disrupted. In other words, Ming naval power prevented Hideyoshi from isolating the theater of war and from denying the Chinese the means to wage war. Korean naval power was also important, especially the actions of Adm. Yi Sunsin and the introduction of ironclad "Turtle Boats" that could close with the large Japanese ships and pummel them with cannon. In the final naval engagement of the Imjin War, the Battle of Noryang Point (露梁海战, 16 December 1598), a combined Sino-Korean force of 150 ships and more than fifteen thousand men routed a larger Japanese force with superior seamanship and gunnery and completely wrecked the Japanese attempts to withdraw their forces from the peninsula intact.[87]

In the longer term, however, Wanli undermined this great strategic success achieved in Korea when he tried to make the widely unpopular and grossly inefficient fiscal expedients of the 1590s permanent even after the crises in Korea and elsewhere had passed. By 1604 Wanli's antistatist adversaries that later coalesced into the Donglin Faction (东林党) had finally blunted his efforts to permanently insinuate the state into the maritime trade sector. In the relative peace of the 1600s, few saw the merits of continuing the emergency measures implemented during the 1590s, especially when the political environment had swung away from the statist agenda with its demands for revenue to the southern literati, who wanted the keep the state out of the southern economy. Factionalism and the opprobrium leveled at Wanli's policy initiatives hampered the court's ability to deal with frontier threats and maintain the impressive military edge that the Ming had acquired in the 1590s. Military success was followed by a disastrous retreat from innovative fiscal policy and a forward-looking maritime policy. The Donglin were ultimately purged by the powerful eunuch Grand Secretary Wei Zhongxian (魏忠贤), contributing even further to the factional infighting and self-destructive pathologies that paralyzed the late Ming.[88] By the 1630s the Ming court would find itself revenue-poor and militarily weak in the face of growing internal and external threats while ruling over a domestic economy that was both huge and directly tied to the immense global movement of wealth. Nevertheless, although nowhere near as ostentatious or spectacular as the Zheng He enterprise, the Ming developed impressive naval capabilities in the late sixteenth century, capabilities that I would argue were appropriate to a large continental empire with a long coastline and extensive overseas trade linkages. The problem was that because of the ideological inclinations of the Ming elite and the systemic flaws in the Ming fiscal apparatus, the dynasty could not sustain that level of effort. This opened the way for new contenders to amass maritime power beyond the reach of the faltering Ming state.

The Rise and Fall of the Zheng Family

Following the Imjin War, the Ming lapsed into a general attitude of benign neglect toward the sea and returned to the pattern of investing regional officials with authority over maritime affairs. Counterpiracy operations continued, and there were some naval skirmishes arising from European and Japanese efforts to seize bases on Taiwan and the Pescadores, including a short and successful naval war against the Dutch in the early 1620s, but for a wide variety of reasons the court's attention lay elsewhere. The maritime sector nonetheless remained very dynamic and proved critical in delaying the ultimate Ming collapse. Moreover, as will be seen in Bruce Elleman's chapter in this volume, the final Ming defeat on Taiwan would have been impossible were it not for the Qing's success in leveraging Chinese seafaring and warfare expertise. The convergence of maritime dynamism and official neglect in turn allowed for the emergence of powerful commercial/military forces beyond Ming control in the early seventeenth century, most notably the Zheng family.

The founder of the Zheng family's pirate/merchant/official empire was Zheng Zhilong (郑芝龙), a Fujianese raised in the Portuguese enclave of Macau where he was baptized a Catholic.[89] Zheng began his merchant/pirate career in southern Japan under the tutelage of Li Dan (李旦), the Chinese headman at Hirado (平户) and the dominant figure in the illicit Hirado-Xiamen trade. Because of the continued Ming ban on Sino-Japanese trade, the Japanese ports at Hirado, Nagasaki, and Tanegashima (种子岛) were hotbeds of smuggling and of Western–Asian collaboration.[90] After Li's death in 1625, Zheng was involved in the battle to take over Li's business interests and his fleet. In this struggle, Zheng cultivated an ambiguous alliance with the Dutch East India Company on Taiwan. The Dutch were particularly eager to expand their access to the China market and to break the hold that the Portuguese and Spanish had on regional trade. As a privateer attacking Iberian shipping and as a commercial and diplomatic conduit to the Ming, Zheng Zhilong could apparently help them on both these objectives.[91] By the late 1620s Zheng dominated the trade between Taiwan and Fujian, and the Ming had not only pardoned him for his predatory past but had also offered him an official title and command of counterpiracy in the Taiwan straits area.[92] By the late 1630s and early 1640s, Zheng Zhilong was probably the most powerful Chinese individual operating in Asian waters, and he is emblematic of the ambivalent place of China's seafaring culture in the late Ming. In a sense, the Ming was outsourcing its maritime security. The trading post that the Dutch established in southern Taiwan as well as the cession of Macau to the Portuguese are also clear indicators that the Ming was perfectly content to outsource the management of trade entrepôts to non-Chinese, who then attracted Chinese merchants, sailors, and craftsmen to make these entrepôts economically viable. This was the case not only in Taiwan and Macau but also farther offshore in Manila, Malacca, Batavia, and Japan. The arrival of the Europeans in Asian waters had empowered the Chinese seagoing population, not displaced it. Zheng Zhilong is therefore indicative of the kind of economic and military power that one man was able to gather in this ungoverned space beyond China's shores, which explains the Ming's desire to co-opt him.

The state to which Zheng had shifted his allegiance, however, was rapidly unraveling. A series of hugely destructive rebellions across northern and central China had severely weakened the Ming. At the same time, the Manchu's new Qing dynasty—proclaimed in 1636—began to make incursions across the Great Wall and even threatened Beijing in the late 1630s. In April 1644 a rebel army entered the capital, and the Ming emperor committed suicide. The rebel interregnum lasted only a few weeks as Manchu and former Ming forces retook the capital. In the meantime, fragments of the court fled south where they set up a temporary government at Nanjing, with the Prince of Fu as "Protector of the State" and later as the Hongguang (弘光) emperor. Plans for consolidating in the south and even retaking the north rapidly disintegrated in the face of mounting debt, strategic incoherence, and political infighting. Qing forces took Nanjing in June 1645 and drove the emperor to flight.

The Ming collapse placed Zheng Zhilong on the horns of a dilemma: support the scattering Ming or surrender to the Qing as so many Ming officials and military commanders were doing. Zheng initially accepted command of the defenses of Ming-held Fuzhou and at one point tried to enlist Japanese military support for the Ming cause. At Fuzhou the Ming regent, the Prince of Tang (later Longwu emperor, 隆武), lavished emoluments on Zheng and even "adopted" his son Zheng Sen and gave the young man the new name of Zheng Chenggong (郑成功) and the title of Lord of the Imperial Surname (国姓爷, better known as Koxinga). Imperial indulgence notwithstanding, as the Qing began massing forces in 1645 for an assault on the port city, Zheng shifted allegiance and allowed the Manchus to capture Fuzhou and slaughter the emperor and his family.[93]

Zheng Zhilong's defection split the Zheng family. As the elder Zheng was transported to Beijing, Zheng Chenggong took up the Ming banner. During the late 1640s he built up his own power base and harassed Qing forces along the coast. In the process, he supplanted his uncles and brothers as claimants to the Zheng legacy. By the mid-1650s Zheng controlled much of the Fujian coast and was planning a massive amphibious assault on the Lower Yangzi region, possibly involving 250,000 troops and more than two thousand ships. Zheng's power forced the Qing to try to arrange his defection from the Ming, and Manchu emissaries delivered letters from Zheng Zhilong to persuade his son to abandon the Ming cause; instead, Zheng Chenggong used the time that these negotiations bought him to prepare for his Yangzi campaign.

Zheng's northern offensive was truly audacious in both scale and objectives. Delayed by bad weather and other mishaps, the offensive effectively began in 1658, and by August 1659 Zheng's forces were laying siege to Nanjing. The audacity of the campaign was also its undoing. Supplying such a force so far inland exhausted Zheng's resources, and he was playing to the Qing's strengths as a land power. By late 1659 the Ming loyalist forces had been routed on land, and Zheng fled by sea to his base at Xiamen (夏门). Although he remained unassailable at sea, Zheng's coastal bases were now vulnerable to Qing offensives. In 1661, therefore, Zheng left Xiamen and sailed to southern Taiwan where his impressive naval forces besieged the Dutch colony at Castle Zeelandia.[94] The Dutch finally surrendered after nine months, and Zheng became undisputed master of the very successful Sino-Dutch colony on Taiwan. He even contemplated seizing Manila farther to the south. Throughout these campaigns, Zheng remained fanatically loyal to the Ming cause, but essentially, his was a completely independent domain.[95] In 1661 Zheng Zhilong was executed by the Manchus, and the Ming cause suffered yet another setback when the latest imperial claimant was captured. Reeling from these two blows, Zheng Chenggong succumbed to a combination of physical and mental ailments and died in June 1662, leaving his son Zheng Jing (郑经) to inherit his maritime empire.[96]

In the near term, there was little that the Qing could do to oust the Zhengs from Taiwan. The Manchus were uncomfortable with the sea and skeptical of those naval commanders that they could recruit; the two assaults they attempted in 1664 and 1665 were aborted. In addition, the Qing had yet to consolidate its control on the mainland and could ill afford the costs of an amphibious assault whereas others in officialdom argued for following the Ming policy of essentially ignoring Taiwan. The new dynasty nonetheless tried to impose economic sanctions on Taiwan and ordered an evacuation of the Fujian coast, but these met with mixed results because much of Taiwan's trade was with Japan and European traders unaffected by Qing prohibitions. In addition, beginning in 1673 the Qing was convulsed by the Revolt of the Three Feudatories (三藩). Hoping to capitalize on Qing setbacks, Zheng Jing sent forces from Taiwan to retake bases along the Fujian coast. By 1680, however, the Qing had regained the upper hand, defeated most of the rebellion on land, and driven the Zheng forces out of Fujian.

By 1681 the resurgent Qing was at last able to set its sights on Taiwan and finally eliminate the last major impediment to its rule. For this daunting undertaking, the Qing turned to Shi Lang (施琅), a former commander in the Zheng family who had defected to the Qing after Zheng Jing had ordered the slaughter of his family. Shi Lang was particularly methodical in his preparations for his final campaign against the Zhengs. Moreover, the Qing plan was not simply military. In 1682 the Fujian viceroy offered amnesty to all Zheng forces, leading to large defections from Taiwan back to Fujian. This and well-placed bribes gradually undermined the Zheng position on Taiwan. Moreover, Shi Lang held off on a direct invasion of Taiwan and instead forced the Zheng navy to contest at the Penghu (Pescadores) archipelago in the middle of the Taiwan Strait. Shi Lang's force of several hundred ships and more than twenty thousand troops met a much depleted Zheng force at the Battle of Penghu (澎湖海战) in July 1683. Shi's decisive victory in that battle led in turn to the capitulation of the Zheng family in September 1683 and to the formal annexation of Taiwan into the Qing polity (as a prefecture of Fujian Province). This direct incorporation of Taiwan into official mainland administration was a step that neither the Ming nor any previous dynasty had ever attempted.[97] Thus, in one final naval engagement, the diminishing hopes of restoring the Ming were finally extinguished.

Conclusion

My purpose in this chapter has not been to prove that Ming China was a sea power in the modern sense of the term. Throughout the dynasty, the strategic foci were consistently continental. At times the maritime sphere was elevated to a strategic priority, as was the case under Yongle in the early fifteenth century and in the Jiajing and Wanli reigns of the late sixteenth and early seventeenth centuries, but the sea was never a consistent priority. That was an eminently workable attitude for Ming China. It would have been ill advised to transform the Ming into a sea power; continental issues rightly prevailed. Notwithstanding these geostrategic realities, however, the endurance of a dynamic maritime sector—despite all the Ming's efforts to contain it—and the gravitational pull that the China market had on regional and global trade meant that Ming China retained all the fundaments of sea power: wealth, raw materials, market access, technological acumen, and native talent. Under the leadership of an audacious emperor, or in times of major threat, the Ming could leverage this latent potential, as it did with the Zheng He voyages and in the Wokou crises and the Imjin War.

The problem was that the Ming, barring a dramatic overhaul of its fiscal apparatus, could not consistently fund and manage a navy. A systemic reform would have to overcome significant precedent and institutional inertia, a process that would take time that the dynasty could ill afford in times of crisis. The other option was direct state penetration of the commercial or maritime economies, as Wanli had implemented in the 1590s. Both of these courses of action would only have been possible over a sustained period with the accession of the southern literati who both staffed the imperial bureaucracy and were increasingly involved in commerce, and with it, foreign trade. That accession was improbable given the vested interests of the elite in keeping the state out of the commercial and maritime economies and in preventing the court from circumventing their role in society. After Wanli, no emperor appears to have had the will or the opportunity to change the state of affairs or to contest the potent ideological arguments that the literati deployed to rein in statist ambitions. Therefore, despite abundant latent potential for sea power, the Ming state was ideologically and institutionally handicapped when it came converting that potential into actual maritime power.

Those impediments also prevented the Ming from striking a balance between continental and maritime power. In the late sixteenth century the Ming was temporarily able to build and maintain the kinds of naval forces appropriate to its new strategic geography, but within a few decades it had fallen back to outsourcing maritime security to the likes of Zheng Zhilong. By the 1630s Ming control on the continent had decayed so badly and factional in-fighting had become so endemic that the best the dynasty could do was attach itself to these maritime princes rather than co-opt the maritime sector as it had done in the previous century. At that point, not even the powerful Zheng clan could save the Ming as a viable continental regime. As we will see, the Qing inherited many of the Ming's institutional and ideological handicaps and carried them through into the nineteenth century, when the dangers and opportunities of the maritime world were of a completely new magnitude.

Finally, there is a prevailing notion that whatever maritime character Ming China possessed—especially in the all-too-brief burst of navalism in the early fifteenth century—was an aberration from a tradition of continentalist isolationism. I would assert instead that China's tragic maritime history of the last two centuries has been the aberration and that China is now returning to the more natural balance between the continental and the maritime that characterized the period from the Southern Song to the mid-Qing. The ways in which Ming China interacted with its neighbors and with the global economy, especially in the late sixteenth century, are therefore highly relevant to China's current maritime transformation and mean that maritime China in the twenty-first century will look much more like that of the Ming era than that of the late Qing or early PRC. If this is the case, then the implications are far ranging and deserving of very careful examination. Despite more than a century of foreign domination and subsequent decades of mismanagement under the PRC government during the Maoist Era, contemporary China still retains many of the same fundaments of maritime power that the Ming enjoyed. Over the past thirty years Beijing has gradually loosened the bonds that kept this dynamism in check, and the Chinese nation has reaped both the benefits and the liabilities of hitching its fortunes to maritime trade. The answer to the question of whether the PRC can avoid the systemic flaws and ideological impediments that prevented the Ming from legitimately and consistently harnessing China's maritime potential to the benefit of Chinese security and prosperity will likely define the history of Asia in the twenty-first century.

Notes

1. See John E. Wills Jr., "Maritime China from Wang Chih to Shih Lang: Themes in Peripheral History," in Jonathan Spence and John E. Wills, eds., *From Ming to Ch'ing: Conquest, Region, and Continuity in Seventeenth-century China* (New Haven, CT: Yale University Press, 1979), 201–38; and Robert Gardella, "The Maritime History of Late Imperial China: Observations on Current Concerns and Recent Research," *Late Imperial China* 6, no. 2 (December 1985): 48–66. One recent book argues that the post–Zheng He retreat meant that "China played no role in the sixteenth- and seventeenth-century struggle for hegemony in Asia." Given the Ming performance in the Imjin War, that assertion does not bear much scrutiny. Jakub J. Grygiel, *Great Powers and Geopolitical Change* (Baltimore: Johns Hopkins University Press, 2006), 123–63. For the revisionist view see Gang Deng, *Maritime Sector, Institutions, and Sea Power of Premodern China* (Contributions in Economics and Economic History) (Westport, CT: Greenwood Press, 1999).

2. 秦大树, 谷艳雪, [Qin Dashu and Gu Yanxue], "越窑的外销及相关问题 *Yueyao de waixiao ji xiangguan wenti* [On the Inter-relation between Porcelains and Export Production]," in 沈琼华 [Shen Qionghua] 主编 [ed.], 中国越窑高峰论坛论文集 *Zhongguo yueyao gaofeng luntan lunwenji* [Collected Essays on the Apogee of Chinese Porcelain Production] (北京 [Beijing]: 文物出版社 [Cultural Relics Publishing], 2008), 177–206.

3. 龍江船厰志 [*Longjiang Chuanchang Zhi*], by 李昭祥 [Li Zhaoxiang], contains descriptions and dimensions for the large vessels built at the imperial yards in Nanjing. 闽省水师各标镇协营战哨船只图说 [*Minsheng Shuishi Gebiao Zhen Xieying Zhanshao Zhitu Shuo*] contains illustrations, dimensions, and schematics for the smaller coastal defense ships constructed in Fujian province. Mao Yuanyi's 1621 compilation covers the entire array of late Ming military technology and tactics. 茅元儀 [Mao Yuanyi], 武備志 *Wubei zhi* [Treatise on Armament Technology], 22 Vols. (台北, 中華民國 [Taipei, Republic of China]: 華世出版社 [China World Press], 1987).

4. 张铁牛, 高晓星 [Zhang Tieniu and Gao Xiaoxing], 中国古代海军史 *Zhongguo Gudai haijun shi* [*Ancient Chinese Naval History*] (北京[Beijing]: 解放军出版社 [People's Liberation Army Press], 2006), 117–47.

5. Ibid., 147–60.

6. Both Marco Polo and Ibn Battutah wrote at length and admiringly of the size, diversity, and sophistication of Chinese ships. Joseph Needham, Wang Ling, and Lu Gwei-Djen, *Science and Civilisation in China*, Vol. 4, *Physics and Physical Technology*, Part III. Civil Engineering and Nautics (Cambridge, U.K.: Cambridge University Press, 1971), 379–477 and 561–87.

7. Ibid., 678–95; and Zhang and Gao, *Ancient Chinese Naval History*, 176–206.

8. Zhang and Gao, *Ancient Chinese Naval History*, 191–92. For more on medieval gunpowder weaponry, see Joseph Needham, with Ho Ping-Yu, Lu Gwei-djen, and Wang Ling, *Science and Civilisation in China*, Vol. 5, *Chemistry and Chemical Technology*,

Part 7. Military Technology; the Gunpowder Epic (Cambridge, U.K.: Cambridge University Press, 1987).

9. The best English source for this campaign is Edward L. Dreyer, "The Poyang Campaign, 1363: Inland Naval Warfare in the Founding of the Ming Dynasty," in Frank A. Kierman Jr. and John K. Fairbank, eds., *Chinese Ways in Warfare* (Cambridge, MA: Harvard University Press, 1974), 202–40. See also Peter Lorge, "Water Forces and Naval Operations," in David A. Graff and Robin Higham, eds., *A Military History of China* (Boulder, CO: Westview Press, 2002), 89–91; José Din Ta-san and Francisco F. Olesa Muñido, *El Poder naval chino: Desde sus orígenes hasta la caída de la Dinastía Ming* (Barcelona: Ariel, 1965); and Zhang and Gao, *Ancient Chinese Naval History*, 160–67.

10. Edward L. Dreyer, *Early Ming China: A Political History, 1355–1435* (Stanford, CA: Stanford University Press, 1982), 61–64.

11. One estimate puts the Ming naval forces in 1370 at 1,200 warships and more than 130,000 men. 杨金森范中义 [Yang Jinsen and Fan Zhongyi], 中国海防史上册, 1368–1644, *Zhongguo haifang shi: Shangce* [History of Chinese Coastal Defense, 1368–1644 vol. 1], (北京 [Beijing]: 海洋出版社 *Haiyang chubanshe* [Ocean Press], 2005), 91.

12. All Ming emperors were patrilineal descendants of Zhu Yuanzhang, and all shared the family name Zhu. Historiographical convention is usually to refer to an emperor by his reign title, sometimes by his given name, or by his posthumous temple name; thus Zhu Yuanzhang (given name) is referred to as the Hongwu emperor (reign name), or Ming Taizu (honorific temple name); Zhu Di is the Yongle emperor, or Ming Chengzu; and Zhu Yijun is the Wanli emperor, or Ming Shenzong. I will use reign titles for the most part when discussing later Ming emperors and primarily use the given names for Zhu Yuanzhang and Zhu Di, which follows the historio-graphical convention for founding emperors.

13. Dreyer, "Poyang Campaign," 223; and "Liao Yung-chung" and "Y̧ T'ung-hai" in L. Carrington and Fang Chaoying, eds., *Dictionary of Ming Biography, 1364–1644* (New York: Columbia University Press, 1976), 909–10 and 1618–21.

14. John W. Dardess, *Confucianism and Autocracy: Professional Elites in the Founding of the Ming Dynasty* (Berkeley: University of California Press, 1983).

15. Timothy Brook has persuasively shown the limits of Ming policy in limiting commerce. In fact, early Ming infrastructure projects and the state's lack of attention in the market actually encouraged trade. Timothy Brook, *The Confusions of Pleasure, Commerce and Culture in Ming China* (Berkeley: University of California Press, 1999).

16. 王日根 [Wang Rigen], "明代海防建设与倭寇, 海贼的炽盛 *Mingdai haifang jianshe yu wokou, haizei de chisheng* [Coastal Defense and the Rampancy of Japanese Pirates during the Ming Dynasty]," 中国海洋大学学报 (社会科学版) [*Journal of China Oceans University* (Social Sciences Edition)], no. 4 (2004): 13–18.

17. Edward L. Dreyer, *Zheng He: China and the Oceans in the Early Ming Dynasty, 1405–1433* (Library of World Biography Series) (New York: Longman, 2007), 15–16.

18. Dreyer, *Zheng He*, 40.

19. Yang and Fan, 57–95.

20. Ibid., 22–23 and 57–65.

21. Frederick W. Mote, "The Rise of the Ming Dynasty, 1330–1367," in Frederick W. Mote and Denis Twitchett, eds., *The Cambridge History of China*, Vol. 7: *The Ming Dynasty, 1368-1644*, Part I (Cambridge, U.K.: Cambridge University Press, 1988), 29–37.

22. 李未醉, 李魁海, [Li Weizui and Li Kuihai], "明代海禁政策及其对中暹经贸关系的影响 *Mingdai haijin zhengce jiqi dui Zhong-Xian jingmao guanxi de yingxiang* [The Ming Dynasty's Maritime Prohibition Policy and Its Impact on Sino-Siamese Trade]," 兰州学刊 [*Lanzhou Academic Journal*] (May 2004): 253–55.

23. Dreyer, *Early Ming China*, 55–57; see also 陈文石 [Chen Wenshi], "明代卫所的军 *Mingdai weisuo de jun* [The Troops of the Ming Dynasty's Wei-suo System]," 中央研究院史语所集刊 [Collected Papers of the Academia Sinica's History and Literature Section] 48, no. 2 (June 1977): 222–62; 洪淑湄 [Hong Shumei] "明代的海防经营 *Mingdai de haifang jingying* [The Management of the Ming Dynasty's Coastal Defenses]," 史学会刊 [*Journal of Historiography*] 19 May 1989: 231–32; and 刘金祥 [Liu Jinxiang], "明代卫所缺伍的原因探析 *Mingdai weisuo quewu de yueyin tanxi* [An Examination and Analysis of the Causes for the Shortage of Soldiers in the Ming Dynasty's Wei-suo System]," 北方论丛 [The Northern Forum], May 2003, 71–74.

24. Edward L. Dreyer, "Military Origins of Ming China," in Frederick W. Mote and Denis Twitchett, eds., *The Cambridge History of China*, Volume 7: *The Ming Dynasty, 1368-1644*, Part I (Cambridge, U.K.: Cambridge University Press, 1988), 104.

25. Dreyer, *Early Ming China*, 78. The influence of the *wei-suo* system would later be seen in Han-era "agricultural garrisons" (屯田), Qing-era "military colonies" (兵屯), and even the PRC-era "construction corps" (e.g., the Xinjiang Production-Construction Corps [XPCC, 新疆生产建设兵团]). The latter organizations, designed to settle, render agriculturally self-sufficient, and develop economically remote regions (e.g., Heilongjiang, Inner Mongolia, and Xinjiang) while engaging in border defense and preparing to resist potential invaders, are testimony to both subsequent civilian coastal development and the PRC's largely continental focus throughout the Cold War.

26. Wang Rigen, *Coastal Defense*, 13–14.

27. The dispersal of the coastal garrisons can likely be explained by the shortage of land for very large colonies and the inherently decentralized nature of the pirate threat. In peacetime the manpower complement for each *wei* and *suo* were supposed to be reduced to caretaker and maintenance levels. Zhang and Gao, *Ancient Chinese Naval History*, 206–20. See also "Tang He yu mingchu dongnan haifang [Tang He and Southeastern Coastal Defense in the Early Ming]," in 吳智和編 [Wu Zhihe, ed.], 明史研究論叢 [*Collection of Ming Historical Research*], Vol. II (台北 [Taibei]: 大立出版社 [Dali Publishing], 1984), 145–221; and 孔东 [Kong Dong], "明代卫所

制度之研究 *Mingdai weisuo zhidu zhi yanjiu* [Research into the Ming Dynasty's Wei-suo System]," 文史学报 [*Journal of Literature & History*], no. 2 (July 1976).

28. 于志嘉 [Yu Zhijia], "明代江西卫所屯田 *Mingdai Jiangxi weisuo tuntian* [The Wei-suo Military Farms of Ming Dynasty Jiangxi]," 中央研究院史语所集刊 [*Collected Papers of the Academia Sinica's History and Literature Section*], 67, no. 3 (September 1996): 654–742; 于志嘉 [Yu Zhijia], "明代江西卫所军役的演变 *Mingdai Jiangxi weisuo junyi de yanbian* [The Evolution of Military Service in the Wei-suo of Ming Dynasty Jiangxi]," 中央研究院史语所集刊 [*Collected Papers of the Academia Sinica's History and Literature Section*] 68, no. 1 (March 1997): 1–53; and 黄中青 [Huang Zhongqing], 明代海防的水寨与游兵—浙闽粤沿海岛屿防卫的建置与解体 *Mingdai haifang de shuizhai yu youbing—Zhe-Ming-Yue yanhai daoyu fangwei de jianzhi yu jueti* [The Ming Dynasty Coastal Defense System's Riverine Defenses and Water Forces—The Establishment and Decline of Coastal and Island Defense in Zhejiang, Fujian and Guangdong] (台北 [Taibei]: 中国文化大学史学研究所硕士论文 [Master's thesis, Chinese Cultural University Department of History], 1996).

29. 陈仁锡着 [Chen Renxi, ed.], "太祖高皇帝宝训 *Taizu Gaohuangdi baoxun* [The Precious Injunctions of Emperor Ming Taizu]," 皇明世法录 *Huangmingshi falu* [*Political Encyclopedia of the Ming Dynasty*], Vol. 6 (台北 [Taibei]: 学生书局 [Student Press], 1965), 164. For the early Ming campaigns against offshore bases, see John D. Langlois Jr., "The Hung-wu Reign, 1368–1398," in Frederick W. Mote and Denis Twitchett, eds., *The Cambridge History of China*, Vol. 7: *The Ming Dynasty, 1368–1644* (Cambridge, U.K.: Cambridge University Press, 1988), Part I, 168–69.

30. Dreyer, *Early Ming China*, 102.

31. 陈文石 [Chen Wenshi], 明洪武嘉靖间的海禁政策 *Ming Hongwu Jiajing jian de haijin zhengce* [*The Ming Maritime Prohibition Policy during the Wanli and Jiajing Eras*] (台北 [Taibei]: 国立台湾大学文史丛刊 [National Taiwan University Literature and History Series], 1988).

32. Many readers may be frustrated with the brevity of this section of the chapter. In my defense, the Zheng He voyages are by now very familiar, and in some cases controversial, territory. See Gavin Menzies' very problematic *1421: The Year China Discovered the World* (New York: Bantam, 2003) as well as Robert Finlay's "How Not to (Re)Write World History: Gavin Menzies and the Chinese Discovery of America," *Journal of World History* 15, no. 2 (June 2004): 229–42. The best work in English to date on the voyages is Dreyer, *Zheng He*. I strongly recommend it to all those interested in a scholarly treatment of these argosies. In addition, one purpose of the current chapter is to look beyond the very long shadow of Zheng He to see more of the other maritime dimensions of the Ming.

33. Many readers may be more familiar with the Wade-Giles system's rendering of Cheng Ho than with the pinyin Zheng He. Despite the different renderings, the pronunciation is the same.

34. Dreyer is quite right to warn us not to try to see these voyages as purely analogous to Western and especially Mahanian conceptions of sea power. Rather we must see them for what they are in the context of early Ming history: regional trade and notions of diplomacy. Dreyer, *Zheng He*, 3–4.

35. Jianwen was unaccounted for, and some have speculated that one motivation for the later voyages was to track down the fugitive emperor. Most serious scholarship assumes that the emperor died in the fire that consumed the palace during Zhu Di's attack. Dreyer, *Zheng He*, 20–21.

36. Chen Xuan remained a person of power and influence throughout Yongle's reign. He oversaw the critical grain transport system from the Yangzi valley to the garrisons of North China and later was the principal architect of a program of canal building that contributed to a mercantile boom in the Ming and the reopening of the southern portion of the Grand Canal. See "Ch'en Hsüan," in L. Carrington and Fang Chaoying, eds., *Dictionary of Ming Biography, 1364–1644* (New York: Columbia University Press, 1976), 157–59; see also Fan Jinmin, "The Social Background of the Emergence of Regional Merchant Groups in the Ming Dynasty," *Frontiers of History in China* 2, no. 3 (July 2007): 345–78.

37. "Ch'en Hsüan," 157.

38. Jung-pang Lo, "The Decline of the Early Ming Navy," *Oriens extremus* 5 (1958): 150–51.

39. Needham, Wang and Lu, *Science and Civilisation in China*, 484. See also 鲍彦邦 [Bao Yanbang], 明代漕运研究 *Mingdai caoyun yanjiu [A Study of Grain Transport in the Ming Dynasty]* (广州 [Guangzhou]: 暨南大学出版社 [Jinan University Press], 1996).

40. "Cheng Ho," in L. Carrington and Fang Chaoying, eds., *Dictionary of Ming Biography, 1364–1644* (New York: Columbia University Press, 1976), 194–200; and Dreyer, *Zheng He*, 22.

41. Dreyer, *Zheng He*.

42. The name Sanfoqi comes from the old maritime empire of Sri Vijaya, which used to have its capital at Palembang. By the time of Zheng He, Palembang was still prominent but in terminal decline and only a shadow of its former self with the rise of first the Majapahit Empire on Java and then the Malacca Sultanate. The use of the old name for the location is simply an instance of the Chinese not catching up with the times.

43. The series in China's official navy newspaper to commemorate the six hundredth anniversary of Zheng He's voyages offers a recent example of this. See, for example, 徐起 [Xu Qi], "敦睦友邻—郑和下西洋对中国和平崛起得启示 [A Friendly Neighbor Promoting Friendly Relations: The Inspiration of Zheng He's Voyages to the West in China's Peaceful Rise]," 人民海军 [*People's Navy*], 12 July 2005, 3.

44. 唐明伟 [Tang Mingwei], "郑和靠什么推行和平外交 [How Did Zheng He Carry Out Peaceful Diplomacy?]," 解放军报 [*Liberation Army Daily*], 4 August 2008, 10.

45. There was an element of coercion in the Ming show of force. When later a group of heavily armed (European) ships showed up on the Chinese coast to seek trade liberalization, it would be called "gunboat diplomacy." In addition, the Malacca Sultanate consciously cultivated its relationship with the Ming to deter threats from the Thai Kingdom of Ayutthaya, then on the ascendant in mainland Southeast Asia.

46. For a typical People's Republic of China (PRC) interpretation of the purpose and tone of the voyages see 薛克翘 [Xue Keqiao], "纪念郑和下西洋六百周年 *Jinian Zheng He xiaxiyang liubai zhounian* [Commemorating the Sixth Hundredth Anniversary of Zheng He's Voyages to the Western Ocean]," 当代亚太 [*Contemporary Asia-Pacific Studies*] (January 2005): 3–7. This is just one of dozens, if not hundreds, of similar articles that appeared in 2005 to commemorate the six hundredth anniversary of Zheng He's first voyage. Joseph Needham also downplayed the military aspects of the voyages in his *Science and Civilisation* series. Dreyer provides a cogent rebuttal to both Needham and to contemporary Chinese interpretations. Dreyer, *Zheng He*, 28–30.

47. I am in agreement with Dreyer on this point, but others have argued for both a prominent economic motivation for the voyages and significant long-term economic benefits arising from the missions. See especially Lo Jung-p'ang's classic "The Decline of the Early Ming Navy," and 陆韧 [Lu Ren], "试论郑和下西洋的商贸活动 *Shilun Zheng He xiaxiyang de shangmao huodong* [Comments on Commerce and Trade Activity during the Zheng He Expeditions to the Western Ocean]," 海交史研究 [*Maritime History Studies*] 1 (2005): 22–30.

48. Dreyer, *Zheng He*, 34.

49. Geoff Wade has argued that part of the Ming movement seaward had to do in part with looking for allies against a potential Mongol threat. In addition, popular Chinese history also couched in terms of Yongle trying to track down the Jianwen emperor who apparently escaped toward the South Sea. This was to eliminate a potential threat to Yongle's position. However, given Yongle's consolidation of power, this fear largely subsided by the 1430s. Geoff Wade, "Ming China and Southeast Asia in the 15th Century: A Reappraisal," paper presented at the Workshop on Southeast Asia in the 15th Century: The Ming Factor, 1–2 May 2003, Singapore.

50. During the Napoleonic Era the operational life of a ship in Britain's Royal Navy did not exceed thirty years, with about ten years between major refits. That is the case even with the copper bottom sheathing and sophisticated dockyards that the British employed. This leads me to conclude that many, if not all of, the ships built for Zheng He in the early 1400s were no longer seaworthy by the 1430s, and that the last batch of treasure ships that had been ordered in 1418 were also approaching the end of their operational life.

51. Wills, "Maritime China," 201–38.

52. Ramon H. Myers, "How did the Modern Chinese Economy Develop? A Review Article," *The Journal of Asian Studies* 50 (August 1991): 604–28.

53. This is an interesting parallel to the PRC government's post-1978 retreat from centralized control of the economy and renewed focus on continental and maritime infrastructure development.

54. The Mongols remained a significant security concern on the northern frontier, but after a brief, albeit destructive, incursion by the Oirat Mongols into North China in 1449, they no longer were a threat to the stability of the dynasty. Frederick W. Mote, "The T'u'-Mu Incident of 1449," in Frank A. Kierman Jr. and John K. Fairbank, eds., *Chinese Ways in Warfare* (Cambridge, MA: Harvard University Press, 1974),

243–72. This is not to say that all was well in Ming China in the late fifteenth century; plagues, famines, and extreme of weather were commonplace. William S. Atwell, "Time, Money, and the Weather: Ming China and the 'Great Depression' of the Mid-Fifteenth Century," *The Journal of Asian Studies* 61, no. 1 (February 2002): 83–113.

55. 吴摭 [Wu Lu], "明初卫所制度之崩溃, *Mingchu weisuo zhidu de bengkui* [The Collapse of the Early Ming Wei-suo System]," 吴摭文集第一卷, *Wu Lu wenji diyijuan* [*The Collected Works of Wu Lu*, Vol. I] (天津 [Tianjin]: 天津人民出版社 [Tianjin People's Press], 1988).

56. Brook, *The Confusions of Pleasure*.

57. Atwell, "Time," 100.

58. James Geiss, "The Chia-ching Reign, 1522–1566," in Frederick W. Mote and Denis Twitchett eds., *The Cambridge History of China*, Vol. 7: *The Ming Dynasty, 1368–1644* (Cambridge: Cambridge University Press, 1988), Part I, 490–504. For the evolution of the antimaritime prohibition argument see 施瀚文 [Shi Hanwen], "浅谈明清时期开放海外贸易思想的发展及其历史导向 *Qiantan Ming-Qing shiqi kaifang haiwai maoyi sixiang de fazhan jiqi lishi daoxing* [On the Development of Ideas about Opening Overseas Trade in Ming and Qing Dynasties and Its Historical Direction]," 湖南财经高等专科学校学报 [*The Journal of the Hunan College of Finance and Economics*] 20, no. 1 (February 2004): 13–15.

59. 肖智慧 [Xiao Zhihui], "明朝中晚期私人海上贸易的地位 *Mingchao zhong wanqi siren haishang maoyi de diwei* [The Status of Private Maritime Trade in the Mid-to-Late Ming Dynasty]," 宜宾学院学报 [*The Journal of the Yibin University*] (8 August 2005): 41–43; and 吴光会, 向远莉 [Wu Guanghui and Xiang Yuanli], "明朝私人海外贸易刍议 *Mingchao siren haiwai maoyi* [On Private Maritime Trade in the Ming Dynasty]," 唐山师范学院学 [*The Journal of Tangshan Teachers College*] 27 no. 3 (May 2005): 76–79.

60. Zhengde had been on a campaign in the south ostensibly to suppress the ill-fated rebellion of the Prince of Ning. The granting of such an audience appears to be a complete reversal of Ming policy vis-à-vis the Portuguese because coastal officials in Guangdong and Fujian were dead-set against opening to the Europeans. Zhengde, however, was notorious for bizarre and extortionate schemes; the emperor may have seen some possible profit to be had from relations with the Portuguese. Geiss, "The Cheng-te Reign," 423–36.

61. See 元邦建, 袁桂秀 [Yuan Bangjian and Yuan Guixiu], 澳门史略, *Aomen Shilue* [*A Brief History of Macau*] (香港 [Hong Kong]: 中流出版社 [Midstream Press], 1988). See also Chang T'ien-tse, *Sino-Portuguese Trade from 1514 to 1644: A Synthesis of Portuguese and Chinese Sources* (Leiden: Brill, 1934). The *Shenzong shilu* contains several references to the various engagements of the 1521–22 Sino-Portuguese War. See 明实录, 神宗实录 *Ming shilu, Shenzong shilu* [*The Veritable Records of the Ming Dynasty, The Veritable Records of the Shenzong Emperor*] (133 Vols. + 21 Vols. of appendices), Reprint (台北 [Taibei]: 中央研究院历史语言研究所 [Academia Sinica Institute of History and Linguistics], 1961–66).

62. For a detailed history of the dynamics of coastal piracy in this era, see Robert J. Antony, *Like Froth Floating on the Sea: The World of Pirates and Seafarers in Late Imperial South China* (Berkeley: University of California Berkeley, 2003); and So Kwan-wai, *Japanese Piracy in Ming China during the 16th Century* (East Lansing: Michigan State University Press, 1975).

63. Hu Zongxian is an ancestor of China's current president, Hu Jintao (胡锦涛).

64. Wang Rigen, *Coastal Defense*, 15–18.

65. See "Ch'i Chi-kuang," in L. Carrington and Fang Chaoying, eds., *Dictionary of Ming Biography, 1364–1644* (New York: Columbia University Press, 1976), 220–24.

66. Kenneth M. Swope, "Cutting Dwarf Pirates Down to Size: Amphibious Warfare in Sixteenth Century East Asia," paper presented at the Naval History Symposium, U.S. Naval Academy, Annapolis, Maryland, 20–22 September 2007, Maochun Yu, ed. (Annapolis, MD: Naval Institute Press, forthcoming, 2009). For more on Qi Jiguang, see also Ray Huang, *1587, A Year of No Significance* (New Haven, CT: Yale University Press, 1981), 156–88.

67. "Lin Feng," in L. Carrington and Fang Chaoying, eds., *Dictionary of Ming Biography, 1364–1644* (New York: Columbia University Press, 1976), 917. See also 陳荊和 [Chen Jinghe], 十六世紀之菲律賓華僑 *Shiliu shiji zhi feilupin huaqiao* [*The Overseas Chinese in the Philippines during the Sixteenth Century*] (Hong Kong: Southeast Asian Studies Section, New Asia Research Institute, 1963), 31–41.

68. During the siege Lin offered to make peace with the Spanish and help them to conquer China. Some Spaniards were willing to consider that rather fanciful notion, but in reality throughout the early years of Manila it was the Spanish who were worried about a Chinese amphibious invasion; Chen, *Shiliu shiji*, 44–47.

69. Swope, "Dwarf Pirates."

70. There is some evidence to indicate that a warming of relations between the Ming and the Portuguese, who as noted earlier had been repulsed in the 1520s, culminating in Beijing accession to a Portuguese trading enclave in Macau, were rewards bestowed upon the Europeans for their help against the Wokou.

71. Hideyoshi's ultimate goal was to conquer Ming China rather than be a servant to a Chinese hegemon.

72. "Letters from Francisco Tello to Felipe II," in Emma H. Blair and James. A. Robertson, eds., *The Philippine Islands, 1493–1898*, 55 Vols. (Cleveland, OH: Arthur H. Clark, 1903–1909), Vol. X, 162.

73. I arrived at this number by using a standard weight of 40g of silver per tael. This is a conservative estimate because taels varied in weight from a low of about 33g to a high of 40g. William S. Atwell, "Notes on Silver, Foreign Trade, and the Late Ming Economy," *Ch'ing-shih wen-t'i* 8, no. 3 (December 1977); and "International Bullion Flows and the Chinese Economy," *Past and Present* 95 (1982): 89–90.

74. In addition to these vast quantities of silver, the Manila trade also introduced New World crops, which had an enormous impact on Chinese agriculture and demographic development.

75. See, in particular Brook, *The Confusions of Pleasure*; and Craig Clunas, *Superfluous Things: Material Culture and Social Status in Early Modern China* (Cambridge, U.K.: Polity, 1991).

76. See in particular the work of Ray Huang, especially his *1587, A Year of no Significance* and his "Lung-ch'ing and Wan-li Reigns, 1567–1620," in Frederick W. Mote and Denis Twitchett, eds., *The Cambridge History of China*, Vol. 7: *The Ming Dynasty, 1368–1644* (Cambridge, U.K.: Cambridge University Press, 1988), Part I, 511–84.

77. For the most comprehensive account of these wars and their costs, see Kenneth M. Swope Jr., "The Three Great Campaigns of the Wanli Emperor, 1592–1600: Court, Military, and Society in Late Sixteenth-Century China," unpublished PhD diss., University of Michigan, 2001.

78. See William H. McNeill, *The Age of Gunpowder Empires, 1450–1800* (Washington D.C.: American Historical Association, 1989); and Geoffrey Parker, *The Military Revolution: Military Innovation and the Rise of the West, 1500–1800* (Cambridge, U.K.: Cambridge University Press, 1996). For more on the weaponry and ships employed by the Ming in the late sixteenth century, see Zhang and Gao, *Ancient Chinese Naval History*, 176–206.

79. My use of the terms "statist" and "antistatist" as well as my discussion of Wanli's war with his officials over the intendant system are drawn from Harrison Stewart Miller, "State Versus Society in Late Imperial China, 1572–1644," unpublished PhD diss., Columbia University, 2001.

80. Geiss, "The Chia-ching Reign," 509.

81. 樊树志 [Fan Shuzhi], "万历年间的朝鲜战争 *Wanli nianjian de Chaoxian zhanzheng* [The Korean War of the Wanli Era]," 复旦学报 (社会科学版) [*Fudan Journal* (Social Sciences Edition)] 6 (2003): 96–102.

82. Early in the struggle it also appeared likely that the war in Korea might spill over into Southeast Asia. For example, in 1591 and 1592, Hideyoshi made the first southern feint by dispatching emissaries to Manila to demand Spanish obeisance to him and support for his war against Ming China. Not long after, the Ming emperor Wanli promised King Sonjo of Choson that he would also marshal aid from Siam and the Spanish Philippines, among other regional powers. While little materialized from these gestures in terms of formal alliances, it does show a cognizance among the major players of the international implications of the war in Korea along with a recognition that each party was likely to be heavily reliant on foreign trade to finance their efforts and on foreign military expertise and technology to out do their adversaries on land and at sea. The Spanish, for their part, managed to avoid direct involvement in the war, and seemed to hold the greatest concern over Japanese aggression to the south, including the capture of Taiwan as a flanking maneuver around the Ming. Their decision to lean toward the Ming seems to have been based primarily on the economic calculations of their lucrative trade with China. 李光涛 [Li Guangtao], comp., 朝鲜壬辰倭祸史料 *Chaoxian renchen wohuo shiliao* [*Historical Materials on the Imjin War*], 5 Vols. (台北 [Taibei]: 中央研究院历史语言研究所 [Academia Sinica's Institute of History and Linguistics], 1970), 29.

83. Eunuch mining tax collectors enjoyed only limited success in meeting the extraordinary demands of the wars of the 1590s and may have done more harm than good by contributing to greater factionalism in the empire. See Ray Huang, "The Ming Fiscal Administration," in Dennis Twitchett and F. W. Mote, eds. *The Cambridge History of China*, Vol. VIII, *The Ming Dynasty*, Part 2 (Cambridge, U.K.: Cambridge University Press, 1988), 106–71; and Richard von Glahn, *Fountain of Fortune: Money and Monetary Policy in China, 1000–1700* (Berkeley: University of California Press, 1996).

84. Kenneth Swope estimates that the Chinese spent between seven and eight million taels on the Imjin War. Tapping into just 10 percent of the bullion flow from Manila would have significantly offset that debt. Personal communication, March 2008.

85. It was primarily the Dutch and Portuguese that had the greatest impact on the actual fighting. Here, however, Kenneth Swope has challenged the conventional wisdom on simple West–East technology flows by showing how advanced and innovative Chinese gun-making was in the late sixteenth century. He suggests a much more dialectical relationship and multidirectional flows of military technology. Kenneth M. Swope, "Crouching Tigers, Secret Weapons: Military Technology Employed during the Sino-Japanese-Korean War, 1592–1598," *The Journal of Military History* 69, no. 1 (January 2005): 11–41.

86. Swope, "Dwarf Pirates."

87. See Stephen Turnbull, *Samurai Invasion: Japan's Korean War* (New York: Cassel, 2002), 226; and Zhang and Gao, *Ancient Chinese Naval History*, 263–69. Also see their 张铁牛, 高晓星 [Zhang Tieniu and Gao Xiaoxing], "露梁海战 中朝联军水师大胜日本水军 *Luliang haizhan Zhong-Chao lianjun shuishi dasheng Riben shuijun* [The Battle of Noryang: The Great Victory of the Sino-Korean Combined Navies over the Japanese Navy]," 军营文化天地 [*Barracks Culture*] 3 (2006): 25.

88. John W. Dardess, *Blood and History in China: The Donglin Faction and Its Repression, 1620–1627* (Honolulu: University of Hawai'i Press, 2003).

89. C. R. Boxer, "The Rise and Fall of Nicholas Iquan," *T'ien Hsia Monthly* 11 no. 5 (1941): 401–39.

90. Seiichi Iwao, "Li Tan, Chief of the Chinese Residents at Hirado, Japan, in the Last Days of the Ming Dynasty," *Memoirs of the Research Department of the Toyo Bunko* 17 (1958): 27–83. See also 李金明 [Li Jinming], "16世纪漳泉贸易港与日本的走私贸易 [The Smuggling Trade between the ports of Zhangzhou and Quanzhou and Japan in the 16th Century]," 海交史研究 [*Maritime History Studies*] 2 (2006): 70–74; 崔来廷 [Cui Laiting], "16世纪东南中国海上走私贸易探析 [Maritime Smuggling Trade in the Southeast China Sea during the Sixteenth Century]," 南洋问题研究 [*Southeast Asian Affairs*] (April 2005): 92–98; and 孟庆梓 [Meng Qingzi], "明代的倭寇与海商 [Japanese Pirates and Chinese Sea Traders in the Ming Dynasty]," 承德民族师专学报 [*Journal of the Chengde Teachers College for Nationalities*] 25, no. 1 (March 2005): 51–52.

91. 李德霞 [Li Dexia], "17世纪初荷兰在福建沿海的骚扰与通商 [Dutch Harassment and Trade along Fujian Coast in the Early 17th Century]" 海交史研究 [*Maritime History Studies*] 1 (2004): 59–69; and 卢建一 [Lu Jianyi], "明代海禁政策与福

建海防 *Mingdai haijin zhengce yu Fujian haifang* [The Ming Dynasty's Maritime Prohibition Policies and Fujian's Coastal Defenses]," 福建师范大学学报 (哲学社会科学版) [*The Journal of Fujian Normal University* (Philosophy and Social Sciences Edition)] 2 (1992): 21–24.

92. Tonio Andrade, "The Company's Chinese Pirates: How the Dutch East India Company Tried to Lead a Coalition of Pirates to War against China, 1621–1662," *Journal of World History* 15 (2004): 415–44.

93. Lynn A. Struve, "The Southern Ming, 1644–1662," in Dennis Twitchett and F. W. Mote, eds., *The Cambridge History of China*, Vol. VIII, *The Ming Dynasty*, Part 2 (Cambridge, U.K.: Cambridge University Press, 1988), 663–76; and Wills, "Maritime China."

94. Struve, "Southern Ming," 710–25.

95. For the dynamics of Sino-Dutch interaction in this period, see three works by Tonio Andrade, "Pirates, Pelts, and Promises: The Sino-Dutch Colony of Seventeenth-Century Taiwan and the Aboriginal Village of Favorolang," *Journal of Asian Studies* 64, no. 2 (2005): 295–320; "The Company's Chinese Pirates: How the Dutch East India Company Tried to Lead a Coalition of Pirates to War against China, 1621–1662," *Journal of World History* 15 (2004): 415–44; and *How Taiwan Became Chinese: Dutch, Spanish, and Han Colonization in the Seventeenth Century* (New York: Columbia University Press, 2006).

96. For more on the era of Zheng rule on Taiwan, see John Robert Shepherd, *Statecraft and Political Economy on the Taiwan Frontier 1600–1800* (Stanford, CA.: Stanford University Press, 1993), 91–104.

97. Shi Lang's feats are a popular metaphor for the future reunification of China and Taiwan. 王政尧 [Wang Zhengyao], "'南堂诗钞'与施琅收复台湾, '*Nantang shichao*' *yu Shi Lang shoufu Taiwan* ['The Collected Poems of the Southern Pavilion' and Shi Lang's Recovery of Taiwan]," 北京社会科学 [*Beijing Social Sciences*], no. 2 (2002): 31–36.

RUSSIA

Frontier 1689-1859
Settled by Treaty of Nerchinsk

Frontier 1757-1864

OUTER MONGOLIA

XINJIANG

INNER
MONGOLIA

GANSU

QINGHAI

XIZANG
(TIBET)

SICHUAN

INDIA

Qing China, c. 1911

	Territory Ceded to Russia
	Provincial boundary
	Great Wall
	Canal
	River

0   250   500 Kilometers

0   250   500 Miles

YUNNAN

ANNAM

Albajin

HEILONGJIANG

Dongjiang

OUTER MONGOLIA

FENGTIAN

JILIN

INNER MONGOLIA

Haishengwei
(Vladivostok)

(SHENGJING)

ZHILI

Sea of
Japan

KOREA

JAPAN

Beijing

Port Arthur
(Lüshun)

Dalian

*"Beiyang"
(Northern) Fleet*

Yantai

Weihai

Qingdao

SHANXI

Wei River

SHANDONG

North
Sea

Yellow
Sea

**Grand
Canal**

Huang River

JIANGSU

SHAANXI

HENAN

Huai River

Nanjing

Shanghai

ANHUI

Hangzhou

*"Nanyang"
(Southern) Fleet*

HUBEI

Yangzi River

Wuhan

Ningbo

ZHEJIANG

Taizhou

East
China
Sea

Wenzhou

JIANGXI

HUNAN

FUJIAN

Fuzhou

*Fuzhou
Fleet*

UIZHOU

Quanzhou

Danshui

Jilong

Xiamen
(Amoy)

TAIWAN

Pacific
Ocean

GUANGXI

GUANGDONG

Guangzhou
(Canton)

Shantou

Tainan

**Guangzhou
Fleet**

Penghudao

Hong
Kong

anoi

Leizhou
Bay

Leizhou

South
China
Sea

Qiongzhou

PHILIPPINES

Bruce A. Elleman

The Neglect and Nadir of Chinese Maritime Policy under the Qing

*Now here is the reason why people are dazzled by the name of England. Because
her vessels are sturdy and her cannons fierce, they call her powerful. . . . Yet they
do not know that the warships of the said barbarians are very heavy, taking water
to the depth of tens of feet. These vessels are successful only on the outer seas; it
is their specialty to break the waves and sail under great winds. If we refrained
from fighting with them on the sea, they would find no opportunity to take
advantage of this skill. Once within the harbor, their vessels become unwieldy.
They can scarcely move in shallow waters or near sand bars. Hence, when their
merchant vessels enter the port, they must employ natives as pilots, paying them
with great sums of money. How much more this applies to the warships!*

> —*Commissioner Lin Zexu to the emperor,*
> *disparaging British ships (24 September 1839)*

AS EMPHASIZED IN THIS GENERALLY DISMISSIVE 1839 REPORT to
the Manchu emperor from Commissioner Lin Zexu, the Qing official in
charge of eliminating foreign-traded opium, China placed a premium on
naval vessels that could navigate canal, riverine, and coastal waters, not on
the deep-sea ships favored by the British and other foreign maritime pow-

ers. In fact, coastal defense (海防, *haifang* had long been a priority of the ruling dynasty but was focused mainly on defending China's littorals and inland waterways rather than on navies battling on the high seas. Its goals were threefold: to fight off marauding pirates from raiding China's coastline, to halt foreign attempts to claim Chinese territory, and to oppose efforts by either rebellious Chinese factions or ambitious tributaries to use naval forces to usurp the imperial throne. To many Chinese, the arrival of the British seemed to fit within the parameters previously set by several other Asian countries—such as Japan and Vietnam—that had constantly carried out petty raids and piracy but had tried and failed to invade China's littorals and inland waterways from the sea.

To explain the maritime transformation of Qing China, it is useful to divide the dynasty into four periods. During the first, from 1644–1839, after a short period during which naval forces helped consolidate Manchu control by retaking Taiwan, the Qing emperors were primarily concerned with continental wars, in particular wars of subjugation against Mongols, Muslims, and Tibetans, as well as keeping Russian expansionism at bay. To strengthen their minority control over Han China, the Qing divided their military into separate Manchu and Han divisions and further divided the naval forces into separate regional fleets, which was intended to weaken potential military rivals. Finally, to control recalcitrant foreigners, the Manchus forced all foreign merchants to trade at the southern cities of Canton (now Guangzhou) and Macau, where Beijing could impose increasingly harsh trade restrictions during times of trouble. None of these Qing policies required a robust naval force, so the Chinese navy gradually atrophied over time.

During the second (1839–42) and third (1843–64) periods, the Manchus and foreigners clashed over several issues, including the detrimental outward flow of China's silver supplies due to the foreign opium trade; the threat of oceangoing shipping competing with China's extensive river and canal-based trade system, thereby undermining China's traditional tax structure; and the potential loss of Beijing's monopoly over foreign trade. After 1842 the Manchus were gradually forced to change their policies. Following a second disastrous naval war with Great Britain and France known as the Second Opium War or Arrow War (1856–60), the Qing court finally realized that it needed to begin the task of modernizing China's naval forces.

Finally, in the fourth period, from 1865–95, the Manchus gradually attempted to reform and build up China's navy, but they began too late and their progress was too slow. China's navy was quickly defeated by Japan's equally modern but better trained and led naval forces during the first Sino-

Japanese War (1894–95). China's 1895 maritime defeat doomed its navy to obscurity, with the exception of a brief and largely ineffectual resurgence under the Nationalist government after World War II, until the more recent growth and expansion of the People's Liberation Army Navy (PLAN).

Period One: 1644–1839

When the Manchus invaded southward and conquered Beijing in 1644, they took possession of a China that had been a maritime nation from time immemorial; during the Han dynasty (221 BC–AD 202), a Chinese fleet even met and defeated a Vietnamese fleet at sea in AD 42, which is the first recorded international high seas battle in Asia.[1] A need for a naval fleet to protect China's coastline declined, however, when the Sui Dynasty completed the Grand Canal in AD 605–10, with the new canal linking the Yangzi River commercial centers with northern cities such as Luoyang, and later Beijing. The completion of the Grand Canal meant that the bulk of China's domestic north–south trade could be conducted exclusively inland, far from any sea-going maritime threats, and the kinds of ships that were most useful along shallow canals—flat-bottomed junks—were not safe venturing deep out to sea. Whoever controlled the Grand Canal could dominate China's major domestic trade routes. Seagoing trade with Southeast Asia remained crucial, however, and in fact increased in importance as the Silk Road gradually fell into decline beginning in the ninth century.[2]

Following the collapse of the Ming dynasty in 1644, mixed Han-Mongol-Manchu military forces under Manchu control invaded northern China and slowly moved southward. In reaction, a group of Ming loyalists led by Zheng Chenggong (1624–62), known in the West as Koxinga,[3] decided to retreat to Taiwan, which had been taken by the Dutch in 1624. In April 1661 Koxinga's twenty-five-thousand-man force moved from Jinmen (Quemoy) to the Penghu Islands to Taiwan, based on the strategy: "Clear away a thorny path to drive out the Dutch barbarians." After making an amphibious landing at Luermen (鹿耳門) on a river near the village of Tucheng, on 29 April 1661, Koxinga's forces surrounded the Dutch Fort Zeelandia at Anping near the modern-day city of Tainan. After a nine-month siege, the fortress capitulated and Koxinga took control over the island in return for allowing the Dutch to leave Taiwan unharmed. Although he opposed the central government in Beijing, Koxinga is variously described by contemporary PLAN sources as a "patriotic general," a "Chinese national hero," and as a military leader who "commanded landing operations to expel the Dutch colonizers and recover Taiwan."[4]

Koxinga followed his military success over the Dutch by establishing an opposition government in Tainan and basing his troops on Taiwan. He also supported a massive program of Han Chinese immigration from Fujian province; many of today's native Taiwanese can trace their family line back to this exodus, just as many mainland-born Taiwanese came to the island in 1949. Although Koxinga intended to continue his anti-Manchu offensive from Taiwan, he died soon afterward in 1662. Koxinga's successors held out against the Qing another twenty years, but Taiwan finally fell to a Qing fleet of three hundred warships and twenty thousand troops commanded by Adm. Shi Lang (1621–96) in 1683, fifty-nine years after it had been lost to the Dutch.[5] The 16–17 July 1683 Battle of Penghu (澎湖海战) once again emphasized the strategic importance of controlling offshore islands.

The Qing continued to support a strong navy. For example, a century later, Qing maritime forces successfully intervened in Taiwan to put down a rebellion (1787–88). After these threats to China's maritime security disappeared, however, scarce resources were usually redirected away from the sea to China's continental borders. Therefore, although the Manchus retained control over Taiwan, it remained a remote backwater with little economic or strategic significance before the nineteenth century.

Arguably of even greater importance to the maritime threat was the Qing conquest of vast inland territories, including Mongolia, Xinjiang, and Tibet, and its opposition to the Russian advance to the north. Russia had interacted with Asia for more than eight hundred years, ever since the first Mongol hordes had swept through Russia and dominated Moscow, halted only by the swamplands bordering the Baltic. The Russians took the first steps eastward under Ivan the Terrible, who made Russia a Eurasian power in 1584 by extending his realm from the White Sea all the way to Siberia. During the early 1600s, Russians began to settle western Siberia. By the late 1630s, they founded the settlement of Udsk on the Sea of Okhotsk. This rapid Russian expansion soon led to friction with Qing China, which had long assumed that these territories were either theirs outright or were tributaries.

The first official contacts occurred in 1618, when a Russian trade expedition reached Beijing. During the mid-1600s, Russian explorers moved into the strategic Amur River Valley, which had the only arable land in the eastern Siberian interior and a river that offered the only major east–west transportation route in northeast Asia. In 1650, one of these explorers, Erofei Pavlovich Khabarov, built a fort at Albazin. From this fort he and his men moved far down the Amur River, fighting with the natives on the way. Khabarov ordered a second fortress, Achansk, built near the mouth of the Songhua (Sungari) River, which flows into the Amur. These actions quickly drew China's attention, and Manchu forces attacked Achansk on 24 March 1652. Although outnumbered, the Russians routed the Manchus.

The Russian position remained tenuous, and clashes continued between 1655 and 1658 when a Manchu force defeated the Russians. Nevertheless, Russian settlers continued to move into the Amur Valley. In the 1670s, the Russian government created a protectorate over Albazin. The first official Russian delegation, under Nikolai Milescu-Spafarii, reached Beijing in 1676 but failed to open diplomatic relations. Faced with ever-growing Russian immigration, the Manchus sent an expedition in the early 1680s to expel them from the Amur Valley. Although Chinese forces managed to retake Albazin, the Russians soon returned in even greater numbers.

Border talks opened at Nerchinsk in 1689 between Fedor Golovin and two members of the Qing imperial household, Songgotu and Tong Guogang. The talks resulted in the 27 August 1689 Treaty of Nerchinsk, China's first treaty with a European power, which remained in effect for the next 170 years. Superior Qing forces in the Amur basin forced a Russian withdrawal, although Russia acquired all the vast lands west and north of the Argun River. This treaty also provided Russia with valuable trading privileges, particularly for sable and black fox pelts, which Moscow monopolized. In the 20 August 1727 Treaty of Bura much of the disputed border was set whereas the 21 October 1727 Treaty of Kiakhta opened two border towns to trade. These trade centers were in some ways the continental precursors to the treaty ports that the Western powers would establish in coastal China more than a century later.[6]

Because Russia was a continental power, China treated it differently from the Western maritime powers. Administratively, Russians were categorized with the other un-Sinicized barbarians populating the northern frontiers. Whereas the Ming Dynasty had handled all Sinicized barbarians through the Bureau of Receptions of the Board of Rites, the Manchus established the Court of Colonial Affairs (理藩院, *Lifanyuan*) to deal with their Inner Asian neighbors. This status, in combination with the treaties of Nerchinsk and Kiakhta, gave Russia diplomatic privileges not shared by other Europeans. In addition to the right to send emissaries directly to Beijing, Russia maintained a permanent ecclesiastical mission that served as a quasi-embassy and language school. The other powers would not gain formal diplomatic privileges in the capital until 1860, after fighting and winning two wars against

China; in 1861, Prince Gong oversaw the establishment of the Foreign Office (总理衙门, *Zongli Yamen/Tsungli Yamen*) to administer China's foreign relations with Europe and the United States.

In the late seventeenth and early eighteenth centuries, China's strategic focus remained continental, not maritime, including two Qing campaigns to suppress the Zunghar Mongols in the far northwest during 1755, the suppression of the Turkic Muslims in the Tarim Basin to the south during 1755–57, two campaigns to repress uprisings of the Jinchuan minority in Sichuan province in 1747–49 and 1771–76, unsuccessful efforts to subjugate Burma in 1766–70 and Vietnam in 1788–89, and attempts to expel the Nepalese (Gurkhas) from Tibet during 1790–92. Government funding for these continental campaigns diverted tax money away from the coast, which might have otherwise been spent on the navy. Prior to the outbreak of the First Opium War in 1839, these continental threats were considered more dangerous to the Chinese Empire than any conceivable foreign maritime threat, in particular because Russia was eager to expand even farther into Mongolia and Xinjiang.

Another important factor in explaining why China did not undergo a maritime transformation was the composition of the Qing military. After 1644 the Qing segregated the military by race, with eight Banners each of Manchu, Han, and Mongol troops. The Banners were spread throughout China, with especially large garrisons of Manchu cavalry located in sensitive frontier regions in the north and in major cities along the Yangzi River to protect the canal system. By contrast, the inferior infantry and navy were composed mainly of Han Chinese, who were assigned to garrisons along China's lengthy coastline and throughout southern China, far from Beijing. Regional fleets were purposefully left weak, and many naval officers were assigned to their posts because of academic success in the Imperial exams, rather than for any real knowledge of military or naval affairs.[7]

By the end of the eighteenth century, when European merchants first began to arrive in force, the number of loyal Bannermen was estimated at a quarter of a million men whereas Han Chinese troops were 660,000.[8] Because so few of China's premier troops were assigned to coastal areas, the Qing coastal defense navy was not particularly proficient. This meant that in terms of organization, force distribution, and the comparative backwardness of their weaponry and ships, the Han Chinese navy could not compete effectively with its Western counterparts, who were appearing in Chinese waters in ever-greater numbers.

A third factor inhibiting maritime transformation was the restrictions put on foreign trade, which could only be conducted legally in the southern city of Canton, the capital of Guangdong Province (although it continued without legal recognition in the Portuguese colony of Macau). Prior to the First Opium War (1839–42), the Qing navy focused its attention mainly on China's immediate neighbors, especially Japan and Vietnam, the only two Asian countries that had successfully repelled Chinese naval forces in the past. When under attack, the Chinese navy had traditionally halted the maritime invaders by blocking harbors with log booms and chains strung from a row of floating junks. The Chinese could also stop a naval foe by utilizing offshore islands, many of them outfitted with impregnable—at least, by premodern standards—fortresses armed with cannons. Foreign trade in Canton could also be halted by the Chinese government, and Beijing could simply wait until the attackers gradually weakened and dispersed; after the threat was gone, normal trade could then be resumed.

Prior to the nineteenth century, the maritime threat from the sea remained largely regional; thus, it could be managed by a small, Han-dominated naval force, which depended mainly on defensive strategies, such as trade embargoes. Qing coastal defense strategies included three key elements: (a) keeping maritime threats at arm's length versus fighting continental enemies in wars of extermination; (b) garrisoning less dependable Han Chinese divisions in the south and southeast to protect the coast versus assigning loyal Manchu Bannermen to protect the vulnerable borders and the Grand Canal; and (c) adopting trade restrictions and defensive coastal strategies rather than utilizing more offensive strategies.

Although extremely effective against regional enemies, these three elements had a negative impact on how Chinese strategic thinkers were to face the newly emerging threat from Europe. After centuries of battling Asian fleets, the Qing navy proved to be particularly ill prepared for the arrival of the deep-sea European navies. Exacerbating these strategic limitations was the fact that the comparative backwardness of the Han-dominated Chinese navy was to some degree intentional, since China's Manchu rulers were well aware that any weapon they provided to the Han troops might one day be turned against them during a mutiny.[9] Therefore, keeping China's naval forces weak and divided had positive benefits for Manchu rule. Such domestic security concerns ultimately created the ingredients for an international military disaster during the early nineteenth century, when Chinese naval forces first encountered the West in battle.

Period Two: 1839–42

When European maritime traders first began to arrive in China, they were accepted into the preexisting government-controlled tributary system, in which China was the superior and other states were considered inferior. Foreign trade was centered in Canton (with some nevertheless occurring in Macau), foreign goods were delivered internally within China by road and canal, and commerce was monopolized by government-licensed merchants who were under the authority of Chinese officials reporting directly to Beijing. This system undermined any need for a vibrant oceanic trade that would have required the protection of a large and powerful Chinese navy. It had also worked well until the early nineteenth century, when Britain's increasing military power—due in large part to the ongoing Industrial Revolution in Europe—for the first time allowed European navies to challenge China's maritime supremacy. Chinese officials, due to their natural conservatism and inability to act collectively, were largely unwilling to recognize that this change required an active military response on the part of the Qing dynasty.

The Han Chinese navy in the early nineteenth century was specifically designed and trained to fight domestic rebellion, protect the canal system by barricading China's river system against pirates, and embargo and discipline small numbers of unruly foreign merchants. It had not been a truly offensive force for well over a hundred years, arguably since the Qing reclaimed Taiwan with a naval expedition in 1683. Having never faced a maritime threat equal, much less superior, to its own power, the Chinese navy was not designed, equipped, or trained to fight a major conflict against a European power, much less the world's premier naval power at that time—Great Britain.

The spark that ignited the First Opium War was a severe silver shortage in China caused by the financing of an ongoing military campaign in Xinjiang, Western China.[10] The Qing emperor's response was not to halt all trade in opium, just the foreign trade, which had contributed to the silver drain. However, the strategy that China chose—embargoing foreign trade with Great Britain and with the other foreign merchants—backfired because it was perceived as a unilateral attempt to disrupt free trade. European merchants who came by sea, especially the Dutch and the British, had long been advocates of free trade and had even fought wars, including the Napoleonic Wars, to uphold their right to trade.

Britain's quest for free trade was at the heart of the First Opium War, but the Chinese official in charge of enforcing the opium restriction,

Commissioner Lin Zexu, grossly underestimated the value of the China trade to Britain. Not surprisingly, Lin failed to realize that Sino-British trade tensions might lead to war, in part due to his underestimation of the economic influence the East India Company and other China merchants could exert over the British government. On 25 August 1839, the British representative, Capt. Charles Elliot, protested the Chinese decision to halt trade and agreed to buy the foreign opium in the name of the British crown, thus making it British property when it was turned over to Chinese officials for destruction. This title transfer later gave the British government the legal right to demand financial restitution from China.

After the foreign merchants were ousted from Canton, the British trade ships did not go home as China expected but instead gathered near a small, waterless, and almost completely barren offshore island called Hong Kong. The seagoing British ships could already dominate the blue water and littorals off China's coastline. By using Hong Kong as a base, however, British naval forces were soon able to focus their attention on invading into China's river systems and eventually even dominating the well-protected canals, which lay at the heart of China's coastal defense.

A second point of tension besides the prohibition on the opium trade was the foreign desire to conduct seagoing trade between south and north. In the early nineteenth century, a dispute raged in China over whether rice tribute from the south should be transported along the Grand Canal or by sea, and the Qing emperor backed the Grand Canal. The sea route was more direct, more reliable, and therefore cheaper, and from 1824–27, the sea route temporarily predominated because of extensive silting in the canals. But the Qing emperor, knowing that the livelihoods of so many government officials depended on the canal fees paid by the tribute ships, and that central government revenues were also linked to these fees, supported repairs to reopen the canal. To encourage use of the Grand Canal, the government enforced strict limits on the sea trade. While oceangoing ships could deliver northern goods, such as salt, to the south, they could not legally bring back southern goods, like rice, to the north. As a result, many seagoing ships returned north empty.

The decision to subsidize the Grand Canal trade undercut China's seagoing trade, a situation foreigners resented. But if oceangoing commerce did increase, it would largely be at the expense of the internal canal trade and could disrupt millions of boatmen, not to mention the provincial authorities whose income was based on the trade tax. To ensure domestic stability and to further his own domestic control over trade, the Qing emperor consistently opposed any radical changes to this traditional canal-based trade system. Similar to seagoing trade, however, the canal trade was vulnerable at certain "choke points" where the different trade routes met and interconnected. One such choke point was near Zhenjiang, where the Grand Canal intersected the Yangzi River, and another was the city of Tianjin, near the northern terminus of the Grand Canal.

To retain its monopoly over foreign trade, it was in the Chinese government's interest to keep foreign traders isolated as much as possible in Canton and Macau. As a result, China's trade system was innately unequal because Eurasian countries that sent tributary missions to China, such as missions from Russia, were allowed to visit and trade in Beijing and were regulated by one organization, the Court of Colonial Affairs (理蕃院, *Lifanyuan*). Meanwhile, maritime nations were kept far from the capital and were administered by another board, the Board of Rites (禮部, *Libu*).[11] Because threats to China's security tended to come from the north and west, continental countries were treated with greater deference. Maritime countries had never before presented a danger to China's ruling dynasties and so were treated as inferiors. The Western maritime nations chafed at this unequal treatment.

What these dual trade systems meant for Europe's major seafaring nations, such as Great Britain, was that they remained isolated in the south, thousands of miles from China's political center in Beijing, while Russia had its own representatives in Beijing. Britain had earlier sent an embassy under Lord Macartney in 1793 to Beijing to rectify this situation, but their request to have a representative in the capital was denied. Commercial factors also played a role because the price of northern goods was significantly higher in the south due to shipping fees and canal taxes. British merchants, in particular, were eager to open up new markets for European goods in North China, as well as to seek lower prices for Chinese goods by going directly to the source of production. Therefore, Russia's ability to send representatives to Beijing was perceived as grossly unfair because this gave Russian merchants greater access to northern goods. Not surprisingly, the British, who were in competition with Russia in other parts of the world, were the first to stand up and oppose what to them seemed to be unequal treatment.

According to Commissioner Lin Zexu, the first stage of the Opium War was a standoff; the British ships may have dominated offshore islands and the coastal waters, but the Chinese continued to control the river entrances and access to the canals. Because China's coastal cities were retained and these were the locations where most of the trade took place, the Chinese believed that their defensive strategy was succeeding. Based on this stalemate, the

British and Chinese negotiated an interim treaty that temporarily ended the conflict. Although the image of the Chinese coastal defense was tarnished, to many officials it appeared that China withstood the foreign assault. Chinese officials remained generally dismissive of the British navy. For example, Yuqian, governor of Jiangsu province, wrote as late as 12 September 1840 that the foreign ships could easily run aground on sand bars, their guns were not accurate because the "ships toss up and down with the waves," and they were susceptible to fire: "If our soldiers attack them with fire, their ships can be burned outright."[12]

By March 1840, however, after a renewal of conflict and following the Sino-British naval encounter at the Battle of Chuanbi on 3 November 1839, Lin Zexu gradually began to change his mind about the utility of the foreign ships. For the first time, Lin advocated the "study of Western techniques" so China could "build and send a cannon-bearing fleet abroad to suppress and punish" the enemy. Because of his modernizing efforts, Lin was later lauded for being the "first person in modern China to open his eyes and look at the world."[13] Lin's views on coastal defense also changed radically. He began to advocate a three-tiered strategy to defeat the British: (1) adopt a "use defense for the sake of war" (以守为战, *yishouweizhan*) strategy, (2) build a modern navy, and (3) arouse the masses to conduct coastal defense.[14] According to another account: "Lin was not only the first modern Chinese statesman who advocated the purchase of western guns and ships, but also the first 'scholar-general' who actually used them to any extent in his army and navy."[15]

Lin Zexu recognized that Chinese ships were no match for the British vessels in size, number, or strength. Therefore, the Chinese navy's best strategy was to stay out of deep water, where the British had the advantage, and to focus instead on protecting the entrances to China's harbors and ports. To do this properly the Chinese must first fix old cannon emplacements, build new long-range batteries, and string metal chains and wooden rafts across the harbor entrances to deny British ships entry. Second, it was necessary to build larger ships and train better sailors. Third, they needed to construct fire ships and conduct night raids to destroy the "barbarian ships." Fourth, they must surround the enemy positions and defend the perimeter, thereby protracting the conflict. Finally, by exacerbating preexisting British tensions with other Western nations, such as the Russians and perhaps even the French, the Chinese could weaken the British resolve.[16]

As part of this plan, Lin proposed the creation of a modernized navy. He reasoned that because China's coastline was so long and harbors so numerous, it would be impossible to defend every one of them from foreign aggression. Therefore, after creating a modern fleet, the Chinese could attack and defeat the enemy on the open sea, which in Lin's vision really meant littoral waters, rather than true "blue" water. Lin's four cornerstones for a modern Chinese navy were "good weapons," "skill and experience," "courage and strength," and the ability of Chinese sailors to "work with one mind." His construction plans were equally ambitious, and he advocated building one hundred large ships, fifty medium ships, and fifty small ships, with a thousand cannon and a specially trained crew of one thousand navigators and helmsmen. Lin further advised practicality: "When making a cannon seek usefulness, when building a ship seek strength."[17]

Unlike many previous Chinese theoreticians of coastal defense, Lin was in a position to put his theories into practice. In line with his views, he strengthened the Chinese forts and strung large chains across the entrance to Canton harbor. He also sponsored the creation of peasant militias to fight the British. But it was his plan to create a modern Chinese navy that was by far the most revolutionary. As shown in a letter written by Lin on 24 October 1840, his respect for foreign ships had increased to the point where he tacitly admitted that "our junks and guns are no match for theirs."[18]

As Sino-British hostilities erupted anew in 1841, the Chinese government largely ignored Lin Zexu's abortive attempts to build a modern navy based on analyzing and reproducing Western technology. Instead, due to constant bureaucratic hesitation to accept new and even more onerous financial burdens, Chinese officials naturally turned to examples from Chinese history to strengthen traditional coastal defense techniques. These included Chinese attempts to cut off the British from local supplies of food and freshwater. It also included denying them direct access to Chinese rivers and canals. Finally, it was widely assumed that the British forces could be defeated if only they could be tempted to fight on the land, which would play to China's strengths. For all of these reasons, China's earliest efforts to build a modern navy lost momentum before they had even begun.

Beijing's assumptions of its own invincibility were wrong on all counts. In fact, the British introduction of new naval technology in the form of iron flat-bottomed boats with built-in watertight compartments, when joined with recent improvements in water-resistant cartridge rifles, allowed the British to demonstrate their military dominance over both the sea and the land. This allowed them to breach China's coastal defenses and gain direct access to the crucial river and canal systems where China's most strategic choke points were located.

Recognizing the key role played by the Grand Canal, the British ignored China's political center to the North during the final campaign of the war and struck instead at China's commercial heart along the Yangzi River. The 19 June 1842 fall of Shanghai gave British forces unimpeded access to the Yangzi River. On 17 August 1842, Qiying, the Imperial Commissioner in charge of the peace negotiations, reported that more than eighty foreign ships had dominated the Yangzi River, captured the canal, and "cut off our communications between the North and the South." This choke point was indeed crucial because without grain supplies from the south, the capital in Beijing could not be sustained. Therefore, Qiying urged the emperor to agree to necessary concessions and a huge indemnity: "The ships of the barbarians are sturdy and their cannons fierce. Previously this was only hearsay. But now we have been on their ships and personally have seen their cannons. After this experience, we are the more convinced that we cannot control them by force."[19] With China's primary trade route in British hands, the Qing emperor was forced to negotiate peace.

The failure of China's traditional coastal defense shocked the emperor. After all, during the first stage of the war, China's coastal cities appeared impervious to foreign attack. On 5 June 1842, however, in the final days of the Opium War, the emperor began to despair of his troops, stating: "As to the officers and soldiers in the army, there is a current belief among them that the sturdy ships and fierce cannons of the barbarians are irresistible. Hence, they gave up fighting the moment they saw the enemies on the battlefield."[20] With no effective military alternatives, the emperor agreed to negotiations. His official representatives signed the Treaty of Nanjing on 29 August 1842.

The Treaty of Nanjing gave the British greater trade privileges and more access to China's interior through Shanghai and the other treaty ports. This facilitated the continued sale of foreign opium which, although not legalized by the treaty, remained commonly bought and sold. This in turn reignited the silver drain that was the original source of the trade conflict. Beijing also permanently ceded the offshore island of Hong Kong to Great Britain. Although this island was steep, had no freshwater, and was located far to the south, thousands of miles from Beijing, Britain's control over any offshore island gave it a permanent base of operations both to extend its trade empire and from which British ships could threaten China militarily. As shown by Koxinga's attempt to use Taiwan to oppose the Qing, even the smallest offshore island could potentially become a significant threat to China's coastal defense. The Opium War was a clear military and strategic victory for

England, and an equally momentous defeat for China, albeit not largely recognized by Chinese as such at the time.

Period Three: 1843–64

To most Chinese, the Opium War appeared to be only a temporary setback because the foreign enemy had retreated after Beijing agreed to sign the Treaty of Nanjing, and traditionally the emperor could rescind any treaties that worked to China's disadvantage. However, new coastal defense strategies had to be developed to take into account the new threats from abroad. Lin Zexu's ambitious proposals for building a modern navy had failed in part because he misunderstood the British free trade objectives. Lin early on labeled the British as merely a Western version of China's earlier "Japanese pirates" (倭寇, *wokou*). Accordingly, "for Lin and his venerators, the British remained, from beginning to end, but another species of 'pirate' 'sea marauder' [海寇, *haikou*], incapable of sustained penetration of the empire's inner fastness, and tied, by their own immediate needs for cash and supplies, to the smuggler-dominated southeastern littoral."[21]

Following China's defeat in the Opium War, there were a number of new naval theorists who recognized the value of Western technology and advocated its adoption. Immediately after the Opium War, Wei Yuan (1794–1857) wrote his famous work "Plans for Maritime Defense." Criticizing the British ships as too heavy for use in China's rivers and canals, he "suggested that the British steam paddle-wheel ships were not efficient." The key was to lure them into areas they were not suited for because "they were vulnerable and helpless if their wheels were damaged by gunfire or clogged by weeds and rushes."[22]

But Wei Yuan further wrote that China must actively "adopt barbarian technology to control the barbarians." This included studying Western ships, guns, troop selection, troop training, and methods for supporting troops, so as to reform completely the Chinese army. To accomplish this task quickly and easily, he recommended using profits from China's lucrative foreign trade to build shipyards and munitions factories. Wei Yuan further envisioned a modernized Chinese fleet of one hundred ships, like the earlier Ming navy, manned by a total force of thirty thousand men. This fleet would be stationed during peacetime at various ports throughout China but could be brought together in times of war to fight together as a single fleet.[23]

Another important representative of the so-called advocate Chinese resistance school of coastal defense during the Opium War era was Yao Ying (1785–1853). Yao's particular focus was the coastal defense of Taiwan, which—

like Hong Kong—was in danger of falling to foreign aggressors. He acknowledged that defending Taiwan was made particularly difficult because it was far from the mainland, isolated by oceans, had a long coastline, and had numerous unprotected harbors. Like his contemporaries, Lin Zexu and Wei Yuan, Yao emphasized aggressive coastal defense, building a modern fleet, and utilizing the common people as a self-defense force. Unlike these other theorists, however, who saw China as working from a position of strength, Yao acknowledged the foreigners' superiority in attacking Taiwan and counseled the use of cunning and deception: "Lure the enemy in and strand them, use a narrow pass and ambush them."[24]

During and immediately after the First Opium War, Lin Zexu, Wei Yuan, and Yao Ying all agreed that China needed to adopt military and naval reforms. Most importantly, Chinese troops needed to acquire foreign technology and adapt foreign methods to create a strong coastal defense. To build an effective coastal defense force, they advocated ambitious construction programs to establish a strong Chinese navy and to train local militia troops. Finally, they supported realistic policies emphasizing highly coordinated defensive, rather than offensive, naval strategies. These defensive policies relied in turn on denying foreigners access to harbors, eventually running them aground or luring them into ambushes.

Although these Chinese maritime theorists advocated a more active coastal defense strategy with the defensive goal of halting the intrusion of the Western countries, the Qing court largely failed to heed their advice. Within ten years most of southern and central China was embroiled in civil war; from 1851–64 the Taiping rebels, based in Nanjing, tried but failed to mobilize Han Chinese support to overthrow the Manchu dynasty in Beijing. It was during the mid- to late 1850s that China and the Western powers—primarily Great Britain and France—once again disagreed over their various treaty rights. During the 1856–60 Arrow War, also known as the Second Opium War, China proved equally unprepared to face the fact that Western naval supremacy could play a decisive role in deciding this conflict in the foreigners' favor.[25] On 28 December 1857, the Bombardment of Canton led to the taking of the city, while the 25 June 1859 Dagu Repulse near Tianjin proved to be a short-lived Chinese victory before the British and French regrouped and sent an expedition to Beijing. While the city was not taken, the European-style Qing summer palace of Yuanmingyuan (圓明園) was looted and burned to punish the Manchus for mistreating foreign prisoners.

While China was fighting maritime battles, it could not focus on the continental threats. At the height of the Arrow War, Nikolai N. Murav'ev, the Russian governor-general of Eastern Siberia, and Yishan, the Manchu military governor of the Manchurian province of Heilongjiang, negotiated the Treaty of Aigun setting the Russo-Chinese border along the Amur and Ussuri rivers. When the Russians negotiated the Treaty of Beijing in 1860, it set the Xinjiang border, and the 1864 Treaty of Tarbagatai transferred to Russia an estimated 350,000 square miles of territory—the equivalent of France and Germany combined. Under the treaties of Aigun, Beijing, and Tarbagatai, Russia acquired 665,000 square miles of territory, or almost five times the total area of Japan.[26]

During the early 1860s the Chinese government attempted to acquire modern ships from abroad to defeat the Taipings. In 1863 the inspector general of the Imperial Maritime Customs, Horatio Nelson Lay, and a British naval officer working for China, Sherard Osborne, helped to negotiate the purchase of seven modern steamships and one supply ship from Britain. Referred to as the Lay–Osborne fleet, these ships were intended to protect foreign trade from Taiping-supported piracy; according to Lay's original plan, therefore, the ships would remain under the control of the foreign-staffed Imperial Maritime Customs, not the Chinese government. To this end, he appointed Captain Osborne in command of the Chinese fleet for a term of four years.

The planned fleet was cancelled, however, when the Qing government insisted that they should be able to appoint the commander in chief; Osborne would be his assistant and would have authority only over the foreign naval officers. This plan was unacceptable to the British, who feared that a truly modern and Westernized Chinese fleet might one day be directed against them. When it appeared that the ships might fall completely under China's authority, the plan was cancelled. The ships were recalled en route and returned to Bombay, India, from where they eventually returned to Britain.

This incident was roundly condemned by China as yet one more example of poor treatment by the West. As one Chinese naval historian later commented, China had been forced to "spend money to buy humiliation" because it was not allowed the right to command its own fleet.[27] Although this plan ultimately failed, the Lay–Osborne fleet was—on paper if not in fact—China's first attempt at procuring a modern navy. If this effort had been made in the 1840s, instead of the 1860s, China's subsequent naval history, and perhaps even its national history, might have been very different.

Period Four: 1865–94

China lost crucial time after the First Opium War by refusing to adopt Western technology, weapons, and naval strategy in order to modernize. Instead, perhaps in an attempt to retain scarce financial resources, Chinese officials were ordered to look back throughout China's own history for appropriate models for coastal defense. However, time did not stand still, and the British, Continental European, and American navies continued to develop. Only after the Taipings were defeated in 1864 did Beijing begin the process of building a modern navy.

Credit for the development of the Chinese navy largely goes to regional administrators, including Zuo Zongtang, the founder of the Fuzhou dockyard, and to Li Hongzhang, who was the governor-general of the northern province of Zhili during 1870–95 and was a primary sponsor of China's naval modernization. New taxes on local commerce were adopted to pay for this rapid militarization; in 1853, for example, the *likin* tax (厘金, *lijin*) was first adopted in Yangzhou, and it "was quickly adopted throughout the provinces to defray military expenses."[28] The reliance on regional initiatives, however, also meant that efforts at naval modernization efforts often lacked broader coordination across China.

Beginning in 1866 Zuo Zongtang insisted that China begin building her own modernized ships. With the support of Prosper Marie Giquel, a French official, Zuo helped create the Fuzhou dockyard, which began to build modern Chinese warships along Western lines. The French government was interested in assisting this effort to offset a possible British offer as well as because of new concerns posed by Japan's southward expansion toward Okinawa. In 1867, with Zuo's backing, a naval academy and shipbuilding center were established with French help in Fuzhou, in Fujian province. Other naval academies were soon established in Tianjin, Nanjing, and Huangpu (Whampoa) near Canton. Over the next six and a half years the French-built Fuzhou dockyard constructed fifteen ships, including one 250-horsepower corvette that weighed in at almost 1,400 tons.[29] However, officer training did not keep pace, and many Chinese naval officers did not have extensive experience at sea, which helps to explain China's apparent inability to exploit its new naval equipment successfully.

In 1870 Li Hongzhang became governor-general of Zhili province. During the 1870s he revived Chinese plans for naval modernization, arguing that the Arrow War had proven Beijing to be more vulnerable from the coast than from its northwestern inland frontiers. In 1875 Li received funds to purchase

Naval Operations in and Around Qing China

- `– – – – –` Province boundary (pre-1907)
- `▬▬▬` Great Wall
- `⊔⊔⊔⊔⊔` Canal
- `———` River

0   125   250 Kilometers

0   125   250 Miles

ZHILI

SHENGJING

KOREA

Beijing

Dalian

Tianjin

Port Arthur
(Lüshun)

**Dagu Repulse
(1859)**

**Battle of the Yalu
(1894)**

Yantai

Weihai

**Japanese Seizure
of Weihai
(1895)**

Qingdao

**Japanese Seizure
of Port Arthur
(1894)**

SHANXI

SHANDONG

Wei River

Yellow
Sea

Huang   River

**Grand
Canal**

JIANGSU

SHAANXI

HENAN

Huai River

**Yangzi Campaign
(1841-42)**

Nanjing

Shanghai

Yangzi River

HUBEI

ANHUI

Hangzhou

Ningbo

East
China
Sea

Wuhan

ZHEJIANG

Taizhou

Wenzhou

**French Blockade
of Taiwan
(1884-85)**

JIANGXI

FUJIAN

**French Halted
Near Danshui
(1884)**

HUNAN

**Battle of Fuzhou
(1884)**

Fuzhou

**French Occupation
of Jilong (1884)**

GUIZHOU

Quanzhou

Danshui

Jilong

Xiamen
(Amoy)

TAIWAN

GUANGXI

Guangzhou
(Canton)

Shantou

**Luermen Landing
(1661)**

**Zeelandia/Tainan
Captured by Zheng
Chenggong (1662)**

Macau

Penghu

Hong
Kong

**Battle of Penghu
(1683)**

**French Seizure
of Penghu (1885)**

Hanoi

Leizhou
Bay

**Japanese Annexation
of Penghu and Taiwan
Island (1895-1945)**

Leizhou

**Bombardment
of Canton (1857)**

Qiongzhou

South
China Sea

**Battle of Chuanbi
(1839)**

PHILIPPINES

ships from abroad, but it was far less money than that allocated for inland border defense. Li's navy would become known as the Beiyang Fleet, based in Lüshun (Port Arthur) on the Liaodong Peninsula, and at Weihaiwei on the Shandong Peninsula, guarding the sea approaches to Beijing. The Qing eventually ordered the development of three other fleets: the Guangdong Fleet based at Canton, the Nanyang Fleet based on the Yangzi River, and the Fuzhou Fleet based at Fuzhou Naval Yard in southeast China. In a policy parallel to the creation of provincial armies, each fleet remained administratively separate from the others so that a single military leader could not mutiny and turn the entire navy against the Manchus.

Meanwhile, the Imperial Maritime Customs focused on collecting fees on European goods imported into China. Initially, 40 percent of this revenue was devoted to paying off the indemnities imposed by the 1860 Treaties of Beijing, but after 1866 the entire account went to the central government. In practice, however, the customs revenue was often retained by foreigners to pay off China's foreign loans or indemnities, such as the particularly onerous 1901 Boxer Indemnity (庚子賠款). Still, the foreign customs income from Shanghai soon became a major source of central governmental revenues, especially for emergency military funding such as Zuo Zongtang's extremely expensive reconquest of Xinjiang during the 1870s. Following the traditional Han strategy of pitting one barbarian against another, the Manchus leveraged the customs income from trade with the West to fund the military expedition to decimate the Muslim resistance.

In 1871 Russia occupied the Ili Valley in western Xinjiang to prevent the ongoing Muslim Rebellion (1862–78) from spreading into its territory. But Russia's goal in taking Ili was not just defensive but also part of its rapid expansion into Central Asia. After the founding of the city of Vernyi in 1854, the Russians absorbed Tashkent in 1865, the Uzbek Khanate of Bukhara in 1868, the Uzbek Khanate of Khiva in 1873, and the Uzbek Kokand Khanate in 1876. The Russian administrative system incorporated these areas as the governor-generalship of Turkestan, established in 1867; the Central Asian border provinces of Semipalatinsk established in 1854; of Syr Darya and Semireche, both established in 1867; and three others in Uralsk, Turgai, and Akhmolinsk, established in 1868. In June 1871 the governor-general of Russian Turkestan ordered Russian troops to cross the Sino-Russian border to occupy Ili, and in 1873 Russia formally incorporated the area into the Russian provincial system as Kuldzha Province.

To quell the Muslim rebellion, China deployed large forces under Zuo Zongtang and, much to Russia's surprise, restored order. However, the

Russians were not eager to relinquish control over Xinjiang's mountain passes because they gave Russia the strategic advantage in dealing with China and provided direct trade routes with Gansu, Shaanxi, and Mongolia. Therefore, the Russian price for withdrawal was high. Russia proposed that it retain control of the strategic Muzart Pass; acquire trading privileges throughout Xinjiang, Mongolia, and beyond the Great Wall into the heart of China; and receive a 5-million-ruble indemnity to defray the occupation costs. The Russians also claimed the right to navigate the Songhua River, in Manchuria, as far inland as Boduna (Potuna). China's diplomatic representative, Chonghou, agreed to these terms when he signed the Treaty of Livadia on 2 October 1879. As soon as China's government understood the treaty terms, however, it immediately repudiated the agreement. The resulting diplomatic scandal threatened to end in a war between Russia and China.

Although Chonghou appears to have reported regularly to officials in Beijing on his ten-month-long negotiations, when officials in Beijing finally read the treaty's contents, the court refused to ratify it. Russia had thousands of troops stationed near Ili and deployed twenty-three warships to Chinese waters, but China had even more soldiers in theater because Zuo Zongtang had recently put down the Muslim rebellion. The Qing put their most famous officers from the Taiping suppression in key positions and even hired the former leader of the Ever-Victorious Army, Charles Gordon, to provide military advice.

Diplomacy prevailed when Russia agreed to accept a new negotiator, Marquis Zeng Jize (Tseng Chi-tse), who was serving as China's minister to Great Britain at the time. The negotiations in St. Petersburg were acrimonious, but in the end Russia accepted a large indemnity instead of an expensive war and restored most of the disputed territory for a 9-million-ruble indemnity. Russia curtailed its demands for more extensive trade privileges and dropped the provision concerning navigation rights on the Songhua River. As a result, the 24 February 1881 Treaty of St. Petersburg superseded the Treaty of Livadia. This halted, temporarily at least, Russian expansion into China.

Despite the increased indemnity, the Chinese widely regarded the Treaty of St. Petersburg as a diplomatic victory because they had made one of the most powerful European nations back down. In reality, the treaty reinforced the precedent of diplomacy conducted not with a sound military and naval strategy but with the purse. China's repeated payments of large indemnities to mollify foreign powers ultimately retarded its own internal economic development. In 1884, soon after the Treaty of St. Petersburg, the Chinese government made Xinjiang a regular province and incorporated it into the Chinese administrative system.

During this same period of continental tensions, Li Hongzhang led a group of progressive Qing officials to push for building a forty-eight-ship navy, arguing persuasively that Beijing was now more vulnerable mainly from the coast, not from the western borderlands. But because of the Russian threat in Xinjiang, the Qing continued to allocate most military funds to frontier and not coastal defense. Naval funds were wasted on incompatible equipment divided among the regional fleets. Also, when the Manchu Court decided in 1874 to build a new Summer Palace to replace the one destroyed during the Second Opium War, it siphoned off funds formerly earmarked for naval development. Some of China's precious naval funds were thus expended on the construction of a ceremonial marble boat.

Li Hongzhang persevered, however, in forming the Beiyang Navy in China's northern waters, which is the region he administered.[30] Li obtained the court's permission to purchase ships from abroad beginning in 1875, right after China was forced to cede Okinawa to Japan, but only two million taels were set aside for this task. This amounted to just a fraction of the sums the Qing were spending during those same years in Xinjiang.[31] With limited funds, Li had to make the decision whether China should build ships herself or should buy them from British, French, and German shipbuilders. Because of his indecision, by the early 1880s the various Chinese regional fleets were far from being standardized and experienced great difficulty working together as a single unit. As Rawlinson has observed, "In that disordered buy-and-build situation, there was no plan, no grasp of the problem. There were only varying degrees of hostility to China's several external foes. Much money was spent, but with little effect. The variety of equipment, which reflected the political compartmentalization of the coast, contributed to the lack of coordinated action and grand strategy. Li Hongzhang only added confusion with his wily and opportunistic purchasing of ships and arms."[32]

During this period Hong Kong coastal defense theorist Wang Dao began to examine China's maritime concerns, even suggesting that China "become intimate with England, resist Russia, protect Taiwan, guard against Japan." In a letter to Li Hongzhang, Wang recommended retaining China's economic power even while cultivating her national power. To do this, he recommended emulating England by building railroads, adopting electricity, and building factories. This would allow China to fight off the greater challenges posed by Russia and Japan.[33]

In particular, Wang Dao was one of the first Chinese to recognize the value of armored ships. He advocated acquiring a fleet composed of many smaller ships to offset the West's large ships. His reasons included the lower price, with the total investment divided over many ships rather than just one or two; the ability for these ships to gang up on an opponent; a smaller ship's superior usefulness in shallow waters; and easy retreat into coastal areas and up China's many rivers. Wang Dao suggested forming four fleets based in Manchuria, Shandong, Shanghai, and Amoy. He optimistically stated "if one fleet does not win, call in another. . . . If the second fleet does not win, call in the third, and thereby enforce a steadfast and indomitable will."[34]

Wang Dao's advice to purchase many small ships was largely ignored by the Chinese government, which sought to buy several large ships instead, and for its own protection kept the naval fleets geographically separate and organizationally distinct from each other. By 1882 the Qing navy consisted of approximately fifty steamships of various sizes and designs. While half of these had been built in China, at either the Shanghai or Fuzhou shipyard, the other half had been purchased from abroad. For example, four gunboats and two 1,350-ton cruisers were on order from England, while two other Stettin-type warships and a steel cruiser were on order from Germany. To man these large ships, by the late 1880s a small number of Chinese students either visited or studied abroad at the Royal Navy College in Greenwich, England; at the École de Construction at Cherbourg, France; and at the U.S. Naval War College in Newport, Rhode Island.

Ding Richang (1823–82), another well-known coastal defense strategist, disagreed with Wang Dao on where these fleets should be based. He advocated the creation of three fleets based at Canton, at the mouth of the Yangzi River, and on the Shandong peninsula at Weihaiwei. A successful coastal defense strategy would depend on proper training of sailors, promoting maritime industry, and an understanding that gaining and keeping the Chinese people's "heart" was the secret of successfully defending China. From a strategic point of view, retaining control over Taiwan was essential, Ding emphasized, in particular from the threat of Japanese aggression.[35]

Beijing initially decided to build three fleets based at Canton, at the Fuzhou Naval Yard in southeast China, and in the north along the approaches to the Bohai Gulf. The three fleets later grew to four fleets based at Canton, Fuzhou, and Shanghai, and then the northern fleet was divided even further between Weihaiwei and Port Arthur. Initially the bulk of these forces were in the south, which ignored Wang Dao's advice to locate two of his three fleets in the north. Also, instead of working closely with each other, each fleet was

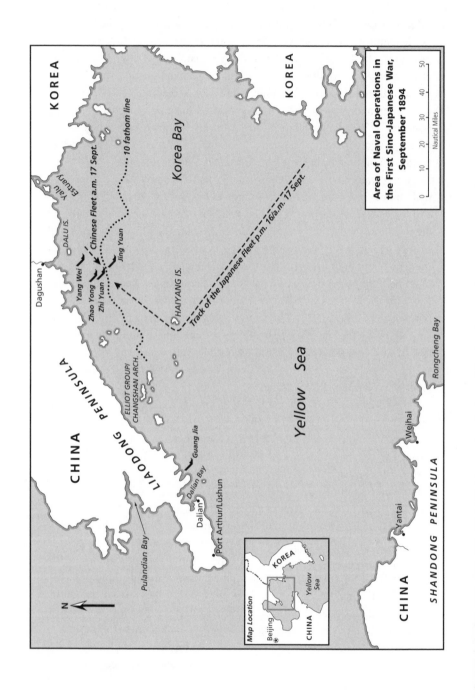

KOREA

KOREA

Korea Bay

Yalu Estuary

DALU IS.

Chinese Fleet a.m. 17 Sept.

10 fathom line

Jing Yuan

Yang Wei

Zhao Yong

Zhi Yuan

Dagushan

HAIYANG IS.

Track of the Japanese Fleet p.m. 16/a.m. 17 Sept.

CHINA

LIAODONG PENINSULA

ELLIOT GROUP/
CHANGSHAN ARCH.

Guang Jia

Dalian Bay

Dalian

Port Arthur/Lüshun

Pulandian Bay

Yellow Sea

Rongcheng Bay

Weihai

Yantai

SHANDONG PENINSULA

CHINA

N

Area of Naval Operations in
the First Sino-Japanese War,
September 1894

0   10   20   30   40   50

Nautical Miles

Map Location

KOREA

Beijing

CHINA

Yellow
Sea

administered and staffed separately, and they each had distinct geographic responsibilities that touched but did not overlap. Instead of forcing each fleet to assist its neighbor in times of trouble, this structure ensured that the separate fleets could not join and rebel against the central government because mutiny was a constant threat.[36]

Not surprisingly, considering Li Hongzhang's political influence in Beijing, many of the best and most modern ships found their way into Li's northern fleet, which never saw any action in the 1884–85 Sino-French conflict. In fact, according to one view, the "southernmost provinces were invariably treated as entities completely separate from the central and northern sections of the country."[37] Fear that he might lose control over his fleet would later lead Li to refuse urgent requests that his ships be sent southward to aid the imperiled Fuzhou fleet in 1884. Li claimed that moving his fleet southward would have left northern China undefended from Japanese aggression, but his decision has generally been criticized as a sign of China's provincial-minded thinking. By refusing to assist the south, China's total naval strength was greatly weakened, allowing their French opponents to pick off the southern fleets in detail.

By 1883, at the outset of the Sino-French war, China's newly modernized navy, especially in southern China, was poorly manned and armed. Although China's Western-made ships were state of the art, training on how to use these ships effectively was haphazard and little progress had been made adopting Western naval strategy. Most of the officers had little or no experience at sea. For example, according to one estimate, only eight of the fourteen ship captains who saw action in the upcoming Sino-French war had received any modern training at all.[38] As mentioned earlier, there was also little, if any, coordination between the various fleets in north and south China. This meant that at any one time the French naval forces opposed only a fraction of China's total navy. For these reasons, French naval dominance in the upcoming conflict was virtually ensured.

In 1884–85 China tried and failed to halt France's efforts to make Vietnam its colony. On 23 August 1884 a French fleet of eight ships destroyed the Fuzhou Fleet in port in "The Battle of Fuzhou" (馬江海战). The French then proceeded to blockade the Nanyang Fleet on the Yangzi River, cutting the flow of tribute grain up the Grand Canal to the capital. They also attacked Jilong, Taiwan, and eventually occupied the city in 1884, but their advance inland was halted near Danshui. Adopting a blockade of Taiwan, the French took the Penghus during March 1885, and held them for the final four months of the war to use them as a negotiating chip. Because the Beiyang

Fleet in North China ignored the requests by the Nanyang Fleet in the south for assistance, the French navy never faced the most modern elements of the Chinese navy. On 9 June 1885 Beijing capitulated, ceding Vietnam to France in return for regaining the Penghus and halting the French blockade of Taiwan.

France's victory underscored China's weakness and perhaps spurred on Japan's later attempts to expand into Korea. Beginning with the Meiji Restoration of 1868, the Japanese rapidly modernized and Westernized their navy. In the late summer of 1894 the Japanese fleet had been trying to engage a very reluctant Beiyang Fleet, which the Japanese intercepted near the Yalu River convoying troops to Korea. The fleets were roughly equivalent, with the Chinese possessing greater firepower and the Japanese greater speed. In the 17 September 1894 "Battle of the Yalu" (黄海海战, lit. Battle of the Yellow Sea), Japan gained a clear victory when it sank four out of the ten Chinese ships, losing none of its own. Corruption had left China's fleet supplied with ordnance of the wrong caliber and with defective powder, neutralizing its superior firepower. Insubordination and the inability to execute basic naval formations had permitted the Japanese fleet repeatedly to broadside the Chinese fleet.

The Battle of the Yalu demonstrated that modern naval equipment can be useless without the Westernized training that allows forces to coordinate together as a unit.[39] While Qing China was willing, albeit grudgingly, to purchase Western naval equipment, it refused to send large numbers of students abroad to adopt the intellectual processes and the educational system that had made these systems so effective in the West. Because of its defeat in battle at Port Arthur by the Japanese on 21 November 1894, and the later blockade and destruction of the Beiyang Fleet in February 1895 by the Japanese navy at Weihaiwei, China lost its formerly unquestioned position as the greatest maritime nation in Asia. Like the French before them, Japanese forces took the Penghus and invaded Taiwan but unlike the French did not return these islands. The April 1895 Treaty of Shimonoseki, which ended the war, made Korea a Japanese protectorate and ceded permanently to Japan the island of Taiwan and the Penghus.

Although the Qing dynasty attempted to adopt a series of belated naval reforms in 1907, and even created a separate Ministry of the Navy in December 1910, the Wuhan uprising of 10 October 1911 succeeded in overthrowing the central government, in part at least, because of a naval mutiny by the very forces sent by Beijing to put down the rebellion.[40] As a result, the Qing government abdicated power in 1912 in favor of a Western-style constitutional democracy, but this ushered in almost forty years of turmoil and civil war before the next government to unify all of China, the People's Republic of China, could begin the long and tortuous road toward maritime transformation.

Conclusion

China's defeat in the First Opium War finally shook selected Chinese officials from their continental mindset and maritime complacency, which had been based on a strong centralized government, weak maritime enemies, and effective coastal defense based on full control of the canals, rivers, coastline, and littoral waters. The founding of a British base of operations on Hong Kong, in particular, created a new strategic threat to China's coastal defense, while the opening of other coastal cities to foreign trade eliminated Beijing's trade monopoly and gradually undermined China's traditional canal trade.

Fearful of losing their own tenuous hold on power, China's Manchu leaders largely ignored the advice of their own naval theorists and refused to adopt major naval reforms. Only following Beijing's defeat in the Second Opium War and the end of the Taiping Rebellion did the Qing rulers belatedly decide to build a modern navy. However, China's naval reforms would prove to be too little, too late, and by the 1890s, Japan had been able to leverage its highly successful Meiji reforms to forge ahead of its much larger, but more cumbersome and tradition-bound, Chinese neighbor. Emboldened by its newfound military powers, the Japanese navy soundly defeated China's Beiyang fleet, taking permanent control of Taiwan as part of the peace terms and stripping China of its formerly unquestioned status as maritime hegemon in East Asia. Meanwhile, major European powers—including France, Germany, and Russia—took advantage of Beijing's naval weakness to increase their territorial concessions at China's expense, which undermined Qing power even more.[41]

Arguably, China's maritime defeats were directly due to the Qing decision not to modernize and Westernize its navy following the First Opium War. In the final analysis, the longer the Manchus delayed adopting comprehensive reforms, the more China fell behind. Instead of deciding—as its island neighbor Japan did in 1868—to reform rapidly and to adopt immediately a thoroughly modern and Western-style oceangoing navy, the Qing rulers adopted a series of largely reactive and ultimately ineffectual coastal defense strategies. Unlike Japan, however, which was protected by the sea and had a relatively homogenous population, the Manchus could not ignore numerous continental threats, most importantly from Russia, nor could they modernize their army and navy without being concerned that the dominant Han Chinese population might use these new weapons to overthrow them. Added to these very real fears was an increasingly decentralized and overly bureaucratic state apparatus that made the adoption of comprehensive reforms difficult, if not impossible. To this day, due in part to this series of poor maritime decisions, China has yet to reclaim its formerly unrivaled influence throughout East Asian waters.

Notes

Epigraph: P. C. Kuo, *A Critical Study of the First Anglo-Chinese* War (Shanghai, China: The Commercial Press, Ltd, 1935), 250–51.

1. Lo Jung-pang, *China as a Sea Power* (UC Davis Archives, unpublished manuscript, 1957); "international" in this case refers to Han versus a non-Han opponent, such as Vietnam.

2. For more on this issue and other related trade questions during this early period of Chinese trade with Southeast Asia, see Qi Dongfang, "Maritime Trade and Tang Dynasty Yangzhou"; Ke Fengmei, "A Study of 'The Record of the Xiangying Temple' Stele from Putian—A Synopsis of Findings"; and Chen Kuo-tung, "Archeological Finding and Its Connection with Chinese Exort Ceramics," papers presented at the *Symposium on the Chinese Export Ceramic Trade in Southeast Asia*, 12–14 March 2007, Asia Research Institute, National University of Singapore.

3. This transliteration comes from his Ming title "Lord of the Imperial Surname," which in the Chinese Wade-Giles transliteration system reads as "Kuo Hsing Yeh."

4. 杨志本 [Yang Zhiben, ed.], 中国海军百科全书 [*China Navy Encyclopedia*], vol. 2 (Beijing: 海潮出版社 [Sea Tide Press], 1998), 1912–14.

5. Shi advocated the integration of Taiwan into Qing administration. Following Shi's victory, Taiwan formally became a prefecture of China's Fujian province. See Andrew Erickson and Andrew Wilson, "China's Aircraft Carrier Dilemma," in Andrew Erickson, Lyle Goldstein, William Murray, and Andrew Wilson, eds., *China's Future Nuclear Submarine Force* (Annapolis, MD: Naval Institute Press, 2007), 260.

6. Mark Mancall, *China at the Center: 300 Years of Foreign Policy* (New York: Free Press, 1984), 57.

7. Frank A. Kierman Jr. and John K. Fairbank, eds., *Chinese Ways of Warfare* (Cambridge, MA: Harvard University Press, 1974); of course, this was not always the case, as shown by the highly successful military careers of nineteenth century Han officials such as Zuo Zongtang and Li Hongzhang.

8. Ralph L. Powell, *The Rise of Chinese Military Power, 1895–1912* (Princeton, NJ: Princeton University Press, 1955), 8–13.

9. Bruce A. Elleman, "The *Chongqing* Mutiny and the Chinese Civil War, 1949," in Christopher Bell and Bruce Elleman, eds., *Naval Mutinies of the Twentieth Century: An International Perspective* (London: Frank Cass, 2003), 232–45.

10. James A. Millward, *Beyond the Pass: Economy, Ethnicity, and Empire in Qing Central Asia, 1759–1864* (Stanford, CA: Stanford University Press, 1998), 146–47.

11. Mancall, *China at the Center*, 17–20, 77.

12. P.C. Kuo, *Critical Study*, 251–61.

13. Gideon Chen, *Lin Tse-hsu: Pioneer Promoter of the Adoption of Western Means of Maritime Defense in China* (New York: Paragon Book Gallery, 1961), 31.

14. Yang Zhiben, ed., *China Navy Encyclopedia*, 1268–69.

15. Chen, *Lin Tse-hsu*, 31.

16. Yang Zhiben, ed., *China Navy Encyclopedia*, 1268–68.

17. Ibid.

18. P. C. Kuo, *Critical Study*, 268.

19. Ibid., 296–99.

20. Ibid., 288–92.

21. James M. Polachek, *The Inner Opium* War (Cambridge, MA: Harvard University Press, 1992), 140.

22. Yang Zhiben, ed., *China Navy Encyclopedia*, 1727–28.

23. Ibid.

24. Ibid., 1814–5.

25. Douglas Hurd, *The Arrow War: An Anglo-Chinese Confusion, 1856–1860* (New York: Macmillan Company, 1967), 205–41.

26. S. C. M. Paine, *Imperial Rivals: China, Russia, and Their Disputed Frontier* (Armonk, NY: M. E. Sharpe, 1993), 252.

27. Yu Zufan, *The Real Record of the Chinese Fleet* (*Zhongguo Jiandui Shi Lu*) (Shenyang, China: Chunfeng Literature and Arts Publishing House, 1997), 9–12.

28. Philip A. Kuhn, *Rebellion and Its Enemies in Late Imperial China: Militarization and Social Structure, 1796–1864* (Cambridge, MA: Harvard University Press, 1970), 91.

29. Gideon Chen, *Tso Tsung T'ang: Pioneer Promoter of the Modern Dockyard and the Woollen Mill in China* (New York: Paragon Book Gallery, 1961), 14–35.

30. Thomas L. Kennedy, "Li Hung-chang and the Kiangnan Arsenal, 1860–1895," in Samuel C. Chu and Kwang-Ching Liu, eds., *Li Hung-chang and China's Early Modernization* (Armonk, NY: M. E. Sharpe, 1994), 197–214; Stanley Spector, *Li Hung-chang and the Huai Army: A Study in Nineteenth-Century Chinese Regionalism* (Seattle: University of Washington Press, 1964).

31. Bruce A. Elleman, *Modern Chinese Warfare, 1795–1989* (London: Routledge Press, 2001), 66.

32. John L. Rawlinson, *China's Struggle for Naval Development, 1839–1895* (Cambridge, MA: Harvard University Press, 1967), 63–81.

33. Lam Kai Yin, "A Study of Wang Dao's Idea of Coastal Defense" ("*Wang Dao de Haifang Sixiang*"), *Modern Chinese History Studies* (*Jindaishi Yenjiu*), no. 2 (1999): 136–50.

34. Ibid.

35. Yang Zhiben, ed., *China Navy Encyclopedia*, 226–27.

36. L.C. Arlington, *Through the Dragon's Eyes: Fifty Years' Experience of a Foreigner in the Chinese Government Service* (New York: Richard R. Smith Inc., 1931), 61–63; that the Manchus were correct to be concerned was best shown by the 1911 naval mutiny at Wuhan that helped overthrow the Qing dynasty.

37. Richard N. J. Wright, *The Chinese Steam Navy, 1862–1945* (London: Chatham, 2000), 14.

38. Rawlinson, *China's Struggle*, 94.

39. Bruce A. Elleman, "Western Advisors and Chinese Sailors in the 1894–1895 Sino-Japanese War," in John Reeve and David Stevens, eds., *The Face of Naval Battle* (Crows Nest, Australia: Allen & Unwin, 2003), 55–69.

40. Edward Dryer, *China at War, 1901–1949* (London: Longman Group, 1995), 34.

41. S. C. M. Paine, "The Triple Intervention and the Termination of the First Sino-Japanese War," in Bruce A. Elleman and S. C. M. Paine, eds., *Naval Coalition Warfare: From the Napoleonic War to Operation Iraqi Freedom* (London: Routledge, 2008), 75–85.

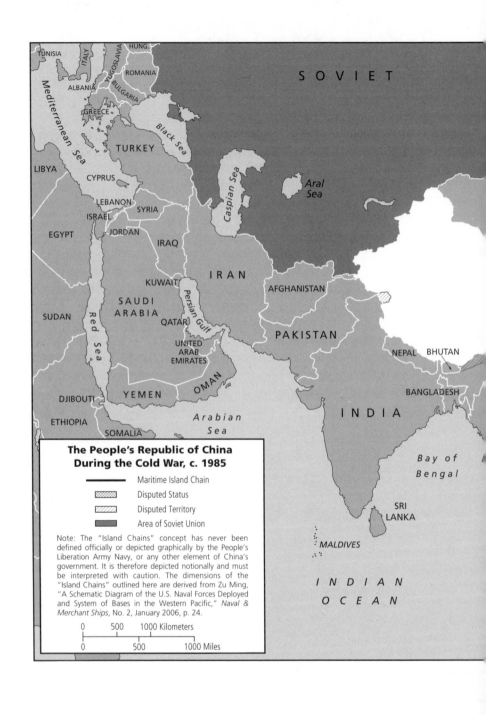

TUNISIA
ITALY
YUGOSLAVIA
HUNG.
ROMANIA
ALBANIA
BULGARIA
GREECE
SOVIET
Mediterranean Sea
Black Sea
TURKEY
LIBYA
CYPRUS
Caspian Sea
Aral Sea
LEBANON
SYRIA
ISRAEL
JORDAN
EGYPT
IRAQ
IRAN
AFGHANISTAN
KUWAIT
Persian Gulf
SAUDI ARABIA
QATAR
PAKISTAN
NEPAL
BHUTAN
SUDAN
Red Sea
UNITED ARAB EMIRATES
OMAN
BANGLADESH
DJIBOUTI
YEMEN
INDIA
ETHIOPIA
SOMALIA
Arabian Sea

The People's Republic of China During the Cold War, c. 1985

———— Maritime Island Chain

▨ Disputed Status

▨ Disputed Territory

▨ Area of Soviet Union

Note: The "Island Chains" concept has never been defined officially or depicted graphically by the People's Liberation Army Navy, or any other element of China's government. It is therefore depicted notionally and must be interpreted with caution. The dimensions of the "Island Chains" outlined here are derived from Zu Ming, "A Schematic Diagram of the U.S. Naval Forces Deployed and System of Bases in the Western Pacific," *Naval & Merchant Ships*, No. 2, January 2006, p. 24.

0   500   1000 Kilometers

0   500   1000 Miles

Bay of Bengal

SRI LANKA

MALDIVES

INDIAN OCEAN

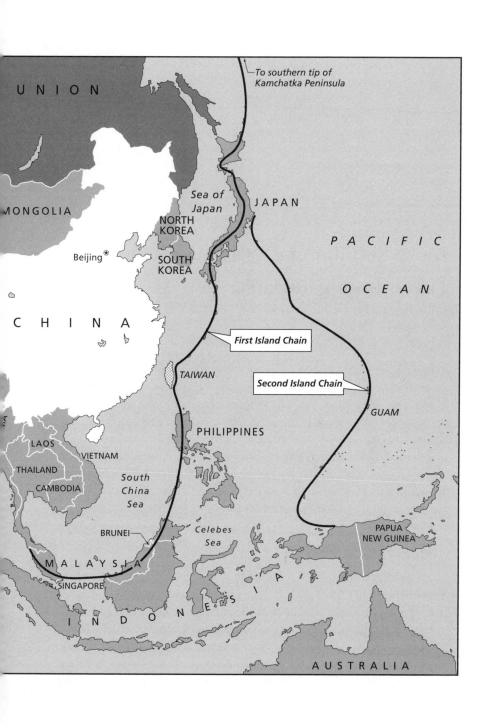

Bernard D. Cole

More Red than Expert: Chinese Sea Power during the Cold War

THE COMMUNIST VICTORY ON THE MAINLAND of China in 1949 was an army victory; the People's Liberation Army (PLA) was unable to project power across even the narrow Taiwan Strait. The army continued as the dominant service within the PLA throughout the Cold War, although Beijing recognized the maritime concerns posed by 14,000 kilometers (km) of coastline and thousands of islands, both occupied and claimed. This chapter will focus on the Chinese strategic military view during the Cold War years, from 1949 to 1991, to gain an understanding of the PLA Navy's role and status: Why did the army continue to dominate the PLA and Beijing's strategic military view?

The Early Years: 1949–54

Even after losing the civil war in 1949 to the PLA, Chiang Kai-shek's Republic of China Navy (ROCN) was capable of stopping the PLA at the mainland's water's edge.[1] The ROCN also continued raiding coastal installations, landing agents, attacking merchant craft and fishing vessels, and threatening invasion on a larger scale. The new government in Beijing sought to defend its coastline and island territories against both the United States and the Kuomintang (KMT) regime on Taiwan. Coastal defense was emphasized in January 1950 in the creation of a new "East China Military Command," headquartered in Shanghai and deploying more than 450,000 men.

Beijing tasked these troops with defending China's coast against "imperialist aggression from the sea," continuing the fight against Chiang's forces, and helping with economic reconstruction.[2] The first People's Republic of China (PRC) naval force, the East China People's Navy, was established on 1 May 1949 as part of this command. Most of this maritime force consisted of the former KMT Second Coastal Defense Fleet, which defected to the new Beijing regime.[3] China's communist leadership justified the new navy as needed "to safeguard China's independence, territorial integrity and sovereignty against imperialist aggression . . . to destroy the sea blockade of liberated China, to support the land and air forces of the people's liberation Army in defense of Chinese soil and to wipe out all remnants of the reactionary forces."[4]

A Chinese navy was also assigned missions of establishing law and order on coastal and riverine waters, assisting the army capture of offshore islands still occupied by the KMT, and preparing for the conquest of Taiwan. The Chinese Communist Party's (CCP) politburo further charged the new navy with "defending both [eastern and southeastern] China coasts and the Yangtze River."[5] The East China Navy's first commander (and simultaneously political commissar) was Gen. Zhang Aiping.

Zhang Aiping was typical of early PRC naval leadership. He was a product of revolutionary China who had spent his entire career as a ground commander and was transferred to the new navy for reasons of political reliability and a proven combat record, rather than for any particular naval experience. In fact, this trend continued throughout the Cold War; the most innovative People's Liberation Army Navy (PLAN) commander, Liu Huaqing, spent almost his entire career as an army officer before his appointment to head the navy in 1982. After six distinguished years in that position, Liu reverted to being a general, becoming vice-chairman of the Central Military Commission (CMC).[6]

Among Zhang Aiping's first acts, in August 1949, were establishing a naval staff college at Nanjing, organizing a rudimentary maintenance and logistical infrastructure, and in September visiting Moscow to obtain Soviet assistance for the new force. The PLAN was then officially established in May 1950.[7] The Chinese wanted a defensive force that would be inexpensive to build and could be quickly manned and trained.[8]

An effective, if limited, new Chinese navy was created in 1949–50, but the success occurred in a strategic environment of "lean to one side" expounded by Mao Zedong (毛泽东, Mao Tse-tung) in June 1949, when he announced

that "[we will] ally ourselves with the Soviet Union . . . and form an international united front."⁹ Mao's decision to ally with the Soviet Union in opposition
to the United States was based in significant part on his fear that Washington
would intervene with military forces in China's civil war, even after the government of Chiang Kai-shek (蔣介石, Jiang Jieshi) had fled to Taiwan.¹⁰
His strategic goal was to avoid armed confrontation with the United States.
Furthermore, Beijing's national security concerns were focused on combating
remaining KMT resistance on the mainland and consolidating CCP control
throughout the new PRC, particularly in Xinjiang Province and Tibet.

Importing the Young School

Soviet financial, material, and advisory assistance to the PLAN was
obtained by Zhang Aiping and Mao Zedong during their 1949–50 visits to
Moscow. China's leaders planned to use half of an initial Soviet loan of $300
million to purchase naval equipment; the new PLAN also ordered two new
cruisers from Great Britain and attempted to obtain surplus foreign warships
through Hong Kong, efforts that were negated by the outbreak of the Korean
War in June 1950.¹¹ Hence, China acquired mostly small vessels suitable to
combat ROCN threats to mainland coastal installations.

Soviet advisors assigned to China brought with them Moscow's "Young
School" of maritime strategy, which emphasized coastal defense by a navy of
small surface craft and submarines. The Young School had developed in the
Soviet Union shortly after World War I, based on conditions particular to
postrevolutionary Russia:

1. A new regime that was under military and political attack by several
   capitalist countries and had not completely quelled domestic fighting;

2. A regime, furthermore, that *expected* to be besieged and attacked by
   capitalist nations, with amphibious attack a current fact and future
   threat, especially from "the ultimate bastion of imperialism, the
   United States";¹²

3. A navy that was in disarray and almost entirely manned by captured
   or defecting former enemy personnel;

4. Budgetary shortages that limited the amount available to spend on
   expensive naval systems;

5. Lack of an industrial infrastructure to produce indigenously modern
   naval armaments; and

6. A maritime frontier hemmed in by adversarial fleets and bases.

These conditions also applied to China in 1949, as did the problem of a very weak modern maritime tradition.

The Soviet Union sent an initial cadre of 500 naval advisors to China in 1950; between 1,500 and 2,000 had arrived by 1953. These advisors paralleled the Chinese chain of command from Beijing headquarters to individual ships and squadrons, providing the means for inculcating Soviet naval doctrine throughout the new navy. Large numbers of Chinese officers, including the officer who succeeded Zhang Aiping as commander of the PLAN, Gen. Xiao Jingguang, received training in the Soviet Union.[13] Xiao was an early associate of Mao Zedong, was twice a student in Moscow, and spoke fluent Russian; he was both "an excellent administrator" and "a staunch Maoist who could be counted upon to adhere to whatever line the chairman espoused."[14]

China initially obtained four old Soviet submarines, two destroyers, and a large number of patrol boats. The new force also included approximately ten corvettes, forty ex-U.S. landing craft, and several dozen miscellaneous river gunboats, minesweepers, and yard craft, all seized from the Nationalists.[15] The Soviets also helped establish a large shore-based infrastructure, including shipyards, naval colleges, and extensive coastal fortifications.[16]

Mao Zedong considered the capture of Taiwan "an inseparable part of his great cause of unifying China."[17] Hence, Beijing wanted to establish a navy capable of helping the PLA conquer the offshore islands still occupied by the KMT. This campaign was to lead to the invasion of Taiwan in the summer of 1951. Although Mao lacked experience in naval warfare, he quickly learned that a successful campaign against Taiwan would require adequate amphibious training, naval transportation, "guaranteed air coverage," and the cooperation of a "fifth column" on the island—requirements that still apply.[18]

Chinese fear of American aggression was heightened in June 1950, when President Harry Truman ordered the U.S. Seventh Fleet into the Taiwan Strait at the outset of the Korean War as a means of preventing either side from attacking the other.[19] Beijing understood that Truman was committing the United States to the defense of Taiwan—after having refused to do so for many months, thus placing American military might back into the Chinese civil war.[20] Beijing also appreciated the United States' complete air and sea superiority in the western Pacific Ocean.

Beijing's fear of U.S. aggression was reinforced in February 1953 when President Dwight Eisenhower withdrew the U.S. fleet from the Taiwan Strait, thus "unleashing" Nationalist forces on Taiwan to attack China.[21] In December 1953 Mao Zedong assigned the PLAN three priority missions: (1) eliminate KMT naval interference and ensure safe navigation for China's

The Naval Situation Along China's Coast, c. 1950

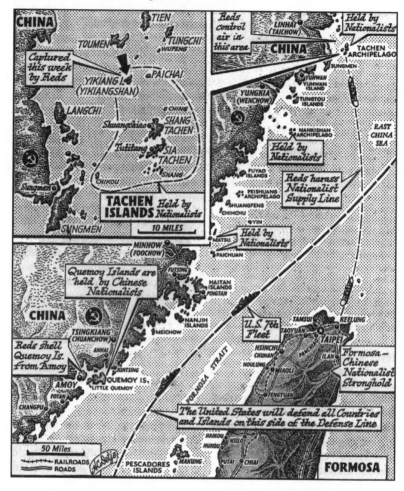

maritime commerce; (2) prepare to recover Taiwan; and (3) oppose aggression from the sea.[22] Among the problems faced by the PRC's young navy was the lack of trained personnel and amphibious ships, as demonstrated in the very spotty record of assaults on KMT-held coastal islands. The PLAN also lacked air power and was still in the process of establishing a maintenance and logistical infrastructure. None of these problems should have been unexpected, but they remained unresolved for the PLAN throughout the Cold War and were exacerbated by Moscow's withdrawal of support in 1959–60.

Consolidating Control over Coastal Waters and Offshore Islands: 1955–59

The Korean War presented mixed naval lessons to China. The amphibious landing at Inchon in September 1950 was a major turning point of the war, and allied command of the sea allowed free employment of aircraft carriers and battleships to bombard Chinese and North Korean forces. The UN forces suffered at least one significant maritime defeat, however, when a planned amphibious assault on the east coast port of Hungnam in October 1950 had to be canceled because of North Korean naval mine warfare. Overall, however, Korea was not significantly a maritime conflict, and the PLA's success in land and air battles in Korea contributed to a continued reliance on a defensive, coastal navy in support of an army serving as China's primary military arm.

This post–Korean War conclusion apparently was not unanimous among PLA commanders; after witnessing firsthand in Korea the effects of modern weaponry, some PLA leaders advocated modifying Mao's theory of "People's War" to one of "People's War under Modern Conditions." Their ability to build a PLA on this principle, however, was limited by the necessity to continue conforming to Maoist ideology. This meant a continued concentration on large ground formations with the navy remaining in a supporting role.

China had relied on Soviet nuclear forces to counter the American nuclear threat during the 1950s. Stresses in the alliance with Moscow became more divisive as the decade progressed, however, in part because Mao Zedong was determined that China develop its own nuclear deterrent. The extraordinary resource requirements of the nuclear weapons program contributed to the lack of resources for the Chinese navy during the late 1950s and 1960s.

Operational missions for the PLAN during the mid- and late 1950s continued to focus on KMT attacks against the mainland and on capturing islands still held by Taiwan. The decade was marked by two Taiwan Strait crises, in 1954–55 and in 1958, that featured PRC bombardments of the Taiwan-occupied islands of Kinmen and Mazu.

In neither of these crises did Beijing intend to capture these islands, but the incidents drew the United States more firmly into the conflict between China and Taiwan, and emphasized the PLAN's comparative weakness.[23] The decade ended with Chinese possession of all the disputed islands except Kinmen, Mazu, the Penghus, and of course Taiwan.[24] Notably, the PLA did capture the Dachen Islands in 1954, a campaign that took advantage of superior PLA air power and a well-coordinated amphibious assault.[25] It was the most sophisticated demonstration of naval power by the PLAN to date. The PLA also stopped most of the raids on the mainland as well as attacks on merchant and fishing vessels.[26]

The PLAN was not the only maritime force organized by the PRC. The Public Security Force established maritime units in 1955 that were responsible for guarding ports, rivers, and the fishing fleets. Ironically, in carrying out these duties, the Public Security Force often operated farther out to sea than did the PLAN. Naval district defense units were also organized and tasked with inshore coastal defense in cooperation with the army.[27]

The navy's air force, the People's Liberation Army Navy Air Force (PLANAF), was organized in 1952 with a mission of supporting antisurface ship and antisubmarine defensive operations.[28] The initial force consisted of 80 aircraft, including MiG-15 jet fighters, Il-28 jet bombers (a model still active), and propeller-driven Tu-2 strike aircraft. The PLANAF had grown to approximately 470 aircraft by 1958 but remained operationally subservient to PLA Air Force (PLAAF) commanders.[29]

The North Sea Fleet included the majority of the PLAN's submarine force, perhaps because it was the fleet nearest the U.S. naval forces based in Japan.[30] The East Sea Fleet, headquartered in Ningbo, was the busiest and most important in the PLAN because it faced the American-supported KMT forces. The Taiwan Strait crises of 1954–55 and 1958 occurred in this fleet's area of responsibility. The South Sea Fleet, after Hainan was taken from KMT forces in 1950 and the Vietnamese-French War ended in 1954, faced a hostile Southeast Asia Treaty Organization alliance but a relatively quiet maritime situation. By 1960, ten years after its founding, the PLAN had been organized, sent to sea, and proven itself as an effective coastal defense force.

A New Situation: 1960–76

The 1960s were marked by major foreign and domestic events that further constrained China's development of a seagoing navy. Most important internationally was the split with the Soviet Union, signaled during Nikita Khrushchev's October 1959 meeting with Mao Zedong in Beijing, and dramatically executed in mid-1960 when Soviet advisors (and their plans) were withdrawn from China. The navy suffered with the rest of the PLA when military development projects were left in turmoil.

Other significant events abroad in the early 1960s included war with India, the reemerging Vietnam conflict, turmoil in the new African states, and revolutionary movements throughout Southeast Asia. None of these major international events was maritime in nature; they did not provide justification for improving the PLAN but rather served to limit naval modernization. Maoist orthodoxy continued to dominate strategic thinking. Minister of Defense Lin Biao may have wanted to change the situation by instituting a policy of technological development (albeit with "politics in command") but he did not succeed: the decade ended with Lin coming down solidly on the side of "politics," writing "long live the victory of people's war."[31]

America's involvement in Vietnam, and Taiwan's failure to act on its invasion rhetoric, meant that China faced no serious overseas threat in the 1960s.[32] By the end of the decade, however, relations with the Soviet Union had deteriorated to the point of armed conflict over Zhenbao Island in the Amur River in 1969. The massive Soviet threat that emerged during the 1960s and the PLA's lack of mobility drove China's national security strategy to continue focusing on very large ground forces with a coastal navy in support. The former ally was now the enemy; soon the United States would be China's ally.

Beijing viewed the Soviet navy at this time as a serious amphibious invasion threat. This estimate probably owed more to the history of threats and invasions from the north, and to the Soviet Union's proximity to Beijing and the economic resources of northeastern China, than it did to Soviet Pacific fleet amphibious forces.[33]

Domestically, the Great Proletarian Cultural Revolution (GPCR), lasting from approximately 1966 to 1976 in China, made any significant naval developments extremely difficult to achieve. The PLAN continued to serve as an extension of the army, and modernization was limited because People's War doctrine portrayed technology and weaponry as insignificant compared to revolutionary soldiers imbued with Mao's ideology.

Mao was determined, however, that China join the nuclear club. Despite the ideological turmoil of the late 1950s and the 1960s, Beijing invested heavily in developing nuclear-armed missiles and the nuclear-powered submarines to launch them. The PLAN's limited role was modified by the development during the latter decade of nuclear-powered attack and ballistic missile submarines that later entered the fleet between 1970 and 1991.[34] These were national rather than PLAN systems, however, and did not significantly increase the navy's ability to obtain the military resources necessary for modernization.[35]

The GPCR seriously hampered technological development in general for a full decade (1966–76); even the relatively sacrosanct missile, submarine, and nuclear weapons programs were affected.[36] PLAN modernization was made even more difficult during this decade by the program restrictions and personnel losses resulting from the political maelstrom.[37]

PLAN modernization was still hamstrung at the end of the GPCR in 1976 by the "Gang of Four": Mao's widow, Jiang Qing; Yao Wenyuan; Zhang Chungqiao; and Wang Hongwen. Jiang led an attack on naval missile development and Zhang expressed the gang's antinavy position while supporting the "continentalist view."[38] This continuing political turmoil meant that the necessary modernization of China's naval strength—in organization, systems acquisition, doctrine, and mission definition—fell victim to transitory but still far-reaching ideological constraints. The period only finally ended with the trial of the Gang of Four in 1981; this era saw in effect a continuation of the post–Korean War shackles placed on the PLA by Mao and his followers at the expense of Peng Dehuai and other more objective generals. Politics continued to suppress professionalism.

Despite this attitude and a lack of resources for major conventional force development, however, the PLAN had moved into the missile age by 1970, deploying a Soviet-designed ballistic missile submarine and ten Soviet-built patrol boats armed with cruise missiles.[39] The relatively rapid downfall of the Gang of Four, which marked the end of the GPCR, allowed the consolidation of these earlier moves.

After the Great Proletarian Cultural Revolution

Mao Zedong reportedly directed the development of a modern navy in May 1975 at a meeting of the CMC.[40] He may have been reacting both to the Soviet threat and to the development of a powerful navy by China's ancient protagonist, Japan. In fact, defending against possible Soviet amphibious assault from the northeast continued to be the PLAN's first priority in the 1970s. Other missions included combating criminal activities such as smuggling, piracy, and illegal immigration; sea and air rescue; and safety of navigation.

China believed itself threatened by the Soviet naval revolution that occurred in the 1970s even though that phenomenon was defensive in motivation and aimed primarily at the United States and its North Atlantic Treaty Organization allies. China was a significant national security concern of Moscow's as well, a perception recognized by Beijing. When the Soviet Union demonstrated its new global naval power in the 1975 *Okean* exercises, Moscow's position as China's most serious threat was strengthened in Beijing.[41]

The Soviet naval threat to Chinese interests in the late 1970s and 1980s included sea lines of communications vital to Beijing's rapidly increasing merchant marine because Soviet maritime forces maintained continual naval presence in the Indian Ocean and North Arabian Sea. The Soviet Pacific fleet almost doubled in size during the 1970s and was upgraded by the assignment of Moscow's latest combatants, including nuclear-powered and nuclear-armed surface ships and submarines. Soviet merchant and fisheries ships were also omnipresent in Pacific waters historically vital to China's economic interests.

Several factors continued to impede development of a large, modern Chinese navy. First were the political aftershocks of the GPCR; after the Gang of Four were arrested in October 1976, Premier Hua Guofeng seemed to move away from a strictly continentalist position, at least so far as to emphasize the PLAN's nuclear deterrent mission.[42] But Hua and Deng Xiaoping then contested for the leadership of post-Mao China, a struggle not resolved until 1980 when Deng emerged on top.

Second, the 1979 conflict with Vietnam was strictly a land contest. The PLA's poor performance during this war underlined the need for the reform of and investment in China's land forces. With the backing of moderate military leaders, Deng Xiaoping had once again become chief of the PLA general staff in July 1977. Deng simultaneously became a vice chairman of the party CMC, which effectively placed him firmly in command of the PLA, including operational and administrative issues. He further cemented his position in 1981 when he assumed the position of CMC chairman and yielded his chief of staff position to Gen. Yang Dezhi. Now firmly in command, Deng led the PLA down the path of military modernization, which included reducing the military's political role.

Given the need to improve the army's capability, after 1980 Deng reemphasized the navy's role as a coastal defense force, a view retained throughout the first half of the decade. "Our navy," Deng asserted, "should conduct coastal operations. It is a defensive force. Everything in the construction of the navy must accord with this guiding principle."[43] While this limited the attention and resources given to naval modernization in the 1980s, the PLAN did benefit from the increased priority China's leaders gave to improving the nation's military posture.

Third, and linked to the first factor above, the turmoil in China's economic and social structures lasted beyond the end of the GPCR. In particular, this turmoil affected China's military–industrial complex, hindering modernization efforts by the PLA. Fourth, the triangular play among China, the Soviet Union, and the United States meant that by 1980 Beijing could rely on the world's largest and most modern navy to counter the Soviet maritime threat. This argued against China developing a similar force. Furthermore, given the U.S.-Japan security treaty, Beijing could subsume any concern about future Japanese aggression within its strategic relationship with Washington.[44]

Major changes in China's domestic and international situation in the 1980s soon altered Beijing's view of the PLAN, however, and maritime power became a more important instrument of national security strategy. Beijing's second maritime priority, after countering the threat posed by the Soviet Union, was to secure offshore territorial claims.

Taiwan was the most significant of these, but the South China Sea was also important. Although successful action against South Vietnamese naval forces in 1974 resulted in Chinese possession of the disputed Paracel Islands, this fight indicated that other claimants to the islands and reefs of the South China Sea would not accede meekly to Beijing's territorial claims. Furthermore, the Soviet naval base at Cam Ranh Bay was flourishing as the 1970s ended. These factors contributed to a significant change in the South Sea Fleet's organization: the Marine Corps, first formed in 1953 but disbanded in 1957, was reestablished in 1980 as an amphibious assault force and assigned to the southern fleet. The PLAN's newer amphibious ships were concentrated in the south, and that fleet's training regimen began including "island seizing" exercises. In 1980, for instance, a major fleet exercise in the South China Sea focused on the seizure and defense of islands in the Paracels.[45]

The South Sea Fleet's capabilities improved as the PLAN's force structure in the 1980s became increasingly based on Chinese-built warships. Although still heavily reliant on Soviet designs, the Luda-class guided missile destroyers, Jianghu-class frigates, and Houjian-class fast-attack missile boats marked a significant increase in China's maritime capability.[46] The submarine force included the first Chinese-built nuclear-powered attack submarines as well as about sixty conventionally powered boats. A seaborne nuclear deterrent force continued under development following Mao's earlier declaration that the navy had to be built up "to make it dreadful to the enemy."[47]

Deng Xiaoping's Navy

The increasing coastal concentration of China's burgeoning economy in the 1980s provided rationale for naval expansion and modernization. Furthermore, the resources necessary for a modernized PLAN became increasingly available as a result of China's dramatic economic development and increasing wealth. Recovery from the GPCR, well under way by 1985, included a reinvigorated if more decentralized military–industrial complex.

Three events contributed prominently to the development of China's navy during the 1980s. The first was Deng's evaluation of the military at an expanded CMC meeting in 1975, describing it as "overstaffed, lazy, arrogant, ill-equipped, and ill-prepared to conduct modern warfare."[48] This opinion was strengthened by the PLA's poor performance during the 1979 conflict with Vietnam. Although the postconflict improvements chiefly benefited the land forces, Chinese leaders apparently also recognized the need for modernizing the navy, even as a supporting force to the army.[49]

The second factor was the 1985 strategic decision that the Soviet Union no longer posed a major threat to China in terms of global nuclear war, and that in the future the PLA would have to be prepared instead for "small wars on the periphery" of the nation.[50] The emphasis on a peripheral and, to a significant extent, maritime paradigm rather than a continental strategic paradigm improved the PLAN's position for obtaining resources within the PLA.

The third factor, and perhaps most important, was the rise to prominence of Gen. Liu Huaqing. Liu had been schooled in the Soviet Union, served most of his career in the science and technology arms of the PLA (where he had worked for Marshal Nie Rongzhen), and was close to Deng Xiaoping.[51] Liu's appointment to head the navy was unusual because he held substantive (general/admiral) rank senior to that (lieutenant-general/vice-admiral) normally held by the PLAN commander. Hence, his promotion showed a determination by Beijing to improve the navy. Liu came to his appointment as PLAN commander as an experienced and politically well connected administrator. His emphasis was on the development paradigm that had focused much of his previous career, which was just what the navy required at this time.

Liu exerted a strong influence on naval developments as navy commander from 1982–87, and then vice-chairman of the CMC until 1997. He is best known for promulgating a three-stage maritime strategy for China that provided justification on which PLAN officers and other navalists could base plans for a larger, more modern navy. More important were his accomplishments in reorganizing the navy, reestablishing the marine corps, upgrading bases and research and development facilities, and restructuring the navy's school system.[52] Although the island chain paradigm (as depicted in the map accompanying this chapter) is often cited as evidence of Liu Hauqing's status as a strategist, it is more likely that he delineated the three-stage construct to support the PLAN's claims on an increased share of the PLA's budget and to impress China's leaders with the positive role the navy could play in attaining vital national security objectives. Liu is sometimes described as "China's Mahan," but it is more correct to describe him as "China's Zumwalt," as the admiral who began the critically required modernization of the navy.

China's widening maritime concerns and increased budget resources in the 1980s also raised interest in a stronger navy. PLAN modernization proceeded along three paths—indigenous construction, foreign purchase, and reverse engineering—just as in Li Hongzhang's "self-strengthening" navy of a hundred years earlier. The 1980s program proceeded at a measured pace, however; Beijing did not embark on a major naval building program.

Construction included guided missile destroyers and frigates, replenishment-at-sea ships, conventionally and nuclear-powered attack submarines, and support craft including missile-tracking ships and officer-training vessels. The PLAN also acquired its only Xia-class fleet ballistic missile submarine. The successful submerged launch in 1988 of the Julang-1 (JL-1) intermediate-range ballistic missile from this submarine meant that China for the first time could deploy nuclear strategic weapons at sea.[53]

Foreign purchases were concentrated in the West, with the United States selling China a small number of modern ship engines and torpedoes; Western European nations also sold Beijing weapons and sensor systems. Protecting offshore petroleum assets, other seabed minerals, and fisheries received increased attention.[54]

The PLAN demonstrated its increasing capability in other maritime missions during this decade. China invested in four large space-surveillance ships to support its growing military and commercial space program; these ships conducted the first long-range PLAN deployments in support of space launches in 1980. Task forces supported scientific expeditions to the Arctic and Antarctic, and the PLAN's first foreign port visit was conducted in 1985 when two East Sea Fleet ships visited Bangladesh, Sri Lanka, and Pakistan. The midshipmen training ship *Zheng He* became the first PLAN vessel to visit the United States when it made a 1989 port call to Hawaii.

After the Cold War

Beijing continued to expand and modernize the navy it had begun building in the 1970s, but still at a measured pace. The PLAN also engaged in a series of long-range deployments throughout East and South Asia, as well as deploying a three-ship task group to the Western Hemisphere in 1998, visiting the United States, Mexico, Peru, and Chile. Foreign purchases of improved ships, submarines, and aircraft made headlines for the PLAN when China acquired *Sovremenny*-class DDGs, Kilo-class submarines, and Su-27 fighters from Russia.

Conclusion

Imperial China for the most part ignored the sea except for specific problems, such as those with Japanese pirates and the sixteenth-century Dutch incursions in Taiwan. Republican China had to focus on civil war and the Japanese invasion, which were both almost entirely land wars. Early on, the communist regime recognized the need to deal with maritime issues, but only after thirty years and a dramatically altered international situation did Beijing recognize the need for a significant navy. China during the Cold War based its national security strategy on border security and shoring up its national sovereignty. The past century of foreign intervention and periodic civil war was much in the leadership's mind. After 1960 the focus was on the Soviet continental threat, and relatively scant attention was paid the navy.

Following the end of the Cold War, however, Beijing has considered "the ocean as its chief strategic defensive direction" because "China's political and economic focus lies on the coastal areas[, and] for the present and a fairly long period to come, [its] strategic focus will be in the direction of the sea."[55] The Chinese navy that began in the early 1990s building for the twenty-first century owes a good deal to a renewed recognition of the importance of the maritime element in China's national security.

Chinese naval development during the Cold War was constrained by very limited contact with other navies; the Soviet and, to a lesser extent, Eastern European navies were the role model and source of modernization. Lacking was the stimulation in maritime theory and equipment availability provided by interaction with the world's other naval forces. Russia was by far the most pervasive influence on the development of naval thought in the PRC.[56] Chinese post–Cold War naval efforts were made possible by China's post–Cold War explosion of economic growth; in this sense, China's naval efforts have been Mahanian—closely linked to national economic development.[57]

Although the Chinese government did not hesitate during the Cold War to employ naval force in pursuit of national security goals, these efforts achieved limited success—witness the events of 1950, 1954–55, and 1958—although those of 1974 and 1988 in the South China Sea were more productive. China has historically employed naval force over issues of sovereignty—about national control of specific islands or provinces. Employment of naval forces during the Cold War was almost always related to sovereignty issues involving Taiwan, the offshore islands, and South China Sea claims, especially the Paracel and Spratly islands.

Historically, national security policymakers in Beijing have viewed the navy as a useful instrument of state policy but one that cannot by itself achieve important objectives such as completing the unification of China, defending its coasts and rich economic areas, and securing the wealth of the ocean. This view was particularly strong during the half-century of the Cold War, from 1949 to 1991. The navy achieved recognition as an important strategic necessity in the eyes of China's leaders only after the breakup of the Soviet Union and the dramatically increased availability of financial resources that followed the Cold War.

Surveying the record of the PLAN during the Cold War offers several possible implications for China and its present navy. This history reveals a naval service viewed by its military and civilian masters as an organization with the primary mission of supporting army forces. Beijing's maritime concerns were defensive; the United States was first considered the likely enemy, and then the Soviet Union. The Chinese navy of those years was dominated by Russian platforms, equipment, and strategy and was accorded low priority in national defense considerations, especially in budget allocations. The PLAN had only a very limited role in the nation's nuclear deterrent structure.

China's navy suffered from the depredations of the post–Korean War ideological madness that affected the nation at large, a period marked by the GPCR. The end of this calamitous event allowed the PLAN to regain some equanimity but it remained near the bottom of military modernization priorities. This position never significantly changed for China's navy before the mid-1990s, although the leadership of Liu Huaqing played a crucial role in an apparent perceptual change on the part of China's leaders towards their country's navy. The PLAN at least gained strategic stature under Liu and positioned it to make the strides so notable in the late twentieth and early twenty-first century.

The PLAN's Cold War characteristics resulted from the Chinese strategic situation of the time; many of them continue to mark the character of the PLAN in the twenty-first century but with significant modification. Most importantly, the Chinese navy today is no longer restricted to a role of supporting ground forces; budget allocations, maritime strategic sophistication, and operational employment all evidence a more traditional naval force. Reliance on Russian sources for platforms and equipment is much reduced while an increased nuclear deterrent role is apparently under rapid development. Perhaps most significantly, while the navy's primary role is still viewed as defensive, the change in military balances among China, Russia, and the United States have led Beijing to realize the value of its navy as an effective means of carrying out national security goals, especially with respect to possible Taiwan scenarios.

Notes

The ideas in this paper are those of the author alone. They do not represent the policy or analyses of the National Defense University, Department of Defense, or any other organization of the U.S. government.

1. The Nationalist retreat was one of the largest and fastest maritime relocation programs in modern history, almost equaling the 3 million Vietnamese "boat people" exodus that began in the mid-1970s, and dwarfing the more well-known Aliyah Bet movement to Palestine that included only about 100,000 people. As a result, from 1949–58 the population of Taiwan grew from 7.7 to 9.8 million; http://www.zum.de/whkmla/region/china/taiwan19451949.html.

2. PLAN Vice-Commander Zhou Xihan, 1957, quoted in David G. Muller Jr., *China as a Maritime Power* (Boulder, CO: Westview Press, 1983), 47. See also Shu Guang Zhang, *Mao's Military Romanticism: China and the Korean War, 1950–1953* (Lawrence: University Press of Kansas, 1995), 48.

3. Larry M. Wortzel, "The Beiping-Tianjin Campaign of 1948–49: The Strategic and Operational Thinking of the People's Liberation Army," paper prepared for the U.S. Army War College's Strategic Studies Institute, Carlisle, PA, n.d. Chart 1 points out that by July 1949 the PLA actually included seventy-seven "naval vessels." Hanrahan describes the Nationalist contribution to this force as "twenty-five vessels ranging from LCTs to destroyers, representing an estimated one-fourth of the total Nationalist naval force"; Gene Z. Hanrahan, "Report on Red China's New Navy," U.S. Naval Institute *Proceedings* 79 (August 1953): 847.

4. Gen. Zhang Aiping, quoted in Hanrahan, "Report on Red China's New Navy," 848.

5. Quoted in Shu Guang Zhang, *Mao's Military Romanticism*, 51.

6. The reverse also occurs. The author's conversation with Qingdao Garrison, DCOS for Militia and Reserve Affairs, in May 2000 involved a long discussion with a PLA "senior colonel," who had spent the previous twenty-two years as a senior captain in the PLAN; his transfer to the army came about because of his expertise as an engineer.

7. Muller, *China as a Maritime Power*, 46–54, provides a useful description of the beginnings of the PLAN.

8. About two thousand former Republic of China naval personnel who defected to the Communist regime in 1949 formed the core of the nascent PLAN. See Muller, *China as a Maritime Power*, 13.

9. Quoted in Chen Jian, *China's Road to the Korean War: The Making of the Sino-American Confrontation* (New York: Columbia University Press, 1994), 64.

10. See ibid., 64–65; see also Chen Xiaolu, "China's Polity toward the United States, 1949–1955," in Harry Harding and Yuan Ming, eds., *Sino-American Relations: 1945–1955* (Wilmington, DE: SR Books, 1989): 185, 188.

11. He Di, "'The Last Campaign to Unify China': The CCP's Unmaterialized Plan to Liberate Taiwan, 1949–1950," *Chinese Historians* 5 (Spring 1992): 8. This article is probably the most complete account of this period's PLAN activities connected with

the Taiwan Strait islands. The author works at the Institute of American Studies of the Chinese Academy of Social Sciences and presumably had good access to PLA archives while researching this article.

12. Vladimir Lenin, cited in Bruce W. Watson, "The Evolution of Soviet Naval Strategy," in Bruce W. Watson and Peter M. Dunn, eds., *The Future of the Soviet Navy: An Assessment to the Year 2000* (Boulder, CO: Westview Press, 1986), 115.

13. Muller, *China as a Maritime Power*, 15. More than a hundred PLA officers were sent to study at the Voroshilov Naval Institute in 1951 while 275 officers studied at the Soviet submarine squadron at Lushun; Andrew Nien-Dzu Yang, "From a Navy in Blue towards a Blue Water Navy: Shaping PLA Navy Officer Corps (1950–1999)," paper prepared for the Center for Naval Analyses conference on "The PLA Navy: Past, Present and Future Prospects," Washington, D.C., April 2000, p. 4.

14. Swanson also notes that Xiao had attended the same school as Mao, in Changsha; Bruce Swanson, *The Eighth Voyage of the Dragon: A History of China's Quest for Seapower* (Annapolis, MD: Naval Institute Press, 1982), 194.

15. Blackman provides these numbers, but they should be treated only as estimates; Raymond V. B. Blackman, ed., *Jane's Fighting Ships: 1955–56* (London: Jane's Fighting Ships Publishing Co., 1956), 151ff.

16. Swanson, *Eighth Voyage*, 196; Swanson also describes such massive projects as a fortified "250-mile, 10-foot-wide communication trench paralleling the southern bank of the Yangtze River from Wusong to Jiujiang up river. . . . A similar trench was constructed along the coast south of Shanghai for about 200 miles"; 187.

17. He Di points out that the date for assaulting Taiwan was postponed by Mao several times as PLA failures against various offshore islands emphasized the additional time required to prepare for a successful, large-scale amphibious assault; He Di, "'The Last Campaign to Unify China,'" 2.

18. Ibid., 4.

19. For Truman's decision to reposition the Seventh Fleet, see Robert J. Donovan, *Tumultuous Years: The Presidency of Harry S. Truman, 1949–1953* (New York: W. W. Norton, 1982), 206. For a good account of administration thinking (Truman, Acheson, Bohlen, et al.) about the implementation of NSC-68, which effectively rearmed the United States for the Cold War and potential global war with Soviet-led communist forces, see ibid., 241ff: "On the last day of July 1950, Truman and Acheson had a talk about grand strategy. The eyes of the American people were glued to Korea. . . . The president and the secretary of state fixed their gaze on the Rhine and the Elbe."

20. Mao Zedong, "Speech Delivered at the Eighth Meeting of the Government Council of the People's Republic of China (28 June 1950), in Jerome Ch'en, ed., *Mao*, Gerald Emanuel Stearn, gen. ed., *Great Lives Observed* (Englewood Cliffs, NJ: Prentice-Hall, 1969), 115.

21. Fred L. Israel, eds., "Dwight D. Eisenhower, First Annual message," *The State of the Union Messsages of the Presidents, 1790–1966*, vol. III, *1905–1966* (New York: Chelsea House Publishers, 1967), 3015. Eisenhower, in his 2 February 1953 State of the Union

Address to Congress, commented that "since the 'Red Chinese' had intervened in the Korean War, he felt no longer any need to 'protect' them from an invasion by. . . . Chiang K'ai-shek." See also Leonard Mosley, *Dulles: A Biography of Eleanor, Allen, and John Foster Dulles and Their Family Network* (New York: Dial Press, 1978), 305.

22. Swanson, *Eighth Voyage*, 187.

23. Thomas J. Torda describes these early battles, which included PLA successes as well as failures; Thomas J. Torda, "Struggle for the Taiwan Strait: A 50th-Anniversary Perspective on the First Communist-Nationalist Battles for China's Offshore Islands and Their Significance for the Taiwan Strait Crises," unpublished manuscript, 1999, in the possession of the author. For a tabular summation of the PLAN's warfighting efforts during this period, see Alexander Huang, "The Evolution of the PLA Navy and Its Early Combat Experiences," paper presented at the Center for Naval Analyses Conference on the People's Liberation Army Navy, Washington, DC, April 2000, 3. Gordon Chang and He Di document this (pp. 1504, 1510) but also point out (n7, n8) that Chiang Kai-shek used the shelling to pressure U.S. secretary of state John Foster Dulles into signing the Mutual Security Treaty with the "Republic of China"; Gordon H. Chang and He Di, "The Absence of War in the U.S.-China Confrontation over Quemoy and Matsu in 1954–1955: Contingency, Luck or Deterrence?" *American Historical Review* 8, no. 5 (December 1993).

24. Other islands remained under Taiwan's control, including the Penghus just off the southwestern Taiwan coast, and the Pratas Islands and Itu Abba in the South China Sea.

25. Chang and He describe this action during which "10,000 PLA troops . . . overwhelmed 1,086 Kuomingtang soldiers"; Gordon H. Chang and He Di, "The Absence of War in the U.S.-China Confrontation over Quemoy and Matsu in 1954–1955: Contingency, Luck, or Deterrence?" *The American Historical Review* 98 (December 1993): 1514.

26. Some Taiwan attacks on the mainland continued into the 1960s. These naval campaigns are addressed by Xiaobing Li, "PLA Attacks and Amphibious Operations during the Taiwan Straits Crises of 1954–1958," paper presented at the CNA Conference on the PLA's Operational History, Alexandria, Virginia, June 1999. For a detailed description of PLAN combat actions, see Alexander Huang, "The PLA Navy at War, 1949–1999: From Coastal Defense to Distant Operations," paper presented at the CNA Conference on the PLA's Operational History, Alexandria, Virginia, June 1999.

27. Swanson points out these forces' similarities to imperial predecessors; Swanson, *Eighth Voyage*, 204.

28. Little open-source information is available about PLANAF assets; a reasonable assumption is that the navy's air arm has flown the older variants of the same aircraft flown by the PLAAF; Kenneth W. Allen, Glenn Krumel, and Jonathan D. Pollack, *China's Air Force Enters the 21st Century* (Santa Monica, CA: RAND, 1995), 205 n11. Allen, Krumel, and Pollack provide a useful description of PLA aircraft acquisition programs in Appendix E, pp. 221–29.

29. Swanson, *Eighth Voyage*, 205.

30. The PLAN submarine bases were perhaps influenced by Soviet advisors. During discussions with the Allies in the 1940s and with Mao in 1950, Stalin had expressed interest in establishing a Soviet submarine base at Port Arthur (Luda).

31. Swanson, *Eighth Voyage*, 236.

32. Presumably, the United States would have come to Taiwan's defense had the PRC tried to take advantage of the American preoccupation with Vietnam by attacking the island, but the Great Proletarian Cultural Revolution (GPCR) was even more of a preoccupation for Beijing.

33. Blackman credits the Soviet navy with just four large (4,000 tons displacement) amphibious ships, and eighty smaller (600–1,000 tons) vessels, but these were spread out among all of the Soviet Union's four fleets; Raymond V. B. Blackman, ed., *Jane's Fighting Ships, 1970–1971* (London: Jane's Yearbooks, 1971), 610.

34. China built two Xia-class fleet ballistic missile submarines, patterned on the U.S. *George Washington*–class/Soviet Hotel-class; Richard Sharpe, ed., *Jane's Fighting Ships: 1995–96* (London: Butler and Tanner, 1996), 114.

35. See John Wilson Lewis and Xue Litai, *China's Strategic Seapower* (Stanford, CA: Stanford University Press, 1984), 206ff.

36. Even Zhou Enlai was unable to completely protect these programs; see Lewis and Xue, 231, 236.

37. This conclusion is supposition, but I base it on global naval developments during the decade. Except for the evolution of maritime nuclear power, the PLAN missed or was very late joining the developments in most warfare areas: guided missiles in antiair, antisurface, and antisubmarine warfare; automation and computerization of command and control; the expansion of shipborne helicopters; automation of gunnery and sensor systems; and even the advent of automation and gas turbine technology in ship propulsion. O'Donnell lists the PLAN's Political Commissar, chief operations officer, the East Sea Fleet commander, two deputy commanders, and two Fleet Political Commissars among the "120 senior naval officers and thousands of lower ranking personnel [who] were purged"; John R. O'Donnell, "An Analysis of Major Developmental Influences on the People's Liberation Army-Navy and Their Implication for the Future," Master's thesis (Ft. Leavenworth, KS: U.S. Army Command and General Staff College, 1995), 42.

38. Lewis and Xue, *China's Strategic Seapower*, 147–148, 223.

39. The PLAN also included more than thirty other submarines, a collection of assorted foreign-built destroyers and escort vessels (Soviet, Japanese, U.S., British, Canadian, and Italian), and more than four hundred Chinese-built patrol craft, some of them hydrofoils and most armed with torpedoes; Blackman, ed., *Jane's Fighting Ships: 1970–71*, 61ff.

40. Foreign Broadcast Information Service (FBIS) reports, cited in Muller, *China as a Maritime Power*, 154.

41. Bernard D. Cole, *The Great Wall at Sea: China's Navy Enters the 21st Century* (Annapolis, MD: Naval Institute Press, 2001), 24.

42. Hua's decision is discussed in Lewis and Xue, *China's Strategic Seapower*, 223.

43. Quoted in ibid., 224.

44. The most memorable expression of this factor was by Lt. Gen. Henry Stackpole, USMC, commander of the Third Marine Expeditionary Force on Okinawa, who described the United States as "a cap in the [Japanese] bottle"; quoted in Fred Hiatt, "Marine General: U.S. Troops Must Stay in Japan," *Washington Post*, 27 March 1990, A14.

45. Tai Ming Cheung, *Growth of Chinese Naval Power: Priorities, Goals, Missions, and Regional Implications* (Singapore: Institute of Southeast Asian Studies, 1990), 28. China's marine corps had been disestablished in 1957 as "unnecessary." The concentration of amphibious forces in the South rather than the East Sea Fleet may reveal the PLAN's attitude—ambivalent at best—toward the very difficult task of conducting an amphibious assault against Taiwan.

46. John E. Moore, ed., *Jane's Fighting Ships: 1976–77* (New York: Franklin Watts, 1977), 100ff. The PLAN also included the first Chinese range-instrument ships for tracking guided missile flights, and the first Chinese-built amphibious transports.

47. Muller, *China as a Maritime Power*, 171.

48. Deng Xiaoping, "Speech at an Enlarged Meeting of the Military Commission of the Party Central Committee," 14 July 1975, in Joint Publications Research Service, *China Reports*, no. 468 (31 October 1983): 14–22, cited in Paul H. B. Godwin, "Change and Continuity in Chinese Military Doctrine: 1949–1999," paper presented at the CAPS-RAND Conference on the PLA, Washington DC, 1999, p. 23.

49. Alfred D. Wilhelm Jr., *China and Security in the Asian Pacific Region through 2010*, CRM 95-226 (Alexandria, VA: Center for Naval Analyses, 1996), 42.

50. Ibid., 32ff.

51. Liu had worked for Deng on at least two previous occasions. In 1956 Party general-secretary Deng Xiaoping appointed Nie as both head of the Scientific Planning Commission and director of the defense industry and equipment program; Nie became a vice-premier and "Zhou Enlai's principal agent in all scientific and technical policy making"; John Wilson Lewis and Xue Litai, *China Builds the Bomb* (Stanford, CA: Stanford University, 1988), 50, 51.

52. Liu's accomplishments are summed up in Wilhelm, *China and Security*, 43.

53. See Lewis and Xue, *China's Strategic Seapower*, for the best account of the development of the FBM and JL-1 programs. A successful 1982 launch was made from a submerged platform, a 1985 attempt from the *Xia* failed, and a 1988 attempt succeeded. The *Xia* itself apparently has been a failure, never operating on a regular basis. Richard Sharpe, ed., *Jane's Fighting Ships, 1999–2000* (London: Jane's Publishing Group, 1999), 115, reports the "rumor" that a second boat of this class may have been built but lost in a fire before it went to sea. There is also a report that *Xia* may have recently been overhauled in preparation for joining the fleet.

54. See, for instance, Michael Leifer, "Chinese Economic Reform and Defense Policy: The South China Sea Connection," paper presented at the IISS/CAPS

Conference, Hong Kong, July 1994; and John W. Garver, "China's Push through the South China Sea: The Interaction of Bureaucratic and National Interests," *China Quarterly* (December 1992): 1019, 1022.

55. Lt.-Gen. Mi Zhenyu, PLA, "A Reflection on Geographic Strategy," Beijing *Zhongguo Junshi Kexue [China Military Science]*, no. 1 (February 1998): 6–14, in FBIS-CHI-98-208.

56. "On balance, it is evident that the evolving Russian model of military ethic and style, especially on the issues of military role, commander authority, and strategy, has been the most important European influence to alter traditional Chinese perspectives." William H. Whitson, with Huang Chen-hsia, *The Chinese High Command: A History of Communist Military Politics, 1927–71* (New York: Praeger, 1973), 473.

57. China's rapidly growing stake in global maritime trade may also be in part due to Taiwan's early development of large-scale container ships, made possible by the fact that in 1949 "the Nationalists had taken with them much of the Chinese navy, as well as the large ships of the merchant marine." John Franklin Copper, *Taiwan: Nation-state or Province* (Boulder, CO: Westview Press, 3rd ed., 1999), 46–47.

PART IV

China in
Comparative Perspective

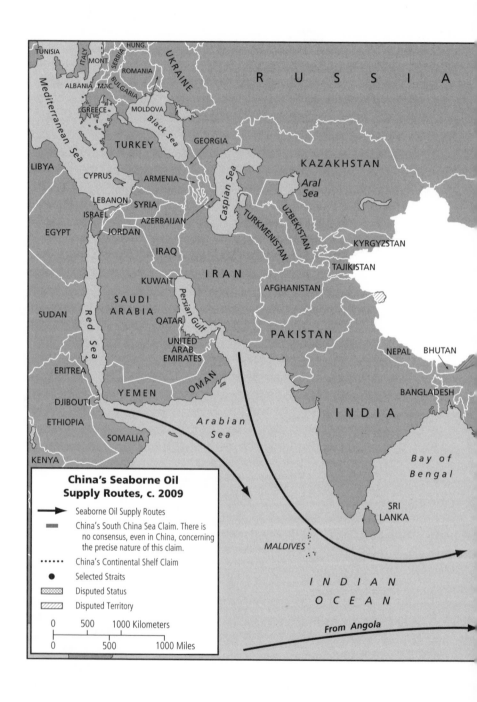

China's Seaborne Oil Supply Routes, c. 2009

→ Seaborne Oil Supply Routes

▬ China's South China Sea Claim. There is no consensus, even in China, concerning the precise nature of this claim.

····· China's Continental Shelf Claim

● Selected Straits

▨ Disputed Status

▨ Disputed Territory

| 0 | 500 | 1000 Kilometers |
| 0 | 500 | 1000 Miles |

From Angola

Gabriel Collins and Michael Grubb

Strong Foundation: Contemporary Chinese Shipbuilding Prowess

IN AN ADDRESS TO THE PEOPLE'S LIBERATION ARMY (PLA) delegation to the 10th National People's Congress, Chinese president Hu Jintao
proclaimed that "we should actively explore new ways and new methods
for combining military with civilian production . . . economically, and in
science and technology."[1] Moving toward this goal, China's shipbuilding
industry has undergone a remarkable transformation since Deng Xiaoping
initiated defense conversion to commercial production nearly thirty years
ago. From producing a mere 220,000 deadweight tons (dwt) of commercial shipping in 1980, People's Republic of China (PRC) shipyards turned out
more than 13 million tons in 2006 and are on pace to exceed 20 million tons
annually by 2010. Targeting even further growth, PRC officials have set a goal
of becoming the world's commercial shipbuilding leader by 2015.[2] Indications
of China's improving shipbuilding prowess have also begun to emerge in the
military arena, with several new classes of modern surface combatants and
submarines commissioned by the PLA Navy in recent years.

The staggering growth in PRC commercial shipbuilding output and
advances in indigenous naval construction underscore shipbuilding's growing role as a key driver in China's economic and military development and
are indicative of a rising maritime culture within China. Here China's mari-

time development path is somewhat different from that of other nations that have previously endeavored to become maritime powers. The Soviet Union, Meiji Japan, and Wilhelmian Germany built their navies first and then promoted merchant marine development. Thus the relationship was based on a "push" from the state, rather than a "pull" in which commercial interests led the way and then the state stepped in to create the capacity to protect these new commercial maritime interests. China is following a different path marked by an emphasis on commercial maritime development, with naval development trailing. If China continues to expand its naval forces, the drivers will include a mix of a desire for status in the international community and a perceived need to defend economic interests, but the single most prominent element will be that Beijing's policymakers are struggling to keep up with China's dynamic commercial mariners. In this sense China's maritime and naval development path may better approximate the successful path of the United States than the failed efforts of the USSR, Meiji Japan, or pre–World War I Germany. China's current maritime transformation is led largely by an exceedingly dynamic commercial maritime sector, which is in turn creating ample synergies for naval development.

Chinese seaborne trade is expected to reach one trillion dollars annually by 2020, much of which will be carried on Chinese-built, -owned, and -operated merchant vessels.[3] Building a foundation for this comprehensive maritime growth, the PRC central government recently affirmed shipbuilding as a "strategic industry" in need of "special oversight and support," reinforcing the central role shipbuilding will play in future Chinese maritime development.[4]

This chapter will briefly trace the history of shipbuilding in China, focusing on how the industry was able to successfully transform itself from a defense-focused socialist monolith into a thriving commercial enterprise. The current structure and output of the PRC shipbuilding industry will be reviewed, highlighting the increasingly complex mix of control and influence within the Chinese shipbuilding industry among the PRC State Council, Central Military Commission, local authorities, private entities, and international corporations. We will then present a more detailed examination of how China's impressive commercial shipbuilding growth may—or may not—translate into similarly significant improvements in Chinese naval development. Finally, the strategic aspects of PRC shipbuilding development will be discussed, and possible indicators and implications of a commercial-to-military shift in PRC shipbuilding priorities will be offered.

Chinese Shipbuilding from Zheng He to Deng Xiaoping

As highlighted by the voyages of Adm. Zheng He's fleets into the Indian Ocean and Red Sea between 1405 and 1433 (discussed in detail in Andrew Wilson's contribution to this volume), shipbuilding in imperial China was capable of formidable feats. These impressive armadas numbered more than 2,100 vessels built around large treasure ships (宝船, *baochuan*) that dwarfed European ships of the day. Technologically advanced, the *baochuan* possessed, centuries before their Western counterparts, such innovations as navigational compasses, hull compartmentalization, and gunpowder weapons.[5] Chinese shipbuilding diminished in the centuries following Zheng He's exploits, however, as successive dynasties focused on continental interests and threats. As a result, technological innovation remained at the level of the traditional wooden sailing vessel ("junk") until the arrival of Europeans in the nineteenth century. The increasing presence of Western ships in Chinese waters quickly created a demand for modern maritime infrastructure, and European firms assisted in building shipyards in Amoy (Xiamen), Canton (Guangzhou), Foochow (Fuzhou), Port Arthur (Lushun), Shanghai, Tsingtao (Qingdao), and Weihai. Many of these yards included modern dry docks, and Europeans were instrumental in introducing metal shipbuilding techniques and steam propulsion technology to China.[6] The Kiangnan Arsenal and Dockyard (today's Jiangnan Shipyard) in Shanghai, founded in 1865, quickly established itself as one of China's premier shipbuilders. It produced China's first steel-hulled ship in 1868 (complete with a locally built steam boiler), several 7,000-gross-ton ships for the United States' Dollar Line in 1908, and six Yangtze River gunboats for the U.S. Navy in the late 1920s.[7] Despite intermittent successes, however, consistent political, economic, and social turmoil prevented any sustained indigenous shipbuilding development in China, leaving the industry virtually dormant when the People's Republic was founded in 1949.

The dawn of the Communist era brought fresh life to China's shipbuilding industry, with shipbuilding and other heavy industry development figuring prominently in the first and second Five-Year Plans. Much of the industry's revitalization in the 1950s was driven by the PRC's strategic alliance with the Soviet Union. Through a series of agreements beginning with the Chinese-Soviet Treaty of Friendship, Alliance, and Mutual Assistance signed in 1950, the Soviet Union poured significant technical assistance into the revitalization of China's shipbuilding industrial base. Shipbuilding facilities at Dalian and Lushun were returned to Chinese control (they had been occupied by the Soviets since the end of World War II), and most of China's other major shipyards were modernized with Soviet assistance.[8] This included a special Soviet project to establish a "Chinese Severodvinsk" in Huludao, a critical step in China's nascent nuclear submarine program.[9]

These infrastructure improvements, key technology transfers, design assistance, and license production agreements allowed the PRC to produce four Chengdu-class frigates in the late 1950s (largely based on the Soviet Riga-class), as well as numerous small torpedo boats, minesweepers, and auxiliary vessels. PRC shipyards also returned to commercial production during this period, producing a limited number of small cargo and passenger ships, fishing vessels, and tugboats with Soviet technical assistance. Despite a small output of new merchant tonnage, commercial production was still secondary to military priorities, and some 360,000 traditional "junks" continued to form the backbone of China's merchant trading fleet as they had done for the past six centuries.[10]

The steady improvement in PRC shipbuilding capabilities through the 1950s came to an abrupt end in 1960 with the Sino-Soviet split. The removal of Soviet technical advisors and access to Soviet-made subcomponents revealed wide gaps in PRC self-sufficiency, and military shipbuilding was quickly limited to continuation of obsolete Soviet designs still on hand from previous years. Commercial production ground to a virtual halt, with less than a dozen oceangoing ships built in the early 1960s.[11] To address the disarray, the Sixth Ministry of Machine Building was established in 1963 to consolidate control of national shipbuilding activities under one coordinating organization. This important initiative aimed to promote shipbuilding industrial development and greater technological self-sufficiency, but the purging of local management and technical expertise during the Cultural Revolution derailed most of these efforts.[12] Likewise, the diversion of resources to relocate defense-related industries inland as part of Mao Zedong's *sanxian* ("Third Front" or "Third Line") strategic defense plan of the 1960s negatively affected Chinese shipbuilding development for well over a decade.[13]

The critical impetus for today's tremendous growth in China's shipbuilding industry finally came in the late 1970s, when Deng Xiaoping consolidated power within the Chinese Communist Party and initiated his policy "reform and opening up" to the outside world (改革开放, *gaige kaifang*). This comprehensive reform initiative set out to develop China's stagnant economy by importing foreign technology and ideas, promoting export trade, and transforming China's unproductive defense industries into viable commercial enterprises through a process of "defense conversion."[14]

RUSSIA

Heilongjiang

Jilin

Inner Mongolia

Liaoning
(6 yards)

NORTH
KOREA

Sea of
Japan

Beijing

Beijing
(★)

Tianjin
(4 yards)

Hebei
(1 yard)

Shanxi

Shandong
(21 yards)

SOUTH
KOREA

Yellow
Sea

aanxi

Henan

Jiangsu
(50 yards)

ongoing

rds)

Hubei
(5 yards)

Anhui
(5 yards)

Shanghai
(14 yards)

Zhejiang
(59 yards)

Jiangxi
(6 yards)

East
China
Sea

Pacific
Ocean

Hunan

Fujian
(17 yards)

zhou

TAIWAN
(Status Disputed)

Guangxi
Zhuang
(4 yards)

Guangdong
(17 yards)

South
China
Sea

Hainan

PHILIPPINES

JAPAN

In May 1982 the Fifth National Congress directed the elimination of the Sixth Ministry of Machine Building, and established the China State Shipbuilding Corporation (CSSC) in its place. More than just a bureaucratic name change, this decision "corporatized" all state shipbuilding activities under CSSC and authorized a degree of market-based economic autonomy previously unprecedented under the communist economic system. CSSC's mandate included direct control of 153 organizations that ranged from shipyards to technical research and design universities; authority over virtually all military and commercial shipbuilding and repair; power to conduct joint ventures with foreign companies; and ability to negotiate export sales through the newly established China Shipbuilding Trading Company.[15]

Viewed broadly, the shipbuilding development strategy chosen by CSSC during this early period is similar to those that propelled Japan to remarkable shipbuilding successes in the 1950s–60s, and South Korea in the late 1970s–90s. As did Japan and South Korea in the early stages of their development, China targeted shipbuilding as a pillar industry for national economic development and stimulant to growth in other heavy industrial sectors (e.g., steel). It leveraged labor cost advantages, imported critical technology and manufacturing best practices from world shipbuilding leaders, and targeted export sales as a means of obtaining hard currency to fuel further economic development.[16] Despite these general similarities, however, parallels with Japan or Korea begin to break down when viewed more closely. The economic structures of the Japanese *keiretsu* and Korean *chaebol* business networks varied among themselves, and both were dissimilar to the Chinese *jituan*-style business conglomerate that took shape in the CSSC. Furthermore, Japanese and Korean shipbuilders were fundamentally capital-accumulating corporations operating in a regulated market economy from the very start of their development. Conversely, CSSC remained answerable to the central government and operated as a rare "corporate" entity within a communist planned economy struggling to transform itself.[17]

Regardless of the degree to which foreign development models were used, the ability of the Chinese shipbuilding industry to successfully negotiate the process of defense conversion is still noteworthy. This is especially so when considering the relative lack of success that Chinese aerospace and other formerly defense-focused industries have displayed when attempting to enter commercial markets. There are several key reasons for the successful transformation of Chinese shipbuilding. First, the economic liberalization and bureaucratic freedom of movement afforded CSSC came well ahead of other industrial sectors. Although CSSC was formed in July 1982, the Ministry of Aerospace Industry was not "corporatized" into the China Aviation Industry Corporation (AVIC) until 1993.[18] By this time, CSSC had largely completed its shift to a commercial focus, with 80 percent of its output dedicated to the civil sector by 1992 and many subsidiaries completely transitioned out of military production.[19]

Second, the shift from a military to a commercial focus for Chinese shipbuilding was aided by the relatively small technological hurdles involved. The Luda-class destroyers, Jianghu-class frigates, and Ming-class submarines built in the early 1980s were only modest improvements on Soviet designs dating back to the 1950s and were technologically closer to commercial vessels than military ships by Western standards of the day. Furthermore, most shipyards engaged in military construction already had at least some basic experience in building commercial ships.

Third, CSSC's early commitment to the international market provided critical exposure to commercial business practices and experience dealing with foreign companies. CSSC moved quickly to obtain foreign assistance in modernizing its shipyards for commercial production, signing partnerships with Mitsubishi Heavy Industries and British Shipbuilders to upgrade the Jiangnan and Dalian shipyards. These technical assistance agreements built upon successful license production deals signed with major Western marine diesel engine manufacturers in the 1970s, and they were accompanied by cooperative agreements with British and Hong Kong–based companies to help market Chinese-built ships on the international market. Western ship classification societies were allowed to inspect and provide technical certifications for Chinese-built ships for the first time, and in 1983 the China Ship Inspection Bureau formally adopted technical standards approved by Lloyd's Register, a critical quality-control step required to attract potential buyers on the international market.[20] Shortly thereafter, CSSC deputy director Pan Zengxi noted that "a ship is a commodity that must be sold according to the market situation," clearly appreciating the dynamics of the new economic paradigm PRC shipbuilding had entered.[21]

The fourth key factor in shipbuilding's successful defense conversion was a healthy balance of domestic and export demand. Export sales were explicitly targeted as means of generating hard currency (required to purchase higher technology subcomponents from abroad and sustaining long-term growth), but the latent demand in China's domestic merchant fleet also played a vital role in facilitating the conversion of the PRC's shipbuilding industry. Having received little attention in previous decades, only 18 percent of China's merchant fleet was built domestically as of 1986, and the vast majority of China's international trade was carried in chartered or foreign-flagged ships.[22] The opening of the Chinese economy increased the demand for maritime trade, and the PRC merchant marine expanded from 955 ships totaling 6.8 million gross tons in 1980 to 1,948 ships totaling 13.9 million gross tons in 1990.[23] Chinese shipyards were still too immature in capacity and capability to provide many of the large tankers and containerships needed in the national fleet, but the steady domestic demand for small to mid-size shipping provided China's shipyards with a vital source of orders while the industry gradually overcame the challenges of breaking into the international market.[24]

Fifth, geography played a notable facilitating role in the successful conversion and growth of China's shipbuilding industry. The industry paid a heavy price for the ill-conceived "Third Front" initiative of the 1960s, but the obvious geographic restraints in building deep-draft ships somewhat minimized the effects of the inland industrialization movement (especially when compared to other defense sectors). The largest and most productive of China's shipyards remained along the coast, near the business centers of Shanghai, Dalian, Guangzhou, and Hong Kong that have fuelled much of China's economic rise over the past three decades.[25]

Finally, the competitive price advantage gained from plentiful cheap labor cannot be overlooked as a significant factor in the transformation of PRC shipbuilding. The seemingly endless supply of inexpensive labor aided Chinese shipbuilders' entrance into the competitive international shipbuilding market 25 years ago and remains a significant marketing advantage today. As of 2002 the average wage for a shipyard worker in the PRC was estimated to be $325 per month, as compared to $1,400, $1,800, and $2,400 per month in South Korea, Japan, and Western Europe, respectively.[26] Although a sizable portion of this labor cost advantage is offset by other production inefficiencies in Chinese shipyards (to be discussed later), the ready availability of inexpensive labor played a significant role in China's shipbuilding development and is likely to continue to do so for the foreseeable future.

Having maneuvered successfully through the minefields of defense conversion, the PRC shipbuilding industry was well positioned as the global shipbuilding market emerged from its deep recession of the late 1980s. PRC shipyard commercial output crossed the one million tons per year mark in 1993 (with roughly 50 percent of tonnage built for export), propelling China to third position in global commercial shipbuilding behind Japan and South Korea by 1995. As the twentieth century drew to a close, China had emerged as a new commercial shipbuilding force and was poised for yet more unprecedented growth in the new century.

Ship Production as Percentage of Total Deadweight Tons
(Displacement Unloaded), 1999–2006

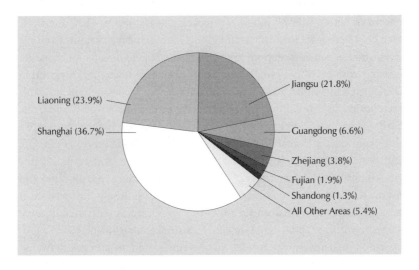

Liaoning (23.9%)

Shanghai (36.7%)

Jiangsu (21.8%)

Guangdong (6.6%)

Zhejiang (3.8%)

Fujian (1.9%)

Shandong (1.3%)

All Other Areas (5.4%)

China's Shipbuilding Industry Today

In the past decade, China's shipbuilding industry structure has undergone major changes. In 1999 the main state builder, CSSC, was split in two.
A range of private shipyards have also arisen and could account for nearly 50
percent of Chinese ship production by 2010.

CSSC and CSIC Shipyards

CSSC remained the principal shipbuilding organization in China until
July 1999, when it was divided into two separate entities. CSSC remained
in control of most shipyards and related subsidiaries in Shanghai and south
of the Yangtze, and the China Shipbuilding Industrial Corporation (CSIC)
was established and given control of shipbuilding operations in the northern half of the country. Currently both serve as umbrella organizations for a
wide range of shipyards, marine subcomponent manufacturing companies,
research and design institutes, and a limited number of nonshipbuilding
related business.[27] CSSC and CSIC are considered major state-owned enterprises, and both report to the PRC State Council through the State-owned
Assets Supervision and Administration Commission.[28]

The partition of CSSC was part of a larger antimonopoly initiative by PRC leadership. State-owned monopolies like CSSC were broken up, and a limited amount of free-market competition was introduced to help promote reform and innovation within each defense industrial sector. CSSC and CSIC each hold significant investment and capital management autonomy from the state, and the two corporations are allowed to compete directly for domestic government contracts as well as on the international market.[29] Competition is facilitated by similar industrial capabilities within each conglomerate, with each having similar commercial and military product lines. CSSC and CSIC both actively seek foreign and domestic contracts for highly competitive ship types such as containerships and very large crude oil carriers (VLCCs), and yards within each organization produce submarines and advanced surface combatants. Considering the high degree of product specialization and overall noncompetitive nature of the PRC aerospace industry, the presence of healthy competition between state-owned shipbuilders is somewhat unusual and noteworthy within China's defense industrial establishment.[30]

Additional incentives for self-improvement and technical innovation also reside within the business structures of CSSC and CSIC themselves. Major shipyards under CSSC and CSIC are further subdivided into several large shipyard group companies. These companies, such as the Hudong-Zhonghua Group under CSSC and the Dalian Shipbuilding Industry Group under CSIC, each manage subsidiary shipyards and largely function as independent corporate entities. Day-to-day operations and most contract bidding are handled directly by the shipyards, with the CSSC and CSIC front offices dealing in more macro-level resource management and large-scale (or high profile) business issues. As part of efforts to become more globally competitive, CSSC and CSIC have also accelerated efforts to become publicly traded corporations. Many subsidiary shipyard companies within CSSC and CSIC are listed on stock exchanges in Shanghai and Hong Kong (shares of Guangzhou Shipyard International have been publicly traded since 1993), and CSSC has launched a comprehensive three-phase plan to increase public offerings across its entire organization. CSSC's diesel engine builder Hudong Heavy Machinery recently went public with 400 million shares valued at more than 12 billion renminbi (RMB) (1.5 billion USD), which one CSSC executive characterized as "just a first step" in the process of incorporating CSSC's core business units.[31]

The business structure changes and incorporation initiatives by CSSC and CSIC are aimed at improving competitive and management practices within China's state-owned shipyards but, in true capitalist fashion, are also intended to help finance China's long-term plan for growth in shipbuilding. The Party Central Committee and State Council identified shipbuilding as a key industry for development in 2000, and in May 2002 Chinese premier Zhu Rongji challenged the country's shipbuilders "to propel the country to world No. 1 status." Following this direction, the State Commission of Science, Technology, and Industry for National Defense set a target of 2015 for China to become the world's leading shipbuilder.[32] This is a lofty goal, considering that China accounted for 13.8 percent of gross tonnage built globally in 2005, substantially short of the 35.0 percent and 37.7 percent shares held by Japan and South Korea.[33]

To provide the infrastructure capacity to support increased output and market share, a significant portion of CSSC and CSIC financial resources have been devoted to expanding China's shipbuilding industrial base. The funding for infrastructure expansion has come from a mix of state subsidies, tax exemptions, reinvested profits, and private-sector financing. Highlighting the shifting nature of the Chinese economy, the state-run *China Daily* reported that "the central government supports large shipbuilding companies issuing corporate bonds or going public [to raise funds for] for shipbuilding infrastructure construction," an idea simply unimaginable in the prereform era.[34]

Through these initiatives CSIC has invested in expansions of its Dalian and Bohai Shipbuilding Heavy Industry facilities, and its Qingdao Beihai Shipbuilding Heavy Industry shipyard recently started construction on two new 500,000 dwt building docks. Similarly, CSSC has multibillion dollar projects under way to build massive new "shipbuilding bases" on Changxing Island in Shanghai and Longxue Island in Guangzhou.[35] These expansion projects are aimed at increasing China's capabilities for building more technically complex ships, especially in such high-value sectors as large containerships, very large or ultra large crude carriers (VLCC/ULCCs), liquefied natural gas (LNG) tankers, and cruise ships. If all plans are completed, CSSC and CSIC will combine to add roughly 12 million dwt of production capacity, carrying China to its official goal of 24 million tons, or 35 percent of world total shipbuilding capacity, by 2015.[36]

Shipping Conglomerate, Joint Venture, and Private Enterprise Yards

The development of China's shipbuilding industry has not been limited to CSSC and CSIC. Twenty-six shipyards under CSSC and CSIC cognizance account for nearly 70 percent of China's commercial output by deadweight, but these represent only 12 percent of the total number of shipyards engaged in new construction since the CSSC/CSIC division in 1999. This percentage falls even lower when considering the scores of additional Chinese shipyards that only engage in ship repair activities and therefore do not regularly appear in new ship construction statistics.

Beyond CSSC and CSIC, the PRC State Council also has jurisdiction over a large number of smaller shipyards administered by provincial and local governments, as well as over numerous shipyards run by China's national shipping conglomerates. The exact number of provincial and local shipyards is not known because many new yards have opened and others have merged or changed names as free market reforms reach the lower levels of the Chinese economy. Some are managed as highly organized group corporations that cater to international customers while others are merely upstart "beach yards" with relatively little infrastructure or government oversight.[37] Illustrating this disparity, the highly reputable Fujian Mawei Shipbuilding is currently building a series of small containerships for German clients, while one Chinese analyst recently described lesser provincial yards as "heavily in debt, not organized, technologically backwards, and having weak risk management capacity."[38] Regardless of administrative structure and individual performance, when taken in aggregate, provincial and local yards play an important and growing role in Chinese shipbuilding. They have produced 1,168 new ships totaling more than 5.1 million dwt since 1999 (10.7 percent of the PRC total), more than double the total provincial and local yard output from 1982 to 1999.[39]

Unlike the variety at provincial and local levels, the shipyards controlled by China's shipping lines more closely resemble the shipyard group companies within CSSC and CSIC. Historically, shipping company yards focused on maintenance and repair of their own vessels, but in recent years they are increasingly moving into new construction to supply their own fleets and other domestic customers as well as international buyers. The China Changjiang (Yangtze) National Shipping Group is the third-largest fully state-owned shipbuilder behind CSSC and CSIC, producing 128 new ships totaling 1.4 million dwt since 1999. It operates four new construction and numerous ship repair yards along the Yangtze River, mostly in the inland provinces of Hubei and Anhui.

China's other major national shipping conglomerates, the China Shipping (Group) Company and China Ocean Shipping Company (COSCO), also operate their own shipyards. China Shipping controls five shipyards in Shanghai and Guangzhou under its China Shipping Industry Company

(CIC) subsidiary, all of which specialize in ship repair work.[40] COSCO operates major facilities in Dalian, Nantong, and Guangzhou that similarly focus on ship repair and conversion, but unlike CIC, COSCO also engages in new ship construction. The Nantong-COSCO KHI Ship Engineering Company (NACKS) shipyard is a fifty-fifty joint venture between COSCO and Kawasaki Heavy Industries of Japan and is one of China's leading commercial shipbuilders. It builds for the COSCO fleet as well as international customers, producing 3.7 million dwt since 1999 (7.7 percent of China's total), with more than 1.1 million tons delivered in 2006 alone.[41]

The success of NACKS highlights a growing trend toward more joint venture and private enterprise companies in China's shipbuilding industry. Prior to 1999 there were only two joint venture shipyards operating in China: the Yantai Raffles Shipyard, a joint venture established in 1994 between the China National Petroleum Company, the Yantai City Mechanical Industrial Company, and the Brian Chang Group of Singapore; and Shanghai Edward Shipbuilding, a 1997 joint venture between CSSC and Hansa Shipbuilding of Germany.[42] In 1999 the Ninth People's Congress approved a constitutional amendment officially affirming the importance of the private sector to China's economy, and the government openly encouraged shipyards to pursue joint venture development following the bifurcation of CSSC.[43]

Foreign investment in most joint ventures was initially limited to a 49 percent share, and agreements included mandatory provisions ensuring foreign technology transfer into Chinese shipyards as a result of any partnership. Foreign companies were limited to noncontrolling interests in new ship construction and low-speed marine diesel engine production but were allowed to establish wholly owned marine equipment factories in China.[44] These restrictions were relaxed somewhat following China's admission to the World Trade Organization in 2001, which required the gradual opening of the Chinese economy to foreign direct investment and foreign corporate ownership across all sectors.[45]

Foreign shipbuilders have been quick to exploit the opening of the Chinese market, eager to reap the benefits of China's low-cost labor pool to offset the rising competition from Chinese shipbuilders. Virtually all Singaporean shipbuilding and repair companies have established joint ventures or wholly owned subsidiaries in China, and major shipbuilders from Japan and South Korea have likewise entered the Chinese market in force. Tsuji Heavy Industries and the Tsuneishi Group of Japan, as well as Samsung Heavy Industries and Daewoo Shipbuilding of South Korea, have established hull block fabrication facilities in China and have had limited success obtaining authorization for full ship construction at their Chinese subsidiaries.[46] In total, eight joint venture, private enterprise, and foreign-owned shipyards have delivered ships by the end of 2006, and six additional non-state-owned yards have ships on order as of January 2007.[47]

This is not to imply that the Chinese shipbuilding industry is heading toward a wave of multinational corporate ownership. To the contrary, the PRC government recently pulled in the reins on foreign investment in Chinese shipbuilding. Limitations on foreign shipbuilding investment were retightened in September 2006, again limiting foreign companies to 49 percent shares in Chinese shipyards, diesel engine, and crankshaft manufacturing enterprises. Additionally, foreign companies "must also transfer their expertise to local partners through the establishment of technology centers."[48] The state-run *Shanghai Daily* characterized these regulations instituted by the PRC Commission of Science, Technology, and Industry for National Defense (COSTIND) as a move "to both maintain control over the fledgling [shipbuilding] industry and tap overseas know-how," and noted that "a 49 percent ceiling in foreign ownership means ship manufacturing falls into the central government's 'strategic' industry category and needs special oversight and support."[49] These restrictions clearly illustrate the limit to which the PRC government is willing to let Chinese shipbuilding move toward Western-style corporate business models, and it reiterates the strategic overtones of shipbuilding development in China. The rollback of foreign investment limits is also likely to further questions by European and other shipbuilding competitors over Chinese compliance with WTO regulations, questions that are likely to only increase as China captures a growing share of the world shipbuilding market.[50]

PLA Shipyards

The smallest, least significant economically, and least understood element of China's shipbuilding industrial structure is a group of shipyards directly controlled by the People's Liberation Army (PLA). Unlike China's other state-owned shipyards, which are under the jurisdiction of the State Council, PLA shipyards answer to the General Armaments Department of the Central Military Commission. Little open source data is available to describe the exact capabilities of the PLA shipyards or the full scope of their work. Maintenance and repair of PLA Navy vessels constitutes a core competency, but at least five PLA yards have engaged in some degree of commercial shipbuilding at various times over the past twenty-five years. Currently,

PLA Navy Factory 4807 in Fu'an and Navy Factory 4808 in Qingdao remain active in commercial new construction, with both building small chemical and oil products tankers for Greek and Saudi buyers.[51]

China's Shipbuilding Geography: Concentration and Dispersion

As one might expect, the vast majority of China's shipbuilding output comes from the country's coastal provinces.[52] China's eleven coastal provinces are home to 90.7 percent of the shipyards engaged in new construction since 1999, accounting for 91.9 percent of the total ships produced and 97.6 percent of the tonnage output by deadweight. Within the coastal areas, China's shipbuilding output is even further concentrated. Just three areas, Shanghai, Liaoning, and Jiangsu, produced more than 80 percent of China's total deadweight tonnage since 1999. Fourteen shipyards in Shanghai accounted for 36.7 percent of total tonnage, and the shipyards of Liaoning and Jiangsu Provinces accounted for 23.9 and 21.8 percent, respectively. Of note, 83 percent of Liaoning's tonnage output came from the two yards of the Dalian Shipbuilding Industry (Group) Co., China's largest shipbuilder by deadweight.

Despite the coastal concentration of tonnage output, the dispersion of China's shipbuilding infrastructure to include several inland provinces is also noteworthy. Some of this dispersion is an unnatural holdover from Mao Zedong's "Third Front" initiative of the 1960s, but most of China's shipyards along the Yangtze River continue to operate for legitimate economic reasons. The Yangtze has long been navigable for oceangoing vessels as far as Wuhan in Hubei Province, some six hundred miles upriver from Shanghai; completion of the Three Gorges Dam in 2008 extended navigability farther inland to Chongqing. Smaller vessels use the river extensively as far as 1,600 miles inland. Consequently, the Yangtze represents an important commercial transportation link similar to the Danube in Europe and Mississippi River in the United States; Chinese vice premier Huang Ju recently announced a 15 billion RMB (1.85 billion USD) government initiative to further develop "shipbuilding standardization" and other shipping-related activities along this vital inland waterway.[53] Currently the Yangtze's shipbuilding significance is highlighted by Song-class submarine construction at CSIC's Wuchang Shipyard in Wuhan, and China Changjiang National Shipping Groups' commercial construction at four yards along the river. The latter includes the Damen Yichang Shipyard in Hubei Province, a recently formed joint venture between Changjiang National and the Damen Shipbuilding Group of the Netherlands to build ships for export.[54]

The shipbuilding infrastructure along China's other rivers is not nearly as significant at that of the Yangtze but does include numerous shipyards along the Yellow River in Shandong Province and the Pearl River in the south of China. As China continues to promote expanding access to the Mekong River for oceangoing ships, further development of inland shipbuilding or repair infrastructure is a future possibility.[55]

Shipbuilding Output by Ship Type

For many years after China's shipbuilding industry emerged in the 1980s, the types of ships built were of relatively low complexity. Commercially, the majority of China's shipbuilding output was composed of dry bulk carriers, small tankers, and general cargo ships. On the naval side, shipbuilding through the 1980s was dominated by Luda-class destroyers, Jianghu I/II-class frigates, and Ming-class diesel submarines, all of which were obsolescent by Western standards at the time of their commissioning.

The diversity and complexity of China's commercial shipbuilding output has steadily increased over the past twenty-five years. China has moved into the lucrative international markets for large containerships and VLCC/ULCCs, and CSSC's Hudong-Zhonghua Shipbuilding is poised to deliver the first Chinese-built LNG tanker in 2007.[56] The ability of Chinese shipyards to build these larger, more complex ships can largely be attributed to a blending of growing domestic experience with a fair amount of foreign technology, but it is also a product of investments in expanded and modernized shipbuilding infrastructure.

Prior to 1995 China did not have a building dock large enough to construct VLCCs or other large types of commercial ships. A 300,000 dwt dock at Dalian Shipbuilding's No. 2 Yard (formerly "Dalian New Shipbuilding Heavy Industry") delivered the first Chinese-built VLCC in 2002, and since then eight additional VLCC-sized building docks have been added in China.[57] With current shipyard expansion projects, China's VLCC dock total is expected to reach thirty by 2015. This dwarfs the current nine in Japan and is more than double the number in South Korea (the two countries that have previously dominated the global VLCC market).[58] VLCCs will occupy in China's output as more of these new large building facilities come online in coming years, and output will trend toward a mix of increasingly complex ships officially targeted in China's National Medium-and-Long Term Plan of the Shipbuilding Industry:

- High tech, high function, and special ships, and large ships with 100,000 dwt and above.

- Passenger ships, Ro-Ro passenger ships, passenger-cargo ships, and train ferries.

- LPG ships and LNG ships with a handling capacity of 5,000 cm and above.

- Container ships with a capacity of 3,000 TEU and above.

- Large deep-sea fishing boats, marine drill vessels, oil rigs, marine floating production storage and offloading (FPSO) structures and other offshore engineering equipment.[59]

China's move toward producing larger, more complex ships has not been limited to the commercial sector. When CSIC received China's first order for VLCCs in 1999, its general manager reportedly remarked that it was a godsend for Chinese shipbuilders because they "had long had two dreams— to build military aircraft carriers, and huge crude oil carriers."[60] Although China has yet to build an aircraft carrier, it now possesses building docks capable of doing so and has demonstrated significant progress in building more complex naval ships over the past decade.[61] Recent years have seen the Luyang II-class (Type 052C) air-defense destroyer emerge from Jiangnan Shipyard, Jiangkai-class (Type 054) "stealth" frigates from the Hudong and Guangzhou Huangpu Shipyards, and two new classes of nuclear-powered submarines from Bohai Shipbuilding Heavy Industries in Huludao. All of these classes represent notable advances in technology and complexity over previous Chinese warships, and each of these shipyards are engaged in both military and commercial construction.

Viewed holistically, the cumulative effects of China's improved commercial shipbuilding prowess have undoubtedly benefited China's naval development to some degree. As discussed previously, most of China's shipyards have undergone significant infrastructure improvements, and the large volume of foreign commercial sales provides China's shipyards (and central government) with the resources necessary to better train and equip their workforce for naval construction. Beyond these generalizations, it becomes far more difficult to quantify the degree to which commercial success has benefited Chinese naval development. While some fundamental aspects of ship design and construction are inherent to any ship type, the unique design requirements and operational characteristics of warships often cause military shipbuilding to quickly diverge from the harsh economic demands of building tankers and container ships for an internationally competitive commercial market.[62]

To understand better the implications of China's commercial shipbuilding development on naval modernization, the remainder of the chapter will focus on five key shipbuilding process and technology areas that have potential for significant civil–military overlap: advanced ship production methods, systems integration, metallurgy, propulsion, and commercial off-the-shelf technologies. Examining China's indigenous capabilities in these key areas will offer a more refined look into China's commercial shipbuilding progress beyond the volume measurement of tonnage output, and more importantly, will provide insight into how advances in these areas may (or may not) affect the pace of future Chinese naval development.

PRC Shipbuilding Technical and Human Abilities

Although international commercial sales currently account for the vast majority of tonnage output, the recent emergence of Luyang II–class (Type 052C) air-defense destroyers, Jiankai-class (Type 054) "stealth" frigates, and two new classes of nuclear-powered submarines from PRC shipyards raises questions regarding the degree to which China's commercial shipbuilding prowess is contributing to modernization of the PLA Navy. All of these classes represent notable advances in technology and complexity over previous Chinese warships, and the shipyards that produced them are simultaneously engaged in both military and commercial construction.

Viewed holistically, the cumulative effects of China's improved commercial shipbuilding abilities have undoubtedly benefited China's naval development to some degree. Chinese yards are now employing advanced modular construction methods, building ship equipment such as engines under license, and rapidly gaining experience in hull fabrication. The top tier Chinese shipyards such as Shanghai Waigaoqiao are also moving beyond being "copy shops" and have begun forging long-term relationships with ship owners. A key component in establishing these long-term ties is creating "feedback" loops in which yards query ship owners about improvements they would like made to various ship types and then use their growing internal design abilities to innovate and incorporate desired changes into future ship designs.

Human Factors

Technical gains are diminished if they are not accompanied by similar growth of indigenous human capital able to harness new shipbuilding technology. This includes the engineering skills required to drive innovation in research and design, the craftsman-level technical skills required to build high-quality ships, as well as the business management skills required to efficiently operate large manufacturing organizations. These human skills are generally portable across shipbuilding sectors and therefore stand to directly affect both commercial and military shipbuilding development.

Thus far these human capital and management issues have hindered the progress of Chinese shipbuilding development. Western and Chinese sources rate the overall productivity of Chinese shipyards as roughly one sixth that of Japanese or South Korean commercial yards, with some more detailed estimates placing PRC shipbuilders even further behind world leaders. Chinese shipbuilding productivity is further hampered by a disproportionately large workforce, estimated to be roughly twice as manpower-intensive as commercial competitors in Japan and South Korea.[63]

To a certain degree, the large size of the Chinese shipbuilding workforce is a matter of policy. Providing employment for China's massive population is a key role for state-owned shipbuilders, especially in major coastal cities flooded with workers migrating from rural areas. Furthermore, for political reasons, many shipyards remain burdened with communist-style employment policies that severely limit or even prohibit the firing of workers. These practices provide obvious negative incentives for increasing productivity and efficiency, as summarized by a Dalian Shipbuilding executive's observation that "it's difficult to control the workers if they get paid whether they work or not."[64]

Productivity issues are not limited to the worker level. Many Chinese shipyards reportedly still lack efficient human resource management and suffer from similar front office deficiencies in material management, scheduling, systematic quality control measures, and industrial safety management. These deficiencies are reflected in continuing quality and on-time delivery performance rated below that of Japanese, South Korean, and European shipbuilders, as well as serious concern displayed by some Western ship owners over a general disregard for worker safety at some Chinese shipyards. Western industry officials interviewed stressed the wide disparity in performance and business practices between small provincial and large state-owned Chinese shipyards, but doubts were expressed as to the ability of even well-established CSSC/CISC yards to generate real profits in light of inconsistent internal cost control practices. This assessment is also evident in the remarks of a senior PRC government official, who recently stated that "the [shipyard] productivity gap offsets China's advantage in cheap labor."[65]

Viewed narrowly, it can be safely surmised that these same productivity and management issues will continue to have similar negative effects on naval shipbuilding in China. The bloated workforce at Chinese shipyards does not help productivity, but from a wider perspective, the large number of shipyard workers may have a secondary strategic effect that actually benefits the PLA Navy. China's shipyards are exposing a growing number of Chinese workers to shipbuilding, improving technical skills, and helping foster a better awareness of the seas in a country long lacking a robust maritime culture. Furthermore, China's sizable shipbuilding workforce includes a growing number of college graduates. Chinese universities produce approximately fifteen hundred naval architects per year, and when combined with students studying overseas, China now meets (or exceeds) its competitors in the number of college graduates entering the workforce with shipbuilding-related technical degrees.[66]

Conclusion

At the time of Zheng He's Ming Dynasty voyages, China boasted some of the world's most advanced shipbuilding and marine technology and could have become a major sea power in addition to a great land power. Its leaders specifically decided not to pursue such a course, however, and halted China's maritime rise. Over the next few centuries, Western powers—first European and later North American—and Japan caught up to and far surpassed these early Chinese achievements. China sought to defend its sovereignty and interests against their predations, but it was too internally disorganized, had too little national power and capabilities, and was too far behind to catch up. Unable to control its own destiny, China did ultimately gain some support from European colonial powers and American merchants determined to protect their newly acquired commercial advantages in China from Japanese encroachment. China had the opportunity to acquire some Western shipbuilding facilities and technologies, but it lacked the skilled labor and technology base to effectively indigenize these assets.

Efforts by Chinese officials to reform their nation in the mold of Meiji Japan were thwarted by an imperial system that was self-centered, out of touch with modern science and technology, and insensitive to the changes then convulsing East Asia—all of which contributed to the downfall of the Qing Dynasty and the overthrow of the imperial system in 1911. The turmoil of the ensuing civil war and (after 1931) conflict with Japan precluded any consolidation of or improvements in China's dispersed and primitive ship-building sector. The communist regime brought to power in 1949 initially secured significant Soviet shipbuilding technology, facilities, and expertise. Complications in the Sino-Soviet alliance of the early Cold War terminated this assistance by 1960, however; and internal politics diverted even focus on this rudimentary and incomplete infrastructure until normalization of relations with the United States and Deng Xiaoping's consolidation of power in 1978 under the banner of modernization and economic development.

In the three decades since, the question of China's ability to rise again as a great sea power has been closely tied to its commercial shipbuilding development—hence the focus of this chapter. Already Beijing is demon-strating an ability to sustain its maritime influence that the Soviet Union and other land powers cum sea powers rarely or never did. It is scarcely conceiv-able that Beijing will once again scrap its fleets and turn inward to autar-kic continental isolation. Yet China still has a long way to go if it hopes to become a great maritime power in the mold of Holland, Great Britain, or the United States. All three maritime powers dominated all levels of commercial shipbuilding when they ruled the waves, not only based on comprehensive national strength but also on personnel quality and, perhaps most impor-tantly, on innovation ability.

Where Dutch, British, and American ships were the most innovative and commercially viable in their respective eras of hegemony, modern China has yet to make any such contribution. Building simpler types of ships at lowest price will not be sufficient to allow China to challenge the United States for maritime dominance—even in maritime East Asia. If China masters more sophisticated shipbuilding technologies, however, new strategic commercial and naval possibilities will emerge that could enable Beijing to reshape the regional maritime order and even to contend for a greater role in a world in which North American commercial ship production has virtually ended and that of Europe has largely eroded. The process of globalization, which has linked the world's economies together, enables China to challenge elements of U.S. maritime dominance through commercial means in a way that was not previously possible.

Notes

The opinions and assessments expressed in this analysis are the authors' only and should not be considered official U.S. government assessments or policies. A more detailed and technical version of this chapter has been published as "A Comprehensive Survey of China's Dynamic Shipbuilding Industry: Commercial Development and Strategic Implications," *China Maritime Study*, no. 1 (Newport, RI: Naval War College/China Maritime Studies Institute, August 2008).

1. Hu Jintao, quoted in Cao Zhi and Li Xuanliang, "Authorized Released by Two Session," *Xinhua*, 11 March 2006, OSC-CPP20060311001006.

2. Derived from new construction and order book statistics in Lloyd's Register–Fairplay, Ltd., *Register of Ships*, *Sea*-web database, http://www.sea-web.com (hereafter cited as Lloyd's *Sea*-web database).

3. Xu Qi, "Maritime Geostrategy and the Development of the Chinese Navy in the 21st Century," trans. Andrew Erickson and Lyle Goldstein, *Naval War College Review* 59, no. 4 (Autumn 2006): 47–67.

4. "China to Limit Foreign Investment in Shipyards," *Shanghai Daily*, 19 September 2006, http://www.shanghaidaily.com/article/?id=292385&type=business.

5. Bruce Swanson, *Eighth Voyage of the Dragon: A History of China's Quest for Sea Power* (Annapolis, MD: Naval Institute Press, 1982), 25–28. The exact size of the *baochuan* is disputed, with estimates ranging from 180 to 440 feet long. By comparison, Christopher Columbus's *Santa Maria* was 85 feet long. See James R. Holmes and Toshi Yoshihara, "Soft Power at Sea: Zheng He and China's Maritime Strategy," U.S. Naval Institute *Proceedings* 132, no. 10 (October 2006): 34–38, n7.

6. Richard N. J. Wright, *The Chinese Steam Navy: 1862–1945* (London: Chatham Publishing, 2000), 21–29; John L. Rawlinson, *China's Struggle for Naval Development: 1839–1895* (Cambridge, MA: Harvard University Press, 1967), 41–62 and 145–48.

7. Wright, *Chinese Steam Navy*, 21–23; Rawlinson, *China's Struggle*, 41–41 and 146–46; Kemp Tolley, *Yangtze Patrol: The U.S. Navy in China* (Annapolis, MD: Naval Institute Press, 1971), 177–83; and the Jiangnan Shipyard (Group) Co. Ltd, http://www.jnshipyard.com.cn/en/indexmain_e.htm. Of note, the river gunboats built at Kiangnan (Jiangnan) included the USS *Luzon* (PG-47), on which Richard McKenna served and based much of his book *The Sand Pebbles* (later made into a famous movie starring Steve McQueen). The gunboats also included the USS *Panay* (PG-45), which was sunk by Japanese aircraft in 1937. See Tolley, *Yangtze Patrol*, 224, 245–52; Bernard D. Cole, "The Real Sand Pebbles," *Naval History* 14, no. 1 (February 2000): 16–23; and Richard McKenna, *The Sand Pebbles* (New York: Harper & Row, 1962).

8. Daniel Todd, *Industrial Dislocation: The Case of Global Shipbuilding* (London: Routledge, 1991), 216; Irwin Millard Heine, *China's Rise to Commercial Maritime Power* (New York: Greenwood Press, 1989), 36; and Evan S. Medeiros, "Revisiting Chinese Defense Conversion: Some Evidence from the PRC's Shipbuilding Industry," *Issues & Studies* 34, no. 5 (May 1998): 79–101.

9. Mikhail Barabanov, "Contemporary Military Shipbuilding in China," *Eksport Vooruzheniy*, 1 August 2005, OSC-CEP20050811949014. Severodvinsk has been the lead shipbuilder for much of the Soviet/Russian submarine program and was used as a model for developing the Bohai Shipyard in Huludao. All of China's nuclear submarines have subsequently been built at Huludao.

10. David G. Muller Jr., *China as a Maritime Power* (Boulder, CO: Westview Press, 1983), 59; Todd, *Industrial Dislocation*, 216–17; and PRC shipbuilding statistical data extracted from Lloyd's *Sea*-web database.

11. Todd, *Industrial Dislocation*, 217, cites only three ships produced in the PRC from 1961–63 whereas Lloyd's *Sea*-web database lists seven ships totaling only 13,439 deadweight tons built during this same period. Regardless of the exact numbers, viewed in a larger context, output was effectively nonexistent.

12. Medeiros, "Revisiting Chinese Defense Conversion," 84; and Todd, *Industrial Dislocation*, 217.

13. For more on the "Third Front" industrial plan and its effects, see Medeiros, "Revisiting Chinese Defense Conversion," 86–87; and Barry Naughton, "The Third Front: Defense Industrialization in the Chinese Interior," *The China Quarterly*, no. 115 (September 1988): 351–86.

14. According to Deng Xiaoping's famous "16-Character Slogan" on defense conversion, its purpose was to "Combine the military and civil, combine peace and war, give priority to military products, let the civil support the military." See Jorn Brommelhorster and John Frankenstein, ed., *Mixed Motives, Uncertain Outcomes: Defense Conversion in China* (Boulder, CO: Lynne Rienner Publishers, 1997), 20–21. For more on defense conversion, see Paul Humes Folta, *From Swords to Plowshares? Defense Industry Reform in the PRC* (Boulder, CO: Westview Press, 1992); Mel Gurtov, "Swords into Market Shares: China's Conversion of Military Industry to Civilian Production," *The China Quarterly*, no. 134 (June 1993): 213–41; and Medieros, "Revisiting Chinese Defense Conversion."

15. Heine, *China's Rise*, 37–39; and Medeiros, "Revisiting Chinese Defense Conversion," 89. The only shipyards left beyond the control of the CSSC were a few minor yards primarily engaged in ship repair and controlled by the PLA.

16. For more on shipbuilding development in Japan and South Korea, see Takafusa Nakamura, *The Post War Japanese Economy: Its Development and Structure*, trans. Jacqueline Kaminski (Tokyo: University of Tokyo Press, 1981), 71–75; Daniel Todd, *The World Shipbuilding Industry* (New York: St. Martin's Press, 1985), esp. 286–96 and 340–45; and Todd, *Industrial Dislocation*, esp. 136–50 and 183–99.

17. For a comparison of Chinese business conglomerate with those in Japan and South Korea, see Richard J. Latham, "A Business Perspective" in Jorn Brommelhorster and John Frankenstein, ed., *Mixed Motives, Uncertain Outcomes: Defense Conversion in China* (Boulder, CO: Lynne Rienner Publishers, 1997), 151–78, esp. 158–61.

18. Evan S. Medeiros et al., *A New Direction for China's Defense Industry* (Santa Monica, CA: RAND, 2005), 157. For more on the defense conversion and modernization of China's aerospace industry, see Howard O. DeVore, *China's Aerospace and Defense*

Industry (Surry, U.K.: Jane's Information Group, 2000); and Kenneth W. Allen, Glenn Krumel, and Jonathan D. Pollack, *China's Air Force Enters the 21st Century* (Santa Monica, CA: RAND, 1995).

19. Medieros, "Revisiting Chinese Defense Conversion," 90.

20. Todd, *Industrial Dislocation*, 218–21; and Heine, *China's Rise*, 38 and 47–49. The now-dissolved British Shipbuilders was the umbrella organization formed following the nationalization of most of the United Kingdom's shipbuilding industry in the 1970s. The far-reaching deal between British Shipbuilders and CSSC was signed in November 1982, just four months after the formal establishment of CSSC. For more, see Heine, *China's Rise*, 108–9.

21. *Lloyd's List*, 16 August 1985, as quoted in Heine, *China's Rise*, 49.

22. Heine, *China's Rise*, 18 and 37; and Muller, *China as a Maritime Power*, 58–61.

23. Lloyd's Register of Shipping, *Statistical Tables 1992* (London: Lloyd's Register of Shipping, 1992), 30. Statistics do not include ships under 100 gross tons, therefore most "junks" are excluded.

24. Heine, *China's Rise*, 47–48; and Todd, *Industrial Dislocation*, 218.

25. See Medeiros, "Revisiting Chinese Defense Conversion," 86 and 98.

26. *European Industries Shaken Up by Industrial Growth in China: What Regulations Are Required for a Sustainable Economy?* (Brussels: European Metalworkers' Federation, 2006), 57.

27. Nonshipbuilding-related business areas for both companies include the fabrication of large steel structures such as bridges, port machinery, and cargo-handling equipment but also ranges as far as real estate holding companies. For corporate profiles and complete lists of all business units under CSSC and CSIC, see China State Shipbuilding Corp. (CSSC), http://www.cssc.net.cn; and China Shipbuilding Industry Corp. (CSIC), http://www.csic.com.cn.

28. State-owned Assets Supervision and Administration Commission (SASAC), Central Enterprises List, http://www.sasac.gov.cn.

29. Medeiros et al., *A New Direction for China's Defense Industry*, 114–15.

30. The China Aviation Industry Corporation (AVIC) was also divided in 1999, forming AVIC I and AVIC II. There was little overlap in product lines between the two companies and competition was very limited. AVIC I produces mainly combat aircraft, while AVIC II tends to specialize in helicopters. See Medeiros et al., *A New Direction for China's Defense Industry*, 175. In 2008, the AVICs were recombined to avoid resource waste.

31. "CSSC Aims to Be a Shipbuilding Leader Globally," *SinoCast* China Transportation Watch, 14 February 2007. Also see "Asset Injections Boost Listed SOEs," *Xinhua*, 15 February 2007; and "China State Shipbuilding to Incorporate Its Business," *SinoCast* China Transportation Watch, 19 October 2005.

32. "China's Drive toward World Dominance," Wartsilla *Marine News*, March 2005, 4–5; and Farah Song, "China Shipbuilding 'Juggernaut' Gains on Leaders Japan, Korea," Bloomberg.com, 22 March 2005.

33. By deadweight, China accounted for 20 percent world tonnage production, Japan 32 percent, and South Korea 35 percent through 2006. See "Shanghai Company Breaks into Shipbuilding Top 10," *China Daily*, 4 January 2007, http://www.china.org.cn.

34. "Getting Ship-Shape," *China Daily*, 31 December 2003, Hong Kong edition, http://www.chinadaily.com.cn/en/doc/2003-12/31/content_294778.htm.

35. Andrew Cutler, "World Leader by 2015? Shipbuilding in the PRC & the YRD," *Business Guide to Shanghai and the YRD*, October 2005, http://www.hfw.com/l3/new/newl3c075.html; and China State Shipbuilding Corp., http://www.cssc.net.cn/enlish/index.php.

36. "Getting Ship-Shape," *China Daily*, 31 December 2003; and Cai Shun, "Full Steam Ahead," *Beijing Review* 48, no. 10 (10 March 2005): 36.

37. Cutler, "World Leader by 2015?" For an example of a high-end provincially administered shipyard group, see Fujian Shipbuilding Industry Group Co. (FSIGC), http://www.fsigc.com.

38. Zhang Kai, "A Life and Death Test for Jiangsu's Shipbuilding Industry," *Mechanical and Electrical Equipment* 3 (2006): 16.

39. Lloyd's *Sea*-web database. By Lloyd's data, provincial and local shipyards produced 1,939,441 dwt from 1982–99. Statistical accuracy for output from these yards can be questionable in earlier years, but the relative magnitude of increased production from provincial and local shipyards is certainly significant.

40. China Shipping Industry Co. (CIC), http://www.csgcic.com/en/gsjj/index.htm; and Lloyd's *Sea*-web database.

41. Lloyd's *Sea*-web database. For a complete list of COCSO's shipyards, see Barbara Matthews, ed., *World Shipping Directory 2006–2007* (Surry, U.K.: Lloyd's Register–Fairplay, Ltd., 2006), 1,1027–30; and COSCO Group, http://www.cosco.com.

42. Yantai Raffles Shipyard, http://www.yantai-raffles.com/?page_id=4; and Hansa Truhand–Schiffsbeiligungs AG & Co. KG, *Die Unternehmensgruppe* (Corporate Profile), 2004, available at http://www.hansatreuhand.de.

43. Chen Wen, "Fueling the Engine," *Beijing Review* 49, no. 11 (March 2006): 28–32; and "Getting Ship-shape," *China Daily*, 31 December 2003.

44. "Getting Ship-shape," *China Daily*, 31 December 2003. NACKS Shipyard is a fifty-fifty joint venture, illustrating that the 49 percent investment limitation was not inflexible.

45. See "National Shipbuilding Group to Embrace More Opportunities and Challenges," *People's Daily*, 29 January 2002; and "WTO Boosts Ship Building," *People's Daily*, 15 October 2001, http://english.peopledaily.com.cn/english/200110/15/eng20011015_82288.html.

46. "Tsuji Heavy Is First Foreign Yard to Build Ships in China," *Lloyd's List*, 19 July 2006; and the Tsuneishi Corporation, http://www.tsuneishi.co.jp.

47. The exact number of Chinese-owned private shipyards is not clear. Additional privatization at smaller provincial-level yards is also known to be occurring. See

European Industries Shaken Up, 35; "Shipbuilding as One of China's Key Industries," *Toplaterne*, no. 80 (January 2006): 5–8; and "Private Enterprise Shipbuilding Group with Focus on International Customers," *Toplaterne*, no. 80 (January 2006): 16. Both *Toplaterne* articles available at http://www.mak-global.com/news/pdf/ Toplaterne80e.pdf.

48. "China to Limit Foreign Investment in Shipyards," *Shanghai Daily*, 19 September 2006.

49. Ibid.

50. See *European Industries Shaken Up*, 41.

51. Lloyd's *Sea*-web database. The other PLA shipyards that have also previously built commercial ships are PLA Navy Factory 4803 in Shantou, 4806 in Zhoushan, and 4810 in Dalian.

52. The term "province" is used loosely to also include China's direct-controlled munic- ipalities and semiautonomous regions (i.e., Shanghai, Tianjin, and Chongqing municipalities, and the Guangi-Zhuang autonomous region).

53. "Coordination Stressed in Developing the Yangtze River," *Xinhua*, 22 November 2006.

54. Matthew Flynn, "From Two Different Rivers Flow the Same Dreams," *Lloyds's List*, 31 January 2007.

55. See Marwaan Macan-Markar, "Sparks Fly as China Moves Oil up Mekong," *Asia Times Online*, 9 January 2007, http://www.atimes.com/atimes/southeast_asia/ ia09ae01.html.

56. "China to Deliver First Liquefied Natural Gas Ship in September," *Xinhua*, 19 Feb- ruary 2007, OSC-CPP20070219968046.

57. Geoffrey Murray, "China's Largest Shipyard Formed by Merger in Shanghai," *Kyodo News Service* (Tokyo), 13 April 2001, OSC-JPP20010413000153; and Lloyd's *Sea*-web database.

58. "Chinese Shipmakers Threaten Korea's High-Value Builders," *Chosun Iibo* (Seoul), 1 March 2007, OSC-KPP0301971163; and "Current Capacity, Future Outlook for Japanese, Chinese Shipbuilding Industries," *Tokyo Sekai no Kansen*, 9 March 2006, OSC-FEA2006030902654.

59. Wu Qiang, "China Maps out Ambitious Goal for Shipbuilding Industry," *Xinhua*, 24 September 2006. Quoted list of ship types is paraphrased from larger list of goals that also included marine power systems, electronics, and other subcomponent systems. These additional systems are discussed later in the paper.

60. Chen Xiaojin, quoted in Murray, "China's Largest Shipyard."

61. Regarding building docks, the No. 2 Yard at Dalian Shipbuilding includes a drydock measuring 550 by 80 meters. This is smaller than the 658.4 by 141.7 meter drydock no. 12 at Newport News Shipbuilding used for building 102,000-ton *Nimitz*-class carriers but is significantly larger than the 310 by 42.1 meter (following expansion) drydock no. 1 at Babcock Rosyth, currently scheduled to be used for final assembly of the United Kingdom's new 65,000-ton displacement *Queen Elizabeth*–class car- riers. See Mathews, ed., *World Shipping Directory 2006–2007*, 1-1031 and 1-1-1323;

Richard Sunders, ed., *Jane's Fighting Ships 2006–2007* (Surry, U.K.: Jane's Information Group, 2006), 829 and 871; and Richard Beedall, "Future Aircraft Carrier (CVF)," parts 19 and 21, http://navy-matters.beedall.com/cvf1-12.htm.

62. For a complete discussion, see John Birkler et al., *Differences between Military and Commercial Shipbuilding: Implications for the United Kingdom's Ministry of Defense* (Santa Monica, CA: RAND, 2005).

63. *European Industries Shaken Up*, 31; and "Current Capacity, Future Outlook for Japanese, Chinese Shipbuilding Industries," *Tokyo Sekai no Kansen*, 9 March 2006, OSC-FEA2006030902654.

64. Paul Sun Bo, quoted in Stewart Brewer, "China: Building for the Future," Det Norske Veritas *Forum*, 19 July 2006, http://www.dnv.com/industry/maritime/publications anddownloads/publications/maritime_news/2005/6_2005/building_for_the_ future.asp. For a full discussion of employment practices at Chinese shipyards (including case studies), see *European Industries Shaken Up*, esp. 38–40 and 72–74.

65. Zhang Xiangmu, COSTIND, as quoted by Wu Qiang, "China Maps Out Ambitious Goal for Shipbuilding Industry," *Xinhua*, 24 September 2006. For a shipowner/ship-broker perspective on business management issues in China's shipbuilding indus-try, see *Purchasing New Buildings in China: A Practical Guide to the Key Commercial and Legal Considerations* (Neuilly sur Seine, France, and Uxbridge, U.K.: Barry Rogliano Salles Shipbrokers and Curtis Davis Garrard LLP, March 2006).

66. Statistics based on correspondence with a Western naval architecture firm represen-tative operating in China and the Society of Naval Architects and Marine Engineers (SNAME); includes four-year bachelor degrees in naval architecture, ocean engi-neering, and shipbuilding technology.

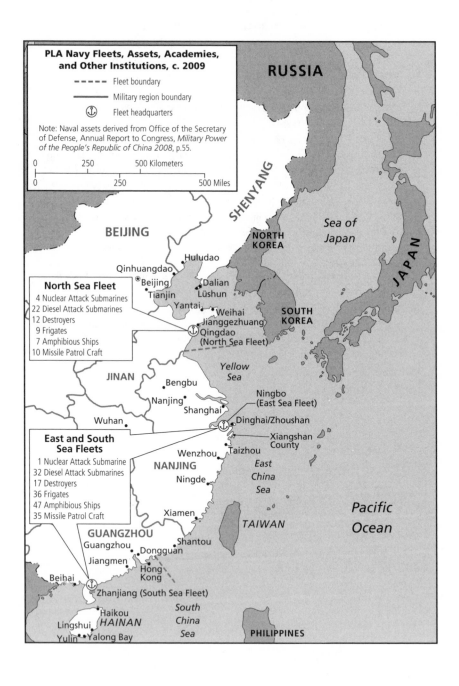

PLA Navy Fleets, Assets, Academies, and Other Institutions, c. 2009

- - - - - Fleet boundary
———— Military region boundary
⚓ Fleet headquarters

Note: Naval assets derived from Office of the Secretary of Defense, *Annual Report to Congress, Military Power of the People's Republic of China 2008*, p.55.

0   250   500 Kilometers

0   250   500 Miles

RUSSIA

SHENYANG

Sea of Japan

JAPAN

BEIJING

NORTH KOREA

Huludao

Qinhuangdao

Beijing   Dalian
Tianjin   Lüshun
Yantai
Weihai
Jianggezhuang
Qingdao
(North Sea Fleet)

SOUTH KOREA

North Sea Fleet
4 Nuclear Attack Submarines
22 Diesel Attack Submarines
12 Destroyers
9 Frigates
7 Amphibious Ships
10 Missile Patrol Craft

Yellow Sea

JINAN

Bengbu

Nanjing
Shanghai

Wuhan

Ningbo
(East Sea Fleet)

Dinghai/Zhoushan

Xiangshan County

East and South Sea Fleets
1 Nuclear Attack Submarine
32 Diesel Attack Submarines
17 Destroyers
36 Frigates
47 Amphibious Ships
35 Missile Patrol Craft

Wenzhou Taizhou

NANJING

Ningde

East China Sea

Xiamen

TAIWAN

Pacific Ocean

GUANGZHOU
Guangzhou Shantou
Dongguan
Jiangmen
Hong Kong

Beihai

Zhanjiang (South Sea Fleet)

Haikou

Lingshui HAINAN

Yulin Yalong Bay

South China Sea

PHILIPPINES

PLA Navy Organizations, Academies, and Units by Fleet and Location

This selective, estimated list of Chinese naval facilities and commands has been compiled from several unclassified sources, including Office of Naval Intelligence, *Handbook on China's Navy 2007*, Jane's, www.sinodefence.com, www.fas.org, www.globalsecurity.org and Google Earth. A *zhidui* is a division-leader level organization (using the PLA's fifteen-grade structure, which is based on army terminology). The best English translation is "flotilla." A *dadui* is a regiment-leader level organization; the best English translation is "squadron."

BEIJING
* Navy Headquarters
- Command Department
- Political Department
- Logistics Department
- Armament Department
* Navy Military Studies Research Institute
* Navy Armament Research Academy

NORTH SEA FLEET
Qingdao
* North Sea Fleet Headquarters
* Submarine Academy
* Support Base
* Naval Aviation Unit
* Air Training Base
* 1st Destroyer Zhidui
* Submarine Zhidui
* Fastboat Zhidui
* Support Vessel Zhidui
* Training Base
Qingdao/Jianggezhuang
* 1st Submarine Base (Nuclear)
Dalian
* Naval Vessel Academy
* 2nd Air Division
* 10th Destroyer Zhidui
* Xiaopingdao Submarine Base
* Naval Garrison
* Testing Area
Lüshun
* Support Base
* 12th Submarine Zhidui
Huludao
* Flight Academy
* Testing Base
* Testing Area
Yantai
* Aviation Engineering Academy
* Naval Aviation Division
Qinhuangdao

* Shanhaiguan Training Base
* Testing Area
Tianjin
* Logistics Academy
Weihai
* Naval Garrison

EAST SEA FLEET
Ningbo
* East Sea Fleet Headquarters
* Submarine Zhidui
* Naval Aviation Unit
* Radar Brigade Unit
* Engineering Command
Dinghai/Zhoushan
* Support Base
* 3rd Destroyer Zhidui
* 6th Destroyer Zhidui
* Operations Support Vessel Zhidui
Shanghai
* Support Base
* 6th Naval Aviation Division
* 5th Landing Ship Zhidui
* Sub Chaser and Frigate Zhidui
* Vessels Training Center
Nanjing
* Command College
* Electronics Engineering Academy
Wuhan
* Engineering University
- Engineering Academy
Bengbu
* Non-Commissioned Officer School
Xiangshan County
* Submarine Zhidui
Taizhou
* Fourth Naval Aviation Division
Wenzhou
* Fastboat Zhidui
Ningde
* Fastboat Zhidui

Xiamen
* Naval Garrison

SOUTH SEA FLEET
Zhanjiang
* South Sea Fleet Headquarters
* 2nd Destroyer Zhidui
* Operations Support Vessel Zhidui
* 1st Marine Brigade
* 164th Marine Brigade
* Testing Area
* Engineering Command Unit
Guangzhou
* Service Arms Command College
* Support Base
Yulin
* Support Base
* 32nd Submarine Unit
Yalong Bay
* Nuclear Submarine Base
Haikou
* Naval Aviation Unit
* 8th Naval Aviation Division
* 11th Fastboat Zhidui
Lingshui
* Naval Airfield
Jiangmen
* Fastboat Zhidui
Shantou
* Naval Garrison
Dongguan
* Training Base
Beihai
* Naval Garrison
Xisha (Paracel Is.)
* Naval Garrison
Nansha (Spratly Is.)
* Patrol District
Hong Kong
* Stonecutter's Island Ship Dadui

Eric A. McVadon

China's Navy Today: Looking toward Blue Water

A NEW AND MUCH MORE CAPABLE CHINESE NAVY, a pillar of China's transformation into a full-fledged maritime power, is being acquired and deployed. It is not yet operationally mature, but its rapid and impressive modernization is making it arguably the only major navy that the United States must undertake special efforts to deter or be able to defeat—suggesting that Sino-American bilateral relations should be designed to bring about maritime cooperation rather than conflict or harmful competition. The feasible alternative to the adversarial relationship that some foresee is partnership on the high seas between the People's Republic of China (PRC) navy and U.S. Navy—a worthy goal to strive for as China undergoes transformation to join the United States as a major maritime nation.

The PRC has moved dramatically over the last decade or so to modernize its naval forces—ships, submarines, aircraft, weapons, electronic systems and other equipment—and is now advancing, albeit somewhat less impressively, in the areas of doctrine, training, command and control, and intelligence support toward making those forces a truly operational modern navy. The Chinese Communist Party (CCP) and the government it pervades have made the major political and programmatic decisions and provided the substantial funding to allow these long-postponed modernization steps. The Chinese military waited patiently for national attainment of economic conditions that would allow greater attention to military modernization. The waiting has now been rewarded. Moreover, technologies and technical assistance in critical areas have become available both through internal advances and from Russia and other external sources.

Dual Incentives for Modernization: Taiwan and Economic Imperative

The incentive to modernize the People's Liberation Army (PLA, the collective term for all of China's armed forces including ground, air, naval, and missile components) has become stronger in the past several years as Chinese leaders have become increasingly concerned about how the government of Taiwan might behave with respect to movement toward independence. However, Beijing also has come to recognize that, quite independent of the Taiwan issue, China should have armed forces that fit the changing China that has clearly become a power—economic, political, and military—not only in its region but globally. Moreover, the realization seems to have sunk in fully with the Chinese leadership that the most important aspect of China's rise, its remarkable national economic growth since 1978, is exceedingly dependent on ocean commerce, including energy supplies (oil and natural gas) arriving by sea. China must become a comprehensive maritime power to protect its governing regime from the feared extreme jeopardy of a severe economic downturn that could result were shipping seriously threatened or disrupted over a sustained period.

China, then, is a twenty-first-century example of a nation that is, of necessity, a forward-looking emerging maritime power. However, the course of development of the navy that is so important to the success of China's maritime transformation remains heavily influenced by senior military officers who have come up through the ranks of the ground forces. Moreover, even China's most senior naval officers lack the full scope of opportunities available to the leaders of other major navies to gain a global view. Despite important openings to the outside world, barriers persist that restrict their ability to interact widely and exchange ideas freely and extensively with other maritime countries—and to bring such ideas back to a receptive home audience. Nevertheless, China's naval and overall maritime transformation is proceeding apace with the prospect that even these persistent barriers will soon be circumvented, brought down, or at least made less onerous.

This modernization of China's navy—the People's Liberation Army Navy (PLAN)—is occurring in a complex, even contradictory, strategic context. Chinese leaders feel compelled to pursue the following strategic objectives:

1. Deter intolerable actions by Taipei or be capable militarily of readily overwhelming Taiwan.

2. Deter, delay, or complicate a U.S. intervention in a Chinese attack on Taiwan.

3. Maintain a stable environment in the region that fosters China's all-important continued national economic growth.

4. Seek a peaceful solution of "the Taiwan problem," including building goodwill toward China among Taiwan's citizens.

5. Maintain good bilateral relations with the United States—the world's only superpower and China's most important trading partner.

6. Promote China's status as a responsible member of the international community through aggressive implementation of its newly progressive and assertive foreign policy.

This new policy has been manifest in Beijing's central role in the establishment of the Shanghai Cooperation Organization (SCO).[1] Other examples include the Six-Party Talks on North Korea's nuclear status and China's role in the Association of Southeast Asian Nations' (ASEAN) expanding circles—all to be discussed later.

China's Desire to Avoid Conflict, to Deter Rather than Defeat

The leaders of an economically successful and internationally active China do not want to jeopardize the nation's prospects for a bright and prosperous future by initiating military conflict with Taiwan and the United States (with conceivable support from its ally Japan); quite the contrary. If, however, the "Taiwan problem" were to become intolerable (as Chinese leaders see it), Beijing would have available an impressive force designed and acquired for this contingency. If that PLA force were effectively deployed, it would be sufficient in terms of hardware (including firepower), if not yet in overall capability, to undertake a two-pronged, PLAN-led campaign against Taiwan and (presumptively though not certainly) U.S. forces in the region. Chinese leaders could conceivably convince themselves that they could subdue Taiwan and compel capitulation before the United States could effectively overcome the barriers the PLA would erect to prompt U.S. intervention.

Put another way, war across the Taiwan Strait is not looming. Nevertheless, Beijing is, by modernizing its military, further ensuring that things will not go awry concerning Taiwan and that its policy of intimidation and military threat will continue to advance the prospects of reunification over the longer term. In a time of American preoccupation with the global war on terrorism, it is all the more appropriate to examine, as this chapter attempts, the principal features of PLA, and specifically PLAN, modernization and what this implies for China as an emerging maritime power. Understanding today's PLAN and how it is changing is important so that the United States can achieve the right balance of deterrence, cooperation, and— we can hope—even partnership on the high seas with the People's Republic of China.

A Maturing but Still Adolescent Navy

The People's Liberation Army Navy might be described as an adolescent navy, with the caution that adolescents can exhibit qualities from juvenile to adult, often acting commendably, occasionally transgressing into the adult world, and maturing unpredictably. To extend the adolescence analogy a bit more, the PLAN is growing remarkably in size and strength, even "bulking up" (in the American vernacular); all remark "how much the PLAN has grown since the last time they saw it."[2]

Simply deploying more modern equipment does not, however, make the PLAN a truly modern operational force. The limits on how the leaders of China and its navy are able to employ their new capabilities reflect significant shortcomings, and success in the effort to overcome them is far from ensured. In other words, the PLAN has matured remarkably insofar as acquiring platforms and equipment (ships, submarines, aircraft, radars, and so on) and weapons (antiship cruise missiles, air defense missiles, torpedoes, and the like) are concerned, but the organization has not matured fully in terms of exercising its forces, developing adequately sophisticated C4ISR,[3] and assembling targeting support needed to make that force fully effective— especially in comparison with its most important, potential adversary, the U.S. Navy.[4]

The Quality of PLAN Leadership

Better educated and more worldly officers are on the way up—if they make it to the top. The PLAN recognizes that to conduct complex joint operations, exercise greatly enhanced and more flexible command and control, and effectively employ modern weapons, it needs a better-educated, more diversely experienced officer corps, and it is striving to acquire those officers, or so it says.[5] PLAN officers are taking more prominent positions in institutions that do strategic thinking; for example, in two firsts in recent years for naval officers, Adm. Zhang Dingfa headed the Academy of Military Science (he then served as the commander of the PLAN until health problems forced his retirement), and Rear Adm. Yang Yi recently served as director of the Institute of Strategic Studies at the National Defense University in Beijing (the only navy officer to hold that job), where he was prolific and respected. The PLAN seeks officers educated in first-rate civilian universities.[6] The emphasis, however, appears to be on specific technical and scientific educations;[7] this approach neglects, it seems, the parallel need for specialists in operations, security issues, strategic studies, and international affairs.[8]

Setting aside specialized education, an important unanswered question is whether the PLAN wants officers who are more able and better educated or more reliably "Red." That is, will competent, forward-thinking officers be selected for flag rank, or will party loyalty and personal connections continue to prevail as the paramount selection criteria?[9] This author has lectured and conferred at the National Defense University and other PLA institutions on several occasions at which the captains and colonels asked all the questions and did all the talking while flag and general officers who were students remained silent—at least in part, it appeared, for fear of being outshone in these lively and insightful discussions. It would seem that at some point the demands of a modern PLA will force the promotion of more of the officers who have all the intelligent questions and original thoughts.

Organizational Impediments

Organization is improving but maybe not yet enough. The PLAN structure has been streamlined: naval aviation no longer stands alone as though an almost separate service, closer ties have been established with the PLAN's marine corps, and there are fewer layers in the chain of command.[10] Nevertheless, as the author has observed and been told, there is still much room for change at the top. As navy officers describe it, there are still many in green uniforms with two or more stars on their shoulders (PLA ground-force generals) who persist in treating the PLAN as mostly an adjunct to the army, and senior officers who, through lack of vision, fail to move decisively toward true joint operations. These generals represent obstacles at a time when real coordination ("jointness") by the PLAN with the 2nd Artillery Corps and the PLAAF would lead to enormous advances in the ability to polish off Taiwan, threaten American intervention capabilities, and keep Japan off balance—as will be explained shortly.

Not Exercising Forces at the Full Potential of Weapon Systems

China's navy is still failing to conduct exercises needed to develop its full potential capability. It continues to operate in the littoral (the "brown" and "green" water rather than the "blue") for the most part. However, the PLAN aspires and is erratically striving to conduct exercises in more distant waters; to make its training more like actual combat; to challenge itself in exercises with active, maneuvering opposition forces; and otherwise to add realism to its training and exercise activity. It has even been so bold as to engage (in August 2005) in a major multiphased exercise with the Russian navy,[11] a notable advance beyond the minor, very basic exercises it has conducted with the French, British, Australian, Pakistani, and Indian navies in recent years.[12] A few years ago the PLAN would not have participated in such exercises at all, fearing not only prying but also embarrassment that its shortcomings and backwardness would be revealed. Chinese naval leaders now seem sufficiently confident in their crews and equipment to seek international partners for exercises. (It is not clear if several unflattering postexercise Russian media reports rejuvenated concerns that bilateral exercises lead to ridicule and embarrassment.)[13]

Still, the import of the Russian-Chinese exercise should not be overstated. It was initially characterized by many as preparation for countering U.S. forces in the region. As it was later more accurately described, however, its primary purpose was to demonstrate that Sino-Russian bilateral relations are strong, especially military-to-military relations and arms sales arrangements. The fact that it was held at all suggests that the Russians are more likely than we might have surmised to provide logistic and possibly intelligence support—specifically, to offer to resupply missiles and spare parts for the key Russian weapon systems that China would employ in combat with Taiwan and the United States.[14]

While the significance of this exercise should not be exaggerated, the PLAN is creeping toward real blue water exercises with composite task forces including surface combatants, submarines, and aviation. So far only in occasional and isolated distant submarine transits does it approximate the task of confronting an enemy, the U.S. Navy, which it might need to keep at arm's length many hundreds of miles from the Chinese coast.[15] In short, the PLAN is not visibly conducting exercises, alone or with other services, that realistically rehearse confrontation with approaching U.S. Navy forces. The United States should be alert to such a development with this new force, a force designed to have the capabilities that could make such operations feasible and that would reflect significant progress in the naval component of Chinese maritime transformation.

The Prospect of Coordinated Joint Attacks from Several Axes

A new aspect of budding maturity, what could facetiously be termed "socialization," is looming and demands attention. It is the prospect that the PLAN and the 2nd Artillery Corps could (and should, from the perspective of enhancing Chinese capabilities) join hands to bolster the nation's capability to attack Taiwan and pose a significantly greater and more diverse threat to the ability of the United States to intervene in the region. The greatly increased number and highly improved accuracy of China's medium- and short-range ballistic missiles (MRBMs and SRBMs), together with information deriving from Chinese strategic and technical writings, strongly suggest that senior Chinese military leaders have recognized the enhancement of naval capabilities that would result from support (coordinated strikes) by ballistic and land-attack cruise missiles. China's MRBMs (the DF-21C) and SRBMs (DF-15 and -11), with conventional warheads, have capabilities well beyond the familiar role of psychological intimidation of Taiwan.[16] Prospective enhanced capabilities stem from the ability of these potent and newly very accurate missile arsenals to neutralize air and missile defenses, suppress Taiwan's offensive and defensive air power, support amphibious and airborne assaults on the island, strike American bases in the region, and possibly inflict heavy damage on Taiwanese naval forces before they could leave port.

The Potential Threat of Ballistic Missiles to Hit Ships

The most important aspect of the increasing ballistic-missile threat is the additional prospect that within a few years China may be able with maneuvering reentry vehicles (MaRVs) to seriously threaten not only American land bases but also carrier strike groups.[17] MaRVed missiles with conventional warheads would maneuver both to enhance warhead survival (defeat missile defenses) and home on mobile (or stationary) targets.[18] The implications for the PLAN of this prospective 2nd Artillery capability are, of course, profound; they include the ability to degrade vital U.S. defense capabilities (including Aegis air and missile defense systems and carrier flight decks). That would allow follow-on attacks by layered, diverse, and appropriately redundant PLAN submarine, air, and surface forces firing large numbers of very modern and capable ASCMs, torpedoes, and even guns, if the earlier attacks succeeded in suppressing most defenses.[19]

This and what follows outline the sort of threat the PLA and PLAN wish to pose to U.S. Navy forces. The precisely focused force that the Chinese have built (and what they have written about its use) leaves no doubt about the concept—although there are grave doubts about their ability to effectively implement it.[20] Even if the technical problems are resolved, hardware does not make a complete capability. The challenge of overall coordination of this dual campaign against Taiwan and the United States would indeed be daunting for a military with no experience in such operations, as will be discussed in more detail later.

The Existing Threat of ASCMs from Submerged Submarines

Whether or how soon the described antiship–ballistic missile threat becomes a factor in the ability of the PLAN to deter, confuse, and delay or, alternatively, confront approaching U.S. Navy forces, the ability to launch lethal antiship–cruise missile (ASCM) attacks is an area where the PLAN is already near or at maturity—even if the capability to detect, identify, and target American forces has not reached a state of consistency and reliability. The PLAN became a cruise missile navy early on as a way of overcoming other deficiencies. Now it must be described as a modern cruise missile navy, at least with respect to the platforms and the lethal, evasive missiles it is deploying.[21] The PLAN's four newest classes of submarines, armed with potent ASCMs, fall just below MaRVed ballistic missiles in the hierarchy of potential or emerging threats to U.S. forces.

At the top of the submarine component of the overall threat are the eight new Kilo-class diesel-electric submarines from Russia that were recently sequentially (and rapidly) delivered to China. These submarines threaten carrier strike groups through their ability to launch, while submerged more than one hundred miles away, the potent SS-N-27B/Sizzler antiship cruise missile.[22] After a subsonic flight to the target area, the SS-N-27B makes a supersonic, sea-skimming, evasive attack.[23] It is described by its marketers and others as part of the best family of cruise missiles in the world and, in the opinion of some, as able to defeat the U.S. Aegis air- and missile-defense system that is central to the defense of carrier strike groups.[24]

The new Shang-class (Type 093) SSNs are possible partners for the new Kilos. The surprisingly rapid construction of follow-on units of this new class of nuclear-powered attack submarine implies special utility in a Taiwan contingency. The Shangs, if they prove sufficiently quiet and fast and are properly equipped with sensors, could be part of the net by which the PLAN locates and identifies approaching U.S. carrier strike groups.[25] If used this way, they could be part of a matrix composed of such detection and reporting means as satellites, merchant ships, and even fishing boats with satellite phones.

Additional Prospects of Multiaxis Attacks

Having served as part of the matrix that detects targets for the ballistic missiles and Kilos, the nuclear-powered Shangs could then join with the Song- and Yuan-class nonnuclear submarines (SSs) in attacks against selected U.S. forces that have suffered by that point, as expected in the sequenced PLA attack concept, significant degradation of their air and missile defenses.[26] These three classes of submarines could carry out, from several attack axes, submerged launches of large salvoes of subsonic—but still very capable—ASCMs. Of course, further follow-on attacks by torpedoes cannot be discounted if they appear to be needed.

China's other new nuclear-powered submarine program, the Jin-class (Project 094) ballistic-missile submarine, is part of China's strategic deterrent—armed with long-range nuclear-tipped submarine-launched ballistic missiles (SLBMs). Nevertheless, it would unavoidably play a role as backdrop in a Taiwan scenario.[27] Although arguably separate from those platforms that directly enhance China's maritime power (as with China's modernized and augmented land-based intercontinental ballistic missiles), this SLBM force enables Beijing to act more confidently in bold undertakings vis-à-vis the United States, knowing that its strategic forces are appropriately redundant and more secure. With the Jins, Beijing is wagering that American missile defenses, even if highly effective, could be saturated, deceived, and depleted—and that Washington would know it. Washington, of course, would have to take into account the fact that it is dealing with a capable nuclear power whose missiles have become very mobile and hard to detect both ashore and at sea.

A Daunting Antisubmarine Warfare Challenge

The success of the PLAN submarine attacks postulated here using submerged-launch antiship cruise missiles depends to some degree on thwarting or coping with U.S. antisubmarine warfare capabilities, primarily aircraft (P-3Cs and to a lesser extent shipborne helicopters) and SSNs. One method by which the Chinese might complicate the antisubmarine warfare (ASW) picture for the Americans would be to use large numbers of submarines, including a score or more of older submarines—Han-class SSNs and Romeo- and Ming-class SSs—which may be noisy but cannot be ignored. In round numbers, the PLAN might—in a campaign where it controls the time to start and is able to ready the crews—be able to deploy more than twenty modern SSNs and SSs and roughly the same number of older submarines.[28] Recall that the long range of the ASCMs carried by the new Kilos mean that those submarines need not come within a hundred miles of the target ships, if targeting information can be obtained remotely and relayed to the "shooter." This greatly expands the areas that American SSNs and P-3Cs would have to search to "sanitize" areas ahead of carrier strike groups. The speed and practically unlimited underwater endurance of the new Shang SSNs could allow them, assuming reasonable lack of noise, to close targets promptly to launch their somewhat shorter-range and subsonic ASCMs after the initial attacks by longer-range and higher-speed ballistic or cruise missiles have degraded defenses.

The role of Taiwan in antisubmarine warfare deserves some attention. Taiwan's current ASW capability is minimal. That capability might improve in the foreseeable future assuming Taiwan, as expected, obtains from the United States the much-discussed P-3Cs, but the quality of that capability will depend on how seriously the Republic of China (ROC) Navy pursues the demanding task of learning how to do antisubmarine warfare with the P-3C aircraft. If it does that well, Taiwan's P-3Cs might offer a measure of help in the big ASW problem that the PLAN could create in the East China Sea and beyond.[29] The Japanese Maritime Self-Defense Force would offer another measure of assistance, if Tokyo were to make a political decision to involve its forces in that way.

All this said, China's diverse, growing, and improving submarine fleet has outpaced existing and even prospective United States, Japanese, and Taiwan ASW in the difficult littoral waters of the region, waters that generally favor submarines seeking to escape detection.[30] Open-ocean areas may be a slightly riskier proposition for the PLAN's submarines, unless they actually achieve the elusive new levels of stealth to which China aspires. Soviet inability to remain undetected was a significant factor in ending the Cold War.

Finding a Way around the Superior U.S. SSNs

The antisurface-warfare roles just described seem the most probable ones for the PLAN's new Shangs. It does not appear likely that the PLAN, inexperienced compared to the U.S. Navy in undersea warfare, would use its few new SSNs—precious to the Chinese but almost certainly not comparable to American SSNs in capability and stealth—in an effort to strip the carrier groups of the submarine protection that the Chinese assume is provided. So far China has conceded that undersea warfare advantage to the United States and has chosen to avoid dueling with the superior American submarines.

By electing to try to develop a land-based ballistic-missile threat against ships at sea, China is pursuing a path that could keep U.S. submarines from thwarting or complicating a critical initial attack on carrier strike groups. In an attack on Taiwan, if the ballistic missile concept is not yet operational, not usable, or fails in execution, the new Kilos with the SS-N-27B, the many other submarines with ASCMs, and the increasingly capable PLA naval air force B-6s, FB-7s, and Su-30MK2s (to be described in more detail later) provide other alternatives that largely avoid American underwater-warfare superiority. The point is that, as the Shang-class SSNs are introduced into the fleet, it seems unlikely that they would be expected to take on American SSNs directly. The naval pillar of China's maritime transformation encompasses major advances in its submarine force, both conventionally and nuclear-powered. It represents a major increase in the submarine threat to the naval forces of adversaries, though as yet it does not offer a challenge to U.S. submarine warfare superiority.

Enough to Make Washington Pause?

In a Taiwan scenario, the intensity and persistence of PLAN attacks on U.S. Navy forces could well be affected by Beijing's perception of the fragility of a government on Taiwan—a Taiwan subjected to a major assault employing everything from ballistic and land-attack cruise missiles to aircraft, special forces, and information warfare of all sorts, and much more. It should be remembered that the primary purpose of denying or delaying access by U.S. forces would be to convince Taipei that waiting for help is futile, that capitulation and negotiation—on Beijing's terms—are the only reasonable option. Success against U.S. forces is therefore important largely for its effect on Taipei's will to fight on. Success in such a conflict would be sweetest for the PLA if the United States never became actively involved. Beijing can hope, at least, that concern about the capabilities of a modernized Chinese force would have led American leaders to delay or withhold carrier strike groups from approaching the Taiwan area.

More Attack Options for the PLAN and Supporting Missile Forces

Returning from strategic considerations to the fight itself, were one to occur, next the Chinese could be expected to deliver against closing U.S. naval forces and possibly other U.S. forces based in the region air-launched antiship cruise missiles once the air defenses of the U.S. strike groups, and possibly regional bases as well, are degraded. So this "layer" in the package of Chinese assault options might be the PLA Navy Air Force, attacking several hundred miles out to sea from China (in some cases possibly much farther) with potent new air-launched ASCMs fired from new aircraft from Russia (the Su-30MK2) and indigenous long-range B-6s (a new version with new antiship missiles) and FB-7 maritime interdiction aircraft, also with new ASCMs.[31] (Note how many times the word *new* appeared, correctly, in that sentence.) Some PLAAF aircraft have similar capabilities. At a minimum, the U.S. Navy would have to be concerned about vulnerability to such an attack and, if it had indeed sustained damage, might feel it had to retreat, knowing these follow-on forces were available. Beijing undoubtedly would anticipate ensuring that such a development was not lost on Taipei.

Surface combatants would be a final layer, if a supposedly casualty-averse Washington and a teetering Taipei have not yet taken the point and succumbed. Cleanup attacks might be intended in such a case with very capable

ASCMs from the several new or upgraded classes of destroyers and frig-ates. These surface warships are led, with respect to lethal firepower, by the Russian *Sovremennyy*s (at least four and possibly more to come) with super-sonic, very evasive SS-N-22 Sunburn ASCMs.[32]

Although China's most potent combatant ship is of Russian origin, much of the modernized surface-combatant force has been and is still being pro-duced indigenously. China has built or is building enough new and modern-ized destroyers and frigates to form several modern surface action groups, each capable of long-range attacks with lethal, although subsonic, ASCMs. Also—and here it is finally beginning to overcome a long-standing short-coming—the PLAN is on the way to acquiring good fleet air defenses using surface-to-air missile systems.[33] Thus, two more significant aspects of mari-time transformation for the PLAN are evident: the capability to construct major components of modern warships in China and the provision to its navy of some measure of fleet air defense.

To capture succinctly the scope of the modernization of the surface com-batant force, it can be said that the Chinese are now building or dramatically upgrading more *classes* of modern destroyers and frigates (these combatants clearly outmatch those of Taiwan) than previous assessments suggested they might acquire combatant *ships* in this decade.[34]

Shortfalls to Overcome

The question that cannot now be answered with confidence is whether such an inescapably visible and inherently slow-moving force of surface combatants (destroyers and frigates), even with dramatically improved air defense, could actually engage even a damaged U.S. force and not be sub-ject to devastating attack by other American strike forces. There are, how-ever, broader uncertainties for the PLAN. As noted, the concepts outlined above emerge from an analysis of the force Beijing is building and from PLA doctrinal and other writing. Beijing has made hard decisions and executed expensive programs in the ongoing surge in modernization of the PLA, with great emphasis on naval, air, and missile forces for such operations as described. But, not to be forgotten, surveillance and targeting support will be needed and extensive disruption of U.S. C4ISR will be highly desirable if this force is to deter or confront American intervention efforts.

To that end, it appears China is making significant efforts to gain a var-ied capability employing assets from space, land, sea (including undersea), and air to locate, identify, track, and target opposing naval forces.[35] China is lagging in this arena; real success in the intelligence, surveillance, and reconnaissance arena could take a decade, but one might make a guess that some rudimentary, if not reliable and consistent, targeting capability could be cobbled together within a couple of years. In other words, there is impending danger that U.S. ships and those of other adversaries could be detected and effectively targeted at very large distances from China. At least equally important is whether China will be able to coordinate, command, and control such operations. The PLAN, although now more realistic and somewhat bolder in its training and exercises, as explained above, has not—with the possible exception of the 2006 surfacing of a Song near the *Kitty Hawk* carrier strike group—touted or otherwise given evidence of rehearsals of encounters with simulated carrier strike groups hundreds of miles east of China, as it might do as part of a deterrence scheme.

There is no doubt about the described PLAN acquisition of modern platforms and threatening weapons, but there remains, as has been seen, much uncertainty as to whether and how promptly the PLAN and the other crucial components of the PLA will make all this capability truly operational. There is, nevertheless, an additional serious question as to whether Beijing would feel compelled in some circumstance to initiate hostilities against Taiwan and to confront U.S. forces even if capabilities and preparations were from its point of view short of optimal.

There is an additional important constraint or limitation facing the PLAN. All of these attack options add up to an exceedingly complex planning and execution challenge for an inexperienced PLA. In the scenario depicted above, the PLA would be conducting two major campaigns simultaneously: one to subdue Taiwan and the other to delay effective American intervention. The campaign against Taiwan, to flesh that out a bit more, would likely include highly accurate initial ballistic missile and precision land-attack cruise missile attacks; antisatellite actions ranging from disruption to destruction using laser energy or kinetic kills (of which both forms were demonstrated or tested in the fall of 2006 and early 2007);[36] special forces, fifth-column sabotage-type actions; information operations, including computer network attacks; major air attacks; and amphibious and airborne assaults to secure lodgments to allow occupation and control of Taiwan.

As already noted, the campaign against the U.S. forces, in addition to being preceded by (or starting with) extensive efforts temporarily to cripple American C4ISR, would consist of ballistic and cruise missile attacks on carrier strike groups and possibly regional U.S. bases, submarine attacks using various forms of antiship cruise missiles, and then selections from such follow-on options as ASCMs from air or surface forces. This would be an extraordinarily demanding array of military missions to be undertaken against a daunting foe by a PLA leadership that has no experience in such combat.

The author's estimate (admittedly more an intuitive personal judgment than a calculation) is that the PLA would quickly succeed against Taiwan but would probably falter against U.S. forces. Against them (assuming they were ordered into the conflict) it would likely encounter surprises, countermeasures, and other capabilities that would likely cause severe reversals. It must also be remembered, however, that China's best strategic and military minds are working on these problems and that Beijing may feel it has to act against Taiwan regardless of how challenging the undertaking may appear, or that its leaders may somehow convince themselves that their forces are more capable and effective than they are in reality.

Beyond "The Taiwan Problem"

The PLA, and especially the PLAN, now seems almost wholly, even obsessively, focused on the Taiwan problem. Two other factors or concerns alluded to earlier should be taken into account. These factors already seem to be seriously intruding into Chinese strategic thinking. First, an emerging China wants to build a military appropriate to the developed major country that it is becoming. Second, and warranting reemphasis here, China's all-important national economic growth, which is also a factor in keeping the Communist Party in power, is dependent on ocean commerce. As the PLAN tries to look beyond Taiwan or to decide what, even now, it should be thinking about besides the Taiwan obsession, it sees as a top priority for China the requirement for a long-term capability to secure sea (and land) routes for the flow of oil and natural gas to China as well as the shipment to and from Chinese ports of other commodities.

Finally a Chinese Aircraft Carrier?

Will we see, for example, development by the PLAN of an organic air capability (some sort of aircraft carrier—although not necessarily resembling those of the U.S. Navy) and a shift to more nuclear attack submarines as well as a real sea-based strategic nuclear capability? A Chinese navy able to carry out the mission to protect ocean commerce would almost certainly have (or need) some form of organic air so it could effectively operate in ocean areas beyond the range of land-based aircraft from China. The organic air would markedly enhance the effectiveness of the force as well as serving to deter a potential disrupter of shipping. Protection of sea-lanes would then be possible far south in the South China Sea, through the Strait of Malacca, even in the Indian Ocean, reaching to the Middle East and its oil as well as in the Pacific as these sea-lanes grow in importance as oil "pipelines." Current shipyard work on the incomplete aircraft carrier *Varyag* may be the start of a move in that direction, unlike so many fanciful Chinese aircraft-carrier sagas and rumors of past decades.[37]

SSNs in Distant Seas?

Another consideration could be a leaning toward submarines with greater range, speed, and independence from land bases. This could mean that nuclear-powered attack submarines, despite the added cost, might be preferred over diesel-electric or even air-independent-propulsion submarines. SSNs are, then, a possible bellwether of PLAN strategic thinking. China is now buying and building three classes of nonnuclear submarines: the Kilos, the Songs, and the Yuans (some speculate about the exact character of the Yuan propulsion system). These submarines, along with the older Mings and remaining Romeos, represent a major investment and will almost certainly constitute a majority of the submarine fleet for the next fifteen years or more. Nevertheless, it will be worthwhile to keep an eye on China's success with the Shang-class nuclear-powered attack submarines to ascertain whether Beijing will feel the need suggested earlier for a faster, more independent force to protect distant sea-lanes, and whether a rising China will follow the American example and increase and diversify its SSN fleet to include land-attack cruise missile capabilities and the ability to insert special forces—or possibly other novel capabilities needed in emerging missions for newly powerful China.

The Features of a Future Chinese Navy

The PLAN has developed in many remarkable ways, but perhaps the biggest tests of maturity will be these possible bold attempts to become a carrier navy and to leap to a new status in the prestigious and unforgiving domain of nuclear submarines—where it had previously faltered. A wide range of options is available with respect to pursuit of a fleet organic (ship-based) aviation arm that would afford protection and provide an extended reconnaissance and strike capability to PLAN forces in distant waters. Despite the high visibility surrounding a possible carrier force, to a significant degree the success or failure of its new nuclear-powered submarines, the Jin ballistic-missile class as well as the Shangs, is likely to determine future decisions for both the Chinese submarine force and for the PLAN more generally.

The organic–air issue may be managed in some nonsensational way, but the outcome of the current nuclear submarine programs could set the tone for a navy that either comes to feel that it ranks with the best or, having "tried out for the pros," finds that once more it has faltered. In any case, it is instructive to imagine particularly intelligent and competent young Chinese naval officers beginning their service. Those junior officers today can see the prospect, at least, of a promising career ahead as a naval aviator or nuclear submariner—as well, of course, as aboard modern surface combatants—in a globally capable "real navy." The prospect of professional challenge and esteem is now roughly comparable to that of an American line-officer counterpart. That in itself is a remarkable and telling change from a few years ago. Then the peak of naval aviation was not even flying first-line (but shore-based) Su-30s but rather aging F-8s from, for example, the Lingshui naval airfield on Hainan to intercept lumbering U.S. surveillance aircraft—a mission the world came to know well on 1 April 2001.[38]

Submarine service in the past was as questionable as shore-based aviation as the core of a navy career. Serving on troubled Chinese submarines previously seemed to many as much a joke as a job. Whatever success the new Chinese submarine force attains will be infectious and will bolster the professionalism of other PLAN components, where newfound pride is thriving as well. The PLAN is not a mature component of a transformed maritime China but has established its potential for that status in the air, on the sea, and, conspicuously, under the sea.

Maritime China Immersed in Maritime Asia's New Regionalism

The new Asia in which a new China will exist is increasingly maritime and regional. Put another way, the Asia that is of interest in this examination is coastal, cosmopolitan Asia, an extensive array of port cities linked by vital sea-lanes, to which China makes a major contribution. The nations that own these world-class major maritime hubs are increasingly integrated, as described in Ellen Frost's new book, *Asia's New Regionalism*.[39] A core circle of regional integration, as she describes, is composed of ASEAN: the ten countries of the Association of Southeast Asian Nations (Indonesia, Malaysia, the

Philippines, Singapore, Thailand, Brunei, Cambodia, Laos, Myanmar, and Vietnam). In Frost's model, borrowed from the organization she describes, the next wider grouping is ASEAN +3, adding Japan, China, and South Korea to the ASEAN 10.[40] A wider grouping, the East Asian Summit, adds India, Australia, and New Zealand.[41] It is noteworthy that China is included in the regional integration described by Frost while the United States is not—as was the case with the Shanghai Cooperation Organization.

There is, however, a grouping that prominently includes the United States. The Six-Party Talks on North Korea's nuclear status include the United States, China, the two Koreas, Japan, and Russia. This grouping is an important manifestation of regionalism, even if it is trans-Pacific, with a non-Asian prominent member—the United States. All the parties are fully engaged, of course, in the ongoing negotiations concerning North Korea. However, these talks hold promise of, or arguably already reflect, a new regional security framework, whether intended or not, especially with respect to the five parties other than North Korea. Criticism of the United States similar to that mentioned for the ASEAN regional groupings is levied by some because Washington seems negligent in not recognizing that the Six-Party Talks process has created this new situation in regional security—a framework inclusive of China and a catalyst for other changes that conceivably include reconsideration of alliance arrangements and even the presence of North Korea in this forum.

A Future China in the Best of All Worlds

It is appropriate to conclude with reminders of why China is making the transformation to a maritime power and the consequences and opportunities thereof—first the domestic factors and then the external picture. As asserted at the outset, China is of necessity becoming a maritime power. This change is both desirable and necessary for China because the continuing stability and the very integrity of the nation depend in significant measure on continued economic growth sustained by expanding, secure, reliable ocean commerce. There is now widespread recognition in China of the need for secure sea-lanes to transport the imports and exports that are vital for continuing essential growth of the economy. The author has been told by Chinese navy colleagues that U.S. Navy Rear Adm. Alfred Thayer Mahan's nineteenth-century works on sea power and seaborne commerce are now a part of the curriculum for the advanced professional military education of rising PLAN officers. Thus the availability of secure ocean commerce is an appreciated and understood critical factor in ensuring continually improving standards of living for crucial components of Chinese society, which in turn translates into societal support of (or at least no strong move to overthrow) the Chinese Communist Party.

It is not excessively dramatic to suggest that this onerous heavy hand, the Party, poised above the Chinese people is tolerated or even accepted by them because life now, compared to that of a few decades back, is quite good for many and at least a bit better for essentially all. Most Chinese who are now prospering do not want to risk possibly chaotic changes in their government and nation. However, there is an expectation among the impatient and unruly Chinese populace that this upward trend in lifestyle will continue. The Party has a full appreciation that unfavorable developments—such as lack of success in the effort to develop the backward, poorer areas of inland China, failure to achieve energy security, or more broadly failure to provide protection of ocean commerce—could become critical factors in economic reversals that could result eventually in the demise of the Party or the division of China. We in the West may not wish the Communist Party well, but we should not seek its demise in the form of a chaotic or shattered China.

With respect to external aspects, for economic reasons Beijing has developed and approved programs and allocated adequate funds to fuel its transformation to a maritime nation, including a modern navy. As a result, China is able to undertake sweeping development of its "oceanic economy" and carry out modernization and expansion of the navy that serves this maritime economy, protects sovereignty and territory, and conducts other traditional and new naval missions. Despite a persisting presence in the PLA top leadership of ground force officers, the PLAN has gained a large share of China's military budget, with the combination of Taiwan and this transformation driving the budget increases.

There are, however, consequences of this transformation, especially its naval aspects, that insidiously reach well beyond the perpetuation of national economic growth and preservation of the Chinese Communist Party just described. China as a global maritime and naval power will be a stronger, more prosperous China. In the eyes of many, that implies a more dangerous China. Consequently, Beijing needs to ensure that a more powerful China neither is nor appears to be a more dangerous China—and Washington can be a partner in this effort, if it is confident that Beijing can be trusted.

A more mature China, as it steps onto the world stage playing a new role, may wish to formulate more mature policies in several areas that would better suit its new status. The easing of tensions in relations with Japan would seem a natural step in the fostering of increased maritime cooperation with neighboring countries. With respect to resolution of the Taiwan issue, a global maritime power may prefer to rely on means other than intimidation and military threats in its conduct as a responsible member of the community of nations. It may conclude that other progressive practices will avoid and even reverse the alienation of Taiwan's citizens and promote a mutually agreeable solution based on self-determination and an objective appraisal of where the best interests of China and Taiwan lie. This fresh approach could rid China of the burden of the "Taiwan problem" or convert the image of China from a highly repulsive autarchic oppressor to a potentially attractive unity partner. The new China that evolves from this transformation can also be justifiably more confident and self-assured domestically than the nation that felt compelled to suppress demonstrations in Tiananmen Square two decades ago.

Of course, China, if its leaders are not bold and enlightened, may shrink from these expansive and beneficent potential manifestations of its new stature, but to do so would impose limits on its own potential to parlay the rising tide of its well-consolidated economic strength and maturing maritime stature into status as a truly responsible regional stakeholder and global power. However, if the tide is prudently taken at the flood, as would nautically befit a major maritime power, this huge country's expansion across the seas could serve as a catalyst for the emergence of a new China that could be proud of much more than just its enhanced maritime and naval prowess.

Notes

Some of the material in this chapter was part of the article "China's Maturing Navy," *Naval War College Review* (Spring 2006): 90–107. The descriptions from that article of PLAN force modernization and attack options remain much the same, but this updated version is also extensively revised and expanded, with most sections rewritten or new in order to address more directly and fully the theme of this book.

1. Possibly the most prominent example of Beijing's new approach to foreign policy is its role in the Six-Party Talks concerning North Korea's nuclear weapon program, where it has worked diligently chairing the sessions and acting behind the scenes to keep the talks going and get Pyongyang to the table. Another less known example is China's leading role in the Shanghai Cooperation Organization, composed of China, Russia, and Kazakstan, Kyrgyzstan, Tajikistan, and Uzbekistan; it represents China's penchant to employ diplomatic and economic (nonmilitary) means to achieve security and stability on its borders. The U.S. alliances in the region originated in the Cold War and include Japan, the Republic of Korea, the Philippines, Thailand, Australia, and New Zealand. China's only security treaty is with the Democratic People's Republic of Korea. The SCO is a recent product of Beijing's diplomatic skills. It has changed from an organization to reconcile border problems to an antiterrorist and economic organization. India, Iran, Pakistan, and Mongolia are SCO observers. The United States is neither a member of the SCO nor an observer. More is said about these groupings near the end of this chapter.

2. For a description of this PLA Navy, Air Force, and 2nd Artillery modernization surge, see the author's testimony on Capitol Hill on 15 September 2005 before the U.S.-China Economic and Security Review Commission, available at www.uscc.org, or at www.ifpa.org/pdf/mcvadon.pdf. For an exhaustive but illuminating description by a non-American source of the PLAN program, see Mikhail Barabanov, "Contemporary Military Shipbuilding in China," *Eksport Vooruzheniy,* 1 FBIS CEP20050811949014, August 2005. This piece (perhaps unexpectedly) is a remarkably accurate and uniquely comprehensive open-source reference on the stunning surge in modernization of the PLAN.

3. C4ISR: command, control, communications, computers, intelligence, surveillance, and reconnaissance.

4. Office of the Secretary of Defense, Military Power of the People's Republic of China 2004, Annual Report to Congress, www.defenselink.mil/pubs/d20040528PRC.pdf), states on page 6: "China has continued to improve its potential for joint operations via development of an integrated command and control network, a new command structure, and improved C4ISR platforms. As in previous years, China's leaders realize that most of the PLA's C4ISR equipment lags generations behind that of the West and are encouraging a new generation of researchers, engineers, and officers to find ways to adapt to the demands of the modern battlefield. The acquisition of advanced C4ISR technology is one of the principal objectives of PRC collection activities."

5. David Shambaugh, *Modernizing China's Military: Progress, Problems, and Prospects* (Berkeley: University of California Press, 2002): "The PLA is still the party's army,

all officers above the rank of senior colonel are party members, and the CCP still institutionally penetrates the military apparatus" (32); "The rules of the game . . . have changed as a result of several developments: [among Shambaugh's listed developments]—Increased professionalism in the senior officer corps and a concomitant decline in the promotion of officers with backgrounds as political commissars" (46–47).

6. Paul H. B. Godwin, "China's Defense Establishment: The Hard Lessons of Incomplete Modernization," in *The Lessons of History: The Chinese People's Liberation Army at 75*, ed. Laurie Burkitt, Andrew Scobell, and Larry M. Wortzel (Carlisle, PA: U.S. Army War College, Strategic Studies Institute, July 2003), 33. Godwin states: "Officer recruitment has been changed to an emphasis on college graduates rather than selecting from the ranks of serving enlisted men and women, and advancement in rank now requires attendance at the appropriate PME schools."

7. Bernard D. Cole, "The Organization of the People's Liberation Army Navy (PLAN)," in *The People's Liberation Army as Organization: Reference Volume v1.0*, ed. James C. Mulvenon and Andrew N. D. Yang (Santa Monica, CA: RAND, 2002), 476. "The PLAN is emulating the U.S. reserve officer-training corps (ROTC) programs for producing well-educated, technically oriented candidate officers."

8. *Xinhua*, 17 August 1999, translated in FBIS-CHI-99–0817: "The Chinese navy plans to recruit about 1,000 officers from non-military universities and colleges yearly beginning this autumn in an effort to meet its need for command and technical talent. . . . [These officers] will account for 40 percent of all naval officers by the year 2010." This was originally cited in Cole, "Organization of the PLAN," 477.

9. Elizabeth Hague, "PLA Leadership in China's Military Regions," in *Civil-Military Change in China: Elites, Institutes, and Ideas after the 16th Party Congress*, ed. Andrew Scobell and Larry Wortzel (Carlisle, PA: U.S. Army War College, Strategic Studies Institute, September 2004). Two extracts from this chapter illustrate that party loyalty, *guanxi* (connections), and a reputation for not rocking the boat remain important in promotion decisions: "Several military region commanders have been promoted . . . to the national level. . . . In all cases they involve a candidate . . . valuable for a national-level position—*even when other factors, such as connections, were a strong factor in a promotion*" (247, emphasis original). Further, "Military leaders reflect PLA priorities, even in some cases when what the leader has to offer is continuity rather than new ideas or techniques" (250).

10. The author and another longtime American specialist on the PLAN were separately told of these organizational changes by knowledgeable PLAN officers.

11. The major exercise with the Russian navy in 2005 was in waters off the Shandong Peninsula. U.S. aircraft carrier strike groups would be very effective operating about 500 nautical miles (nm) from targets. Beijing might consider it prudent to confront the approaching forces at about 1,000 nm. Except for rare submarine patrols, the PLAN still seems to favor exercising in littoral waters rather than in a blue water environment beyond the Ryukyu Islands (Okinawa) that lie south of the Japanese main islands.

12. These exercises with foreign navies consisted of search-and-rescue drills, communications exercises, and even underway replenishment alongside in at least one case; however, conspicuously absent were tactical operations. Later exercises with Thailand and other ASEAN countries also had the goal of fostering bilateral relations, not of achieving operational capability.

13. Nikolay Petrov, "Moscow and Beijing Did Not Mention Their Loses [sic] That They Incurred during the Joint Maneuvers," Moscow Kommersant, FBIS CEP20051013330001, 8 September 2005. The following FBIS reports contain left-handed compliments and question PLA competence: "Chinese Army's 'Iron Discipline' Impresses Russian Defense Minister," Moscow RIA-Novosti, CEP20050825002002, 25 August 2005; "Russia: Results of Joint Military Exercise with China Assessed," Moscow Rossiya television, CEP20050927027016, 24 September 2005; "Russian TV Looks at Military Cooperation with China Post-Exercise," Moscow Zvezda television, CEP20050919027182, 19 September 2005.

14. "China-Russia: PRC Media on Sino-Russian Military Exercises Project Image of Converging Interests in Asia," FBIS Feature, FEA20050831007588, 31 August 2005. This analysis of the August 2005 Russian-Chinese exercise quotes the principal Chinese and Russian generals involved as saying the exercise represented "a major strategic decision of the Russian and Chinese leaders" aimed at deepening "strategic cooperative partnership"—a phrase described by the FBIS analyst as normally used to describe bilateral relations.

15. Richard Halloran, "Chinese Sub Highlights Underseas Rivalries," *Japan Times*, 30 November 2004, available at search.japantimes.co.jp/print/opinion/eo2004/eo20041130a1.htm.

16. Office of the Secretary of Defense, Military Power of the People's Republic of China 2004, Annual Report to Congress, 12–13, www.defenselink.mil/news/Jul2005/d20050719china.pdf. On MRBMs, see Mark A. Stokes, "Chinese Ballistic Missile Forces in the Age of Global Missile Defense: Challenges and Responses," in *China's Growing Military Power: Perspectives on Security, Ballistic Missiles, and Conventional Capabilities*, ed. Andrew Scobell and Larry M. Wortzel (Carlisle, PA: U.S. Army War College, Strategic Studies Institute, September 2002), 113, www.strategicstudies institute.army.mil/pdffiles/PUB59.pdf. The DF-21 family is also called the CSS-5. On SRBMs, see ibid., 116. The DF-15 and DF-11 families are also called the CSS-6 and CSS-7, respectively.

17. Stokes, "Chinese Ballistic Missile Forces," 150 (note).

18. See Eric A. McVadon, *Recent Trends in China's Military Modernization,* written statement prepared for testimony before the U.S.-China Economic and Security Review Commission, 15 September 2005, www.ifpa.org/pdf/mcvadon.pdf. The information was derived from many translated Chinese articles during recent years; sources can be identified for serious researchers.

19. Adm. Lowell E. Jacoby, Director, Defense Intelligence Agency, *Current and Projected National Security Threats to the United States,* statement (excerpted) to the Senate Select Committee on Intelligence, 24 February 2004, www.ransac.org/Official%20 Documents/U.S.%20Government/Intelligence%20Community/492004113202AM. html.

20. For Chinese analysis of challenges involved in realizing the concept, see 主特人: 海军军事学术研究所研究员 李杰 [Special Moderator: Li Jie, Naval Operations Research Center Researcher], "弹道导弹是航母的 '克星' 吗? (上)," [Is the Ballistic Missile a 'Silver Bullet' Against Aircraft Carriers? (Part 1 of 2)], 当代海军 [Modern Navy] (February 2008): 42–44, trans. Lyle Goldstein. The "conversation" in this piece seems to this author an anachronism. Other articles read over the years, but not available to the author any longer, have reflected success in Chinese theoretical work to design a MaRV that can indeed home on a target. This theoretical work, including computer simulations, was done using the concept developed by the United States for use in the Pershing II ballistic missile.

21. See Barabanov, "Contemporary Military Shipbuilding in China," for an open-source catalogue of PLAN modernization efforts.

22. John R. Benedict, "The Unraveling and Revitalization of U.S. Navy Antisubmarine Warfare," Naval War College Review 58, no. 2 (Spring 2005), 93–120. "The recent sale [to China] of eight additional Project 636 Kilos equipped with wake-homing antiship torpedoes and submerged-launch 3M54E Klub-S [the SS-N-27B] antiship cruise missiles is indicative of the transformation of this submarine force. The Project 636 Kilo 'is one of the quietest diesel submarines in the world' [quoting the U.S. Office of Naval Intelligence]; . . . the Klub-S missile has a 220-kilometer maximum range . . . and a terminal speed of up to Mach 3. Such a capability represents a very formidable threat to American and allied surface units" (102).

23. "Club-S / 3M-54E/E1 (SS-N-27) Anti-Ship Cruise Missile," http://www.sinodefence. com/navy/navalmissile/3m54.asp. This and several of the following citations from public sources usefully describe Chinese acquisitions and deployments; the varied character of these sources also illustrates that reasonably accurate descriptions of the ongoing PLA modernization are publicly available. The problem can be culling inaccurate reports; the author is often able to do so by asking knowledgeable PLA officers and through active exchanges with other diligent specialists.

24. "Russia to Deliver SS-N-27 to China," Chinese Defence Today, 29 April 2005, www. sinodefence.com/news/2005/news29-04-05.asp.

25. On quietness and sensors, see Zachary Moss, "Nuclear Submarines Worldwide: Current Force Structure and Future Developments," Bellona Nuclear Naval Vessels, 13 May 2004, www.bellona.no/en/international/russia/navy/northern_fleet/vessels/ 34070.html. On employment, see Globalsecurity.org, www.globalsecurity.org/military/library/report/2005/d20050719china.pdf. The U.S. Defense Department, in its 2005 Annual Report to the Congress: The Military Power of the People's Republic of China, states on page 33: "China is developing capabilities to achieve local sea denial, including . . . developing the Type-093 nuclear attack submarine for missions requiring greater at-sea endurance."

26. "Yuan Class Diesel-Electric Submarine," Chinese Defence Today, www.sinodefence. com/navy/sub/yuan.asp. For the Song class, "Type 039 Song Class Diesel-Electric Submarine," ibid., www.sinodefence.com/navy/sub/039.asp.

27. Jing-Dong Yuan, "Chinese Responses to U.S. Missile Defenses: Implications for Arms Control and Regional Security," *Nonproliferation Review* (Spring 2003): 89, cns.miis.edu/pubs/npr/vol10/101/101yuan.pdf.

28. This is a conservative estimate based on the author's acquaintance over fifteen years with the PLAN submarine force and discussions in recent years with others who have extensive experience concerning that force.

29. With respect to Taiwan's ASW capability and potential, the author drew on numerous exchanges with ROC naval officers and think-tankers over many years, including numerous visits to Taiwan's naval bases since 1996. For judgments on other aspects of the ASW environment, the author relied on his three decades of ASW experience piloting P-2 and P-3 antisubmarine aircraft (the major portion of which was with the U.S. Seventh Fleet in western Pacific waters) and commanding a P-3C squadron in the Pacific Fleet and U.S. and NATO ASW forces in Iceland.

30. The ASW situation for 2003 is described as "few new ASW sensor & weapon capabilities fielded to counter diesel subs in littorals"; Benedict, "Unraveling and Revitalization," 97, fig. 2. The U.S. Navy vice admiral commanding Atlantic submarine and ASW forces is quoted as saying, "Our ASW capabilities can best be described as poor or weak," and the Pacific Fleet commander as warning, "We will need greater ASW capability than we have today. . . . Future technologies are essential to counter the growing submarine threat"; ibid., 99–100.

31. For the Su-30, see Charles R. Smith, "New Chinese Jets Superior, Eagle Loses to Flanker," NewsMax.com, 26 May 2004, www.newsmax.com/archives/articles/2004/5/26/154053.shtml. This article illustrates that open sources were reporting this PLA naval air force acquisition and its antiship role soon after its purchase from Russia was consummated: "China is about to receive 24 advanced Sukhoi Su-30MK2 Flanker fighters from Russia. . . . The new Chinese fighters are reportedly equipped with enhanced anti-ship strike capabilities including the Kh-31 Krypton supersonic anti-ship missile. . . . The PLA Naval Air Corps will deploy the latest batch of Su-30MK2 fighters." For the B-6, see Robert S. Norris and Hans M. Kristensen, "Chinese Nuclear Forces, 2003," *2003 Bulletin of the Atomic Scientists* 59, no. 6 (November/December 2003): 77–80, www.thebulletin.org/article_nn.php?art_ofn=nd03norris. Using the Chinese designation for B-6—that is, H-6— this article states: "Although increasingly obsolete as a modern strike bomber, the H-6 may gain new life as a platform for China's emerging cruise missile capability. The naval air force has used the H-6 to carry the C-601/Kraken anti-ship cruise missile for more than 10 years, and Flight International reported in 2000 that up to 25 H-6s would be modified to carry four new YJ-63 land-attack cruise missiles." For the FB-7, see "JH-7 [Jianhong Fighter-Bomber] [FB-7]/FBC-1," Globalsecurity. org, 27 April 2005, www.globalsecurity.org/military/world/china/jh-7.htm: "China reportedly is developing an improved version of the FB-7. The twin-engine FB-7 is an all-weather, supersonic, medium-range fighter-bomber with an anti-ship mission. Improvements to the FB-7 likely will include a better radar, night attack avionics, and weapons." For ASCMs, see Nuclear Threat Initiative (NTI), *China's Cruise Missile Designations and Characteristics,* 26 March 2003, www.nti.org/db/china/

mimport.htm. This material is produced independently for NTI by the Center for Nonproliferation Studies at the Monterey Institute of International Studies.

32. "Naval Forces," *Strategy Page,* 20 March 2005, www.strategypage.com/htmw/ htsurf/articles/20050320.aspx. This source states: "The primary weapon of the *Sovremennyy* is the SS-N-22 Sunburn, a high-speed sea-skimming missile with a huge 660-pound warhead. The Sunburn is probably the best anti-ship missile in the world." This article is cited primarily to illustrate the widespread reputation of the Sunburn missile as lethal and evasive.

33. "Type 052C Luyang-II Class Missile Destroyer," http://www.sinodefence.com/navy/ surface/type052c_luyang2.asp. "Two Type 052C (NATO codename: Luyang-II class) air defence guided missile destroyers have been built by Jiangnan Shipyard of Shanghai for the PLA Navy. Based on the hull design of the Type 052B (Luyang class) multirole destroyer, the Type 052C features an indigenously developed four-array multifunction phased array radar (PAR) similar to the Aegis AN/SPY-1 equipped by the U.S. Arleigh Burke class and Japanese Kongo class DDG. The ship is also armed with the indigenous HQ-9 air defence missile system, which is believed to be comparable to the Russian S-300F/Rif in performance, and a newly developed anti-ship cruise missile (ASCM) designated YJ-62 (C-602)."

34. "The PLA Navy (PLAN) is engaged in an unprecedented level of construction and acquisition of major surface combatant ships. It currently is deploying seven new major ship classes at one time, building up to two new ships in each class per year. These include the Project 956 *Sovremenny*-class guided-missile destroyer (DDG); the Type 52B [Luyang I-class] DDG; the Type 52C [Luyang II-class], Aegis-like DDG; the Type 54 [Jiangkai-class] guided-missile frigate [NATO class names added]"; U.S.-China Economic and Security Review Commission annual report for 2005, chap. 3, sec. 1, based on testimony of expert witnesses, www.uscc.gov/annual_report/2005/chapter3_sec1.pdf. This list incorrectly implies that China is building the *Sovremennyys* acquired from Russia and omits the new Type 051C Luzhou-class destroyer, which has modern SAMs but lacks the Aegis-like radar. It also lacks a stealthy hull design and, like the *Sovremennyys*, has less modern steam propulsion (rather than the combination of gas turbine and diesel in both classes of Luyangs)— probably to keep costs down.

35. "Acquisition of modern ISR systems remains a critical aspect of Beijing's military modernization. China is developing its ISR capabilities based on domestic components, supplemented by foreign technology acquisition and procurement of complete foreign systems. PLA procurement of new space systems, AEW [airborne early warning] aircraft, long-range UAVs [unmanned aerial vehicles], and over-the-horizon radar will enhance its ability to detect, monitor, and target naval activity in the western Pacific Ocean. It appears, from writings on PLA exercises, that that this system currently lacks integration and that a fused, efficient ISR capability will not be achieved for many years"; Office of the Secretary of Defense, 2004, 43–44. See also Richard A. Bitzinger, "Come the Revolution: Transforming the Asia-Pacific's Militaries," *Naval War College Review* 58, no. 4 (Autumn 2005): 42–43, 46.

36. Kevin Pollpeter, "Motives and Implications behind China's ASAT Test," *China Brief* 7, no. 2 (24 January 2007), Jamestown Foundation, available at http://jamestown.org/publications_details.php?volume_id=422&issue_id=3983&article_id=2371834. Pollpeter states: "The United States government revealed on January 18 that the Chinese military had conducted an anti-satellite (ASAT) missile test against an aging Chinese weather satellite. . . . Yet, the ASAT test is just one of several provocative actions taken by China recently. In August 2006, National Reconnaissance Office Director Donald M. Kerr confirmed that a U.S. satellite had been painted by a Chinese laser."

37. For the saga of China and aircraft carrier acquisition, see Ian Storey and You Ji, "China's Aircraft Carrier Ambitions: Seeking Truth from Rumors," *Naval War College Review* 57, no. 1 (Winter 2004): 77–93.

38. On 1 April 2001, PLAN commander Wang Wei, in a typical two-aircraft reaction to a U.S. surveillance flight, launched along with his flight leader from Lingshui, intercepted, closed dangerously more than once and, then, through a combination of "hot dogging" and poor airmanship, collided from the left and beneath with a U.S. Navy EP-3 over international waters off Hainan Island. He ejected from his badly damaged F-8 aircraft but was not rescued. He had struck the larger aircraft's left outboard propeller, port aileron, and nose. As the author, a twenty-five-year P-3 pilot, understands it, the damaged EP-3 recovered from a dramatic descent caused by the collision and landed at Lingshui without normal flight controls and flaps (and lacking an airspeed indicator because of collision damage to the Pitot-static tube) and with one of its four engines and propellers not only inoperative but also windmilling uncontrollably, producing enormous drag that the pilots had to overcome using physical strength absent the normal hydraulic boost to the controls. (For readers who are aviators, this was a remarkable boost-out, 3-engine, no-flap landing with an overspeeding prop on the disabled outboard engine and no indicated airspeed! It was made at an unfamiliar and potentially hostile airfield; the cockpit was extremely noisy and unpressurized because of damage to the nose of the aircraft. The crew had reason to fear that other, even catastrophic, problems might develop from undetected additional damage.) The crew and aircraft were eventually returned to the United States. U.S. observers believe PRC weaknesses in crisis management were revealed in this incident; the leadership may never have received accurate reports of the circumstances of the collision. This suggests that problems persist in Chinese command and control that go beyond equipment shortcomings.

39. Ellen L. Frost, *Asia's New Regionalism* (Boulder, CO: Lynne Rienner Publishers, Inc., 2008), 1–3. Dr. Frost is an adjunct fellow at the Institute for National Strategic Studies at the U.S. National Defense University. She has held, among other pursuits, senior positions at the departments of State and Defense and with the U.S. Trade Representative.

40. The concentric circle model of the community process with ASEAN at the center, ASEAN +3 at the next band, and the East Asia Summit at the outer band is supported by the Second Joint Statement on East Asia Cooperation Building on the Foundations of ASEAN +3 Cooperation.

41. Frost, *Asia's New Regionalism*, 2.

Andrew S. Erickson and Lyle J. Goldstein

China Studies the Rise of Great Powers

A REMARKABLE CHINESE GOVERNMENT STUDY titled *Daguo Jueqi* (*The Rise of Great Powers*, 大国崛起) attempts to determine the reasons why nine nations (Portugal, Spain, the Netherlands, the United Kingdom, France, Germany, Japan, Russia, and the United States) became great powers. *The Rise of Great Powers* was apparently inspired by a 24 November 2003 Communist Party of China (CPC) Central Committee Political Bureau group session, "Study of Historical Development of Major Countries in the World since the 15th Century," reportedly following a directive from Chinese president Hu Jintao to determine which factors enabled major powers to grow most rapidly.[1] Hu is reported to have said at the session, "China, as a late-coming great nation, should learn from and draw upon the historical experience of the leading nations of the world in their modernization processes, as this will certainly be very beneficial to realizing the strategy of catching up and overtaking the leaders in modernization and achieving the great rejuvenation of the Chinese nation."[2]

Completed in 2006, the study draws on the analyses of many top Chinese scholars (including those at the Chinese Academy of Social Sciences and Beijing University's History Department), interviews with several hundred international political leaders and scholars, and the producers' onsite research in all nine nations. Some of the scholars reportedly briefed the

Politburo concerning their conclusions.³ As a twelve-part program twice broadcast on China Central Television (CCTV) and an eight-volume book series, *The Rise of Great Powers* has enjoyed considerable popular exposure in China.⁴ The first ten thousand copies of the book series sold out almost immediately.⁵ CCTV president Zhao Huayong states that his organization produced the series "for the development of the country, the rejuvenation of the nation."⁶ This chapter will analyze *The Rise of Great Powers* and other relevant Chinese writings for insights into the particular lessons that Beijing is drawing from other nations' previous attempts to master the maritime domain as well as the geopolitical results of those efforts.⁷

The Rise of Great Powers is not the first popular Chinese production to raise the issue of maritime development to the level of national popular discourse. In 1988 CCTV broadcast *He Shang* (*River Elegy*, 河殇), which used the theme of China's early development centering on the Yellow River to criticize "the mentality of a servile, static, and defensive people who always meekly hug to mother earth to eke out a miserable living, rather than boldly venturing forth on the dangerous deep blue sea in search of a freer, more exalted existence."⁸ This ethos, which was quite consistent with the initial "reform and opening up" (改革开放) ethic of the Deng Xiaoping era, challenged viewers to consider: "How can the 'yellow' culture of the earth be transformed into the 'blue' culture of the ocean?"⁹ Like *The Rise of Great Powers*, *River Elegy* suggested that China had much to learn from the West. *River Elegy* was later viewed by Chinese officials as having helped to inspire the 1989 Tiananmen Square demonstrations, however, and was subsequently banned.¹⁰ In this sense, it is significant that the far more sophisticated and intellectually nuanced *Rise of Great Powers* seeks to analyze the ascension to preeminence of foreign powers objectively, even citing the development of Western political systems and institutions as great national strengths rather than focusing on the harm caused by Western exertion of power, as has much Marxist-Leninist propaganda in the past.¹¹ This seemingly daring act appears to have attracted a small amount of controversy, particularly from Chinese leftist hard-liners, but is understandable when one examines the purpose of the series: not to recount past wrongs but to guide China's great power development, which cannot plausibly be linked to slavery or colonization.¹²

The Rise of Great Powers suggests that national power stems from economic development fueled by foreign trade, which can in turn be furthered by a strong navy. To see how the series' developers reached this conclusion, it is worthwhile to examine the initial and later sea powers detailed in the series, especially the land powers that attempted to become sea powers with varying degrees of success.[13] Where appropriate, the views of other Chinese scholars and analysts will also be considered.

Initial Global Sea Powers

To establish a contrast with the world land powers that are the focus of our analysis, we first examine how *The Rise of Great Powers* portrays world sea powers. The earliest examples are Portugal and Spain, which were ultimately limited by their focus on empire, and the Netherlands, which became a global economic juggernaut and appears to offer a model for China in some respects.

Portugal and Spain

Portugal and Spain are assessed by Chinese scholars to have initially realized global power by achieving internal unity at a time when the rest of Europe lacked it, which enabled them to embark on naval expansion.[14] When the land-focused Ottoman Empire blocked Iberian access to the spice trade, strong economic imperative emerged to develop a sea route. As People's Liberation Army Air Force (PLAAF) colonel Dai Xu points out, "Portugal, the first [global] power in modern history, suddenly developed an interest in the sea in 1415 when she conquered Cueta, an important place for transportation between the Mediterranean Sea and the Atlantic Ocean."[15] Portugal achieved technological breakthroughs by inventing new boats and developing navigation science, which helped it to wrest control of trade from Italy and circumnavigate the Cape of Good Hope in 1487. This "national project" was systematically organized. Portugal's future lay in taking "the sea road" (海上之路) and "conquering the vast ocean" (征服大海). Just as China's influence disappeared from the seas, "Portugal's big maritime discoveries . . . [emerged as] a well-conceived and well-organized national strategy."[16]

Spain likewise embarked on maritime expansion. As Colonel Dai points out, "Stimulated by her neighbor Portugal, Spain also withdrew from the endless conquests over the European continent and began her adventure on the sea, initiating the overseas conquests."[17] Spain became a "strong enemy" (强大对手) for Portugal after Queen Isabella seized Granada, thereby ending Islamic attempts at control of the Iberian peninsula and providing the requisite internal unity, "strength" (实力), and "determination" (决心). "On 12 October 1492," the CCTV film series relates, "the Atlantic's strong trade wind sent Columbus' fleet to the new continent it had dreamed to reach, blowing away the invisible barriers that separated all the continents. . . . It was those mariners' passion that cleaved the tranquil blue waters. To pursue wealth, they and their ships, loaded with goods, cannons and other weapons, started the journeys of building big nations."[18] The ability of a unified Spain to value and support Columbus' efforts paid great dividends for national power: "When Columbus with his navigation plan bargained with the Spanish royal court, Queen Isabella accepted his request, even though he was a common man. To finance Columbus' seafaring trip, she even sold the jewelry on her crown. However, what she won back was a crown with even greater luster. It was the laurel of a world overlord."[19]

By the late 1500s, however, Portugal and Spain are assessed to have squandered their great power status by waging wars in the defense of far-flung colonial empires, and importing expensive products, rather than focusing on their own intensive economic development and raising living standards at home. The obvious lesson for China is that naval development in the absence of robust maritime commerce and internal growth is unsustainable. Colonel Dai blames Spain's decline on the neglect of sea power: "With mere foresight, Spain had once chosen the move toward the sea, which benefitted her greatly, but the country did not further develop military theories of marine control, because of her comparatively shallow knowledge of sea power. As a result, not having gone further, the unrivaled fleet had followed the same old road of the Ottomans to ruin—in just 17 years. We can see: an empire declined once its navy failed."[20] Ye Zicheng, a prominent Beijing University scholar whose landpower-centric theories were surveyed in the introductory chapter, draws another lesson: "The rise of the Spanish Empire indeed achieved success through relying on sea power, but the history of Spain also shows that without land power, sea power cannot prop up the international status of a leading power for long."[21]

The Netherlands

The Rise of Great Powers pointedly notes that while Spain and Portugal depended on military force as a key element of their rise as maritime powers, Holland relied on commerce and became a "global commercial empire" (全世界的商业大国). It is quite possible that the authors of the series are using this parallel to frame China's rising maritime power as commercial rather than military in nature.[22]

The Netherlands' rise was driven by commercial maritime development. Export of herring generated significant profits, thereby permitting the con-

struction of canals and turning the loose coalition of city-states run by feudal lords into a "key hub" (集散地), with Rotterdam as the world's premier
port. This infrastructure renaissance, in turn, allowed the Dutch to serve as
middlemen in trade (e.g., of Portuguese gold and spice). More than eighteen
hundred unarmed Dutch ships—lighter, cheaper, and of higher capacity than
their British counterparts—ferried goods throughout Europe. This commerce
in turn fueled the ascendance to power of merchant elites who further supported maritime-oriented policies.

Were the Dutch experience to end here, the lesson for China might be
to pursue trade to the exclusion of politics and naval development. But military technological innovations (e.g., gunpowder) made it impossible for the
Netherlands to escape intra-European power struggles. Later, with fifteen
thousand branches and ten thousand ships, the Dutch East India Company
captured half of world trade. An analyst at Beijing's influential Navy Research
Institute likewise notes that "seventeenth century Holland, with its incomparable 'Chariots on the Sea' opened up colonial regions that spanned as far as
Asia, Africa, America and Oceania, controlling sea channels and four-fifths
of the world's trade volume."[23] Wealthy Amsterdam seized control of Taiwan
and Indonesia (the latter as a colony) and monopolized trade with Japan.
In 1656 Dutch representatives arrived in Beijing and prostrated themselves
before Qing Dynasty emperor Shunzhi. At the time, the Chinese interpreted
this to mean that for the Dutch, "the great interest was making money"
(重大利益赚钱). The ultimate lesson for China from the Dutch experience would seem to be that trade produces wealth and power but that some
degree of naval forces is necessary to safeguard it.

Later Sea Powers

The modern world sea powers surveyed by *The Rise of Great Powers* are
the United Kingdom, Japan, and the United States. The United Kingdom
and the United States are viewed as success stories with valuable lessons for
China, whereas Japan's aggressive attempt to rise rapidly on the seas, despite
its undeniable achievements, is viewed as a terrible failure.

United Kingdom

"How did such a small island transform itself and influence the world?"
asks *The Rise of Great Powers*.[24] Britain, like the United States later, is assessed
to have achieved this rapid accretion of power thanks to economic growth

driven by innovation. "England . . . put great effort into developing a power-ful navy, and defeated Holland through three wars," notes a Chinese military researcher.[25] Elizabeth I helped to catalyze Britain's rise by encouraging pri-vateers to attack Spanish shipping. Anglo-Spanish religious wars ended with British victory in 1588 when Spain's Armada was defeated by lighter ships with better firepower. Spain persisted for five more decades as a great power, but this naval victory clearly marked Britain's rise as a "maritime power" (海上强国).

Much is made of Britain's internal consolidation facilitated by such polit-ical innovations as the Magna Carta, which sustained Britain's great power rise and facilitated rapid economic development. Overseas trade expan-sion, which fueled Britain's rise, was facilitated by Britain's subsequent use of both naval power and the eighteenth century "Navigation Acts" (航海法), intended to give preference to British commercial shipping to eliminate Dutch and French maritime commercial competition. Britain thus won both "the competition for sea power" (海上竞争) and "the competition among the great powers" (大国竞争). This, in turn, enabled London to become a "world power."

The Industrial Revolution, scientific and technical innovation, patents (rule of law), and laissez faire capitalism made Britain the "workshop of the world" and enabled it to defeat rival Napoleonic France, whose military uni-forms and other provisions were British-made. By the time Britain hosted the World's Fair in 1852, it produced more iron products than the rest of world combined, two-thirds of world coal, and 50 percent of world textiles. This achievement marked Britain's zenith, however, and it had already begun slow decline as increasingly unprofitable colonial acquisitions produced imperial overstretch. Following World War II, Britain decided to relinquish its territo-ries to improve national living standards.

For Ye Zicheng, England's rise cannot be ascribed to sea power alone, however:

> The emergence of England as the first world power of truly world-wide significance did not just depend on the development of sea power and its sea power superiority. Without the great revolution, the industrial revolution, and the parliamentary democracy system in England's land space, England would not have had the status of a world power. . . . Britain still has strong sea power today, which to a certain extent props up Britain's great power status, but due to the limitations of the development of its land space, Britain can cer-

tainly not become a powerful land power, or else the strong points of its land power development are not as strong as those of other land powers, hence Britain is now losing and is bound to lose its world power status.[26]

Chinese appraisals of the Falklands War demonstrate a keen awareness of the Royal Navy's weaknesses in that campaign.[27]

Japan

Chinese analysts assess that, like Germany and Russia, Japan suffered from institutional defects that compromised its ability to succeed as a late-modernizer. As with Germany, a policy of external aggression is cited as a major reason for Japan's failure to realize its imperial ambitions. These lessons have been emphasized repeatedly by Chinese policy makers and scholars alike.[28] Qinghua University's Yan Xuetong points out that coordinated containment by other nations can hinder the rise of a great power.[29] Rather than focusing on Japan's anti-Chinese atrocities, however, *The Rise of Great Powers* dwells instead on Japan's constitutional-monarchy-led internal modernization following the Meiji Restoration, which enabled it to avoid Western domination until imperial overstretch provoked war with the United States.[30]

In its "one-hundred-year road to great powerhood" (一百年的大国之路), Japan became the first Asian country to resist Western colonialism, industrialize, and colonize others. In 1853, however, Japan's leaders ultimately decided not to resist the black ships of Admiral Perry when he came to open Japan for trade and to seize control of Pacific shipping routes. Perry believed that Japan might eventually come to rival the United States in terms of national power. This "pressure from abroad and chaos within" (外忧内患) triggered the Meiji Restoration in 1868. Rapid, far-reaching internal reforms commenced. In 1871 forty-nine high officials (more than half Japan's government) joined the Iwakura Mission to visit America and Europe. In Germany they found the model system they sought, one in which the government led industrialization to catch up to earlier modernizers. Chinese analysts note that they listened intently to Bismarck, who declared that despite all the diplomatic niceties, the world was still a place where the strong oppressed the weak.

In addition to importing substantial commercial and military technology, Japan supported small businesses, notably Mitsubishi, which by 1875 had taken over the Tokyo-Shanghai shipping route. Despite rapid, wide-ranging internal reforms culminating in the "Constitution of the Empire of Japan," however, Japan still lagged behind the West. Accordingly, in 1889 Tokyo began to "develop through war" (通过战争来发展). This "militaristic emphasis" occurred under the rubric of "Enrich the Country, Strengthen the Military"—"富国強兵."

The Rise of Great Powers emphasizes that naval development was central to Japan's expansionism: Following the 1895 war, in addition to colonizing Taiwan, the Chinese documentary asserts that Japan took four times as much from China in reparations as annual government expenditure and invested half of that into its own navy. This investment paid off in 1905 with victory in the Russo-Japanese War.[31] Japan then colonized the Korean Peninsula.[32] In World War II, Japan expanded into the Pacific and Indian Oceans.[33] But this progress was short-lived, and the atomic bombing and surrender ceremony on the deck of USS *Missouri* followed in 1945. According to Zhang Wenmu, the Beijing University of Aeronautics & Astronautics scholar whose seapower-centric writings were surveyed in the introductory chapter, "Japan's defeat was to a large extent the result of the Japanese people taking on the United States at sea. Once Japan lost its control of the sea in the Pacific, it was doomed to defeat."[34] A "Peace Constitution" (和平宪法) demoted Japan's emperor to symbolic status and imposed categorical military limitations. Rapid economic growth, however, made Japan the world's third largest economy by 1968 and the second largest today.

In contrast to Zhang Wenmu, Ye Zicheng believes that Japan failed disastrously in World War II because this natural sea power tried to become a land power:

> Japan is relatively distant from the east Asian continent; it is also homogenous, and relatively lacking in natural resources; this aspect has been prone to shape the Japanese nation's independent nature, and another aspect has created the rootless cultural characteristic of the Japanese nation in following the tide. The former aspect meant that Japan very early on refused to join the east Asian system centered on China, and the latter caused the Japanese nation to lose its way and embark on a deviant path in the process of developing sea power, becoming a big scourge to Asian and world peace, and doing tremendous damage to the countries of east Asia, especially China and north and south Korea.[35]

Then, "in 1907 Japan decided to develop both sea and land power, simultaneously developing the navy and the army; the main objective for the army would be to repulse Russia, the land power on the Eurasian continent, while the building of the navy would have the U.S. sea power as the imaginary enemy. It was precisely Japan's continental strategy and strategy of turning itself into a continental country that led to its final defeat. Japan's switch also ended in failure."[36]

United States

The Rise of Great Powers marvels at how the United States became a great power in only 230 years of history, built independently on the base of European civilization enriched with subsequent immigrant contributions from all over the world, protected by a foresighted constitution, and driven by a culture of industry and self-reliance.[37] By 1860 the U.S. economy was already bigger than that of most European powers. The peaceful environment that the United States enjoyed following the Civil War is credited with providing the conditions necessary for it to develop into a superpower. A culture of invention during the second industrial revolution transformed the United States from a student of European technology to an innovator in its own right.[38] By 1894, 118 years after its founding, the United States had become the world's largest economy. According to Wang Jisi, Beijing University professor and president of the Institute of International Strategy under the Party School of the CPC Central Committee, "in 1894 the United States was already the world's number one power."[39]

Meanwhile, as a senior colonel at Beijing's Navy Research Institute concludes, "Mahan's sea power theory directly supported 20th century America's abrupt rise."[40] PLAN senior captain Xu Qi agrees: "[The United States] benefited from the guidance of Mahan's theories of sea power, and unceasingly pressed forward in the maritime direction . . . [thus] establishing a firm foundation for its move into the world's first-rank powers.[41] PLAAF Col. Dai Xu goes even further: "America introduced the term 'sea power' and the United States was also the first country to realize the secret of sea power. Exactly because of holding such a secret, the United States has gradually approached being a superpower and accomplishing world hegemony."[42] Whereas the CCTV film series ignores Mahan's contribution to the rapid rise of American sea power, the book series devotes a section to it. Mahan's writings are reviewed in some detail, with a focus on his complaint that while England and Japan had powerful navies and "China also has a modern 'Beiyang' fleet . . . the U.S. Navy stands twelfth in the world, and must pursue [the others] with force and spirit."[43] Mahan is credited with inspiring Congress to appropriate funds for naval construction in 1890 such that within five years the U.S. Navy was fifth in the world. By 1898, when the United States vanquished the Spanish fleet in Manila Harbor, thus capturing the Philippines, Guam, and Puerto Rico, America's ascension to sea power dominance was indisputable: "500 years before, the Spaniards had found the new continent of America. Now, this rising New World country had defeated its discoverers by revealing its cutting edge battleships to the world for the first time. On the North American continent, this promising youth, obsessed with ambition, sized up the world, and its warships flying star-spangled flags frequently appeared in the world's five oceans. Already, the world could not ignore America's influence."[44]

World War I further stimulated the U.S. economy by generating large-scale European weapons and steel orders and left the United States with 40 percent of the world's wealth. Following President Wilson's subsequent failure to remake the international order, "the United States' geopolitical advantages that allowed it to advance or retreat freely were once again manifested. It shifted its focus back to the American continent and concentrated on its own matters."[45] After World War II, whose naval battles are depicted only briefly, the United States emerged triumphant: "The participation of the United States, as the number one economic and military power, was undoubtedly decisive for the victory of the antifascist war."[46] In the new world order that unfolded at Yalta, "the gross industrial output value of the United States accounted for more than half of the world total and a dollar-centric international financial system was established worldwide," giving the United States "leadership status" (领导地位).[47] Washington "also sent troops to 50 countries and territories around the world and had them stationed there."[48] It began to dominate the international order in a way that was beneficial to itself and, in the latter part of the twentieth century, eventually became a superpower (超级大国). Wang Jisi has cautioned, "Wars did accompany the rise of the United States, but we cannot say it became powerful through war. The notion that the rise of a world power is inevitably accompanied by wars is erroneous."[49]

To Ye Zicheng, the role of land power in America's rise should not be underestimated: "The United States first embarked on the power road by land power expansion and development; the political system established in its early years became the strong and firm foundation for the later United States."[50] Ye posits that nations must develop within their natural endowments, which typically dictate a maritime or continental focus:

One can say that there have been few successful examples in history of switching from sea to land power. The United States may appear now to be an exception. The United States was mainly a land power from its founding up to the 1890s, when it started its switch process and vigorously developed sea power. . . . The United States then became a world power, very strong in both land and sea power. . . . However, the past success of the United States does not mean that it was also successful later. The United States today seems to be starting a second switch. It is not content with only possessing land power on the American continent, but also wants to possess land power on the Eurasian continent and become a sea and land power with land power on both the American and Eurasian continents. . . . Can U.S. success continue? No. This is because U.S. actions have gone far beyond the strategic potential given it by its natural endowment.[51]

Ye predicts that "if land power does not develop well, U.S. influence abroad is bound to greatly shrink, and the so-called U.S. hegemony will ebb away; [but] if no major problems emerge in U.S. land power development, its international influence may be maintained for a very long time.[52]

Land Powers

Land powers are naturally of greatest interest in this book because the focus is how land powers are able or are not able to transition into sea powers. It is therefore worthwhile to examine these cases and see what insights can be gleaned from this comprehensive Chinese survey to gain at least a partial understanding of how the Chinese conceptualize sea power as an element in the rise of great powers and their prospects for transition.

France

In this discussion of French history, the continental nature of its power is emphasized from the start.[53] Indeed, the title of the chapter on France in the main study compilation refers to France as a "continental power" (陆上强权).[54] Louis XIV is credited with building up France's science, technology, and national power to the point that it played a role in the international system at that time comparable to the role played by the United States today.[55]

France's position vis-à-vis sea power arises primarily in the context of analysis of the Napoleonic wars. According to this analysis, Britain was gravely troubled in 1802 when France closed Dutch and Italian ports to British trade and set the shipyards to work with the goal of doubling the size of the French Navy.[56] The Trafalgar victory for England in 1805, noted by the Chinese analysis to have occurred against superior numbers, spelled the end of France's quest to match Britain at sea.[57] Neither Britain nor France could decisively defeat the other's strength, so the Chinese analysis observes that their war became one of blockade and counterblockade—in essence, economic warfare.[58] As PLAN senior captain Xu Qi observes, "At the end of the eighteenth century, Napoleon sought to expel England from the European continent, and toward that end advanced into the Mediterranean on the southern flank and attempted to cut England off from its foreign markets and natural resources by way of the Persian Gulf.[59]

In a dictum with resonance in contemporary Chinese strategy, Napoleon is quoted in *The Rise of Great Powers* as saying to his brother that he intended to "use the land to conquer the sea" (用陆地征服海洋).[60] In evaluating Napoleon's intention to defeat Britain by cutting it off from crucial continental markets, the Chinese analysts do credit France with creating difficulties for Britain in 1807–8. Nevertheless, British sea power is viewed as being decisive in routing the so-called Continental System. By the Chinese account, Napoleon's strategy was defeated because England was a strong naval power that relied on its mighty fleets in the North Sea, the Mediterranean, and even along the French coast, for which France, despite its having conquered much of Western Europe with "military power" (军事力量), remained "without any option" (无可奈何). It is recognized, however, that Britain's financial and industrial prowess were also key to its eventual victory.[61]

There is no further mention of sea power in the discussion of France. Still, France once again found itself the dominant continental power in Europe after World War I.[62] At that time, however, France's role was quickly surpassed because, the Chinese analysis contends, Paris no longer had the will to dominate as had Louis XIV or Napoleon. Likewise, its rapid defeat by Hitler's Germany is put down to a deleterious national sense of being "in no hurry to fight" (快不再战).[63] Indeed, the concept of appeasement has developed its own place in Chinese discourse concerning the use of force.[64]

It is also noted that France and China have enjoyed somewhat similar modern histories and culture. Like Beijing, Paris has "[taken] an independent road" [唯一道路] in the postwar years, developing "an independent industrial system" complete with "aviation and nuclear industries."[65]

Germany

The discussion of German history in *The Rise of Great Powers* has little focus on Germany's shortcomings in the maritime domain. Nevertheless, the analysis is still noteworthy because of the lessons Chinese analysts appear to draw regarding the imperative of national unification, on the one hand, and caution regarding the use of force, on the other.[66]

Germans are depicted as a people who are courageous, tough, and skilled at warfare, owing largely to their history of continuous military conflict.[67] The description of Frederick the Great relates his cold calculations to serve the national interest, noting that this logic could justify breaking any treaty and launching any attack.[68] Indeed, the theme of Prussia's militarization is emphasized when the common adage appears noting that Prussia was not a state with an army but rather an army with a state.[69] After a recounting of the wars of German unification in some detail, Bismarck is described in glowing terms as the principle architect of German unification: "Overall, the unification of Germany represented progress as a historical fact, because it was a requirement of modern development, and Bismarck's activities were in conformity with the wave of modern development."[70] In a depiction with possible significance for Beijing's evaluation of Taiwan's future, it is emphasized that Bismarck succeeded with "iron and blood" (铁与血) where the peaceful revolutionaries of 1848 had failed.

The analysis then turns to explain how Germany turned toward a wayward and self-destructive path in the late nineteenth and early twentieth centuries. While Germany's "military focus" (军事注意) started with Bismarck, he preserved peace in Europe by maintaining the balance of power and not overexpanding. In a shift with some echoes in contemporary Chinese foreign policy (at least from a Western perspective), Berlin under Kaiser Wilhelm is described in 1890 as altering its foreign policy "from a 'continental policy' to a 'global policy'" ("大陆政策" 向 "世界政策"). It is related that German leaders desired "living space," viewed their existing territory as being too small, and also sought a "place in the sun" for Germany. Meanwhile, "the German government continuously increased its military expenditures." The enormous naval building program of Adm. Alfred von Tirpitz is mentioned in this context.[71]

The Chinese discussion of the world wars observes that the earlier wars of German unification had convinced Berlin (wrongly) that another war would also be short.[72] In a thinly veiled critique of democratic norms, the analysis notes that the German decision for war in 1914 was intensely popular.[73] Although Anglo-German commercial rivalry is mentioned as a cause of World War I, it is somewhat surprising that no mention is made of the extensive Anglo-German naval arms race that preceded this conflict.[74] Little is said about German naval power before and during World War II except to note that German submarines "did not achieve their anticipated goal" of knocking Britain out of the war.[75]

Ultimately, this Chinese discussion of Germany's rise as a great power concludes: "Germany's economic development, especially its education and technological development, provide a rich experience for us. However, once Germany had become powerful, it became an upstart, had difficulty in finding its place, and as a result its excess of power was channeled into a path of expansion, belligerence and destruction."[76]

It is recognized that Germany's difficult geostrategic situation—located in the heart of Europe—rendered it subject to intense pressures.[77] But the primary lesson for China of Germany's travails is to "always choose the path of peaceful development."[78] *The Rise of Great Powers* draws a larger lesson for China from the German legacy: "So far there is yet to have any precedence of any emerging big power defeating a hegemonic power directly. The rise and decline of Germany was a historical legacy that all big powers must contemplate deeply. . . . When this emerging big power adopted the parity principle that big European powers were following, it developed rapidly in a peaceful environment and became the leading economic power in Europe. However, just when it attempted to assert its turf under the sun, it met disastrous defeat."[79] Any contradiction between this point and the prior endorsement of Bismarck's belligerent unification policies is not addressed.

Russia

The Chinese discussion of modern Russian history provides the most focused assessment of maritime transformation by a traditional continental power.[80] This analysis concentrates heavily on the leadership of Peter the Great, who is described as being fully dedicated to establishing Russia as a maritime power.[81] According to this history of Russia, Muscovy grew powerful because the city lay proximate to rivers that were crucial thoroughfares for people and goods. Nevertheless, Russia's agrarian economy, as that of a "landlocked country" (内陆国家), was restricted by limited transport routes and so remained backward. "The only way to alter this situation was to capture ports, and for this war was the only option."[82] In fact, during the thirty-six year reign of Peter the Great, Russia fought fifty-three wars.[83]

To reach the sea, Peter needed a strong military to confront the strong power on its northern flank, Sweden, as well as the strong power on its southern flank, the Ottoman Empire. The Chinese analysis observes admiringly that Peter achieved progress in military development at a rapid pace.[84] Peter's time abroad (especially in Holland) was crucial to informing his perspective regarding Russia's relative weaknesses. In a description analogous to contemporary China, Peter is praised for having insisted that Russia open itself to foreign ideas and influences. In particular, he stressed the imperative to study the development of foreign militaries, to import foreign military equipment, and to call upon foreign experts. Russian students were also sent abroad more frequently to study foreign military methods.[85] The discussion also notes Peter's success in creating a foreign policy that complemented his military strategy (e.g., in the Northern War against Sweden, which Russia defeated in 1709).[86] In 1713 Peter built his cosmopolitan, Westernized capital of St. Petersburg on land captured in that war.

A critical component of Peter's broadly successful strategy, according to the Chinese analysis, was the building of Russia's first navy, with its own academy. After his return from Holland, where he personally observed how the European powers were "prosperous and strong" (富强), Peter was utterly determined to seize a port on the Baltic Sea to open Russia to commercial and cultural interaction with Western Europe.[87] He is quoted as saying "our country needs the sea—without a port, we cannot survive."[88] To this end, Peter emphasized the importing of modern shipbuilding and navigation technology. Between 1706 and 1725, Russia launched forty full-size battleships in addition to almost one thousand smaller vessels. With naval power, it is suggested, the Russian state was no longer dependent on a single hand but rather had two hands (land and sea power) with which to fulfill its ambitions.[89] This initial Russian progress is recognized by PLAN senior captain Xu Qi: "As early as the reign of Peter the Great, Russia initiated a military struggle to gain access to the sea. It successively achieved access to seaports along its northern flank and expanded its influence to the Black Sea and the Persian Gulf, even contending for the Black Sea Straits, as well as nibbling at the Balkan Peninsula."[90] While amply crediting Peter for modernizing Russia and establishing it as a sea power, the Chinese analysis also observes that the Russian navy all but disappeared after Peter's death because its capabilities were not maintained.[91]

The role of sea power in Russian history after Peter is not seriously explored in the book series. It is noted that Russia emerged as the dominant European continental power in the wake of Napoleon's demise.[92] Catherine,

who assumed power in 1762, embraced much of Peter's ideology as a proponent of the "Western faction" over the "Slavic faction." Like Peter, she turned
to military conquest to expand Russia's power and influence, seizing a Black
Sea port, Poland, and even Alaska. It is implied that the emancipation of serfs
enabled industrialization and military expansion. In the 1856 Crimean War,
however, Russia is said to have been forced to confront the powerful armored
fleets of Britain and France with mere wooden sailing ships, thereby ensuring
its defeat.[93] Russia's "catastrophic vanquishment" at the hands of the upstart
Japan in 1905 is likewise mentioned, but not described in any detail.[94]

Like Russia, the USSR is described as a power that was continuously striving toward the sea.[95] In the years following the Revolution of 1917, Moscow
used not "military power" (武力) but "national power" (国力) to further
internal development. As this Chinese analysis indicates, however, the Soviet
Union reached the apex of its power in the 1970s but failed at that time to pay
adequate attention to its own people's standard of living, preferring instead
to lavish resources on its military rivalry with the United States.[96] A wide
body of scholarship and policy statements indicate that China is determined
not to repeat this mistake.[97] As Zhou Yan, executive writer-director of the
CCTV documentary series notes, "if a country is economically undeveloped
it will find it very hard to rise."[98]

Not only did the USSR reach parity with the United States in nuclear
weapons, it also exceeded the United States in numbers of tanks. As for the
Soviet Navy, the analysis notes that it was active on all the world's three major
oceans and began to hold global exercises that demonstrated its strength.[99]
Cumulatively, the Russian case is especially interesting for Beijing because it
is a case of a land power with a similar governmental system making a concerted, if ineffectual, effort to transform into a maritime power.

In the view of Ye Zicheng, Moscow's failure stemmed from trying to
become a sea power when it was naturally more of a land power. "The size of
the Soviet Navy ranked second in the world at one time, and was three times
that of the British fleet. Eventually, however, the Soviet Union's switch ended
in failure. Many Soviet aircraft carriers were sold to other countries for scrap,
becoming theme park vehicles. The development of Soviet naval power did
not leave behind any inheritable legacy for Russia, and Russia now remains a
mainly land power."[100] PLAAF colonel Dai Xu has a different interpretation:
Following the collapse of the Soviet Union in 1991, "Russia painfully realized
that no country can be a long-term power without sea power."[101]

Conclusion

The *Rise of Great Powers* project is an ambitious, timely, sophisticated, and surprisingly objective study of one of China's greatest challenges: accomplishing the rise of China without precipitating devastating conflict in the international system. Indeed, *The Rise of Great Powers* reflects China's new technocratic society at its best because it demonstrates a new will and capability to look outward for lessons applicable to China's new situation. And this project does so in a deep and integrated way (over the course of several well-edited volumes prepared by disciplined and focused research teams), rather than a shallow and subjective approach. The overall findings can be summarized as emphasizing the importance of (a) internal unity; (b) market mechanisms; (c) related ideological, scientific, and institutional innovation; and (d) international peace.

This chapter does not attempt a comprehensive summary of the findings of *The Rise of Great Powers*, however. Rather, this chapter surveys the study's notions of sea power to gauge how this project might affect a future Chinese transformation into a full-fledged maritime power. Although *The Rise of Great Powers* does not itself assert direct findings related to sea power (which is in itself an interesting conclusion), the case studies that comprise it nevertheless do make ample observations with respect to maritime power that have been revealed in this research effort.

In studying the rise of Britain, the United States, and Japan, any historical study is likely to question of the role of sea power. As is the case for the rest of this volume, we define "sea power" here to mean not only explicit naval strength but also the commerce and shipping that underpin it. Sea power is not an end in itself but a medium for trade and a source of national security. In some cases, maritime power is useful primarily as a means to trade (as when Portugal's land trade route was cut off by the Ottomans). Yet, as the commercially proficient Dutch discovered painfully, trade must be secured from foreign threats. In this sense, naval power is necessary even if it is not needed for trade per se.

In reviewing British history, for example, it is not surprising that the study emphasizes London's use of the Navigation Acts, coupled with naval power, to eliminate Dutch and French maritime commercial competition. With respect to the United States, the authors of *The Rise of Great Powers* observe that Washington enjoyed "the geopolitical advantages [and by inference the necessary naval power] that allowed it to advance and retreat freely."[102] Similarly, the major investment in naval expansion made by Tokyo after the Sino-Japanese War is described as paying major dividends during the Russo-Japanese War, and especially at the all-important naval victory in the Tsushima Straits.[103] The role of sea power is even more pronounced in other historical case studies. For example, regarding Portugal, *The Rise of Great Powers* notes that just as China's influence disappeared from the seas, "Portugal's big maritime discoveries . . . [emerged as] a well-conceived and well-organized national strategy."[104] Similarly for Spain, Madrid's willingness to support Columbus' maritime discoveries is described as a risky investment with a massive payoff for Spain's national power. Sea power is also discussed in the context of exploring the ascent of various land powers. While Napoleon intended to "use the land to conquer the sea," in the end Paris was left "without any option" to contest Britain's power on the seas.[105] Somewhat contrary to its wider conclusions, the legacy of Bismarck (especially in the context of national unification) is thoroughly praised, but Germany's clumsy attempts to develop and wield naval power are criticized in *The Rise of Great Powers*. The description of Russia's development as a great power may be the most relevant to the maritime transformation question. Indeed, Peter the Great's quest to develop ports for international trade is described as a major impetus for Russia's rise. Ultimately, however, the capability of the USSR to field fleets on all the world's oceans, impressive as it might have been, is discredited in *The Rise of Great Powers* because of its part in Moscow's larger tendency "to lavish resources on its military rivalry with the United States."[106]

Undoubtedly, a major conclusion of *The Rise of Great Powers* is the fundamental value of the market and international trade as drivers for national development and consequently national power. For example, one historian is cited in the study explaining that "only three countries in the past 500 years could claim that they had dominated the world—the Netherlands, Britain and the United States. Like taking part in a relay race, these three countries renewed and developed the market economy."[107] The essential link between maritime commerce and national development is very clear in the context of *The Rise of Great Powers*' exploration of the Netherlands' rise to preeminence: "During the 17th century, the Netherlands, which has an area about half the size of Beijing, created a commercial empire that dominated the world because of the financial and commercial institutions it had created."[108]

Observing in *The Rise of Great Powers* that the Netherlands' commercial power was superseded with remarkable rapidity by the upstart British in part because of a lack of robust naval power, a possible conclusion is certainly that Chinese commercial power cannot develop wholly independently of national military capabilities, including a blue water fleet. PLAN analysts unquestionably view commercial and naval power as creating a virtuous circle: "The booming maritime economy will surely advance and drive the progress of a navy with high-tech. On the other hand, a navy with high-tech can also protect, drive and advance the maritime economy."[109]

In conclusion, then, *The Rise of Great Powers* suggests that developing maritime power is necessary but not sufficient to support the rise of a great power. A great power's rise, which may be underwritten by such other factors as industrialization, innovation, and an effective political system, can support naval development, but naval development only seems to support a great power's rise if it is part of a larger flourishing of economic development and trade. Such nations as Portugal and the Soviet Union tried to further their national power by selectively developing the military component of maritime power but ultimately failed because of a lack of dynamic economic activity. China is clearly avoiding this strategic error; indeed, its commercial maritime development is proceeding much more rapidly and broadly than its naval development. Perhaps in this way China can finally follow the injunction of Li Hongzhang from the Qing-era Self-Strengthening Movement to "place equal emphasis on wealth and strength, use wealth to promote strength, use strength to protect wealth" (富与强并重, 以富促强, 以强保富).[110] By thus balancing economic and military development, China may rise to great power status sustainably and with minimal foreign opposition.

This is a positive sign—for China, the United States, and the rest of the world. Western analysts and officials should welcome the findings of *The Rise of Great Powers* project because it uses sound historical research methods to chart a path for China's peaceful rise—one that is careful to avoid military conflicts that could derail its development path. Still, it must be emphasized that the study's findings also may serve to support China's continued dynamic development of its new maritime inclinations. Further research should be done to see what lessons Chinese leaders take from the series.

Notes

This chapter represents only the authors' personal opinions and not the policies or analyses of the U.S. Navy or any other element of the U.S. government. The authors thank Alexander Liebman for his useful insights.

1. For more on the Central Committee Political Bureau group session, see 袁正明, 主任 [Yuan Zhengming et al.], 中央电视台 "大国崛起"节目组 [China Central Television "Rise of Great Powers" Program Group], 德国 [Germany], vol. 5, "大国崛起"系列丛书 ["Rise of Great Powers" Book Series] (Beijing: 中国民主法制出版社 [China Democratic and Legal Institutions Press], 2006), 205–10. For President Hu Jintao's directive, see Irene Wang, "Propaganda Takes Back Seat in Fêted CCTV Series," *South China Morning Post*, 27 November 2006, OSC# CPP20061127715018. Individuals associated with producing *The Rise of Great Powers*, when quoted in the Chinese media, have often minimized or denied that there is an official connection. See Long Yuqin and Shen Liang, "'The Rise of Great Powers' Has No Special Political Background," 南方周末 [*Southern Weekend*], 30 November 2006, OSC# CPP20061205050002. Also see "The Rise of Nations," *China Daily*, 25 November 2006, OSC# CPP20061125052001. At minimum, however, it must be recognized that the series was produced by China's state-owned media and benefitted from the insights of China's foremost scholars and analysts.

2. Chiang Hsun, "China Explores Secrets of Rise of Great Powers: Institutions, Quality of People, Soft Power," 亚洲周刊 [*AsiaWeek*], no. 49 (10 December 2006): 68–73, OSC# CPP20061207710014.

3. Joseph Kahn, "China, Shy Giant, Shows Signs of Shedding Its False Modesty," *New York Times*, 9 December 2006, www.nytimes.com.

4. Jiang Shengxin, "Why Has the 'Rise of Great Powers' Attracted Such Widespread Attention—A Wen Hui Bao Staff Reporter Interviews Experts and Scholars Who Shed Light on the Reasons for the Ratings Miracle Wrought by a Documentary," *Wen Hui Bao*, 11 December 2006, OSC# CPP20061213050001; Dominic Zigler, "Reaching for a Renaissance," *Economist*, 31 March 2007, 4; Aric Chen, "The Next Cultural Revolution," *Fast Company*, June 2007, 73.

5. Chiang Hsun, "China Explores Secrets," 68–73.

6. Zhao Huayong, "Let History Illuminate Our Future Path," "The Rise of Great Powers" (CCTV website), http://finance.cctv.com/special/C16860/01/index.shtml.

7. For an indication of the range and sophistication of related scholarship, see the recent series in a premier Academy of Military Sciences journal, 中国军事科学 [*China Military Science*] 20, no. 3 (2007); 李效东 [Li Xiaodong], "大国崛起安全战略的历史考察" ["A Historical Review of the Security Strategies of Rising World Powers"], 39–49; 王春生 [Wang Chunsheng], "美国国家安全战略选择探析" ["An Analysis of the Strategic Choices for U.S. National Security"], 50–61; 原颖 [Yuan Ying], "法国国家安全战略钩沉" ["A Study of the Strategic Choices for French National Security"], 62–72; 丁皓, 万伟 [Ding Hao and Wan Wei], "从殖民地走向大国的崛起之路—印度国家安全战略选择" ["The Road from Former Colony to Rising World Power—Strategic Choices for Indian National Security"],

73–84. See also, 张文木 [Zhang Wenmu], "欧美地缘政治格局的历史演变" ["Historical Evolution of Euro-American Geopolitical Patterns"], 中国军事科学 [*China Military Science*] 20, no. 1 (2007): 30–38; 丁一平, 李洛荣, 龚连娣 [Ding Yiping, Li Luorong, and Gong Liandi], 世界海军史 [*The History of World Navies from the Chinese Perspective*] (Beijing: 海潮出版社 [Sea Tide Press], 2000).

8. Chen Fong-Ching and Jin Guantao, *From Youthful Manuscripts to River Elegy: The Chinese Popular Cultural Movement and Political Transformation 1979–1989* (Hong Kong: Chinese University Press, 1997), 221–22.

9. Ibid., 222.

10. Wang, "Propaganda Takes Back Seat." To these national soul-searching historical series might be added 走向共和 [*For the Sake of the Republic*] a fifty-nine-episode Chinese television series that covers the Qing Dynasty's collapse and the Republic of China's founding.

11. Even such sources as the daily newspaper sponsored by the Communist Youth League of the Chinese Communist Party Central Committee emphasize this willingness to learn from abroad. See, for example, 徐百柯 [Xu Baike], "何谓大国? 如何崛起?—电视纪录片 "大国崛起" 总策划麦天枢访谈" ["What Is a Big Power? How Does a Country Spring into Being?—An Interview with Mai Tianshu, Chief Producer of the CCTV Documentary 'Rise of Great Nations'"], 青年报 [*China Youth Daily*], 29 November 2006, http://zqb.cyol.com/content/2006-11/29/content_1591021.htm, OSC# CPP20061130715007.

12. For more on this controversy, see Zhang Shunhong, "Worries Emerge and Linger in the Air—After Watching 'The Rise of Great Nations', *Studies on Marxism*, January 2007, 111–14, OSC# CPP20070726332002; Chiang Hsun, "China Explores Secrets of Rise of Great Powers; He Sanwei, "Opportunity and Right of 'Misinterpretation,'" 南方周末 [*Southern Weekend*], 14 December 2006, OSC# CPP20061214050003.

13. Unless otherwise specified, quotations and summaries in this chapter are derived from the film series 中央电视台十二集大型电视纪录片 [China Central Television Large Scale Documentary No. 12], "大国崛起" ["The Rise of Great Powers"], 2006.

14. Unless otherwise specified, quotations and summaries in this section are derived from "第一集: 海洋时代 (开篇·葡西)" ["Part 1: The Age of the Sea (Introduction, Portugal, and Spain)"], CCTV International, 14 November 2006, www.cctv.com.

15. Col. Dai Xu, PLAAF, "The Rise of World Powers Cannot Do without Military Transformation," 环球时报 [*Global Times*], 15 March 2007, OSC# CPP20070326455002.

16. "Part 12: 第十二集 大道行思 (结篇)" ["The Big Way (Final Part)"], Transcript of the last part of CCTV-2 Program, "The Rise of Great Powers," CCTV, 25 November 2006, www.cctv.com.cn, OSC# CPP20061215071001.

17. Dai Xu, "The Rise of World Powers."

18. "Part 12: The Big Way (Final Part)."

19. Ibid.

20. Dai Xu, "The Rise of World Powers."

21. Ye Zicheng, "China's Peaceful Development: The Return and Development of Land Power," 世界经济与政治 [*World Economics & Politics*], February 2007, 23–31, OSC# CPP20070323329001.

22. Unless otherwise specified, quotations and summaries in this section are derived from "第二集: 小国大业 (荷兰)" ["Part 2: A Small Country's Great Undertaking (Holland)"], CCTV International, 15 November 2006, www.cctv.com.

23. Senior Col. Zhang Wei, "Exploring National Sea Security Theories," 中国军事科学 [*China Military Science*], January 2007, 84–91, OSC# CPP20070621436009.

24. Unless otherwise specified, quotations and summaries in this section are derived from "第三集: 走向现代 (英国上)" ["Part 3: Moving towards Modern Times (England, first part)"]; "第四集: 工业先声 (英国下)" ["Part 4: First Signs of Industry (England, second part)"], CCTV International, 16 and 17 November 2006, www.cctv.com.

25. Zhang Wei, "Exploring National Sea Security Theories," 84–91.

26. Ye Zicheng, "China's Peaceful Development," 23–31.

27. Numerous PRC analyses highlight the relative deficiencies of the United Kingdom's naval air capabilities in this conflict. See, for example, 蒋都庭 [Capt. Jiang Duting, PLA Navy], 海军航空兵 [*Naval Aviation*] (Beijing: New Star Press, 2006), 45; and 张艳明, 周丽娅 [Zhang Yanming and Zhou Liya] "马岛战争: 美英现代海军发展的分水岭" ["The Malvinas War: A Watershed for U.S. and British Naval Development"], 海事达观 [*Maritime Spectacle*], December 2006, 100.

28. Chen Fenglin, "Rise of Modern Powers and Its Historic Revelations," 外交评论 [*Foreign Affairs Review*], 25 October 2006, OSC# CPP20061218508001.

29. Yan Xuetong, quoted in Wang Haijing, "An International Mirror for a Rising China," *Liaowang*, no. 50, 11 December 2006, 56–57, OSC# CPP20061219715005.

30. Unless otherwise specified, quotations and summaries in this section are derived from "第七集: 百年维新 (日本)" ["Part 7: One Hundred Years of Reform and Modernization (Japan)"], CCTV International, 20 November 2006, www.cctv.com.

31. Yuan Zhengming et al., *Japan*, vol. 6, "Rise of Great Powers" Book Series, 136–39.

32. Ibid., 140–41.

33. Ibid., 142.

34. 张文木 [Zhang Wenmu], "Modern China Needs a New Concept of Sea Power," 环球时报 [*Global Times*], 12 January 2007, http://www.people.com.cn/GB/paper68/, OSC# CPP20070201455002.

35. 叶自成 [Ye Zicheng], "Geopolitics from a Greater Historical Perspective," 现代国际关系 [*Contemporary International Relations*], 20 June 2007, OSC# CPP20070712455001.

36. Ibid.

37. Unless otherwise specified, quotations and summaries in this section are derived from "第十集: 新国新梦 (美国上)" ["Part 10: New Country, New Dream (U.S., first part)"]; "第十一集: 危局新政 (美国·下)" ["Part 11: Dangerous Time, New Politics"], CCTV International, 24 November 2006, www.cctv.com.

38. Yuan Zhengming et al., *United States*, vol. 8, "Rise of Great Powers" Book Series, 150.

39. "Wang Jisi and Zhou Yan on the Real Story of the Rise of the Great Powers," Sina. com, 22 November 2006, OSC# CPP20061207038001.

40. Zhang Wei, "Exploring National Sea Security Theories," 84–91.

41. *China Military Science* is published by the PLA's Academy of Military Sciences. Unless otherwise indicated, quotations in this paragraph are from 徐起 [Xu Qi], "21世纪初海上地缘战略与中国海军的发展" ["Maritime Geostrategy and the Development of the Chinese Navy in the Early 21st Century"], 中国军事科学 [*China Military Science*] 17, no. 4 (2004): 75–81. Translation by Andrew Erickson and Lyle Goldstein published in *Naval War College Review* 59, no. 4 (Autumn 2006): 46–67.

42. Dai Xu, "The Rise of World Powers."

43. Yuan Zhengming et al., *United States*, vol. 8, "Rise of Great Powers" Book Series, 141.

44. Ibid.

45. "'Focus' Program: 'Rise of Great Powers'—Episode 11: A New Deal in a Time of Crisis (United States, Part 2)," CCTV, 24 November 2006, www.cctv.com.cn, OSC# CPP20061215071003.

46. Ibid.

47. For World War II and the U.S. emergence as a superpower, see Yuan Zhengming et al., *United States*, vol. 8, "Rise of Great Powers" Book Series, 234–38.

48. "'Focus' Program: 'Rise of Great Powers'—Episode 11: A New Deal in a Time of Crisis (United States, Part 2)," CCTV, 24 November 2006, OSC# CPP20061215071003.

49. "TV Documentary Stimulates More Open Attitude to History, China, the World (part two of two parts)," *Xinhua*, 26 November 2006, OSC# CPP20061126968012.

50. Ye Zicheng, "China's Peaceful Development: The Return and Development of Land Power," *World Economics & Politics*, February 2007, 23–31, OSC# CPP20070323329001.

51. Ibid.

52. Ye Zicheng, "Geopolitics From a Greater Historical Perspective."

53. Unless otherwise specified, quotations and summaries in this section are derived from "第五集 激情岁月 (法国)" ["Part 5: Years of Passion"], CCTV International, 19 November 2006, www.cctv.com.

54. 唐普, 主编 [Tang Pu, ed.], 大国崛起: 以历史的眼光和全球的视野解读15世纪以来9个世界性大国崛起得历史 [*The Rise of Great Powers: Interpreting the History of the Rise of 9 World Powers since the 15th Century from the Viewpoint of History and the Global Field of Vision*] (Beijing: 人民出版社 [People's Press], 2006), 185.

55. Yuan Zhengming et al., *France*, vol. 4, "Rise of Great Powers" Book Series, 39.

56. Tang Pu, ed., *The Rise of Great Powers*, 214.

57. Ibid., 215.

58. Ibid., 217.

59. Unless otherwise indicated, quotations in this paragraph are from Xu Qi, "Maritime Geostrategy and the Development of the Chinese Navy," 75–81.

60. Tang Pu, ed., *The Rise of Great Powers*, 217.

61. Ibid., 217.

62. Ibid., 231.

63. Ibid., 232.

64. For example, one well-known Chinese scholar used the term "appeasement" to describe China's present policies vis-à-vis Taiwan, suggesting that Beijing would have to resort to force or become the victim of further bullying. Interview, Beijing, March 2007.

65. "Part 5: Years of Passion."

66. Unless otherwise specified, quotations and summaries in this section are derived from "第六集: 帝国春秋 (德国)" ["Part 6: An Empire's Spring and Autumn (Germany)"], CCTV International, 19 November 2006, www.cctv.com.

67. Tang Pu, ed., *The Rise of Great Powers*, 237.

68. Ibid., 250.

69. Ibid., 251.

70. Ibid., 264.

71. Ibid., 266.

72. Ibid., 268.

73. Ibid., 267.

74. Ibid., 139.

75. Ibid., 273.

76. Ibid., 265.

77. Ibid., 276.

78. Ibid., 277.

79. "Part 12: The Big Way (Final Part)."

80. Unless otherwise specified, quotations and summaries in this section are derived from "第八集: 寻道图强 (俄国)" ["Part 8: Searching for the Way, Seeking Strength"]; "第九集: 风云新途 (苏联)" ["Part 9: Unstable Situation, New Way"], CCTV International, 22 and 23 November 2006, www.cctv.com.

81. "Part 12: The Big Way (Final Part)."

82. Tang Pu, ed., *The Rise of Great Powers*, 335.

83. Yuan Zhengming et al., *Russia*, vol. 7, "Rise of Great Powers" Book Series, 9.

84. Tang Pu, ed., *The Rise of Great Powers*, 339.

85. Ibid., 337.

86. Ibid., 339.

87. Ibid., 336–37.

88. Yuan Zhengming et al., *Russia*, vol. 7, "Rise of Great Powers" Book Series, 38.

89. Ibid., 39.

90. Unless otherwise indicated, quotations in this paragraph are from Xu Qi, "Maritime Geostrategy and the Development of the Chinese Navy," 75–81.

91. Yuan Zhengming et al., *Russia*, vol. 7, "Rise of Great Powers" Book Series, 15.

92. Tang Pu, ed., *The Rise of Great Powers*, 352.

93. Ibid., 354.

94. Ibid., 359.

95. Yuan Zhengming et al., *Russia*, vol. 7, "Rise of Great Powers" Book Series, 39.

96. Tang Pu, ed., *Rise of Great Powers*, 371.

97. See, for example, 王辑思 [Wang Jisi], "苏美争霸的历史教训和美中国的崛起新道路" ["The Historic Lesson of the U.S.-Soviet Contest for Hegemony and China's Peaceful Rise"], essay in 中国和平崛起新道路 [*China's Peaceful Rise: The New Path*] (Beijing: 中共中央党校国际战略研究所 [Central Committee of the CCP Party School International Strategy Research Institute], April 2004).

98. "Wang Jisi and Zhou Yan on the Real Story of the Rise of the Great Powers," Sina.com, 22 November 2006, OSC# CPP20061207038001.

99. Tang Pu, ed., *The Rise of Great Powers*, 372.

100. Ye Zicheng, "Geopolitics from a Greater Historical Perspective."

101. Dai Xu, "The Rise of World Powers."

102. "'Focus' Program: 'Rise of Great Powers'—Episode 11: A New Deal in a Time of Crisis (United States, Part 2)," CCTV, 24 November 2006, www.cctv.com.cn, OSC# CPP20061215071003.

103. See Yuan Zhengming et al., *Japan*, vol. 6, "Rise of Great Powers" Book Series, 136–39.

104. "Part 12: The Big Way (Final Part)."

105. Tang Pu, ed., *Rise of Great Powers*, 217.

106. Ibid., 371.

107. "Part 12: The Big Way (Final Part)."

108. Ibid.

109. Liu Jiangping and Zhui Yue, "Management of the Sea in the 21st Century: Whither the Chinese Navy?," 当代海军 [*Modern Navy*], 1 June 2007, 6–9, OSC# CPP20070628436012.

110. 杨毅, 主编 [Yang Yi, chief editor], 国家安全战略研究 [*Research on National Security Strategy*] (Beijing: 国防大学出版社 [National Defense University Press], 2007), 319. This concept is related to another slogan from the Self-Strengthening Movement (洋务运动 or 自强运动), "Rich Country, Strong Army" (富国强兵). This concept was appropriated by Japan, initially with great success and later with devastating strategic failure.

Carnes Lord

China and Maritime Transformations

Continentalist China to the Communist Revolution

THE PEOPLE'S REPUBLIC OF CHINA (PRC) is in the process of an astonishing transformation. The explosive growth of China's industrial economy over the last several decades is the most obvious component of this transformation. No less remarkable, however, is China's turn to the sea. With the notable exception of the early Ming, Chinese governments have traditionally emphasized land power over sea power because of nearly constant continental threats and concerns about internal rebellion.[1] Of course, ordinary Chinese living on its extensive coastline took to the sea for their livelihood, but the economy of China was fundamentally rooted in its soil. To the extent that the Chinese engaged in commercial activities, they did so primarily with a view to the large and largely self-sufficient internal market, readily accessible through China's great navigable river systems as well as its many seaward ports. Moreover, prior to 1840, the Chinese faced fewer sustained security threats on their ocean flank than on their sprawling continental frontier. Apart from chronic piracy, few naval powers in the vicinity posed a significant threat.[2] Historically, the security threat that preoccupied China's leaders was its exposure to raiding or invasion by the steppe nomads of Inner Asia. This threat was always latent and sometimes serious: Several Chinese dynasties succumbed to the horsemen of the north. The strategic culture formed by this history and political geography was therefore a profoundly continentalist one.[3]

Throughout most of the last two centuries, this strategic culture retained its power. In the nineteenth century, Qing China proved incapable of meeting the maritime challenge posed by the modern navies of the Western powers, even as it conquered vast new territories on its Inner Asian periphery. In the First Opium War (1839–42), a British fleet penetrating to the heart of China's riverine network threatened to shut down its internal commerce, thus forcing the regime to sue for peace; it was at this time that Britain acquired Hong Kong. In the 1880s, defeat of China's nascent fleet at the hands of the French sealed the end of its traditional influence in Indochina. By the last decade of the century, in spite of their acquisition of significant naval capabilities, the Chinese proved no match for their rapidly modernizing island neighbor and suffered humiliating defeat in the Sino-Japanese War of 1895, leading to a Japanese protectorate in Korea and the loss of Taiwan.[4] Pressed by the Russians from the north as well as by the Western maritime powers (including Germany), the imperial court was forced to accede to rising demands for commercial and territorial concessions. Popular resistance to these developments culminated in 1900 in the Boxer Rebellion, a series of spontaneous acts of violence against Western interests that the court tried to use to its advantage. The result was a lengthy occupation of the imperial capital itself by forces of the Western powers and further humiliation for the regime. In 1905 China suffered terribly but without recourse as the Russo-Japanese War was waged on its land territory and in nearby waters, in part over access to strategically located Port Arthur. All of these developments would fatally weaken the foundations of the dynasty and indeed the legitimacy of the empire itself.

The fall of the Qing in 1911 led to a long period of internal instability. Local warlords contended with the Kuomintang movement under Jiang Jieshi (Chiang Kai-shek), the Communists under Mao Zedong (Mao Tse-tung), and (beginning in 1931) the Japanese army in a complex struggle for control of the territories bequeathed by imperial China. The eventual Communist victory in 1949 restored it to unity—except for Taiwan and some smaller offshore islands held by the retreating Kuomintang. This legacy of China's civil war, which of course persists today, has changed fundamentally the political and strategic geography of China and the thinking of China's Communist elites concerning her security: No longer could the nation turn its back on its seaward frontier. Nevertheless, for a variety of reasons, it is only recently that these changes have had the transformative effect on Chinese security behavior that might have been predicted decades ago.

Continentalism under the People's Republic

The first reason for the slowness of change in Chinese security behavior is that the outlook of the ruling elites of the Chinese Communist Party was formed by the experience of land warfare, conventional as well as guerrilla; few of the party's leading commanders knew anything about naval warfare or the advanced technologies critical to modern naval (or air) combat. Although Mao initiated plans for an invasion of Taiwan in 1951, it was quickly discovered that this lay well beyond current or foreseeable PRC capabilities;[5] furthermore, Chinese involvement in the Korean War diverted resources and the attention of the leadership to ground combat. The border war against India in 1962, in which the Chinese performed well but against an unprepared Indian Army in uniquely difficult terrain, was another example of Maoist China's continental focus. What progress Beijing was able to make in building up a modern navy virtually from scratch was only possible with technical assistance provided by the Soviet Union.

A second factor has to do with the PRC's changing relationship with Communist Russia. The Communist seizure of power in China led immediately (in 1950) to the formation of a political–military alliance with the USSR—a development of immense significance that (together with the expulsion of the Japanese from mainland China at the end of World War II) provided the Chinese a degree of security on their landward frontiers, which they had rarely enjoyed in their long history. However, the solidity of this alliance was less than it first appeared. It became clear in the course of the 1960s that the greatest security threat to China was in fact that posed by the Soviet Union itself. In 1969 the two nuclear-armed Communist powers carried on a series of border skirmishes in Siberia that might well have sparked a larger conflict (the Soviets at this time appear to have contemplated a preemptive attack on China's nuclear forces and facilities). By the end of the Cold War, both countries maintained substantial conventional forces along their common border. Given the severe underdevelopment of the Chinese economy (not to mention the devastating effects of decades of internal warfare as well as Mao's ill-conceived and, indeed, insane domestic policies), China's military resources were sharply constrained; its ground forces had to be accorded top priority. Moreover, once Soviet technical assistance to the Chinese had ended in 1960, it was evident that modernization of the technology-driven components of the People's Liberation Army (PLA) could not be accomplished anytime soon.

A third factor was the poor showing of Chinese ground forces in the short war against communist Vietnam in 1979. This was only the third conflict directly involving the PRC since the Korean War at the beginning of the 1950s, but it seemed to reconfirm the continuing strategic salience of China's landward frontiers. The war convinced the Chinese leadership—notably Deng Xiaoping, who emerged as Mao's successor by 1978[6]—that China urgently needed to reform and upgrade its ground forces. Accordingly, Deng was led to reemphasize the modest role that was to be played by the navy in the PRC's future security posture—coastal defense. It may also be that Beijing's functional entente with the United States during this period allowed the People's Republic to take a more relaxed view of the not inconsiderable potential threat posed by the Soviet Navy in Asian waters than might otherwise have been the case.[7]

All of this soon began to change, however. With the end of the Cold War and the collapse of the Soviet Union, China no longer faced an existential threat on its Inner Asian frontier. Instead, its primary security concerns were clearly in the process of shifting to the maritime domain. In the first instance, territorial disputes in offshore waters with various regional states took on increasing salience, beginning with the PRC's clash with Vietnam over the Paracel Islands in the South China Sea in 1974. Second, the evolution of Taiwan's domestic politics in a democratic direction was threatening to move the Republic of China away from its long-standing "One China" policy toward de facto and even de jure independence. At the same time, the apparent willingness of the United States to act as Taiwan's protector, in spite of its normalization of relations with the PRC in the 1970s and the quasi-alliance of the two countries in the 1980s, forced the Chinese to face the eventual prospect of engaging the U.S. Navy in a conflict in East Asian waters. Finally, the rapid growth of the Chinese economy as a result of the bold reforms instituted by Deng and pursued by his successors made comprehensive modernization of China's naval forces a feasible objective of Chinese Communist military policy for the first time ever.

Maritime Elements in Imperial China

Looking at China's current maritime transformation in historical perspective, it is possible to overstate the extent to which Chinese strategic culture (if indeed such a thing exists) has been inexorably continentalist.[8] The great exception apparently proving this generalization is of course the well-known voyages of the eunuch admiral Zheng He in the early fifteenth century. Under the Ming emperor Yongle and Zheng He, a palace favorite, the Chinese undertook an ambitious program of ship construction and maritime infrastructure development. Between the years 1405 and 1433, Zheng He commanded seven major expeditions, typically consisting of hundreds of ships and tens of thousands of men, which showed the Ming flag in the Straits of Malacca, the Indian Ocean, the Persian Gulf, and East Africa. The fleet included warships mounting cannon and "treasure ships," of which the largest may have been 440 feet in length and displaced more than twenty thousand tons; vessels on this scale dwarfed anything known in the West to that time.[9] These vast and no doubt expensive enterprises do not seem to have brought commensurate benefit to the empire, however, and the impetus behind them quickly flagged not long after the death of Yongle. The mandarins of the imperial bureaucracy seem to have opposed them as risky and wasteful; in the century following, imperial edicts attempted to discourage long-distance maritime commerce, and Zheng He's navy was not maintained.

Nevertheless, a case can be made that conventional historiography of this period has overstated later Ming neglect of the maritime domain.[10] For that matter, older Chinese naval and maritime activities have not received the attention they deserve. The Southern Song Dynasty (1127–1279) actually had a seaport (Hangzhou, on the lower Yangzi River) as its capital—a city greatly admired by Marco Polo when he visited it; its large shipyards supported a significant naval force. When the Mongols overthrew the Song, their Yuan Dynasty (1271–1368) inherited these naval assets and accompanying nautical skills, enabling them to launch major (albeit unsuccessful) amphibious expeditions—in fact, they are thought to be the largest such operations in all of the Middle Ages—against Japan, Vietnam, and Java. Chinese shipbuilding technology and naval armament made significant advances in the fourteenth century, as did the skills of Chinese mariners in astronomy, cartography, and the magnetic compass. Moreover, the Ming Dynasty first established itself by defeating its rivals in southern China largely by naval power. The decisive battle of Lake Poyang (1363) involved hundreds of warships on both sides, larger than all but a few sea battles in earlier or, for that matter, later times. Riverine operations like this, too often slighted in conventional naval historiography, are of central importance to the maritime history of China in particular. Finally, commercial activity beyond China's territorial waters was far from unknown in the earlier eras of its imperial history.

Nevertheless, it remains true that in the decisive respect—which is to say from the perspective of China's imperial center—China has been primarily a continental power since its remote beginnings, and especially so in modern times. The question this volume sets out to address is whether or to what extent China's persisting political and strategic geography and the continentalist strategic culture it helped to form will constrain the nation's development as a maritime power today. In coming to grips with this question, it is well to step back from the Chinese case and take a long view of the subject.

Geography and Technology

It is necessary at the outset to say something about a basic premise of much of our analysis: geography matters.[11] Contemporary security studies all too commonly dismiss the importance of geography for the strategic outlook and fate of nations: modern technology, it is said, erases distance and eliminates or greatly reduces the traditional military advantages afforded by natural barriers on the land or at sea. That there is something to this is of course undeniable, yet this just as surely overstates the importance of technology relative to other factors conditioning the employment of military power. During the eighteenth century, the French (and Spanish) built ships that were technically as good, and sometimes even better, than their British equivalents, but they were regularly thrashed by the British navy in numerous fleet encounters. As for the persisting if unobtrusive presence of geographic considerations in the employment of military power today, a helpful point of reference is Britain's war with Argentina over the Falkland/Malvinas Islands in the South Atlantic in 1982. The large technical and operational advantages enjoyed by the British in this encounter barely compensated for the liabilities imposed on them by the need to project significant military power over many thousands of miles of open ocean. It is telling that the Chinese have made a special study of this episode (one of the few major naval battles of the last half century) for what it can teach about the limits to the ability of the United States to project combat power over the vast distances of the Pacific Ocean against a regional state determined to deny it "access."[12]

In any event, much can be learned about the prospects for maritime transformation in contemporary China from an examination of attempted maritime transformations in the past. This includes an excursion to the deep past that is somewhat unusual in studies of this kind. In fact, however, the cases we have looked at from the pre-Christian era are of unusual interest. This is true above all because the only cases in the entire historical record of successful *and enduring* maritime transformations are from this period: Persia and Rome.

Successful Maritime Transformations: Persia and Rome

The Persian Empire—founded by Cyrus the Great in the sixth century BC and destroyed by Alexander the Great in the fourth—was the largest state in antiquity before Rome. The epic struggles between Persia and the city-states of classical Greece form the backdrop to what is perhaps the most remarkable cultural flowering in human history, and a defining moment in the rise of what we have come to call the West. Not surprisingly, the Persians have not come off well in the historiography of this period, dominated as it has been by European writers. In particular, the Persian Empire has traditionally been viewed through the optic of the notion of "oriental despotism" and hence in stark contrast to Greece as the birthplace of republican freedom. In fact, however, Persia was an empire of a new kind, one having more in common with Rome than with the brutal, domineering empires of the ancient Near East that preceded it.[13] One of the secrets to its success was an imperial ideology of inclusion and tolerance that reconciled defeated peoples to its rule and fostered stability throughout its vast domains. This provides a key element of the explanation for the Persians' successful turn to the sea. Persia's swift rise as a commercial maritime and naval power in the eastern Mediterranean at the turn of the fifth century BC would not have been possible without the empire's ability to co-opt the nautical skills and manpower of sea-faring allies or dependents on its maritime periphery, especially the Phoenicians (but also the East Greeks). In addition, though, it is important to acknowledge the sheer scale of the resources available to the Persians to build and maintain naval vessels in quantities that could not be remotely matched by their adversaries. Moreover, by initiating the practice of paying ships' crews, the Persians were able to man these large fleets and keep them at sea for longer periods. In the scale and economic dynamism of these efforts, one sees potential parallels to China.

Rome's maritime transformation began during the two so-called Punic Wars against the Carthaginians in the third century BC.[14] Carthage (near modern Tunis), originally settled by Phoenician colonists as a trading outpost, grew over time into a maritime-based empire dominating the western Mediterranean. Though situated only a few miles from the sea and with the benefit of a good port, Rome by contrast remained for centuries an agriculturalist community, and its nascent empire was confined to the Italian peninsula. (Compare China in these respects.) In the inevitable collision between the two most powerful states in the region over control of the rich island of Sicily, Rome also looked for help to maritime allies, in this case the Etruscans and the Greeks of southern Italy. (This pattern would later repeat itself in Rome's relationship with the maritime states Pergamum and Rhodes.) And yet Rome went further than the Persians ever did in developing indigenous naval capabilities. With the ruthless determination that characterized everything they did in the military sphere, the Romans built and manned with their own citizens large fleets that could and did challenge the Carthaginians at sea until they finally prevailed. Roman ship construction and technology seems to have been generally inferior to that of Carthage, and their deficiencies in basic nautical skills led to repeated disasters at the hands of the elements. As in the case of many continental powers turning to the sea, Roman sailors remained essentially embarked soldiers, and Roman naval tactics little more than infantry tactics adapted to a new medium. But the Romans' commitment to relying on their own resources for mastery of the sea rather than on potentially unreliable allies was unshakeable. On one telling occasion, reconstitution of the Roman fleet after a devastating storm was underwritten by the private wealth of leading citizens when available state funds proved inadequate. In the end, the Romans vanquished all rival naval powers and turned the Mediterranean into a Roman lake. It remained that way for some four centuries. During this extended Pax Romana, maritime commerce flourished throughout the Mediterranean—the ancient equivalent of an era of globalization under the protection of a great-power naval policing force.

Even in the cases of Persia and Rome, however, it would be difficult to argue that a maritime transformation was fully realized. At the least, one would have to say that in both cases the imprint of an originally continentalist mindset was never completely effaced. The Persians never really used their navy as an offensive instrument, in the style of their Athenian adversaries, and they tended to avoid meeting engagements with enemy fleets in open water. Rather, they specialized in what today would be called joint maritime operations, in which their fleet provided logistic support and flank protection for large Persian armies advancing along an enemy's coast. In the Roman case, repeated failure to defeat the Carthaginians at sea led the Romans to shift their approach in the Sicilian (and later in the African) theater to landward operations against ports; the Mithridatic War was fought the same way. The Romans were also slow to establish permanent fleets (this occurred only under the empire) and a regime of maritime policing; one result was the persistence of a serious piracy threat in the western Mediterranean down to the first century BC. After that had happened, though, it seems fair to say that an enduring maritime transformation had taken hold.

Understanding Failed Maritime Transformations

With the two (partial) exceptions just discussed, the historical record has not been kind to powers attempting maritime transformations. In all of the other cases studied in this volume, remarkable efforts were made by national leaders to create and project naval and maritime power, sometimes with real success for limited periods. Invariably, however, what was achieved in the longer run seems never to have been commensurate with these efforts. In at least one case (Imperial Germany), the decision to go to sea was a strategic disaster. What factors account for the relative failure of these ventures?

To properly understand all of these cases, it is essential to begin with the brute facts of political and strategic geography. Second, we need to look at the economic dimension of statecraft as it relates to maritime power, taking into account both the resource base of the state and the extent to which it depended on or was affected by overseas commerce and trade. Third, we need to assess the strategic outlook and objectives of the ruler or ruling elite as shaped by these and other factors. This analysis must pay particular attention to how statesmen understand and assess the trade-offs between land and naval strength. Fourth, we shall look at the role of individual leadership in effecting a maritime transformation, in relationship to political, bureaucratic, or cultural forces that may pose obstacles to it. Fifth, we shall consider the various material and operational handicaps to be overcome in a maritime transformation. Finally, some attention (if necessarily limited) needs to be paid to naval strategy and operational art as a reflection of these various factors.

It will not always be possible to make definitive (or even tentative) judgments on these matters in particular cases given the limited evidence of the historical record, particularly in some of the older cases. As several of our authors have suggested, it would not be surprising if continentalist states were less than scrupulous in documenting their naval and maritime activities. It is also necessary to point out that comparison is made difficult by the fact that the cases span periods of time that vary considerably, including some extremely long periods (notably, Ming China, France, and Russia). The level of detail in each case study therefore varies accordingly. With these caveats in mind, it seems possible nevertheless to make some illuminating and suggestive comparisons.

Political and Strategic Geography

What we have been calling continentalist powers have been more or less disadvantaged by their geographic situation. Of the cases studied here, Russia (and later the Soviet Union) as well as Germany particularly belong to the former category. Russia's very restricted access to the sea and to global sea lines of communication, its lack of good ice-free ports, and the necessity of wide dispersal of its naval assets have been and remain fundamental limiting problems. In the case of Germany, in spite of its good ports and a history of maritime commercial activity going back to the Hanseatic League of the Middle Ages, the exposure of its land borders to attack by multiple adversaries over many centuries was decisive in forming its continentalist outlook. In addition, Germany's access to the oceans was handicapped by choke points (notably, the English Channel and the approaches to the Baltic) controlled by unfriendly powers.[15] These more severely disadvantaged powers have sometimes engaged in ambitious strategic projects designed to change the stubborn facts of geography in their favor—thus, classically, Peter the Great's successful effort to bring Russian power to the shores of the Baltic and Black Sea and found the city of St. Petersburg to provide Russia a "window" on European culture and commerce. Construction of the Kiel Canal across the Jutland Peninsula was intended to free Germany from dependence on the Danish straits.

The role of geography in the other cases studied is more ambiguous. Sparta lacked good ports and ready access to timber for shipbuilding, but more decisive for its continentalist orientation was (as in the Roman or Chinese cases) its agrarian economy coupled with a distinctive culture that was devoted to the cultivation of the martial arts of the Greek infantryman. This culture in turn reflected the political geography of Sparta's landward neighborhood, where a number of smaller but still powerful states in combination could pose a serious danger to it.[16] The Ottomans were almost wholly a land power prior to their occupation of Constantinople, which, however, provided both an incomparable strategic base for the projection of naval power and maritime and shipbuilding skills; these enabled the Ottomans to go to sea and eventually expel Venice from the Aegean. Nevertheless, the main vector of Ottoman expansion remained the Balkans, and continuing multiple threats along its long land borders made of its naval capabilities a dispensable luxury. But France is perhaps the most puzzling case.[17] With its ample shoreline, good harbors, large population, and significant commerce from early times, it is surprising that the French did not more effectively establish themselves as a maritime people over the centuries, in spite of building an extensive overseas empire. Part of the explanation clearly lies with the preoccupation of French leaders with their landward borders from at least the time of Louis XIV. It may have had something to do with the centralization of the French state and the fact that Paris is not a maritime city. Moreover, for the French, with three distinct maritime frontiers in the homeland (a particular problem once the British controlled the Straits of Gibraltar) as well as distant colonial theaters that were difficult to defend in any case, the development of strategically effective naval power may well have been seen not so much as a luxury but as essentially beyond their reach.

Of all these cases, the one most reminiscent of China is France. Common to both are not only good ports and ready access to the sea but an inland capital and a system of inland waterways that lessened the nation's dependence on seagoing commerce. Furthermore, like France, China has three relatively distinct maritime frontiers and a history of less than optimal coordination between fleets stationed in each (this was a major cause of China's naval defeats by France in the South China Sea in the 1880s and by Japan in its northern waters in 1895). Both countries have a history of fitful (to say the least) naval development together with skepticism or outright hostility toward naval power or maritime expansion among important elements of its elite. And in both cases, the most compelling explanation for this is longstanding elite preoccupation with threats to—or opportunities afforded by—the landward frontier.

The Economic Dimension

The geostrategic outlook of great powers is shaped not only by geography proper but also by economic factors—notably, the availability of natural resources and patterns of production (agriculture versus commerce principally). For states that are not self-sufficient in basic resources, long-distance trade may be vital to their survival, and the protection of trade routes accordingly seen as a key to national security. The aggregate wealth created by natural resources and production sustains a certain level of population, which in turn translates into military capability. Furthermore, military effectiveness depends on a marriage of a state's manpower with appropriate military equipment or technology. In more advanced societies, self-sufficiency in the latter requires an industrial base and the availability of technical skills in the population. Throughout history, but especially in more recent times, navies in particular were expensive to build and maintain. This helps to explain why some states that might otherwise have been geographically positioned to exploit naval power have failed to do so.

Sparta is the limiting case in this discussion.[18] Sparta's feudal agricultural system did not produce a significant surplus, and the Spartans not only did not pursue commercial gain but were actively hostile to it. For this (and other) reasons, Sparta suffered chronic shortages in military manpower. Because of the absence of a robust commercial maritime sector, the country lacked skilled mariners or shipbuilding capability. Accordingly, when faced with war with a maritime empire such as Athens, Sparta had few alternatives to relying on allied naval assistance—and ultimately the generous financial support of the Persian Empire.

Persia is perhaps another limiting case. Persia's success in transforming itself into a maritime power was owing to two things above all: appropriation of the nautical skills and maritime infrastructure of its Phoenician and East Greek subjects; and very ample imperial revenues—made possible by the possession (and, not least important, relatively effective administration) of vast territories but also by Persia's growing dominance of maritime commerce in the eastern Mediterranean. The Ottoman case has similarities to the Persian (both empires occupied much of the same area). The Ottomans also enjoyed substantial revenues from their conquered lands while seeking to secure their central role in overland trade to Asia (the "Silk Road").

In the French, German, Russian, and Soviet cases, national wealth was, for the most part, sufficient to permit the creation of large navies. But the necessity of maintaining at the same time large ground force establishments, together with deficiencies in commercial infrastructure and marine skills in the population as well as the geostrategic constraints just discussed, made it difficult to sustain strategically significant naval forces over time or to employ them effectively. The case of France is again curious in this context. Of the four (partial) maritime transformations France can be said to have experienced since the seventeenth century, the first was a function of various private interests (fishing, trading, privateering, and missionary) rather than the French state. Throughout its history, in fact, the central authorities harbored at best a lukewarm attitude toward the projection of French power and presence overseas, and they largely failed to harness in a coherent imperial policy the considerable resources potentially at their disposal.

Strategic Outlook/Objectives

The strategic outlook of states throughout history is shaped by domestic as well as international circumstances.[19] Foremost among the domestic imperatives operating on statesmen at most times is the preservation of the existing regime or form of government. This has important implications for maritime transformation. As we have seen, Chinese dynasties could be and were overthrown by nomadic warriors from Inner Asia; although naval power did play a significant role in the rise of the Ming Dynasty, it generally posed no such threat, thus powerfully reinforcing China's continentalist orientation. Other domestically conditioned strategic objectives include the fostering of maritime exploration, resource exploitation, and commerce for the benefit of a politically favored elite or class. These objectives can serve as a powerful driver of state action and transformation. However, states sometimes have conflicting strategic imperatives that result in inconsistent policies or strategic paralysis. Among our cases, Germany is perhaps the best example of this, though France too must be mentioned.

Ancient Sparta is a telling example of the pervasive influence of the regime survival imperative on strategic behavior. For the Spartan ruling elite, the central requirement of Sparta's security situation was to safeguard the system of agricultural serfdom underpinning its unique way of life, especially because any serf ("Helot") revolt threatened Spartan control of the rich lands belonging to the formerly independent state of Messenia. This requirement dovetailed with Sparta's traditional foreign policy priorities: maintaining its hegemonic alliance system in the Peloponnese and keeping at bay its chief local rival, Argos. Unfortunately, the growing Athenian threat could not be managed through the projection of land power alone given the protection Athens' extensive fortifications afforded the city and its ports. To challenge Athens at sea, however, created existential difficulties for the regime. The xenophobic Spartans were traditionally reluctant to allow their citizens to travel extensively abroad and interact with foreigners out of (amply justified) fear of corrupting outside influences, but expeditionary warfare against the Athenian Empire required just this. Secondly, Athenian naval dominance opened the Peloponnese to seaward raiding and, in the worst case, a possible lodgment by the Athenians in Spartan territory that it was feared could spark desertions or a full-scale revolt by the Helots. When this in fact occurred (at Pylos in Messenia), Sparta sued for peace. These fears would prove an important limiting factor in Sparta's later (and very brief) maritime transformation.

Apart from such domestic considerations, it is frequently difficult for states to balance and prioritize strategic objectives when they pose multiple and potentially conflicting challenges. Faced with opportunities for expansion in the Balkans and the Aegean, the Ottomans do not seem to have paid sufficient attention to the rising threat to their domination of the trade routes to Asia from Portuguese penetration of the Indian Ocean. When Louis XIV built the largest navy in the world at the turn of the eighteenth century, he did so without any clear sense of how it should be used strategically to support French expansion or commercial interests either in Europe or in the New World. In the late nineteenth century the Germans, in a similar spirit, poured enormous resources into a "risk fleet" intended to challenge British naval superiority but without developing any clear strategic objectives that it should serve, without analyzing trade-offs between this navy and the land forces that were essential to protecting Germany's exposed borders, and without calculating the adverse diplomatic consequences that resulted from it. Soviet Russia similarly embarked on an extremely expensive program of naval construction to counter American global naval mastery while striving for superiority in conventional forces in Europe and in nuclear strike capabilities. Both the German and Soviet efforts seem to have been motivated as much by vague notions of national prestige as by any strategic concept, and it seems unlikely that, at the conventional level, at least, the Soviet navy could have achieved much more against the United States in a hot war than the German navy did against Britain during World War I, leaving aside the nuclear dimension of this competition.

In any case, it would be wrong to leave the impression that great powers always make fine calculations concerning their strategic objectives and the best way to pursue them. In older eras, the vanity or personal obsession of a prince (Louis XIV, Peter the Great, Kaiser Wilhelm) may largely account for a continental state suddenly taking to the sea. In recent times, more relevant is the influence of what may be called navalist ideology. The impact of the teachings of Alfred Thayer Mahan concerning "the influence of sea power on history" on the thinking of the German naval leadership and, indeed, the Kaiser himself at the turn of the twentieth century is well known. Mahan also had a marked and equally unfortunate influence on Japanese naval thought.[20] Today, the one place in the world where Mahan is seriously read and studied is the People's Republic of China.[21]

Leadership

We come now to what is perhaps the most critical factor enabling (or frustrating) maritime transformations. If continentalist powers typically face formidable political, bureaucratic, and cultural obstacles to maritime transformation, strong political leadership would seem essential to overcoming them.[22] Although direct evidence is lacking, leadership was clearly indispensable in the successful maritime transformations of Persia (under three strong and energetic kings) and Rome (under the collective leadership of a disciplined martial elite). In the case of Sparta, inconsistent leadership helps account both for the temporary success and ultimate failure of its maritime transformation. Strong individuals and unconventional leaders (Lysander, notably) were essential to Spartan successes in developing and projecting naval power, but the parochialism and arrogance of Sparta's elite undermined its wartime diplomacy and ultimately sealed the doom of its maritime empire. In the case of the Ottomans, Mehmed the Conqueror played a key role in their rapid and successful turn to the sea, but his energetic navalist leadership does not seem to have been sustained or adequately institutionalized.

Again, the case of France is particularly instructive. With the partial exceptions of Richilieu and Louis XIV, the French monarchy consistently showed little appreciation or understanding of the navy or of the value of overseas empire, a phenomenon that carried over as well into the Napoleonic period. This being the case, the French were never able to consistently overcome the multiple obstacles to maritime transformation that characterized their politics and culture. Weakness and disorganization in the central government (even under the Sun King himself) was a chronic problem; anticommercial and anti-imperial attitudes were widespread among the elite; a weak financial system (in contrast with Britain) hobbled naval construction and supply; and relations between the navy and the army were consistently poor or nonexistent.

Imperial Russia of course offers the unique example of Peter the Great, who among other things travelled to the West to familiarize himself with advanced naval technologies and founded a maritime capital to foster trade and naval development. As with the Ottomans, however, it is fair to say that this level of navalist-oriented leadership was not matched subsequently, although the naval and maritime industrial reforms initiated in the middle of the nineteenth century by Grand Duke Konstantin Nikolaevich deserve special mention in this context.[23] In the German case, the Mahan-inspired naval buildup of the late nineteenth century would simply not have happened without the aggressive leadership of Adm. Alfred von Tirpitz and the enthusiastic support of Kaiser Wilhelm, overriding a military establishment completely dominated by the army. Perhaps the most interesting aspect of this case is Tirpitz's relentless and very successful propaganda and political action campaigns on behalf of increased naval expenditures and a navalist strategic culture. In the Soviet case, a similar role was played by Adm. Sergei Gorshkov.[24] As for the Soviet leadership, Stalin became a committed supporter of a large blue water fleet and intervened actively in the naval doctrinal debates of the 1930s—indeed, to the point of ending them by purging officers on both sides. Postwar Soviet leaders, however, were much less favorable to the navy, especially after the emergence of nuclear weapons seemed to call into question the continuing utility of large surface combatants. In many respects, even in the golden age of Gorshkov, the navy remained the odd man out in a military establishment dominated by the ground and missile forces.[25]

Material and Operational Handicaps

In all of the cases studied, various material and operational handicaps helped to limit, thwart, or reverse maritime transformations. It is not obvious that many or even most of these handicaps could not have been remedied given adequate leadership and a commitment of resources, but for whatever reason they were not.

Despite being a coastal state, Sparta had little else going for her—no maritime commerce or infrastructure to speak of, few good harbors, lack of skilled seamen, lack of ready access to timber and other materials for naval construction, and, of course not least, inadequate resources to fix or obviate any of these problems on its own. Fortunately, the Spartans had maritime allies they could call upon to provide significant numbers of ships, and eventually they were able to secure funding from Persia sufficient to allow them to build and man a fleet that could challenge the Athenians. The Ottomans also suffered initially from a lack of shipbuilding and other maritime skills. With the capture of Constantinople, they inherited a strategic naval base with important maritime infrastructure; they also seem to have benefitted from technical assistance in various forms from European (especially Italian) naval architects. Their great failure, however, was their inability or unwillingness to make the transition from rowed galleys to sailing ships. While well suited to the waters of the Mediterranean, galleys could not negotiate the open ocean; thus the Ottomans could not effectively oppose the

Portuguese when they pushed into the Indian Ocean in pursuit of an alternate trade route to the riches of Asia.[26] In the case of the French, by contrast, they were generally fully a match for the British in the quality of their ship construction. However, they seem to have lagged in nautical skills; in addition, they suffered from an inadequate supply system and poor naval infrastructure—notably, in the West Indies. The Germans also suffered from inadequate infrastructure relative to the ambitious shipbuilding program they undertook. Like the French, the Germans seem to have consistently lacked confidence in their sea-faring skills vis-à-vis the British, leading to an overly conservative approach to fleet operations; the performance of the Soviet navy in World War II revealed a similar problem.

In the Russian case, technological backwardness relative to the Western powers was a central problem in naval development from the early nineteenth century through World War II. The Russians (and the Soviets in the 1920s and 30s) went to considerable lengths to import modern naval vessels and technologies from the West but ran into many political obstacles along the way. After the Communist revolution, the Soviets had to rely for some time on former Czarist officers who remained politically suspect, and technological and operational naval skills were in short supply. While an impressive naval infrastructure was created in the Baltic theater during the nineteenth century, this was a key limitation for the Russians in the Black Sea.

Naval Strategy and Operational Art

To what extent did these factors have a negative impact on the actual performance of continentalist states in naval warfare? Are there patterns in the conduct of naval strategy and operations that can be discerned over time?

It is illuminating in this context to revisit the successful cases. Although both the Persians and the Romans were able to transform themselves into effective naval powers, it is fair to say that their performance in naval combat was almost certainly not as consistently impressive as in the case of maritime-oriented states such as Athens, Carthage, Britain, or the United States. The Persians classically suffered crushing defeat at Salamis at the hands of the Athenians. They tended to avoid direct fleet-on-fleet encounters in favor of joint operations in support of expeditionary land forces; after several unsuccessful engagements with the Carthaginian fleet, the Romans did likewise. The Ottomans also avoided direct encounters with the Venetian fleet after losing every battle in their first war with that power. The main function of their fleet was to transport armies for amphibious-style operations to seize ports and maritime choke points as part of a larger strategy of sea denial as distinct from sea control. In fact, the Ottomans developed a distinctive style of naval warfare suited to their continentalist strategic culture. Of particular note are their series of amphibious and littoral warfare operations to seize offshore islands in the Mediterranean. This continental approach to sea power has parallels in China's own campaigns (1949–55) that expelled the Nationalists from all offshore islands save Taiwan, the Penghus, Jinmen, and Mazu.[27]

Russia's disastrous encounters with the technologically superior British and French navies in the Crimean War led it to recognize that it had to make major adjustments in naval strategy, operations, and fleet structure. Under the reforming leadership of Grand Duke Konstantin Nikolaevich, the Russians replaced their obsolete sailing ships-of-the-line with an innovative system for defense of their exposed Baltic flank resting on coastal fortifications, sea mines, and fast gunboats; in addition, they developed a class of modern cruiser/frigates for commerce raiding. The French pursued at different times and sometimes simultaneously three types of naval strategies vis-à-vis Britain: to strike the British homeland in a major cross-channel invasion; to engage it in overseas theaters; and to raid its commerce. None of these strategies proved effective. In the late nineteenth century, a group of French naval thinkers (the "Young School") was the first to articulate a naval posture based on the third of these approaches as the most cost-effective strategy for a second-tier naval power such as France under modern conditions.

This thinking presaged the German embrace of submarine warfare against the allied powers in the two world wars. That said, the Germans never really developed a fully conscious doctrine or strategy based on this lethal new weapon. In fact, German naval planning for both wars remained bound to the orthodox Mahanian paradigm of major fleet encounters, and the Germans resorted to the U-boat commerce-raiding option only when the Mahanian approach had plainly faltered; as a result, they never had enough submarines in either conflict to implement such a strategy effectively.[28]

In the early Soviet period, there was a similar tension between proponents of a large Mahan-style surface fleet and (another) Young School advocating primary reliance on submarines, mines, and land-based naval aircraft employed in a "partisan" or guerrilla-style operational mode. Eventually, at the direction of Stalin, a fusion of these approaches emerged, but one strongly weighted toward a large surface fleet, including aircraft carriers as well as battleships. This ambitious building program was stillborn on the outbreak of World War II. Although this approach was revisited briefly after the war, with the death of Stalin and the advent of nuclear weapons, a strong current of opinion in the Soviet leadership came to hold that large surface naval vessels were essentially obsolete. This led to a revival of the original Young School strategic concept of reliance on submarines and land-based naval aviation supplemented with light surface forces for missile strikes against American aircraft carriers and coastal defense. By the 1970s, however, under the far-sighted and energetic leadership of Admiral Gorshkov, the pendulum swung the other way, toward the idea of a very robust balanced navy including a significant component of larger surface combatants capable of maintaining a global peacetime presence and prepared to wage conventional war at sea against the United States and its allies. It is more than doubtful, however, that this approach was any more economically sustainable in the long term than the grandiose building programs proposed by some Soviet naval officers and embraced by Stalin both before and after World War II. In any case, with the collapse of the Soviet Union in 1991, the point became moot. Over the last quarter century, the proud Gorshkov-era Soviet fleet has rusted away, and Russia today is no longer a serious sea power.

The Case of China Today

There is no need to belabor here the dramatic nature of contemporary China's ongoing maritime transformation. Other contributors to this volume have detailed the rapid buildup of the People's Liberation Army Navy (PLAN) over the last decade and the radically enhanced capabilities that the Chinese military in general can now bring to bear against the maritime forces of the United States and its regional allies, as well as the impressive rise of China's military and commercial ship-building industry.[29] The question is how to interpret these developments. A key point that must be made at the outset is that the Chinese themselves are evidently not entirely of one mind in this regard. Indeed, there appears to be an ongoing debate within the Chinese national security community concerning the meaning and limits of China's turn to the sea. Voices continue to be heard defending China's traditional continentalist orientation and expressing skepticism about the wisdom and affordability of acquiring a world-class navy. Debates also rage over lesser issues such as the need for aircraft carriers or a conventionally balanced surface fleet more generally. Yet it is fair to say that the overall climate of opinion in China today is more favorable to maritime transformation than at any time in its long history.[30]

Let us review briefly the various factors that condition the success or failure of maritime transformations as they relate to the case of China, in the past and today. Geography, as we have noted, is a brute fact; geography is difficult—though not impossible—to alter (the Chinese did so when they built the Grand Canal and the Great Wall). It is tempting to say that nothing in the geographical situation of China as such prevents it from becoming a maritime power, as the experience of early imperial China (in the Song, Yuan, and Ming periods) attests. Conversely, there were some good reasons why premodern Chinese officials often looked on the sea more as a barrier than as a highway.[31] Weather is a factor easily overlooked, but typhoons along China's coasts can be devastating to shipping and maritime infrastructure.[32] The Taiwan Strait is a notoriously hazardous maritime passage—no doubt one of the reasons Taiwan was long considered by many Chinese not fully a part of China, at least in a formal administrative sense.[33] Moreover, as is repeatedly emphasized by Chinese commentators today, it is not quite correct to say that China's littorals form an unimpeded highway to the world ocean. Rather, as the Chinese see it today, China's maritime geography has always been disadvantaged by the existence of a series of "island chains"— the first running the length of its coasts, from Japan through Taiwan and the Philippines to Malaysia—that has been dominated throughout most of its history by other powers. The island chains have become a fixture of contemporary Chinese geostrategic thinking.[34] That there is some reality to this notion cannot be denied.[35]

It is nevertheless true that China's main problem has always been the vulnerability of its landward borders, which imposed a priority of armies over navies in its security policy and conditioned the mentality of its elites. Today China faces no real threat in this regard. Yet tempting as it may be to assume this change in China's political geography is a permanent one, it would be shortsighted to do so. The interests of China and Russia today may largely coincide, but there can be no guarantee that this will remain the case for the indefinite future; it is not difficult to imagine scenarios of potential conflict. It is also well to recall that China has fought wars with two other militarily potent neighboring states within living memory (India and Vietnam). Perhaps of greater immediate importance, however, is the internal threat to the integrity of China itself posed by ethnic minority groups. The recent rioting throughout Tibet (and in other Chinese provinces with a significant Tibetan population) has provided a graphic reminder of the continuing salience of this issue. But perhaps more worrisome still for the longer term are the Uighurs of Xinjiang province in China's far west, a Turkic Muslim people that has already shown itself susceptible to the appeal of radical Islamism. In general, while the fall of the Soviet Union may be said to have stabilized China's northern border, it also destabilized China's western border, allowing as it did the formation of independent, ethnically Turkic successor states in Central Asia. The level of official Chinese concern over this situation should not be underestimated.

With respect to the economic dimension, it is evident that this has been a very important—possibly the most important—factor driving China's current maritime transformation. China's great industrial boom of recent years has disproportionately benefited its coastal provinces, thus helping to shift the country's strategic center of gravity further from the landward frontiers. This development has also created a new geostrategic vulnerability to seaward attack—made very concrete by the imposing American (and Japanese) naval presence in the western Pacific. Furthermore, China's leadership is increasingly concerned over the country's growing dependence on overseas sources of natural resources, especially energy. This has provided it strong incentives to insert China fully into the globalized trading system of today, which in turn has important implications (although the Chinese themselves do not seem wholly in agreement as to just what they are) for China's naval development. The Chinese seem convinced of the classic Mahanian thesis that commerce and sea power are inextricably intertwined.[36] Finally, there is the obvious but inescapable point that the newfound wealth of the Chinese state accruing from its industrial and commercial development is putting within its reach for the first time a strategically competitive navy and capabilities for global power projection. As the ancient Persians were the first to demonstrate, large revenues can buy large navies. The question is whether the acquisition of such capabilities by China would in fact be wise given other pressing demands on the state's coffers as well as possible adverse international repercussions.[37]

This brings us back to the question of how China's leaders or ruling elites interpret their current situation. We earlier emphasized the importance for all states at all times of the imperative of regime preservation. There is ample evidence that this is a major preoccupation of China's leadership today just as it was in times past. No sharp line distinguishes this concern for regime preservation from China's interest in external security because it has frequently been foreign invasion that has destroyed the legitimacy of dynasties (the "mandate of heaven," in the classic Chinese phrase) and led to their overthrow. As just suggested, the Chinese also have a lively and well-grounded fear of internal threats to the order and unity of the nation. The current Communist regime is no different in this respect from China in imperial times. However, there is little doubt that the current Chinese leadership differs from that of the imperial past by a greater sensitivity to the economic underpinnings of domestic tranquility and the security of the regime, reflecting among other things the legitimating myth of Marxism-Leninism. Hence the clear priority the leadership had long placed on economic development of the country at the expense of military modernization.

There can also be little question that these priorities have been adjusted very recently to reflect a determination by the leadership to reclaim a place for China in the world as a great power with a modern military establishment. The strength of this determination—anchored as it is in a resurgent popular nationalism that has virtually replaced communism as the regime's legitimizing ideology—should not be underestimated. Imperial China's "century of humiliation" at the hands of the Western maritime powers remains the single most important historical point of reference for the Chinese leadership. From this perspective, China's turn to the sea is seen as mandatory, not optional (as could be argued was the case for the Ottomans, Russia, and Germany, for example.) The next question is whether or to what extent the ongoing buildup of Chinese naval and other modern military capabilities reflects a clear strategic vision and set of choices or, as in the case of the former Soviet Union, a dubious and economically unsustainable attempt to play the global superpower. With respect to the navy in particular, it is necessary to ask whether China's apparent decision to break with tradition and build a strategically competitive navy reflects a coherent strategy or something more like the challenge posed by late imperial Germany to Britain's mastery of the sea. It is not possible to answer either question with confidence at the present time, but we will return to the latter question in a moment.

Returning to the issue of leadership, it is apparent from the history surveyed in this volume that leadership has been a key factor enabling—but also frustrating—maritime transformations in the past. Ming China's brief maritime golden age was brought to its climax by two men, the Emperor Yongle and Adm. Zheng He. By the same token, declining activity in the maritime domain under the later Ming Dynasty was exacerbated by imperial preoccupation with continental challenges coupled with the opposition of the imperial bureaucracy to state penetration of the maritime economy. Under the Qing Dynasty, navalist elements within the state bureaucracy were unable to carry through promising programs of reform and naval building in the face of the maritime threat posed by the European powers owing primarily to incompetence and disinterest at the center.[38] During the Cold War, the leadership of the PLA as well as the Communist Party itself remained overwhelmingly army-centric. Only toward the end of this period did the PLAN come into its own, and this occurred largely through the efforts of one man, Adm. Liu Huaqing, during his long tenure as commander of the PLAN and then as vice chairman of the key policy board overseeing the entire Chinese military. Today there are ample indications of the elevated status of the PLAN in the eyes of China's political leadership as well as of the institutionalization of a navalist or maritime outlook within the PLAN and to some extent beyond it. Nevertheless, it would be well not to discount entirely the legacy of China's centuries-old continentalist culture or the residual ground-forces bias within the PLA as a factor affecting Chinese strategic decision making, particularly at a time when China's leaders are vividly reminded of the fragility of their hold on large parts of the country's periphery.

Little needs to be said here of the material and operational handicaps that have helped derail Chinese maritime transformation in the past because there is every reason to think that the contemporary Chinese have overcome most of them or at least are well along in the process of doing so. This is not to say that Chinese naval technology or shipbuilding skills are yet or will soon be completely on a par with the advanced West, but only that whatever shortcomings remain in these areas should not act as a fatal obstacle in the larger process of maritime transformation. In an interesting parallel with the Ottomans, Imperial China was fundamentally disadvantaged in its maritime encounter with the West in the nineteenth century by the fact that it had never developed a truly ocean-going naval vessel: Like the Ottoman galley, the Chinese junk was optimized for use in littoral waters (and rivers). There is little reason to believe that any such critical disparity exists currently. Of course, the Chinese (like the Persians and Ottomans) have benefited greatly in recent years by their ability to acquire advanced naval and other military systems from other countries, especially Russia. But they have also shown themselves capable at reverse engineering and adapting such systems to their own needs. Not many years ago, many observers doubted whether the Chinese would ever be able to build, maintain, or operate effectively a modern submarine force. Though of course the PLAN has not yet met the test of actual undersea warfare, few now would agree with this assessment.[39] As we have seen, deficiencies in training and general professionalism remain a problem in China's shipbuilding industry; nevertheless, China has risen to a dominant position in the global shipbuilding business.[40] Similar limitations affect the PLAN, but the Chinese are well aware of them and seem determined to fix them.[41]

To speculate at length about the current Chinese approach to naval strategy and operational art would take us too far afield, but several points may be made. In the first place, there is a great deal of evidence that the ongoing buildup of Chinese naval and maritime capabilities has one very sharp and relatively limited strategic focus: the Taiwan problem. China is in the process of developing and fielding capabilities that are optimized for a scenario in which Taiwan declares its independence of China and the United States is poised to come to its aid in the event of a PRC military response. This strategy is heavily reliant on short- and medium-range conventionally armed missiles both to neutralize Taiwan's defenses and to deter or defeat American carrier battle groups approaching the island from the east; its submarine force would also contribute importantly to the second task. Conversely, however, there is also reason to think that the Chinese are looking beyond the Taiwan problem.[42]

As mentioned earlier, Chinese navalists have become avid students of the American naval strategist Alfred Thayer Mahan. Writing at the dawn of the modern American navy in the late nineteenth century, Mahan preached the gospel of sea power as an unappreciated yet essential factor in the rise of great powers and as a vital safeguard of their overseas commercial interests. Mahan pointed to the importance of protecting sea lines of communication to markets abroad, and argued that sea-faring nations needed to establish a network of overseas bases or refueling stations that would enable their navies to perform this function effectively. He argued that maritime powers needed to be prepared to field a powerful fleet of capital ships capable of maintaining command of the sea ultimately through defeat of the adversary's navy in a climactic confrontation. While the Chinese government has not officially embraced such views, these views are espoused by many prominent military writers and academics in the PRC today, and they seem to be exercising some influence over China's naval planning. Although it is unlikely that the Chinese think they can or should prepare to challenge the United States in the foreseeable future in a head-to-head clash of major surface forces in the Pacific, they show clear signs of moving away from a maritime strategy heavily reliant on submarines and land-based air and missile attack—a strategy reminiscent of the Young School approach popular at one time in both France and the Soviet Union—toward one more balanced in the direction of major surface combatants. Recently the Chinese have shown notable new interest in developing an aircraft carrier after much inconclusive internal debate on this subject. It is significant that at least part of the rationale for moving in this direction is a newly felt need (in the aftermath of the recent Indonesian tsunami disaster) for China to have a capability for intervention in humanitarian crises comparable to that of the United States. The conspicuous revival of interest in contemporary China in the exploits of the Ming admiral Zheng He strongly suggests that the Chinese are increasingly coming to appreciate the "soft power" dimension of navies, but it is difficult for a submarine-centric navy to project soft power or influence effectively.

However this may be, the Chinese leadership clearly resonates with Mahan's ideas concerning commerce protection and the importance of sea lines of communication. As China has become more dependent on oil supplies from the Persian Gulf and Africa in recent years, it is plainly worried about a potential threat to its oil tankers in transit through the Strait of Malacca and the Indian Ocean.[43] In good Mahanian fashion, China appears to be in the process of helping to develop facilities of various kinds in friendly countries throughout this region, particularly Burma and Pakistan.[44] In the latter, Beijing has invested $1 billion in the construction of a deep-water port at Gwadar; when completed, such a facility could have significant military functions as well, depending on the future direction of China's relationship with both Pakistan and India.[45] Chinese motives and intentions with regard to this so-called string of pearls strategy have been the subject of much speculation.[46] It is presently far from clear whether or to what extent China will shape its future naval planning and procurement around the requirement to project Chinese naval power in the direction of the Middle East.[47] But the least that can be said is that emerging evidence of a firm Chinese commitment to developing a permanent maritime infrastructure of this sort would be a strong sign that China's maritime transformation is here to stay.

The extent to which Chinese maritime-oriented commentators also focus on the sea itself as a resource-rich environment is worth noting. The Chinese are very sensitive to issues of sovereignty over ocean areas for precisely this reason; in particular, they have been aggressive in pushing territorial claims affecting ownership of gas and oil deposits in the South and East China seas.[48] Fishing is another area highly relevant in this context. But the Chinese also seem seized by the prospect of the seabed as a future source of mineral resources.[49] More broadly, China's burgeoning seaborne trade and consequent growing reliance on maritime imports of energy and raw materials may gradually motivate Beijing to more actively safeguard its sea lines of communication.

How, then, should one finally assess China's contemporary turn to the sea? While I have sounded a number of cautionary notes, especially concerning the enduring pull of China's continentalist past as it relates to threats to the country's internal stability and its landward borders, it seems reasonable to conclude that China has very likely turned the corner on a genuine maritime transformation, in the sense that we have been using that term in this volume. If that proves indeed to be the case, it would be a remarkable if not singular event in the history of the last two millennia.

As we have seen, however, even the successful cases of maritime transformation identified here—ancient Persia and Rome—retained an imprint of their original continentalist orientation after they had become full-fledged maritime powers. Perhaps the most interesting issue in the contemporary Chinese case is whether or to what extent the Chinese maritime transformation will simply mirror the experience of classic maritime powers such as Britain or the United States—or instead reveal (as the Chinese like to say) distinctive "Chinese characteristics." In any event, it is certain we have not yet seen the end of a process that could fundamentally transform not only China as a whole but also the shape of global politics in the decades to come.

Notes

1. During the Song, Yuan, Ming, and early Qing dynasties, sea power was relatively important and carefully cultivated, even if to varying degrees. The Ming and Qing navies were quite powerful at times, and maritime mercantile exchange was significant for much of Chinese history.

2. As Andrew Wilson's chapter in this volume explains, sea power was important in several conflicts involving China, including the Imjin War, the defeat of the Mongols, Yongle's usurpation, and the fall of the Ming.

3. For an insightful and nuanced general account, see John Curtis Perry, "Imperial China and the Sea," in Toshi Yoshihara and James R. Holmes, eds., *Asia Looks Seaward: Power and Maritime Strategy* (Westport, CT: Praeger Security International, 2007), 17–31. Of particular importance is Perry's stress on the more maritime orientation of southern as opposed to northern China.

4. See the extensive discussion in Bruce Elleman's chapter in this volume.

5. Mao's optimism regarding a Taiwan invasion stemmed in part from the Communists' successful landing operation on Hainan Island (海南岛登陆战役) in March–May 1950, which had succeeded where the previous year's attempted invasion of Jinmen had failed. In retrospect, it would become clear that several critical differences from Hainan rendered Taiwan invulnerable to Communist takeover: lack of communist guerillas, determination of the Nationalists to defend it, sheer distance by water from the mainland, and protection by the presence of the U.S. Seventh Fleet.

6. Deng managed to sideline Mao's handpicked successor, Hua Guofeng, more or less completely by 1980, but it was clear that Deng was in charge by 1978—hence China's opening and reform. This was despite the fact that Deng's rank at the time was only vice premier.

7. As suggested by Bernard Cole in this volume.

8. On this general subject see Alastair I. Johnston, *Cultural Realism: Strategic Culture and Grand Strategy in Chinese History* (Ithaca, NY: Cornell University Press, 1995); Michael D. Swaine and Ashley J. Tellis, *Interpreting China's Grand Strategy: Past, Present, and Future* (Santa Monica, CA: RAND, 2000).

9. See notably the account of Edward L. Dreyer, *Zheng He: China and the Oceans in the Early Ming Dynasty, 1405–1433* (New York: Longman, 2007).

10. This argument is developed by Andrew Wilson in this volume.

11. The case for this general proposition is ably made by Jakub J. Grygiel, *Great Powers and Geopolitical Change* (Baltimore: The Johns Hopkins University Press, 2006), a comparative study of Venice, the Ottoman Empire, and Ming China.

12. Lyle J. Goldstein, "China's Falklands Lessons," *Survival* 50, no. 3 (June 2008): 65–82. Easily overlooked is the fact that today's high-technology militaries require a level of logistics support for power projection that would have been unimaginable to states in the pre-industrial era. For the classic World War II American experience, see Worrall R. Carter, *Beans, Bullets, and Black Oil* (Washington, DC: U.S.

Government Printing Office, 1953).

13. Properly emphasized by Gregory Gilbert in this volume. In fact, this was already recognized by the ancient Greeks. See Xenophon's semifictional account of the founding of the Persian Empire, *The Education of Cyrus*, trans. Wayne Ambler (Ithaca: Cornell University Press, 2001).

14. Eckstein, this volume.

15. Of particular interest in this connection is Wolfgang Wegener, *The Naval Strategy of the World War*, ed. Holger H. Herwig (Annapolis, MD: Naval Institute Press, 1989).

16. Sparta's position of hegemony in the Peloponnese and Greece more generally was in fact overthrown by a coalition led by Thebes in a decisive land battle at Leuctra, 371 BC.

17. Ably dissected by Pritchard in this volume.

18. Strauss, this volume.

19. See, for example, Richard Rosecrance and Arthur J. Stein, eds., *The Domestic Bases of Grand Strategy* (Ithaca, NY: Cornell University Press, 1993).

20. James Holmes and Toshi Yoshihara, "Japan's Postwar Maritime Thought: If Not Mahan, Who?" *Naval War College Review* 59, no. 3 (Summer 2006): 23–51.

21. See, for example, A.T. 马汉 [A.T. Mahan], 安常容, 成忠勤 译 [An Changrong and Cheng Zhongqin, translators], 张志云, 卜允德 校 [Zhang Zhiyun and Bu Yunde, proofreaders], 海权对历史的影响, 1660–1783 [*The Influence of Sea Power upon History, 1660–1783*] (Beijing: 解放军出版社 [People's Liberation Army Press], 2006); 刘华清 [Liu Huaqing], 刘华清回忆录 [*The Memoirs of Liu Huaqing*] (Beijing: People's Liberation Army, 2004), 432–33; 丁一平, 李洛荣, 龚连娣 [Ding Yiping, Li Luorong, and Gong Liandi], 世界海军史 [*The History of World Navies from the Chinese Perspective*] (Beijing: 海潮出版社 [Sea Tide Press], 2000), 309, 343–48; 徐起 [Xu Qi], "21世纪初海上地缘战略与中国海军的发展" ["Maritime Geostrategy and the Development of the Chinese Navy in the Early Twenty-first Century"], 中国军事科学 (*China Military Science*) 17, no. 4 (2004): 75–81; 朗丹阳, 刘分良 [Lang Danyang and Liu Fenliang], "海陆之争的历史检视" ["Historical Exploration into the Land-Sea Dispute"], 中国军事科学 [*China Military Science*], no. 1 (2007): 39–46. The publications of James Holmes and Toshi Yoshihara, recognized Western authorities on this subject, include *Chinese Naval Strategy in the 21st Century: The Turn to Mahan* (London: Routledge, 2007); "China and the Commons: Angell or Mahan?" *World Affairs* 163, no. 4 (Spring 2006): 1–20; "China's 'Caribbean' in the South China Sea," *SAIS Review of International Affairs* 26, no. 1 (Winter–Spring 2006): 79–92; "Command of the Sea with Chinese Characteristics," *Orbis* 49, no. 4 (Fall 2005): 677–94; and "The Influence of Mahan upon China's Maritime Strategy," *Comparative Strategy* 24, no. 1 (January–March 2005): 23–51.

22. For a general discussion see Carnes Lord, *The Modern Prince: What Leaders Need to Know Now* (New Haven: Yale University Press, 2003).

23. Kipp, this volume.

24. Notably, through a series of widely publicized articles in the 1970s, later collected in his book *The Sea Power of the State* (New York: Pergamon, 1980). For a Russian precedent, consider also Konstantin Nikolaevich's promotion of the Imperial Navy through the official journal *Morskoi Sbornik* (Kipp, pp. 162 above)—in fact, the same journal used by Gorshkov over a century later.

25. Vego, this volume.

26. Grygiel, this volume.

27. Chinese discussions of potential future campaigns to coerce Taiwan often employ the concept of "using the land to control the sea" (以陆制海). This might involve, for example, operating aircraft from nearby airfields because China lacks an aircraft carrier or using land-launched missiles and artillery.

28. Herwig, this volume.

29. Surveyed by Collins and Grubb, this volume.

30. On the aircraft carrier issue, see, for example, Andrew S. Erickson, "Can China Become a Maritime Power?" in Toshi Yoshihara and James R. Holmes, *Asia Looks Seaward: Power and Maritime Strategy* (Westport, CT: Praeger Security International, 2007), 90–92, as well as Andrew S. Erickson and Andrew R. Wilson, "China's Aircraft Carrier Dilemma," *Naval War College Review* 59 (Autumn 2006): 13–46. For a cogent statement of the case for China's turn to the sea by a PRC official, see Xu Qi, "Maritime Geostrategy and the Development of the Chinese Navy," 47–67. For further details, see Erickson and Goldstein, Introduction, this volume.

31. As this chapter and the Elleman and Wilson chapters have pointed out, the sea appeared as more of a barrier in terms of received Chinese historiography (popular Chinese and Western perceptions about Chinese maritime history) today than may have actually been the case. Even if central governments saw the sea as a barrier, merchants (sometimes sanctioned by or in collaboration with the center) often did see the sea as a highway.

32. It was a "divine wind" (*kamikaze*) that famously thwarted the Mongol/Yuan invasion of Japan in 1281. Consider the lethal effects of Mediterranean storms on naval vessels in ancient times in spite of the more protected situation of that body of water—and in spite of the fact that such vessels rarely ventured far from land.

33. For a fascinating discussion of this larger issue see Alan M. Wachman, *Why Taiwan? Geostrategic Rationales for China's Territorial Integrity* (Stanford, CA: Stanford University Press, 2007).

34. While the term may have originated in response to the U.S. force posture in East Asia beginning in the 1950s, it was more recently popularized by former PLAN commander Liu Huaqing. See Liu Huaqing, *The Memoirs of Liu Huaqing*, 437; Alexander Huang, "The Chinese Navy's Offshore Active Defense Strategy: Conceptualization and Implications," *Naval War College Review* 47, no. 3 (Summer 1994): 18; Bernard D. Cole, *The Great Wall at Sea: China's Navy Enters the Twenty-first Century* (Annapolis, MD: Naval Institute Press, 2001), 165–68.

35. When an eighteen-ship task group sailed to the previously surveyed Fiji Islands area to retrieve the instrument package from China's first successful DF-5/CSS-4 ICBM test on 18 May 1980, it was the first major instance of Chinese maritime power projection since Zheng He's voyages and the first ever beyond the First Island Chain into the Western Pacific.

36. See, for example, the recent book by two Chinese naval officers, 郝廷兵, 杨志荣 [Hao Tingbing and Yang Zhirong], 海上力量与中华民族的伟大复兴 [*Sea Power and the Chinese Nation's Mighty Resurgence*] (Beijing: National Defense University Press, 2005), 33–37.

37. It is very likely no accident that the account of Imperial Germany in the officially inspired Chinese study *The Rise of Great Powers* fails even to mention the Anglo-German naval arms race as a cause of World War I. See Erickson and Goldstein, this volume.

38. See Elleman, this volume.

39. See notably Andrew S. Erickson, Lyle J. Goldstein, William Murray, and Andrew R. Wilson, eds., *China's Future Nuclear Submarine Force* (Annapolis, MD: Naval Institute Press, 2007).

40. Collins and Grubb, this volume.

41. See the comments of McVadon, this volume, highlighting PLAN deficiencies in officer education and training and, in the technological arena, C4ISR (command, control, communications, computers, intelligence, surveillance, and reconnaissance).

42. See McVadon, this volume, for an overall assessment.

43. See, for example, John Garofano, "China-Southeast Asia Relations: Problems and Prospects," in Toshi Yoshihara and James R. Holmes, ed., *Asia Looks Seaward: Power and Maritime Strategy* (Westport, CT: Praeger Security International, 2007), ch. 9.

44. 林锡星 [Li Xixing], "中缅石油管道设计中的美印因素" ["The Influence of the U.S. and India on the Sino-Myanmar Oil Pipeline Proposal"], 东南亚研究 [Southeast Asian Studies], no. 5 (2007): 34.

45. For an article that emphasizes the strategic significance of China's assistance in the construction of Gwadar, see Xu Qi, *Maritime Geostrategy and the Development of the Chinese Navy.*

46. The term "String of Pearls" was apparently first applied to China in a report titled "Energy Futures in Asia" by the defense contractor Booz-Allen-Hamilton. This report was commissioned in 2005 by the U.S. Department of Defense's Office of Net Assessment. See also Ross Munro, "China's Strategy towards Countries on its Land Borders," final report of study commissioned by the Director of Net Assessment of the Office of the Secretary of Defense (McLean, VA: Booz Allen Hamilton, August 2006).

47. For studies that suggest that China has not thus far developed bases in the Indian Ocean, see Gurpreet S. Khurana, "China's 'String of Pearls' in the Indian Ocean and its Security Implications," *Strategic Analysis* 32, no. 1 (January 2008): 1–39;

Andrew Selth, "Burma, China and the Myth of Military Bases," *Asian Security* 3, no. 3 (September 2007): 279–307.

48. See, for example, Peter Dutton, "Carving up the East China Sea," *Naval War College Review* 60 (Spring 2007): 49–72.

49. Note the specific reference to this in Xu Qi, "Maritime Geostrategy and the Development of the Chinese Navy," 62.

Abbreviations and Acronyms

ASCM	antiship cruise missile
ASW	antisubmarine warfare
C_4ISR	command, control, communications, computers, intelligence, surveillance, and reconnaissance
CCP	Chinese Communist Party
CIC	China Shipping Industry Company
CMC	Central Military Commission
COSCO	China Ocean Shipping Company
CSIC	China Shipbuilding Industry Corporation
CSSC	China State Shipbuilding Corporation
dwt	deadweight tons
GM	Goldmark
GPCR	Great Proletarian Cultural Revolution
KMT	Kuomintang
LNG	liquefied natural gas
PLA	People's Liberation Army
PLAAF	PLA Air Force
PLAN	People's Liberation Army Navy
PRC	People's Republic of China
RKKA	Workers' and Peasants' Red Army
RMA	Revolution in Military Affairs
SCO	Shanghai Cooperation Organization
SSBN	nuclear-powered ballistic missile submarine
VLCC	very large crude oil carriers

About the Contributors

DR. BERNARD D. COLE (CAPTAIN, USN, RET.) is professor of international history at the National War College in Washington, D.C., where he concentrates on the Chinese military and Asian energy issues. He previously served thirty years as a surface warfare officer in the Navy, all in the Pacific. He commanded USS *Rathburne* (FF 1057) and Destroyer Squadron 35, and he served as a naval gunfire liaison officer with the Third Marine Division in Vietnam, as plans officer for Commander-in-Chief Pacific Fleet, and as special assistant to the Chief of Naval Operations for Expeditionary Warfare. Dr. Cole has written numerous articles and book chapters; his published books are *Gunboats and Marines: The U.S. Navy in China* (1982); *The Great Wall at Sea: China's Navy Enters the 21st Century* (2001); *Oil for the Lamps of China: Beijing's 21st Century Search for Energy* (2003); Taiwan's Security: *History and Prospects* (2006); and *Sealanes and Pipelines: Energy Security in Asia* (2008). Dr. Cole earned an AB in history from the University of North Carolina, an MPA (National Security Affairs) from the University of Washington, and a PhD in history from Auburn University.

MR. GABRIEL COLLINS was an OSD/ONA research fellow in the U.S. Naval War College's China Maritime Studies Institute (CMSI) from 2006–8. He is an honors graduate of Princeton University (2005, AB politics) and is proficient in Mandarin Chinese and Russian. His primary research areas are Chinese and Russian energy policy, maritime energy security, Chinese shipbuilding, and Chinese naval modernization. Mr. Collins' energy- and shipping-related work has been published in *Oil & Gas Journal, Jane's Intelligence*

Review, Geopolitics of Energy, Proceedings, Naval War College Review, The National Interest, Hart's Oil & Gas Investor, LNG Observer, and *Orbis.*

DR. ARTHUR M. ECKSTEIN is a professor of history at the University of Maryland, College Park. He is a specialist in the history of Roman imperial expansion. He has published fifty major scholarly articles and four books, the latest of which is *Rome Enters the Greek East: From Anarchy to Hierarchy in the Hellenistic Mediterranean, 230–170 BC* (Blackwell, 2008). He is also currently coediting an edition of the great history of the rise of Rome to world power written by Polybius (ca. 150 BC).

DR. BRUCE A. ELLEMAN received his BA degree from UC Berkeley in 1982, MA and Harriman Institute Certificate at Columbia University in 1984, followed by the MPhil in 1987, East Asian Certificate in 1988, and PhD in 1993. In addition, he completed the MSc in international history at the London School of Economics in 1985, and the MA in national security and strategic studies (with distinction) at the U.S. Naval War College in 2004. He is research professor in the Maritime History Department, Center for Naval Warfare Studies, U.S. Naval War College, and author of *Waves of Hope: The U.S. Navy's Response to the Tsunami in Northern Indonesia* (Naval War College Press, 2007); co-editor with S. C. M. Paine of *Naval Coalition Warfare: From the Napleonic War to Operation Iraqi Freedom* (Routledge, 2008), and *Naval Blockades and Seapower: Strategies and Counter-strategies, 1805–2005* (Routledge, 2006); *Japanese-American Civilian Prisoner Exchanges and Detention Camps, 1941– 45* (Routledge, 2006); co-editor with Christopher Bell of *Naval Mutinies of the Twentieth Century: An International Perspective* (Frank Cass, 2003); *Wilson and China: A Revised History of the Shandong Question* (M. E. Sharpe, 2002); *Modern Chinese Warfare, 1795–1989* (Routledge, 2001); co-editor with Stephen Kotkin of *Mongolia in the Twentieth Century: Landlocked Cosmopolitan* (M. E. Sharpe, 1999); and *Diplomacy and Deception: The Secret History of Sino-Soviet Diplomatic Relations, 1917–1927* (M. E. Sharpe, 1997). Several of Dr. Elleman's books have been translated into foreign languages, including a Chinese translation of *Modern Chinese Warfare: Jindai Zhongguo de junshi yu zhanzheng* (Elite Press, 2002) and a Czech translation of the Naval Mutiny book: *Námoøní vzpoury ve dvacátém století: mezinárodní souvislosti* (BBart, 2004).

DR. GREGORY P. GILBERT completed BE and MEngSc degrees at the University of Adelaide in 1984 and 1988, respectively. He worked for the Australian Department of Defence (Navy) as a naval design engineer for eleven years; this included work at Cockatoo Island Dockyard, Garden Island Dockyard, the New Submarine Project (*Collins* class), Directorate of Marine Engineering Design, and Naval Support Command's In-Service Design Section. He then worked as a defense consultant specializing in naval systems from 1996 until 2004. While working in the engineering field, he pursued a second career in the humanities, receiving his BA degree in ancient history from the University of New England, Australia in 1996, MA at Macquarie University Australia in 1999, followed by a PhD, also at Macquarie University in 2004. His broad research interests include the archaeology and anthropology of warfare, Egyptology, international relations—the Middle East, maritime strategy, and naval history. As an archaeologist, he has excavated with international teams in Egypt at the sites of Helwan, Hierakonpolis, Koptos, and Sais. He directed the Qift Regional Expedition (Koptos) in Egypt between 2000 and 2004. He is presently a research fellow attached to the University of Durham, United Kingdom and a visiting fellow with the Australian National University. Dr. Gilbert is the author of *Weapons, Warriors and Warfare in Early Egypt* (Oxford, 2004) and *Ancient Egyptian Sea Power and the Origin of Maritime Forces* (in press) and is now researching a similar work on ancient Persian sea power. He has contributed to numerous journals and edited works on wide-ranging subjects and has edited *Australian Naval Personalities: Lives from the Australian Dictionary of Biography* (Sea Power Centre, 2006). Since the beginning of 2005 he has contributed to the development of Australia's maritime strategy and furthered his naval historical interests at the Sea Power Centre, Canberra, Australia.

LT. CDR. MICHAEL C. GRUBB, USN, is a submarine officer currently assigned as the engineering officer on USS *Pennsylvania* (Blue) (SSBN 735). He has previously served on USS *Miami* (SSN 755) and the staff of Destroyer Squadron Twenty Two. His sea tours have included two deployments to the Arabian Gulf in support of maritime security operations and one strategic deterrence patrol. He earned a BSE in naval architecture and marine engineering from the University of Michigan in 2000 and an MA in national security and strategic studies (with highest distinction) from the U.S. Naval War College in 2007. His academic research at the Naval War College focused on merchant shipping and shipbuilding, and has been published in the *Naval War College Review* and U.S. Naval Institute *Proceedings*.

DR. JAKUB J. GRYGIEL is the George H. W. Bush Assistant Professor of International Relations at the Paul H. Nitze School of Advanced International Studies of The Johns Hopkins University (Washington, D.C.). He has previously worked as a consultant for the Organisation for Economic Co-operation and Development (OECD, Paris) and the World Bank (Washington, D.C.), and has been an international security commentator for the Swiss newspaper *Giornale del Popolo* (Lugano, Ticino). His first book, *Great Powers and Geopolitical Change*, was published in 2006 by Johns Hopkins University Press. His writings on international relations and security studies have appeared in *The American Interest, Journal of Strategic Studies, Orbis, Commentary, Joint Force Quarterly*, and *Political Science Quarterly*. He earned a PhD and an MPA from Princeton University, and a BSFS summa cum laude from Georgetown University.

DR. HOLGER H. HERWIG holds a dual position at the University of Calgary as professor of history and Canada Research Chair in the Centre for Military and Strategic Studies. He received his BA (1965) from the University of British Columbia and his MA (1967) and PhD (1971) from the State University of New York at Stony Brook. Dr. Herwig taught at Vanderbilt University in Nashville, Tennessee, from 1971 until 1989 and served as head of the Department of History at Calgary from 1991 until 1996. He was a visiting professor of strategy at the Naval War College, Newport, Rhode Island, in 1985–86 and the Andrea and Charles Bronfman Distinguished Visiting Professor of Judaic Studies at The College of William & Mary, Williamsburg, Virginia, in 1998. A Fellow of the Royal Society of Canada and of the Alexander von Humboldt Foundation in Bonn, Germany, Dr. Herwig has held major research grants from the Humboldt Foundation, the National Endowment for the Humanities, NATO, the Rockefeller Foundation, and the Social Sciences and Humanities Research Council of Canada. Dr. Herwig has published more than a dozen books, including the prize-winning *The First World War: Germany and Austria-Hungary 1914–1918*. He translated, edited, and wrote an introduction to *The Naval Strategy of the World War*, edited by Wolfgang Wegener, in the Naval Institute Press series Classics of Sea Power. He has co-authored *Deadly Seas, The Destruction of the Bismarck*, and *One Christmas in Washington*. In 2002 Dr. Herwig joined James Cameron for three weeks in the Atlantic to produce "James Cameron's Expedition: Bismarck" for the Discovery Channel.

DR. JACOB W. KIPP is the deputy director of the School of Advanced Military Studies (SAMS) of the U.S. Army Training and Doctrine Command at Ft. Leavenworth, Kansas. Prior to joining SAMS in 1986, he served as director of the Foreign Military Studies Office from 2003 to 2006. Dr. Kipp was born in Harrisburg, Pennsylvania, and graduated from Shippensburg State College in 1964 with a BS in secondary education. He received his PhD in Russian History from the Pennsylvania State University in 1970. He has conducted extensive archival research and publications on the history of the Imperial Russian and Soviet Navies. In 1971 he joined the History Department of Kansas State University, where he taught Russian, Soviet, East European, and Military and Naval History. In 1985 he was promoted to the rank of full professor. In 1986 he joined the newly founded Soviet Army Studies Office (SASO) at Ft. Leavenworth as a senior analyst. In 1990 SASO became the Foreign Military Studies Office (FMSO). As senior analyst, Dr. Kipp lead research efforts on Soviet military doctrine, perestroika and military reform, ethnonationalism in Eastern Europe and the former Soviet Union, and the revolution in military affairs. Dr. Kipp has published extensively in military and naval history. His works include eight books, more than forty articles in professional journals, and forty chapters in books. He has also been actively involved in editorial work as associate editor of *Military Affairs*, *Aerospace Historian*, and the *Journal of Slavic Military Studies*, and as editor of *European Security*. He also serves on the editorial board of the modern War Studies Series of the University Press of Kansas. Dr. Kipp is married to Dr. Maia A. Kipp, emeritus professor of theater and film at the University of Kansas.

REAR ADM. ERIC A. MCVADON, USN (RET.), concluded his thirty-five years of naval service as the U.S. defense and naval attaché at the American Embassy in Beijing 1990–92. A consultant on East Asian security affairs, he works extensively with the U.S. policy and intelligence communities and the Department of Defense, directly and indirectly. He is also the director of Asia-Pacific Studies at the Institute for Foreign Policy Analysis and a non-resident fellow at the Atlantic Council of the United States. His naval career encompassed extensive experience in air antisubmarine warfare and politico-military affairs, including service as the NATO and U.S. subunified commander in Iceland and assignments on the Navy Staff, in the Office of the Secretary of Defense, and with the Chairman of the Joint Chiefs of Staff. He also commanded a P-3C squadron and the naval station in Iceland. Admiral McVadon, a designated naval aviator, is a 1958 graduate of Tulane University and has a master's degree in international affairs from George Washington

University. He is a distinguished graduate of the Naval Postgraduate School, Naval War College (Command & Staff), and National War College. His recent publications include an article titled "China and the United States on the High Seas" in *China Security*, Autumn 2007; a chapter titled "China's Maturing Navy" in the 2007 book *China's Future Nuclear Submarine Force*, and an article with the same title in the *Naval War College Review*, Spring 2006. His testimony and prepared statements in September 2005 and March 2007 on PLA modernization and implications for the United States before the U.S.-China Economic and Security Review Commission are available at http://www.uscc.gov. He and his wife, Marshall, both from Baton Rouge, Louisiana, live and work in Great Falls, Virginia.

DR. JAMES PRITCHARD is Professor Emeritus of History at Queen's University, Kingston, Canada, where he taught history for thirty-two years. He was educated at schools in Ottawa, London, and Toronto, and after studying in France earned his PhD in history in 1971 at the University of Toronto. He is the author of *Louis XV's Navy, 1748–1762: A Study in Organization and Administration* (McGill-Queen's University Press, 1987) and *Anatomy of a Naval Disaster: The 1746 French Naval Expedition to North America* (McGill–Queen's University Press 1995), which was awarded the Keith Matthews Prize by the Canadian Nautical Research Society and received a John Lyman Book Award from the North American Society for Oceanic History. His most recent book, *In Search of Empire: The French in the Americas, 1670–1730* (Cambridge University Press, 2004) was awarded the Wallace K. Ferguson Prize of the Canadian Historical Association. It appeared in paperback in 2007. He is currently writing a history of the Canadian shipbuilding industry during World War II.

DR. BARRY STRAUSS is professor of history and classics at Cornell University with specialties in ancient history and in military and naval history. His numerous books, articles, and reviews have been translated into six foreign languages. His latest book is *The Trojan War: A New History* (Simon & Schuster, 2006), which was preceded by *The Battle of Salamis, the Naval Encounter that Saved Greece—and Western Civilization* (Simon & Schuster, 2004), which was named by the *Washington Post* as one of the best books of 2004. Among his other books are *Fathers and Sons in Athens* (Princeton University Press, 1993), *The Anatomy of Error: Ancient Military Disasters and their Lessons for Modern Strategists* (with Josiah Ober; St. Martins, 1990), *Athens after the Peloponnesian War* (Cornell University Press, 1986), and two coedited collections of essays: *War and Democracy: A Comparative Study of the Korean War and the Peloponnesian War* (with David McCann; M. E. Sharpe, 2001) and *Hegemonic Rivalry: From Thucydides to the Nuclear Age* (with Richard Ned Lebow; Westview, 1991). He is currently writing a book on Spartacus. A frequent interviewee on PBS, NPR, the History Channel, and the Discovery Channel, Strauss has published op-ed pieces in such newspapers as the *Washington Post* and the *L.A. Times*. He holds fellowships from the National Endowment for the Humanities, the American School of Classical Studies at Athens, the German Academic Exchange Service, and the Korea Foundation. He received Cornell's Clark Distinguished Teaching Award. He holds a BA in history from Cornell and an MA and PhD in history from Yale. He lives in Ithaca, New York, with his wife and children.

DR. MILAN VEGO holds a BA in Naval Science from the former Yugoslav Academy (1961) and a Master Mariner's license (1973). He served for twelve years as an officer in the former Yugoslav Navy and for four years as 2nd officer (deck) in the former West German merchant marine before obtaining political asylum in the United States in February 1976. He also holds a BA in Modern History (1970) and an MA in U.S./Latin American History (1973) from Belgrade University, and a PhD in Modern European History from George Washington University (1981). Dr. Vego was an adjunct professor at the George Washington University (1983), former Defense Intelligence College (1985–91), and at the War Gaming and Simulations Center, National Defense University, Washington, D.C. (1989–91) before joining the Naval War College faculty in August 1991. He was also a senior fellow at the Center for Naval Analyses, Alexandria, Virginia (1985–87), and the former Soviet Army Studies Office (SASO), U.S. Army Combined Center, Ft. Leavenworth, Kansas (1987–89). Dr. Vego has published seven books: *Soviet Navy Today* (1986); *Soviet Naval Tactics* (1992); *The Austro-Hungarian Naval Policy 1904–1914* (1996); *Naval Strategy and Operations in Narrow Seas* (1st ed., 1999; 2nd ed., 2003; Spanish edition in 2003); *Operational Warfare* (2001); *The Battle for Leyte, 1944: Allied and Japanese Plans, Preparations, and Execution* (2006); and *Joint Operational Warfare* (2007). Dr. Vego has also published about 280 articles in various professional journals and magazines.

DR. ANDREW R. WILSON is professor of strategy and policy at the United States Naval War College. Professor Wilson is a graduate of the University of California Santa Barbara; he received his PhD in history and East Asian, languages from Harvard University. Prior to joining the Naval War College faculty in 1998 he taught courses in Chinese history at Wellesley College and at Harvard University. He is the author of numerous articles on Chinese military history, Chinese sea power, and Sun Tzu's *Art of War*. He has also published two books on the Chinese overseas, a monograph, *Ambition and Identity: Chinese Merchant-Elites in Colonial Manila, 1885–1916*, and an edited volume, *The Chinese in the Caribbean*. Recently he has been involved with editing *China's Future Nuclear Submarine Force*, a multivolume history of the China War, 1937–45, and a conference volume titled *War, Virtual War and Society*; and he is completing a new translation of Sun Tzu's *Art of War*.

The Editors

DR. ANDREW S. ERICKSON is an assistant professor in the Strategic Research Department at the U.S. Naval War College and a founding member of the department's China Maritime Studies Institute (CMSI). He is an associate in research at Harvard University's Fairbank Center for Chinese Studies, a fellow in the National Committee on U.S.–China Relations' Public Intellectuals Program (2008–11), and a member of the Council for Security Cooperation in the Asia–Pacific (CSCAP). Erickson previously worked for Science Applications International Corporation (SAIC) as a Chinese translator and technical analyst. He has also worked at the U.S. Embassy in Beijing, the U.S. Consulate in Hong Kong, the U.S. Senate, and the White House. Proficient in Mandarin Chinese and Japanese, he has traveled extensively in Asia. Erickson received his PhD and MA in international relations and comparative politics from Princeton and graduated magna cum laude from Amherst College with a BA in history and political science. His research, which focuses on East Asian defense, foreign policy, and technology issues, has been published widely in such journals as *Orbis*, *Journal of Strategic Studies*, and *Joint Force Quarterly*. Erickson is coeditor of, and a contributor to, the Naval Institute Press book series, Studies in Chinese Maritime Development: *China Goes to Sea* (2009), *China's Energy Strategy* (2008), *China's Future Nuclear Submarine Force* (2007); as well as the Naval War College Newport Paper, *China's Nuclear Modernization*.

DR. LYLE J. GOLDSTEIN is an associate professor in the Strategic Research Department of the Naval War College in Newport, Rhode Island, and director of NWC's China Maritime Studies Institute (CMSI), which was established in October 2006. Proficient in Chinese and Russian, Professor Goldstein has conducted extensive field research in both China and Russia.

His research on Chinese defense policies, especially concerning naval development, has been published in *China Quarterly, International Security, Jane's Intelligence Review, Journal of Strategic Studies,* and *Proceedings.* Professor Goldstein's first book, which compared proliferation crises and focused particularly on Chinese nuclear strategy, was published by Stanford University Press in 2005. He earned a PhD from Princeton University in 2001 and has an MA from Johns Hopkins SAIS. Dr. Goldstein has also worked in the Office of the Secretary of Defense.

DR. CARNES LORD, professor of military and naval strategy in the Strategic Research Department of the Center for Naval Warfare Studies, U.S. Naval War College, is a political scientist with broad interests in international and strategic studies, national security organization and management, and political philosophy. He has held a number of positions in the U.S. government, including director of international communications and information policy on the National Security Council staff (1981–83), assistant to the vice president for national security affairs (1989–91), and distinguished fellow at the National Defense University (1991–93). Dr. Lord has taught political science at Yale University, the University of Virginia, and the Fletcher School of Law and Diplomacy and was director of international studies at the National Institute for Public Policy. He is the author of, among other works, *The Presidency and the Management of National Security* (1988), *The Modern Prince: What Leaders Need to Know Now* (2003), and *Losing Hearts and Minds? Strategic Influence and Public Diplomacy in the Age of Terror* (2006).

Index